MORE PRAISE FROM ACROSS THE NATION FOR THE JOBBANK SERIES...

"If you are looking for a job ... before you go to the newspapers and the help-wanted ads, listen to Bob Adams, publisher of *The Metropolitan New York JobBank.*"

-Tom Brokaw, *NBC*

"Help on the job hunt ... Anyone who is job-hunting in the New York area can find a lot of useful ideas in a new paperback called *The Metropolitan New York JobBank* ..."

-Angela Taylor, *New York Times*

"For those graduates whose parents are pacing the floor, conspicuously placing circled want ads around the house and typing up resumes, [*The Carolina JobBank*] answers job-search questions."

-*Greensboro News and Record*

"Because our listing is seen by people across the nation, it generates lots of resumes for us. We encourage unsolicited resumes. We'll always be listed [in *The Chicago JobBank*] as long as I'm in this career."

-Tom Fitzpatrick, Director of Human Resources
Merchandise Mart Properties, Inc.

"Job-hunting is never fun, but this book can ease the ordeal ... [*The Los Angeles JobBank*] will help allay fears, build confidence, and avoid wheel-spinning."

-Robert W. Ross, *Los Angeles Times*

"I read through the 'Basics of Job Winning' and 'Resumes' sections [in *The Dallas-Fort Worth JobBank*] and found them to be very informative, with some positive tips for the job searcher. I believe the strategies outlined will bring success to any determined candidate."

-Camilla Norder, Professional Recruiter
Presbyterian Hospital of Dallas

"Through *The Dallas-Fort Worth JobBank,* we've been able to attract high-quality candidates for several positions."

-Rob Bertino, Southern States Sales Manager
CompuServe

"*The Seattle JobBank* is an essential resource for job hunters."

-Gil Lopez, Staffing Team Manager
Battelle Pacific Northwest Laboratories

"Job hunters can't afford to waste time. *The Minneapolis-St. Paul JobBank* contains information that used to require hours of research in the library."

-Carmella Zagone
Minneapolis-based Human Resources Administrator

"*The Florida JobBank* is an invaluable job-search reference tool. It provides the most up-to-date information and contact names available for companies in Florida. I should know -- it worked for me!"

-Rhonda Cody, Human Resources Consultant
Aetna Life and Casualty

"*The Phoenix JobBank* is a first-class publication. The information provided is useful and current."

-Lyndon Denton
Director of Human Resources and Materials Management
Apache Nitrogen Products, Inc.

"*The Boston JobBank* provides a handy map of employment possibilities in greater Boston. This book can help in the initial steps of a job search by locating major employers, describing their business activities, and for most firms, by naming the contact person and listing typical professional positions. For recent college graduates, as well as experienced professionals, *The Boston JobBank* is an excellent place to begin a job search."

-Juliet F. Brudney, Career Columnist
Boston Globe

"No longer can jobseekers feel secure about finding employment just through want ads. With the tough competition in the job market, particularly in the Boston area, they need much more help. For this reason, *The Boston JobBank* will have a wide and appreciative audience of new graduates, job changers, and people relocating to Boston. It provides a good place to start a search for entry-level professional positions."

-Journal of College Placement

"Packed with helpful contacts, *The Houston JobBank* empowers its reader to launch an effective, strategic job search in the Houston metropolitan area."

-Andrew Ceperley, Director
College of Communication Career Services
The University of Texas at Austin

"*The San Francisco Bay Area JobBank* ... is a highly useful guide, with plenty of how-to's ranging from resume tips to interview dress codes and research shortcuts."

-A.S. Ross, *San Francisco Examiner*

What makes the JobBank series the nation's premier line of employment guides?

With vital employment information on thousands of employers across the nation, the JobBank series is the most comprehensive and authoritative set of career directories available today.

Each book in the series provides information on **dozens of different industries** in a given city or area, with the primary employer listings providing contact information, telephone and fax numbers, addresses, Websites, a summary of the firm's business, and in many cases descriptions of the firm's typical professional job categories, the principal educational backgrounds sought, internships, and the fringe benefits offered.

In addition to the **detailed primary employer listings,** JobBank books give telephone numbers and addresses for **thousands of additional employers,** as well as information about executive search firms, placement agencies, and professional associations.

All of the reference information in the JobBank series is as up-to-date and accurate as possible. Every year, the entire database is thoroughly researched and verified by mail and by telephone. Adams Media Corporation publishes **more local employment guides more often** than any other publisher of career directories.

In addition, the JobBank series features current information about the local job scene -- **forecasts on which industries are the hottest** and **lists of regional professional associations,** so you can get your job hunt started off right.

The JobBank series offers **33 regional titles**, from Minneapolis to Houston, and from Boston to San Francisco. All of the information is organized geographically, because most people look for jobs in specific areas of the country.

A condensed, but thorough, review of the entire job search process is presented in the chapter **The Basics of Job Winning**, a feature which has received many compliments from career counselors. In addition, each JobBank directory includes a section on **resumes and cover letters** the *New York Times* has acclaimed as "excellent."

The JobBank series gives job hunters the most comprehensive, timely, and accurate career information, organized and indexed to facilitate the job search. An entire career reference library, JobBank books are the consummate employment guides.

Top career publications from Adams Media Corporation

The JobBank Series:
each JobBank book is $16.95

The Atlanta JobBank, 1999
The Austin/San Antonio JobBank, 2nd Ed.
The Boston JobBank, 1999
The Carolina JobBank, 5th Ed.
The Chicago JobBank, 1999
The Connecticut JobBank, 1st Ed.
The Dallas-Fort Worth JobBank, 1999
The Denver JobBank, 11th Ed.
The Detroit JobBank, 8th Ed.
The Florida JobBank, 1999
The Houston JobBank, 10th Ed.
The Indiana JobBank, 2nd Ed.
The Las Vegas JobBank, 2nd Ed.
The Los Angeles JobBank, 1999
The Minneapolis-St. Paul JobBank, 10th Ed.
The Missouri JobBank, 2nd Ed.
The Northern New England JobBank, 1st Ed.
The New Jersey JobBank, 1st Ed.
The New Mexico JobBank, 1st Ed.
The Metropolitan New York JobBank, 1999
The Upstate New York JobBank, 1st Ed.
The Ohio JobBank, 1999
The Greater Philadelphia JobBank, 1999
The Phoenix JobBank, 7th Ed.
The Pittsburgh JobBank, 2nd Ed.
The Portland JobBank, 2nd Ed.
The Salt Lake City JobBank, 1st Ed.
The San Francisco Bay Area JobBank, 1999
The Seattle JobBank, 1999
The Tennessee JobBank, 4th Ed.
The Virginia JobBank, 2nd Ed.
The Metropolitan Washington DC JobBank, 1999
The Wisconsin JobBank, 1st Ed.

The JobBank Guide to Computer & High-Tech Companies ($16.95)

The JobBank Guide to Health Care Companies ($16.95)

The National JobBank, 1999
(Covers the entire U.S.: $350.00 hc)

The JobBank Guide to Employment Services, 1998-1999
(Covers the entire U.S.: $199.00 hc)

Other Career Titles:

The Adams Cover Letter Almanac ($10.95)
The Adams Electronic Job Search Almanac, 1999 ($10.95)
The Adams Executive Recruiters Almanac ($16.95)
The Adams Job Interview Almanac ($12.95)
The Adams Jobs Almanac, 1999 ($16.95)
The Adams Resume Almanac ($10.95)
America's Fastest Growing Employers, 2nd Ed. ($16.00)
Career Shifting ($9.95)
Cold Calling Techniques, 3rd Ed. ($7.95)
College Grad Job Hunter, 4th Ed. ($14.95)
The Complete Resume & Job Search Book for College Students ($10.95)
Cover Letters That Knock 'em Dead, 3rd Ed. ($10.95)
Every Woman's Essential Job Hunting & Resume Book ($10.95)
The Harvard Guide to Careers in the Mass Media ($7.95)
High Impact Telephone Networking for Job Hunters ($6.95)
How to Become Successfully Self-Employed, 2nd Ed. ($9.95)
How to Get a Job in Education, 2nd Ed. ($15.95)
The Job Hunter's Checklist ($5.95)
The Job Search Handbook ($6.95)
Knock 'em Dead, 1999 ($12.95)
The Lifetime Career Manager ($20.00 hc)
The MBA Advantage ($12.95)
The Minority Career Book ($9.95)
The National Jobline Directory ($7.95)
The New Rules of the Job Search Game ($10.95)
Outplace Yourself ($15.95)
Over 40 and Looking for Work? ($7.95)
Reengineering Yourself ($12.95)
The Resume Handbook, 3rd Ed. ($7.95)
Resumes That Knock 'em Dead, 3rd Ed. ($10.95)
Richard Beatty's Job Search Networking ($9.95)
300 New Ways to Get a Better Job ($7.95)

Adams JobBank FastResume Suite (CD-ROM)
(Please call for details.)

If you are interested in variations of JobBank company profiles in electronic format for job search or sales mailings, please call **800/872-5627x317** or e-mail us at **jobbank@adamsonline.com**.

To order books, please send check or money order (including $4.50 for postage) to:
Adams Media Corporation, 260 Center Street, Holbrook MA 02343.
(Foreign orders please call for shipping rates.) Discounts available for standing orders.

Ordering by credit card? Just call **800/USA-JOBS** (In Massachusetts, call 781/767-8100). Fax: **800/872-5687**.
Please check your favorite retail outlet first.

—VISIT OUR WEBSITE—
http://www.careercity.com

2nd Edition

THE Indiana JobBank

Managing Editor: Steven Graber

Assistant Managing Editor: Marcie DiPietro

Senior Editor: Michelle Roy Kelly

Senior Associate Editor: Heidi E. Sampson

Associate Editor: Jayna S. Stafford

Editorial Assistants: Thom Blackett
Heather L. Vinhateiro
Jennifer M. Wood

Editorial Intern: Jason S. Spratley

Adams Media Corporation
HOLBROOK, MASSACHUSETTS

Published by Adams Media Corporation
260 Center Street, Holbrook, MA 02343

Manufactured in the United States of America.

Because addresses and telephone numbers of smaller companies change rapidly, we recommend you call each company and verify the information before mailing to the employers listed in this book. Mass mailings are not recommended.

While the publisher has made every reasonable effort to obtain and verify accurate information, occasional errors are inevitable due to the magnitude of the database. Should you discover an error, or if a company is missing, please write the editors at the above address so that we may update future editions.

ISBN: 1-58062-099-X
ISSN: 1099-0178

This book is available at quantity discounts for bulk purchases.
For information, call 800/872-5627.

Visit our exciting job and career site at http://www.careercity.com

TABLE OF CONTENTS

SECTION ONE: INTRODUCTION

SECTION TWO: THE JOB SEARCH

SECTION THREE: PRIMARY EMPLOYERS

INTRODUCTION

HOW TO USE THIS BOOK

Right now, you hold in your hands one of the most effective job-hunting tools available anywhere. In *The Indiana JobBank*, you will find a wide array of valuable information to help you launch or continue a rewarding career. But before you open to the book's employer listings and start calling about current job openings, take a few minutes to learn how best to use the resources presented in *The Indiana JobBank*.

The Indiana JobBank will help you to stand out from other jobseekers. While many people looking for a new job rely solely on newspaper help-wanted ads, this book offers you a much more effective job-search method -- direct contact. The direct contact method has been proven twice as effective as scanning the help-wanted ads. Instead of waiting for employers to come looking for you, you'll be far more effective going to them. While many of your competitors will use trial and error methods in trying to set up interviews, you'll learn not only how to get interviews, but what to expect once you've got them.

In the next few pages, we'll take you through each section of the book so you'll be prepared to get a jump-start on your competition.

Basics of Job Winning

Preparation. Strategy. Time-management. These are three of the most important elements of a successful job search. *Basics of Job Winning* helps you address these and all the other elements needed to find the right job.

One of your first priorities should be to define your personal career objectives. What qualities make a job desirable to you? Creativity? High pay? Prestige? Use *Basics of Job Winning* to weigh these questions. Then use the rest of the chapter to design a strategy to find a job that matches your criteria.

In *Basics of Job Winning,* you'll learn which job-hunting techniques work, and which don't. We've reviewed the pros and cons of mass mailings, help-wanted ads, and direct contact. We'll show you how to develop and approach contacts in your field; how to research a prospective employer; and how to use that information to get an interview and the job.

Also included in *Basics of Job Winning*: interview dress code and etiquette, the "do's and don'ts" of interviewing, sample interview questions, and more. We also deal with some of the unique problems faced by those jobseekers who are currently employed, those who have lost a job, and college students conducting their first job search.

Resumes and Cover Letters

The approach you take to writing your resume and cover letter can often mean the difference between getting an interview and never being noticed. In this section, we discuss different formats, as well as what to put on (and what to leave off) your resume. We review the benefits and drawbacks of professional resume writers, and the importance of a follow-up letter. Also included in this section are sample resumes and cover letters which you can use as models.

CD-ROM Job Search

Jobseekers who are looking for an edge against the competition may want to check out these CD-ROM products.

The Employer Listings

Employers are listed alphabetically by industry, and within each industry, by company names. When a company does business under a person's name, like "John Smith & Co.," the company is usually listed by the surname's spelling (in this case "S"). Exceptions occur when a company's name is widely recognized, like "JCPenney" or "Howard Johnson Motor Lodge." In those cases, the company's first name is the key ("J" and "H" respectively).

The Indiana JobBank covers a very wide range of industries. Each company profile is assigned to one of the industry chapters listed below.

Accounting and Management Consulting
Advertising, Marketing, and Public Relations
Aerospace
Apparel, Fashion, and Textiles
Architecture, Construction, and Engineering
Arts and Entertainment/Recreation
Automotive
Banking/Savings and Loans
Biotechnology, Pharmaceuticals, and Scientific R&D
Business Services and Non-Scientific Research
Charities and Social Services
Chemicals/Rubber and Plastics
Communications: Telecommunications and Broadcasting
Computer Hardware, Software, and Services
Educational Services
Electronic/Industrial Electrical Equipment
Environmental and Waste Management Services
Fabricated/Primary Metals and Products
Financial Services
Food and Beverages/Agriculture
Government
Health Care: Services, Equipment, and Products
Hotels and Restaurants
Insurance
Legal Services
Manufacturing: Miscellaneous Consumer
Manufacturing: Miscellaneous Industrial
Mining/Gas/Petroleum/Energy Related
Paper and Wood Products
Printing and Publishing
Real Estate
Retail
Stone, Clay, Glass, and Concrete Products
Transportation/Travel
Utilities: Electric/Gas/Water
Miscellaneous Wholesaling

Many of the company listings offer detailed company profiles. In addition to company names, addresses, and phone numbers, these listings also include contact names or hiring departments, and descriptions of each company's products and/or services. Many of these listings also feature a variety of additional information including:

Common positions - A list of job titles that the company commonly fills when it is hiring, organized in alphabetical order from Accountant to X-ray Technician. Note: Keep in mind that *The Indiana JobBank* is a directory of major employers in the area, not a directory of openings currently available. Many of the companies listed will be hiring, others will not. However, since most professional job openings are filled without the placement of help-wanted ads, contacting the employers in this book directly is still a more effective method than browsing the Sunday papers.

Educational backgrounds sought - A list of educational backgrounds that companies seek when hiring.

Benefits - What kind of benefits packages are available from these employers? Here you'll find a broad range of benefits, from the relatively common (medical insurance) to those that are much more rare (health club membership; child daycare assistance).

Special programs - Does the company offer training programs, internships, or apprenticeships? These programs can be important to first time jobseekers and college students looking for practical work experience. Many employer profiles will include information on these programs.

Parent company - If an employer is a subsidiary of a larger company, the name of that parent company will often be listed here. Use this information to supplement your company research before contacting the employer.

Number of employees - The number of workers a company employs.

Company listings may also include information on other U.S. locations and any stock exchanges the firm may be listed on.

Because so many job openings are with small and mid-sized employers, we've also included the addresses and phone numbers of such employers. While none of these listings include any additional hiring information, many of them do offer rewarding career opportunities. These companies are found under each industry heading. Within each industry, they are organized by the type of product or service offered.

A note on all employer listings that appear in *The Indiana JobBank*: This book is intended as a starting point. It is not intended to replace any effort that you, the jobseeker, should devote to your job hunt. Keep in mind that while a great deal of effort has been put into collecting and verifying the company profiles provided in this book, addresses and contact names change regularly. Inevitably, some contact names listed herein have changed even before you read this. We recommend you contact a company before mailing your resume to ensure nothing has changed.

At the end of each industry section, we have included a directory of other industry-specific resources to help you in your job search. These include: professional and industrial associations, many of which can provide employment advice and job-search help; magazines that cover the industry; and additional directories that may supplement the employer listings in this book.

Employment Services

Immediately following the employer listings section of this book are listings of local employment services firms. Many jobseekers supplement their own efforts by contracting "temp" services, headhunters, and other employment search firms to generate potential job opportunities.

This section is a comprehensive listing of such firms, arranged alphabetically under the headings Temporary Employment Agencies, Permanent Employment Agencies, and Executive Search Firms. Each listing includes the firm's name, address, telephone number, and contact person. Most listings also include the industries the firm specializes in, the type of positions commonly filled, and the number of jobs filled annually.

Index

The Indiana JobBank index is a straight alphabetical listing.

THE JOB SEARCH

THE BASICS OF JOB WINNING: A CONDENSED REVIEW

This chapter is divided into four sections. The first section explains the fundamentals that every jobseeker should know, especially first-time jobseekers. The following three sections deal with special situations faced by specific types of jobseekers: those who are currently employed, those who have lost a job, and college students.

THE BASICS:
Things Everyone Needs to Know

Career Planning

The first step to finding your ideal job is to clearly define your objectives. This is better known as career planning (or life planning if you wish to emphasize the importance of combining the two). Career planning has become a field of study in and of itself.

If you are thinking of choosing or switching careers, we particularly emphasize two things. First, choose a career where you will enjoy most of the day-to-day tasks. This sounds obvious, but most of us have at one point or another been attracted by a glamour industry or a prestigious job title without thinking of the most important consideration: Would we enjoy performing the everyday tasks the position entails?

The second key consideration is that you are not merely choosing a career, but also a lifestyle. Career counselors indicate that one of the most common problems people encounter in job-seeking is that they fail to consider how well-suited they are for a particular position or career. For example, some people, attracted to management consulting by good salaries, early responsibility, and high-level corporate exposure, do not adapt well to the long hours, heavy travel demands, and constant pressure to produce. Be sure to ask yourself how you might adapt to not only the day-to-day duties and working environment that a specific position entails, but also how you might adapt to the demands of that career or industry choice as a whole.

Choosing Your Strategy

Assuming that you've established your career objectives, the next step of the job search is to develop a strategy. If you don't take the time to develop a strategy and lay out a plan, you may find yourself going in circles after several weeks of randomly searching for opportunities that always seem just beyond your reach.

The most common job-seeking techniques are:

- following up on help-wanted advertisements
- using employment services
- relying on personal contacts
- contacting employers directly (the Direct Contact method)

Many professionals have been successful in finding better jobs using each one of these approaches. However, the Direct Contact method boasts twice the success rate of the others. So unless you have specific reasons to believe that other strategies would work best for you, Direct Contact should form the foundation of your job search.

If you prefer to use other methods as well, try to expend at least half your effort on Direct Contact, spending the rest on all of the other methods combined. Millions of other jobseekers have already proven that Direct Contact has been twice as effective in obtaining employment, so why not benefit from their experience?

Setting Your Schedule

With your strategy in mind, the next step is to work out the details of your search. The most important detail is setting up a schedule. Of course, since job searches aren't something most people do regularly, it may be hard to estimate how long each step will take. Nonetheless, it is important to have a plan so that you can monitor your progress.

When outlining your job search schedule, have a realistic time frame in mind. If you will be job-searching full-time, your search could take at least two months or more. If you can only devote part-time effort, it will probably take at least four months.

You probably know a few currently employed people who seem to spend their whole lives searching for a better job in their spare time. Don't be one of them. If you are presently working and don't feel like devoting a lot of energy to job-seeking right now, then wait. Focus on enjoying your present position, performing your best on the job, and storing up energy for when you are really ready to begin your job search.

The first step in beginning your job search is to clearly define your objectives.

Those of you who are currently unemployed should remember that job-hunting is tough work physically and emotionally. It is also intellectually demanding work that requires you to be at your best. So don't tire yourself out by working on your job campaign around the clock. At the same time, be sure to discipline yourself. The most logical way to manage your time while looking for a job is to keep your regular working hours.

If you are searching full-time and have decided to choose several different contact methods, we recommend that you divide up each week, designating some time for each method. By trying several approaches at once, you can evaluate how promising each seems and alter your schedule accordingly. But be careful -- don't judge the success of a particular technique just by the sheer number of interviews you obtain. Positions advertised in the newspaper, for instance, are likely to generate many more interviews per opening than positions that are filled without being advertised.

If you are searching part-time and decide to try several different contact methods, we recommend that you try them sequentially. You simply won't have enough time to put a meaningful amount of effort into more than one method at once. Estimate the length of your job search, and then allocate so many weeks or months for each contact method, beginning with Direct Contact.

And remember that all schedules are meant to be broken. The purpose of setting a schedule is not to rush you to your goal but to help you periodically evaluate how you're progressing.

The Direct Contact Method

Once you have scheduled your time, you are ready to begin your search in earnest. If you decide to begin with the Direct Contact method, the first step is to develop a checklist for categorizing the types of firms for which you'd like to work. You might categorize firms by product line, size, customer type (such as industrial or consumer), growth prospects, or geographical location. Your list of important criteria might be very short. If it is, good! The shorter it is, the easier it will be to locate a company that is right for you.

Now you will want to use this *JobBank* book to assemble your list of potential employers. Choose firms where *you* are most likely to be able to find a job. Try matching your skills with those that a specific job demands. Consider where your skills might be in demand, the degree of competition for employment, and the employment outlook at each company.

Separate your prospect list into three groups. The first 25 percent will be your primary target group, the next 25 percent will be your secondary group, and the remaining names you can keep in reserve.

After you form your prospect list, begin work on your resume. Refer to the Resumes and Cover Letters section following this chapter to get ideas.

Once your resume is complete, begin researching your first batch of prospective employers. You will want to determine whether you would be happy working at the firms you are researching and to get a better idea of what their employment needs might be. You also need to obtain enough information to sound highly informed about the company during phone conversations and in mail correspondence. But don't go all out on your research yet! You probably won't be able to arrange interviews with some of these firms, so save your big research effort until you start to arrange interviews. Nevertheless, you should plan to spend several hours researching each firm. Do your research in batches to save time and energy. Start with this book, and find out what you can about each of the firms in your primary target group. Contact any pertinent professional associations that may be able to help you learn more about an employer. Read industry

The more you know about a company, the more likely you are to catch an interviewer's eye. (You'll also face fewer surprises once you get the job!)

publications looking for articles on the firm. (Addresses of associations and names of important publications are listed after each industrial section of employer listings in this book.) Then try additional resources at your local library. Keep organized, and maintain a folder on each firm.

If you discover something that really disturbs you about the firm (they are about to close their only local office), or if you discover that your chances of getting a job there are practically nil (they have just instituted a hiring freeze), then cross them off your prospect list. If possible, supplement your research efforts by contacting individuals who know the firm well. Ideally you should make an informal contact with someone at that particular firm, but often a direct competitor, or a major supplier or customer, will be able to supply you with just as much information. At the very least, try to obtain whatever printed information the company has available -- not just annual reports, but product brochures and any other printed materials that the firm may have to offer, either about its operations or about career opportunities.

DEVELOPING YOUR CONTACTS: NETWORKING

Some career counselors feel that the best route to a better job is through somebody you already know or through somebody to whom you can be introduced. These counselors recommend that you build your contact base beyond your current acquaintances by asking each one to introduce you, or refer you, to additional people in your field of interest.

The theory goes like this: You might start with 15 personal contacts, each of whom introduces you to three additional people, for a total of 45 additional contacts. Then each of these people introduces you to three additional people, which adds 135 additional contacts. Theoretically, you will soon know every person in the industry.

Of course, developing your personal contacts does not work quite as smoothly as the theory suggests because some people will not be able to introduce you to anyone. The further you stray from your initial contact base, the weaker your references may be. So, if you do try developing your own contacts, try to begin with as many people that you know personally as you can. Dig into your personal phone book and your holiday greeting card list and locate old classmates from school. Be particularly sure to approach people who perform your personal business such as your lawyer, accountant, banker, doctor, stockbroker, and insurance agent. These people develop a very broad contact base due to the nature of their professions.

Getting the Interview

Now it is time to arrange an interview, time to make the Direct Contact. If you have read many books on job-searching, you may have noticed that most of these books tell you to avoid the personnel office like the plague. It is said that the personnel office never hires people; they screen candidates. Unfortunately, this is often the case. If you can identify the appropriate manager with the authority to hire you, you should try to contact that person directly. However, this will take a lot of time in each case, and often you'll be bounced back to personnel despite your efforts. So we suggest that initially you begin your Direct Contact campaign through personnel offices. If it seems that the firms on your prospect list do little hiring through personnel, you might consider some alternative courses of action.

The three obvious means of initiating Direct Contact are:

- Showing up unannounced
- Mail (postal or electronic)
- Phone calls

Cross out the first one right away. You should never show up to seek a professional position without an appointment. Even if you are somehow lucky enough to obtain an interview, you will appear so unprofessional that you will not be seriously considered.

Mail contact seems to be a good choice if you have not been in the job market for a while. You can take your time to prepare a letter, say exactly what you want, and of course include your resume. Remember that employers receive many resumes every day. Don't be surprised if you do not get a response to your inquiry, and don't spend weeks waiting for responses that may never come. If you do send a letter, follow it up (or precede it) with a phone call. This will increase your impact, and because of the initial research you did, will underscore both your familiarity with and your interest in the firm.

Another alternative is to make a "cover call." Your cover call should be just like your cover letter: concise. Your first statement should interest the employer in you. Then try to subtly mention your familiarity with the firm. Don't be overbearing; keep your introduction to three sentences or less. Be pleasant, self-confident, and relaxed. This will greatly increase the chances of the person at the other end of the line developing the conversation. But don't press. If you are asked to follow up with "something in the mail," this signals the conversation's natural end. Don't try to prolong the conversation once it has ended, and don't ask what they want to receive in the mail. Always send your resume and a highly personalized follow-up letter, reminding the addressee of the phone conversation. *Always* include a cover letter if you are asked to send a resume.

Always include a cover letter if you are asked to send a resume.

Unless you are in telephone sales, making smooth and relaxed cover calls will probably not come easily. Practice them on your own, and then with your friends or relatives.

If you obtain an interview as a result of a telephone conversation, be sure to send a thank-you note reiterating the points you made during the

DON'T BOTHER WITH MASS MAILINGS OR BARRAGES OF PHONE CALLS

Direct Contact does not mean burying every firm within a hundred miles with mail and phone calls. Mass mailings rarely work in the job hunt. This also applies to those letters that are personalized -- but dehumanized -- on an automatic typewriter or computer. Don't waste your time or money on such a project; you will fool no one but yourself.

The worst part of sending out mass mailings, or making unplanned phone calls to companies you have not researched, is that you are likely to be remembered as someone with little genuine interest in the firm, who lacks sincerity -- somebody that nobody wants to hire.

HELP WANTED ADVERTISEMENTS

Only a small fraction of professional job openings are advertised. Yet the majority of jobseekers -- and quite a few people not in the job market -- spend a lot of time studying the help wanted ads. As a result, the competition for advertised openings is often very severe.

A moderate-sized employer told us about their experience advertising in the help wanted section of a major Sunday newspaper:

It was a disaster. We had over 500 responses from this relatively small ad in just one week. We have only two phone lines in this office and one was totally knocked out. We'll never advertise for professional help again.

If you insist on following up on help wanted ads, then research a firm before you reply to an ad. Preliminary research might help to separate you from all of the other professionals responding to that ad, many of whom will have only a passing interest in the opportunity. It will also give you insight about a particular firm, to help you determine if it is potentially a good match. That said, your chances of obtaining a job through the want ads are still much smaller than they are with the Direct Contact method.

conversation. You will appear more professional and increase your impact. However, unless specifically requested, don't mail your resume once an interview has been arranged. Take it with you to the interview instead.

Preparing for the Interview

Once the interview has been arranged, begin your in-depth research. You should arrive at an interview knowing the company upside-down and inside-out. You need to know the company's products, types of customers, subsidiaries, parent company, principal locations, rank in the industry, sales and profit trends, type of ownership, size, current plans, and much more. By this time you have probably narrowed your job search to one industry. Even if you haven't, you should still be familiar with the trends in the firm's industry, the firm's principal competitors and their relative performance, and the direction in which the industry leaders are headed.

Dig into every resource you can! Read the company literature, the trade press, the business press, and if the company is public, call your stockbroker (if you have one) and ask for additional information. If possible, speak to someone at the firm before the interview, or if not, speak to someone at a competing firm. The more time you spend, the better. Even if you feel extremely pressed for time, you should set aside several hours for pre-interview research.

> **You should arrive at an interview knowing the company upside-down and inside-out.**

If you have been out of the job market for some time, don't be surprised if you find yourself tense during your first few interviews. It will probably happen every time you re-enter the market, not just when you seek your first job after getting out of school.

Tension is natural during an interview, but knowing you have done a thorough research job should put you more at ease. Make a list of questions that you think might be asked in each interview. Think out your answers carefully and practice them with a friend. Tape record your responses to the problem questions. If you feel particularly unsure of your interviewing skills, arrange your first interviews at firms you are not as interested in. (But remember it is common courtesy to seem enthusiastic about the possibility of working for any firm at which you interview.) Practice again on your own after these first few interviews. Go over the difficult questions that you were asked.

Interview Attire

How important is the proper dress for a job interview? Buying a complete wardrobe of Brooks Brothers pinstripes or Donna Karan suits, donning new wing tips or pumps, and having your hair styled every morning are not enough to guarantee you a career position as an investment banker. But on the other hand, if you can't find a clean, conservative suit or won't take the time to wash your hair, then you are just wasting your time by interviewing at all.

Top personal grooming is as important as finding appropriate clothes for a job interview. Careful grooming indicates both a sense of thoroughness and self-confidence. This is not the time to make a statement -- take out the extra earrings and avoid any garish hair colors not found in nature. Women should not wear excessive makeup, and both men and women should refrain from wearing any perfume or cologne (it only takes a small spritz to leave an allergic interviewer with a fit of sneezing and a bad impression of your meeting). Men should be freshly shaven, even if the interview is late in the day, and men with long hair should have it pulled back and neat.

Men applying for any professional position should wear a suit, preferably in a conservative color such as navy or charcoal gray. It is easy to get away with wearing the same dark suit to consecutive interviews at the same company; just be sure to wear a different shirt and tie for each interview.

Women should also wear a businesslike suit. Professionalism still dictates a suit with a skirt, rather than slacks, as proper interview garb for women. This is usually true even at companies where pants are acceptable attire for female employees. As much as you may disagree with this guideline, the more prudent time to fight this standard is after you land the job.

SKIRT VS. PANTS:
An Interview Dilemma

For those women who are still convinced that pants are acceptable interview attire, listen to the words of one career counselor from a prestigious New England college:

I had a student who told me that since she knew women in her industry often wore pants to work, she was going to wear pants to her interviews. Almost every recruiter commented that her pants were "too casual," and even referred to her as "the one with the pants." The funny thing was that one of the recruiters who commented on her pants had been wearing jeans!

The final selection of candidates for a job opening won't be determined by dress, of course. However, inappropriate dress can quickly eliminate a first-round candidate. So while you shouldn't spend a fortune on a new wardrobe, you should be sure that your clothes are adequate. The key is to dress at least as formally or slightly more formally and more conservatively than the position would suggest.

What to Bring

Be complete. Everyone needs a watch, a pen, and a notepad. Finally, a briefcase or a leather-bound folder (containing extra, *unfolded*, copies of your resume) will help complete the look of professionalism.

Sometimes the interviewer will be running behind schedule. Don't be upset, be sympathetic. There is often pressure to interview a lot of candidates and to quickly fill a demanding position. So be sure to come to your interview with good reading material to keep yourself occupied and relaxed.

The Interview

The very beginning of the interview is the most important part because it determines the tone for the rest of it. Those first few moments are especially crucial. Do you smile when you meet? Do you establish enough eye contact, but not too much? Do you walk into the office with a self-assured and confident stride? Do you shake hands firmly? Do you

BE PREPARED:
Some Common Interview Questions

Tell me about yourself...

Why did you leave your last job?

What excites you in your current job?

Where would you like to be in five years?

How much overtime are you willing to work?

What would your previous/present employer tell me about you?

Tell me about a difficult situation that you faced at your previous/present job.

What are your greatest strengths?

What are your greatest weaknesses?

Describe a work situation where you took initiative and went beyond your normal responsibilities.

Why do you wish to work for this firm?

Why should we hire you?

make small talk easily without being garrulous? It is human nature to judge people by that first impression, so make sure it is a good one. But most of all, try to be yourself.

Often the interviewer will begin, after the small talk, by telling you about the company, the division, the department, or perhaps, the position. Because of your detailed research, the information about the company should be repetitive for you, and the interviewer would probably like nothing better than to avoid this regurgitation of the company biography. So if you can do so tactfully, indicate to the interviewer that you are very familiar with the firm. If he or she seems intent on providing you with background information, despite your hints, then acquiesce.

But be sure to remain attentive. If you can manage to generate a brief discussion of the company or the industry at this point, without being forceful, great. It will help to further build rapport, underscore your interest, and increase your impact.

> **The interviewer's job is to find a reason to turn you down; your job is to not provide that reason.**
>
> -John L. LaFevre, author, *How You Really Get Hired*
>
> Reprinted from the 1989/90 *CPC Annual,* with permission of the National Association of Colleges and Employers (formerly College Placement Council, Inc.), copyright holder.

Soon (if it didn't begin that way) the interviewer will begin the questions, many of which you will have already practiced. This period of the interview usually falls into one of two categories (or somewhere in between): either a structured interview, where the interviewer has a prescribed set of questions to ask; or an unstructured interview, where the interviewer will ask only leading questions to get you to talk about yourself, your experiences, and your goals. Try to sense as quickly as possible in which direction the interviewer wishes to proceed. This will make the interviewer feel more relaxed and in control of the situation.

Remember to keep attuned to the interviewer and make the length of your answers appropriate to the situation. If you are really unsure as to how detailed a response the interviewer is seeking, then ask.

As the interview progresses, the interviewer will probably mention some of the most important responsibilities of the position. If applicable, draw parallels between your experience and the demands of the position as detailed by the interviewer. Describe your past experience in the same manner that you do on your resume: emphasizing results and achievements and not merely describing activities. But don't exaggerate. Be on the level about your abilities.

The first interview is often the toughest, where many candidates are screened out. If you are interviewing for a very competitive position, you will have to make an impression that will last. Focus on a few of your greatest strengths that are relevant to the position. Develop these points carefully, state them again in different words, and then try to summarize them briefly at the end of the interview.

Often the interviewer will pause toward the end and ask if you have any questions. Particularly in a structured interview, this might be the one chance to really show your knowledge of and interest in the firm. Have a list prepared of specific questions that are of real interest to you. Let your questions subtly show your research and your knowledge of the firm's activities. It is wise to have an extensive list of questions, as several of them may be answered during the interview.

Getting a job offer is a lot like getting a marriage proposal. Someone is not going to offer it unless they're pretty sure you're going to accept it.

-Marilyn Hill,
Associate Director,
Career Center,
Carleton College

Do not turn your opportunity to ask questions into an interrogation. Avoid reading directly from your list of questions, and ask questions that you are fairly certain the interviewer can answer (remember how you feel when you cannot answer a question during an interview).

Even if you are unable to determine the salary range beforehand, do not ask about it during the first interview. You can always ask about it later. Above all, don't ask about fringe benefits until you have been offered a position. (Then be sure to get all the details.)

Try not to be negative about anything during the interview (particularly any past employer or any previous job). Be cheerful. Everyone likes to work with someone who seems to be happy.

Don't let a tough question throw you off base. If you don't know the answer to a question, simply say so -- do not apologize. Just smile. Nobody can answer every question -- particularly some of the questions that are asked in job interviews.

Before your first interview, you may be able to determine how many rounds of interviews there usually are for positions at your level. (Of course it may differ quite a bit even within the different levels of one firm.) Usually you can count on attending at least two or three interviews, although some firms are known to give a minimum of six interviews for all professional positions. While you should be more relaxed as you return for subsequent interviews, the pressure will be on. The more prepared you are, the better.

Depending on what information you are able to obtain, you might want to vary your strategy quite a bit from interview to interview. For instance, if the first interview is a screening interview, then be sure a few of your strengths really stand out. On the other hand, if later interviews are primarily with people who are in a position to veto your hiring, but not to push it forward, then you should primarily focus on building rapport as opposed to reiterating and developing your key strengths.

If it looks as though your skills and background do not match the position the interviewer was hoping to fill, ask him or her if there is another division or subsidiary that perhaps could profit from your talents.

After the Interview

Write a follow-up letter immediately after the interview, while it is still fresh in the interviewer's mind (see the sample follow-up letter format found in the Resumes and Cover Letters chapter). Then, if you haven't heard from the interviewer within a week, call to stress your continued interest in the firm, and the position, and request a second interview.

THE BALANCING ACT:

Looking for a New Job While Currently Employed

For those of you who are still employed, job-searching will be particularly tiring because it must be done in addition to your normal work responsibilities. So don't overwork yourself to the point where you show up to interviews looking exhausted and start to slip behind at your current job. On the other hand, don't be tempted to quit your present job! The long hours are worth it. Searching for a job while you have one puts you in a position of strength.

Making Contact

If you're expected to be in your office during the business day, then you have additional problems to deal with. How can you work interviews into the business day? And if you work in an open office, how can you even call to set up interviews? As much as possible you should keep up the effort and the appearances on your present job. So maximize your use of the lunch hour, early mornings, and late afternoons for calling. If you keep trying, you'll be surprised how often you will be able to reach the executive you are trying to contact during your out-of-office hours. You can catch people as early as 8 a.m. and as late as 6 p.m. on frequent occasions.

Scheduling Interviews

Your inability to interview at any time other than lunch just might work to your advantage. If you can, try to set up as many interviews as possible for your lunch hour. This will go a long way to creating a relaxed atmosphere. But be sure the interviews don't stray too far from the agenda on hand.

Lunchtime interviews are much easier to obtain if you have substantial career experience. People with less experience will often find no alternative to taking time off for interviews. If you have to take time off, you have to take time off. But try to do this as little as possible. Try to take the whole day off in order to avoid being blatantly obvious about your job search, and try to schedule two to three interviews for the same day. (It is very difficult to maintain an optimum level of energy at more than three interviews in one day.) Explain to the interviewer why you might have to juggle your interview schedule -- he/she should honor the respect you're

> **Try calling as early as 8 a.m. and as late as 6 p.m. You'll be surprised how often you will be able to reach the executive you want during these times of the day.**

showing your current employer by minimizing your days off and will probably appreciate the fact that another prospective employer is interested in you.

References What do you tell an interviewer who asks for references? Just say that while you are happy to have your former employers contacted, you are trying to keep your job search confidential and would rather that your current employer not be contacted until you have been given a firm offer.

IF YOU'RE FIRED OR LAID OFF:

Picking Yourself Up and Dusting Yourself Off

If you've been fired or laid off, you are not the first and will not be the last to go through this traumatic experience. In today's changing economy, thousands of professionals lose their jobs every year. Even if you were terminated with just cause, do not lose heart. Remember, being fired is not a reflection on you as a person. It is usually a reflection of your company's staffing needs and its perception of your recent job performance and attitude. And if you were not performing up to par or enjoying your work, then you will probably be better off at another company anyway.

Be prepared for the question "Why were you fired?" during job interviews.

A thorough job search could take months, so be sure to negotiate a reasonable severance package, if possible, and determine what benefits, such as health insurance, you are still legally entitled to. Also, register for unemployment compensation immediately. Don't be surprised to find other professionals collecting unemployment compensation -- it is for everyone who has lost their job.

Don't start your job search with a flurry of unplanned activity. Start by choosing a strategy and working out a plan. Now is not the time for major changes in your life. If possible, remain in the same career and in the same geographical location, at least until you have been working again for a while. On the other hand, if the only industry for which you are trained is leaving, or is severely depressed in your area, then you should give prompt consideration to moving or switching careers.

Avoid mentioning you were fired when arranging interviews, but be prepared for the question "Why were you fired?" during an interview. If you were laid off as a result of downsizing, briefly explain, being sure to reinforce that your job loss was not due to performance. If you were in fact fired, be honest, but try to detail the reason as favorably as possible and portray what you have learned from your mistakes. If you are confident one of your past managers will give you a good reference, tell the interviewer to contact that person. Do not to speak negatively of your past employer and try not to sound particularly worried about your status of being temporarily unemployed.

Finally, don't spend too much time reflecting on why you were let go or how you might have avoided it. Think positively, look to the future, and be sure to follow a careful plan during your job search.

THE COLLEGE STUDENT:
How to Conduct Your First Job Search

While you will be able to apply many of the basics covered earlier in this chapter to your job search, there are some situations unique to the college student's job search.

Gaining Experience

Perhaps the biggest problem college students face is lack of experience. Many schools have internship programs designed to give students exposure to the field of their choice, as well as the opportunity to make valuable contacts. Check out your school's career services department to see what internships are available. If your school does not have a formal internship program, or if there are no available internships that appeal to you, try contacting local businesses and offering your services -- often, businesses will be more than willing to have any extra pair of hands (especially if those hands are unpaid!) for a day or two each week. Or try contacting school alumni to see if you can "shadow" them for a few days, and see what their day-to-day duties are like. Either way, try to begin building experience as early as possible in your college career.

What do you do if, for whatever reason, you weren't able to get experience directly related to your desired career? First, look at your previous jobs and see if there's anything you can highlight. Did you supervise or train other employees? Did you reorganize the accounting system, or boost productivity in some way? Accomplishments like these demonstrate leadership, responsibility, and innovation -- qualities that most companies look for in employees. And don't forget volunteer activities and school clubs, which can also showcase these traits.

THE GPA QUESTION

You are interviewing for the job of your dreams. Everything is going well: You've established a good rapport, the interviewer seems impressed with your qualifications, and you're almost positive the job is yours. Then you're asked about your GPA, which is pitifully low. Do you tell the truth and watch your dream job fly out the window?

Never lie about your GPA (they may request your transcript, and no company will hire a liar). You can, however, explain if there is a reason you don't feel your grades reflect your abilities, and mention any other impressive statistics. For example, if you have a high GPA in your major, or in the last few semesters (as opposed to your cumulative college career), you can use that fact to your advantage.

On-Campus Recruiting

Companies will often send recruiters to interview on-site at various colleges. This gives students a chance to get interviews at companies that may not have interviewed them otherwise, particularly if the company schedules "open" interviews, in which the only screening process is who is first in line at the sign-ups. Of course, since many more applicants gain interviews in this format, this also means that many more people are rejected. The on-campus interview is generally a screening interview, to see if it is worth the company's time to invite you in for a second interview. So do everything possible to make yourself stand out from the crowd.

The first step, of course, is to check out any and all information your school's career center has on the company. If the information seems out of date, call the company's headquarters and ask to be sent the latest annual report, or any other printed information.

Many companies will host an informational meeting for interviewees, often the evening before interviews are scheduled to take place. DO NOT MISS THIS MEETING. The recruiter will almost certainly ask if you attended. Make an effort to stay after the meeting and talk with the company's representatives. Not only does this give you an opportunity to find out more information about both the company and the position, it also makes you stand out in the recruiter's mind. If there's a particular company that you had your heart set on, but you weren't able to get an interview with them, attend the information session anyway. You may be able to convince the recruiter to squeeze you into the schedule. (Or you may discover that the company really isn't suited for you after all.)

Try to check out the interview site beforehand. Some colleges may conduct "mock" interviews that take place in one of the standard interview rooms. Or you may be able to convince a career counselor (or even a custodian) to let you sneak a peek during off-hours. Either way, having an idea of the room's setup will help you to mentally prepare.

Be sure to be at least 15 minutes early to the interview. The recruiter may be running ahead of schedule, and might like to take you early. But don't be surprised if previous interviews have run over, resulting in your 30-minute slot being reduced to 20 minutes (or less). Don't complain; just use whatever time you do have as efficiently as possible to showcase the reasons *you* are the ideal candidate.

LAST WORDS

A parting word of advice. Again and again during your job search you will be rejected. You will be rejected when you apply for interviews. You will be rejected after interviews. For every job offer you finally receive, you probably will have been rejected a multitude of times. Don't let rejections slow you down. Keep reminding yourself that the sooner you go out and get started on your job search, and get those rejections flowing in, the closer you will be to obtaining the job you want.

RESUMES AND COVER LETTERS

When filling a position, a recruiter will often have 100-plus applicants, but time to interview only a handful of the most promising ones. As a result, he or she will reject most applicants after only briefly skimming their resumes.

Unless you have phoned and talked to the recruiter -- which you should do whenever you can -- you will be chosen or rejected for an interview entirely on the basis of your resume and cover letter. Your cover letter must catch the recruiter's attention, and your resume must hold it. (But remember -- a resume is no substitute for a job search campaign. *You* must seek a job. Your resume is only one tool.)

RESUME FORMAT:
Mechanics of a First Impression

The Basics

Recruiters dislike long resumes, so unless you have an unusually strong background with many years of experience and a diversity of outstanding achievements, keep your resume length to one page. If you must squeeze in more information than would otherwise fit, try using a smaller typeface or changing the margins.

Keep your resume on standard 8-1/2" x 11" paper. Since recruiters often get resumes in batches of hundreds, a smaller-sized resume may get lost in the pile. Oversized resumes are likely to get crumpled at the edges, and won't fit easily in their files.

First impressions matter, so make sure the recruiter's first impression of your resume is a good one. Print your resume on quality paper that has weight and texture, in a conservative color such as white, ivory, or pale gray. Use matching paper and envelopes for both your resume and cover letter.

Getting it on Paper

Modern photocomposition typesetting gives you the clearest, sharpest image, a wide variety of type styles, and effects such as italics, bold-facing, and book-like justified margins. It is also much too expensive for many jobseekers. And improvements in laser printers mean that a computer-generated resume can look just as impressive as one that has been professionally typeset.

A computer or word processor is the most flexible way to type your resume. This will allow you to make changes almost instantly and to store different drafts on disk. Word processing and desktop publishing systems also offer many different fonts to choose from, each taking up different amounts of space. (It is generally best to stay between 9-point and 12-point font size.) Many other options are also available, such as bold-facing for emphasis, justified margins, and the ability to change and manipulate spacing.

The end result, however, will be largely determined by the quality of the printer you use. You need at least "letter quality" type for your resume. Do not use a "near letter quality" or dot matrix printer. Laser printers will generally provide the best quality.

Household typewriters and office typewriters with nylon or other cloth ribbons are *not* good enough for typing your resume. If you don't have access to a quality word processor, hire a professional who can prepare your resume with a word processor or typesetting machine.

Don't make your copies on an office photocopier. Only the personnel office may see the resume you mail. Everyone else may see only a copy of it, and copies of copies quickly become unreadable. Either print out each copy individually, or take your resume to a professional copy shop, which will generally offer professionally-maintained, extra-high-quality photocopiers and charge fairly reasonable prices.

Proof with Care

Whether you typed it yourself or paid to have it produced professionally, mistakes on resumes are not only embarrassing, but will usually remove you from further consideration (particularly if something obvious such as your name is misspelled). No matter how much you paid someone else to type, write, or typeset your resume, *you* lose if there is a mistake. So proofread it as carefully as possible. Get a friend to help you. Read your draft aloud as your friend checks the proof copy. Then have your friend read aloud while you check. Next, read it letter by letter to check spelling and punctuation.

If you are having it typed or typeset by a resume service or a printer, and you can't bring a friend or take the time during the day to proof it, pay for it and take it home. Proof it there and bring it back later to get it corrected and printed.

> **The one piece of advice I give to everyone about their resume is: Show it to people, show it to people, show it to people. Before you ever send out a resume, show it to at least a dozen people.**
>
> -Cate Talbot Ashton,
> Associate Director,
> Career Services,
> Colby College

If you wrote your resume on a word processing program, also use that program's built-in spell checker to double-check for spelling errors. But keep in mind that a spell checker will not find errors such as "to" for "two" or "wok" for "work." It's important that you still proofread your resume, even after it has been spell-checked.

Types of Resumes

The two most common resume formats are the functional resume and the chronological resume (examples of both types can be found at the end of this chapter). A functional resume focuses on skills and de-emphasizes job titles, employers, etc. A functional resume is best if you have been out of the work force for a long time and/or if you want to highlight specific skills and strengths that your most recent jobs don't necessarily reflect.

Choose a chronological format if you are currently working or were working recently, and if your most recent experiences relate to your desired field. Use reverse chronological order. To a recruiter your last job and your latest schooling are the most important, so put the last first and list the rest going back in time.

Organization

Your name, phone number, and a complete address should be at the top of your resume. Try to make your name stand out by using a slightly larger font size or all capital letters. Be sure to spell out everything -- never abbreviate St. for Street or Rd. for Road. If you are a college student, you should also put your home address and phone number at the top.

Next, list your experience, then your education. If you are a recent graduate, list your education first, unless your experience is more important than your education. (For example, if you have just graduated from a teaching school, have some business experience, and are applying for a job in business, you would list your business experience first.)

Keep everything easy to find. Put the dates of your employment and education on the left of the page. Put the names of the companies you worked for and the schools you attended a few spaces to the right of the dates. Put the city and state, or the city and country, where you studied or worked to the right of the page.

This is just one suggestion that may work for you. The important thing is simply to break up the text in some way that makes your resume visually attractive and easy to scan, so experiment to see which layout works best for your resume. However you set it up, stay consistent. Inconsistencies in fonts, spacing, or tenses will make your resume look sloppy. Also, be sure to use tabs to keep your information vertically lined up, rather than the less precise space bar.

RESUME CONTENT:
Say it with Style

Sell Yourself

You are selling your skills and accomplishments in your resume, so it is important to inventory yourself and know yourself. If you have achieved something, say so. Put it in the best possible light. But avoid subjective statements, such as "I am a hard worker" or "I get along well with my coworkers." Just stick to the facts.

While you shouldn't hold back or be modest, don't exaggerate your achievements to the point of misrepresentation. Be honest. Many companies will immediately drop an applicant from consideration (or fire a current employee) if inaccurate information is discovered on a resume or other application material.

Keep it Brief Write down the important (and pertinent) things you have done, but do it in as few words as possible. Your resume will be scanned, not read, and short, concise phrases are much more effective than long-winded sentences. Avoid the use of "I" when emphasizing your accomplishments. Instead, use brief phrases beginning with action verbs.

While some technical terms will be unavoidable, you should try to avoid excessive "technicalese." Keep in mind that the first person to see your resume may be a human resources person who won't necessarily know all the jargon -- and how can they be impressed by something they don't understand?

Also, try to keep your paragraphs at six lines or shorter. If you have more than six lines of information about one job or school, put it in two or more paragraphs. The shorter your resume is, the more carefully it will be examined. Remember: Your resume usually has between eight and 45 seconds to catch an employer's eye. So make every second count.

Job Objective A functional resume may require a job objective to give it focus. One or two sentences describing the job you are seeking can clarify in what capacity your skills will be best put to use.

Examples: An entry-level position in the publishing industry.
A challenging position requiring analytical thought and excellent writing skills.

Don't include a job objective in a chronological resume. Even if you are certain of exactly what type of job you desire, the presence of a job objective might eliminate you from consideration for other positions that a recruiter feels are a better match for your qualifications. But even though you may not put an objective on paper, having a career goal in mind as you write can help give your resume a sense of direction.

Work Experience Some jobseekers may choose to include both "Relevant Experience" and "Additional Experience" sections. This can be useful, as it allows the jobseeker to place more emphasis on certain experiences and to de-emphasize others.

Emphasize continued experience in a particular job area or continued interest in a particular industry. De-emphasize irrelevant positions. Delete positions that you held for less than four months (unless you are a very recent college grad or still in school). Stress your results, elaborating on how you contributed in your previous jobs. Did you increase sales, reduce costs, improve a product, implement a new program? Were you promoted? Use specific numbers (i.e., quantities, percentages, dollar amounts) whenever possible.

Mention all relevant responsibilities. Be specific, and slant your past accomplishments toward the position that you hope to obtain. For example, do you hope to supervise people? If so, then state how many people, performing what function, you have supervised.

Education

Keep it brief if you have more than two years of career experience. Elaborate more if you have less experience. If you are a recent grad with two or more years of college, you may choose to include any high school activities that are directly relevant to your career. If you've been out of school for awhile, list post-secondary education only.

Mention degrees received and any honors or special awards. Note individual courses or research projects you participated in that might be relevant for employers. For example, if you are an English major applying for a position as a business writer, be sure to mention any business or economics courses.

USE ACTION VERBS

How you write your resume is just as important as *what* you write. The strongest resumes use short phrases beginning with action verbs. Below are a few action verbs you may want to use. (This list is not all-inclusive.)

achieved	developed	integrated	purchased
administered	devised	interpreted	reduced
advised	directed	interviewed	regulated
analyzed	discovered	invented	reorganized
arranged	distributed	launched	represented
assembled	eliminated	maintained	researched
assisted	established	managed	resolved
attained	evaluated	marketed	restored
budgeted	examined	mediated	restructured
built	executed	monitored	revised
calculated	expanded	negotiated	scheduled
collaborated	expedited	obtained	selected
collected	facilitated	operated	served
compiled	formulated	ordered	sold
completed	founded	organized	solved
computed	generated	participated	streamlined
conducted	headed	performed	studied
consolidated	identified	planned	supervised
constructed	implemented	prepared	supplied
consulted	improved	presented	supported
controlled	increased	processed	tested
coordinated	initiated	produced	trained
created	installed	proposed	updated
designed	instituted	provided	upgraded
determined	instructed	published	wrote

Highlight Impressive Skills Be sure to mention any computer skills you may have. You may wish to include a section entitled "Additional Skills" or "Computer Skills," in which you list any software programs you know. An additional skills section is also an ideal place to mention fluency in a foreign language.

Personal Data This section is optional, but if you choose to include it, keep it very brief (two lines maximum). A one-word mention of hobbies such as fishing, chess, baseball, cooking, etc., can give the person who will interview you a good way to open up the conversation. It doesn't hurt to include activities that are unusual (fencing, bungee jumping, snake-charming) or that somehow relate to the position or the company you're applying to (for instance, if you are a member of a professional organization in your industry). Never include information about your age, health, physical characteristics, marital status, or religious affiliation.

References The most that is needed is the sentence, "References available upon request," at the bottom of your resume. If you choose to leave it out, that's fine.

HIRING A RESUME WRITER:
Is it the Right Choice for You?

If you write reasonably well, it is to your advantage to write your own resume. Writing your resume forces you to review your experience and figure out how to explain your accomplishments in clear, brief phrases. This will help you when you explain your work to interviewers.

If you write your resume, everything will be in your own words -- it will sound like you. It will say what you want it to say. If you are a good writer, know yourself well, and have a good idea of which parts of your background employers are looking for, you should be able to write your own resume better than anyone else can. If you decide to write your resume yourself, have as many people review and proofread it as possible. Welcome objective opinions and other perspectives.

> **Those things [marital status, church affiliations, etc.] have no place on a resume. Those are illegal questions, so why even put that information on your resume?**
>
> -Becky Hayes, Career Counselor
> Career Services, Rice University

When to Get Help If you have difficulty writing in "resume style" (which is quite unlike normal written language), if you are unsure of which parts of your background you should emphasize, or if you think your resume would make your case better if it did not follow one of the standard forms outlined either here or in a book on resumes, then you should consider having it professionally written.

There are two reasons even some professional resume writers we know have had their resumes written with the help of fellow professionals. First, they may need the help of someone who can be objective about their background, and second, they may want an experienced sounding board to help focus their thoughts.

If You Hire a Pro

The best way to choose a writer is by reputation -- the recommendation of a friend, a personnel director, your school placement officer, or someone else knowledgeable in the field.

Important questions:

- "How long have you been writing resumes?"
- "If I'm not satisfied with what you write, will you go over it with me and change it?"
- "Do you charge by the hour or a flat rate?"

There is no sure relation between price and quality, except that you are unlikely to get a good writer for less than $50 for an uncomplicated resume and you shouldn't have to pay more than $300 unless your experience is very extensive or complicated. There will be additional charges for printing.

Few resume services will give you a firm price over the phone, simply because some resumes are too complicated and take too long to do for a predetermined price. Some services will quote you a price that applies to almost all of their customers. Once you decide to use a specific writer, you should insist on a firm price quote before engaging their services. Also, find out how expensive minor changes will be.

COVER LETTERS:
Quick, Clear, and Concise

Always mail a cover letter with your resume. In a cover letter you can show an interest in the company that you can't show in a resume. You can also point out one or two skills or accomplishments the company can put to good use.

Make it Personal

The more personal you can get, the better. If someone known to the person you are writing has recommended that you contact the company, get permission to include his/her name in the letter. If you have the name of a person to send the letter to, address it directly to that person (after first calling the company to verify the spelling of the person's name, correct title, and mailing address). Be sure to put the person's name and title on both the letter and the envelope. This will ensure that your letter will get through to the proper person, even if a new person now occupies this position. But even if you don't have a contact name and are simply addressing it to the "Personnel Director" or the "Hiring Partner," definitely send a letter.

Type cover letters in full. Don't try the cheap and easy ways, like using a computer mail merge program, or photocopying the body of your letter and typing in the inside address and salutation. You will give the impression that you are mailing to a host of companies and have no particular interest in any one.

Cover letter do's and don'ts

- *Do* keep your cover letter brief and to the point.
- *Do* be sure it is error-free.
- *Don't* just repeat information verbatim from your resume.
- *Don't* overuse the personal pronoun "I."
- *Don't* send a generic cover letter -- show your personal knowledge of and interest in that particular company.
- *Do* accentuate what you can offer the company, not what you hope to gain from them.

FUNCTIONAL RESUME

(Prepared on a word processor and laser printed.)

ELIZABETH HELEN LaFRANCE
129 Shoreline Drive
Harbor Point OH 45822
419/555-6652

Objective

A position as a graphic designer commensurate with my acquired skills and expertise.

Summary

Extensive experience in plate making, separations, color matching, background definition, printing, mechanicals, color corrections, and personnel supervision. A highly motivated manager and effective communicator. Proven ability to:

- **Create Commercial Graphics**
- **Produce Embossed Drawings**
- **Color Separate**
- **Control Quality**
- **Resolve Printing Problems**
- **Analyze Customer Satisfaction**

Qualifications

Printing:
Knowledgeable in black and white as well as color printing. Excellent judgment in determining acceptability of color reproduction through comparison with original. Proficient at producing four- or five-color corrections on all media, as well as restyling previously reproduced four-color artwork.

Customer Relations:
Routinely work closely with customers to ensure specifications are met. Capable of striking a balance between technical printing capabilities and need for customer satisfaction through entire production process.

Specialties:
Practiced at creating silk screen overlays for a multitude of processes including velo bind, GBC bind, and perfect bind. Creative design and timely preparation of posters, flyers, and personalized stationery.

Personnel Supervision:
Skillful at fostering atmosphere that encourages highly talented artists to balance high-level creativity with maximum production. Consistently meet or beat production deadlines. Instruct new employees, apprentices, and students in both artistry and technical operations.

Experience

Graphic Arts Professor, Ohio State University, Columbus OH (1987-1993).
Manager, Design Graphics, Lima OH (1993-present).

Education

Massachusetts Conservatory of Art, Ph.D. 1987
University of Massachusetts, B.A. 1984

CHRONOLOGICAL RESUME

(Prepared on a word processor
and laser printed.)

RANDALL ELLIS
557 Pine Street
Seattle, WA 98404
(206) 555-6584

EXPERIENCE

THE CENTER COMPANY — Seattle, WA
Systems Programmer — 1993-present

- Develop and maintain over 100 assembler modules.
- Create screen manager programs, using Assembler and Natural languages, to trace input and output to the VTAM buffer.
- Install and customize Omegamon 695 and 700 on IBM mainframes.
- Develop programs to monitor complete security control blocks, using Assembler and Natural.
- Produce stand-alone IPLs and create backrests on IBM 3380 DASD.

INFO TECH, INC. — Seattle, WA
Technical Manager — 1991-1993

- Designed and managed the implementation of a network providing the legal community with a direct line to Supreme Court cases, using Clipper on IBM 386s.
- Developed a system which catalogued entire library inventory, using Turbo Pascal on IBM AT.
- Used C to create a registration system for university registrar on IBM AT.

EDUCATION

SALEM STATE UNIVERSITY — Salem, OR
B.S. in Computer Science. — 1989
M.S. in Computer Science. — 1991

COMPUTER SKILLS

- Programming Languages: C, C++, Assembler, COBOL, Natural, Turbo Pascal, dBASE III+, and Clipper.
- Software: VTAM, Complete, TSO, JES 2, ACF 2, Omegamon 695 and 700, and Adabas.
- Operating Systems: MVS/XA, MVS/SP, MS-DOS, and VMS.

FUNCTIONAL RESUME

(Prepared on an office-quality typewriter.)

MEAGHAN O'LEARY
703 Mulberry Avenue
Chicago, IL 60601
(312) 555-8841

OBJECTIVE:
To contribute over eight years of experience in promotion, communications, and administration to an entry-level position in advertising.

SUMMARY OF QUALIFICATIONS:
- Performed advertising duties for small business.
- Experience in business writing and communications skills.
- General knowledge of office management.
- Demonstrated ability to work well with others, in both supervisory and support staff roles.
- Type 75 words per minute.

SELECTED ACHIEVEMENTS AND RESULTS:

Promotion:
Composing, editing, and proofreading correspondence and PR materials for own catering service. Large-scale mailings.

Communication:
Instruction; curriculum and lesson planning; student evaluation; parent-teacher conferences; development of educational materials. Training and supervising clerks.

Computer Skills:
Proficient in MS Word, Lotus 1-2-3, Excel, and Filemaker Pro.

Administration:
Record-keeping and file maintenance. Data processing and computer operations, accounts receivable, accounts payable, inventory control, and customer relations. Scheduling, office management, and telephone reception.

WORK HISTORY:
Teacher; Self-Employed (owner of catering service); Floor Manager; Administrative Assistant; Accounting Clerk.

EDUCATION:
Beloit College, Beloit, WI, BA in Education, 1987

CHRONOLOGICAL RESUME

(Prepared on a word processor
and laser printed.)

PAUL K. NORTON
16 Charles Street
Marlborough CT 06447
203/555-9641

EDUCATION

Keene State College, Keene NH
Bachelor of Arts in Elementary Education, 1995
- Graduated *magna cum laude*
- English minor
- Kappa Delta Pi member, inducted 1993

EXPERIENCE

September 1995-Present

Elmer T. Thienes Elementary School, Marlborough CT
Part-time Kindergarten Teacher
- Instruct kindergartners in reading, spelling, language arts, and music.
- Participate in the selection of textbooks and learning aids.
- Organize and supervise class field trips and coordinate in-class presentations.

Summers 1993-1995

Keene YMCA, Youth Division, Keene NH
Child-care Counselor
- Oversaw summer program for low-income youth.
- Budgeted and coordinated special events and field trips, working with Program Director to initiate variations in the program.
- Served as Youth Advocate in cooperation with social worker to address the social needs and problems of participants.

Spring 1995

Wheelock Elementary School, Keene NH
Student Teacher
- Taught third-grade class in all elementary subjects.
- Designed and implemented a two-week unit on Native Americans.
- Assisted in revision of third-grade curriculum.

Fall 1994

Child Development Center, Keene NH
Daycare Worker
- Supervised preschool children on the playground and during art activities.
- Created a "Wishbone Corner," where children could quietly look at books or take a voluntary "time-out."

ADDITIONAL INTERESTS

Martial arts, skiing, politics, reading, writing.

GENERAL MODEL FOR A COVER LETTER

Your mailing address
Date

Contact's name
Contact's title
Company
Company's mailing address

Dear Mr./Ms. _________:

Immediately explain why your background makes you the best candidate for the position that you are applying for. Describe what prompted you to write (want ad, article you read about the company, networking contact, etc.). Keep the first paragraph short and hard-hitting.

Detail what you could contribute to this company. Show how your qualifications will benefit this firm. Describe your interest in the corporation. Subtly emphasizing your knowledge about this firm and your familiarity with the industry will set you apart from other candidates. Remember to keep this letter short; few recruiters will read a cover letter longer than half a page.

If possible, your closing paragraph should request specific action on the part of the reader. Include your phone number and the hours when you can be reached. Mention that if you do not hear from the reader by a specific date, you will follow up with a phone call. Lastly, thank the reader for their time, consideration, etc.

Sincerely,

(signature)

Your full name (typed)

Enclosure (use this if there are other materials, such as your resume, that are included in the same envelope)

SAMPLE COVER LETTER

16 Charles Street
Marlborough CT 06447
March 16, 1999

Ms. Lia Marcusson
Assistant Principal
Jonathon Daniels Elementary School
43 Mayflower Drive
Keene NH 03431

Dear Ms. Marcusson:

Janet Newell recently informed me of a possible opening for a third grade teacher at Jonathon Daniels Elementary School. With my experience instructing third-graders, both in schools and in summer programs, I feel I would be an ideal candidate for the position. Please accept this letter and the enclosed resume as my application.

Jonathon Daniels' educational philosophy that every child can learn and succeed interests me, since it mirrors my own. My current position at Elmer T. Thienes Elementary has reinforced this philosophy, heightening my awareness of the different styles and paces of learning and increasing my sensitivity toward special needs children. Furthermore, as a direct result of my student teaching experience at Wheelock Elementary School, I am comfortable, confident, and knowledgeable working with third-graders.

I look forward to discussing the position and my qualifications for it in more detail. I can be reached at 203/555-9641 evenings or 203/555-0248 weekdays. If I do not hear from you before Tuesday of next week, I will call to see if we can schedule a time to meet. Thank you for your time and consideration.

Sincerely,

Paul K Norton

Paul K. Norton

Enclosure

GENERAL MODEL FOR A FOLLOW-UP LETTER

Your mailing address
Date

Contact's name
Contact's title
Company
Company's mailing address

Dear Mr./Ms.__________:

Remind the interviewer of the reason (i.e., a specific opening, an informational interview, etc.) you were interviewed, as well as the date. Thank him/her for the interview, and try to personalize your thanks by mentioning some specific aspect of the interview.

Confirm your interest in the organization (and in the opening, if you were interviewing for a particular position). Use specifics to re-emphasize that you have researched the firm in detail and have considered how you would fit into the company and the position. This is a good time to say anything you wish you had said in the initial meeting. Be sure to keep this letter brief; a half-page is plenty.

If appropriate, close with a suggestion for further action, such as a desire to have an additional interview, if possible. Mention your phone number and the hours that you can be reached. Alternatively, you may prefer to mention that you will follow up with a phone call in several days. Once again, thank the person for meeting with you, and state that you would be happy to provide any additional information about your qualifications.

Sincerely,

(signature)

Your full name (typed)

• CD-ROM JOB SEARCH

Jobseekers who are looking for any edge they can find may want to check out the following selected CD-ROM products. Since most of these databases cost upwards of $500, and are designed for use by other businesses or libraries, don't expect to find these at your local software store. Of course, not all libraries will have all of these resources. Depending on how technologically advanced your library is, you may find only one or two of these electronic databases. Call your library to find out what electronic resources it has available. Many of these databases can also be found in the offices of career counselors or outplacement specialists, and are used as part of your service.

ADAMS JOBBANK FASTRESUME SUITE
260 Center Street
Holbrook MA 02343
800/872-5627
The CD-ROM version of the best-selling *JobBank* series contains 22,000 detailed profiles of companies in all industries, 1,800 executive search firms, and 1,100 employment agencies. For most companies, you will find the name, address, company description, and key contact name. The database also lists common professional positions and information on benefits for most companies. You can search the database by company name, state, industry, and job title. Calling itself a "total job search package," the CD-ROM also creates personalized resumes and cover letters and offers advice on job interviews, including over 100 sample interview questions and answers. *Adams JobBank FastResume Suite* CD-ROM is for Windows®98, Windows®95, and Windows®3.1.

AMERICAN BIG BUSINESS DIRECTORY
5711 South 86th Circle
P.O. Box 27347
Omaha NE 68127
800/555-5211
Provides profiles of 160,000 privately and publicly held companies employing over 100 people. The CD-ROM contains company descriptions which include company type, industry, products, and sales information. Also included are contact names for each company, with a total of over 340,000. You can search the database by industry, SIC code, sales volume, employee size, or zip code.

AMERICAN MANUFACTURER'S DIRECTORY
5711 South 86th Circle
P.O. Box 27347
Omaha NE 68127
800/555-5211
Made by the same company that created *American Big Business Directory*, *American Manufacturer's Directory* lists over 531,000 manufacturing

companies of all sizes and industries. The directory contains product and sales information, company size, and a key contact name for each company. The user can search by region, SIC code, sales volume, employee size, or zip code.

BUSINESS U.S.A.
5711 South 86th Circle
P.O. Box 27347
Omaha NE 68127
800/555-5211
Also from the makers of *American Big Business Directory* and *American Manufacturer's Directory*, this CD-ROM contains information on 10 million U.S. companies. The profiles provide contact information, industry type, number of employees, and sales volume. Each listing also indicates whether the company is public or private, as well as providing information about the company's products. There are a number of different search methods available, including key words, SIC code, geographic location, and number of employees.

CAREER SEARCH - INTEGRATED RESOURCE SYSTEM
21 Highland Circle
Needham MA 02194-3075
617/449-0312
Career Search is a database which contains listings for over 490,000 privately and publicly held companies. It has contact information, including names of human resources professionals or other executives, for companies of virtually all sizes, types, and industries. The database can be searched by industry, company size, or region. This product is updated monthly.

COMPANIES INTERNATIONAL
835 Penobscot Building
645 Griswald Street
Detroit MI 48226
800/877-GALE
Produced by Gale Research Inc., this CD-ROM is compiled from *Ward's Business Directory* and the *World's Business Directory*, and contains information on more than 300,000 companies worldwide. You can find industry information, contact names, and number of employees. Also included is information on the company's products and revenues. The database can be searched by industry, company products, or geographic location.

CORPTECH DIRECTORY
12 Alfred Street, Suite 200
Woburn MA 01801-1915
800/333-8036
The *CorpTech Directory* on CD-ROM contains detailed descriptions of over 45,000 technology companies. It also lists the names and titles of nearly 155,000 executives -- CEOs, sales managers, R&D managers, and human resource professionals. World Wide Web and e-mail addresses are also available. In

addition to contact information, you can find detailed information about each company's products or services and annual revenues. The *CorpTech Directory* also lists both the number of current employees, and the number of employees one year ago. Some companies also list the number of employees they project having in one year. You can search the database by type of company, geographic location, or sales revenue. This product is updated quarterly.

DISCOVERING CAREERS & JOBS
835 Penobscot Building
645 Griswald Street
Detroit MI 48226
800/877-GALE
Provides overviews on 1,200 careers, 1,000 articles from trade publications, and contact information for professional associations. This CD-ROM also contains self-assessment tests, college profiles, and financial aid data.

DISCOVERING CAREERS & JOBS PLUS
835 Penobscot Building
645 Griswald Street
Detroit MI 48226
800/877-GALE
This CD-ROM gives users contact information on more than 45,000 companies, with 15,000 in-depth profiles and 1,000 company history essays. In addition, the product also provides profiles and application procedures for all major two- and four-year U.S. colleges and universities.

DUN & BRADSTREET MILLION DOLLAR DISC PLUS
3 Sylvan Way
Parsippany NJ 07054
800/526-0651
This CD-ROM provides information on over 400,000 companies in virtually every industry. About 90 percent of the companies listed are privately held, and all have at least $3 million in annual sales or at least 50 employees. Each company's listing includes the number of employees, sales volume, name of the parent company, and corporate headquarters or branch locations. The *Million Dollar Disc Plus* also provides the names and titles of top executives, as well as biographical information on those executives, including education and career background. Searches can be done by location, industry, SIC code, executive names, or key words in the executive biographies. This directory is updated quarterly.

**ENCYCLOPEDIA OF ASSOCIATIONS:
NATIONAL ORGANIZATIONS OF THE U.S.**
835 Penobscot Building
645 Griswald Street
Detroit MI 48226
800/877-GALE

Contains descriptions and contact information for nearly 23,000 national organizations. You can search by association name, geographic location, and key words. This CD-ROM is available in both single- and multi-user formats.

GALE BUSINESS RESOURCES CD-ROM
835 Penobscot Building
645 Griswald Street
Detroit MI 48226
800/877-GALE
This two CD-ROM set contains detailed profiles on certain industries and covers the major companies in each industry, with statistics on over 200,000 businesses nationwide. You can search by company name, industry type, products, and more. This product is available in both single- and multi-user formats.

HARRIS INFOSOURCE NATIONAL
2057 East Aurora Road
Twinsburg OH 44087
800/888-5900
This directory of manufacturers profiles thousands of companies. Although the majority of the companies listed are located in the United States, there are also listings for some Canadian businesses. The listings include the number of employees, plant size, and sales revenue, as well as the names and titles of top executives. This CD-ROM is updated annually and can be purchased in smaller regional or state editions.

MOODY'S COMPANY DATA
99 Church Street
New York NY 10007
800/342-5647
Moody's Company Data is a CD-ROM which has detailed listings for over 10,000 publicly traded companies. In addition to information such as industry, company address, and phone and fax numbers, each listing includes the names and titles of its top officers, including the CEO, president, and vice president; company size; number of shareholders; corporate history; subsidiaries; and financial statements. Users can conduct searches by region, SIC codes, industry, or earnings. This CD-ROM is updated monthly.

STANDARD & POOR'S REGISTER
65 Broadway
8th Floor
New York NY 10004
800/221-5277
The CD-ROM version of this three-volume desk reference provides the same information as its printed companion. The database lists over 55,000 companies, including more than 12,000 public companies. In addition to contact information, which includes the names and titles of over 500,000 executives, you can find out about each company's primary and secondary sources of

business, annual revenues, number of employees, parent company, and subsidiaries. When available, the *Standard & Poor's Register* also lists the names of banks, accounting firms, and law firms used by each company. Also, the directory provides biographies of more than 70,000 top executives, which include information such as directorships held and schools attended. There are 55 different search modes available on the database. You can search geographically, by zip code, industry, SIC code, or stock symbol. You can also limit your search to only private or only public companies. This directory is updated quarterly.

PRIMARY EMPLOYERS

ACCOUNTING AND MANAGEMENT CONSULTING

Accounting and management consulting firms are facing more competitive pressures than ever, coupled with declining profits. Competition is forcing accounting firms to redesign the services they offer, cut costs significantly, and upgrade their recruiting efforts to attract more highly-skilled accountants. Fortunately, innovations in tax software and other technologies have made accounting practices more efficient.

The nation's largest and most dominant accounting firms are focusing more on management consulting, and revenues in the consulting arena have grown significantly. The split of Arthur Andersen into a separate division, Andersen Consulting, reflects a trend that will continue to transform the larger accounting firms and push some business customers toward these smaller divisions or toward private firms.

The largest firms are continuing to create partnerships worldwide, and some of the smaller firms are following suit. The majority of the mid-sized accounting firms, however, concentrate on maintaining strong regional client relationships. According to Inc. *magazine, while some accounting firms will be forced out of business due to competition, many have responded by specializing in a particular area.*

ARTHUR ANDERSEN & COMPANY
111 Monument Circle, Suite 4300, Bank One Center Tower, Indianapolis IN 46204. 317/634-3210. **Contact:** Dick Cult, Director of Human Resources. **World Wide Web address:** http://www.arthurandersen.com. **Description:** One of the largest certified public accounting firms in the world. Arthur Andersen's four key practice areas include Audit and Business Advisory, Tax and Business Advisory, Business Consulting, and Economic and Financial Consulting. Arthur Andersen is a segment of the Arthur Andersen Worldwide Organization, one of the leading providers of professional services in the world. With over 380 worldwide locations, the global practice of its member firms is conducted through two business units: Arthur Andersen and Andersen Consulting, which provides global management and technology consulting. **Corporate headquarters location:** Chicago IL. **Number of employees worldwide:** 91,000.

BLUE & COMPANY LLC
P.O. Box 80069, Indianapolis IN 46280-0069. 317/848-8920. **Fax:** 317/573-2458. **Contact:** Pamela J. Fogle, Director of Human Resources. **World Wide Web address:** http://www.blueandco.com. **Description:** A public accounting and consulting firm with specialties in health care, manufacturing, construction, wholesale distribution, litigation support, and retirement planning. **Common positions include:** Accountant/Auditor; Consultant. **Educational backgrounds include:** Accounting. **Benefits:** 401(k); Disability Coverage; Life Insurance; Medical Insurance; Savings Plan; Tuition Assistance. **Special programs:** Internships. **Internship information:** Internships are offered January through April. Resumes should be sent to the above address. **Corporate headquarters location:** This Location. **Other U.S. locations:** KY. **Listed on:** Privately held. **Number of employees at this location:** 130. **Number of employees nationwide:** 200.

DELOITTE & TOUCHE
10 West Market Street, Suite 3000, Indianapolis IN 46204. 317/464-8600. **Contact:** Mr. Denny Faurote, Human Resources Manager. **World Wide Web address:** http://www.dttus.com.

Description: An international firm of certified public accountants, providing professional accounting, auditing, tax, and management consulting services to widely diversified clients. Deloitte & Touche operates more than 500 offices throughout the world, and has a specialized program consisting of some 25 national industry groups and 50 functional (technical) groups that cross industry lines. Groups are involved in various disciplines, including accounting, auditing, taxation management advisory services, small and growing businesses, mergers and acquisitions, and computer applications.

ERNST & YOUNG
One Indiana Square, Suite 3400, Indianapolis IN 46204. 317/681-7000. **Contact:** Human Resources. **World Wide Web address:** http://www.ey.com. **Description:** A certified public accounting firm. Ernst & Young also provides its clients with management consulting services. The consulting staff is comprised of more than 1,000 consultants and support staff worldwide, and is involved in such fields as data processing, financial modeling, financial feasibility studies, production planning and inventory management, management sciences, health care planning, human resources, and cost accounting and budgeting systems. Ernst & Young provides services to numerous industries, including health care, finance, insurance, manufacturing, retailing, government, utilities, and transportation. **Number of employees nationwide:** 8,000. **Number of employees worldwide:** 16,000.

GEORGE S. OLIVE AND COMPANY
201 North Illinois Street, Suite 700 South, Indianapolis IN 46204. 317/383-4000. **Contact:** J. Thomas Porter, Director of Human Resources. **Description:** A full-service, certified public accounting agency. **Corporate headquarters location:** This Location.

Note: Because addresses and telephone numbers of smaller companies can change rapidly, we recommend you call each company to verify the information below before inquiring about job opportunities. Mass mailings are not recommended.

Additional small employers:

ACCOUNTING, AUDITING, AND BOOKKEEPING SERVICES

Capz Sapper & Miller
11711 N Meridian Street, Carmel IN 46032-4534. 317/580-2100.

Ciproms
8770 Purdue Road, Indianapolis IN 46268-1120. 317/870-0480.

Crowe Chizek & Company
301 S Main Street, Suite 400, Elkhart IN 46516-3101. 219/295-1991.

Crowe Chizek & Company
PO Box 7, South Bend IN 46624-0007. 219/232-3992.

Crowe Chizek & Company
2100 Market Tower, 10 W Market, Indianapolis IN 46204. 317/632-8989.

Ernst & Young
2300 Fort Wayne National Bank, Fort Wayne IN 46802. 219/424-2233.

Harding Shymanski & Company
PO Box 3677, Evansville IN 47735-3677. 812/464-9161.

KPMG Peat Marwick
135 N Pennsylvania Street, Indianapolis IN 46204-2400. 317/636-5592.

Medcor Data Inc.
8015 Castleton Road, Indianapolis IN 46250-2004. 317/849-1379.

Merchants Choice Card
8309 W 109th Avenue, Crown Point IN 46307-8848. 219/365-3095.

Outsource Receivables Services
8019 Castleton Road, Indianapolis IN 46250-2004. 317/570-0055.

PricewaterhouseCoopers
PO Box 82002, Indianapolis IN 46282. 317/639-4161.

Whipple & Company Professional
PO Box 40368, Indianapolis IN 46240-0368. 317/469-7776.

BUSINESS CONSULTING SERVICES

Atec Associates
5150 East 65th Street, Indianapolis IN 46220-4817. 317/849-4990.

Coresource Inc.
2828 Enterprise Drive, Anderson IN 46013-9663. 765/778-8511.

Data Bank USA
803 S Calhoun St, Suite 100, Fort Wayne IN 46802-2305. 219/424-1711.

DMA
6610 Mutual Drive, Fort Wayne IN 46825-4236. 219/484-8631.

Forethought Group Inc.
One Forethought Center, Batesville IN 47006-1279. 812/934-7910.

Kelsington General Inc.
228 W Lincoln Highway, Schererville IN 46375-1854. 219/791-4819.

Lambic Telcom Inc.
1502 Magnavox Way, Suite 240, Fort Wayne IN 46804-1564. 219/436-5973.

Press Ganey Associates Inc.
404 Columbia Street, South Bend IN 46601-2364. 219/232-3387.

Teletron Inc.
1921 Liberty Dr, Bloomington IN 47403-5146. 812/336-1300.

For more information on career opportunities in accounting and management consulting:

Associations

AMERICAN ACCOUNTING ASSOCIATION
5717 Bessie Drive, Sarasota FL 34233. 941/921-7747. World Wide Web address: http://www.aaa-edu.org. An academically-oriented accounting association that offers two quarterly journals, a semi-annual journal, a newsletter, and a wide variety of continuing education programs.

AMERICAN INSTITUTE OF CERTIFIED PUBLIC ACCOUNTANTS
1211 Avenue of the Americas, New York NY 10036. 212/596-6200. World Wide Web address: http://www.aicpa.org. A national professional organization for all CPAs. AICPA offers a comprehensive career package to students.

AMERICAN MANAGEMENT ASSOCIATION
1601 Broadway, New York NY 10019. 212/586-8100. Provides a variety of publications, training videos, and courses, as well as an Information Resource Center, which provides management information, and a library service.

ASSOCIATION OF GOVERNMENT ACCOUNTANTS
2200 Mount Vernon Avenue, Alexandria VA 22301. 703/684-6931. World Wide Web address: http://www.rutgers.edu/accounting/raw/aga. Serves financial management professionals and offers continuing education workshops.

ASSOCIATION OF MANAGEMENT CONSULTING FIRMS
521 Fifth Avenue, 35th Floor, New York NY 10175. 212/697-9693. World Wide Web address: http://www.amcf.org.

THE INSTITUTE OF INTERNAL AUDITORS
249 Maitland Avenue, Altamonte Springs FL 32701. 407/830-7600. World Wide Web address: http://www.theiia.org. Publishes magazines and newsletters. Provides information on current issues, a network of more than 50,000 members in 100 countries, and professional development and research services. Also offers continuing education seminars.

INSTITUTE OF MANAGEMENT ACCOUNTANTS
10 Paragon Drive, Montvale NJ 07645. 201/573-9000. World Wide Web address: http://www.rutgers.edu/accounting/raw/ima. Offers a Certified Management Accountant Program, periodicals, seminars, educational programs, a research program, a financial management network, and networking services. The association has about 80,000 members and 300 local chapters.

INSTITUTE OF MANAGEMENT CONSULTANTS
521 Fifth Avenue, 35th Floor, New York NY 10175. 212/697-8262. World Wide Web address: http://www.imc.org. Offers certification programs, professional development, and a directory of members.

NATIONAL ASSOCIATION OF TAX PRACTITIONERS
720 Association Drive, Appleton WI 54914-1483. 414/749-1040. World Wide Web address: http://www.natptax.com. Offers seminars, research, newsletters, preparer worksheets, state chapters, insurance, and other tax-related services.

NATIONAL SOCIETY OF ACCOUNTANTS
1010 North Fairfax Street, Alexandria VA 22314. 703/549-6400. World Wide Web address: http://www.nsacct.org. Offers professional development services, government representation, a variety of publications, practice aids, low-cost group insurance, annual seminars, and updates for members on new tax laws.

Magazines

CPA JOURNAL
The New York State Society, 530 Fifth Avenue, 5th Floor, New York NY 10036. 212/719-8300. Monthly.

CPA LETTER
American Institute of Certified Public Accountants, 1211 Avenue of the Americas, New York NY 10036. 212/596-6200. World Wide Web address: http://www.aicpa.org/pubs/cpaltr.

THE FINANCE AND ACCOUNTING JOBS REPORT
Career Advancement Publications, Jamestown NY. World Wide Web address: http://www.jobsreports.net. This publication is dedicated to finance and accounting professionals who are looking for a job. Each issue includes several hundred job openings in the United States and abroad. This report also offers subscribers networking opportunities through its contact and referral program.

JOURNAL OF ACCOUNTANCY
American Institute of Certified Public Accountants, 1211 Avenue of the Americas, New York NY 10036. 212/596-6200.

MANAGEMENT ACCOUNTING
Institute of Management Accountants, 10 Paragon Drive, Montvale NJ 07645. 201/573-9000.

Online Services

ACCOUNTANTS FORUM
Go: Aicpa. A CompuServe forum sponsored by the American Institute of Certified Public Accountants.

FINANCIAL/ACCOUNTING/INSURANCE JOBS PAGE
http://www.nationjob.com/financial. This Website provides a list of financial, accounting, and insurance job openings.

JOBS IN ACCOUNTING
http://www.cob.ohio-state.edu/dept/fin/jobs/account.htm#Link7. Provides information on the accounting profession, including salaries, trends, and resources.

MANAGEMENT CONSULTING JOBS ONLINE
http://www.cob.ohio-state.edu/dept/fin/jobs/mco/mco.html. Provides information and resources for jobseekers looking to work in the field of management consulting.

ADVERTISING, MARKETING, AND PUBLIC RELATIONS

Professionals in advertising, marketing, and public relations face an industry that is constantly changing and extremely competitive due to the high salaries it commands. Growth is forecast for all areas of advertising through 2000; and the public relations sector is projected to be one of the fastest growing.

Advertising executives are reporting that certain trends are dictating the industry's direction. Perhaps the most prominent is a renewed emphasis on corporate branding and the strategy of advertising products to individual consumers rather than larger groups or corporations. Business Week *cites growing consumer spending as a positive factor creating a boom in the advertising market.*

Publishers Information Bureau reports that although ad receipts were up by 8 percent in 1996, ad pages were down. Even so, magazines and newspapers continue to be the popular source of advertising and should continue to prosper well into the next decade. Although the cost of television ad time has not increased significantly over the last few years, networks are subtly trying to crowd more ads into programming. In 1998, the networks were expected to collect $14 billion in ad sales, 5.5 percent above 1997.

The latest trend in advertising is on the Internet. Companies are investing in "pop-up ads" that are linked to Websites related to the types of products and services they offer. This method of advertising is popular because it allows companies to target wider audiences and it provides consumers with easy access to information about specific advertisers. Online advertisers are also using well known search engines as springboards to their sites, but at great expense. It costs millions of dollars for companies to have their logos displayed on these high-traffic areas of the Web.

Direct mail is another successful area of the industry. According to U.S. News and World Report, *in 1997 consumers spent $244 billion in response to direct mail advertisers, including $48 billion on catalog merchandise. The growth in this sector is fueled by newer, more precise data-collection databases, and the volume of "junk mail" is expected to triple in the next decade.*

ASHER AGENCY, INC.
P.O. Box 2535, Fort Wayne IN 46801. 219/424-3373. **Contact:** Tom Borne, President. **Description:** An advertising agency.

BATES U.S.A.
117 East Washington Street, Indianapolis IN 46204. 317/686-7800. **Contact:** Beverly Helm, Director of Human Resources. **World Wide Web address:** http://www.batesusa.com. **Description:** An advertising agency. **Corporate headquarters location:** New York NY.

CALDWELL VANRIPER, INC.
1314 North Meridian, Indianapolis IN 46202. 317/632-6501. **Contact:** Human Resources. **World Wide Web address:** http://www.cvr.com. **Description:** An advertising agency.

JUHL MARKETING COMMUNICATIONS
3930 Edison Lakes Parkway, Mishawaka IN 46545. 219/271-5621. **Fax:** 219/271-8200. **Contact:** Linda Touree, Office Manager. **World Wide Web address:** http://www.juhl.com. **Description:** An advertising and public relations agency. **NOTE:** Entry-level positions are offered. **Common positions include:** Account Manager; Advertising Account Executive; Editor; Graphic Artist; Graphic Designer; Public Relations Specialist; Technical Writer/Editor. **Educational backgrounds include:** Art/Design; Communications; Marketing; Public Relations. **Benefits:** 401(k); Dental Insurance; Disability Coverage; Life Insurance; Medical Insurance. **Number of employees at this location:** 25.

KELLER CRESCENT COMPANY, INC.
1100 East Louisiana Street, Evansville IN 47711. 812/464-2461. **Fax:** 812/426-7668. **Contact:** Mr. Chris Feagans, Vice President of Human Resources. **Description:** A marketing communications company offering advertising, media, public relations, sales promotion, audio/visual production, and marketing services, as well as printing and packaging facilities. **Common positions include:** Accountant/Auditor; Advertising Clerk; Broadcast Technician; Buyer; Clerical Supervisor; Computer Programmer; Credit Manager; Customer Service Representative; Design Engineer; Designer; General Manager; Human Resources Manager; Market Research Analyst; MIS Specialist; Multimedia Designer; Public Relations Specialist; Purchasing Agent/Manager; Quality Control Supervisor; Services Sales Representative; Technical Writer/Editor; Typist/Word Processor; Video Production Coordinator. **Educational backgrounds include:** Art/Design; Communications; Computer Science; Marketing. **Benefits:** 401(k); Dental Insurance; Disability Coverage; Employee Discounts; Life Insurance; Medical Insurance; Pension Plan; Profit Sharing; Savings Plan; Tuition Assistance. **Other area locations:** Indianapolis IN. **Other U.S. locations:** St. Louis MO. **Operations at this facility include:** Administration; Manufacturing; Sales. **Listed on:** Privately held. **Annual sales/revenues:** More than $100 million. **Number of employees at this location:** 500. **Number of employees nationwide:** 600.

Note: Because addresses and telephone numbers of smaller companies can change rapidly, we recommend you call each company to verify the information below before inquiring about job opportunities. Mass mailings are not recommended.

Additional small employers:

DIRECT MAIL ADVERTISING SERVICES

Advo Inc.
5517 West Minnesota Street, Indianapolis IN 46241-3821. 317/879-4710.

Mid-America Mailers Inc.
PO Box 646, Hammond IN 46325-0646. 219/933-0137.

MISC. ADVERTISING SERVICES

Burkhart Advertising Inc.
PO Box 536, South Bend IN 46624-0536. 219/233-2101.

Directory Composition
6970 Corporate Drive, Indianapolis IN 46278-1928. 317/297-4926.

Dow Theory Forecasts
7412 Calumet Ave, Suite 100, Hammond IN 46324-2622. 219/931-6480.

MZD
1800 N Meridian Street, Indianapolis IN 46202-1443. 317/924-6271.

Titan Advertising Inc.
8650 Commerce Park Place, Indianapolis IN 46268-3126. 317/228-9684.

TMP/Worldwide Inc.
7030 Pointe Inverness Way, Fort Wayne IN 46804-7930. 219/432-0948.

Whiteco Metrocom
1000 E 80th Pl, Merrillville IN 46410. 219/769-6601.

Whiteco Metrocom
1770 W 41st Ave, Crown Point IN 46307. 219/980-1147.

PUBLIC RELATIONS SERVICES

Dialamerica Marketing Inc.
2634 E 10th Street, Bloomington IN 47408-2666. 812/331-2212.

For more information on career opportunities in advertising, marketing, and public relations:

<u>Associations</u>

ADVERTISING RESEARCH FOUNDATION
641 Lexington Avenue, 11th Floor, New York NY 10174. 212/751-5656. Fax: 212/319-5265. E-mail address: email@arfsite.org. World Wide Web address: http://www.arfsite.org. A nonprofit organization comprised of advertising, marketing, and media research companies. For institutions only.

AMERICAN ASSOCIATION OF ADVERTISING AGENCIES
405 Lexington Avenue, 18th Floor, New York NY 10174. 212/682-2500. World Wide Web address: http://www.commercepark.com/aaaa. Offers educational and enrichment benefits such as publications, videos, and conferences.

AMERICAN MARKETING ASSOCIATION
250 South Wacker Drive, Suite 200, Chicago IL 60606. 312/648-0536. World Wide Web address: http://www.ama.org. An association with nearly 45,000 members worldwide. Offers a reference center, 25 annual conferences, and eight publications for marketing professionals and students.

THE DIRECT MARKETING ASSOCIATION
1120 Avenue of the Americas, New York NY 10036-6700. 212/768-7277. World Wide Web address: http://www.the-dma.org. This association offers monthly newsletters, seminars, and an annual telephone marketing conference.

INTERNATIONAL ADVERTISING ASSOCIATION
521 Fifth Avenue, Suite 1807, New York NY 10175. 212/557-1133. Fax: 212/983-0455. E-mail address: iaa@ibnet.com. World Wide Web address: http://www.iaaglobal.org. Over 3,600 members in 89 countries. Membership includes publications; professional development; congresses, symposia, and conferences; annual report and membership directory; and worldwide involvement with governments and other associations. Overall, the organization looks to promote free speech and the self-regulation of advertising.

LEAGUE OF ADVERTISING AGENCIES
2 South End Avenue #4C, New York NY 10280. 212/945-4991. Seminars available for agency principals.

MARKETING RESEARCH ASSOCIATION
1344 Silas Deane Highway, Suite 306, Rocky Hill CT 06067. 860/257-4008. World Wide Web address: http://www.mra-net.org. Publishes several magazines and newsletters.

PUBLIC RELATIONS SOCIETY OF AMERICA
33 Irving Place, New York NY 10003-2376. 212/995-2230. World Wide Web address: http://www.prsa.org. Publishes three magazines for public relations professionals.

Directories

AAAA ROSTER AND ORGANIZATION
American Association of Advertising Agencies, 405 Lexington Avenue, 18th Floor, New York NY 10147. 212/682-2500.

DIRECTORY OF MINORITY PUBLIC RELATIONS PROFESSIONALS
Public Relations Society of America, 33 Irving Place, New York NY 10003-2376. 212/995-2230.

O'DWYER'S DIRECTORY OF PUBLIC RELATIONS FIRMS
J. R. O'Dwyer Company, 271 Madison Avenue, Room 600, New York NY 10016. 212/679-2471.

PUBLIC RELATIONS CONSULTANTS DIRECTORY
American Business Directories, Division of American Business Lists, 5711 South 86th Circle, Omaha NE 68127. 402/593-4500.

STANDARD DIRECTORY OF ADVERTISING AGENCIES
Reed Reference Publishing Company, P.O. Box 31, New Providence NJ 07974. Toll-free phone: 800/521-8110.

Magazines

ADVERTISING AGE
Crain Communications, 740 North Rush Street, Chicago IL 60611. 312/649-5200. World Wide Web address: http://www.adage.com.

ADWEEK
BPI, 1515 Broadway, 12th Floor, New York NY 10036-8986. 212/536-5336. World Wide Web address: http://www.adweek.com.

BUSINESS MARKETING
Crain Communications, Inc., 740 North Rush Street, Chicago IL 60611. 312/649-5200. World Wide Web address: http://www.netb2b.com.

JOURNAL OF MARKETING
American Marketing Association, 250 South Wacker Drive, Suite 200, Chicago IL 60606. 312/648-0536.

THE MARKETING NEWS
American Marketing Association, 250 South Wacker Drive, Suite 200, Chicago IL 60606. 312/648-0536. A biweekly magazine offering new ideas and developments in marketing.

PR REPORTER
PR Publishing Company, P.O. Box 600, Exeter NH 03833. 603/778-0514. World Wide Web address: http://www.prpublishing.com.

PUBLIC RELATIONS NEWS
Phillips Business Information, Inc., 1201 Seven Locks Road, P.O. Box 61130, Potomac MD 20859-61130. 301/424-3338. Fax: 301/309-3847. World Wide Web address: http://www.phillips.com.

Newsletters

PUBLIC RELATIONS CAREER OPPORTUNITIES
1575 I Street NW, Suite 1190, Washington DC 20005. 202/408-7904. Fax: 202/408-7907. World Wide Web address: http://www.careeropps.com/prcareer1. Contact: James J. Zaniello, Managing Director. Newsletter listing public relations, public affairs, special events, and investor positions nationwide compensating above $35,000 annually. Available on a subscription basis, published 24 times a year.

Published on behalf of the Public Relations Society of America. Company also publishes other newsletters, including *CEO Job Opportunities Update* and *ASAE Career Opportunities* (for the American Society of Association Executives).

Online Services

ADVERTISING & MEDIA JOBS PAGE
http://www.nationjob.com/media. This Website offers advertising and media job openings that can be searched by a variety of criteria including location, type of position, and salary. This site also offers a service that will perform the search for you.

DIRECT MARKETING WORLD'S JOB CENTER
http://www.dmworld.com. Posts professional job openings for the direct marketing industry. This site also provides a career reference library, a list of direct marketing professionals, and a list of events within the industry.

MARKETING CLASSIFIEDS ON THE INTERNET
http://www.marketingjobs.com. Offers job listings by state, resume posting, discussions with other marketing professionals, links to other career sites, and company home pages.

AEROSPACE

Strong growth is predicted for the aerospace industry, where demand for commercial planes is high and suppliers are scrambling to keep up. The Aerospace Industries Association projected that profit margins would get a significant boost in 1998. Commercial aircraft shipments were expected to be primarily responsible, and healthy growth was also expected for space launch vehicles, large transport aircraft, small business jets, and helicopters.

ALLIEDSIGNAL AEROSPACE
BENDIX ENGINE CONTROLS DIVISION
717 North Bendix Drive, South Bend IN 46620. 219/231-3000. **Contact:** Donald McCundiff, Director of Human Resources. **World Wide Web address:** http://www.alliedsignal.com/aerospace. **Description:** Manufactures aircraft engine controls and subsystems, aircraft electronics systems, and aircraft equipment. **Parent company:** AlliedSignal Corporation.

ALLIEDSIGNAL LANDING SYSTEMS
3520 Westmoor Street, South Bend IN 46628-1373. 219/231-2000. **Contact:** Human Resources. **Description:** Manufactures wheels, brakes, and other related aircraft parts. **Parent company:** AlliedSignal Corporation serves a broad spectrum of industries through its more than 40 strategic businesses, which are grouped into three sectors: Aerospace, Automotive, and Engineered Materials. AlliedSignal is one of the nation's largest industrial organizations and has 115,000 employees in over 30 countries.

ITT AEROSPACE/COMMUNICATIONS DIVISION
P.O. Box 3700, Fort Wayne IN 46801-3700. 219/487-6151. **Contact:** Mike E. Evans, Senior Technical Recruiter. **World Wide Web address:** http://www.ittind.com. **Description:** Maintains fully-equipped facilities for research, engineering, manufacturing, and product support in the fields of voice and data battlefield communications, aerospace navigation, and weather satellite imagine/IR sensors. ITT Aerospace/Communications operates as a division of ITT Defense & Electronics Inc. **Common positions include:** Accountant/Auditor; Buyer; Computer Programmer; Draftsperson; Electrical/Electronics Engineer; Human Resources Manager; Industrial Engineer; Mechanical Engineer; Physicist; Quality Control Supervisor; Software Engineer; Systems Analyst. **Educational backgrounds include:** Accounting; Computer Science; Engineering. **Benefits:** 401(k); Dental Insurance; Disability Coverage; Life Insurance; Medical Insurance; Pension Plan; Tuition Assistance. **Corporate headquarters location:** New York NY. **Other U.S. locations:** San Diego CA; Clifton NJ. **Parent company:** ITT Corporation is a diversified, global enterprise engaged in three major business areas: Financial and Business Services, which includes ITT Hartford, ITT Financial Corporation, and ITT Communications and Information Services, Inc.; Manufactured Products, which includes ITT Automotive, ITT Defense and Electronics, Inc., and ITT Fluid Technology Corporation; and Sheraton Hotels (ITT Sheraton Corporation). **Listed on:** New York Stock Exchange. **Number of employees at this location:** 2,100. **Number of employees nationwide:** 2,800.

LOCKHEED MARTIN
P.O. Box 2232, Fort Wayne IN 46801. 219/434-5000. **Contact:** Human Resources. **Description:** This location manufactures and services control systems for aircraft. Overall, Lockheed Martin provides turnkey systems development, engineering services, and space flight mission support for civil and commercial space programs worldwide. The company supports both space and ground-based systems, with an emphasis on command and control, data storage, and processing systems. **Corporate headquarters location:** Bethesda MD.

TRI-MANUFACTURING
333 South Third Street, Terre Haute IN 47807. 812/234-1591. **Contact:** Human Resources. **E-mail address:** tri@aol.com. **Description:** Engaged in a variety of sheet metal work, primarily for the aerospace industry.

TWIGG CORPORATION
659 East York Street, Martinsville IN 46151. 765/342-7126. **Fax:** 765/342-1553. **Contact:** Human Resources. **E-mail address:** twigg@reliable-net.net. **World Wide Web address:** http://www.twiggcorp.com. **Description:** Manufactures military and commercial jet engine parts.

For more information on career opportunities in aerospace:

Associations

AMERICAN INSTITUTE OF AERONAUTICS AND ASTRONAUTICS
1801 Alexander Bell Drive, Reston VA 20191. World Wide Web address: http://www.aiaa.org. Membership required. Publishes six journals and books.

NATIONAL AERONAUTIC ASSOCIATION OF USA
1815 North Fort Myer Drive, Suite 700, Arlington VA 22209. 703/527-0226. World Wide Web address: http://www.naa.ycg.org. Publishes a magazine. Membership required.

PROFESSIONAL AVIATION MAINTENANCE ASSOCIATION
636 I Street, Suite 300, Washington DC 20001-3736. World Wide Web address: http://www.pama.org. Members' resumes are distributed to companies who advise the organization of employment opportunities. Many local chapters also provide job referrals. Members have access to the Worldwide Membership Directory.

APPAREL, FASHION, AND TEXTILES

Employment in the apparel and textiles industry has been hurt by advances in labor-saving technology. Machinery such as computer-controlled cutters, semi-automatic sewing machines, and automated material handling systems continues to reduce the need for apparel workers.

Increased overseas production of apparel and textiles has also decreased the need for domestic workers who perform sewing functions. In fact, the U.S. Department of Commerce projected that imports would grow by about 9.2 percent in 1998. The industry has responded by attempting to develop niche markets, strong brand names, and faster customer response systems, according to Monthly Labor Review. *Despite these efforts, over 1 million U.S. textile and apparel jobs were eliminated between 1973 and 1997, and the U.S. Department of Labor expects employment to decline steadily through the year 2000.*

M. FINE & SONS MANUFACTURING COMPANY, INC.
P.O. Box 258, New Albany IN 47150. 812/944-6441. **Contact:** Human Resources. **Description:** Manufactures and distributes men's work clothes and leisure apparel.

HART SCHAFFNER & MARX
1420 Wabash Avenue, Rochester IN 46975. 219/223-3125. **Contact:** Human Resources. **Description:** Manufactures clothing. **Parent company:** Hartmarx Corporation sells men's clothing under the Austin Reed and Tommy Hilfiger labels and manufactures women's clothing and sportswear under the brand names Austin Reed and Hickey-Freeman. The company conducts direct marketing and catalog sales operations worldwide.

LOGO ATHLETICS, INC.
8677 Logo Athletics Court, Indianapolis IN 46219. 317/895-7000. **Contact:** Human Resources Department. **Description:** Manufactures sports apparel featuring licensed team logos including those for most major professional and collegiate sports teams.

NINE WEST GROUP
P.O. Box 95, Vevay IN 47043. 812/427-3317. **Contact:** Human Resources. **Description:** Manufactures Nine West brand shoes.

REGAL RUGS, INC.
P.O. Box 926, North Vernon IN 47265. 812/346-3601. **Fax:** 812/346-7112. **Contact:** Human Resources. **World Wide Web address:** http://www.regalrug.com. **Description:** A manufacturer of rugs. **Common positions include:** Accountant/Auditor; Blue-Collar Worker Supervisor; Credit Manager; Customer Service Representative; Designer; Human Resources Manager; Industrial Engineer; Operations/Production Manager; Purchasing Agent/Manager; Quality Control Supervisor. **Educational backgrounds include:** Business Administration; Communications; Engineering; Marketing. **Benefits:** 401(k); Dental Insurance; Disability Coverage; Employee Discounts; Life Insurance; Medical Insurance; Pension Plan; Savings Plan; Tuition Assistance. **Parent company:** Redicut, Inc. (England). **Operations at this facility include:** Administration; Manufacturing; Research and Development; Service. **Number of employees at this location:** 300. **Number of employees nationwide:** 450.

TRANS-APPAREL GROUP
P.O. Box 700, Michigan City IN 46360. 219/879-7341. **Contact:** Personnel. **Description:** A manufacturer of men's slacks. Trans-Apparel Group has a nationwide sales force. The company formerly operated under the name Jaymar-Ruby, Inc. **Common positions include:**

Accountant/Auditor; Advertising Clerk; Blue-Collar Worker Supervisor; Customer Service Representative; Financial Analyst; Industrial Engineer. **Educational backgrounds include:** Accounting; Business Administration; Computer Science; Finance. **Benefits:** Disability Coverage; Employee Discounts; Life Insurance; Medical Insurance; Tuition Assistance. **Corporate headquarters location:** This Location. **Operations at this facility include:** Manufacturing.

Note: *Because addresses and telephone numbers of smaller companies can change rapidly, we recommend you call each company to verify the information below before inquiring about job opportunities. Mass mailings are not recommended.*

Additional small employers:

FOOTWEAR

Nine West Group Inc.
615 West Franklin Street, Osgood IN 47037-9807. 812/689-4162.

Nine West Group Inc.
805 East Street, Madison IN 47250-3210. 812/265-3931.

MEN'S AND BOYS' CLOTHING

Berne Apparel Company Inc.
PO Box 309, Berne IN 46711-0309. 219/589-3136.

Indiana Knitwear Corporation
PO Box 9, B St, Greenfield IN 46140-1535. 317/462-4413.

Midwest Embroidery Inc.
3431 William Richardson Drive, South Bend IN 46628-9477. 219/273-2300.

NARROW FABRIC AND OTHER SMALLWARES MILLS

Indiana Ribbon Inc.
PO Box 355, Wolcott IN 47995-0355. 219/279-2113.

NONWOVEN FABRICS

Fiber Bond Corporation
110 Menke Road, Michigan City IN 46360-6530. 219/879-4541.

WATERPROOF OUTERWEAR

Nasco Industries Incorporated
PO Box 427, Washington IN 47501-0427. 812/254-7393.

For more information on career opportunities in the apparel, fashion, and textiles industries:

Associations

AMERICAN APPAREL MANUFACTURERS ASSOCIATION
2500 Wilson Boulevard, Suite 301, Arlington VA 22201. 703/524-1864. World Wide Web address: http://www.americanapparel.org. Publishes numerous magazines, newsletters, and bulletins for the benefit of employees in the apparel manufacturing industry.

AMERICAN TEXTILE MANUFACTURERS INSTITUTE
Office of the Chief Economist, 1130 Connecticut Avenue, Suite 1200, Washington DC 20036. 202/862-0500. Fax: 202/862-0570. World Wide Web address: http://www.atmi.org. The national trade association for the domestic textile industry. Members are corporations only.

THE FASHION GROUP INTERNATIONAL, INC.
597 Fifth Avenue, 8th Floor, New York NY 10017. 212/593-1715. World Wide Web address: http://www.fgi.org. A nonprofit organization for professional women in the fashion industries (apparel, accessories, beauty, and home). Offers career counseling workshops 18 times per year.

INTERNATIONAL ASSOCIATION OF CLOTHING DESIGNERS
475 Park Avenue South, 9th Floor, New York NY 10016. 212/685-6602. Fax: 212/545-1709.

Directories

AAMA DIRECTORY
American Apparel Manufacturers Association, 2500 Wilson Boulevard, Suite 301, Arlington VA 22201. 703/524-1864. A directory of publications distributed by the American Apparel Manufacturers Association.

APPAREL TRADES BOOK
Dun & Bradstreet Inc., One Diamond Hill Road, Murray Hill NJ 07974. 908/665-5000.

FAIRCHILD'S MARKET DIRECTORY OF WOMEN'S AND CHILDREN'S APPAREL
Fairchild Publications, 7 West 34th Street, New York NY 10001. 212/630-4000.

Magazines

ACCESSORIES
Business Journals, 50 Day Street, P.O. Box 5550, Norwalk CT 06856. 203/853-6015.

AMERICA'S TEXTILES
Billiam Publishing, 555 North Pleasant Bark Drive, Suite 132, Greenville SC 29607. 864/242-5300.

APPAREL INDUSTRY MAGAZINE
Shore Verone Inc., 6255 Barfield Road, Suite 200, Atlanta GA 30328-4300. 404/252-8831. World Wide Web address: http://www.aimagazine.com.

BOBBIN MAGAZINE
Bobbin Publishing Group, P.O. Box 1986, 1110 Shop Road, Columbia SC 29202. 803/771-7500.

TEXTILE HILIGHTS
American Textile Manufacturers Institute, Office of the Chief Economist, 1801 K Street NW, Suite 900, Washington DC 20006. A quarterly publication.

WOMEN'S WEAR DAILY (WWD)
Fairchild Publications, 7 West 34th Street, New York NY 10001. 212/630-4000. World Wide Web address: http://www.wwd.com.

Online Services

THE INTERNET FASHION EXCHANGE
http://www.fashionexch.com. An excellent site for those industry professionals interested in apparel and retail. The extensive search engine allows you to search by job title, location, salary, product line, industry, and whether you want a permanent, temporary, or freelance position. The Internet Fashion Exchange also offers career services such as recruiting and outplacement firms that place fashion and retail professionals.

ARCHITECTURE, CONSTRUCTION, AND ENGINEERING

Building on its success in the mid-'90s, the construction industry is flourishing. Approximately 7.1 million workers were employed in the industry in 1997, a record year according to U.S. Industry and Trade Outlook 1998. *While the nation's booming economy has encouraged new construction projects across the country, the Associated Builders and Contractors Association is predicting a shortage of 250,000 workers each year into the next decade.*

For job seekers who choose construction, the best opportunities will be in projects at electric utilities, educational facilities, and water supply facilities. In 1998, housing starts were expected to total 1.41 million, a 1 percent increase over 1997. Construction is likely to remain strongest in the Midwest and the South. Building trade workers such as architects, bricklayers, concrete masons, and sheet metal workers will see only average growth in their industries through 2005.

In engineering, the best opportunities through 2005 are in the civil, industrial, and electrical sectors. Aerospace engineers will continue to face fierce competition and chemical engineers will have more opportunities with companies that focus on developing specialty chemicals.

AEROQUIP CORPORATION
10801 U.S. Highway 24 East, New Haven IN 46774. 219/748-6000. **Contact:** Human Resources. **World Wide Web address:** http://www.aeroquip-vickers.com. **Description:** Manufactures air conditioning and heating equipment.

BURGESS & NIPLE, LTD.
201 North Illinois, Capitol Center, Suite 2250, Indianapolis IN 46204. 317/237-2760. **Contact:** Human Resources. **E-mail address:** burnip@burnip.com. **Description:** An engineering and architecture firm offering study, analysis, and design services. The company's programs include waterworks, wastewater, industrial services, hydropower, energy conservation, transportation, HVAC, systems analysis, and geotechnical services. **Common positions include:** Architect; Civil Engineer. **Corporate headquarters location:** Columbus OH.

CALUMET CONSTRUCTION CORPORATION
1247 169th Street, Hammond IN 46324. 219/844-9420. **Contact:** Human Resources. **Description:** A general industrial contractor.

CONSOLIDATED FABRICATIONS
3851 Ellsworth Street, Gary IN 46408. 219/884-6150. **Contact:** Human Resources. **Description:** A mechanical contracting company for industrial applications including the repair of oil refineries and chemical plants. Consolidated Fabrications also manufactures and repairs tanks and pressure valves.

CONTINENTAL ELECTRIC COMPANY
P.O. Box 2710, Gary IN 46403. 219/938-3460. **Physical address:** 9501 East Fifth Avenue, Gary IN. **Contact:** Human Resources. **Description:** Provides electrical contracting services to residential and industrial clients.

CROSSMAN COMMUNITIES, INC.
9202 North Meridian Street, Suite 300, Indianapolis IN 46260. 317/843-9514. **Contact:** Linda Hitchcock, Human Resources. **World Wide Web address:** http://www.croscom.com. **Description:** A holding company which operates through subsidiaries that design, develop, and build single-family detached homes. **Number of employees nationwide:** 170.

DEUPEL DEMARS
1919 North Meridian, Indianapolis IN 46202. 317/924-9192. **Contact:** Gil Hammand, Personnel Director. **Description:** Engages in construction management and general contracting. **Common positions include:** Accountant/Auditor; Civil Engineer; Construction Contractor; Cost Estimator; Electrical/Electronics Engineer; Mechanical Engineer. **Educational backgrounds include:** Accounting; Engineering. **Benefits:** 401(k); Dental Insurance; Disability Coverage; Life Insurance; Medical Insurance; Pension Plan; Tuition Assistance. **Corporate headquarters location:** This Location. **Operations at this facility include:** Administration. **Number of employees at this location:** 100. **Number of employees nationwide:** 180.

FAIRMONT HOMES, INC.
P.O. Box 27, Nappanee IN 46550. 219/773-7941. **Contact:** Human Resources. **Description:** Manufactures sectional housing, modular homes, and recreational vehicles sold nationwide. **Common positions include:** Accountant/Auditor; Advertising Clerk; Blue-Collar Worker Supervisor; Buyer; Computer Programmer; Construction and Building Inspector; Customer Service Representative; Draftsperson; Electrical/Electronics Engineer; Electrician; Financial Analyst; General Manager; Industrial Engineer; Industrial Production Manager; Management Trainee; Manufacturer's/Wholesaler's Sales Rep.; Mechanical Engineer; Operations/Production Manager; Purchasing Agent/Manager; Quality Control Supervisor; Software Engineer; Systems Analyst. **Benefits:** 401(k); Life Insurance; Medical Insurance; Savings Plan. **Corporate headquarters location:** This Location. **Other U.S. locations:** Montevideo MN. **Listed on:** Privately held. **Number of employees at this location:** 2,400. **Number of employees nationwide:** 2,700.

JM FOSTER INC.
P.O. Box M-750, Gary IN 46401. 219/949-4020. **Contact:** Human Resources. **Description:** A general contracting firm involved in bridge, road, and industrial construction.

GARY STEEL PRODUCTS CORPORATION
2700 East Fifth Avenue, Gary IN 46402. 219/885-3232. **Contact:** Human Resources. **Description:** Manufactures air distribution products for the heating and air conditioning industry.

THE GILBERT COMPANY
P.O. Box 1032, Muncie IN 47308-1032. 765/284-4461. **Contact:** Human Resources. **Description:** A construction contracting firm specializing in pipeline, sewer, and marine projects.

GROUPE SCHNEIDER
252 North Tippecanoe Street, Peru IN 46970. 765/472-3381. **Contact:** Human Resources. **Description:** Possesses global expertise in electrical contracting, industrial engineering, and construction. Its five major operating companies include Jeumont-Schneider Industrie, Merlin Gerin, Spie Batignolles, Square D, and Telemecanique.

HAGERMAN CONSTRUCTION CORPORATION
P.O. Box 10690, Fort Wayne IN 46853-0690. 219/424-1470. **Contact:** Human Resources. **Description:** A commercial and industrial building contractor.

HOME-CREST CORPORATION
P.O. Box 595, Goshen IN 46527. 219/533-9571. **Contact:** Human Resources. **Description:** Manufactures wooden kitchen cabinets.

HUBER, HUNT & NICHOLS, INC.
P.O. Box 128, Indianapolis IN 46206. 317/241-6301. **Physical address:** 2450 South Tibbs Avenue, Indianapolis IN 46241. **Contact:** Human Resources. **World Wide Web address:** http://www.hhn.com. **Description:** A construction firm performing work throughout the

continental U.S. **NOTE:** Please direct resumes to your department of interest. **Common positions include:** Civil Engineer; Construction Contractor; Electrical/Electronics Engineer; Industrial Engineer; Mechanical Engineer. **Educational backgrounds include:** Construction; Engineering. **Corporate headquarters location:** This Location.

INTERNATIONAL STEEL REVOLVING DOOR CO.
2124 North Sixth Avenue, Evansville IN 47710. 812/425-3311. **Toll-free phone:** 800/745-4726. **Fax:** 812/426-2682. **Contact:** David Wu, Personnel. **Description:** Designs and builds custom revolving doors and also performs metal stamping. Founded in 1963. **Common positions include:** Account Manager; Administrative Assistant; Chief Financial Officer; Controller; Cost Estimator; Database Manager; Design Engineer; Draftsperson; Electrician; Financial Analyst; Industrial Production Manager; Sales Representative. **Educational backgrounds include:** Business Administration; Computer Science; Engineering. **Benefits:** Life Insurance; Medical Insurance; Savings Plan; Tuition Assistance. **Special programs:** Internships; Apprenticeships. **Corporate headquarters location:** This Location. **Parent company:** Evansville Metal Products. **Operations at this facility include:** Divisional Headquarters; Manufacturing. **Listed on:** Privately held. **Annual sales/revenues:** $5 - $10 million. **Number of employees at this location:** 100.

KAWNEER COMPANY, INC.
751 International Drive, Franklin IN 46131. 317/738-2600. **Contact:** Human Resources. **Description:** Manufactures and markets nonresidential architectural building products such as storefronts, building entrances, facings, window framing, and curtain wall systems. **Parent company:** Alumax is one of the largest aluminum producers in North America. The company operates more than 90 plants and facilities in the United States, Canada, and Western Europe. **Number of employees worldwide:** 14,000.

LIBERTY HOMES, INC.
P.O. Box 35, Goshen IN 46527-0035. 219/533-0431. **Contact:** Human Resources. **World Wide Web address:** http://www.libertyhomesinc.com. **Description:** Designs, manufactures, and sells single section and multisectional homes.

MILLER BUILDING SYSTEMS, INC.
P.O. Box 1283, Elkhart IN 46515. 219/295-1214. **Contact:** Barb Frye, Human Resources. **Description:** The company designs, manufactures, and markets prefabricated buildings. **Subsidiaries include:** Miller Structures, Inc. and Miller Telecom Services, Inc. Miller Structures serves both the modular and mobile office market, as well as (through its Residential Division) the modular housing market. Miller Telecom is responsible for telecommunication shelters and pre-cast concrete assemblies for prisons, hazardous waste, and material confinement structures. Miller Structures' main clients are firms that sell, lease, and rent modular and mobile office structures, as well as residential housing builders and dealers. The main market for Miller Telecom is end users with specific requirements for specialized applications. **Number of employees nationwide:** 360.

NEW ALBANY COMPONENT & TRUSS
56 Galt Street, New Albany IN 47150. 812/945-2155. **Contact:** Human Resources. **Description:** Manufactures structural wooden trusses and other construction components.

SCHULT HOMES CORPORATION
P.O. Box 151, Middlebury IN 46540. 219/825-5881. **Contact:** Mike Worrell, Director of Human Resources. **World Wide Web address:** http://www.schulthome.com. **Description:** One of the nation's oldest and largest producers of manufactured housing, Schult Homes Corporation operates 10 manufacturing facilities throughout the United States.

SUPERIOR ENGINEERING CORPORATION
2345 167th Street, Hammond IN 46323. 219/844-7030. **Contact:** Human Resources. **Description:** Offers structural, electrical, and mechanical engineering services.

THERMA-TRU CORPORATION
108 Mutzfeld Road, Butler IN 46721. 219/868-5811. **Contact:** Human Resources. **Description:** Manufactures fiberglass doors and steel doors.

UNITED TECHNOLOGIES CARRIER
P.O. Box 70, Indianapolis IN 46206. 317/243-0851. **Contact:** Salaried Human Resources. **World Wide Web address:** http://www.carrier.utc.com. **Description:** A commercial manufacturer of HVAC equipment. **Parent company:** United Technologies provides high-technology products and support services to customers in the aerospace, building, military, and automotive industries worldwide. Products include large jet engines, temperature control systems, elevators and escalators, helicopters, and flight systems. The company markets its products under a variety of brand names including Carrier, Hamilton Standard, Otis, Pratt & Whitney, and Sikorsky. Production facilities are located in the U.S., Latin America, Mexico, Canada, Australia, Europe, and Asia.

WATERFURNACE INTERNATIONAL
9000 Conservation Way, Fort Wayne IN 46809. 219/478-5667. **Fax:** 219/478-3029. **Contact:** Lisa Weston, Human Resources. **World Wide Web address:** http://www.waterfurnace.com. **Description:** WaterFurnace is one of North America's leading manufacturers and distributors of geothermal heating and cooling systems for residential and commercial applications. WaterFurnace products are sold and serviced through a network of commercial representatives and residential authorized dealers, and supported by independent distributors and regional direct-sales branches throughout the United States, Canada, and Australia. **Parent company:** WFI Industries, Ltd. **Operations at this facility include:** Administration; Distribution; Manufacturing; Marketing; Research and Development.

WEIL-McLAIN
500 Blaine Street, Michigan City IN 46360-2388. 219/879-6561. **Contact:** Human Resources. **Description:** Manufactures heating equipment including boilers for the home construction and industrial markets.

Note: Because addresses and telephone numbers of smaller companies can change rapidly, we recommend you call each company to verify the information below before inquiring about job opportunities. Mass mailings are not recommended.

Additional small employers:

ARCHITECTURAL SERVICES

BSA Design
9365 Counselors Row, Indianapolis IN 46240-6418. 317/819-7878.

CSO Architects Engineers Interiors
9100 Keystone Crossing, Indianapolis IN 46240-2154. 317/848-7800.

Fanning/Howey Associates Inc.
3750 Priority Way South D, Indianapolis IN 46240-3815. 317/848-0966.

Gibraltar Design Inc.
9102 North Meridian Street, Indianapolis IN 46260-1809. 317/580-5777.

Interdesign Group Incorporated
141 E Ohio Street, Indianapolis IN 46204-2128. 317/263-9655.

Ratio Interiors
107 S Pennsylvania St, Indianapolis IN 46204-3667. 317/633-4040.

RQAW Corporation
4755 Kingsway Dr, Ste 400, Indianapolis IN 46205-1545. 317/255-6060.

Schmidt Associates Inc.
320 E Vermont St, Indianapolis IN 46204-2126. 317/263-6226.

Troyer Group Inc.
550 Union St, Mishawaka IN 46544-2340. 219/259-9976.

BRIDGE, TUNNEL, AND HIGHWAY CONSTRUCTION

Superior Construction Co. Inc.
PO Box M888, Gary IN 46401-0888. 219/886-3728.

Traylor Brothers Inc.
835 N Congress Ave, Evansville IN 47715-2452. 812/477-1542.

CONCRETE WORK

Custom Concrete Company Inc.
2816 West 193rd Road, Westfield IN 46074-9225. 317/896-2885.

CONSTRUCTION MATERIALS WHOLESALE

Firestone Building Products
525 Congressional Boulevard, Carmel IN 46032. 317/575-7000.

Mulzer Crushed Stone Inc.
Cate Sandy Quarry, Leavenworth IN 47137. 812/739-2929.

ELECTRICAL WORK

Gaylor Electric
PO Box 1192, Carmel IN 46032-6192. 317/843-0577.

Indianapolis Electric Company Inc.
241 S State Avenue, Indianapolis IN 46201-3960. 317/636-3391.

Intelex Inc.
335 Ridge Point Drive, Carmel IN 46032-2572. 317/816-6900.

JWP/HYRE Electric Company of Indiana Inc.
2655 Garfield Avenue, Highland IN 46322-1609. 219/923-6100.

Koontz-Wagner Electric Company
3801 Voorde Drive, South Bend IN 46628-1643. 219/232-2051.

Long Electric Company Inc.
1310 S Franklin Road, Indianapolis IN 46239-1119. 317/356-2455.

Meade Electric Company Inc.
1825 Summer Street, Hammond IN 46320-2237. 219/932-2100.

Miller-EADS Company Inc.
PO Box 55234, Indianapolis IN 46205-0234. 317/545-7101.

Stelko Electric Inc.
PO Box 1101, Kokomo IN 46903-1101. 765/452-2090.

Sycamore Engineering Inc.
PO Box 1056, Terre Haute IN 47808-1056. 812/232-0968.

The L.E. Myers Co.
PO Box 51710, Indianapolis IN 46251-0710. 317/787-8264.

Town & Country Electric Inc.
PO Box 562, Tell City IN 47586-0562. 812/547-7362.

Trans Tech Electric Inc.
PO Box 3915, South Bend IN 46619-0915. 219/272-9673.

ENGINEERING SERVICES

Alt & Witzig Engineering Inc.
3405 West 96th Street, Indianapolis IN 46268-1102. 317/875-7000.

American Consulting Engineers
4165 Millersville Road, Indianapolis IN 46205-2966. 317/547-5580.

ATC Group Services Inc.
8665 Bash Street, Indianapolis IN 46256-1202. 317/577-1761.

Atsi Inc.
9200 Calumet Ave, Suite N500, Hammond IN 46321-2885. 219/836-8490.

Bayer Becker Engineers
1230 Belleview Drive, Lawrenceburg IN 47025-1350. 812/537-9064.

Beam Longest & Neff Inc.
8126 Castleton Road, Indianapolis IN 46250-2007. 317/849-5832.

Bernardin Lochmueller & Company
6200 Vogel Road, Evansville IN 47715-4006. 812/479-6200.

Bonar Group
616 South Harrison Street, Fort Wayne IN 46802-1602. 219/424-0318.

Brockway Associates
PO Box 584, Michigan City IN 46361-0584. 219/872-0635.

Butler-Fairman & Seufert Inc.
9405 Delegates Row, Indianapolis IN 46240-3805. 317/573-4615.

Cole Associates Inc.
2211 E Jefferson Boulevard, South Bend IN 46615-2607. 219/236-4400.

Compression Inc.
7752 Moller Road, Indianapolis IN 46268-4163. 317/228-2200.

Crew Technical Services
1631 W Thompson Road, Indianapolis IN 46217-9349. 317/788-5858.

Diversified Systems Inc.
3939 West 56th Street, Indianapolis IN 46254-1501. 317/299-9547.

Fink Roberts & Petrie Inc.
3307 West 96th Street, Indianapolis IN 46268-1106. 317/872-8400.

GE Industrial Systems
7200 Eagle Crest Boulevard, Evansville IN 47715-8154. 812/469-9700.

HNTB Corporation
111 Monument Cir, Suite 1200, Indianapolis IN 46204-5100. 317/636-4682.

Jacob's Engineering Group Inc.
2601 Fortune Circle E 200, Indianapolis IN 46241-5548. 317/248-8222.

KMC Controls
PO Box 497, New Paris IN 46553-0497. 219/831-5170.

Lockwood Greene Company of Indiana
11590 North Meridian Street, Carmel IN 46032-6954. 317/571-3290.

Meca Engineering Corporation of America
5539 Indianapolis Boulevard, East Chicago IN 46312-3918. 219/397-0100.

Multiple Engineering
4982 West State Road 32, Anderson IN 46011-1574. 765/642-4973.

Orbital Engineering Inc.
3800 179th Street, Hammond IN 46323-3035. 219/989-3300.

Project Associates Inc.
PO Box 15395, Evansville IN 47716-0395. 812/473-2424.

RDS
6330 E 75th St, Ste 302, Indianapolis IN 46250-2708. 317/577-2255.

RW Armstrong & Associates
2801 S Pennsylvania St, Indianapolis IN 46225-2322. 317/786-0461.

Sieco Inc.
PO Box 407, Columbus IN 47202-0407. 812/372-9911.

Technology Service Corporation
116 W 6th St, Ste 200, Bloomington IN 47404-3927. 812/336-7576.

Three I Engineering Inc.
PO Box 6562, Evansville IN 47719-0562. 812/423-6800.

United Consulting Engineers
1625 North Post Road, Indianapolis IN 46219-1923. 317/895-2585.

Woolpert
7140 Waldemar Dr, Indianapolis IN 46268-2183. 317/299-7500.

GENERAL CONTRACTORS

Davis Homes
3755 E 82nd St, Suite 120, Indianapolis IN 46240-2423. 317/595-2800.

Estridge Group Inc.
PO Box 277, Carmel IN 46032-0277. 317/846-7311.

Kelly Construction of Indiana
PO Box 4158, Lafayette IN 47903-4158. 765/474-1800.

GENERAL INDUSTRIAL CONTRACTORS

Ancon Construction Company
PO Box 825, Goshen IN 46527-0825. 219/533-9561.

Arc Construction Company
PO Box 2660, Evansville IN 47728-0660. 812/426-0481.

Casteel Construction Corporation
23186 Ireland Road, South Bend IN 46614-4407. 219/289-6347.

Dallman Industrial Corporation
933 North Illinois Street, Indianapolis IN 46204-1053. 317/634-7774.

Deig Brothers
PO Box 6429, Evansville IN 47719-0429. 812/423-4201.

Dunlap General & Mechanical Contractors
PO Box 328, Columbus IN 47202-0328. 812/376-3021.

FBI Buildings Inc.
3823 West 1800 Street, Remington IN 47977-8831. 219/261-2157.

Force Construction Company
990 North National Road, Columbus IN 47201-7854. 812/372-8441.

Gibraltar Mausoleum Construction Company
9102 N Meridian Street, Indianapolis IN 46260-1809. 317/846-7525.

Graycor Industrial
6500 North U.S. Highway 231, Rockport IN 47635-9061. 812/362-7104.

Hunter Corporation
270 Steel Drive, Chesterton IN 46304-1038. 219/787-8058.

Kettelhut Construction Inc.
PO Box 5000, Lafayette IN 47903-5000. 765/447-2181.

Koetter Construction Inc.
7393 Pete Andres Road, Floyds Knobs IN 47119-8812. 812/923-9873.

Kvaerner Songer Inc.
264 Steel Drive, Chesterton IN 46304-1038. 219/787-8422.

Oberle & Associates Inc.
PO Box 9, Richmond IN 47374-4241. 765/966-7715.

Reinke Construction Corp.
1216 West Sample St, South Bend IN 46619-3832. 219/287-1561.

RL Turner Corporation
PO Box 40, Zionsville IN 46077-0040. 317/873-2712.

Robert Henry Corporation
PO Box 1407, South Bend IN 46624-1407. 219/232-2091.

Shiel-Sexton Company Inc.
8035 Castleton Rd, Indianapolis IN 46250-2004. 317/842-4941.

Smock Fansler Corporation
2910 W Minnesota St, Indianapolis IN 46241-4525. 317/248-8371.

Summit Construction Co. Inc.
PO Box 88126, Indianapolis IN 46208-0126. 317/634-6112.

Tonn & Blank
126 East 5th Street, Michigan City IN 46360-3307. 219/879-7321.

Ziolkowski Construction Inc.
PO Box 1106, South Bend IN 46624-1106. 219/287-1811.

HEAVY CONSTRUCTION

Atlas Excavating Inc.
1270 Washington Avenue, Frankfort IN 46041-2134. 765/654-9373.

Electricom Inc.
PO Box 319, Paoli IN 47454-0319. 812/723-2626.

Henckels & McCoy
PO Box 1067, Elkhart IN 46515-1067. 219/264-1121.

John Reynolds & Sons
PO Box 186, Orleans IN 47452-0186. 812/865-3232.

Miller Pipeline Corporation
PO Box 34141, Indianapolis IN 46234-0141. 317/293-0278.

SM&P Utility Resources Inc.
518 Herriman Ct, Noblesville IN 46060-4363. 317/636-7555.

Underground Utilities Group Inc.
PO Box 66, Ellettsville IN 47429-0066. 812/876-3511.

MASONRY, STONEWORK, AND PLASTERING

Beeler Beeler Associates Masonry Company Inc.
519 E Highway 131, Clarksville IN 47129-1729. 812/283-9385.

MISC. SPECIAL TRADE CONTRACTORS

Brandenburg Industrial Services Company
PO Box 908, Gary IN 46401. 219/881-0200.

Campbell Contracting Inc.
5273 Lakeview Parkway South, Indianapolis IN 46268-4111. 317/328-4440.

Midwest Pipe Coating Inc.
PO Box 609, Schererville IN 46375-0609. 219/322-4564.

Poindexter Excavating Inc.
PO Box 36399, Indianapolis IN 46236-0399. 317/823-6837.

Specialty Systems of Indiana
302 S State Ave, Indianapolis IN 46201-3900. 317/269-3600.

PLUMBING, HEATING, AND A/C

American Residential Services of Indiana Inc.
1915 W 18th Street, Indianapolis IN 46202-1016. 317/630-2100.

Amex Construction Company Inc.
1636 Summer Street, Hammond IN 46320-2232. 219/937-6100.

Frank E. Irish Inc.
PO Box 11108, Indianapolis IN 46201-0108. 317/636-2337.

Herrman & Goetz Inc.
225 S Lafayette Boulevard, South Bend IN 46601. 219/282-2596.

Ivey Mechanical Company
PO Box 68759, Indianapolis IN 46268-0759. 317/873-0915.

JO Mory Inc.
PO Box 128, South Milford IN 46786-0128. 219/351-2221.

McDaniel Fire Systems Inc.
PO Box 70, Valparaiso IN 46384-0070. 219/462-0571.

Real Mechanical Inc.
475 Gradle Dr, Carmel IN 46032-2535. 317/846-9299.

RT Moore Mechanical Contractors
6340 La Pas Trail, Indianapolis IN 46268-2511. 317/291-1052.

Sterling Boiler
PO Box 8004, Evansville IN 47716-8004. 812/479-5447.

Tri-State Fire Protection Inc.
PO Box 70, Newburgh IN 47629-0070. 812/853-9229.

PLUMBING, HEATING, AND A/C EQUIPMENT WHOLESALE

Airtron Inc.
5150 Elmwood Avenue, Indianapolis IN 46203-5913. 317/783-3101.

Landis & Staefa Inc.
6002 Corporate Way, Indianapolis IN 46278-2923. 317/293-8880.

ROAD CONSTRUCTION

Brooks Construction Company
PO Box 9560, Fort Wayne IN 46899-9560. 219/478-1990.

Milestone Contractors
PO Box 1496, Lafayette IN 47902-1496. 765/742-1081.

Milestone Contractors
5950 S Belmont Street, Indianapolis IN 46217-9757. 317/788-6885.

Sellersburg Stone
PO Box 2428, Clarksville IN 47131-2428. 812/282-1349.

ROOFING, SIDING, AND SHEET METAL WORK

Crown Corr Inc.
PO Box 1750, Highland IN 46322-0750. 219/949-8080.

Midland Engineering Company
PO Box 1019, South Bend IN 46624-1019. 219/272-0200.

Preferred Inc.
500 Wolfe Dr, Fort Wayne IN 46825-5253. 219/483-8383.

Sink & Edwards
PO Box 1686, Indianapolis IN 46206-1686. 317/633-7614.

SURVEYING SERVICES

Schneider Corporation
PO Box 26068, Indianapolis IN 46226-0068. 317/898-8282.

For more information on career opportunities in architecture, construction, and engineering:

Associations

AACE INTERNATIONAL: THE ASSOCIATION FOR ADVANCEMENT OF COST ENGINEERING
209 Prairie Avenue, Suite 100, Morgantown WV 26505. 304/296-8444. Toll-free phone: 800/858-2678. Fax: 304/291-5728. World Wide Web address: http://www.aacei.org. A membership organization which offers *Cost Engineering*, a monthly magazine; employment referral services; technical reference information and assistance; insurance; and a certification program accredited by the Council of Engineering Specialty Boards. Toll-free number provides information on scholarships for undergraduates.

AMERICAN ASSOCIATION OF ENGINEERING SOCIETIES
1111 19th Street NW, Suite 403, Washington DC 20036-3690. 202/296-2237. World Wide Web address: http://www.aaes.org. A multidisciplinary organization of professional engineering societies. American Association of Engineering Societies publishes reference works, including *Who's Who in Engineering*, *International Directory of Engineering Societies*, and the *Thesaurus of Engineering and Scientific Terms*, as well as statistical reports from studies conducted by the Engineering Workforce Commission.

AMERICAN CONSULTING ENGINEERS COUNCIL
1015 15th Street NW, Suite 802, Washington DC 20005. 202/347-7474. Fax: 202/898-0068. World Wide Web address: http://www.acec.org. A national organization of more than 5,000 member firms. Offers *Last Word*, a weekly newsletter; *American Consulting Engineer* magazine; life and health insurance programs; books, manuals, video- and audiotapes, and contract documents; conferences and seminars; and voluntary peer reviews.

AMERICAN INSTITUTE OF ARCHITECTS
1735 New York Avenue NW, Washington DC 20006. 202/626-7300. Toll-free phone: 800/365-2724. World Wide Web address: http://www.aia.org. Contact toll-free number for brochures.

AMERICAN INSTITUTE OF CONSTRUCTORS
466 94th Avenue North, St. Petersburg FL 33702. 813/578-0317. World Wide Web address: http://www.aicnet.org.

AMERICAN SOCIETY FOR ENGINEERING EDUCATION
1818 N Street NW, Suite 600, Washington DC 20036. 202/331-3500. World Wide Web address: http://www.asee.org. Publishes magazines and journals including the *Journal of Engineering Education*.

AMERICAN SOCIETY OF CIVIL ENGINEERS
1801 Alexander Bell Drive, Reston VA 20191-4400. Toll-free phone: 800/548-2723. World Wide Web address: http://www.asce.org. A membership organization which offers subscriptions to *Civil Engineering* magazine and *ASCE News,* discounts on various other publications, seminars, video- and audiotapes, specialty conferences, an annual convention, group insurance programs, and pension plans.

AMERICAN SOCIETY OF HEATING, REFRIGERATING AND AIR CONDITIONING ENGINEERS
1791 Tullie Circle NE, Atlanta GA 30329. 404/636-8400. Fax: 404/321-5478. World Wide Web address: http://www.ashrae.org. A society of 50,000 members which offers handbooks, a monthly journal, a monthly newspaper, discounts on other publications, group insurance, continuing education, and registration discounts for meetings, conferences, seminars, and expositions.

AMERICAN SOCIETY OF LANDSCAPE ARCHITECTS
636 I Street NW, Washington DC 20001. 202/686-2752. World Wide Web address: http://www.asla.org. Check out the Website's Joblink for listings of employment opportunities.

AMERICAN SOCIETY OF MECHANICAL ENGINEERS
345 East 47th Street, New York NY 10017. 212/705-7722. World Wide Web address: http://www.asme.org. Handles educational materials for certified engineers, as well as scholarships.

AMERICAN SOCIETY OF NAVAL ENGINEERS
1452 Duke Street, Alexandria VA 22314. 703/836-6727. World Wide Web address: http://www.jhuapl.edu/ASNE. Holds symposiums based on technical papers. Publishes a journal and newsletter bimonthly.

AMERICAN SOCIETY OF PLUMBING ENGINEERS
3617 Thousand Oaks Boulevard, Suite 210, Westlake CA 91362-3649. 805/495-7120. Provides technical and educational information.

AMERICAN SOCIETY OF SAFETY ENGINEERS
1800 East Oakton Street, Des Plaines IL 60018-2187. 847/699-2929. Jobline service available at ext. 243. Fax: 847/296-3769. World Wide Web address: http://www.asse.org. A membership organization offering *Professional Safety,* a monthly journal; educational seminars; an annual professional development conference and exposition; technical publications; certification preparation programs; career placement services; and group and liability insurance programs.

ASSOCIATED BUILDERS AND CONTRACTORS
1300 North 17th Street, 8th Floor, Arlington VA 22209. 703/812-2000. World Wide Web address: http://www.abc.org. Sponsors annual career fair.

ASSOCIATED GENERAL CONTRACTORS OF AMERICA, INC.
1957 E Street NW, Washington DC 20006. 202/393-2040. World Wide Web address: http://www.agc.org. A full-service construction association of subcontractors, specialty contractors, suppliers, equipment manufacturers, and professional firms. Services include government relations, education and training, jobsite services, legal services, and information services.

THE ENGINEERING CENTER (TEC)
One Walnut Street, Boston MA 02108-3616. 617/227-5551. Contact: Abbie Goodman. World Wide Web address: http://www.engineers.org. An association that provides services for many engineering membership organizations.

ILLUMINATING ENGINEERING SOCIETY OF NORTH AMERICA
120 Wall Street, 17th Floor, New York NY 10005-4001. 212/248-5000. World Wide Web address: http://www.iesna.org. An organization for industry professionals involved in the manufacturing, design, specification, and maintenance of lighting systems. Conference held annually. Offers a Technical Knowledge Examination.

JUNIOR ENGINEERING TECHNICAL SOCIETY
1420 King Street, Suite 405, Alexandria VA 22314-2794. 703/548-JETS. Fax: 703/548-0769. E-mail address: jets@nae.edu. World Wide Web address: http://www.asee.org/jets. A nonprofit, educational society promoting interest in engineering, technology, mathematics, and science. Provides information to high school students and teachers regarding careers in engineering and technology.

NATIONAL ACTION COUNCIL FOR MINORITIES IN ENGINEERING
350 Fifth Avenue, New York NY 10118. 212/279-2626. Offers scholarship programs for students. World Wide Web address: http://www.nacme.org.

NATIONAL ASSOCIATION OF HOME BUILDERS
1201 15th Street NW, Washington DC 20005. 202/822-0200. World Wide Web address: http://www.nahb.com. A trade association promoting safe and affordable housing. Provides management services and education for members.

NATIONAL ASSOCIATION OF MINORITY ENGINEERING
1133 West Morse Boulevard, Suite 201, Winter Park FL 32789. 407/647-8839.

NATIONAL ELECTRICAL CONTRACTORS ASSOCIATION
http://www.necanet.org. Provides information on hiring and trade shows. The association also publishes a magazine called *Electrical Contractor.*

NATIONAL SOCIETY OF BLACK ENGINEERS
1454 Duke Street, Alexandria VA 22314. 703/549-2207. World Wide Web address: http://www.nsbe.org. A nonprofit organization run by college students. Offers scholarships, editorials, and magazines.

NATIONAL SOCIETY OF PROFESSIONAL ENGINEERS
1420 King Street, Alexandria VA 22314-2794. 703/684-2800. Call 703/684-2830 for scholarship information for students. Fax: 703/836-4875. World Wide Web address: http://www.nspe.org. Membership includes the monthly magazine *Engineering Times;* continuing education; scholarships and fellowships; and health and life insurance programs.

SOCIETY OF AMERICAN REGISTERED ARCHITECTS
303 South Broadway, Suite 322, Tarrytown NY 10591. 914/631-3600. Fax: 914/631-1319. World Wide Web address: http://www.sara-national.org.

SOCIETY OF FIRE PROTECTION ENGINEERS
7315 Wisconsin Avenue, Bethesda MD 20814. 301/718-2910. Fax: 301/718-2242. World Wide Web address: http://www.sfpe.org. A professional society which offers members reports, newsletters, *Journal of Fire Protecting Engineering,* insurance programs, short courses, symposiums, tutorials, an annual meeting, and engineering seminars.

Directories

DIRECTORY OF ENGINEERING SOCIETIES
American Association of Engineering Societies, 1111 19th Street NW, Suite 403, Washington DC 20036. 202/296-2237.

DIRECTORY OF ENGINEERS IN PRIVATE PRACTICE
National Society of Professional Engineers, 1420 King Street, Alexandria VA 22314-2794. 703/684-2800. $50.00. Lists members and companies.

Magazines

THE CAREER ENGINEER
National Society of Black Engineers, 1454 Duke Street, Alexandria VA 22314. 703/549-2207.

CHEMICAL & ENGINEERING NEWS
American Chemical Society, 1155 16th Street NW, Washington DC 20036. 202/872-4600. World wide Web address: http://www.acs.org.

COMPUTER-AIDED ENGINEERING
Penton Publishing, 1100 Superior Avenue, Cleveland OH 44114. 216/696-7000.

EDN CAREER NEWS
Cahners Publishing Company, 275 Washington Street, Newton MA 02158. 617/964-3030. World Wide Web address: http://www.cahners.com.

ENGINEERING TIMES
National Society of Professional Engineers, 1420 King Street, Alexandria VA 22314. 703/684-2800.

NAVAL ENGINEERS JOURNAL
American Society of Naval Engineers, 1452 Duke Street, Alexandria VA 22314. 703/836-6727. Subscription: $48.00.

Online Services

ARCHITECTURE AND BUILDING FORUM
Go: Arch. A CompuServe discussion group for architectural professionals.

ARCHITECTURE AND LANDSCAPE ARCHITECTURE JOBS
http://www.clr.toronto.edu/VIRTUALLIB/jobs.html. This Website provides job openings for architects and landscape architects, as well as links to other related sites.

HOT JOBS! - CONSTRUCTION
http://www.kbic.com/construction.htm. Provides construction employment opportunities organized by job title.

P.L.A.C.E.S. FORUM
Keyword: places. A discussion group available to America Online subscribers who are professionals in the fields of architecture, construction, and engineering.

ARTS AND ENTERTAINMENT/RECREATION

Diversity is the trend in the entertainment industry. Recently, Business Week *reported that media corporations and entertainment powerhouses are trying to gain revenue by creating new divisions. These companies have originated record labels, online services, movie studios, theme parks, and cable networks. As a result, the market is oversaturated and profits are falling.*

A recent study predicted that the average television viewer will gain almost 1,000 channel choices by the time that digital compression of television is complete and the linking of TVs to the Internet becomes an option. With the creation of new channels comes more competition and as a result, programming costs have hit the roof. In an attempt to ease the sting of losing Seinfeld, *NBC reportedly agreed to pay close to $900 million to renew* ER *(its highest-rated show) for three years. Look for movie makers to create more distinct products that attract consumers in all areas. Fox and Paramount struck a golden iceberg with* Titanic, *which has spawned book tie-ins, a best-selling soundtrack, and a $30 million sale to NBC for the television rights.*

Broadway completed its most successful season ever in June 1997, with ticket sales slightly over $1 billion. Prosperity on The Great White Way is a direct result of focused industrywide ad campaigns and easier ticket accessibility. Productions are linking with larger corporations like Continental Airlines to promote themselves and the strategy is working.

Fans of professional sports continue to spend money on their teams and 1999 should be no exception. The National Football League has closed a highly profitable television contract. Major League Baseball has expanded by two more teams and is climbing back from its slump of the mid-'90s with the help of interleague play. The National Hockey League also has plans to expand, with four new teams possible by the year 2000. On the other hand, National Basketball Association officials reported that 13 of the 29 teams in the league lost money in 1997, in part due to an inefficient salary cap and escalating demands for franchise players.

All this adds up to survival of the fittest for jobseekers in the entertainment field. Across much of the industry costs are being cut and joint ventures continue. Those with business savvy and a flair for marketing may find some solid opportunities.

BALLET INTERNATIONALE
502 North Capitol Avenue, Suite B, Indianapolis IN 46204. 317/637-8979. **Fax:** 317/637-1637. **Contact:** Barbara A. Turner, Managing Director. **Description:** A professional ballet company that performs nationally. **Special programs:** Internships. **Corporate headquarters location:** This Location. **Operations at this facility include:** Administration; Sales. **Number of employees at this location:** 45.

BRADFORD WOODS OUTDOOR CENTER
5040 State Road 67 North, Martinsville IN 46151. 765/342-2915. **Contact:** Ms. Kim Nunn, Human Resources. **World Wide Web address:** http://www.indiana.edu/~bradford. **Description:** Offers environmental education and recreation programs for a diverse range of visitors. Bradford Woods is affiliated with Indiana University. **Special programs:** Internships.

THE CHILDREN'S MUSEUM OF INDIANAPOLIS
3000 North Meridian Street, Indianapolis IN 46206. 317/924-5431. **Contact:** Human Resources. **World Wide Web address:** http://www.childrensmuseum.org. **Description:** An interactive museum dedicated to helping children understand and enjoy the world. Founded in 1925. **Common positions include:** Accountant/Auditor; Buyer; Computer Programmer; Customer Service Representative; Designer; Editor; Education Administrator; Electrician; Financial Analyst; Graphic Artist; Human Resources Manager; Human Service Worker; Librarian; Library Technician; Preschool Worker; Public Relations Specialist; Purchasing Agent/Manager; Teacher/Professor; Wholesale and Retail Buyer. **Educational backgrounds include:** Accounting; Art/Design; Communications; Education; Finance; Liberal Arts; Marketing. **Benefits:** 403(b); Dental Insurance; Disability Coverage; Employee Discounts; Leave Time; Life Insurance; Medical Insurance; Pension Plan; Savings Plan; Tuition Assistance. **Special programs:** Internships. **Operations at this facility include:** Research and Development; Sales; Service. **Listed on:** Privately held. **Number of employees at this location:** 360.

DIGITAL AUDIO DISC CORPORATION
1800 North Fruitridge Avenue, Terre Haute IN 47804. 812/462-8100. **Contact:** Human Resources. **World Wide Web address:** http://www.sonydisc.com. **Description:** Produces audio compact discs and laser discs. **Parent company:** Sony.

INDIANA REPERTORY THEATRE
140 West Washington Street, Indianapolis IN 46204. 317/635-5277. **Contact:** Employment. **World Wide Web address:** http://www.indianarep.com. **Description:** A theatre operating from October to May of each year. Founded in 1971. **NOTE:** Jobseekers interested in administrative positions should contact Jane Robison. Those interested in production positions should contact the Production Manager, Kent Newbold.

THE INDIANAPOLIS ZOO
1200 West Washington Street, Indianapolis IN 46222. 317/630-2041. **Contact:** Human Resources. **World Wide Web address:** http://www.indyzoo.com. **Description:** The Indianapolis Zoo's collection includes a hoofed animal complex, a display garden, an education center, and a library.

Note: Because addresses and telephone numbers of smaller companies can change rapidly, we recommend you call each company to verify the information below before inquiring about job opportunities. Mass mailings are not recommended.

Additional small employers:

AMUSEMENT AND RECREATION SERVICES

Discovery Zone
3720 E 82nd Street, Indianapolis IN 46240-2422. 317/577-1839.

Splash Down Dunes Inc.
150 E US Highway 20, Porter IN 46304-9561. 219/929-1181.

ENTERTAINMENT GROUPS

Bertelsmann Music Group
6550 East 30th Street, Indianapolis IN 46219-1102. 317/542-6000.

RCA Records
6550 East 30th Street, Indianapolis IN 46219-1102. 317/542-6354.

PROFESSIONAL SPORTS CLUBS AND PROMOTERS

Indiana Pacers Basketball Team
300 East Market Street, Indianapolis IN 46204-2603. 317/263-2100.

Indianapolis Colts
PO Box 535000, Indianapolis IN 46253-5000. 317/297-2658.

VIDEO TAPE PRODUCTION AND DISTRIBUTION

Full Perspective Video
6902 Hawthorn Park Drive, Indianapolis IN 46220-3911. 317/579-0400.

For more information on career opportunities in arts, entertainment, and recreation:

Associations

AMERICAN ASSOCIATION OF MUSEUMS
1575 I Street NW, Suite 400, Washington DC 20005. 202/289-1818. Fax: 202/289-6578. World Wide Web address: http://www.aam-us.org. Publishes *AVISO*, a monthly newsletter containing employment listings for the entire country.

AMERICAN CRAFTS COUNCIL
72 Spring Street, New York NY 10012-4019. 212/274-0630. Operates a research library. Publishes *American Crafts* magazine.

AMERICAN DANCE GUILD
31 West 21st Street, New York NY 10010. 212/627-3790. Holds an annual conference with panels, performances, and workshops. Operates a job listings service (available at a discount to members).

AMERICAN FEDERATION OF MUSICIANS
1501 Broadway, Suite 600, New York NY 10036. 212/869-1330. World Wide Web address: http://www.afm.org.

AMERICAN FILM INSTITUTE
2021 North Western Avenue, Los Angeles CA 90027. 213/856-7706. Toll-free phone: 800/774-4AFI. World Wide Web address: http://www.afionline.org. Membership is required, and includes a newsletter; members-only discounts on events, seminars, workshops, and exhibits; and two free tickets and discounts at the AFI Theater in Washington DC.

AMERICAN MUSIC CENTER
30 West 26th Street, Suite 1001, New York NY 10010-2011. 212/366-5260. Fax: 212/366-5265. World Wide Web address: http://www.amc.net. A nonprofit research and information center for contemporary music and jazz. Provides information services and grant programs.

AMERICAN SOCIETY OF COMPOSERS, AUTHORS, AND PUBLISHERS (ASCAP)
One Lincoln Plaza, New York NY 10023. 212/621-6000. World Wide Web address: http://www.ascap.com. A membership association which licenses members' work and pays members' royalties. Offers showcases and educational seminars and workshops. The society also has an events hotline: 212/621-6485.

AMERICAN SYMPHONY ORCHESTRA LEAGUE
1156 15th Street NW, Suite 800, Washington DC 20005. 202/776-0212. World Wide Web address: http://www.symphony.org.

AMERICAN ZOO AND AQUARIUM ASSOCIATION
Oglebay Park, Wheeling WV 26003. 304/242-2160. E-mail address: azaoms@aol.com. World Wide Web address: http://www.aza.org. Publishes a monthly newspaper with employment opportunities for members.

AMERICANS FOR THE ARTS
One East 53rd Street, 2nd Floor, New York NY 10022. 212/223-2787. World Wide Web address: http://www.artsusa.org. A nonprofit organization for the literary, visual, and performing arts. Supports K-12 education and promotes public policy through meetings, forums, and seminars.

ASSOCIATION OF INDEPENDENT VIDEO AND FILMMAKERS
625 Broadway, 9th Floor, New York NY 10012. 212/807-1400. World Wide Web address: http://www.aivf.org.

THE CENTER FOR THE STUDY OF SPORT IN SOCIETY
360 Huntington Avenue, Suite 161 CP, Boston MA 02115. 617/373-4025. World Wide Web address: http://www.sportinsociety.org. Develops programs and provides publications on the interaction of sports and society.

NATIONAL ARTISTS' EQUITY ASSOCIATION
P.O. Box 28068, Central Station, Washington DC 20038-8068. 202/628-9633. A national, nonprofit organization dedicated to improving economic, health, and legal conditions for visual artists.

NATIONAL ENDOWMENT FOR THE ARTS
1100 Pennsylvania Avenue NW, Washington DC 20506. 202/682-5400. World Wide Web address: http://www.arts.endow.gov.

NATIONAL RECREATION AND PARK ASSOCIATION
22377 Belmont Ridge Road, Ashburn VA 20148. 703/858-0784. Fax: 703/8580794. World Wide Web address: http://www.nrpa.org. A national, nonprofit service organization. Offers professional development and training opportunities in recreation, parks, and leisure services. Publishes a newsletter and magazine that offer employment opportunities for members only.

PRODUCERS GUILD OF AMERICA
400 South Beverly Drive, Suite 211, Beverly Hills CA 90212. 310/557-0807. Fax: 310/557-0436. World Wide Web address: http://www.producersguild.com. Membership is required, and includes credit union access; subscription to *P.O.V. Magazine* and the association newsletter; attendance at the organization's annual Golden Laurel Awards and other events; and special screenings of motion pictures at the time of the Academy Awards.

Directories

ARTIST'S MARKET
Writer's Digest Books, 1507 Dana Avenue, Cincinnati OH 45207. 513/531-2222.

BLACK BOOK ILLUSTRATION
The Black Book, 10 Astor Place, 6th Floor, New York NY 10003. 212/539-9800. World Wide Web address: http://www.blackbook.com.

BLACK BOOK PHOTOGRAPHY
The Black Book, 10 Astor Place, 6th Floor, New York NY 10003. 212/539-9800. World Wide Web address: http://www.blackbook.com.

PLAYERS GUIDE
165 West 46th Street, New York NY 10036. 212/869-3570.

ROSS REPORTS TELEVISION
Billboard Publications, Inc., 1515 Broadway, New York NY 10036-8986. 212/764-7300.

Magazines

AMERICAN CINEMATOGRAPHER
American Society of Cinematographers, 1782 North Orange Drive, Hollywood CA 90028. 213/969-4333. World Wide Web address: http://www.cinematographer.com.

ARTFORUM
65 Bleecker Street, New York NY 10012. 212/475-4000. World Wide Web address: http://www.artforum.com.

AVISO
American Association of Museums, 1575 I Street NW, Suite 400, Washington DC 20005. 202/289-1818.

BACK STAGE
Billboard Publications, Inc., 1515 Broadway, New York NY 10036-8986. 212/764-7300. World Wide Web address: http://www.backstage.com.

BILLBOARD
Billboard Publications, Inc., 1515 Broadway, New York NY 10036-8986. 212/764-7300. World Wide Web address: http://www.billboard.com.

CRAFTS REPORT
300 Water Street, Wilmington DE 19801. 302/656-2209. World Wide Web address: http://www.craftsreport.com.

DRAMA-LOGUE
P.O. Box 38771, Los Angeles CA 90038. 213/464-5079.

HOLLYWOOD REPORTER
5055 Wilshire Boulevard, 6th Floor, Los Angeles CA 90036. 213/525-2000. World Wide Web address: http://www.hollywoodreporter.com.

VARIETY
245 West 17th Street, 5th Floor, New York NY 10011. 212/337-7001. Toll-free phone: 800/323-4345.

WOMEN ARTIST NEWS
300 Riverside Drive, New York NY 10025. 212/666-6990.

Online Services

AMERICAN CAMPING ASSOCIATION
http://www.aca-camps.org/. Provides listings of jobs at day and overnight camps for children and adults with special needs.

ARTJOB
Gopher://gopher.tmn.com/11/Artswire/artjob. Provides information on jobs, internships, and conferences in theater, dance, opera, and museums. This site is only accessible through America Online.

COOLWORKS
http://www.coolworks.com/. Provides links to 22,000 job openings in national parks, summer camps, ski areas, river areas, ranches, fishing areas, cruise ships, and resorts. This site also includes information on volunteer openings.

VISUAL NATION ARTS JOBS LINKS
http://fly.hiwaay.net/%7Edrewyor/art_job.html. Provides links to other sites that post arts and academic job openings and information.

AUTOMOTIVE

In the face of fierce competition both in the U.S. and abroad, automotive manufacturers have been forced to lower car prices, grant low interest-rate financing, and offer better deals on leasing. With consumer confidence at a dramatic high, this presents a strong buyer's market, but according to Business Week, *auto consumers are also more discriminating than ever.*

In fact, J.D. Power & Associates forecasted a 2 percent drop in 1998 automotive prices, even though the "Big Three" -- General Motors Corporation, Chrysler Corporation, and Ford Motor Corporation -- had made significant price cuts in 1997. Used car prices are also projected to decline further, and leasing remains a popular alternative to traditional car purchasing.

AM GENERAL CORPORATION
105 North Niles Avenue, South Bend IN 46617. 219/237-6222. **Contact:** Human Resources. **Description:** Manufactures the Hummer, an oversized truck built primarily for the military, but also for an increasing number of consumers. AM General began production in 1983, and has sold more than 100,000 trucks to the military since then.

AM GENERAL CORPORATION
1300 McKinley Highway, Mishawaka IN 46544. 219/256-1581. **Contact:** Human Resources. **Description:** Manufactures the Hummer, an oversized truck built primarily for the military, but also for an increasing number of consumers. AM General began production in 1983, and has sold more than 100,000 vehicles to the military since then.

ADESA CORPORATION
310 East 96th Street, Suite 400, Indianapolis IN 46240. 317/815-1100. **Contact:** Steve Kotz, Director of Human Resources. **World Wide Web address:** http://www.adesa.com. **Description:** Auctions used cars and other vehicles to franchised auto dealerships. Adesa also provides auto reconditioning and vehicle transport services. **Number of employees nationwide:** 2,750.

ALPHABET INC.
JCI DIVISION
700 Industrial Drive, Portland IN 47371. 219/726-6501. **Contact:** Mr. Kline Bryan, Human Resources Manager. **Description:** Manufactures wire harnesses for automobiles.

ALPINE ELECTRONICS MANUFACTURING OF AMERICA
421 North Emerson Avenue, Greenwood IN 46143. 317/881-7700. **Contact:** Mark King, Human Resources Director. **Description:** Manufactures car stereos and accessories. **Common positions include:** Electrical/Electronics Engineer; Mechanical Engineer.

ARVIN EXHAUST
101 Center Street, Greenwood IN 46143. 317/881-2551. **Contact:** Human Resources. **Description:** Manufactures stainless steel tubing for the automotive industry. **Parent company:** Arvin Industries, Inc. has 11 operating companies engaged in manufacturing and research and development serving the automotive, consumer, government, and industrial markets.

ARVIN SANGO, INC.
2905 Wilson Avenue, Madison IN 47250. 812/265-2888. **Contact:** Human Resources Manager. **Description:** Manufactures automotive exhaust systems. **Common positions include:** Accountant/Auditor; Industrial Engineer; Mechanical Engineer.

BORG-WARNER AUTOMOTIVE
5401 Kilgore Avenue, Muncie IN 47304. 765/286-6100. **Contact:** Employment Department. **World Wide Web address:** http://www.bwa-auto.com. **Description:** Manufactures automotive equipment.

THE BUDD COMPANY
PLASTICS DIVISION
2620 Marion Drive, Kendallville IN 46755. 219/347-5973. **Contact:** Human Resources. **World Wide Web address:** http://www.buddcompany.com. **Description:** This location manufactures car parts. Overall, The Budd Company is a diversified transportation manufacturing firm with three primary operating segments. Automotive Products Group manufactures products such as auto body parts, frames, wheels, and brakes. Industrial Products Group manufactures railway cars, truck trailers, iron castings, plastic auto parts, and specialized fibers and nylon for industrial products. International Group has facilities in West Germany, France, Argentina, and Mexico.

CAMBRIDGE INDUSTRIES
501 Northridge Drive, Shelbyville IN 46176. 317/392-8000. **Contact:** Brian Woehler, Human Resources Manager. **Description:** Manufactures automotive parts.

CHRYSLER CORPORATION
CASTING PLANT
2401 South Reed, Kokomo IN 46904. 765/454-1000. **Contact:** Employment Office. **World Wide Web address:** http://www.chrysler.com. **Description:** Produces cars, trucks, minivans, and sport-utility vehicles for customers in more than 100 countries. In North America, the company markets vehicles through three divisions: Chrysler/Plymouth, Dodge/Dodge Truck, and Jeep/Eagle. Founded in 1924. **NOTE:** In May 1998, Chrysler Corporation and Daimler-Benz (Germany) announced plans to merge. The two will combine to form a new company called DaimlerChrysler. **Corporate headquarters location:** Highland Park MI. **Subsidiaries include:** Chrysler Financial Corporation provides financing for Chrysler's dealers and customers. Pentastar Transportation Group, Inc. includes Thrifty Rent-A-Car System, Inc. and Dollar Systems, Inc. Chrysler Technologies Corporation manufactures high-technology electronic products.

CHRYSLER CORPORATION
INDIANAPOLIS FOUNDRY
1100 South Tibbs Avenue, Indianapolis IN 46241. **Contact:** Personnel. **Description:** Produces cars, trucks, minivans, and sport-utility vehicles for customers in more than 100 countries. **NOTE:** In May 1998, Chrysler Corporation and Daimler-Benz (Germany) announced plans to merge. The two will combine to form a new company called DaimlerChrysler. This firm does not accept unsolicited resumes. Please only respond to advertised openings.

COACHMEN INDUSTRIES, INC.
601 East Beardsley Avenue, Elkhart IN 46514. 219/262-0123. **Contact:** Human Resources. **World Wide Web address:** http://www.coachmen.com. **Description:** Produces recreational vehicles, such as motor homes, travel trailers, camping trailers, truck campers, and van campers. The company also manufactures parts and supplies for its vehicles. **NOTE:** Please send resumes to Human Resources, 423 North Main, P.O. Box 30, Middlebury IN 46540. 219/825-8258. **Corporate headquarters location:** This Location.

COACHMEN RECREATIONAL VEHICLES, INC.
423 North Main Street, P.O. Box 30, Middlebury IN 46540. 219/825-5821. **Contact:** Human Resources. **World Wide Web address:** http://www.coachmenrv.com. **Description:** Manufactures recreational vehicles, such as motor homes, travel trailers, camping trailers, truck campers, and van campers. **Corporate headquarters location:** Elkhart IN. **Parent company:** Coachmen Industries, Inc.

COOPER AUTOMOTIVE
402 Royal Road, Michigan City IN 46360. 219/872-5150. **Contact:** Human Resources. **World Wide Web address:** http://www.cooperauto.com. **Description:** This location is primarily an automotive assembly plant. **Common positions include:** Accountant/Auditor; Computer

Programmer; Draftsperson; Management Trainee; Mechanical Engineer; Systems Analyst. **Educational backgrounds include:** Accounting; Business Administration; Computer Science; Engineering; Marketing. **Benefits:** Dental Insurance; Disability Coverage; Employee Discounts; Life Insurance; Medical Insurance; Pension Plan; Savings Plan; Tuition Assistance. **Corporate headquarters location:** Houston TX. **Parent company:** Cooper Industries. **Operations at this facility include:** Divisional Headquarters.

CUMMINS ENGINE COMPANY, INC.
P.O. Box 3005, Columbus IN 47202. 812/377-5000. **Contact:** Amberly Schrink, Human Resources. **World Wide Web address:** http://www.cummins.com. **Description:** One of the world's leading producers of diesel engines for heavy-duty trucks, engine parts, and powertrain systems for the mining, military, construction, transportation, agriculture, and industrial markets. **Corporate headquarters location:** This Location. **Listed on:** New York Stock Exchange. **Number of employees nationwide:** 26,000.

CURTIS COACH
1400 West Main Street, Mitchell IN 47446. 812/849-3131. **Contact:** Human Resources. **Description:** Manufactures school and commercial bus bodies. **Common positions include:** Accountant/Auditor; Blue-Collar Worker Supervisor; Designer; Draftsperson; Electrical/ Electronics Engineer; Human Resources Manager; Industrial Engineer; Mechanical Engineer; Purchasing Agent/Manager. **Educational backgrounds include:** Business Administration; Engineering; Finance; Marketing. **Benefits:** 401(k); Dental Insurance; Disability Coverage; Life Insurance; Medical Insurance; Savings Plan. **Corporate headquarters location:** This Location. **Other U.S. locations:** Richmond IN. **Operations at this facility include:** Administration; Manufacturing; Sales. **Listed on:** Privately held. **Number of employees at this location:** 577. **Number of employees nationwide:** 645.

DELPHI/DELCO ELECTRONIC SYSTEMS
One Corporate Center, P.O. Box 9005, Kokomo IN 46904-9005. 765/451-5011. **Contact:** Personnel. **World Wide Web address:** http://www.delphiauto.com. **Description:** Produces automotive starting, generating, and ignition systems, as well as a wide variety of related parts and systems. **Corporate headquarters location:** This Location. **Parent company:** General Motors produces cars, trucks, and buses to be sold worldwide. The firm has 152 facilities operating in 26 states and 93 cities in the United States and 13 plants in Canada, and also has assembly, manufacturing, distribution, sales, and warehousing operations in 37 other countries.

EATON CORPORATION
P.O. Box 308, Winamac IN 46996. 219/946-3163. **Contact:** Human Resources. **World Wide Web address:** http://www.eaton.com. **Description:** This location manufactures automotive switches for a variety of vehicle applications. Overall, Eaton Corporation designs, manufactures, and sells electronic and electromechanical devices to automotive, appliance, and air conditioning and refrigeration manufacturers.

EATON CORPORATION
CLUTCH DIVISION
201 Brandon Street, Auburn IN 46706. 219/925-3800. **Contact:** George Campbell, Human Resources Director. **World Wide Web address:** http://www.eaton.com. **Description:** This location manufactures automotive clutches. Overall, Eaton Corporation manufactures electronic and electromechanical control components and systems including motor starters, programmable controllers, and automated and push-button material handling systems. Eaton Corporation also manufactures golf grips and vehicle components including brakes, axles, superchargers, and steering systems. Founded in 1905. **Corporate headquarters location:** Cleveland OH. **Number of employees worldwide:** 55,000.

EXCEL INDUSTRIES, INC.
1120 North Main Street, Elkhart IN 46514. 219/264-2131. **Contact:** Michael Paquette, Human Resources Director. **Description:** Designs, manufactures, and supplies window and door systems to the combined automobile, light truck and van, bus, heavy truck, and recreational vehicle markets in North America. Product categories include automotive windows and doors, automotive regulators,

mass transit/RV/heavy truck, and plastic products. Founded in 1928. **Other area locations:** LaGrange IN; Mishawaka IN. **Other U.S. locations:** Jacksonville FL; Bowling Green KY; Fulton KY; Toledo OH; Lawrenceburg TN; Pikeville TN. **International locations:** Aurora, Ontario. **Number of employees nationwide:** 3,100.

FEDERAL-MOGUL CORPORATION
2845 West State Road 28, Frankfort IN 46041. 765/654-8761. **Contact:** Personnel Department. **World Wide Web address:** http://www.federal-mogul.com. **Description:** This location manufactures oil seals for the automotive industry. Overall, Federal-Mogul is a manufacturer of cylindrical and tapered roller bearings, bushings, sleeve bearings, ball bearings, thrust washers, and related products for the automotive industry. The company also produces and distributes precision parts to original equipment manufacturers, and replacement parts such as fuel systems, suspension parts, and lighting and electrical products to worldwide markets. Brand names of manufactured goods include Federal-Mogul, Glyco, Bruss, National, Mather, and Signal-Stat. **Corporate headquarters location:** Southfield MI. **Number of employees nationwide:** 12,000.

FEDERAL-MOGUL CORPORATION
LIGHTING, ELECTRICAL & FUEL SYSTEMS DIVISION
101 Industrial Boulevard, Logansport IN 46947. 219/722-6141. **Fax:** 219/722-5297. **Contact:** Human Resources Manager. **World Wide Web address:** http://www.federal-mogul.com. **Description:** This location manufactures electrical lighting systems for tractor-trailers, and electrical and diesel fuel pumps for the automotive industry. Overall, Federal-Mogul is a manufacturer of cylindrical and tapered roller bearings, oil seals, bushings, sleeve bearings, ball bearings, thrust washers, and related products for the automotive industry. The company also produces and distributes precision parts to original equipment manufacturers and replacement parts such as fuel systems, suspension parts, and lighting and electrical products to worldwide markets. Brand names of manufactured goods include Federal-Mogul, Glyco, Bruss, National, Mather, and Signal-Stat. **Common positions include:** Accountant/Auditor; Blue-Collar Worker Supervisor; Buyer; Computer Programmer; Customer Service Representative; Draftsperson; Electrical/Electronics Engineer; Electrician; Financial Analyst; Human Resources Manager; Industrial Engineer; Management Trainee; Marketing Specialist; Mechanical Engineer; Operations/Production Manager; Purchasing Agent/Manager; Quality Control Supervisor. **Educational backgrounds include:** Accounting; Business Administration; Computer Science; Engineering; Finance; Liberal Arts; Marketing. **Benefits:** 401(k); Dental Insurance; Disability Coverage; Life Insurance; Medical Insurance; Pension Plan; Savings Plan; Stock Option; Tuition Assistance. **Corporate headquarters location:** Southfield MI. **Operations at this facility include:** Administration; Manufacturing; Research and Development; Sales. **Listed on:** New York Stock Exchange. **Number of employees at this location:** 600. **Number of employees nationwide:** 12,000.

FLEETWOOD MOTOR HOMES, INC.
1031 U.S. Highway 224 East, P.O. Box 31, Decatur IN 46733. 219/728-2121. **Contact:** Doug Hormann, Personnel Director. **World Wide Web address:** http://www.fleetwood.com. **Description:** Produces recreational vehicles and manufactured housing with operations in the U.S., Canada, and Germany. The company's recreational vehicles are primarily motor homes sold under the brand names: American Eagle, Coronado, Bounder, Flair, and PaceArrow. Fleetwood also manufactures a variety of trailers and campers, and owns subsidiaries which offer financial services and supplies. The company has an 80 percent interest in Niesmann & Bischoff, a motor home manufacturer in Germany.

FREUDENBERG-NOK
P.O. Box 150, Ligonier IN 46767. 219/894-7183. **Contact:** Human Resources. **World Wide Web address:** http://www.freudenberg-nok.com. **Description:** Manufactures vibration control parts, such as engine mounts for automobiles.

GECOM CORPORATION
1025 Barachel Lane, Greensburg IN 47240. 812/663-0515. **Fax:** 812/663-2230. **Contact:** Joe Bausback, Recruiting Manager. **Description:** A QS-9000 certified automotive parts supplier to Honda, Toyota, Chrysler, Mazda, Isuzu, and other OEMs. GECOM manufactures opener and latch

assemblies. Founded in 1987. **NOTE:** Entry-level positions and second and third shifts are offered. **Common positions include:** Account Representative; Accountant/Auditor; Administrative Assistant; Administrative Manager; Applications Engineer; Assistant Manager; Blue-Collar Worker Supervisor; Budget Analyst; Buyer; Chief Financial Officer; Claim Representative; Computer Operator; Computer Programmer; Customer Service Representative; Database Manager; Design Engineer; Education Administrator; Electrician; Financial Analyst; General Manager; Human Resources Manager; Industrial Engineer; Industrial Production Manager; Librarian; Manufacturing Engineer; Marketing Manager; Marketing Specialist; Mechanical Engineer; Operations/Production Manager; Project Manager; Purchasing Agent/Manager; Quality Control Supervisor; Registered Nurse; Secretary; Systems Analyst; Systems Manager; Transportation/Traffic Specialist; Typist/Word Processor. **Benefits:** 401(k); Dental Insurance; Disability Coverage; Medical Insurance; Tuition Assistance. **Special programs:** Training. **Corporate headquarters location:** This Location. **Other U.S. locations:** Southfield MI. **International locations:** Nirasaki, Japan. **Parent company:** Mitsui Kinzoku. **Operations at this facility include:** Administration; Manufacturing; Service. **Listed on:** Privately held. **Annual sales/revenues:** More than $100 million. **Number of employees at this location:** 1,500. **Number of employees nationwide:** 2,150.

GENERAL MOTORS CORPORATION
P.O. Box 388, Indianapolis IN 46206. 317/269-5830. **Contact:** Personnel. **World Wide Web address:** http://www.gm.com. **Description:** This location stamps metal for pick-up trucks. Overall, General Motors Corporation is one of the world's largest full-line vehicle manufacturers. The company also has substantial interests in information technology, electronics, and finance. GM conducts business through six different sectors. North American Automotive Operations includes Sales/Service Groups (Buick, Cadillac, Chevrolet, GMC Truck, Oldsmobile, Pontiac, and Saturn) and Vehicle Development Groups (Powertrain, Truck Group, Small Car Group, and Midsize/Luxury Car Group). Delphi Automotive Systems consists of Delphi Chassis Systems, Delphi Packard Electric Systems, Delphi Energy & Engine Management Systems, Delphi Saginaw Steering Systems, Delphi Harrison Thermal Systems, Delphi Interior & Lighting Systems, Delphi Automotive Systems European Region, Delphi Automotive Systems Asia/Pacific Region, and Delphi Automotive Systems South America. International Operations include GM Europe (GME), Asia Pacific Operations (APO), and Latin America, Africa, Middle East Operations (LAAMO). General Motors Acceptance Corporation (GMAC) provides financing and insurance to GM customers and dealers, consists of North American Operations, International Operations, Motors Insurance Corporation, and GMAC Mortgage Group. Electronic Data Systems Corporation (EDS) applies information technologies to more than 8,000 customers globally in the communications, energy/chemical, insurance, public sector, travel and transportation, financial services, manufacturing, and retail industries. GM Hughes Electronics Corporation is involved in automotive electronics, telecommunications and space electronics, and defense electronics. Founded in 1908. **Corporate headquarters location:** Detroit MI.

GENERAL MOTORS CORPORATION
C-P-C GROUP
2400 West Second Street, Marion IN 46952. 765/668-2000. **Contact:** Personnel. **World Wide Web address:** http://www.gm.com. **Description:** One of the world's largest full-line vehicle manufacturers. The company also has substantial interests in information technology, electronics, and finance. GM conducts business through six different sectors. North American Automotive Operations includes Sales/Service Groups (Buick, Cadillac, Chevrolet, GMC Truck, Oldsmobile, Pontiac, and Saturn) and Vehicle Development Groups (Powertrain, Truck Group, Small Car Group, and Midsize/Luxury Car Group). Delphi Automotive Systems consists of Delphi Chassis Systems, Delphi Packard Electric Systems, Delphi Energy & Engine Management Systems, Delphi Saginaw Steering Systems, Delphi Harrison Thermal Systems, Delphi Interior & Lighting Systems, Delphi Automotive Systems European Region, Delphi Automotive Systems Asia/Pacific Region, and Delphi Automotive Systems South America. International Operations include GM Europe (GME), Asia Pacific Operations (APO), and Latin America, Africa, Middle East Operations (LAAMO). General Motors Acceptance Corporation (GMAC) provides financing and insurance to GM customers and dealers, consists of North American Operations, International Operations, Motors Insurance Corporation, and GMAC Mortgage Group. Electronic Data Systems Corporation (EDS) applies information technologies to more than 8,000 customers globally in the

communications, energy/chemical, insurance, public sector, travel and transportation, financial services, manufacturing, and retail industries. GM Hughes Electronics Corporation is involved in automotive electronics, telecommunications and space electronics, and defense electronics. Founded in 1908. **Corporate headquarters location:** Detroit MI.

GENERAL MOTORS CORPORATION
DELPHI ENERGY AND ENGINE MANAGEMENT SYSTEMS
2900 South Scatterfield Road, Anderson IN 46013. 765/646-2000. **Contact:** Human Resources. **World Wide Web address:** http://www.gm.com. **Description:** This location manufactures and distributes auto storage batteries. Overall, General Motors Corporation is one of the world's largest full-line vehicle manufacturers. The company also has substantial interests in information technology, electronics, and finance. GM conducts business through six different sectors. North American Automotive Operations includes Sales/Service Groups (Buick, Cadillac, Chevrolet, GMC Truck, Oldsmobile, Pontiac, and Saturn) and Vehicle Development Groups (Powertrain, Truck Group, Small Car Group, and Midsize/Luxury Car Group). Delphi Automotive Systems consists of Delphi Chassis Systems, Delphi Packard Electric Systems, Delphi Energy & Engine Management Systems, Delphi Saginaw Steering Systems, Delphi Harrison Thermal Systems, Delphi Interior & Lighting Systems, Delphi Automotive Systems European Region, Delphi Automotive Systems Asia/Pacific Region, and Delphi Automotive Systems South America. International Operations include GM Europe (GME), Asia Pacific Operations (APO), and Latin America, Africa, Middle East Operations (LAAMO). General Motors Acceptance Corporation (GMAC) provides financing and insurance to GM customers and dealers, consists of North American Operations, International Operations, Motors Insurance Corporation, and GMAC Mortgage Group. Electronic Data Systems Corporation (EDS) applies information technologies to more than 8,000 customers globally in the communications, energy/chemical, insurance, public sector, travel and transportation, financial services, manufacturing, and retail industries. GM Hughes Electronics Corporation is involved in automotive electronics, telecommunications and space electronics, and defense electronics. Founded in 1908. **Corporate headquarters location:** Detroit MI.

GENERAL MOTORS CORPORATION
DELPHI INTERIOR AND LIGHTING SYSTEMS
2915 Pendleton Avenue, Anderson IN 46016-4849. 765/644-5511. **Contact:** Human Resources. **World Wide Web address:** http://www.gm.com. **Description:** This location manufactures headlamps, tail lights, and interior lighting systems. Overall, General Motors Corporation is one of the world's largest full-line vehicle manufacturers. The company also has substantial interests in information technology, electronics, and finance. GM conducts business through six different sectors. North American Automotive Operations includes Sales/Service Groups (Buick, Cadillac, Chevrolet, GMC Truck, Oldsmobile, Pontiac, and Saturn) and Vehicle Development Groups (Powertrain, Truck Group, Small Car Group, and Midsize/Luxury Car Group). Delphi Automotive Systems consists of Delphi Chassis Systems, Delphi Packard Electric Systems, Delphi Energy & Engine Management Systems, Delphi Saginaw Steering Systems, Delphi Harrison Thermal Systems, Delphi Interior & Lighting Systems, Delphi Automotive Systems European Region, Delphi Automotive Systems Asia/Pacific Region, and Delphi Automotive Systems South America. International Operations include GM Europe (GME), Asia Pacific Operations (APO), and Latin America, Africa, Middle East Operations (LAAMO). General Motors Acceptance Corporation (GMAC) provides financing and insurance to GM customers and dealers, consists of North American Operations, International Operations, Motors Insurance Corporation, and GMAC Mortgage Group. Electronic Data Systems Corporation (EDS) applies information technologies to more than 8,000 customers globally in the communications, energy/chemical, insurance, public sector, travel and transportation, financial services, manufacturing, and retail industries. GM Hughes Electronics Corporation is involved in automotive electronics, telecommunications and space electronics, and defense electronics. Founded in 1908. **Corporate headquarters location:** Detroit MI.

GENERAL MOTORS CORPORATION
GM FORT WAYNE TRUCK AND BUS
12200 Lafayette Center Road, Roanoke IN 46783. 219/673-2000. **Contact:** Human Resources. **World Wide Web address:** http://www.gm.com. **Description:** This location manufactures trucks.

Overall, General Motors Corporation is one of the world's largest full-line vehicle manufacturers. The company also has substantial interests in information technology, electronics, and finance. GM conducts business through six different sectors. North American Automotive Operations includes Sales/Service Groups (Buick, Cadillac, Chevrolet, GMC Truck, Oldsmobile, Pontiac, and Saturn) and Vehicle Development Groups (Powertrain, Truck Group, Small Car Group, and Midsize/Luxury Car Group). Delphi Automotive Systems consists of Delphi Chassis Systems, Delphi Packard Electric Systems, Delphi Energy & Engine Management Systems, Delphi Saginaw Steering Systems, Delphi Harrison Thermal Systems, Delphi Interior & Lighting Systems, Delphi Automotive Systems European Region, Delphi Automotive Systems Asia/Pacific Region, and Delphi Automotive Systems South America. International Operations include GM Europe (GME), Asia Pacific Operations (APO), and Latin America, Africa, Middle East Operations (LAAMO). General Motors Acceptance Corporation (GMAC) provides financing and insurance to GM customers and dealers, consists of North American Operations, International Operations, Motors Insurance Corporation, and GMAC Mortgage Group. Electronic Data Systems Corporation (EDS) applies information technologies to more than 8,000 customers globally in the communications, energy/chemical, insurance, public sector, travel and transportation, financial services, manufacturing, and retail industries. GM Hughes Electronics Corporation is involved in automotive electronics, telecommunications and space electronics, and defense electronics. Founded in 1908. **Corporate headquarters location:** Detroit MI.

GREAT DANE TRAILERS, INC.
P.O. Box 350, Brazil IN 47834. 812/443-4711. **Contact:** Larry Stunkel, Human Resources Director. **Description:** Manufactures flatbed and refrigerated trailers, and truck and van bodies.

GROTE INDUSTRIES
P.O. Box 1550, Madison IN 47250. 812/273-2121. **Physical address:** 2600 Lanier Drive, Madison IN. **Contact:** Human Resources. **World Wide Web address:** http://www.grote.com. **Description:** Manufactures vehicular lighting products.

GUARDIAN AUTOMOTIVE
1900 South Center Street, Auburn IN 46706. 219/925-5656. **Contact:** Human Resources. **Description:** Produces flat glass for automotive windshields.

GUARDIAN AUTOMOTIVE
P.O. Box 5109, Evansville IN 47716-5109. 812/477-6151. **Contact:** Larry Gerbig, Human Resources Director. **Description:** Manufactures automotive trim.

LIBBEY-OWENS-FORD COMPANY
300 Northridge Drive, Shelbyville IN 46176. 317/392-7000. **Contact:** Human Resources. **Description:** A diversified manufacturer of fluid power and fluid systems components, automotive glass, flat and tinted glass products, and decorative laminates and molded plastics.

MONACO COACH CORPORATION
P.O. Box 4313, Elkhart IN 46517. 219/295-8060. **Contact:** Human Resources. **Description:** One of the nation's leading manufacturers of high-line motor coaches. The company has five distinct lines: the Windsor, the Dynasty, the Executive, the Crowne Royale Signature Series, and Royale Coach bus conversions. Monaco offers its customers a high level of after-sale service and support, including company-sponsored rallies, membership in one of its two owners' clubs, and a subscription to *Lifestyles*, its owners' magazine. **Corporate headquarters location:** Junction City OR.

NAVISTAR INTERNATIONAL TRANSPORTATION
5565 Brookville Road, Indianapolis IN 46219. 317/352-4500. **Contact:** Human Resources. **World Wide Web address:** http://www.navistar.com. **Description:** A large manufacturer of large- and medium-sized heavy duty trucks, chassis, and mid-range diesel engines. Other operations include financing for dealers and customers, service operations, and replacement parts distribution. The company operates seven production facilities in the U.S. and one in Canada, and sells its products throughout more than 70 countries.

PREFERRED TECHNICAL GROUP/DANA CORPORATION
303 North Jackson Street, Andrews IN 46702. 219/786-3371. **Contact:** Human Resources. **Description:** Manufactures electrical engine equipment. **Parent company:** Echlin, Inc. is a producer of automotive products which are primarily used as replacement parts. These products include brakes and engine system parts, clutches, pumps, gears and chains, steering and suspension components, windshield wiper blades and related parts, and gaskets. The company also manufactures non-automotive products for industrial uses, and wire, cable, and security access control products for commercial uses.

ROYALE COACH BY MONACO
1330 Wade Drive, Elkhart IN 46514. 219/262-9278. **Contact:** Human Resources. **Description:** This location is a manufacturing and conversion facility for the Royale Coach bus line. **Corporate headquarters location:** Junction City OR. **Parent company:** Monaco Coach Corporation is one of the nation's leading manufacturers of high-line motor coaches. The company has five distinct lines: the Windsor, the Dynasty, the Executive, the Crowne Royale Signature Series, and Royale Coach bus conversions. Monaco offers its customers a high level of after-sale service and support, including company-sponsored rallies, membership in one of its two owners clubs, and a subscription to Lifestyles, its semi-monthly owners magazine.

SKYLINE CORPORATION
2520 Bypass Road, Elkhart IN 46514. 219/294-6521. **Contact:** Human Resources. **Description:** Designs, produces, and distributes manufactured mobile homes and recreational vehicles, such as travel trailers, park models, mini motor homes, and fifth wheels. **Corporate headquarters location:** This Location. **Listed on:** New York Stock Exchange.

STANT MANUFACTURING, INC.
1620 Columbia Avenue, Connersville IN 47331. 765/825-3121. **Contact:** Human Resources. **Description:** This location is a manufacturing facility. Overall, Stant Corporation is a holding company whose subsidiaries design, manufacture, and distribute a broad range of automotive parts and tools including windshield washing and wiping systems, fuel tank caps, engine thermostats, and other accessories. **Parent company:** Stant Corporation.

STARCRAFT AUTOMOTIVE GROUP, INC.
2703 College Avenue, Goshen IN 46528. 219/533-1105. **Contact:** Human Resources. **World Wide Web address:** http://www.starcraftcorp.com. **Description:** Specializes in upscale, custom vehicles and is one of the largest conversion van manufacturers in the United States. In addition to converting full-size vans and minivans, the company customizes pick-up trucks and sport-utility vehicles. Starcraft Automotive sells its products through a network of approximately 900 authorized automotive dealers worldwide. **Corporate headquarters location:** This Location. **Listed on:** NASDAQ.

STARCRAFT RV, INC.
P.O. Box 458, Topeka IN 46571. 219/593-2550. **Fax:** 219/593-2579. **Contact:** Barbara Babcock, Personnel Department. **Description:** Manufactures recreational vehicles. Starcraft's products include fold-down camping trailers, truck campers, travel trailers, and fifth-wheel trailers. **Common positions include:** Accountant/Auditor; Blue-Collar Worker Supervisor; Buyer; Computer Programmer; Credit Manager; Draftsperson; General Manager; Industrial Production Manager; Manufacturer's/Wholesaler's Sales Rep.; Operations/Production Manager; Purchasing Agent/Manager; Quality Control Supervisor. **Educational backgrounds include:** Accounting; Computer Science; Engineering; Liberal Arts; Marketing. **Benefits:** 401(k); Dental Insurance; Disability Coverage; Life Insurance; Medical Insurance. **Corporate headquarters location:** Goshen IN. **Parent company:** Jayco, Inc. **Operations at this facility include:** Administration; Manufacturing; Research and Development; Sales; Service. **Listed on:** NASDAQ. **Number of employees at this location:** 300.

SUPREME INDUSTRIES, INC.
P.O. Box 463, Goshen IN 46527. 219/642-3070. **Contact:** Human Resources. **Description:** A manufacturer and distributor of specialized truck bodies. The company also installs the bodies and other equipment on truck chassis.

UNIVERSAL TOOL AND STAMPING COMPANY, INC.
P.O. Box 100, Butler IN 46721-0100. 219/868-2147. **Contact:** Personnel. **Description:** Manufactures automotive jacks.

UTILIMASTER CORPORATION
65266 State Road 19, P.O. Box 585, Wakarusa IN 46573. 219/862-4561. **Contact:** Human Resources. **World Wide Web address:** http://www.utilimaster.com. **Description:** A manufacturer of truck and bus bodies.

WABASH NATIONAL CORPORATION
P.O. Box 6129, Lafayette IN 47903. 765/448-1591. **Contact:** Chuck Fish, Vice President of Human Resources. **World Wide Web address:** http://www.wncwabash.com/wabash. **Description:** Designs, manufactures, and markets standard and customized truck trailers including dry freight vans, refrigerated trailers, and bimodal vehicles, as well as parts and related equipment. Wabash markets its products through dealers to truckload and less-than-truckload common carriers, private fleet operators, household moving and storage companies, package carriers, and intermodal carriers including railroads. Founded in 1985. **Common positions include:** Accountant/Auditor; Blue-Collar Worker Supervisor; Buyer; Computer Programmer; Draftsperson; Electrical/Electronics Engineer; Human Resources Manager; Industrial Engineer; Licensed Practical Nurse; Mechanical Engineer; Purchasing Agent/Manager; Systems Analyst; Transportation/Traffic Specialist. **Educational backgrounds include:** Accounting; Computer Science; Engineering. **Benefits:** 401(k); Dental Insurance; Disability Coverage; Life Insurance; Medical Insurance; Pension Plan; Profit Sharing; Tuition Assistance. **Corporate headquarters location:** This Location. **Operations at this facility include:** Administration; Manufacturing. **Listed on:** New York Stock Exchange. **Number of employees at this location:** 2,700.

WABASH TECHNOLOGIES
1375 Swan Street, Huntington IN 46750. 219/426-0611. **Contact:** Human Resources. **Description:** Manufactures sensors, coils, and other electronic parts and equipment for use in the automotive industry.

WALBRO AUTOMOTIVE CORPORATION
P.O. Box 350, Ligonier IN 46767. 219/894-3163. **Contact:** Human Resources. **Description:** Engaged in product design, brazed assemblies, precision stamping, refrigeration products, and auto parts. **Common positions include:** Accountant/Auditor; Administrator; Blue-Collar Worker Supervisor; Buyer; Computer Programmer; Credit Manager; Draftsperson; Human Resources Manager; Industrial Designer; Mechanical Engineer; Operations/Production Manager; Purchasing Agent/Manager; Quality Control Supervisor. **Benefits:** Dental Insurance; Disability Coverage; Life Insurance; Medical Insurance; Pension Plan; Tuition Assistance. **Corporate headquarters location:** Auburn Hills MI.

***Note:** Because addresses and telephone numbers of smaller companies can change rapidly, we recommend you call each company to verify the information below before inquiring about job opportunities. Mass mailings are not recommended.*

Additional small employers:

AUTOMOTIVE REPAIR SHOPS

Dickinson Fleet Services LLC
4709 West 96th Street, Indianapolis IN 46268-1118. 317/872-4542.

Kinro Inc.
1206 Eisenhower Drive South, Goshen IN 46526-5357. 219/533-8337.

AUTOMOTIVE STAMPINGS

Benteler Automotive Corporation
910 Eisenhower Drive South, Goshen IN 46526-5351. 219/534-1499.

Challenge Tool & Manufacturing
PO Box 306, New Haven IN 46774-0306. 219/749-9558.

Duffy Tool & Stamping Inc.
3401 West 8th Street, Muncie IN 47302-1912. 765/288-1931.

General Motors-Powertrain
105 GM Drive, Bedford IN 47421-1558. 812/279-7200.

Heritage Products Inc.
2000 Smith Avenue, Crawfordsville IN 47933-1080. 765/364-9002.

Kauffman Products Inc.
1092 3rd Avenue SW, Carmel IN 46032-2524. 317/574-9009.

PK USA Inc.
PO Box 420, Shelbyville IN 46176-0420. 317/398-6909.

Steel Parts Corporation
PO Box 700, Tipton IN 46072-0602. 765/675-2191.

Textron Automotive Company
PO Box 559, Morristown IN 46161-0559. 765/763-7212.

Tower Automotive-Kendallville
221 S Progress Dr W, Kendallville IN 46755-3264. 219/347-4100.

Vincennes Manufacturing Company
2525 N 6th St, Vincennes IN 47591-2405. 812/882-9520.

INDUSTRIAL VEHICLES AND MOVING EQUIPMENT

American Lifts
PO Box 524, Greensburg IN 47240-0524. 812/663-4085.

Crown Commercial Products
PO Box 840, Greencastle IN 46135-0840. 765/653-4240.

Gleason Industrial Products
612 East Reynolds Street, Goshen IN 46526-4050. 219/533-1141.

Toyota Industrial Equipment Manufacturing Inc.
PO Box 2487, Columbus IN 47202-2487. 812/342-0060.

MOTOR VEHICLE EQUIPMENT WHOLESALE

American Fabricating Company
PO Box 548, Boonville IN 47601-0548. 812/897-6560.

Balkamp Inc.
PO Box 421268, Indianapolis IN 46242-1268. 317/244-7241.

Cooper Automotive
8325 N Norfolk Street, Indianapolis IN 46268-1695. 317/228-5300.

Fort Wayne Vehicle Auction
3600 East Washington Boulevard, Fort Wayne IN 46803-1546. 219/422-9577.

Indianapolis Auto Auction
2950 East Main Street, Plainfield IN 46168-2723. 317/838-8000.

Indianapolis Car Exchange Incorporated
5161 South Indianapolis Road, Whitestown IN 46075-9377. 317/769-7777.

Jasper Engine & Transmission Exchange
PO Box 650, Jasper IN 47547-0650. 812/482-1041.

JRV Supply Company
2174 N State Road 257, Otwell IN 47564-8756. 812/354-6300.

Kesler-Schaefer Auto Auction
PO Box 53203, Indianapolis IN 46253-0203. 317/297-2300.

Lavanture Products Company
PO Box 2088, Elkhart IN 46515-2088. 219/264-0658.

Louisville Auto Auction Inc.
PO Box 827, Jeffersonville IN 47131-0827. 812/283-0734.

Piston Service Company
PO Box 421252, Indianapolis IN 46242-1252. 317/240-2000.

Wolfes Evansville Auto Auction
PO Box 2409, Evansville IN 47728-0409. 812/425-4576.

MOTOR VEHICLES AND EQUIPMENT

Acadia
PO Box 29, Ligonier IN 46767-0029. 219/894-7125.

Advance Mixer Inc.
PO Box 80070, Fort Wayne IN 46898-0070. 219/497-0728.

Aisin USA Manufacturing Inc.
1700 East 4th Street, Seymour IN 47274-4309. 812/523-1969.

Allomatic Products Company
PO Box 267, Sullivan IN 47882-0267. 812/268-0322.

AM General Corporation
711 W Chippewa Avenue, South Bend IN 46614-3711. 219/280-7100.

Amcast Automotive
PO Box 705, Fremont IN 46737-0705. 219/495-5602.

Amcast Automotive/Gas City
6231 East 500 South, Marion IN 46953-9539. 765/674-0618.

Arvin North American Auto Division
PO Box 577, Franklin IN 46131-0577. 317/736-7111.

Atwood Mobile Products
PO Box 1927, Elkhart IN 46515-1927. 219/522-7891.

Auburn Gear Inc.
400 Auburn Drive, Auburn IN 46706-3400. 219/925-3200.

Bendix
1850 Riverfork Drive, Huntington IN 46750-9004. 219/356-9720.

Bennington
52791 County Road 113, Elkhart IN 46514-9614. 219/264-6336.

Bremen Technologies
425 Industrial Drive, Bremen IN 46506-2111. 219/546-3791.

Carlisle Motion Control Systems
1031 E Hillside Drive, Bloomington IN 47401-6586. 812/336-3811.

Carpenter Industries Inc.
1100 Industries Road, Richmond IN 47374-9761. 765/965-4000.

CF Gomma USA Inc.
643 W Ellsworth Street, Columbia City IN 46725-2301. 219/248-5607.

Challenger Escaper
PO Box 1107, Elkhart IN 46515-1107. 219/522-3035.

Chrysler New Castle Machining & Forge
1817 I Avenue, New Castle IN 47362-2611. 765/521-1600.

Cooper Automotive
100 Progress Way West, Avilla IN 46710-9669. 219/897-2962.

Custom Form Manufacturing Inc.
2100 Industrial Parkway, Elkhart IN 46516-5433. 219/522-2856.

Dana Corporation
PO Box 245, Churubusco IN 46723-0245. 219/693-2111.

Dana Corporation
PO Box 390, Mishawaka IN 46546-0390. 219/259-9933.

Dana Corporation
PO Box 5002, Marion IN 46952. 765/664-1281.

Delco Remy America Inc.
1524 Jackson Street, Anderson IN 46016-1621. 765/643-8068.

Dexter Axle
PO Box 467, North Manchester IN 46962. 219/982-4047.

Dexter Axle
PO Box 250, Elkhart IN 46515-0250. 219/295-1900.

Dexter Axle
PO Box K, Fremont IN 46737-0780. 219/495-5100.

Dexter Axle
PO Box 108, Albion IN 46701-0108. 219/636-2195.

Diamet Corporation
PO Box 2189, Columbus IN 47202-2189. 812/379-4606.

Diamond Chain Company
PO Box 7045, Indianapolis IN 46207-7045. 317/638-6431.

Discovery Vans & Trucks
53387 Ada Drive, Elkhart IN 46514-9212. 219/264-0602.

Donaldson Company Inc.
3260 West State Road 28, Frankfort IN 46041-8721. 765/659-4766.

Elsa Corporation
1240 South State Road 37, Elwood IN 46036-3100. 765/552-5200.

Enkei America Inc.
2900 Inwood Drive, Columbus IN 47201-9758. 812/342-2000.

Explorer Van Company
PO Box 4527, Warsaw IN 46581-4527. 219/267-7666.

Fairfield Manufacturing Company
PO Box 7940, Lafayette IN 47903-7940. 765/474-3474.

Federal-Mogul Corporation
PO Box 399, Mooresville IN 46158-0399. 317/831-3830.

Fibre Body Industries Inc.
10324 W Highway 36, Modoc IN 47358. 765/853-5105.

FMC
1849 Sabine Street, Huntington IN 46750-2454. 219/356-2410.

Four Winds International Corporation
PO Box 1486, Elkhart IN 46515-1486. 219/293-0606.

Franklin Power Products Incorporated
PO Box 667, Franklin IN 46131-0667. 317/738-2117.

General Products Angola Corporation
1411 Wohlert Street, Angola IN 46703-1062. 219/665-8441.

Gladiator
PO Box 1647, Elkhart IN 46515-1647. 219/295-7178.

GNU Inc.
2252 Industrial Drive, Valparaiso IN 46383-9511. 219/464-7813.

Granger Manufacturing
13065 Anderson Road, Granger IN 46530-9283. 219/277-6984.

Griner Engineering Inc.
2500 North Curry Pike, Bloomington IN 47404-1431. 812/332-2220.

GW Bartlett Company Inc.
PO Box 1673, Muncie IN 47308-1673. 765/289-1586.

Hayes Lemmerz International Inc.
PO Box 769, Huntington IN 46750-0769. 219/356-7001.

Heartland Automotive Inc.
PO Box 648, Greencastle IN 46135-0648. 765/653-4263.

Hendrickson Suspension
101 South Progress Drive W, Kendallville IN 46755-3262. 219/347-3402.

Hendrickson Trailer
180 Mount Zion Road, Lebanon IN 46052-8186. 765/482-0207.

Hilldale Tool & Manufacturing
PO Box 249, Hamilton IN 46742-0249. 219/488-3546.

HPA Monon Corporation
One Water Tower Drive, Monon IN 47959. 219/253-6621.

Indiana Heat Transfer Inc.
500 W Harrison Street, Plymouth IN 46563-1324. 219/936-3171.

IPT
PO Box 68, B St, Greenfield IN 46140-1540. 317/462-3015.

Jaytec Inc.
555 Industrial Drive, Portland IN 47371-9399. 219/726-8023.

KS Bearings
PO Box 319, Greensburg IN 47240-0319. 812/663-3401.

KYP Industries Inc.
PO Box 490, Franklin IN 46131-0490. 317/736-7774.

Machine-Rite Products
1775 E U.S. Highway 20, Lagrange IN 46761-9501. 219/463-2116.

Modine Manufacturing Company
239 Factory Street, La Porte IN 46350-2624. 219/362-7041.

MOR/RYDE International Inc.
PO Box 579, Elkhart IN 46515-0579. 219/293-1581.

NAC Inc.
PO Box 966, North Vernon IN 47265-0966. 812/346-2115.

Nachi Technology Inc.
PO Box 250, Greenwood IN 46142-0250. 317/535-5000.

New Energy
PO Box 4413, Elkhart IN 46514-0413. 219/264-7511.

Newmar Corporation
PO Box 30, Nappanee IN 46550-0030. 219/773-7791.

NSU Corporation
8757 Colorado Street, Merrillville IN 46410-7204. 219/947-7616.

Perfect Circle Products
PO Box 1446, Richmond IN 47375-1446. 765/935-7800.

Pierce Company Inc.
PO Box 2000, Upland IN 46989-2000. 765/998-2712.

PI Porter Automotive Inc.
19635 US Highway 31 N, Westfield IN 46074-9685. 317/867-0234.

Rexhall Industries Inc.
29391 US Highway 33, Elkhart IN 46516-1427. 219/825-5661.

Rieter Automotive North America
790 W Commercial Ave, Lowell IN 46356-2249. 219/696-5253.

Ryobi Die Castings USA Inc.
800 W Mausoleum Rd, Shelbyville IN 46176-9719. 317/398-3398.

Schwitzer US Inc.
PO Box 80, Indianapolis IN 46206-0080. 317/328-3190.

Simpson Industries
PO Box 477, Bluffton IN 46714-0477. 219/824-2360.

Simpson Industries
PO Box 615, Fremont IN 46737-0615. 219/495-4315.

Sintering Technologies Inc.
PO Box 588, Greensburg IN 47240-0588. 812/663-5058.

Sprague Devices
PO Box 389, Michigan City IN 46361-0389. 219/872-7295.

Strick Corporation
301 N Polk St, Monroe IN 46772-9703. 219/692-6121.

Subaru-Isuzu Automotive Inc.
PO Box 5689, Lafayette IN 47903-5689. 765/449-1111.

Sure Start Division
4760 Kentucky Ave, Indianapolis IN 46221-3530. 317/856-8213.

Talbert Manufacturing Inc.
1628 W State Road 114, Rensselaer IN 47978-7266. 219/866-7141.

Tiara Motor Coach Division
1135 Kent St, Elkhart IN 46514-1741. 219/264-6543.

Tower Automotive-Auburn
801 W 15th St, Auburn IN 46706-2030. 219/925-5113.

Tower Automotive-Corydon
3301 Cline Rd NW, Corydon IN 47112-6907. 812/738-5600.

Toyota Motor Manufacturing of Indiana
4000 Tulip Tree Dr, Princeton IN 47670-2300. 812/387-2000.

Transwheel Corporation
PO Box 997, Huntington IN 46750-0997. 219/358-8660.

Union City Body Company LP
PO Box 190, Union City IN 47390-0190. 765/964-3121.

United Technologies Automotive
PO Box 500, Grabill IN 46741-0500. 219/627-3656.

Universal Bearings Inc.
PO Box 38, Bremen IN 46506-0038. 219/546-2261.

US Cargo Inc.
17645 Commerce Dr, Bristol IN 46507-9209. 219/848-1335.

Valeo Inc.
1100 Barachel Ln, Greensburg IN 47240-1200. 812/663-8541.

Ventra Corporation
PO Box 3009, Columbus IN 47202-3009. 812/378-0028.

Viking Engineering Company
PO Box 727, Hammond IN 46325-0727. 219/844-1123.

Visteon
3120 16th St, Bedford IN 47421-3514. 812/275-5961.

Visteon Climate Control Systems
4747 Western Ave, Connersville IN 47331-9706. 765/825-7551.

Walbro Automotive Corporation
1200 Baker Dr, Ossian IN 46777-9106. 219/622-7900.

Walker Manufacturing Company
1101 Eisenhower Dr, Goshen IN 46526. 219/534-3515.

Wells Cargo Inc.
PO Box 728, Elkhart IN 46515-0728. 219/264-9661.

For more information on career opportunities in the automotive industry:

Associations

AMERICAN AUTOMOBILE MANUFACTURERS ASSOCIATION
1401 H Street NW, Suite 900, Washington DC 20005. 202/326-5500. Fax: 202/326-5567. World Wide Web address: http://www.aama.com. A trade association. Sponsors research projects, distributes publications, and reviews social and public policies pertaining to the motor vehicle industry and its customers.

ASSOCIATION OF INTERNATIONAL AUTOMOBILE MANUFACTURERS, INC.
1001 North 19th Street, Suite 1200, Arlington VA 22209. 703/525-7788. World Wide Web address: http://www.aiam.org.

AUTOMOTIVE SERVICE ASSOCIATION
1901 Airport Freeway, Suite 100, P.O. Box 929, Bedford TX 76095. 817/283-6205. World Wide Web address: http://www.asashop.org. Works with shops to find workers. Publishes a monthly magazine with classified advertisements.

AUTOMOTIVE SERVICE INDUSTRY ASSOCIATION
25 Northwest Point Boulevard, Suite 425, Elk Grove Village IL 60007-1035. 847/228-1310. World Wide Web address: http://www.aftmkt.com/asia. Members are manufacturers and distributors of automobile replacement parts. Sponsors a trade show. Publishes educational guidebooks and training manuals.

Directories

AUTOMOTIVE NEWS MARKET DATA BOOK
Crain Communications, Automotive News, 1400 Woodbridge Avenue, Detroit MI 48207-3187. 313/446-6000.

WARD'S AUTOMOTIVE YEARBOOK
Ward's Communications, Inc., 3000 Town Center, Suite 2750, Southville MI 48075. 248/357-0800.

World Wide Web address: http://www.wardsauto.com.

Magazines

AUTOMOTIVE INDUSTRIES
Cahners Business Information, 201 King of Prussia Road, Radnor PA 19089. 610/964-4000.

AUTOMOTIVE NEWS
Crain Communications, 1400 Woodbridge Avenue, Detroit MI 48207-3187. 313/446-6000.

WARD'S AUTO WORLD
WARD'S AUTOMOTIVE REPORTS
Ward's Communications, Inc., 3000 Town Center, Suite 2750, Southville MI 48075. 248/357-0800. World Wide Web address: http://www.wardsauto.com.

BANKING/SAVINGS AND LOANS

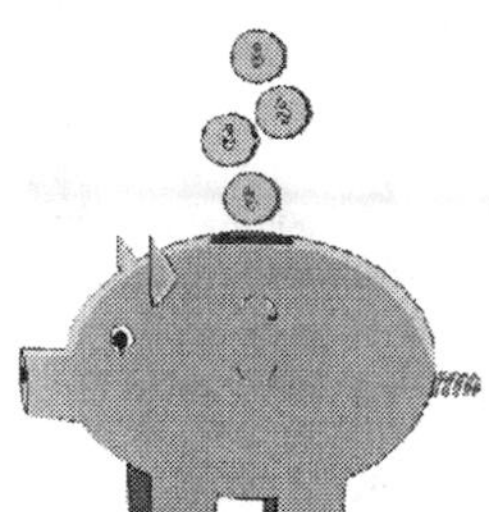

The banking industry is still plagued by uncertainty heading into 2000. Mergers and acquisitions continue to be the norm, the Asian crisis looms abroad, and the Year 2000 computer glitch is causing concerns for many banks. Although most banks remain unscathed and continue to prosper, some are still losing ground to security houses and financial divisions of large corporations.

According to the Federal Deposit Insurance Corporation, 156 new bank charters were granted in 1996, 165 in 1997, and 89 applications were still pending at the end of December 1997. More and more consumers are choosing to take their money out of banking conglomerates and are giving their business to smaller, more personalized community banks. In fact, Business Week *reports that even analysts in the field are beginning to lose faith in the promised efficiency of the mega-mergers of 1997.*

A successful banking trend is automation. Automated teller machines will begin to offer more services like check cashing and printouts of account information. Jobseekers will find less opportunities for bank tellers and more opportunities for call center customer service representatives. The Bureau of Labor Statistics expects bank tellers to lose 152,000 jobs by 2005 and projects numerous layoffs for bank office workers and managers.

ALLIANCE BANK
P.O. Box 1217, Vincennes IN 47591. 812/882-9310. **Contact:** Human Resources. **Description:** A full-service savings bank.

AMBANK INDIANA, N.A.
302 Main Street, Vincennes IN 47591. 812/882-3050. **Contact:** Richard Fox, Human Resources Manager. **World Wide Web address:** http://www.ambk.com. **Description:** A full-service bank providing credit card services. **Subsidiaries include:** American National Bank.

AMERIANA BANK
P.O. Box H, New Castle IN 47362. 765/529-2230. **Contact:** James Moyer, Human Resources. **Description:** A savings and loan bank. **Parent company:** Ameriana Bancorp.

AMERICAN NATIONAL BANK
110 East Main Street, Muncie IN 47305. 765/747-7575. **Contact:** Jim Convy, Vice President of Human Resources. **World Wide Web address:** http://www.accessanb.com. **Description:** A bank which offers commercial banking and other related financial services. **Parent company:** ANB Corporation.

AMERICAN SAVINGS BANK, SSB
8230 Hohman Avenue, Munster IN 46321. 219/836-5870. **Contact:** Michael Mellon, Assistant Vice President. **Description:** A full-service bank.

BANK ONE INDIANAPOLIS, N.A.
111 Monument Circle, Suite IN1-0071, Indianapolis IN 46277. 317/321-7969. **Contact:** Human Resources. **Description:** A full-service bank. **Common positions include:** Accountant/Auditor; Bank Officer/Manager; Branch Manager; Financial Analyst; Loan Officer; Management Trainee; Systems Analyst. **Educational backgrounds include:** Accounting; Business Administration;

Communications; Computer Science; Economics; Finance; Liberal Arts; Marketing. **Benefits:** 401(k); Dental Insurance; Disability Coverage; Life Insurance; Medical Insurance; Pension Plan; Savings Plan; Tuition Assistance. **Special programs:** Internships. **Corporate headquarters location:** Columbus OH. **Other U.S. locations:** Nationwide. **Parent company:** Banc One Corporation (Columbus OH) is one of the nation's largest bank holding companies. Banc One operates an affiliate network of over 75 banks with more than 1,500 banking locations. In addition, Banc One operates corporations involved in data processing, venture capital, investment and merchant banking, trust, brokerage, investment management, leasing, mortgage banking, consumer finance, and insurance. **Operations at this facility include:** Regional Headquarters. **Listed on:** New York Stock Exchange. **Number of employees at this location:** 75,000.

CITIZENS FINANCIAL SERVICES
1720 45th Avenue, Munster IN 46321. 219/924-1720. **Contact:** Human Resources. **Description:** A commercial bank.

CITIZENS NATIONAL BANK
P.O. Box 778, Evansville IN 47705-0778. 812/464-3400. **Contact:** Charlotte Kohlman, Human Resources Director. **World Wide Web address:** http://www.citizensonline.com. **Description:** A full-service bank. **Parent company:** CNB Bancshares is a regional, multibank holding company which owns eight commercial banks, one savings bank, and one consumer finance company. Other subsidiaries of CNB include Citizens National Bank of Evansville with more than 20 locations; Peoples Bank and Trust, headquartered in Madisonville KY (seven locations); CNB Bank of Kentucky, headquartered in Shively KY (two locations); Valley Bank, headquartered in Terre Haute IN (10 locations); Citizens Bank of Jasper, headquartered in Jasper IN (two locations); Citizens Bank of Central Indiana, headquartered in Greenwood IN (13 locations); Citizens Bank of Henderson County, headquartered in Henderson KY (six locations); and Peoples Security Finance Company, headquartered in Madisonville KY (18 locations).

CITIZENS NATIONAL BANK
P.O. Box 159, Tell City IN 47586-0159. 812/547-2355. **Physical address:** 529 Main Street, Tell City IN 47586. **Contact:** Barbara Morrison, Human Resources Manager. **World Wide Web address:** http://www.citizensonline.com. **Description:** A full-service bank. **Parent company:** CNB Bancshares is a regional, multibank holding company which owns eight commercial banks, one savings bank, and one consumer finance company. Other subsidiaries of CNB include Citizens National Bank of Evansville with more than 20 locations; Peoples Bank and Trust, headquartered in Madisonville KY (seven locations); CNB Bank of Kentucky, headquartered in Shively KY (two locations); Valley Bank, headquartered in Terre Haute IN (10 locations); Citizens Bank of Jasper, headquartered in Jasper IN (two locations); Citizens Bank of Central Indiana, headquartered in Greenwood IN (13 locations); Citizens Bank of Henderson County, headquartered in Henderson KY (six locations); and Peoples Security Finance Company, headquartered in Madisonville KY (18 locations).

COMMUNITY BANK
COMMUNITY BANK SHARES OF INDIANA, INC.
P.O. Box 939, New Albany IN 47151. 812/944-2224. **Contact:** Diane Murphy, Human Resources Director. **Description:** A full-service savings and loan bank. **Corporate headquarters location:** This Location. **Parent company:** Community Bank Shares of Indiana, Inc. (also at this location).

FARMERS BANK
P.O. Box 129, Frankfort IN 46041. 765/654-8731. **Contact:** Human Resources. **World Wide Web address:** http://www.abetterbank.com. **Description:** A full-service commercial bank. **Parent company:** Farmers Bancorp.

FIRST INDIANA BANK
1300 Windhorst Way, Greenwood IN 46143. 317/269-1200. **Contact:** Human Resources. **World Wide Web address:** http://www.firstindiana.com. **Description:** A full-service bank. **Common positions include:** Accountant/Auditor; Bank Officer/Manager; Branch Manager; Credit Manager; Securities Sales Representative. **Educational backgrounds include:** Accounting; Business Administration; Finance; Marketing. **Benefits:** Dental Insurance; Disability Coverage; Employee

Discounts; Life Insurance; Medical Insurance; Pension Plan. **Corporate headquarters location:** This Location. **Parent company:** First Indiana Corporation (also at this location) is a holding company whose principal subsidiary is First Indiana Bank. The corporation is engaged primarily in retail banking and lending through 29 banking centers including Evansville-based Mid-West Federal Savings Bank, First Federal Savings and Loan of Rushville, and Mooresville Savings Bank. In addition, the corporation has six mortgage services offices in central Indiana. One Mortgage Corporation, a subsidiary, operates offices in Florida and North Carolina. First Indiana Corporation's other subsidiaries, One Insurance Agency, One Investment Corporation, and One Property Corporation, are engaged in insurance sales, investments, and full-service securities brokerage. **Operations at this facility include:** Administration; Divisional Headquarters; Sales. **Listed on:** NASDAQ. **Number of employees at this location:** 450. **Number of employees nationwide:** 550.

FIRST MERCHANTS BANK N.A.
200 East Jackson Street, Muncie IN 47308. 765/747-1500. **Contact:** Human Resources. **Description:** A bank. First Merchants Bank, with more than $820 million in fiduciary assets at market value, operates one of the largest trust departments in Indiana. **Parent company:** First Merchants Corporation provides service through 21 offices located in Delaware, Madison, and Henry Counties in Indiana. Subsidiaries of First Merchants, including Pendleton Banking Company and First United Bank, conduct a full range of banking activities including commercial, industrial, consumer and real estate lending, deposit and investment services, and other banking services.

FIRST SOURCE CORPORATION
P.O. Box 1602, South Bend IN 46634. 219/235-2000. **Contact:** Dan Craft, Human Resources Director. **World Wide Web address:** http://www.1scsource.com. **Description:** A commercial bank holding company.

FORT WAYNE NATIONAL BANK
110 West Berry Street, P.O. Box 110, Fort Wayne IN 46801. 219/426-0555. **Contact:** Dave Swanson, Vice President of Human Resources. **Description:** A commercial bank offering a variety of consumer checking and savings services. **Corporate headquarters location:** This Location. **Parent company:** Fort Wayne National Corporation.

GERMAN AMERICAN BANK
P.O. Box 810, Jasper IN 47547. 812/482-1314. **Contact:** Human Resources. **Description:** A full-service bank.

GREENFIELD BANKING COMPANY
10 East Main Street, Greenfield IN 46140. 317/462-1431. **Contact:** Human Resources. **Description:** A commercial banking company with six regional branches. **Parent company:** Greenfield Bancshares.

HOME FEDERAL BANCORP
222 West Second Street, Seymour IN 47274. 812/522-1592. **Contact:** Human Resources. **Description:** A holding company for a savings and loan bank.

HORIZON BANK
P.O. Box 800, Michigan City IN 46361. 219/879-0211. **Contact:** Human Resources. **Description:** Provides commercial banking services.

INDIANA FEDERAL CORPORATION
63 South Lafayette Street, Valparaiso IN 46383. 219/462-4131. **Contact:** April Wolford, Human Resources Director. **Description:** A commercial bank holding company.

INDIANA UNITED BANCORP
201 North Broadway, Greensburg IN 47240. 812/663-4711. **Contact:** Human Resources. **Description:** A financial services holding company, whose subsidiaries perform savings and commercial banking activities.

IRWIN FINANCIAL CORPORATION
500 Washington Street, Columbus IN 47201. 812/376-1020. **Contact:** Human Resources. **World Wide Web address:** http://www.irwinunion.com. **Description:** A diversified financial services company with operations in commercial banking, credit card services, insurance services, mortgage banking, investment services, and other financial activities.

LAFAYETTE SAVINGS BANK
101 Main Street, Lafayette IN 47902. 765/742-1064. **Contact:** Human Resources. **World Wide Web address:** http://www.lsbank.com. **Description:** A savings and loan bank.

LAKE CITY BANK
P.O. Box 1387, Warsaw IN 46581-1387. 219/267-6144. **Contact:** Human Resources. **World Wide Web address:** http://www.lakecitybank.com. **Description:** A bank which performs commercial banking operations, credit card services, and mortgage banking services.

MFB FINANCIAL CORPORATION
P.O. Box 528, Mishawaka IN 46546-0528. 219/255-3146. **Contact:** Human Resources. **Description:** A holding company for a savings and loan bank.

MERCANTILE NATIONAL BANK OF INDIANA
5243 Hohman Avenue, Hammond IN 46320. 219/932-8220. **Contact:** Human Resources. **Description:** A commercial bank.

NBD BANK
One Indiana Square, Mail Stop 7193, Indianapolis IN 46266. 317/266-6000. **Contact:** Human Resources Department. **Description:** NBD Bank is a full-service bank and one of the largest bank holding companies in the country. The company also conducts payment processing activities. **Subsidiaries include:** NBD Indiana, Inc.

NATIONAL CITY BANK
101 West Washington Street, Indianapolis IN 46255. 317/267-7554. **Fax:** 317/267-6156. **Contact:** Human Resources. **World Wide Web address:** http://www.national-city.com. **Description:** A bank. **Common positions include:** Accountant/Auditor; Adjuster; Bank Teller; Clerical Supervisor; Order Clerk; Receptionist; Secretary; Typist/Word Processor. **Educational backgrounds include:** Accounting; Business Administration; Finance; Liberal Arts. **Benefits:** Dental Insurance; Disability Coverage; Employee Discounts; Life Insurance; Medical Insurance; Pension Plan; Profit Sharing; Savings Plan; Tuition Assistance. **Corporate headquarters location:** Cleveland OH. **Other U.S. locations:** Lexington KY; Louisville KY; Akron OH; Columbus OH; Dayton OH; Toledo OH. **Operations at this facility include:** Regional Headquarters. **Listed on:** New York Stock Exchange. **Number of employees at this location:** 1,785. **Number of employees nationwide:** 20,200.

NATIONAL CITY BANK
P.O. Box 730, Kokomo IN 46903. 765/457-5551. **Physical address:** 200 West Mulberry Street, Kokomo IN 46901. **Contact:** Ms. Sandy Kaselonis, Human Resources Director. **World Wide Web address:** http://www.national-city.com. **Description:** A full-service savings bank.

NORWEST BANK
P.O. Box 960, Fort Wayne IN 46801. 219/461-6000. **Contact:** Human Resources. **World Wide Web address:** http://www.norwest.com. **Description:** A full-service bank. **Parent company:** Norwest Corporation is one of the largest domestic bank holding companies and operates 583 branches in 15 states in the northwestern U.S. The bank offers corporate and community banking services, credit card products, trust, investment services, and insurance. Subsidiaries provide consumer financial, commercial financial, mortgage banking, venture capital, and data processing services.

OLD NATIONAL BANCORP
420 Main Street, Evansville IN 47708. 812/464-1434. **Contact:** Human Resources. **World Wide Web address:** http://www.oldnational.com. **Description:** Old National Bancorp is a $4.4 billion

multibank holding company. Old National provides a comprehensive range of financial services including commercial and retail banking, trust, brokerage, correspondent banking, and insurance. **Corporate headquarters location:** This Location.

PEOPLES BANK & TRUST COMPANY
130 East Market Street, Indianapolis IN 46204. 317/237-8072. **Contact:** Human Resources. **Description:** A commercial bank.

PEOPLES BANK SB
9204 Columbia Avenue, Munster IN 46321. 219/836-9690. **Contact:** Human Resources. **Description:** A savings and loan bank.

PEOPLES FEDERAL SAVINGS BANK
P.O. Box 231, Auburn IN 46706. 219/925-2500. **Contact:** Human Resources. **Description:** A savings and loan bank. **Parent company:** Peoples Bancorporation.

PERMANENT FEDERAL BANK
P.O. Box 1227, Evansville IN 47706. 812/428-6800. **Contact:** Human Resources. **Description:** A savings and loan bank that performs savings and loan operations, insurance services, brokerage services, and other financial activities.

TERRE HAUTE FIRST NATIONAL BANK
P.O. Box 2122, Terre Haute IN 47802. 812/238-6000. **Contact:** Human Resources Department. **Description:** Terre Haute First National Bank is engaged in savings and loan banking. **Parent company:** First Financial Corporation of Indiana.

UNITED FIDELITY BANK, FSB
700 South Green River Road, Evansville IN 47715. 812/424-0921. **Contact:** Human Resources. **Description:** Services of United Fidelity Bank include savings deposits, which the bank then invests in consumer installment loans, commercial loans for owner-occupied one- to four-family homes in Indiana, and in investment and money market securities. **Subsidiaries include:** The bank also owns, develops, builds, rents, and manages affordable housing projects through Village Management Corporation, Village Community Development Corporation, and Village Housing Corporation.

Note: Because addresses and telephone numbers of smaller companies can change rapidly, we recommend you call each company to verify the information below before inquiring about job opportunities. Mass mailings are not recommended.

Additional small employers:

COMMERCIAL BANKS

NBD Bank
PO Box 2345, Fort Wayne IN 46801-2345. 219/427-8333.

NBD Bank
PO Box 1686, Elkhart IN 46515-1686. 219/524-3000.

PNC National Bank
201 Main St, Lafayette IN 47901-1277. 765/423-0689.

Valley American Bank & Trust Co.
PO Box 328, South Bend IN 46624-0328. 219/237-4733.

Valley American Bank & Trust Co.
310 W McKinley Ave, Mishawaka IN 46545-5602. 219/256-6121.

CREDIT UNIONS

Finance Center Federal Credit Union
PO Box 26501, Indianapolis IN 46226-0501. 317/543-5800.

Purdue Employees Federal Credit Union
PO Box 1950, Lafayette IN 47996-1950. 765/743-9660.

Teachers Credit Union
PO Box 1395, South Bend IN 46624-1395. 219/232-8011.

SAVINGS INSTITUTIONS

Mutual Federal Savings Bank
PO Box 551, Muncie IN 47308-0551. 765/747-2800.

Peoples Bank
9204 Columbia Ave, Hammond IN 46321-3517. 219/836-9828.

Union Federal Savings Bank Indiana
PO Box 6054, Indianapolis IN 46206-6054. 317/269-4700.

For more information on career opportunities in the banking/savings and loans industry:

Associations

AMERICA'S COMMUNITY BANKERS
900 19th Street NW, Suite 400, Washington DC 20006. 202/857-3100. World Wide Web address: http://www.acbankers.org. A trade association representing the expanded thrift industry. Membership is limited to institutions.

AMERICAN BANKERS ASSOCIATION
1120 Connecticut Avenue NW, Washington DC 20036. 202/663-5221. World Wide Web address: http://www.aba.com. Provides banking education and training services, sponsors industry programs and conventions, and publishes articles, newsletters, and the *ABA Service Member Directory*.

BANK ADMINISTRATION
One North Franklin, Suite 1000, Chicago IL 60606. Toll-free phone: 800/323-8552. World Wide Web address: http://www.bai.org.

Directories

AMERICAN BANK DIRECTORY
Thomson Financial Publications, 1770 Breckenridge Parkway, Suite 500, Duluth GA 30136. 770/381-2511.

MOODY'S BANK AND FINANCE MANUAL
Moody's Investors Service, Inc., 99 Church Street, 1st Floor, New York NY 10007-2701. 212/553-0300. World Wide Web address: http://www.moodys.com.

RANKING THE BANKS/THE TOP NUMBERS
American Banker, Inc., One State Street Plaza, New York NY 10004. 212/803-6700. World Wide Web address: http://www.americanbanker.com.

Magazines

ABA BANKING JOURNAL
American Bankers Association, 1120 Connecticut Avenue NW, Washington DC 20036. 202/663-5221. World Wide Web address: http://www.aba.com.

BANKERS MAGAZINE
Warren, Gorham & Lamont, Park Square Building, 31 St. James Avenue, Boston MA 02116-4112. 617/423-2020.

JOURNAL OF COMMERCIAL BANK LENDING
Robert Morris Associates, 1650 Market Street, Suite 2300, Philadelphia PA 19103. 215/446-4000.

Online Services

JOBS FOR BANKERS!
http://www.bankjobs.com/. This site provides access to a database of over 6,000 banking-related job openings. Jobs for Bankers! is run by Careers Inc. This Website also includes a resume database.

JOBS IN COMMERCIAL BANKING
http://www.cob.ohio-state.edu/dept/fin/jobs/commbank.htm. Provides information and resources for jobseekers looking to work in the field of commercial banking.

NATIONAL BANKING NETWORK: RECRUITING FOR BANKING AND FINANCE
http://www.banking-financejobs.com/. Offers a searchable database of job openings in banking and financial services. The database is searchable by region, keyword, and job specialty.

BIOTECHNOLOGY, PHARMACEUTICALS, AND SCIENTIFIC R&D

The forecast is bright for the biotechnology industry, with the advent of new technologies in drug research and a heightened demand for prescription drugs of all types. Analysts from Cowen & Company predicted a healthy sales increase of about 12 percent in 1998, up from 8 percent in 1997. In effect, marketing costs were also expected to rise.

Large drug companies are preparing to release a plethora of new products and continue to face competition from generic drug makers. Advances in genetic research offer promising new developments, but capitalizing on them requires significant investment. Therefore, those companies with bigger research budgets currently dominate. However, a trend is developing whereby large drug companies form partnerships with smaller biotechnology firms that provide them with research services. Often, these partnerships allow a drug to move through the trial process faster, therefore gaining FDA approval much sooner.

Among the industry leaders in breakthrough drug development is Merck & Company, Inc., which plans to introduce new painkillers; antidepressants; and drugs for asthma, arthritis, and male pattern baldness. Other drug manufacturers anticipate new drugs for hepatitis-B as well as new AIDS drug combinations. In addition, drug-delivery companies are working to improve the ways in which drugs are absorbed by the body.

BAYER CORPORATION
P.O. Box 40, Elkhart IN 46515. 219/264-8111. **Physical address:** 1884 Miles Avenue, Elkhart IN 46514. **Contact:** Connie Dunn, Human Resources Director. **World Wide Web address:** http://www.bayerus.com. **Description:** Produces citric acid monitoring systems for blood and urine, over-the-counter cold remedy products, and vitamins.

BINDLEY WESTERN INDUSTRIES, INC.
4212 West 71st Street, Indianapolis IN 46268. 317/298-9900. **Contact:** Thomas J. Weakley, Human Resources. **Description:** Distributes prescription pharmaceuticals to drug stores, hospitals, clinics, and other health care providers. The company also distributes non-pharmaceutical products including health and beauty aids.

BIVONA INC.
5700 West 23rd Avenue, Gary IN 46406. 219/989-9150. **Contact:** Human Resources. **Description:** Manufactures and distributes medical supplies.

CENTRAL INDIANA REGIONAL BLOOD CENTER
3450 North Meridian Street, Indianapolis IN 46208. 317/927-1611. **Fax:** 317/927-1743. **Contact:** Jennifer Bosler, Senior Human Resources Coordinator. **World Wide Web address:** http://www.donor-link.org. **Description:** A nonprofit blood center and one of the nation's largest blood banking institutions, providing blood services as well as bone and tissue products. Founded in 1952. **Common positions include:** Accountant; Administrative Assistant; Applications Engineer; Assistant Manager; Auditor; Clinical Lab Technician; Computer Operator; Computer Programmer; Consultant; Customer Service Representative; Database Manager; Emergency Medical Technician; Graphic Artist; Graphic Designer; Human Resources Manager; Licensed Practical Nurse; Medical Records Technician; MIS Specialist; Operations Manager; Production Manager; Public Relations Specialist; Quality Control Supervisor; Registered Nurse; Systems

Analyst; Systems Manager; Technical Writer/Editor. **Educational backgrounds include:** Accounting; Biology; Chemistry; Computer Science; Health Care; Marketing. **Benefits:** Dental Insurance; Disability Coverage; Employee Discounts; Flexible Schedule; Job Sharing; Life Insurance; Medical Insurance; Pension Plan; Public Transit Available; Savings Plan; Tuition Assistance. **Annual sales/revenues:** $11 - $20 million. **Number of employees at this location:** 200. **Number of employees nationwide:** 400.

DOW AGROSCIENCES LLC
9330 Zionsville Road, Indianapolis IN 46268. 317/337-3000. **Contact:** Human Resources Department. **World Wide Web address:** http://www.dowagro.com. **Description:** Produces a variety of agricultural products including herbicides and insecticides. Founded in 1989. **NOTE:** Entry-level positions are offered. **Company slogan:** Improving the quality of life around the world. **Common positions include:** Administrative Assistant; Attorney; Biochemist; Biological Scientist; Chemist; Computer Programmer; Credit Manager; Financial Analyst; MIS Specialist; Paralegal; Secretary; Systems Analyst. **Educational backgrounds include:** Biology; Business Administration; Chemistry; Computer Science; Finance. **Benefits:** 401(k); Dental Insurance; Disability Coverage; Flexible Schedule; Life Insurance; Medical Insurance; Pension Plan; Profit Sharing; Savings Plan; Tuition Assistance. **Special programs:** Internships; Training. **Office hours:** Monday - Friday, 7:30 a.m. - 4:30 p.m. **Corporate headquarters location:** This Location. **Other U.S. locations:** Nationwide. **International locations:** Worldwide. **Parent company:** Dow Chemical Company. **Operations at this facility include:** Administration; Research and Development; Sales; Service.

ELI LILLY AND COMPANY
Lilly Corporate Center, Indianapolis IN 46285. 317/277-7731. **Contact:** Human Resources. **World Wide Web address:** http://www.lilly.com. **Description:** Discovers, develops, manufactures, and sells a broad line of human health products and pharmaceuticals, such as diagnostic products; monoclonal antibody-based diagnostic tests for colon, prostate, and testicular cancer; medical devices; patient vital-signs measurement and electrocardiograph systems; implantable cardiac pacemakers, and other related medical systems; and anti-infectives and diabetic care products. The company also produces animal health products such as animal antibiotics and special animal feed additives. **Common positions include:** Biological Scientist; Biomedical Engineer; Chemical Engineer; Chemist; Civil Engineer; Computer Programmer; Electrical/Electronics Engineer; Financial Analyst; Industrial Engineer; Mechanical Engineer; Statistician; Systems Analyst. **Educational backgrounds include:** Biology; Chemistry; Computer Science; Economics; Engineering; Finance; Marketing. **Benefits:** Dental Insurance; Disability Coverage; Life Insurance; Medical Insurance; Pension Plan; Profit Sharing; Savings Plan. **Corporate headquarters location:** This Location. **Operations at this facility include:** Administration; Manufacturing; Research and Development; Sales. **Listed on:** New York Stock Exchange. **Number of employees nationwide:** 30,000.

ELI LILLY AND COMPANY
10500 South State Road 63, Clinton IN 47842. 765/832-4400. **Recorded jobline:** 800/892-9121. **Contact:** Human Resources. **World Wide Web address:** http://www.lilly.com. **Description:** Discovers, develops, manufactures, and sells a broad line of human health products and pharmaceuticals, such as diagnostic products; monoclonal antibody-based diagnostic tests for colon, prostate, and testicular cancer; medical devices; patient vital-signs measurement and electrocardiograph systems; implantable cardiac pacemakers, and other related medical systems; and anti-infectives and diabetic care products. The company also produces animal health products such as animal antibiotics and special animal feed additives. **NOTE:** Jobseekers must call the jobline for application procedures. **Operations at this facility include:** Manufacturing; Research and Development.

ELI LILLY AND COMPANY
P.O. Box 708, Greenfield IN 46140-2714. **Contact:** Human Resources. **Description:** Discovers, develops, manufactures, and sells a broad line of human health products such as diagnostic products; monoclonal antibody-based diagnostic tests for colon, prostate, and testicular cancer; medical devices; patient vital-signs measurement and electrocardiograph systems; implantable cardiac pacemakers, and other related medical systems; anti-infectives and diabetic care products;

and produces animal health products such as animal antibiotics and special animal feed additives. **NOTE:** This firm does not accept unsolicited resumes. Please only respond to advertised openings.

ELI LILLY AND COMPANY
P.O. Box 685, Lafayette IN 47902. **Contact:** Personnel. **Description:** Discovers, develops, manufactures, and sells a broad line of human health products and pharmaceuticals, such as diagnostic products; monoclonal antibody-based diagnostic tests for colon, prostate, and testicular cancer; patient vital-signs measurement and electrocardiograph systems; implantable cardiac pacemakers, and other related medical systems; anti-infectives and diabetic care products; and produces animal health products such as animal antibiotics and special animal feed additives. **NOTE:** This firm does not accept unsolicited resumes. Please only respond to advertised openings.

MEAD JOHNSON NUTRITIONAL GROUP
2400 West Lloyd Expressway, Evansville IN 47721. 812/429-5000. **Contact:** Employment Department. **Description:** Engaged in the research, manufacture, and marketing of pharmaceutical and nutritional products. **Common positions include:** Accountant/Auditor; Biological Scientist; Biomedical Engineer; Chemical Engineer; Chemist; Computer Programmer; Electrical/Electronics Engineer; Financial Analyst; Human Resources Manager; Industrial Engineer; Manufacturer's/Wholesaler's Sales Rep.; Mechanical Engineer; Quality Control Supervisor; Statistician; Systems Analyst; Technical Writer/Editor. **Educational backgrounds include:** Accounting; Chemistry; Computer Science; Engineering; Marketing; MBA. **Benefits:** Dental Insurance; Employee Discounts; Medical Insurance; Pension Plan; Savings Plan. **Corporate headquarters location:** New York NY. **Parent company:** Bristol-Myers Squibb Company.

SERADYN INC.
1200 Madison Avenue, Indianapolis IN 46225. 317/266-2000. **Contact:** Personnel. **World Wide Web address:** http://www.seradyn.com. **Description:** This location manufactures medical test kits. Overall, Seradyn consists of three distinct divisions: Diagnostics, Particle Technology, and Photovolt. **Common positions include:** Accountant/Auditor; Biological Scientist; Buyer; Chemist; Computer Programmer; Customer Service Representative; Department Manager; Draftsperson; Electrical/Electronics Engineer; General Manager; Manufacturer's/ Wholesaler's Sales Rep.; Mechanical Engineer; Quality Control Supervisor. **Educational backgrounds include:** Biochemistry; Biology; Chemistry; Engineering; Immunology; Marketing. **Benefits:** Dental Insurance; Disability Coverage; Life Insurance; Medical Insurance; Savings Plan; Tuition Assistance. **Corporate headquarters location:** This Location. **Parent company:** Mitsubishi Chemical Corporation. **Listed on:** Privately held. **Number of employees nationwide:** 150.

SHIRE RIDGEWOOD
5767 Thunderbird Road, Indianapolis IN 46236. 317/823-6878. **Contact:** Human Resources. **Description:** Manufactures pharmaceutical preparations. **NOTE:** Please send resumes to Human Resources, P.O. Box 6497, Florence KY 41022.

***Note:** Because addresses and telephone numbers of smaller companies can change rapidly, we recommend you call each company to verify the information below before inquiring about job opportunities. Mass mailings are not recommended.*

Additional small employers:

MEDICAL LABORATORIES

Corning Pharmaceutical Laboratories
8211 Scicor Drive, Indianapolis IN 46214-2942. 317/271-1200.

Mid-America Clinical Laboratories
PO Box 19163, Indianapolis IN 46219-0163. 317/355-5263.

Northern Indiana Medical Lab
PO Box 8600, Michigan City IN 46361-8600. 219/872-5521.

Park View Health Systems Lab
328 Ley Road, Fort Wayne IN 46825-5220. 219/482-5834.

Pathologists Associated
PO Box 7002, Muncie IN 47308-7002. 765/284-7795.

PHARMACEUTICAL PREPARATIONS

Schwarz Pharmaceutical Manufacturing
1101 C Ave W, Freeman Field, Seymour IN 47274. 812/523-3457.

For more information on career opportunities in biotechnology, pharmaceuticals, and scientific R&D:

Associations

AMERICAN ASSOCIATION FOR CLINICAL CHEMISTRY
2101 L Street NW, Suite 202, Washington DC 20037-1526. 202/857-0717. Toll-free phone: 800/892-1400. World Wide Web address: http://www.aacc.org. International scientific/medical society of individuals involved with clinical chemistry and other clinical lab science-related disciplines.

AMERICAN ASSOCIATION OF COLLEGES OF PHARMACY
1426 Prince Street, Alexandria VA 22314-2841. 703/739-2330. World Wide Web address: http://www.aacp.org. An organization composed of all U.S. pharmacy colleges and over 2,000 school administrators and faculty members. Career publications include *Shall I Study Pharmacy?*, *Pharmacy: A Caring Profession*, and *A Graduate Degree in the Pharmaceutical Sciences: An Option For You?*

AMERICAN ASSOCIATION OF PHARMACEUTICAL SCIENTISTS
1650 King Street, Suite 200, Alexandria VA 22314-2747. 703/548-3000. World Wide Web address: http://www.aaps.org.

THE AMERICAN COLLEGE OF CLINICAL PHARMACY (ACCP)
3101 Broadway, Suite 380, Kansas City MO 64111. 816/531-2177. World Wide Web address: http://www.accp.com. Operates ClinNet jobline at 412/648-7893 for members only.

AMERICAN PHARMACEUTICAL ASSOCIATION
2215 Constitution Avenue NW, Washington DC 20037-2985. 202/628-4410. World Wide Web address: http://www.aphanet.org.

AMERICAN SOCIETY FOR BIOCHEMISTRY AND MOLECULAR BIOLOGY
9650 Rockville Pike, Bethesda MD 20814-3996. 301/530-7145. Fax: 301/571-1824. World Wide Web address: http://www.faseb.org/asbmb. A nonprofit scientific and educational organization whose primary scientific activities are in the publication of the *Journal of Biological Chemistry* and holding an annual scientific meeting. Also publishes a career brochure entitled *Unlocking Life's Secrets: Biochemistry and Molecular Biology*.

AMERICAN SOCIETY OF HEALTH SYSTEM PHARMACISTS
7272 Wisconsin Avenue, Bethesda MD 20814. 301/657-3000. World Wide Web address: http://www.ashp.org. Provides pharmaceutical education. Updates pharmacies on current medical developments. Offers a service for jobseekers for a fee.

BIOMEDICAL RESEARCH INSTITUTE
355 K Street, Chula Vista CA 91911-1209. 619/793-2750. Fax: 619/427-2634. A nonprofit organization which promotes scientific research and education and provides annual scholarships to students. Maintains a national Institutional Review Board.

BIOTECHNOLOGY INDUSTRY ORGANIZATION (BIO)
1625 K Street NW, Suite 1100, Washington DC 20006-1604. 202/857-0244. Fax: 202/857-0237. World Wide Web address: http://www.bio.org. Represents agriculture, biomedical, diagnostic, food, energy, and environmental companies.

NATIONAL PHARMACEUTICAL COUNCIL
1894 Preston White Drive, Reston VA 20191. 703/620-6390. Fax: 703/476-0904. An organization of research-based pharmaceutical companies. Fax requests to the attention of Pat Adams, Vice President of Finance and Administration.

Directories

DRUG TOPICS RED BOOK
Medical Economics Company, 5 Paragon Drive, Montvale NJ 07645. 201/358-7200.

Magazines

DRUG TOPICS
Medical Economics Company, 5 Paragon Drive, Montvale NJ 07645. 201/358-7200.

PHARMACEUTICAL ENGINEERING
International Society of Pharmaceutical Engineers, 3816 West Linebaugh Avenue, Suite 412, Tampa FL 33624. 813/960-2105. World Wide Web address: http://www.ispe.org.

Online Services

MEDZILLA
E-mail address: info@medzilla.com. World Wide Web address: http://www.medzilla.com. Lists job openings for professionals in the fields of biotechnology, health care, medicine, and science related industries.

SCI.MED.PHARMACY
A networking discussion group focusing on the pharmaceutical field.

SCI.RESEARCH.CAREERS
A networking group discussing various careers relating to scientific research.

BUSINESS SERVICES AND NON-SCIENTIFIC RESEARCH

Standard & Poor's *forecasted 7.5 percent growth across the board for the business services industry in 1998. This sector covers a broad range of services, from adjustment and collection to data processing. While the outlook varies depending on the service, in general, the business services sector is among the fastest-growing in the nation. Increasingly, companies are outsourcing functions like data processing to outside firms.*

Steady consolidation across many industries continued to result in a greater need for services in 1998, from temporary help to consulting and engineering services. Security firms expect a significant boost in employment through the year 2005, due to increased concern about crime and vandalism, and the surge in commercial use of sophisticated computer equipment and guards trained to operate such equipment.

HUDSON INSTITUTE
P.O. Box 26-919, Indianapolis IN 46226. 317/545-1000. **Contact:** Human Resources Department. **World Wide Web address:** http://www.hudson.org/hudson. **Description:** A conservative research organization. The institute's work includes The Joint Hungarian-International Blue Ribbon Commission, which works to promote capitalism in Hungary; the Modern Red Schoolhouse, which works to improve elementary and high school education; and the Competitiveness Center, which promotes research and debate on issues such as legal reform, trade and investment liberalization, and job training.

MERIDIAN FINANCIAL CORPORATION
9265 Counselor's Row, Suite 106, Indianapolis IN 46240. 317/722-2000. **Contact:** Human Resources Department. **Description:** Meridian Financial Corporation provides commercial leasing of restaurant equipment, office equipment, computers, and transportation equipment for other companies.

WALKER INFORMATION
3939 Priority Way South Drive, Indianapolis IN 46240. 317/843-3939. **Contact:** Mark Sherman, Human Resources Director. **World Wide Web address:** http://www.walkernet.com. **Description:** Walker Information provides marketing research and data collection. Walker Information uses a variety of methods to collect information from its clients' customers including questionnaires and telephone interviewing.

Note: *Because addresses and telephone numbers of smaller companies can change rapidly, we recommend you call each company to verify the information below before inquiring about job opportunities. Mass mailings are not recommended.*

Additional small employers:

ADJUSTMENT AND COLLECTION SERVICES

CSC Credit Services
PO Box 1180, Anderson IN 46015-1180. 765/649-4251.

CREDIT REPORTING SERVICES

Credit Bureau of La Porte Inc.
PO Box 67, La Porte IN 46350-5559. 219/326-8334.

DETECTIVE, GUARD, AND ARMORED CAR SERVICES

B&W Security Academy
504 Broadway, Suite 828, Gary IN 46402-1936. 219/882-7771.

Blue Line Security Systems
PO Box 17072, Indianapolis IN 46217-0072. 317/784-7103.

Burns International Security Services
4913 Illinois Road, Suite 5, Fort Wayne IN 46804-1167. 219/436-5570.

Burns International Security Services
3737 N Meridian Street, Indianapolis IN 46208-4348. 317/923-5368.

Charles L. Brown Associates
PO Box 501997, Indianapolis IN 46250-6997. 317/577-0046.

Clark Security
PO Box 38, Evansville IN 47701-0038. 812/424-2448.

DBS Executive Security
1803 Lincoln Way West, Mishawaka IN 46544-1622. 219/254-7100.

Industrial Security Management
5475 Broadway, Merrillville IN 46410-1647. 219/884-7775.

Magnum Security Services Inc.
601 South Bend Avenue, South Bend IN 46617. 219/232-9653.

Metro Security Forces Inc.
1001 Benham Avenue, Elkhart IN 46516-3343. 219/522-1611.

MSI Security Services
575 N Pennsylvania Street, Indianapolis IN 46204-1526. 317/635-1901.

Murray Guard Inc.
5036 E 10th Street, Indianapolis IN 46201-2864. 317/352-0451.

Pinkerton Security
PO Box 3009, Terre Haute IN 47803-0009. 812/234-3724.

Pinkerton's Inc.
PO Box 14, Evansville IN 47701-0014. 812/477-8295.

Pinkerton's Inc.
1010 Memorial Way, Fort Wayne IN 46805-1368. 219/482-8102.

Pinkerton's Inc.
PO Box 55553, Indianapolis IN 46205-0553. 317/542-0121.

Protection Plus Inc.
2345 S Lynhurst Dr, Indianapolis IN 46241-5100. 317/244-7569.

Stanley Smith Security Inc.
8455 Keystone Crossing, Indianapolis IN 46240-4353. 317/924-4506.

United Protective Services Inc.
PO Box 186, Jeffersonville IN 47131-0186. 812/284-9651.

SECRETARIAL AND COURT REPORTING SERVICES

ISI Services Inc.
PO Box 12913, Fort Wayne IN 46866-2913. 219/423-6650.

SECURITY SYSTEMS SERVICES

ADT Security Services Inc.
12166 North Meridian Street, Carmel IN 46032-4578. 317/848-1181.

ADT Security Services Inc.
1428 S 3rd Street, Terre Haute IN 47802-1010. 812/238-1238.

Allen Protection Services Inc.
5129 Illinois Road, Fort Wayne IN 46804-1172. 219/436-5252.

Employer's Security Inc.
PO Box 1045, Elkhart IN 46515-1045. 219/295-1020.

Security Automation Systems
8001 East 196th Street, Noblesville IN 46060-9091. 317/776-3500.

For more information on career opportunities in miscellaneous business services and non-scientific research:

Associations

AMERICAN SOCIETY OF APPRAISERS
P.O. Box 17265, Washington DC 20041. 703/478-2228. Toll-free phone: 800/ASA-VALU. Fax: 703/742-8471. World Wide Web address: http://www.appraisers.org. An international, nonprofit, independent appraisal organization. ASA teaches, tests, and awards designations.

EQUIPMENT LEASING ASSOCIATION OF AMERICA
4301 North Fairfax Drive, Suite 550, Arlington VA 22203. 703/527-8655. World Wide Web address: http://www.elaonline.com.

NATIONAL ASSOCIATION OF PERSONNEL SERVICES
3133 Mt. Vernon Avenue, Alexandria VA 22305. 703/684-0180. Fax: 703/684-0071. World Wide Web address: http://www.napsweb.org. Provides federal legislative protection, education, certification, and business products and services to its member employment service agencies.

Online Services

INTERNET BUSINESS OPPORTUNITY SHOWCASE
http://www.clark.net./pub/ibos/busops.html. This Website offers links to franchise, small business, and related opportunities.

PLANT MAINTENANCE RESOURCE CENTER
http://www.plant-maintenance.com. A great resource for maintenance professionals offering links to maintenance consultants and vendors; information on conferences; and articles on maintenance.

CHARITIES AND SOCIAL SERVICES

Charitable health organizations have come into the spotlight in recent years. The American Heart Association, the Arthritis Foundation, and the American Lung Association have all volunteered their names (for a fee) to promote the sale of brand name products. Many think that the charities are risking their reputations by choosing one product over another. Even with this controversy, there is still a growing need for professionals to work in charitable organizations. The industry faces a high turnover rate and opportunities are plentiful.

The need for qualified social workers continues to grow as the older population in need of such services increases. Other factors leading to increasing job opportunities include: rising crime and juvenile delinquency; a growing number of mentally ill, AIDS patients, and families in crisis; and the need for more social workers to administer discharge plans at medical facilities.

COMMUNITY CENTERS OF INDIANAPOLIS
615 North Alabama Street, Suite 312, Indianapolis IN 46204. 317/638-3360. **Contact:** Human Resources Department. **Description:** A service organization that operates 14 community service centers in Indianapolis. Services include individual and family counseling, assessment, and referral; emergency assistance, such as food and clothing; housing revitalization; senior citizen activities, hot lunches, a residential facility, and homemaker assistance; transportation for low income seniors and disabled persons to center-related activities; summer youth activities; tutoring and remedial education; outpatient and residential drug and alcohol treatment programs for adolescents; recreation and social development for all ages; training for job readiness and jobseeking skills seminars; well baby clinics, health clinics, and a dental clinic; Women, Infants and Children (WIC) nutrition programs; food stamp distribution; immigration and naturalization assistance; ESL classes; library extensions; meeting places for scout troops, community groups, and Alcoholics Anonymous; and offices for the Indiana State Employment Service. **Number of employees nationwide:** 300.

COMMUNITY HARVEST FOOD BANK
P.O. Box 10967, Fort Wayne IN 46855-0967. 219/447-3696. **Fax:** 219/447-4859. **Contact:** Jane Avery Doswell, Executive Director. **E-mail address:** mjdoswell@secondharvest.org. **Description:** Collects and distributes food donations. The food bank operates as part of a group of over 400 agencies in northeast Indiana and Allen County. Founded in 1983.

EMPLOYMENT ENTERPRISES
P.O. Box 98, Batesville IN 47006. 812/934-4995. **Contact:** Human Resources Department. **Description:** A nonprofit job service that helps people with disabilities find jobs within the community.

GIRL SCOUTS OF LIMBERLOST
2135 Spy Run Avenue, Fort Wayne IN 46805. 219/422-3417. **Contact:** Human Resources. **World Wide Web address:** http://www.girlscouts.com. **Description:** A social service organization aimed at meeting the social and developmental needs of adolescent girls. **Corporate headquarters location:** New York NY. **Parent company:** Girl Scouts USA.

NATIONAL ASSOCIATION FOR COMMUNITY LEADERSHIP
200 South Meridian Street, Suite 340, Indianapolis IN 46225. 317/637-7408. **Contact:** Human Resources. **World Wide Web address:** http://www.communityleadership.org. **Description:** A nonprofit organization fostering leadership programs in 40 cities and towns throughout the U.S.

The work of the organization includes the sponsorship of conferences, seminars, and publications, all aimed at creating leadership organizations nationwide. Founded in 1979.

TRI-CITY COMMUNITY MENTAL HEALTH CENTER
3903 Indianapolis Boulevard, East Chicago IN 46302. 219/791-2315. **Contact:** Human Resources. **Description:** A mental health care facility that primarily provides care on an outpatient basis. Other services include a detoxification unit for adults and residential care for adolescent women. **NOTE:** Resumes for Tri-City Community Mental Health Center must be sent to Geminus, 5281 Fountain Drive, Crown Point IN 46307.

UNITED WAY OF HOWARD COUNTY
210 West Walnut, Room 201, Kokomo IN 46901. 765/457-6691. **Contact:** Michael Spear, President. **Description:** An organization that raises and distributes funds for community service needs. **Special programs:** Internships.

YMCA CAMP POTAWATAMI
P.O. Box 38, South Milford IN 46786. 219/351-2525. **Contact:** Executive Director. **Description:** Provides educational opportunities in a Christian environment. The camp operates as a branch of the YMCA of greater Fort Wayne.

YMCA CAMP TECUMSEH OUTDOOR CENTER
12635 West Tecumseh Road, Brookston IN 47923. 765/564-2898. **Contact:** Susan Jones, Senior Program Director. **Description:** Operates an outdoor education and conference facility used by churches, YMCAs, and businesses. The facility also operates summer resident and day camp programs.

Note: Because addresses and telephone numbers of smaller companies can change rapidly, we recommend you call each company to verify the information below before inquiring about job opportunities. Mass mailings are not recommended.

Additional small employers:

MISC. SOCIAL SERVICES

American Association of Retired Persons
2912 East 83rd Place, Merrillville IN 46410-6414. 219/942-4097.

American Scholarship Foundation
PO Box 971, Madison IN 47250-0971. 812/273-2799.

Area Five Agency On Aging
1801 Smith Street, Suite 300, Logansport IN 46947-1579. 219/722-4451.

CAP
PO Box 188, Covington IN 47932-0188. 765/793-4881.

CICOA
4755 Kingsway Drive, Suite 200, Indianapolis IN 46205-1545. 317/254-5465.

Citizens Action Coalition Inc.
347 W Berry Street, Suite 420, Fort Wayne IN 46802-2241. 219/423-4492.

Community Action Southern Indiana
PO Box 843, Jeffersonville IN 47131-0843. 812/288-6451.

United Way of Central Indiana
PO Box 88409, Indianapolis IN 46208-0409. 317/923-1466.

For more information on career opportunities in charities and social services:

Associations

AMERICAN COUNCIL OF THE BLIND
1155 15th Street NW, Suite 720, Washington DC 20005. 202/467-5081. World Wide Web address: http://www.acb.org. Membership required. Offers an annual conference, a monthly magazine, and scholarships.

CAREER OPPORTUNITIES
1575 I Street NW, Suite 1190, Washington DC 20005-1168. 202/408-7900. Fax: 202/408-7907. World Wide Web address: http://www.careeropps.com. Publishes a newsletter for the American Society of Association Executives. The newsletter lists job openings at associations and nonprofit organizations nationwide and internationally. Each issue is organized by region. All jobs listed are in the $30,000 - $50,000 salary range. Subscription rates for non-members: $57 for 5 issues; $117 for 12 issues; $197 for 24 issues. Subscription rates for members: $57 for 6 issues; $117 for 14 issues; $197 for 28 issues.

CATHOLIC CHARITIES USA
1731 King Street, Suite 200, Alexandria VA 22314. 703/549-1390. World Wide Web address: http://www.catholiccharitiesusa.org. Membership required.

CLINICAL SOCIAL WORK FEDERATION
P.O. Box 3740, Arlington VA 22203. 703/522-3866. A lobbying organization. Offers newsletters and a conference every two years to member organizations.

FAMILY SERVICE ASSOCIATION OF AMERICA
11700 West Lake Park Drive, Park Place, Milwaukee WI 53224. 414/359-1040. World Wide Web address: http://www.fsanet.org. Membership required.

NATIONAL ASSOCIATION OF SOCIAL WORKERS
750 First Street NE, Suite 700, Washington DC 20002-4241. 202/408-8600. World Wide Web address: http://www.naswdc.org.

NATIONAL COUNCIL ON FAMILY RELATIONS
3989 Central Avenue NE, Suite 550, Minneapolis MN 55421. 612/781-9331. Fax: 612/781-9348. Membership required. Publishes two quarterly journals. Offers an annual conference and newsletters.

NATIONAL FEDERATION OF THE BLIND
1800 Johnson Street, Baltimore MD 21230. 410/659-9314. World Wide Web address: http://www.nfb.org. Membership of 50,000 in 600 local chapters. Publishes a monthly magazine.

NATIONAL MULTIPLE SCLEROSIS SOCIETY
733 Third Avenue, New York NY 10017. 212/986-3240. Toll-free phone: 800/344-4867. World Wide Web address: http://www.nmss.org. Publishes a quarterly magazine.

NATIONAL ORGANIZATION FOR HUMAN SERVICE EDUCATION
Brookdale Community College, 765 Newman Springs Road, Lyncroft NJ 07738. 732/842-1900x546.

Online Services

COOLWORKS
http://www.coolworks.com/. This Website includes information on volunteer openings. The site also provides links to 22,000 job openings in national parks, summer camps, ski areas, river areas, ranches, fishing areas, cruise ships, and resorts.

NONPROFIT JOBNET
http://www.nando.net/philant/philant.html. The *Philanthropy Journal*'s site lists jobs in nonprofit associations and philanthropic occupations.

CHEMICALS/RUBBER AND PLASTICS

Growth in the chemicals industry should be rather weak overall, with some sectors faring better than others. Since 1996, the industry has done poorly in terms of growth, trade, and earnings, according to the U.S. Department of Commerce.

The two major industrial consumers of chemicals -- the housing and automotive industries -- both face overall sluggish growth for the next few years. However, a growing market for electronics and electronic components will feed the demand for products such as cleaners, resin, and other specialty chemicals. With production and prices at a low for large-volume industrial chemicals, both the inorganic and organic sectors expected to see minimal growth in 1998.

The demand and production of plastics, on the other hand, continues to grow, especially in the automotive industry. Additionally, industrial use of rubber will expand as the demand for synthetic rubber by the automotive industry increases.

AET PACKAGING FILMS
P.O. Box 5038, Terre Haute IN 47805. 812/466-4277. **Contact:** Ken Baker, Human Resources Manager. **Description:** A leading manufacturer of plastic films for flexible packaging applications. AET's oriented polypropylene film products are used for snack food and candy packaging, labels for bottles and cans, and numerous other packaging, labeling, and overwrap applications. **Common positions include:** Accountant/Auditor; Budget Analyst; Buyer; Chemical Engineer; Clerical Supervisor; Construction Contractor; Draftsperson; Editor; Electrical/Electronics Engineer; Electrician; Emergency Medical Technician; Environmental Engineer; Financial Analyst; General Manager; Human Resources Manager; Industrial Production Manager; Mechanical Engineer; Operations/Production Manager; Quality Control Supervisor; Systems Analyst. **Educational backgrounds include:** Accounting; Business Administration; Chemistry; Computer Science; Engineering; Finance; Marketing. **Benefits:** 401(k); Dental Insurance; Disability Coverage; Life Insurance; Medical Insurance; Profit Sharing; Savings Plan; Tuition Assistance. **Special programs:** Internships. **Corporate headquarters location:** Peabody MA. **Other U.S. locations:** Covington VA. **Parent company:** Applied Extrusion Technologies, Inc. **Operations at this facility include:** Administration; Manufacturing; Research and Development; Sales; Service. **Listed on:** NASDAQ. **Number of employees at this location:** 400. **Number of employees nationwide:** 1,000.

ALCO TEXTRON
1400 South Industrial Drive, Mishawaka IN 46544. 219/256-0277. **Contact:** Human Resources. **Description:** Manufactures injection-molded plastic products, primarily for use in automotive manufacturing.

ALLIEDSIGNAL LAMINATES
P.O. Box 250, Franklin IN 46131. 317/736-6106. **Contact:** Tonya Mohr, Human Resources Director. **Description:** Manufactures copper-clad and unclad plastic laminates. **Parent company:** AlliedSignal Corporation serves a broad spectrum of industries through its more than 40 strategic businesses, which are grouped into three sectors: Aerospace, Automotive, and Engineered Materials. AlliedSignal is one of the nation's largest industrial organizations and has 115,000 employees in over 30 countries.

ALLTRISTA CORPORATION
P.O. Box 5004, Muncie IN 47307-5004. 765/281-5000. **Contact:** Devona Coffey, Human Resources. **Description:** A diversified manufacturer, doing business in a number of product and

service areas including a line of home food preservation products, such as consumer canning jars, jar closures, and related food products; high-barrier, multilayer, co-extruded plastic products, including sheet-formed containers and retort containers; copper-plated zinc penny blanks, cans for use in zinc/carbon batteries, and other industrial zinc products; protective coating application and decorative lithography services; tin-plated steel aluminum and light-gauge rolled products; thermoformed plastic refrigerator door liners, separators, and evaporator trays; injection-molded plastics products; and software and hardware for non-destructive inspection systems. **Corporate headquarters location:** This Location.

BERRY PLASTICS CORPORATION
P.O. Box 959, Evansville IN 47706. 812/424-2904. **Contact:** Personnel. **World Wide Web address:** http://www.berryplastics.com. **Description:** Manufactures and markets plastic packaging products, including caps for aerosol cans and rigid open-top containers.

CARPENTER COMPANY
P.O. Box 2386, Elkhart IN 46515. 219/522-2800. **Physical address:** 195 County Road 15 South, Elkhart IN 46516. **Fax:** 219/522-6340. **Contact:** Matt Fasbender, Personnel Manager. **Description:** A division of one of the world's largest producers of polyurethane foam and comfort cushioning products. Founded in 1948. **NOTE:** Entry-level positions and second and third shifts are offered. **Common positions include:** Administrative Assistant; Blue-Collar Worker Supervisor; Branch Manager; Chemical Engineer; Electrician; Industrial Engineer; Management Trainee; Purchasing Agent/Manager; Quality Control Supervisor. **Educational backgrounds include:** Business Administration; Engineering. **Special programs:** Internships. **Corporate headquarters location:** Richmond VA. **Listed on:** Privately held. **Number of employees nationwide:** 4,600. **Number of employees worldwide:** 6,800.

EAGLE-PICHER INDUSTRIES, INC.
PLASTICS DIVISION
P.O. Box 189, Grabill IN 46741-0189. 219/627-3612. **Contact:** Personnel. **World Wide Web address:** http://www.epcorp.com. **Description:** This location manufactures plastics. Overall, Eagle-Picher is a diversified manufacturer of raw materials for industrial clients.

FIRESTONE INDUSTRIAL PRODUCTS
1700 Firestone Boulevard, Noblesville IN 46060. 317/773-0650. **Contact:** Human Resources. **Description:** Manufactures fabricated rubber products.

FOAMEX INTERNATIONAL, INC.
2211 South Wayne, Auburn IN 46706. 219/925-1073. **Contact:** Debbie Stein, Human Resources. **World Wide Web address:** http://www.foamex.com. **Description:** One of the nation's largest manufacturers of flexible polyurethane foam products. Foamex products are classified into four groups: Cushion foams are used for mattresses, quilting and borders, home and office furniture, computer and electronics packaging, and padding foams for health care; Carpet cushion foams include prime, bonded, sponge rubber, felt carpet cushion, synthetic grass turf, and a variety of textured carpeting and wallcovering. Automotive foams include foams for cushioning and seating, acoustical foams, headliner foams, trim foams, and foams for door panel parts; Technical foams include those for filtration, reservoiring, sound absorption and sound transmission, carburetors, high-speed inkjet printers, speaker grilles, oxygenators, and EKG pads, as well as cosmetic applicators, mop heads, paint brushes, and diapers. **Other U.S. locations:** Nationwide. **International locations:** Canada; Mexico. **Listed on:** NASDAQ. **Stock exchange symbol:** FMXI. **Annual sales/revenues:** More than $100 million. **Number of employees worldwide:** 3,600.

GREAT LAKES CHEMICAL CORPORATION
P.O. Box 2200, West Lafayette IN 47996-2200. 765/497-6100. **Recorded jobline:** 765/497-6377. **Contact:** Human Resources. **World Wide Web address:** http://www.greatlakeschem.com. **Description:** A leading supplier of specialty chemical solutions to customers in plastics, additives, and life sciences. The company also develops performance chemicals for use in fire protection, oil and gas drilling, and recreational water treatment. **NOTE:** Please call the jobline for application procedures before sending a resume. **Corporate headquarters location:** This Location. **Listed on:** New York Stock Exchange.

HAMMOND GROUP, INC.
5231 Hohman Avenue, Hammond IN 46320. 219/931-9360. **Contact:** Human Resources. **World Wide Web address:** http://www.hmndgroup.com. **Description:** This location houses administrative offices. Overall, Hammond Group manufactures lead chemicals and products, under the name Hammond Lead Products, including lead carbonates, silicates, and sulfates for a variety of industries. The company also developed and manufactures a dedusted granular litharge called 400Y. **Corporate headquarters location:** This Location.

HOLM INDUSTRIES INC.
745 South Gardner Street, Scottsburg IN 47170. 812/752-2526. **Fax:** 812/752-3563. **Contact:** Human Resources Manager. **Description:** Involved in the extrusion of plastic, rubber, and vinyl for the appliance and building trade industries. **Common positions include:** Accountant/Auditor; Biological Scientist; Blue-Collar Worker Supervisor; Buyer; Chemical Engineer; Chemist; Claim Representative; Computer Programmer; Cost Estimator; Customer Service Representative; General Manager; Human Resources Manager; Industrial Engineer; Industrial Production Manager; Mechanical Engineer; Operations/Production Manager; Purchasing Agent/Manager; Quality Control Supervisor; Transportation/Traffic Specialist. **Educational backgrounds include:** Business Administration; Chemistry; Communications; Finance; Marketing. **Benefits:** 401(k); Dental Insurance; Disability Coverage; Life Insurance; Medical Insurance; Pension Plan; Tuition Assistance. **Corporate headquarters location:** This Location. **Other U.S. locations:** Hartselle AL; San Diego CA; St. Charles IL; New Ulm MN. **Parent company:** Standard Products. **Operations at this facility include:** Administration; Manufacturing; Research and Development; Sales. **Number of employees at this location:** 700. **Number of employees nationwide:** 1,100.

INDIANA ARMY AMMUNITION PLANT
11452 Highway 62, Charlestown IN 47111. 812/284-7600. **Contact:** Human Resources. **World Wide Web address:** http://www.facilityone.com. **Description:** A stand-by explosives manufacturing facility.

KEIL CHEMICAL
3000 Sheffield Avenue, Hammond IN 46327. 219/931-2630. **Contact:** Human Resources. **Description:** Produces lubricant and gas additives and fire retardants.

GEORGE KOCH & SONS, INC.
10 South 11th Avenue, Evansville IN 47744. 812/465-9600. **Contact:** Human Resources. **Description:** Manufactures paints, varnishes, lacquers, and enamels.

LEVER BROTHERS COMPANY
1200 Calumet Avenue, Hammond IN 46320. 219/659-3200. **Contact:** Human Resources. **World Wide Web address:** http://www.lever.com. **Description:** This location produces a variety of soap and detergent products. Overall, Lever Brothers Company is an international manufacturer and distributor of soaps and cleaning products, specialty foods, toothpastes, and detergents.

LILLY INDUSTRIES
733 South West Street, Indianapolis IN 46225. 317/687-6700. **Contact:** Human Resources. **World Wide Web address:** http://www.lillyindustries.com. **Description:** Formulates, manufactures and sells liquid and powder industrial coatings for use on furniture, doors, paneling, appliances, and auto parts.

NATIONAL STARCH & CHEMICAL
1515 South Drover Street, Indianapolis IN 46221. 317/635-4455. **Contact:** Human Resources. **World Wide Web address:** http://www.nationalstarch.com. **Description:** An industrial chemical manufacturer producing adhesives, resins, starches, and specialty chemicals for the packaging, textile, paper, food, furniture, electronic materials, and automotive markets.

ONEIDA ROSTONE CORPORATION
P.O. Box 7497, Lafayette IN 47903. 765/474-2421. **Fax:** 765/474-8785. **Contact:** Human Resources Manager. **World Wide Web address:** http://www.oneidarostone.com. **Description:** A custom molder of thermoset plastic products for a variety of applications including the automotive

and electric industries. **Common positions include:** Accountant/Auditor; Chemical Engineer; Customer Service Representative; Electrical/Electronics Engineer; Electrician; Environmental Engineer; Human Resources Manager; Industrial Production Manager; Mechanical Engineer; Operations/Production Manager; Purchasing Agent/Manager; Services Sales Representative; Systems Analyst. **Educational backgrounds include:** Chemistry; Computer Science; Engineering. **Benefits:** 401(k); Dental Insurance; Disability Coverage; Employee Discounts; Life Insurance; Medical Insurance; Relocation Assistance; Savings Plan; Tuition Assistance. **Corporate headquarters location:** This Location. **Other U.S. locations:** Nationwide. **Listed on:** Privately held. **Number of employees at this location:** 370.

PRAXAIR SURFACE TECHNOLOGY, INC.
1500 Polco Street, Indianapolis IN 46224. 317/240-2500. **Contact:** Personnel. **Description:** Engaged in the production of metallic coatings. **Parent company:** Praxair, Inc. produces gases and gas production equipment for customers in the aerospace, chemicals, electronics, food processing, health care, glass, metal fabrication, petroleum, primary metals, pulp, and paper markets.

RHODIA CHEMICAL
2000 Michigan Street, Hammond IN 46320. 219/932-7651. **Contact:** Human Resources. **Description:** Produces acid that is mainly used in the manufacturing of gasoline. **Parent company:** Rhone-Poulenc Basic Chemicals.

SYRACUSE RUBBER PRODUCTS, INC.
501 South Sycamore Street, Syracuse IN 46567. 219/457-3141. **Fax:** 219/457-5009. **Contact:** Cari Kline, Human Resources Manager. **Description:** Manufactures molded rubber products. **Common positions include:** Accountant/Auditor; Chemist; Computer Programmer; Draftsperson; Electrical/Electronics Engineer; Electrician; Human Resources Manager; Industrial Engineer. **Educational backgrounds include:** Accounting; Business Administration; Chemistry; Communications; Computer Science; Engineering; Finance. **Benefits:** 401(k); Dental Insurance; Disability Coverage; Employee Discounts; Life Insurance; Medical Insurance; Profit Sharing; Savings Plan; Tuition Assistance. **Special programs:** Internships. **Corporate headquarters location:** Goshen IN. **Other U.S. locations:** Nationwide. **Parent company:** Goshen Rubber Co. **Number of employees at this location:** 330. **Number of employees nationwide:** 1,500.

UNIROYAL-GOODRICH TIRE COMPANY
P.O. Box 277, Woodburn IN 46797. 219/493-8100. **Contact:** Personnel Manager. **Description:** Manufactures tires. **Parent company:** Michelin has operations in the United States, Canada, Mexico, Asia, Europe, Brazil, Nigeria, and Algeria.

VISKASE CORPORATION
102 East Bailie, Kentland IN 47951. 219/474-5101. **Contact:** Human Resources. **Description:** Manufactures cellulose casings and flexible packaging primarily used in the food industry.

WESTERN CONSOLIDATED TECHNOLOGIES
620 East Douglas Street, Goshen IN 46526. 219/533-4126. **Contact:** Human Resources. **Description:** Manufactures molded, extruded, and lathe cut rubber goods.

Note: Because addresses and telephone numbers of smaller companies can change rapidly, we recommend you call each company to verify the information below before inquiring about job opportunities. Mass mailings are not recommended.

Additional small employers:

ADHESIVES AND SEALANTS

Morton Coatings Group
PO Box 647, Warsaw IN 46581-0647. 219/372-2000.

Pipeconx
PO Box 6288, Evansville IN 47719-0288. 812/425-1361.

Shamban Seals
PO Box 176, Fort Wayne IN 46801-0176. 219/749-9631.

Uniroyal Technology Corp.
2001 W Washington St, South Bend IN 46628. 219/246-5000.

Van Ru Inc.
1175 E Diamond Ave, Evansville IN 47711-3903. 812/464-2488.

ALKALIS AND CHLORINE

Olin Brass
PO Box 51519, Indianapolis IN 46251-0519. 317/484-5600.

CHEMICALS AND ALLIED PRODUCTS WHOLESALE

Harcros Chemicals Incorporated
456 Nowlin Avenue, Lawrenceburg IN 47025-1524. 812/537-8620.

Praxair
4400 Kennedy Avenue, East Chicago IN 46312-2715. 219/398-3700.

CHEMICALS AND CHEMICAL PREPARATIONS

Qualicaps
Lilly Corporate Center, Indianapolis IN 46225. 317/276-7030.

CLEANING, POLISHING, AND SANITATION PREPARATIONS

Arden Corporation
PO Box 456, Kendallville IN 46755-0456. 219/347-4388.

Ecolab Inc.
970 East Tipton Street, Huntington IN 46750-1611. 219/356-8100.

INDUSTRIAL INORGANIC CHEMICALS

Criterion Catalyst
1800 E U.S. Highway 12, Michigan City IN 46360-2074. 219/874-6211.

Silberline Manufacturing Co.
PO Box 267, Decatur IN 46733-0267. 219/728-2111.

INDUSTRIAL ORGANIC CHEMICALS

New Energy Corporation
PO Box 2289, South Bend IN 46680-2289. 219/233-3116.

MISC. RUBBER AND PLASTIC PRODUCTS

Hitachi Cable Indiana Inc.
PO Box 6743, New Albany IN 47151-6743. 812/945-9011.

PAINTS, VARNISHES, AND RELATED PRODUCTS

Red Spot Paint & Varnish Company
PO Box 418, Evansville IN 47703-0418. 812/428-9100.

United Coatings
323 West 15th Street, Indianapolis IN 46202-2206. 317/262-1841.

Valspar Corporation
PO Box 10330, Fort Wayne IN 46851-0330. 219/484-9011.

PLASTIC MATERIALS, SYNTHETICS, AND ELASTOMERS

Ampacet Corporation
PO Box 5357, Terre Haute IN 47805-0357. 812/466-5231.

Dow Corning
PO Box 369, Kendallville IN 46755-0369. 219/347-5813.

GE Plastics Division
One Lexan Lane, Mount Vernon IN 47620-9367. 812/831-7000.

Johnson Controls
2501 East 850 North, Ossian IN 46777-9365. 219/622-6222.

Sonoco Products Company
PO Box 440, North Vernon IN 47265-0440. 812/346-1066.

PLASTIC PRODUCTS

Aker Plastics Company Inc.
PO Box 484, Plymouth IN 46563-0484. 219/936-3838.

Alcoa Closure Systems International
1604 Elmore Street, Crawfordsville IN 47933-3121. 765/364-6300.

Ameri-Kart Corporation
PO Box 368, Bristol IN 46507-0368. 219/848-7462.

American Plastic Molding Corporation
PO Box 480, Scottsburg IN 47170-0480. 812/752-2292.

American Window & Glass Inc.
2715 Lynch Road, Evansville IN 47711-2958. 812/464-9400.

Arrowhead Plastic South
PO Box 1585, Muncie IN 47308-1585. 765/286-0533.

Ashland Products Inc.
790 W Commercial Avenue, Lowell IN 46356-2249. 219/696-5950.

Bailey Corporation
PO Box 548, Hartford City IN 47348-0548. 765/348-5780.

BPC Manufacturing
1755 North Oak Road, Plymouth IN 46563-3413. 219/936-9894.

Central Fine Pack Inc.
7707 Vicksburg Pike, Fort Wayne IN 46804-5549. 219/436-7225.

Charleston Corporation
PO Box 1647, Elkhart IN 46515-1647. 219/633-4696.

Como Plastics Corporation
2860 North National Road, Columbus IN 47201-3746. 812/372-8251.

Componx Inc.
PO Box 925, North Vernon IN 47265-0925. 812/346-8567.

Crescent Plastics Inc.
955 E Diamond Avenue, Evansville IN 47711-3407. 812/428-9300.

D&E Components
PO Box 37, Knox IN 46534-0037. 219/772-6278.

Decatur Plastic Products Incorporated
PO Box 965, North Vernon IN 47265-0965. 812/346-5159.

Deflect-O Corporation
PO Box 50057, Indianapolis IN 46250-0057. 317/849-9555.

Dolco Packaging Corporation
PO Box 469, Decatur IN 46733-0469. 219/728-2161.

DSM Engineering Plastics Incorporated
PO Box 3333, Evansville IN 47732-3333. 812/424-3831.

Eagle-Picher Molding
4306 Gibbs Road, Danville IN 46122-8453. 317/839-0427.

Eagle-Picher Plastics Division
PO Box 398, Ashley IN 46705-0398. 219/587-9155.

EFP Corporation
PO Box 2368, Elkhart IN 46515-2368. 219/295-4690.

Elite Enterprises Inc.
2701 S Coliseum Boulevard, Fort Wayne IN 46803-2950. 219/420-1605.

Flair Molded Plastics Inc.
2521 Lynch Road, Evansville IN 47711-2954. 812/425-6155.

Flambeau Products Corporation
PO Box 5067, Columbus IN 47202-5067. 812/372-4899.

Flexible Foam
PO Box 2057, Elkhart IN 46515-2057. 219/294-7694.

Foamex
3005 Commercial Road, Fort Wayne IN 46809. 219/747-7485.

Fowler Specialty Bag
407 South Adeway, Fowler IN 47944-8410. 765/884-1040.

Gaska Tape Inc.
PO Box 1968, Elkhart IN 46515-1968. 219/294-5431.

Gold Shield
PO Box 496, Decatur IN 46733-0496. 219/728-2476.

Hartson-Kennedy Cabinet Top Co.
PO Box 3095, Marion IN 46953-0095. 765/668-8144.

Hedwin Corporation
1209 East Lincoln Way, La Porte IN 46350-3987. 219/326-6565.

IDM
9100 Front Street, Fort Wayne IN 46818-2209. 219/489-3528.

Jasper Plastics
1220 Power Drive, Jasper IN 47549-0001. 812/634-3443.

Key Plastics Inc.
1615 W McDonald Street, Hartford City IN 47348-9259. 765/348-7300.

Key Plastics Inc.
PO Box 427, Ashley IN 46705-0427. 219/587-3224.

Landis Plastics Inc.
PO Box 386, Monticello IN 47960-0386. 219/583-5583.

Landis Plastics Inc.
630 Commerce Drive, Richmond IN 47374-2600. 765/966-1414.

LDM Technologies Inc.
300 S Progress Drive E, Kendallville IN 46755-3266. 219/347-0500.

Letica Corporation
PO Box 693, Fremont IN 46737-0693. 219/495-2000.

Lichter Rubber Products
PO Box 386, Seymour IN 47274-0386. 812/522-5211.

Maax Midwest
1010 W Dewey Street, Bremen IN 46506-2068. 219/546-3298.

Mullinix Packages Inc.
3511 Engle Road, Fort Wayne IN 46809-1117. 219/747-3149.

National Plastics Corporation
5727 Industrial Road, Fort Wayne IN 46825-5127. 219/484-0595.

Nippisun Indiana Corporation
821 W Mausoleum Road, Shelbyville IN 46176-9719. 317/398-2269.

Nyloncraft
616 W McKinley Avenue, Mishawaka IN 46545-5518. 219/256-1521.

Oxford Bath Products
700 International Dr, Franklin IN 46131-9733. 317/736-9945.

Pent Plastics Inc.
PO Box 668, Avilla IN 46710-0668. 219/897-3775.

Plastic Moldings Corporation
PO Box 18, East Enterprise IN 47019-0018. 812/534-3202.

Plastic Moldings Corporation
1451 E State Road 44, Shelbyville IN 46176-1887. 317/392-4139.

Poly Hi Solidur Inc.
2710 American Way, Fort Wayne IN 46809-3011. 219/479-4100.

PRD Inc.
Rur Rte 2, Box 502B, Springville IN 47462-9519. 812/279-8885.

Precise Technologies
4750 Swisher Rd, Lafayette IN 47906-9782. 765/423-2592.

Precision Plastics of Indiana
PO Box 628, Crawfordsville IN 47933-0628. 765/362-0400.

Primex Plastics Corporation
1235 N F St, Richmond IN 47374-2448. 765/966-7774.

Pro Form Inc.
1000 Grove St, Evansville IN 47710-1824. 812/465-4600.

Prodesign
23925 Reedy Dr, Elkhart IN 46514-8316. 219/262-9250.

Salga Inc.
PO Box 65, Fremont IN 46737-0065. 219/495-7788.

Scottsburg Plastics Inc.
1250 S Bond St, Scottsburg IN 47170. 812/752-6224.

Silgan Plastics Corporation
3779 County Rd, Seymour IN 47274. 812/522-0963.

Silgan Plastics Corporation
910 Gerber St, Ligonier IN 46767-2413. 219/894-7931.

Solvay Automotive Inc.
1827 N Bendix Dr, South Bend IN 46628-1602. 219/232-6911.

Sonoco-Crellin Inc.
PO Box 67, Frankfort IN 46041-0067. 765/659-3307.

South Bend Plastics Inc.
1810 Clover Rd, Mishawaka IN 46545-7247. 219/259-1991.

Southcorp USA Inc.
4002 Montdale Dr, Valparaiso IN 46383. 219/462-8915.

Spencer Industries Inc.
PO Box 449, Dale IN 47523-0449. 812/937-4561.

Stelrema Corp.
PO Box 9, Knox IN 46534-0009. 219/772-2103.

Tasus Corp.
300 Daniels Way, Bloomington IN 47404-9772. 812/333-6500.

UTA Bourbon
12340 Elm Rd, Bourbon IN 46504-9608. 219/342-0219.

United Technologies
600 S Kyle Street, Edinburgh IN 46124-1606. 812/526-5551.

Viking Formed Products
PO Box 3300, Elkhart IN 46515-3300. 219/825-8401.

PRINTING INK

General Printing Ink
2642 West State Road 28, Frankfort IN 46041-9193. 765/659-6000.

RUBBER PRODUCTS

AVI
1411 Pidco Drive, Plymouth IN 46563-1352. 219/936-7065.

Bauman Harnish Rubber Company
400 N Taylor Road, Garrett IN 46738-1846. 219/357-3125.

BRC Rubber Group Inc.
PO Box 255, Bluffton IN 46714-0255. 219/824-4501.

BRC Rubber Group Inc.
PO Box 227, Churubusco IN 46723-0227. 219/693-2171.

BRC Rubber Group Inc.
PO Box 145, Montpelier IN 47359-0145. 765/728-8510.

BTR Antivibration Systems Inc.
PO Box 7007, Logansport IN 46947-7007. 219/753-5131.

Connor Corporation
2701 Dwenger Avenue, Fort Wayne IN 46803-1417. 219/424-1601.

Cooper Engineered Products Division
725 W 11th Street, Auburn IN 46706-2022. 219/925-0700.

Freudenberg-NOK Brake Division
PO Box 4452, Scottsburg IN 47170. 812/752-4232.

Goshen Rubber Company Inc.
PO Box 517, Goshen IN 46527-0517. 219/533-1111.

IMCO Inc.
PO Box 444, Huntington IN 46750-0444. 219/356-4810.

Jasper Rubber Products Inc.
PO Box 706, Jasper IN 47547-0706. 812/482-3242.

Ligonier Rubber
PO Box 71, Ligonier IN 46767-0071. 219/894-4121.

Lintec
301 Progress Way, Avilla IN 46710-9668. 219/897-2244.

NISCO
324 Morrow Street, Topeka IN 46571-9076. 219/593-2156.

NISCO
2808 Adams Center Road, Fort Wayne IN 46803. 219/493-7938.

Nishikawa Standard Company
501 High Road, Bremen IN 46506-1040. 219/546-5938.

Sperry Rubber & Plastic Co.
9146 US Rte 52, Brookville IN 47012. 765/647-4141.

Ten Cate Enbi Inc.
1703 McCall Dr, Shelbyville IN 46176-9783. 317/398-3267.

Triangle Rubber
PO Box 95, Goshen IN 46527-0095. 219/533-3118.

UNSUPPORTED PLASTIC PRODUCTS

Formflex
PO Box 158, Bloomingdale IN 47832-0158. 765/498-3900.

Janco Products Inc.
PO Box 1090, Mishawaka IN 46546-1090. 219/255-3169.

Polygon Company
PO Box 176, Walkerton IN 46574-0176. 219/586-3145.

Royalite Thermoplastics
PO Box 958, Warsaw IN 46581-0958. 219/267-7127.

Sabin Corporation
PO Box 788, Bloomington IN 47402-0788. 812/339-2567.

Spartech Plastics
PO Box 757, Richmond IN 47375-0757. 765/935-7541.

For more information on career opportunities in the chemicals/rubber and plastics industries:

Associations

AMERICAN ASSOCIATION FOR CLINICAL CHEMISTRY
2101 L Street NW, Suite 202, Washington DC 20037-1526. 202/857-0717. Toll-free phone: 800/892-1400. World Wide Web address: http://www.aacc.org. International scientific/medical society of individuals involved with clinical chemistry and other clinical lab science-related disciplines.

AMERICAN CHEMICAL SOCIETY
Career Services, 1155 16th Street NW, Washington DC 20036. 202/872-4600. World Wide Web address: http://www.acs.org.

AMERICAN INSTITUTE OF CHEMICAL ENGINEERS
345 East 47th Street, New York NY 10017. 212/705-7338. Toll-free phone: 800/242-4363. World Wide Web address: http://www.aiche.org. Provides leadership in advancing the chemical engineering profession as it meets the needs of society.

CHEMICAL MANAGEMENT & RESOURCES ASSOCIATION
60 Bay Street, Suite 702, Staten Island NY 10301. 718/876-8800. Fax: 718/720-4666. Engaged in marketing, marketing research, business development, and planning for the chemical and allied process industries. Provides technical meetings, educational programs, and publications to members.

CHEMICAL MANUFACTURERS ASSOCIATION
1300 Wilson Boulevard, Arlington VA 22209. 703/741-5000. World Wide Web address: http://www.cmahq.com. A trade association that develops and implements programs and services and advocates public policy that benefits the industry and society.

THE ELECTROCHEMICAL SOCIETY
10 South Main Street, Pennington NJ 08534-2896. An international educational society dealing with electrochemical issues. Also publishes monthly journals.

SOAP AND DETERGENT ASSOCIATION
475 Park Avenue South, 27th Floor, New York NY 10016. 212/725-1262. World Wide Web address: http://www.sdahq.org. A trade association and research center.

SOCIETY OF PLASTICS ENGINEERS
14 Fairfield Drive, P.O. Box 403, Brookfield CT 06804-0403. 203/775-0471. World Wide Web address: http://www.4spe.org. Dedicated to helping members attain higher professional status through increased scientific, engineering, and technical knowledge.

THE SOCIETY OF THE PLASTICS INDUSTRY, INC.
1801 K Street NW, Suite 600K, Washington DC 20006. 202/974-5200. Promotes the development of the plastics industry and enhances public understanding of its contributions while meeting the needs of society.

Directories

CHEMICAL INDUSTRY DIRECTORY
State Mutual Book and Periodical Service, Order Department, 17th Floor, 521 Fifth Avenue, New York NY 10175. 516/537-1104.

CHEMICALS DIRECTORY
Cahners Publishing, 275 Washington Street, Newton MA 02158. 617/964-3030.

DIRECTORY OF CHEMICAL ENGINEERING CONSULTANTS
American Institute of Chemical Engineers, 345 East 47th Street, New York NY 10017. 212/705-7338.

DIRECTORY OF CHEMICAL PRODUCERS
SRI International, 333 Ravenswood Avenue, Menlo Park CA 94025. 650/326-6200. World Wide Web address: http://www.sri.com.

Magazines

CHEMICAL & ENGINEERING NEWS
American Chemical Society, 1155 16th Street NW, Washington DC 20036. 202/872-4600. World Wide Web address: http://www.pubs.acs.org/cen.

CHEMICAL MARKETING REPORTER
Schnell Publishing Company, 80 Brot Street, 23rd Floor, New York NY 10004. 212/791-4267.

CHEMICAL WEEK
888 Seventh Avenue, 26th Floor, New York NY 10106. 212/621-4900. World Wide Web address: http://www.chemweek.com.

COMMUNICATIONS: TELECOMMUNICATIONS AND BROADCASTING

The telecommunications industry was marked by radical changes in 1997, and more consolidation and intense competition among local and long-distance carriers were expected to follow in 1998, according to Business Week. *In reaction to price drops and increased competition across all segments of the industry, mergers and acquisitions have been an industry trend.*

The Telecommunications Act of 1996, coupled with promising new wireless technology, opened the door for major long-distance companies to break into the local phone market within their respective regions, which proved a very costly venture. However, a federal court decision to limit the FCC's regulation over long-distance carriers should give businesses more power over prices and the freedom to enter new territories.

Subscribers of wireless services were expected to increase substantially by the end of 1998, although declining prices of wireless minutes, driven by competition, will likely be detrimental to smaller wireless operators. Meanwhile, a strong demand for data and networking communications equipment will be beneficial to the industry.

Internet technologies continue to transform the telecommunications industry as companies begin to offer long-distance and fax services over the Internet. According to Action Information Services, these services will produce $1 billion in revenues by 2001, although companies must satisfy customers' demands for increasingly faster Internet access.

AMERITECH NETWORK SERVICES
220 North Meridian Street, Room 1788, Indianapolis IN 46204. 317/265-2390. **Contact:** Greg Barth, Staffing Manager. **Description:** Provides technologically-advanced information services. The company serves 12 million business and residential customers throughout the Great Lakes region. **International locations:** New Zealand; Poland. **Parent company:** Ameritech Corporation is one of the largest telephone holding companies in the U.S. Ameritech provides local telephone service to nearly 18 million customers in five mid-western states. The company has an interest in Bell Communications Research with other Bell holding companies. Subsidiaries of Ameritech Corporation include: Ameritech Mobile is a wireless communications company, providing services to 1 million clients and over 500,000 pagers; another subsidiary markets, installs, and provides maintenance services for business equipment; other subsidiaries conduct advertising, publishing, research and development, messaging, financing, and leasing services. **Number of employees nationwide:** 65.

BRIGHTPOINT INC.
6402 Corporate Drive, Indianapolis IN 46278. 317/297-6100. **Contact:** Human Resources. **World Wide Web address:** http://www.brightpoint.com. **Description:** A wholesale distributor of cellular telephones including a variety of brands of vehicle-mounted, transportable, and hand-held portable cellular telephones and accessories, such as batteries, battery eliminators and chargers, antennas, and cases. The company distributes its products to over 2,000 customers including cellular carriers, agents, dealers, and retailers throughout the United States as well as to foreign markets.

EMMIS BROADCASTING CORPORATION
950 North Meridian Street, Suite 1200, Indianapolis IN 46204. 317/266-0100. **Contact:** Carolyn Herald, Personnel Director. **Description:** Owns and operates FM radio stations and publishes a monthly statistical publication for the radio industry. **Corporate headquarters location:** This Location. **Number of employees nationwide:** 825.

GTE NORTH INC.
19845 North U.S. 31, Westfield IN 46074. 317/896-6464. **Contact:** Human Resources. **World Wide Web address:** http://www.gte.com. **Description:** As part of GTE Telephone Operations, GTE North provides communications services ranging from local telephone services to highly-complex voice and data services for industry. GTE is one of the largest publicly-held telecommunications companies in the world, one of the largest U.S.-based local telephone companies, and one of the largest cellular-service providers in the United States. In the U.S., GTE Telephone Operations serves 17.4 million access lines in 28 states. **NOTE:** For hiring information, please contact Human Resources, 8001 West Jefferson Boulevard, Fort Wayne IN 46801. 219/461-2056. **Corporate headquarters location:** Stamford CT. **Other U.S. locations:** Nationwide.

LUCENT TECHNOLOGIES
6612 East 75th Street, Indianapolis IN 46250. 317/845-8980. **Contact:** Human Resources. **World Wide Web address:** http://www.lucent.com. **Description:** Manufactures communications products, including switching, transmission, fiber-optic cable, wireless systems, and operations systems, to supply the needs of telephone companies and other communications service providers.

LUCENT TECHNOLOGIES
2855 North Franklin Road, Indianapolis IN 46219. 317/352-0011. **Contact:** Human Resources. **World Wide Web address:** http://www.lucent.com. **Description:** This location is the Customer Information Center and is responsible for the production and distribution of product manuals and literature. Overall, the company manufactures communications products including switching, transmission, fiber-optic cable, wireless systems, and operations systems.

WISH-TV 8
1950 North Meridian Street, Indianapolis IN 46202. 317/923-8888. **Contact:** Human Resources. **World Wide Web address:** http://www.wish-tv.com/8. **Description:** A CBS affiliate broadcasting throughout central Indiana. **NOTE:** Each department at the station hires its own personnel.

WTIU-TV
400 East Seventh Street, Bloomington IN 47405. 812/855-5900. **Contact:** Human Resources. **World Wide Web address:** http://www.wtiu.indiana.edu/iub. **Description:** A public television station serving south central Indiana. **NOTE:** Hiring is done through Indiana University.

WZPL
MYSTAR COMMUNICATIONS
9245 North Meridian Street, Suite 300, Indianapolis IN 46260. 317/816-4000. **Contact:** Human Resources. **World Wide Web address:** http://www.wzpl.com. **Description:** A contemporary music radio station.

Note: Because addresses and telephone numbers of smaller companies can change rapidly, we recommend you call each company to verify the information below before inquiring about job opportunities. Mass mailings are not recommended.

Additional small employers:

CABLE/PAY TELEVISION SERVICES

American Cablevision Indianapolis
3030 Roosevelt Avenue, Indianapolis IN 46218-3755. 317/632-2288.

Comcast Cable Division
720 Taylor Street, Fort Wayne IN 46802-5144. 219/456-9000.

COMMUNICATIONS EQUIPMENT

GTE
1099 North Meridian Street, Indianapolis IN 46204-1075. 317/630-3630.

Hughes Defense Communications
1010 Production Road, Fort Wayne IN 46808-4106. 219/429-0000.

Ritron Inc.
PO Box 1998, Carmel IN 46032-4998. 317/846-1201.

MISC. COMMUNICATIONS SERVICES

Xerox Connect
9455 Delegates Row, Indianapolis IN 46240-3805. 317/846-5996.

RADIO BROADCASTING STATIONS

WFMS-FM
8120 Knue Rd, Indianapolis IN 46250-1937. 317/842-9550.

WIKY-FM
PO Box 3848, Evansville IN 47736-3848. 812/424-8284.

WNDE-AM
6161 Fall Creek Road, Indianapolis IN 46220-5032. 317/257-7565.

WTHI
PO Box 1486, Terre Haute IN 47808-1486. 812/232-9481.

TELEPHONE COMMUNICATIONS

Ameritech
134 NW 6th Street, Evansville IN 47708-1306. 812/464-6100.

Ameritech Cellular & Paging
9190 Priority Way West Drive, Indianapolis IN 46240-1437. 317/817-9529.

Ameritech of Indiana
116 E Taylor Street, Kokomo IN 46901-4627. 317/556-4200.

Ameritech of Indiana
5858 N College Avenue, Indianapolis IN 46220-2552. 317/252-4253.

GTE Corporation
129 South 2nd Street, Elkhart IN 46516-3114. 219/294-4252.

GTE Mobilenet Incorporated
250 East 96th Street, Indianapolis IN 46240-3730. 317/696-5887.

GTE North Inc.
4027 Beckwith Drive, Fort Wayne IN 46808-4025. 219/428-8611.

GTE North Inc.
PO Box 1547, Terre Haute IN 47808-1547. 812/238-5011.

GTE North Inc.
PO Box 1406, Richmond IN 47375-1406. 765/983-4450.

GTE Telephone Operations
PO Box 1040, Lafayette IN 47902-1040. 765/423-3278.

GTE Telephone Operations
PO Box 2300, Fort Wayne IN 46801-2300. 219/426-2580.

GTE Wireless of the Midwest
250 East 96th St, Suite 175, Indianapolis IN 46240-3730. 317/848-0162.

Hellyer Communications Inc.
8500 Keystone Crossing, Indianapolis IN 46240. 317/252-3000.

Smithville Telephone Company Inc.
300 W Temperance St, Ellettsville IN 47429-1535. 812/876-1212.

United Telephone Company Indiana
PO Box 190, Plymouth IN 46563-0190. 219/936-3879.

Walker Information Inc.
309 Insurance Avenue, Fort Wayne IN 46825-4252. 219/484-9025.

Westel-Indianapolis
8888 Keystone Crossing, Indianapolis IN 46240-4609. 317/575-8900.

TELEVISION BROADCASTING STATIONS

WANE-TV
PO Box 1515, Fort Wayne IN 46801-1515. 219/424-1515.

WEVV-TV Channel 44
44 Main St, Evansville IN 47708-1450. 812/464-4444.

WFFT-TV Channel 55
PO Box 8655, Fort Wayne IN 46898-8655. 219/471-5555.

WFIE-TV
PO Box 1414, Evansville IN 47701-1414. 812/426-1414.

WFYI-TV Channel 20
1401 North Meridian St, Indianapolis IN 46202-2304. 317/636-2020.

WHME-TV Channel 46
61300 Ironwood Road, South Bend IN 46614-9019. 219/291-8200.

WKJG-TV
2633 W State Blvd, Fort Wayne IN 46808-3937. 219/422-7474.

WNDU-TV Channel 16
PO Box 1616, South Bend IN 46634-1616. 219/631-1616.

WNDY
4555 W 16th St, Indianapolis IN 46222-2513. 317/241-2388.

WPTA-TV Inc.
3401 Butler Rd, Fort Wayne IN 46808-3811. 219/483-0584.

WRTV-TV
PO Box 607, Indianapolis IN 46206-0607. 317/635-9788.

WSBT-TV
300 W Jefferson Blvd, South Bend IN 46601-1513. 219/233-3141.

WTBU-TV
4600 Sunset Ave, Indianapolis IN 46208-3443. 317/940-8000.

WTHR-TV Channel 13
PO Box 1313, Indianapolis IN 46206-1313. 317/636-1313.

WTPA-TV
3401 Butler Rd, Fort Wayne IN 46808-3811. 219/483-0584.

WTTV-TV
3490 Bluff Rd, Indianapolis IN 46217-3204. 317/782-4444.

WTVW-TV Channel 7
PO Box 7, Evansville IN 47701-0007. 812/422-1121.

WTWO-TV
PO Box 299, Terre Haute IN 47808-0299. 812/232-9504.

WXIN-TV Channel 59
PO Box 7700, Indianapolis IN 46277-4000. 317/632-5900.

For more information on career opportunities in the communications industries:

Associations

ACADEMY OF TELEVISION ARTS & SCIENCES
5220 Lankershim Boulevard, North Hollywood CA 91601. 818/754-2800. World Wide Web address: http://www.emmys.org.

AMERICAN DISC JOCKEY ASSOCIATION
World Wide Web address: http://www.adja.org. A membership organization for professional disc jockeys that publishes a newsletter of current events and new products.

AMERICAN WOMEN IN RADIO AND TELEVISION, INC.
1650 Tysons Boulevard, Suite 200, McLean VA 22102. 703/506-3290. World Wide Web address: http://www.awrt.org. A national, nonprofit professional organization for the advancement of women who work in electronic media and related fields. Services include *News and Views*, a fax newsletter transmitted biweekly to members; *Careerline*, a national listing of job openings available to members only; and the AWRT Foundation, which supports charitable and educational programs and annual awards.

THE COMPETITIVE TELECOMMUNICATIONS ASSOCIATION (COMPTEL)
World Wide Web address: http://www.comptel.org. A national association providing a wide variety of resources including telecommunications trade shows.

INTERACTIVE SERVICES ASSOCIATION
8403 Colesville Road, Suite 865, Silver Spring MD 20910. 301/495-4955. World Wide Web address: http://www.isa.net.

INTERNATIONAL TELEVISION ASSOCIATION
6311 North O'Connor Road, Suite 230, Irving TX 75309. 972/869-1112. World Wide Web address: http://www.itva.org. Membership required.

NATIONAL ASSOCIATION OF BROADCASTERS
1771 N Street NW, Washington DC 20036. 202/429-5300, ext. 5490. Fax: 202/429-5343. World Wide Web address: http://www.nab.org. Provides employment information.

NATIONAL CABLE TELEVISION ASSOCIATION
1724 Massachusetts Avenue NW, Washington DC 20036-1969. 202/775-3651. Fax: 202/775-3695. World Wide Web address: http://www.ncta.com. A trade association. Publications include *Cable Television Developments*, *Secure Signals*, *Kids and Cable*, *Linking Up*, *Only on Cable*, and *Producers' Sourcebook: A Guide to Program Buyers*.

PROMAX INTERNATIONAL
2029 Century Park East, Suite 555, Los Angeles CA 90067. 310/788-7600. Fax: 310/788-7616. A nonprofit organization for radio, film, television, video, and other broadcasting professionals. Ask for the jobline.

U.S. TELEPHONE ASSOCIATION
1401 H Street NW, Suite 600, Washington DC 20005-2136. 202/326-7300. World Wide Web address: http://www.usta.org. A trade association for local telephone companies.

Magazines

BROADCASTING AND CABLE
Broadcasting Publications Inc., 1705 DeSales Street NW, Washington DC 20036. 202/659-2340.

ELECTRONIC MEDIA
Crain Communications, 220 East 42nd Street, New York NY 10017. 212/210-0100.

Online Services

BROADCAST PROFESSIONALS FORUM
Go: BPForum. A CompuServe discussion group for professionals in radio and television.

CPB JOBLINE
http://www.cpb.org/jobline/index.html. The Corporation for Public Broadcasting, a nonprofit company, operates this site which provides a list of job openings in the public radio and television industries.

JOURNALISM FORUM
Go: Jforum. A CompuServe discussion group for journalists in print, radio, or television.

ON-LINE DISC JOCKEY ASSOCIATION
http://www.odja.com. Provides members with insurance, Internet advertising, a magazine, and networking resources. This site also posts job opportunities.

COMPUTER HARDWARE, SOFTWARE, AND SERVICES

As the computer industry's expansion continues to gain strength in a diverse and competitive marketplace, a plethora of new products and services will open up even more opportunities for employment into the next century.

The demand for software, particularly for education, entertainment, and communications, increased by about 12 percent in 1997, and International Data Corporation projected that global sales of packaged software would grow 12.8 percent in 1998. This fastest-growing segment of the industry continues to be dominated by Microsoft, whose office software products are chosen by over 85 percent of users worldwide. Furthermore, Internet-related software sales are expected to double each year through 2000, according to the U.S. Department of Labor.

Telephone and cable companies are investing in new technologies, including ASDL (asynchronous digital subscriber line), that promise to link users to the Internet at up to 200 times faster than traditional modems. According to Dataquest Inc., 80 percent of the nation's households will have these fast-access technologies available by the year 2001.

Services that aid business customers in areas such as technology strategy, employee training, and Internet access have grown considerably, including IBM Global Services, a division whose revenues account for 25 percent of IBM's overall sales, according to The New York Times. *Meanwhile, mainframe programmers and consultants are being actively hired to correct the "Year 2000 problem" due to anticipated system errors resulting from the year 2000. Personnel are needed who can read old programming codes, and according to Gartner Research, those with the required skills have a good chance at finding highly-paid jobs in this particular area. In effect, many qualified workers from other segments of the computer industry are leaving their current jobs to work as Year 2000 consultants.*

The U.S. Department of Commerce forecasted that the healthy demand for computer systems and networking equipment would boost product shipments by about 10 percent in 1998, especially as businesses upgrade to more powerful PCs. The continued drop in PC prices should also increase sales significantly.

ANALYSTS INTERNATIONAL CORPORATION (AiC)
5750 Castle Creek Parkway North, Suite 259, Indianapolis IN 46250. 317/842-1100. **Contact:** Human Resources. **World Wide Web address:** http://www.analysts.com/indi. **Description:** An international computer consulting firm. AiC assists clients in developing systems in a variety of industries using different programming languages and software. **Corporate headquarters location:** Minneapolis MN. **Number of employees nationwide:** 3,700.

CARLETON INC.
3975 William Richardson Drive, South Bend IN 46628. 219/236-4600. **Fax:** 219/236-4640. **Contact:** Human Resources. **World Wide Web address:** http://www.carletoninc.com.

Description: Develops software for the consumer credit and credit insurance industries. Carleton also sells pre-programmed, hand-held computers.

FISERV, INC.
1818 Commerce Drive, South Bend IN 46628. 219/282-3300. **Contact:** Lora Bentley, Human Resources Manager. **World Wide Web address:** http://www.fiserve.com. **Description:** Develops software for the mortgage industry.

GRAHAM MICROAGE COMPUTER CENTER
5604 Fortune Circle South, Suite G-N, Indianapolis IN 46241. 317/634-8202. **Contact:** Mark Graham, General Manager. **Description:** Sells and services computers for business and educational customers.

HEWLETT-PACKARD COMPANY
217 South Way Boulevard East, Suite 102, Kokomo IN 46902. 765/455-3281. **Contact:** Human Resources. **World Wide Web address:** http://www.hp.com. **Description:** This location is a sales and service office. Overall, Hewlett-Packard is engaged in the design and manufacturing of measurement and computation products and systems used in business, industry, engineering, science, health care, and education. Principal products are integrated instrument and computer systems (including hardware and software), peripheral products, and medical electronic equipment and systems. **NOTE:** Jobseekers should send resumes to Employment Response Center, Event #2498, Hewlett-Packard Company, Mail Stop 20-APP, 3000 Hanover Street, Palo Alto CA 94304-1181. **Corporate headquarters location:** Palo Alto CA. **Other U.S. locations:** Nationwide. **Listed on:** New York Stock Exchange. **Number of employees nationwide:** 93,000.

HURCO COMPANIES, INC.
One Technology Way, Indianapolis IN 46268. 317/293-5309. **Contact:** Judy Summers, Human Resources Manager. **E-mail address:** info@hurco.com. **Description:** Designs, manufactures, and sells computer numerical control (CNC) systems and software, as well as CNC machine tools for the international machine tool industry. Hurco is among the largest U.S. manufacturers of CNC systems for stand-alone machine tools. These CNC systems and software are either integrated with machine tools sold by Hurco or sold to machine tool end users. The company's CNC systems include Autocon Technologies, Inc. (Delta Series) CNC Controls, Ultimax controls and software, and Autobend CNC and press brake gauging systems. Among the company's integrated machine tool products are CNC machining centers and CNC milling machines. Hurco's products are sold through the company's international network of distributors. Industries served include aerospace, computer, defense, medical equipment, farm implement, construction equipment, energy, and transportation.

MICRO DATA BASE SYSTEMS INC.
P.O. Box 2438, West Lafayette IN 47996. 765/463-7200. **Contact:** Human Resources Department. **World Wide Web address:** http://www.mdbs.com. **Description:** Produces database management systems for small computers and artificial intelligence systems. Consulting and applications groups implement customized applications for clients worldwide using the firm's software tools. **Educational backgrounds include:** Accounting; Business Administration; Computer Science; Marketing. **Benefits:** Dental Insurance; Life Insurance; Medical Insurance; Profit Sharing. **Corporate headquarters location:** This Location. **Other U.S. locations:** Shaumburg IL. **Operations at this facility include:** Administration; Computer Programming; Research and Development; Sales; Service.

ONE SOURCE MICRO PRODUCTS, INC.
3305 Lathrop Street, South Bend IN 46628. 219/288-7455. **Contact:** Human Resources. **Description:** A computer hardware wholesaler.

ONTARIO SYSTEMS CORPORATION
1150 West Kilgore, Muncie IN 47305. 765/751-7000. **Contact:** Human Resources. **World Wide Web address:** http://www.ontariosystems.com. **Description:** Develops software for collection agencies and health care providers.

PINNACLE TECHNOLOGY, INC.
P.O. Box 128, Kirklin IN 46050. 765/279-5157. **Fax:** 765/279-8039. **Contact:** Human Resources. **World Wide Web address:** http://www.pinnacletech.com. **Description:** Produces desktop management and security software.

SOFTWARE ARTISTRY
9025 North River Road, Indianapolis IN 46240. 317/843-1663. **Contact:** Human Resources Director. **Description:** Develops, markets, and supports a family of internal and external customer support software. The company's primary product, Expert Advisor, is a complete problem management system that incorporates multiple diagnostic techniques to access a single solutions database to resolve customer problems. **Corporate headquarters location:** This Location. **Listed on:** NASDAQ.

SOFTWARE SYNERGY INC. (SSI)
10000 Allisonville Road, Fishers IN 46038. 317/849-4444. **Contact:** Recruiting Coordinator. **World Wide Web address:** http://www.softsynergy.com. **Description:** A computer consulting firm.

TRUEVISION INC.
7340 Shadeland Station, Indianapolis IN 46256-3919. 317/841-0332. **Contact:** Human Resources. **E-mail address:** jobs@truevision.com. **World Wide Web address:** http://www.truevision.com. **Description:** This location is a technical support and engineering design facility. Overall, Truevision Inc. is a developer of PC digital video cards for desktop video production. **Corporate headquarters location:** Santa Clara CA. **Listed on:** NASDAQ. **Stock exchange symbol:** TRUV.

***Note:** Because addresses and telephone numbers of smaller companies can change rapidly, we recommend you call each company to verify the information below before inquiring about job opportunities. Mass mailings are not recommended.*

Additional small employers:

COMPUTER EQUIPMENT AND SOFTWARE WHOLESALE

AMS
2525 N Shadeland Avenue, Indianapolis IN 46219-1787. 317/357-8643.

Bradford Scott Data Corporation
3901 W 86th Street, Suite 130, Indianapolis IN 46268-1793. 317/876-2065.

DPS
9100 Keystone Crossing, #300, Indianapolis IN 46240. 317/574-4300.

Pulse Computer Systems Inc.
420 NW 5th St, Evansville IN 47708-1322. 812/428-6707.

COMPUTER MAINTENANCE AND REPAIR

Advanced Micro Electronics
Rural Route 1, Box 63l, Vincennes IN 47591-9712. 812/726-4500.

DecisionOne
6620 Parkdale Place, Suite K, Indianapolis IN 46254-4697. 317/299-0213.

Microdyne Corporation
5355 West 76th Street, Indianapolis IN 46268-4166. 317/870-0284.

COMPUTER PROCESSING AND DATA PREPARATION SERVICES

ADP of Indianapolis
3665 Priority Way South Drive, Indianapolis IN 46240-1489. 317/848-7700.

Alverno Administrative Services
1300 Albany Street, Beech Grove IN 46107-1536. 317/783-9341.

American Document Management Group
2707 Rand Road, Indianapolis IN 46241-5504. 317/247-4400.

CDT
2525 N Shadeland Avenue, Indianapolis IN 46219-1787. 317/351-5656.

CSI Valparaiso
PO Box 2300, Valparaiso IN 46384-2300. 219/464-4864.

Custom Data Services Inc.
PO Box 10645, Merrillville IN 46411-0645. 219/769-1670.

Dana Corporation
PO Box 1345, Richmond IN 47375-1345. 765/973-6101.

DCIS
3700 Washington Avenue, Evansville IN 47714-0542. 812/485-6520.

EDS
2900 S Scatterfield Road, Anderson IN 46013-1817. 765/646-2846.

EDS
2925 W Minnesota Street, Indianapolis IN 46241-4550. 317/230-2680.

EDS
1350 Arcadia Drive, Columbus IN 47201-8445. 812/376-3798.

EDS
PO Box 248, Chesterton IN 46304-0248. 219/787-3937.

EDS
2915 Pendleton Avenue, Anderson IN 46016-4848. 765/641-5531.

EDS
2601 Fortune Circle East, Indianapolis IN 46241-5548. 317/240-5575.

EDS
4700 W 10th Street, L1, Indianapolis IN 46222-3277. 317/242-3711.

Image Max
701 Congressional Boulevard, Carmel IN 46032. 317/581-7600.

Integrated Technologies
799 W Michigan Street, Indianapolis IN 46202-5195. 317/274-0707.

Interlogic Holding Inc.
PO Box 2737, Elkhart IN 46515-2737. 219/264-2200.

Old National Service Corporation
PO Box 11010, Evansville IN 47701. 812/464-1200.

Professional Data Dimensions
200 S Meridian St, Ste 200, Indianapolis IN 46225-1076. 317/636-7355.

Rexnord Corporation
PO Box 1006, Indianapolis IN 46206-1006. 317/299-1600.

SCT Corp.
200 E Washington St, Indianapolis IN 46204-3307. 317/327-8619.

Utility Data Corporation
PO Box 1220, Indianapolis IN 46206-1220. 317/263-6331.

COMPUTER SOFTWARE, PROGRAMMING, AND SYSTEMS DESIGN

Baker Hill Corporation
655 West Carmel Drive, Carmel IN 46032-2500. 317/571-2000.

Ceridian EAS
4345 Security Parkway, New Albany IN 47150-9374. 812/941-9360.

Computer Horizons Corporation
1980 E 116th Street, Suite 317, Carmel IN 46032-3517. 317/574-5600.

Disc Support Services
5587 West 73rd Street, Indianapolis IN 46268-2162. 317/328-7400.

IBM Corporation
9465 Counselors Row, Indianapolis IN 46240-3816. 317/844-7750.

Interactive Intelligence Inc.
3500 Depauw Boulevard, Indianapolis IN 46268-1170. 317/872-3000.

Made2Manage Systems Incorporated
9002 Purdue Road, Indianapolis IN 46268-3136. 317/532-7000.

Powerway Inc.
6919 Hillsdale Court, Indianapolis IN 46250-2054. 317/598-1760.

Sagian Inc.
PO Box 78668, Indianapolis IN 46278-0668. 317/328-3588.

Sigma/Micro Corporation
714 North Senate Ave, Indianapolis IN 46202-3112. 317/631-0907.

Tracor Systems Engineering
5001 North State Rd 47, Bloomington IN 47408. 812/333-6291.

Whittman-Hart Inc.
310 E 96th St, Ste 100, Indianapolis IN 46240-3732. 317/575-9696.

MISC. COMPUTER RELATED SERVICES

Avantec Inc.
655 W Carmel Drive, Suite 120, Carmel IN 46032-2500. 317/574-8610.

CSI Indianapolis
3830 S Emerson Avenue, Indianapolis IN 46203-5923. 317/788-4576.

CTG
5875 Castle Creek Parkway, Indianapolis IN 46250-4331. 317/578-5100.

Indecon Inc.
115 W Washington Street, Indianapolis IN 46204-3419. 317/634-9482.

Intracomp Group Incorporated
52303 Emmons Road, South Bend IN 46637-4294. 219/272-9800.

Keller Schroeder & Associates
4920 Carriage Drive, Evansville IN 47715-2578. 812/474-6825.

MID
8720 Castle Creek Parkway, Indianapolis IN 46250-4300. 317/578-8960.

Profound Consulting Incorporated
8335 Allison Pointe Trail, Indianapolis IN 46250-1685. 317/579-5200.

Summit Group Inc.
PO Box 5106, Mishawaka IN 46546-5106. 219/272-8500.

Total Response Inc.
5804 Churchman Bypass, Indianapolis IN 46203-6109. 317/791-1414.

For more information on career opportunities in the computer industry:

__Associations__

AMERICAN INTERNET ASSOCIATION
World Wide Web address: http://www.amernet.org. A nonprofit association providing assistance in the use of the Internet. Membership required.

ASSOCIATION FOR COMPUTING MACHINERY
1515 Broadway, 17th Floor, New York NY 10036. 212/869-7440. World Wide Web address: http://www.acm.org. Membership required.

ASSOCIATION FOR MULTIMEDIA COMMUNICATIONS
P.O. Box 10645, Chicago IL 60610. 312/409-1032. E-mail address: amc@amcomm.org. World Wide Web address: http://www.amcomm.org. A multimedia and Internet association.

ASSOCIATION FOR WOMEN IN COMPUTING
41 Sutter Street, Suite 1006, San Francisco CA 94104. 415/905-4663. E-mail address: awc@acm.org. World Wide Web address: http://www.awc-hq.org. A nonprofit organization promoting women in computing professions.

ASSOCIATION OF INTERNET PROFESSIONALS
1301 Fifth Avenue, Suite 3300, Seattle WA 98101. E-mail address: info@associp.org. World Wide Web address: http://www.associp.org. A nonprofit trade association providing a forum for Internet users and professionals.

BLACK DATA PROCESSING ASSOCIATES
1111 14th Street NW, Suite 700, Washington DC 20005-5603. Toll-free phone: 800/727-BDPA. E-mail address: nbdpa@bdpa.org. World Wide Web address: http://www.bdpa.org. An organization of information technology professionals serving the minority community.

THE CENTER FOR SOFTWARE DEVELOPMENT
111 West St. John, Suite 200, San Jose CA 95113. 408/494-8378. E-mail address: info@center.org. World Wide Web address: http://www.center.org. A nonprofit organization providing technical and business resources for software developers.

COMMERCIAL INTERNET EXCHANGE ASSOCIATION (CIX)
1041 Sterling Road, Suite 104A, Herndon VA 20170. 703/824-9249. E-mail address: helpdesk@cix.org. World Wide Web address: http://www.cix.org. A nonprofit trade association of data internetworking service providers.

HTML WRITERS GUILD
World Wide Web address: http://www.hwg.org. An international organization of Web page writers and Internet professionals.

THE IPG SOCIETY
World Wide Web address: http://www.ipgnet.com. A professional trade association representing programmers internationally.

INFORMATION TECHNOLOGY ASSOCIATION OF AMERICA
1616 North Fort Myer Drive, Suite 1300, Arlington VA 22209. 703/522-5055. World Wide Web address: http://www.itaa.org.

INTERNET DEVELOPERS ASSOCIATION
World Wide Web address: http://www.association.org. A trade association concerned with content development for the Internet.

MULTIMEDIA DEVELOPMENT GROUP
520 Third Street, Suite 225, San Francisco CA 94107. 415/512-3556. Fax: 415/512-3569. E-mail address: info@mdg.org. A nonprofit trade association dedicated to the business and market development of multimedia companies.

THE OPEN GROUP
11 Cambridge Center, Cambridge MA 02142-1405. 617/621-8700. World Wide Web address: http://www.opengroup.org. A consortium concerned with open systems technology in the information systems industry. Membership required.

SOCIETY FOR INFORMATION MANAGEMENT
401 North Michigan Avenue, Chicago IL 60611-4267. 312/644-6610. E-mail address: info@simnet.org. World Wide Web address: http://www.simnet.org. A forum for information technology professionals.

SOFTWARE FORUM
P.O. Box 61031, Palo Alto CA 94306. 415/854-7219. E-mail address: 73771.1176@ compuserve.com. World Wide Web address: http://www.softwareforum.org. An independent, nonprofit organization for software industry professionals.

SOFTWARE PUBLISHERS ASSOCIATION
1730 M Street NW, Suite 700, Washington DC 20036. 202/452-1600. World Wide Web address: http://www.spa.org.

SOFTWARE SUPPORT PROFESSIONALS ASSOCIATION
11858 Bernardo Plaza Court, Suite 101C, San Diego CA 92128. 619/674-4864. World Wide Web address: http://www.sspa-online.com. A forum for service and support professionals in the software industry.

USENIX ASSOCIATION
2560 Ninth Street, Berkeley CA 94710. 510/528-8649. World Wide Web address: http://www.usenix.org. An advanced computing systems professional association for engineers, systems administrators, scientists, and technicians.

WORLD WIDE WEB TRADE ASSOCIATION
World Wide Web address: http://www.web-star.com/wwwta.html. An association promoting responsible use of the World Wide Web.

Magazines

COMPUTER-AIDED ENGINEERING
Penton Publishing, 1100 Superior Avenue, Cleveland OH 44114. 216/696-7000. World Wide Web address: http://www.penton.com/cae.

COMPUTERWORLD, INC.
International Data Group, 500 Old Connecticut Path, Framingham MA 01701. 508/879-0700.

DATA COMMUNICATIONS
McGraw-Hill, 1221 Avenue of the Americas, New York NY 10020. 212/512-2000.

DATAMATION
Cahners Publishing, 275 Washington Street, Newton MA 02158. 617/964-3030. World Wide Web address: http://www.datamation.com.

IDC REPORT
International Data Corporation, 5 Speen Street, Framingham MA 01701. 508/872-8200.

Online Services

COMPUTER CONSULTANTS
Go: Consult. A CompuServe discussion group for computer professionals interested in networking and business development.

COMPUTERWORLD
http://www.computerworld.com. A weekly online newspaper for information sciences professionals. Features the latest news and employment opportunities. *Computerworld* conducts a job search by skills, job level (entry-level or experienced), job title, company, and your choice of three cities and three states. One feature of this site is "CareerMail," a service which e-mails you when a job matches the skills you have submitted online. This site also has corporate profiles, an events calendar, *Computerworld*'s publications, an index of graduate schools, and other informative and educational resources.

IT JOBS
http://www.internet-solutions.com/itjobs/us/usselect.htm. This Website provides links to companies that have job openings in the information technology industry.

JOBSERVE
http://www.jobserve.com. Provides information on job openings in the field of information technology for companies throughout Europe. The site also offers links to numerous company Web pages, resume posting services, and a directory of recruiters.

SELECTJOBS
http://www.selectjobs.com. Post a resume and search the job database by region, discipline, special requirements, and skills on *SelectJOBS.* Once your search criteria has been entered, this site will automatically e-mail you when a job opportunity matches your requests.

THE SOFTWARE JOBS HOMEPAGE
http://www.softwarejobs.com/. This Website offers a searchable database of openings for jobseekers looking in the software industry. The site is run by Allen Davis & Associates.

EDUCATIONAL SERVICES

Job prospects remain favorable in educational services, due to a healthy demand for qualified teachers at all levels. The U.S. Department of Labor projects that over the next 10 years, an additional 2.2 million teaching jobs in elementary and secondary education will be created, and demand will also be strong for college and university faculty, education administrators, school counselors, and kindergarten teachers. Special education teachers are still in strong demand, with a 56 percent projected increase in openings through 2005.

As enrollment swells in elementary and secondary schools, and at higher learning institutions, the growth of operating costs will rise significantly as well, and the U.S. Department of Commerce projects a 1 percent annual cost increase through the year 2000. Among the cost pressures schools face is the implementation of computer technology in the classroom and curriculum changes.

According to Business Week, *colleges and universities, under fiscal constraints, are struggling to meet the challenge of sustaining a high level of teaching and curricula without increasing tuitions to the point that they are unaffordable for the majority of students.*

ITT EDUCATIONAL SERVICES, INC.
5975 Castle Creek Parkway North Drive, Indianapolis IN 46250-0466. 317/594-9499. **Contact:** Personnel. **Description:** Provides post-high school programs, including associate's, bachelor's, and non-degree diploma programs to more than 20,000 students through a system of 54 ITT Technical Institutes located in 25 states. About 70 percent of ITT Technical Institute students are enrolled in electronics engineering technology and related programs, and about 25 percent are enrolled in computer-aided drafting technology (CAD) and related programs.

INDIANA STATE UNIVERSITY/TERRE HAUTE
210 North Seventh Street, Rankin Hall, Terre Haute IN 47809. **Contact:** Human Resources. **Description:** A four-year state university offering associate's, bachelor's, master's (including MBA), and doctoral degrees. Approximately 10,200 undergraduate and 1,500 graduate students attend Indiana State University. **NOTE:** Jobseekers must obtain an application from the university before sending a resume. Resumes without applications will be returned.

INDIANA UNIVERSITY BLOOMINGTON
Bloomington IN 47405. 812/855-4848. **Contact:** Human Resources. **World Wide Web address:** http://www.indiana.edu. **Description:** A branch of the state university. Indiana University Bloomington offers bachelor's, master's (including MBA), first professional, and doctoral degrees. The School of Business and the School of Public and Environmental Affairs are also at this location.

INDIANA UNIVERSITY KOKOMO
2300 South Washington Street, P.O. Box 9003, Kokomo IN 46904-9003. 765/455-9368. **Contact:** Human Resources. **Description:** A branch of the state university.

INDIANA UNIVERSITY NORTHWEST
3400 Broadway, Gary IN 46408. 219/980-6500. **Contact:** Personnel Department. **Description:** A branch of the state university.

INDIANA UNIVERSITY SOUTH BEND
1700 Mishawaka Avenue, South Bend IN 46634. 219/237-4111. **Contact:** John Hundley, Director of Human Resources. **World Wide Web address:** http://www.usb.edu. **Description:** A branch of the state university, offering associate's, bachelor's, and master's degrees (including MBAs). Approximately 5,700 undergraduate and 1,500 graduate students attend Indiana University South Bend.

INDIANA UNIVERSITY SOUTHEAST
4201 Grant Line Road, New Albany IN 47150. 812/941-2000. **Contact:** Ann Lee, Director of Human Resources. **World Wide Web address:** http://www.ius.indiana.edu. **Description:** A branch of the state university.

INDIANA UNIVERSITY/PURDUE UNIVERSITY AT FORT WAYNE
2101 Coliseum Boulevard East, Fort Wayne IN 46805-1499. 219/481-6840. **Contact:** Personnel Department. **World Wide Web address:** http://www.ipsw.indiana.edu. **Description:** Fort Wayne campus of two state universities.

INDIANA UNIVERSITY/PURDUE UNIVERSITY AT INDIANAPOLIS
620 Union Drive, Student Union Building, Room 342, Indianapolis IN 46202. 317/274-7617. **Contact:** Marcia Combs, Employment Coordinator. **Description:** A four-year, state university with professional schools, teaching hospitals, and schools of medicine and dentistry. **Common positions include:** Accountant/Auditor; Architect; Biological Scientist; Biomedical Engineer; Broadcast Technician; Buyer; Chemist; Claim Representative; Clerical Supervisor; Computer Programmer; Counselor; Customer Service Representative; Dental Assistant/Dental Hygienist; Draftsperson; Editor; Education Administrator; EEG Technologist; Electrician; Financial Analyst; Human Resources Manager; Landscape Architect; Librarian; Library Technician; Property and Real Estate Manager; Psychologist; Public Relations Specialist; Purchasing Agent/Manager; Social Worker; Speech-Language Pathologist; Statistician; Systems Analyst; Technical Writer/Editor; Veterinarian. **Educational backgrounds include:** Accounting; Biology; Business Administration; Chemistry; Computer Science; Health Care. **Benefits:** 403(b); Dental Insurance; Disability Coverage; Life Insurance; Medical Insurance; Pension Plan; Tuition Assistance. **Number of employees at this location:** 10,000.

PURDUE UNIVERSITY
1126 Freehafer Hall, West Lafayette IN 47907. 765/494-9687. **Fax:** 765/494-6138. **Contact:** Personnel. **World Wide Web address:** http://www.adpc.purdue.edu/Personnel/job-home.htm. **Description:** Purdue has an enrollment of 64,000 students across five campuses with numerous teaching and research sites statewide. Degrees are offered in the following areas of study: agriculture, consumer and family sciences, education, engineering, health sciences, liberal arts, management, nursing, pharmacy and pharmaceutical sciences, science, technology, and veterinary medicine. **Common positions include:** Accountant/Auditor; Administrative Manager; Agricultural Engineer; Agricultural Scientist; Architect; Biological Scientist; Blue-Collar Worker Supervisor; Budget Analyst; Buyer; Chemical Engineer; Chemist; Civil Engineer; Clerical Supervisor; Clinical Lab Technician; Computer Programmer; Construction and Building Inspector; Construction Contractor; Cost Estimator; Counselor; Draftsperson; Editor; Electrical/Electronics Engineer; Electrician; Financial Analyst; Hotel Manager; Human Resources Manager; Industrial Engineer; Librarian; Library Technician; Management Trainee; Mechanical Engineer; Nuclear Engineer; Public Relations Specialist; Purchasing Agent/Manager; Radiological Technologist; Restaurant/Food Service Manager; Science Technologist; Structural Engineer; Systems Analyst; Technical Writer/Editor; Veterinarian. **Educational backgrounds include:** Accounting; Biology; Business Administration; Chemistry; Communications; Computer Science; Engineering; Finance; Liberal Arts. **Benefits:** Life Insurance; Medical Insurance; Pension Plan; Tuition Assistance. **Special programs:** Internships. **Operations at this facility include:** Administration; Research and Development; Service. **Number of employees at this location:** 10,000.

PURDUE UNIVERSITY/CALUMET
2200 169th Street, Hammond IN 46323. 219/989-2993. **Contact:** Personnel Department. **World Wide Web address:** http://www.purdue.calumet.edu. **Description:** One location of Purdue University.

UNIVERSITY OF EVANSVILLE
1800 Lincoln Avenue, Evansville IN 47722. 812/479-2943. **Toll-free phone:** 800/423-8653. **Fax:** 812/479-2320. **Contact:** Gregory R. Bordfeld, Director of Personnel. **E-mail address:** gb5@evansville.edu. **World Wide Web address:** http://www.evansville.edu. **Description:** A nonprofit, four-year university offering bachelor's and master's degrees. Approximately 3,500 undergraduate and 500 graduate students attend the University of Evansville. Founded in 1854. **NOTE:** The university offers entry-level positions as well as second and third shifts. **Common positions include:** Accountant/Auditor; Administrative Manager; Biochemist; Biological Scientist; Budget Analyst; Chemical Engineer; Chemist; Chief Financial Officer; Civil Engineer; Computer Programmer; Controller; Counselor; Database Manager; Economist; Editor; Editorial Assistant; Education Administrator; Electrician; ESL Teacher; Finance Director; Fund Manager; Geographer; Graphic Artist; Graphic Designer; Human Resources Manager; Internet Services Manager; Librarian; Paralegal; Physician; Psychologist; Public Relations Manager; Purchasing Agent/Manager; Radio/TV Announcer/Broadcaster; Registered Nurse; Secretary; Systems Analyst; Teacher/Professor; Technical Writer/Editor; Vice President. **Educational backgrounds include:** Accounting; Biology; Business Administration; Chemistry; Communications; Computer Science; Economics; Engineering; Finance; Liberal Arts; Marketing; Mathematics. **Benefits:** 403(b); Dental Insurance; Disability Coverage; Flexible Benefits; Life Insurance; Medical Insurance; Pension Plan; Tuition Assistance. **Corporate headquarters location:** This Location. **Operations at this facility include:** Administration. **Listed on:** Privately held. **Annual sales/revenues:** $51 - $100 million. **Number of employees at this location:** 515.

UNIVERSITY OF INDIANAPOLIS
1400 East Hanna Avenue, Indianapolis IN 46227. 317/788-3368. **Contact:** Human Resources. **World Wide Web address:** http://www.uindy.edu. **Description:** A four-year university offering associate's, bachelor's, and master's (including MBA) degrees. Enrollment includes 2,800 undergraduates and 460 graduate students.

UNIVERSITY OF NOTRE DAME
Notre Dame IN 46556. **Contact:** Human Resources. **Description:** A four-year, Catholic, co-educational university offering bachelor's, master's (including MBA), and doctoral degrees. Approximately 7,600 undergraduate and 2,400 graduate students attend the University of Notre Dame. **NOTE:** The university does not accept unsolicited resumes. Please only respond to advertised openings.

***Note:** Because addresses and telephone numbers of smaller companies can change rapidly, we recommend you call each company to verify the information below before inquiring about job opportunities. Mass mailings are not recommended.*

Additional small employers:

CHILD DAYCARE SERVICES

Carey Services Inc.
2724 S Carey Street, Marion IN 46953-3515. 765/668-8961.

COLLEGES, UNIVERSITIES, AND PROFESSIONAL SCHOOLS

Ball State University
2000 W University Avenue, Muncie IN 47306-1022. 765/289-1241.

Bethel College
1001 West McKinley Avenue, Mishawaka IN 46545-5509. 219/259-8511.

Christian Theological Seminary
PO Box 88267, Indianapolis IN 46208-0267. 317/924-1331.

Depauw University
PO Box 37, Greencastle IN 46135-0037. 765/658-4800.

Earlham College
National Road West, Richmond IN 47374. 765/983-1200.

Goshen College
1700 South Main Street, Goshen IN 46526-4724. 219/535-7000.

Hanover College
PO Box 108, Hanover IN 47243-0108. 812/866-7000.

Huntington College
2303 College Avenue, Huntington IN 46750-1237. 219/356-6000.

Indiana Business College
802 North Meridian Street, Indianapolis IN 46204-1108. 317/264-5656.

Indiana Institute of Technology
1600 E Washington Boulevard, Fort Wayne IN 46803-1228. 219/422-5561.

Indiana University East
2325 Chester Boulevard, Richmond IN 47374. 765/973-8201.

Indiana University-Southern
8600 University Boulevard, Evansville IN 47712-3534. 812/464-8600.

Indiana Wesleyan University
4201 S Washington Street, Marion IN 46953-4974. 765/674-6901.

Krannert Graduate School
1310 Krannet Building, Lafayette IN 47907. 765/494-9700.

Manchester College
PO Box 365, North Manchester IN 46962-0365. 219/982-5000.

Marian College
3200 Cold Springs Road, Indianapolis IN 46222-1960. 317/955-6000.

Purdue University-North Central
1401 S US Highway 421, Westville IN 46391-9542. 219/785-5200.

Rose-Hulman Institute of Technology
PO Box 22, Terre Haute IN 47808-0022. 812/877-1511.

Saint Joseph's College
PO Box 889, Rensselaer IN 47978-0889. 219/866-6000.

Saint Mary's College
US 33 N, Notre Dame IN 46556. 219/284-4000.

Saint Mary-of-The-Woods College
1 Saint Mary of The Woods, Saint Mary-of-the-Woods IN 47876. 812/535-5151.

Tri-State University
1 University Ave, Angola IN 46703-1764. 219/665-4100.

Valparaiso University
Valparaiso IN 46383. 219/464-5000.

ELEMENTARY AND SECONDARY SCHOOLS

Adams Central Community Schools
222 W Washington Street, Monroe IN 46772-9436. 219/692-6629.

Amy Beverland Elementary School
11650 Fox Road, Indianapolis IN 46236-8374. 317/823-5228.

Andrean High School
5959 Broadway, Merrillville IN 46410-2617. 219/887-5281.

Argos Community Schools
410 N 1st Street, Argos IN 46501-1014. 219/892-5139.

Arlington High School
4825 N Arlington Avenue, Indianapolis IN 46226-2401. 317/226-4006.

Attica Consolidated School District
205 S College Street, Attica IN 47918-1401. 765/762-3236.

Avon High School
7199 E US Highway 36, Plainfield IN 46168-7968. 317/272-2586.

Bedford Lawrence High School
Box 439, Bedford IN 47421-9111. 812/279-9756.

Belmont High School
1000 E North Adams Drive, Decatur IN 46733-2739. 219/724-7121.

Belzer Middle School
7555 East 56th Street, Indianapolis IN 46226-1358. 317/545-7411.

Ben Davis High School
1200 N Girls School Road, Indianapolis IN 46214-3403. 317/244-7691.

Ben F. Geyer Junior High School
420 E Paulding Road, Fort Wayne IN 46816-1102. 219/425-7343.

Benjamin Harrison Elementary School
3302 W Western Avenue, South Bend IN 46619-3061. 219/289-2896.

Benton Central Junior/Senior High School
4241 E 300 S, Oxford IN 47971-8633. 765/884-1600.

Binford Elementary School
2300 East Second Street, Bloomington IN 47401-5312. 812/330-7741.

Bishop Noll Institute
1519 Hoffman Street, Hammond IN 46327-1764. 219/932-9058.

Blackhawk Middle School
7200 East State Boulevard, Fort Wayne IN 46815-6478. 219/425-7313.

Bloomington High School North
3901 North Kinser Pike, Bloomington IN 47404-1870. 812/330-7724.

Blue River Special Education Co-Operative
1111 W McKay Road, Shelbyville IN 46176-3205. 317/398-4468.

Bluffton Harrison Metro School District
628 South Bennett Street, Bluffton IN 46714-3309. 219/824-2620.

Broad Ripple High School
1115 Broad Ripple Avenue, Indianapolis IN 46220-2036. 317/226-4005.

Canterbury School
3210 Smith Road, Fort Wayne IN 46804-3109. 219/436-0746.

Carmel Junior High School
300 South Guilford Road, Carmel IN 46032-1531. 317/846-7331.

Carroll Consolidated School District
2 South Third Street, Flora IN 46929-1367. 219/967-4113.

Carroll High School
3701 Carroll Road, Fort Wayne IN 46818-9528. 219/637-3161.

Castle High School
PO Box 719, Newburgh IN 47629-0719. 812/853-3331.

Center Grove High School
2717 S Morgantown Road, Greenwood IN 46143-8537. 317/881-0581.

Central High School
5400 N First Avenue, Evansville IN 47710-4110. 812/435-8292.

Central High School
801 N Walnut Street, Muncie IN 47305-1458. 765/747-5260.

Chesterton High School
651 W Morgan Avenue, Chesterton IN 46304-2243. 219/926-2151.

Clay Community School
PO Box 169, Knightsville IN 47857-0169. 812/443-4461.

Clay High School
19131 Darden Road, South Bend IN 46637-3947. 219/272-3400.

Clay Junior High School
5150 E 126th Street, Carmel IN 46033-9746. 317/844-7251.

Columbus East High School
230 South Marr Road, Columbus IN 47201-7267. 812/376-4369.

Columbus North High School
1400 25th Street, Columbus IN 47201-4384. 812/376-4431.

Concord Community High School
59117 Minuteman Way, Elkhart IN 46517-3409. 219/875-6524.

Concordia Lutheran High School
1601 St. Joseph's River Drive, Fort Wayne IN 46805-1433. 219/483-1102.

Craig Middle School
6501 Sunnyside Road, Indianapolis IN 46236-9707. 317/823-6805.

Crawfordsville Community School
1000 Fairview Avenue, Crawfordsville IN 47933-1511. 765/362-2342.

Creston Middle School
10925 Prospect Street, Indianapolis IN 46239-9692. 317/894-8883.

Crown Point High School
401 West Joliet Street, Crown Point IN 46307-3808. 219/663-4885.

Culver Military Academy
1300 Academy Road, Suite 147, Culver IN 46511-1234. 219/842-8181.

DE Gavit Junior/Senior High School
1670 175th Street, Hammond IN 46324-3132. 219/989-7328.

Decatur Central High School
5251 Kentucky Avenue, Indianapolis IN 46221-3616. 317/856-5288.

Decatur Middle School
5108 S High School Road, Indianapolis IN 46221-3606. 317/856-5274.

Discovery Middle School
10050 Brummitt Road, Granger IN 46530-7264. 219/674-6010.

East Chicago Central High School
1100 W Columbus Drive, East Chicago IN 46312-2582. 219/391-4000.

East Noble High School
901 Garden Street, Kendallville IN 46755-2257. 219/347-2032.

Elmhurst High School
3829 Sandpoint Road, Fort Wayne IN 46809-9732. 219/425-7510.

Elwood Community High School
1137 North 19th Street, Elwood IN 46036-1376. 765/552-9854.

Evansville Vanderburgh School
One SE 9th Street, Evansville IN 47708-1821. 812/435-8401.

Fairfield Community School District
67530 U.S. Highway 33, Goshen IN 46526-8552. 219/831-2184.

Fall Creek Valley Middle School
9701 East 63rd Street, Indianapolis IN 46236-7801. 317/823-5490.

Fayette County School
1501 Spartan Drive, Connersville IN 47331-1054. 765/827-0891.

Floyd Junior & Senior High School
6575 Old Vincennes Road, Floyds Knobs IN 47119-9433. 812/923-8811.

Fort Wayne Community Schools
1200 South Clinton Street, Fort Wayne IN 46802. 219/425-7221.

Franklin Central High School
6215 South Franklin Road, Indianapolis IN 46259-9600. 317/862-6646.

Franklin Community High School
625 Grizzly Cub Drive, Franklin IN 46131-1362. 317/738-5700.

Franklin Township Middle School
6019 South Franklin Road, Indianapolis IN 46259-1319. 317/862-2446.

Frederick Douglass School
2020 Dawson Street, Indianapolis IN 46203-4151. 317/226-4219.

Fremont Elementary School
PO Box 625, Fremont IN 46737-0625. 219/495-4385.

Fulton Junior High School
7320 West 10th Street, Indianapolis IN 46214-2514. 317/241-9285.

Garrett Junior/Senior High School
801 East Houston Street, Garrett IN 46738-1662. 219/357-4114.

Gary Community School District
620 East 10th Place, Gary IN 46402-2731. 219/886-6400.

Goshen Middle School
1216 South Indiana Avenue, Goshen IN 46526. 219/533-0391.

GR Clark Middle High School
1921 Davis Avenue, Whiting IN 46394-1820. 219/659-3522.

Hamilton Heights Elementary School
PO Box 400, Arcadia IN 46030-0400. 317/984-3547.

Hamilton Heights Middle School
PO Box 609, Arcadia IN 46030-0609. 317/984-3588.

Hamilton Southeastern Junior High School
12001 Olio Road, Fishers IN 46038-9799. 317/594-4120.

Hammond High School
5926 Calumet Avenue, Hammond IN 46320-2505. 219/933-2442.

Hanover Community School
PO Box 645, Cedar Lake IN 46303-0645. 219/374-5546.

Harrison High School
5701 North 50 West, West Lafayette IN 47906-9736. 765/463-3511.

Harrison High School
211 Fielding Road, Evansville IN 47715-3360. 812/477-1046.

Hebron High School
307 South Main Street, Hebron IN 46341-8909. 219/996-2171.

Heritage Christian School
6401 E 75th Street, Indianapolis IN 46250-2703. 317/849-3441.

Highland High School
9135 Erie Street, Hammond IN 46322-2735. 219/922-5610.

Highland Senior High School
2108 E 200 N, Anderson IN 46012-9475. 765/641-2059.

HL Harshman School
1501 East 10th Street, Indianapolis IN 46201-1909. 317/226-4101.

Hobart High School
36 E 8th Street, Hobart IN 46342-5144. 219/942-8521.

Homestead High School
4310 Homestead Road, Fort Wayne IN 46804-5451. 219/431-2251.

Horace Mann High School
524 Garfield Street, Gary IN 46404-1403. 219/886-1445.

Indiana School For The Blind
7725 North College Avenue, Indianapolis IN 46240-2504. 317/253-1481.

Indiana School For The Deaf
1200 E 42nd Street, Indianapolis IN 46205-2004. 317/924-4374.

Jay County High School
Rural Route 2, Box 245B, Portland IN 47371-9589. 219/726-9306.

Jefferson High School
1801 S 18th Street, Lafayette IN 47905-2011. 765/449-3400.

Jeffersonville High School
2315 Allison Lane, Jeffersonville IN 47130-5818. 812/282-6601.

Jennings High School
Highway 50 West, North Vernon IN 47265. 812/346-5588.

John Marshall Junior High School
10101 E 38th Street, Indianapolis IN 46235-1903. 317/226-4002.

Knox Community Elementary School
210 W Culver Road, Knox IN 46534-2237. 219/772-6273.

Kokomo High School
2501 South Berkeley Road, Kokomo IN 46902-3006. 765/455-8040.

La Porte High School
602 F Street, La Porte IN 46350-5526. 219/362-3102.

Lake Central High School
8400 Wicker Avenue, Saint John IN 46373-9710. 219/365-8551.

Lakeville Junior/Senior High School
69969 U.S. Highway 31, Lakeville IN 46536-9735. 219/784-3151.

LaSalle High School
2701 Elwood Avenue, South Bend IN 46628-2806. 219/234-1083.

Lawrence Central High School
7300 East 56th Street, Indianapolis IN 46226-1306. 317/545-5301.

Lawrence North High School
7802 Hague Road, Indianapolis IN 46256-1754. 317/849-9455.

Lew Wallace High School
415 W 45th Avenue, Gary IN 46408-3927. 219/980-6305.

Linton-Stockton School District
801 1st Street NE, Linton IN 47441-1166. 812/847-6020.

Logansport High School
One Berry Lane, Logansport IN 46947-3901. 219/753-0441.

Loogootee Community School
PO Box 282, Loogootee IN 47553-0282. 812/295-2595.

Lowell Senior High School
2051 E Commercial Avenue, Lowell IN 46356-2115. 219/696-7733.

Madison Heights High School
4610 Madison Avenue, Anderson IN 46013-1316. 765/641-2037.

Manual High School
2405 Madison Avenue, Indianapolis IN 46225-2106. 317/226-4004.

Marian High School
1311 South Logan Street, Mishawaka IN 46544-4701. 219/259-5257.

Marion High School
750 W 26th Street, Marion IN 46953-2929. 765/664-9051.

McCutcheon High School
4951 U.S. Highway 231 South, Lafayette IN 47905-3447. 765/474-1488.

Merrillville Senior High School
276 E 68th Place, Gary IN 46410-3566. 219/736-2390.

Metropolitan School District
7523 South Mooresville Road, Indianapolis IN 46221-9668. 317/856-5265.

Metropolitan School District
4824 Homestead Road, Fort Wayne IN 46804-5461. 219/431-2000.

Metropolitan School District
3801 East 79th Street, Indianapolis IN 46240-3407. 317/845-9400.

Michigan City Junior High School
317 Detroit Street, Michigan City IN 46360-3717. 219/873-2035.

Mishawaka High School
1202 Lincoln Way East, Mishawaka IN 46544-2716. 219/258-3010.

Monroe Central School
Rural Route 1, Box 17A, Parker City IN 47368-9704. 765/468-6868.

Mooresville High School
550 North Indiana Street, Mooresville IN 46158-1220. 317/831-9203.

Morton Senior High School
6915 Grand Avenue, Hammond IN 46323-2587. 219/989-7316.

Mount Tabor Elementary School
800 Mount Tabor Road, New Albany IN 47150-2121. 812/949-4301.

Mount Vernon High School
700 Harriett Street, Mount Vernon IN 47620-2031. 812/838-4356.

Muncie Southside High School
1601 E 26th Street, Muncie IN 47302-5808. 765/747-5320.

Munster High School
8808 Columbia Avenue, Munster IN 46321-2520. 219/836-3200.

New Albany Senior High School
1020 Vincennes Street, New Albany IN 47150-3148. 812/949-4272.

New Castle Senior High School
801 Parkview Drive, New Castle IN 47362-2954. 765/593-6670.

Noblesville High School
18111 Cumberland Road, Noblesville IN 46060-5650. 317/773-4680.

Nora Elementary School
1000 East 91st Street, Indianapolis IN 46240-1612. 317/844-5436.

North Central High School
1801 East 86th Street, Indianapolis IN 46240-2345. 317/259-5301.

North High School
450 McGahn Street, Huntington IN 46750-1310. 219/356-6104.

North Newton Junior/Senior High School
Rural Route 2, Box 111, Morocco IN 47963-9632. 219/285-2252.

North Side High School
475 E State Boulevard, Fort Wayne IN 46805-3321. 219/425-7530.

Northern Community City School
2115 W 500 North, Sharpsville IN 46068-9322. 765/963-2585.

Northrop High School
7001 Coldwater Road, Fort Wayne IN 46825-3607. 219/425-7550.

Northview High School
8401 Westfield Boulevard, Indianapolis IN 46240-2367. 317/259-5421.

Northwest High School
5525 West 34th Street, Indianapolis IN 46224-1301. 317/226-4001.

Orchard School
615 W 64th St, Indianapolis IN 46260-4730. 317/251-9253.

Oregon Davis Junior/Senior High School
Rural Route 2, Box 50, Hamlet IN 46532-9802. 219/867-4561.

Park Tudor School
PO Box 40488, Indianapolis IN 46240-0488. 317/415-2700.

Perry Central Community School District
Old Highway 37, Leopold IN 47551. 812/843-5121.

Perry Elementary School
PO Box 337, Selma IN 47383-0337. 765/282-5615.

Perry Meridian Middle School
202 W Meridian School Rd, Indianapolis IN 46217-2913. 317/865-2704.

Pierce Junior High School
199 E 70th Pl, Merrillville IN 46410-3615. 219/736-4837.

Pike Central Junior/Senior High School
1810 East State Road 56, Petersburg IN 47567-8378. 812/354-8478.

Pike High School
6701 Zionsville Road, Indianapolis IN 46268-2462. 317/291-5250.

Plainfield High School
709 Stafford Rd, Plainfield IN 46168-2269. 317/839-7711.

Portage High School East
6450 US Highway 6, Portage IN 46368-5110. 219/763-8100.

Prairie Heights School
305 S 1150 E, Lagrange IN 46761-9667. 219/351-3214.

Princeton Community High School
PO Box 49, Princeton IN 47670-0049. 812/385-2591.

Raymond Park Middle School
8575 E Raymond St, Indianapolis IN 46239-9426. 317/862-8247.

Rensselaer Central High School
1106 E Grace St, Rensselaer IN 47978-3211. 219/866-5175.

Richmond Community Schools
300 Hub Etchison Parkway, Richmond IN 47374-5339. 765/973-3300.

Rockport-Ohio Elementary School
201 S 6th St, Rockport IN 47635-1315. 812/649-2201.

Salem Community School District
500 N Harrison St, Salem IN 47167-1671. 812/883-4437.

Seeger Memorial Junior/Senior High School
Rural Route 1, Box 143, West Lebanon IN 47991-9767. 765/893-4445.

Shakamak Elementary School
S Fry St, Jasonville IN 47438. 812/665-3550.

Shenandoah School
5100 N Raider Rd, Middletown IN 47356-9797. 765/354-2266.

Shortridge Junior High School
3401 N Meridian St, Indianapolis IN 46208-4436. 317/226-4010.

Snider High School
4600 Fairlawn Pass, Fort Wayne IN 46815-6041. 219/425-7570.

South Bend Community School
635 S Main St, South Bend IN 46601-2223. 219/282-4000.

South Central Community School
9808 S 600 W, Union Mills IN 46382-9600. 219/767-2263.

South Side High School
3601 S Calhoun St, Fort Wayne IN 46807-2006. 219/425-7610.

South Vigo High School
3737 S 7th St, Terre Haute IN 47802-4184. 812/462-4252.

Southern Wells Community School District
9120 S 300 W, Poneto IN 46781-9713. 765/728-5537.

Southwest Dubois County School
PO Box 238, Huntingburg IN 47542-0238. 812/683-3971.

Southwestern Junior/Senior High School
167 S Main Cross St, Hanover IN 47243-9468. 812/866-6230.

Spencer Elementary School
151 E Hillside Ave, Spencer IN 47460-1419. 812/829-2253.

St. Joseph High School
1441 N Michigan St, South Bend IN 46617-1120. 219/233-6137.

Theodore Roosevelt High School
730 W 25th Ave, Gary IN 46407-3525. 219/881-1500.

Thomas Carr Howe High School
4900 Julian Ave, Indianapolis IN 46201-3755. 317/226-4008.

Thompson Elementary School
PO Box 320, Walton IN 46994-0320. 219/626-2525.

Triton School
100 Triton Dr, Bourbon IN 46504-1801. 219/342-2255.

Union County Middle School
488 E State Road 44, Liberty IN 47353-8984. 765/458-7438.

Valparaiso High School
2727 Campbell St, Valparaiso IN 46385-2356. 219/464-1002.

Vermillion Community School District
5551 N Falcon Drive, Cayuga IN 47928-8181. 765/492-4033.

Vigo County School
961 Lafayette Ave, Terre Haute IN 47804-2929. 812/462-4216.

Warren Central High School
9500 E 16th St, Indianapolis IN 46229-2008. 317/898-6133.

Warsaw Community High School
1 Tiger Ln, Warsaw IN 46580-4807. 219/267-5174.

Washington High School
4747 W Washington St, South Bend IN 46619. 219/287-1026.

Wawasee High School
1 Warrior Path, Syracuse IN 46567-9170. 219/457-3147.

Wayne High School
9100 Winchester Rd, Fort Wayne IN 46819-2427. 219/425-7630.

West Noble High School
5094 N US Highway 33, Ligonier IN 46767-9606. 219/894-3191.

Western Boone Junior/Senior High School
1205 N State Road 75, Thorntown IN 46071-9229. 765/482-6143.

Whitko Community School District
PO Box 114, Pierceton IN 46562-0114. 219/594-2658.

Willowcreek Middle School
5962 Central Ave, Portage IN 46368-2903. 219/762-6511.

Wilson Middle School
3100 S Tillotson Ave, Muncie IN 47302-6539. 765/747-5370.

JUNIOR COLLEGES AND TECHNICAL INSTITUTES

Ivy Tech College
7999 S U.S. Highway 41, Terre Haute IN 47802-4845. 812/299-1121.

Ivy Tech College
PO Box 3100, Muncie IN 47307-1100. 765/289-2291.

Ivy Tech College
1534 W Sample St, South Bend IN 46619-3837. 219/289-7001.

Ivy Tech College
PO Box 1763, Indianapolis IN 46206-1763. 317/921-4882.

Ivy Tech College
3116 Canterbury Court, Bloomington IN 47404-1500. 812/332-1559.

Ivy Tech College
8204 Highway 311, Sellersburg IN 47172-1829. 812/246-3301.

Ivy Tech College
4475 Central Avenue, Columbus IN 47203-1868. 812/372-9925.

Ivy Tech College
1440 E 35th Avenue, Gary IN 46409-1401. 219/981-1111.

MISC. SCHOOLS AND EDUCATIONAL SERVICES

Anthis Career Center
203 E Douglas Avenue, Fort Wayne IN 46802. 219/425-7627.

Exceledge Inc.
9123 Holly Lane, Munster IN 46321-3013. 219/838-0740.

For more information on career opportunities in educational services:

__Associations__

AMERICAN ASSOCIATION FOR HIGHER EDUCATION
One DuPont Circle, Suite 360, Washington DC 20036. 202/293-6440. World Wide Web address: http://www.aahe.org.

AMERICAN ASSOCIATION OF SCHOOL ADMINISTRATORS
1801 North Moore Street, Arlington VA 22209-1813. 703/528-0700. Fax: 703/841-1543. World Wide Web address: http://www.aasa.org. An organization of school system leaders. Membership includes a national conference on education; programs and seminars; *The School Administrator,* a monthly magazine; *Leadership News,* a bi-monthly newspaper; *The AASA Professor,* a quarterly publication; and a catalog of other publications and audiovisuals.

AMERICAN FEDERATION OF TEACHERS
555 New Jersey Avenue NW, Washington DC 20001. 202/879-4400. World Wide Web address: http://www.aft.org.

COLLEGE AND UNIVERSITY PERSONNEL ASSOCIATION
1233 20th Street NW, Suite 301, Washington DC 20036. 202/429-0311. World Wide Web address: http://www.cupa.org. Membership required.

NATIONAL ASSOCIATION OF BIOLOGY TEACHERS
11250 Roger Bacon Drive, Suite 19, Reston VA 20190-5202. 703/471-1134. Toll-free phone: 800/406-0775. Fax: 703/435-5582. E-mail address: nabter@aol.com. World Wide Web address: http://www.nabt.org. A professional organization for biology and life science educators.

NATIONAL ASSOCIATION OF COLLEGE ADMISSION COUNSELORS
1631 Prince Street, Alexandria VA 22314. 703/836-2222. World Wide Web address: http://www.nacac.com. An education association of secondary school counselors, college and university admission officers, and related individuals who work with students as they make the transition from high school to post-secondary education.

NATIONAL ASSOCIATION OF COLLEGE AND UNIVERSITY BUSINESS OFFICERS
2501 M Street NW, Suite 400, Washington DC 20037-1308. 202/861-2500. World Wide Web address: http://www.nacubo.org. Association for those involved in the financial administration and management of higher education. Membership required.

NATIONAL COMMISSION FOR COOPERATIVE EDUCATION (NCCE)
360 Huntington Avenue, Suite 384 CP, Boston MA 02115-3770. 617/373-3770. E-mail address: ncce@lynx.neu.edu. Offers free information to students interested in learning more about cooperative education programs.

NATIONAL SCIENCE TEACHERS ASSOCIATION
1840 Wilson Boulevard, Arlington VA 22201-3000. 703/243-7100. World Wide Web address: http://www.nsta.org. Organization committed to the improvement of science education at all levels, preschool through college. Publishes five journals, a newspaper, and a number of special publications. Also conducts national and regional conventions.

NATIONAL SOCIETY FOR EXPERIENTIAL EDUCATION (NSEE)
3509 Haworth Drive, Suite 207, Raleigh NC 27609-7299. 919/787-3263. A membership organization offering publications, conferences, and a resource center. Among the society's publications is *The Experienced Hand: A Student Manual for Making the Most of an Internship*.

Books

HOW TO GET A JOB IN EDUCATION
Adams Media Corporation, 260 Center Street, Holbrook MA 02343. 781/767-8100. World Wide Web address: http://www.adamsmedia.com.

Directories

WASHINGTON EDUCATION ASSOCIATION DIRECTORY
Council for Advancement and Support of Education, 11 DuPont Circle, Suite 400, Washington DC 20036. 202/328-5900. World Wide Web address: http://www.case.org.

Online Services

ACADEMIC EMPLOYMENT NETWORK
http://www.academploy.com. This site offers information for the educational professional. It allows you to search for positions using keywords or location. It also has information on other sites of interest, educational products, certification requirements by state, and relocation services.

THE CHRONICLE OF HIGHER EDUCATION
http://chronicle.com/jobs. This Website provides job listings from the weekly published newspaper *The Chronicle of Higher Education*. Besides featuring articles from the paper, this site also offers employment opportunities. You can search for information by geographic location, type of position, and teaching fields.

EDUCATION & INSTRUCTION JOBS
http://csueb.sfsu.edu/jobs/educationjobs.html. Offers a long list of links to other sites around the country that provide job openings and information for jobseekers looking in education. This site is part of the California State University Employment Board.

EDUCATION FORUM
Go: Edforum. This CompuServe discussion group is open to educators of all levels.

JOBWEB SCHOOL DISTRICTS SEARCH
http://www.jobweb.org/search/schools/. Provides a search engine for school districts across the country. The site is run by the National Association of Colleges and Employers and it also provides information on colleges and career fairs.

THE TEACHER'S LOUNGE
Keyword: teacher's lounge. An America Online discussion group for teachers of kindergarten through the twelfth grade.

VISUAL NATION ARTS JOBS LINKS
http://fly.hiwaay.net/%7Edrewyor/art_job.html. Provides links to other sites that post academic and arts job openings and information.

ELECTRONIC/INDUSTRIAL ELECTRICAL EQUIPMENT

Intense international competition is prompting the U.S. electronics industry to become more globalized. Companies are being forced to seek less expensive materials and labor. Overall, employment in the industry has remained stable at about 551,000 since 1994. Foreign demand for U.S. electronic component exports was expected to reach $48 billion by the end of 1998, a 15.9 percent increase over 1997. Semiconductor manufacturing needs were expected to rise by 18 percent in North America in 1998 and to support this growth the industry continues to invest in new technology and equipment.

U.S. Industry and Trade Outlook 1998 *projects the best opportunities for jobseekers to be in the production of analog and memory ICs, microcomponents, and discrete semiconductors. Industry observers worldwide predict that semiconductor markets will grow at an approximate rate of 15 percent annually through 2005. Sales of printed circuit boards should have seen an increase of 7 percent in 1998. The outlook for the switchgear sector is highly favorable. U.S. electric utilities are expected to spend more than $300 million to automate power substations by 2000; and shipments of switchgear are forecasted to grow at an average rate of 4 to 5 percent through 2000.*

ABB POWER T&D COMPANY, INC.
P.O. Box 2448, Muncie IN 47302. 765/286-9272. **Contact:** Human Resources. **World Wide Web address:** http://www.abb.com. **Description:** Manufactures power and distribution transformers for utility companies.

ALLIEDSIGNAL GUIDANCE DIVISION
400 South Beiger Street, Mishawaka IN 46544. 219/255-2111. **Contact:** Paul Silverman, Human Resources Manager. **World Wide Web address:** http://www.alliedsignal.com. **Description:** Manufactures high-performance supersonic targets, image interpretation systems, and missile guidance systems. **Parent company:** AlliedSignal Corporation serves a broad spectrum of industries through its more than 40 businesses, which are grouped into three sectors: Aerospace; Automotive; and Engineered Materials.

AMERICAN ELECTRONIC COMPONENTS, INC.
P.O. Box 280, Elkhart IN 46514. 219/264-1116. **Contact:** Chuck Lee, Human Resources Manager. **Description:** Designs and manufactures specialized electronic and electrical components including highly-engineered sensors. In addition, the company designs and manufactures high-performance industrial relays, switches, and electromechanical and plastic products. The company's products are sold to major North American automotive OEMs, and to diverse industrial and consumer products manufacturers. Founded in 1935. **Common positions include:** Applications Engineer; Electrical/Electronics Engineer; Manufacturing Engineer; Mechanical Engineer. **Educational backgrounds include:** Engineering. **Benefits:** 401(k); Dental Insurance; Disability Coverage; Life Insurance; Medical Insurance; Tuition Assistance. **Corporate headquarters location:** This Location. **Parent company:** Echlin Corporation. **Listed on:** New York Stock Exchange. **Annual sales/revenues:** $21 - $50 million. **Number of employees at this location:** 550.

BI MONITORING
P.O. Box 1336, Anderson IN 46015. 765/649-6000. **Contact:** Human Resources. **World Wide Web address:** http://www.bi.com. **Description:** A leading provider of electronic home arrest and

jail management systems to corrections agencies worldwide. The company also offers computerized, interactive telephone service and monitoring service for its electronic monitoring systems. BI employs approximately 267 full-time professionals in the following functions: research and development; manufacturing; quality assurance; sales; marketing; product service; account management; monitoring; administration; and management. **Corporate headquarters location:** Boulder CO. **Other U.S. locations:** GA; IL; OH; TX. **Number of employees at this location:** 65.

BELDEN WIRE AND CABLE COMPANY
P.O. Box 1980, Richmond IN 47375-1980. 765/983-5200. **Physical address:** 2200 U.S. Highway 27 South, Richmond IN 47374. **Contact:** Mike Mellinger, Human Resources Manager. **World Wide Web address:** http://www.belden.com. **Description:** Designs and manufactures wire, cable, and cord products. Belden currently serves the computer market with a broad range of multiconductor, coaxial, flat, and fiberoptic cables. Belden cable links virtually every segment of broadcast and cable television, from broadcast studios, to post-production, to satellite transmission centers. Belden's electrical products include power supply cords, electrical motor lead wire, and Canadian building wire. In 1994, Belden formed the Cord Products Division to focus on further increasing revenues in the electrical cord market. Belden also serves the industrial market by providing a broad spectrum of industrial products, ranging from general purpose control cables to highly sophisticated cables for process control.

BELDEN WIRE AND CABLE COMPANY
350 NW N Street, Richmond IN 47374. 765/962-7561. **Contact:** Human Resources. **World Wide Web address:** http://www.belden.com. **Description:** Designs and manufactures wire, cable, and cord products. Belden currently serves the computer market with a broad range of multiconductor, coaxial, flat, and fiberoptic cables. Belden cable links virtually every segment of broadcast and cable television, from broadcast studios, to post-production, to satellite transmission centers. Belden's electrical products include power supply cords, electrical motor lead wire, and Canadian building wire. In 1994, Belden formed the Cord Products Division to focus on further increasing revenues in the electrical cord market. Belden also serves the industrial market by providing a broad spectrum of industrial products, ranging from general purpose control cables to highly sophisticated cables for process control.

BEST ACCESS SYSTEMS
6161 East 75th Street, Indianapolis IN 46250. 317/849-2250. **Contact:** Human Resources. **World Wide Web address:** http://www.bestaccess.com. **Description:** Manufactures and distributes access control and security systems for corporations and institutions worldwide. **Common positions include:** Accountant/Auditor; Computer Programmer; Manufacturer's/Wholesaler's Sales Rep.; Mechanical Engineer; Systems Analyst. **Educational backgrounds include:** Accounting; Business Administration; Communications; Engineering; Marketing. **Benefits:** 401(k); Dental Insurance; Disability Coverage; Life Insurance; Medical Insurance; Tuition Assistance. **Corporate headquarters location:** This Location. **Other U.S. locations:** Nationwide. **Number of employees at this location:** 700. **Number of employees nationwide:** 1,200.

CTS CORPORATION
905 West Boulevard North, Elkhart IN 46514. 219/293-7511. **Contact:** Human Resources. **World Wide Web address:** http://www.ctscorp.com. **Description:** This location houses the administrative offices. Overall, CTS Corporation designs, manufactures, and sells electronic components. **Corporate headquarters location:** This Location. **Listed on:** New York Stock Exchange.

CTS CORPORATION
RESISTOR NETWORKS DIVISION
406 Parr Road, Berne IN 46711. 219/589-3111. **Fax:** 219/589-3243. **Contact:** Sherri Minnich, Human Resources. **World Wide Web address:** http://www.ctscorp.com. **Description:** Manufactures electronic resistor networks. **Parent company:** Dynamics Corporation of America.

CONTROLS INC.
Caller Box 7011, Logansport IN 46947. 219/722-1167. **Fax:** 219/722-3100. **Contact:** Laura Rinehart, Human Resources. **World Wide Web address:** http://www.controls-inc.com. **Description:** Designs and manufactures electronic controls. **Common positions include:**

Accountant/Auditor; Blue-Collar Worker Supervisor; Buyer; Customer Service Representative; Designer; Electrical/Electronics Engineer; Human Resources Manager; Purchasing Agent/Manager; Quality Control Supervisor; Systems Analyst. **Educational backgrounds include:** Engineering; Finance; Marketing. **Benefits:** 401(k); Disability Coverage; Life Insurance; Medical Insurance; Profit Sharing; Savings Plan; Tuition Assistance. **Corporate headquarters location:** This Location. **Operations at this facility include:** Administration; Manufacturing; Sales; Service. **Listed on:** Privately held. **Number of employees at this location:** 200.

CROWN INTERNATIONAL
1718 West Mishawaka Road, Elkhart IN 46517. 219/294-8000. **Fax:** 219/294-8329. **Recorded jobline:** 219/294-8002. **Contact:** Cheryl Crowel, Recruiter. **E-mail address:** cheryl@crownintl.com. **World Wide Web address:** http://www.crownintl.com. **Description:** Manufactures a variety of amplification equipment for the professional audio and industrial markets. The company also manufactures microphones, special computerized test equipment, and transmitters for the broadcast market. **Common positions include:** Accountant/Auditor; Computer Programmer; Designer; Draftsperson; Electrical/Electronics Engineer; Industrial Engineer; Internet Services Manager; Marketing Manager; Mechanical Engineer; Purchasing Agent/Manager; Sales Manager; Secretary; Software Engineer; Systems Analyst; Webmaster. **Educational backgrounds include:** Accounting; Business Administration; Communications; Computer Science; Economics; Engineering; Finance; Liberal Arts; Marketing. **Benefits:** 401(k); Dental Insurance; Disability Coverage; Employee Discounts; Life Insurance; Medical Insurance; Tuition Assistance. **Corporate headquarters location:** This Location. **Operations at this facility include:** Administration; Manufacturing; Research and Development; Sales; Service. **Listed on:** Privately held. **Number of employees at this location:** 900.

ESSEX GROUP, INC.
1601 Wall Street, Fort Wayne IN 46802. 219/461-4000. **Contact:** Dominic Lucenta, Human Resources Manager. **World Wide Web address:** http://www.essexgroup.com. **Description:** Manufactures and distributes electrical cable and insulation products including magnetic and building wires, and telephone cable. **Common positions include:** Accountant/Auditor; Administrator; Attorney; Blue-Collar Worker Supervisor; Buyer; Chemical Engineer; Chemist; Computer Programmer; Credit Manager; Customer Service Representative; Draftsperson; Electrical/Electronics Engineer; Financial Analyst; General Manager; Human Resources Manager; Industrial Engineer; Industrial Production Manager; Manufacturer's/Wholesaler's Sales Rep.; Mechanical Engineer; Metallurgical Engineer; Operations/Production Manager; Purchasing Agent/Manager; Quality Control Supervisor; Software Engineer; Systems Analyst; Transportation/Traffic Specialist. **Educational backgrounds include:** Accounting; Business Administration; Chemistry; Computer Science; Engineering; Finance. **Benefits:** 401(k); Dental Insurance; Disability Coverage; Life Insurance; Medical Insurance; Pension Plan; Savings Plan; Tuition Assistance. **Special programs:** Internships. **Corporate headquarters location:** This Location. **Listed on:** Privately held.

FRANKLIN ELECTRIC COMPANY, INC.
400 East Spring Street, Bluffton IN 46714. 219/824-2900. **Contact:** Personnel. **World Wide Web address:** http://www.fele.com. **Description:** One of the world's largest manufacturers of submersible electric motors, and a leading producer of engineered specialty electric motor products. The principal application for the company's submersible motors is providing electrical power for water and pumping systems, oil wells, and wastewater handling systems. Franklin Electric's specialty electric motor products and electronic controls are used in a wide variety of industrial products including gasoline dispensers, paint sprayers, electric hoists, explosion-proof vapor exhaust fans, vacuum pumping systems, livestock feeding systems, and soft ice cream machines. **Other area locations:** Jonesboro IN. **Other U.S. locations:** Siloam Springs AR; Tulsa OK; Wilburton OK; McFarland WI. **International locations:** Australia; Czech Republic; Germany; Mexico; South Africa. **Number of employees worldwide:** 2,500.

HI-TEK LIGHTING
1615 East Elmore Street, Crawfordsville IN 47933. 765/362-1837. **Contact:** Tom Abbott, Human Resources Director. **Description:** Manufactures a wide variety of light fixtures, including industrial, indoor, and outdoor fixtures.

HUBBELL & RACO ELECTRICAL PRODUCTS, INC.
3902 West Sample Street, South Bend IN 46634. 219/234-7151. **Contact:** Human Resources. **Description:** Manufactures non-current-carrying, electronic wiring devices.

HURCO COMPANIES, INC.
One Technology Way, Indianapolis IN 46268. 317/293-5309. **Contact:** Judy Summers, Human Resources Manager. **E-mail address:** info@hurco.com. **Description:** Designs, manufactures, and sells computer numerical control (CNC) systems and software, as well as CNC machine tools for the international machine tool industry. Hurco is among the largest U.S. manufacturers of CNC systems for stand-alone machine tools. These CNC systems and software are either integrated with machine tools sold by Hurco or sold to machine tool end users. In some cases, the company's products are sold to original equipment manufacturers (OEMs) who combine them with their own machine tools. The company's CNC systems include Autocon Technologies, Inc. (Delta Series) CNC Controls, Ultimax controls and software, and Autobend CNC and press brake gauging systems. Among the company's integrated machine tool products are CNC machining centers and CNC milling machines. Hurco's products are sold through the company's international network of distributors. Clients for the company's products include independent contract manufacturing operations, short-run, precision, tool, die, and mold manufacturers, and specialized production applications within large companies that cut or form metal parts. Industries served include aerospace, computer, defense, medical equipment, farm implement, construction equipment, energy, and transportation.

MAGNETEK, INC.
305 North Briant Street, Huntington IN 46750. 219/356-7100. **Contact:** Human Resources. **World Wide Web address:** http://www.magnetek.com. **Description:** Designs, produces, and markets electrical, electronic, and industrial components and products. The company also offers services and repair support for its components. MagneTek, Inc.'s principal products include a variety of ballasts and transformers for lighting; motors; and control components for motors and generators, systems, and controls. The company's service group rebuilds and repairs large motors, generators, and transformers, primarily for utility companies and industrial manufacturers.

MAGNETEK, INC.
112 East Union Street, P.O. Box 490, Goodland IN 47948. 219/297-3111. **Contact:** Human Resources. **World Wide Web address:** http://www.magnetek.com. **Description:** MagneTek, Inc. is a designer, producer, and marketer of electrical, electronic, and industrial components and products. The company also offers services and repair support for its components. MagneTek, Inc.'s principal products include a variety of ballasts and transformers for lighting; motors; and control components for motors and generators, systems, and controls. The company's service group rebuilds and repairs large motors, generators, and transformers primarily for utility companies and industrial manufacturers.

MALLORY CONTROLS
2831 Waterfront Parkway, Indianapolis IN 46206. 317/328-4032. **Fax:** 317/328-4118. **Contact:** Sula Dippold, Human Resources Representative. **Description:** Manufactures appliance controls and automotive switches. **Common positions include:** Computer Programmer; Design Engineer; Mechanical Engineer. **Educational backgrounds include:** Engineering. **Benefits:** 401(k); Dental Insurance; Disability Coverage; Employee Discounts; Life Insurance; Medical Insurance; Pension Plan; Savings Plan; Tuition Assistance. **Special programs:** Co-ops. **Parent company:** Emerson Electric Co. **Operations at this facility include:** Divisional Headquarters. **Listed on:** New York Stock Exchange. **President:** Lowell Kilgus.

MALLORY CONTROLS
3405 West State Road 28, Frankfort IN 46041. 765/654-5501. **Contact:** Jim Lower, Human Resources Manager. **Description:** An electronics company specializing in electromechanical controls, automotive switches, and timers.

RAYTHEON SYSTEMS COMPANY
1010 Production Road, Mail Stop 10-26, Fort Wayne IN 46808-4106. 219/429-6000. **Fax:** 219/429-4499. **Contact:** Human Resources. **Description:** A leader in the design of military tactical

communications, electronic combat, command and control, and antisubmarine warfare products and systems for the Armed Forces of the United States and Allied Nations. **NOTE:** Entry-level positions are offered. **Company slogan:** Expect great things. **Common positions include:** Computer Programmer; Electrical/Electronics Engineer; Software Engineer. **Educational backgrounds include:** Computer Science; Engineering; Software Development. **Benefits:** 401(k); Dental Insurance; Disability Coverage; Flexible Schedule; Life Insurance; Medical Insurance; Pension Plan; Tuition Assistance. **Special programs:** Internships. **Office hours:** Monday - Friday, 7:30 a.m. - 4:30 p.m. **Corporate headquarters location:** Lexington MA. **Other U.S. locations:** Nationwide. **Parent company:** Raytheon Company. **Operations at this facility include:** Administration; Divisional Headquarters; Manufacturing; Research and Development; Sales. **Annual sales/revenues:** More than $100 million. **Number of employees at this location:** 2,000. **Number of employees nationwide:** 120,000. **Number of projected hires for 1998 - 1999 at this location:** 120.

ROBINSON NUGENT, INC.
P.O. Box 1208, New Albany IN 47151. 812/945-0211. **Toll-free phone:** 800/457-2412. **Fax:** 812/941-3568. **Contact:** Michael W. Schreiweis, Director of Human Resources. **E-mail address:** mikes@robinsonnugent.com. **World Wide Web address:** http://www.robinsonnugent.com. **Description:** Manufactures electronic connectors and integrated circuit sockets for the electronics industry serving the telecommunications, computer, commercial, and industrial markets. Founded in 1952. **Company slogan:** Connect with quality. **Common positions include:** Accountant; Administrative Assistant; Advertising Account Executive; Chief Financial Officer; Computer Operator; Computer Programmer; Controller; Customer Service Representative; Database Manager; Design Engineer; Draftsperson; Electrical/Electronics Engineer; Sales Executive; Sales Manager; Secretary. **Educational backgrounds include:** Accounting; Business Administration; Computer Science; Engineering; Finance; Marketing. **Benefits:** 401(k); Dental Insurance; Life Insurance; Medical Insurance; Pension Plan; Tuition Assistance. **Corporate headquarters location:** This Location. **Other U.S. locations:** Kings Mountain NC; Dallas TX. **Subsidiaries include:** Cablelink, Inc. **Operations at this facility include:** Administration; Manufacturing; Research and Development; Sales; Service. **Listed on:** NASDAQ. **Stock exchange symbol:** RNIC. **Annual sales/revenues:** $51 - $100 million. **Number of employees at this location:** 140. **Number of employees nationwide:** 440. **Number of employees worldwide:** 705. **Number of projected hires for 1998 - 1999 at this location:** 10.

SCHUMACHER ELECTRIC CORPORATION
P.O. Box 39, Rensselaer IN 47978. 219/866-7126. **Contact:** Human Resources. **Description:** Manufactures transformers and automotive battery chargers.

THERMWOOD CORPORATION
P.O. Box 436, Dale IN 47523. 812/937-4476. **Contact:** Human Resources. **World Wide Web address:** http://www.thermwood.com. **Description:** Develops, manufactures, markets, and services computer-controlled industrial systems that perform high-speed machining and routing functions.

TOKHEIM CORPORATION
P.O. Box 360, Fort Wayne IN 46801. 219/470-4600. **Contact:** Human Resources. **Description:** Designs, manufactures, and markets electronic petroleum and monitoring systems such as service station equipment, point-of-sale control systems, card-activated transaction systems, and underground tank monitoring equipment. The company also designs, manufactures, and produces process control automation systems, solid-state time delays, and time and temperature control devices.

UNITED TECHNOLOGIES CORPORATION
ELECTRONIC CONTROLS
3650 West 200 North, Huntington IN 46750. 219/358-0888. **Contact:** Director of Human Resources. **World Wide Web address:** http://www.utc.com. **Description:** This location manufactures electronic controls, primarily used in heating and air conditioning equipment. Overall, United Technologies Corporation provides high-technology products and support services to customers in the aerospace, building, military, and automotive industries worldwide. Its products include large jet engines, temperature control systems, elevators and escalators, helicopters, and

flight systems. The company markets its products under a variety of brand names including Carrier, Hamilton Standard, Otis, Pratt & Whitney, and Sikorsky. **International locations:** Latin America; Mexico; Canada; Australia; Europe; and Asia.

WAVETEK CATV/COMMUNICATIONS
5808 Churchman Bypass, Indianapolis IN 46203. 317/788-5981. **Fax:** 317/788-5999. **Contact:** Human Resources Manager. **Description:** Produces electronic test and management equipment for cable, cellular, two-way, and paging products and markets. **Common positions include:** Computer Programmer; Electrical/Electronics Engineer; Software Engineer; Systems Analyst. **Educational backgrounds include:** Computer Science; Engineering. **Benefits:** 401(k); Daycare Assistance; Dental Insurance; Disability Coverage; Employee Discounts; Life Insurance; Medical Insurance; Tuition Assistance. **Corporate headquarters location:** This Location. **Parent company:** Wavetek Corporation. **Operations at this facility include:** Administration; Manufacturing; Research and Development; Sales; Service. **Listed on:** Privately held. **Annual sales/revenues:** More than $100 million.

WOODS INDUSTRIES
510 Third Avenue SW, Carmel IN 46032. 317/844-7261. **Contact:** Mike Porter, Vice President of Human Resources. **Description:** Manufactures electrical wiring products used in a wide variety of applications.

Note: *Because addresses and telephone numbers of smaller companies can change rapidly, we recommend you call each company to verify the information below before inquiring about job opportunities. Mass mailings are not recommended.*

Additional small employers:

ELECTRIC LIGHTING AND WIRING EQUIPMENT

CMW Inc.
PO Box 2266, Indianapolis IN 46206-2266. 317/634-8884.

Deco Engineering
2700 County Road 75, Butler IN 46721-9400. 219/868-5878.

ESD
PO Box 929, Huntington IN 46750-0929. 219/356-2700.

FCI Berg Electronics
PO Box 547, Franklin IN 46131-0547. 317/738-2800.

Industrial Dielectrics Inc.
PO Box 357, Noblesville IN 46061-0357. 317/773-1766.

Indy Lighting Inc.
12001 Exit 5 Parkway, Fishers IN 46038-9627. 317/849-1233.

Spectrum Products Inc.
6220 Churchman Bypass, Indianapolis IN 46203-6117. 317/791-9721.

The Halex Company
7715 S Homestead Drive, Hamilton IN 46742-9622. 219/488-3531.

Tippecanoe Products
PO Box 337, North Webster IN 46555-0337. 219/834-2818.

Wells-CTI
3502 N Olive Rd, South Bend IN 46628. 219/287-5941.

ELECTRICAL ENGINE EQUIPMENT

Carlisle
Winands Road, Bloomington IN 47401. 812/334-8715.

Delphi Energy & Engine Management Systems
PO Box 502650, Indianapolis IN 46250-7650. 317/579-3700.

Delphi Energy & Engine Management Systems
2620 E 38th Street, Anderson IN 46013-2645. 765/646-7818.

Hazleton Industries Inc.
1202 Gach Road, Princeton IN 47670-9714. 812/386-3307.

Indiana Marine Products Inc.
409 Growth Parkway, Angola IN 46703-9323. 219/665-6112.

Ristance Corporation
1718 N Home St, Mishawaka IN 46545-7237. 219/259-6253.

VDO Control Systems Inc.
813 S Grandstaff Dr, Auburn IN 46706-2044. 219/925-8700.

Wirekraft Industries Inc.
833 Legner St, Bremen IN 46506-1060. 219/546-4680.

ELECTRICAL EQUIPMENT WHOLESALE

Diamond Wire & Cable Company Inc.
PO Box 1710, Fort Wayne IN 46801-1710. 219/461-4880.

Kirby Risk Electrical Supply
PO Box 5089, Lafayette IN 47903-5089. 765/448-4567.

Square D Company
6 Commercial Rd, Huntington IN 46750-8805. 219/356-2060.

ELECTRICAL EQUIPMENT, MACHINERY, AND SUPPLIES

Jasonville Cord Company
121 North Meridian Street,

Jasonville IN 47438-1211. 812/665-2213.

Trans Guard Industries Inc.
PO Box 369, Angola IN 46703-0369. 219/665-9402.

UMM Electronics Inc.
6911 Hillsdale Ct, Indianapolis IN 46250-2054. 317/576-5035.

ELECTRICAL INDUSTRIAL APPARATUS

Huntington Electric Inc.
PO Box 366, Huntington IN 46750-0366. 219/356-0756.

Kreuter Manufacturing Company Inc.
PO Box 158, New Paris IN 46553-0158. 219/831-4626.

Siemens Potter & Brumfield
200 S Richland Creek Dr, Princeton IN 47670-9569. 812/386-1000.

Smith Systems
913 10th St, Elkhart IN 46516-2657. 219/262-4417.

ELECTRONIC CAPACITORS

North American Capacitor Co.
PO Box 489, Greencastle IN 46135-0489. 765/653-3151.

ELECTRONIC COILS AND TRANSFORMERS

Dana Corporation
802 E Short Street, Columbia City IN 46725. 219/244-6183.

Warsaw Coil Co. Inc.
PO Box 1057, Warsaw IN 46581-1057. 219/267-6041.

ELECTRONIC COMPONENTS AND ACCESSORIES

Kimball Electronics Group
PO Box 587, Jasper IN 47547-0587. 812/634-4200.

ELECTRONIC PARTS AND EQUIPMENT WHOLESALE

D&L Communications Inc.
PO Box 8496, Fort Wayne IN 46898-8496. 219/484-0466.

Ingram Entertainment Inc.
7319 Innovation Boulevard, Fort Wayne IN 46818-1371. 219/489-2022.

Nationwide Home Discount Video
2900 E 83rd Place, Gary IN 46410-6414. 219/942-1155.

Telamon Corporation
1000 E 116th St, Carmel IN 46032-3416. 317/818-6888.

MISC. ELECTRONIC COMPONENTS

Aztec Wire Inc.
PO Box 236, Lagrange IN 46761. 219/463-7432.

Central Industries of Indiana
1325 East Virginia Street, Evansville IN 47711-5728. 812/421-0231.

CTS Elkhart
1142 W Beardsley Avenue, Elkhart IN 46514-2224. 219/295-3575.

Dormeyer Industries
Rural Route 2, Box AA1, Rockville IN 47872-9501. 765/569-2061.

Electromation Inc.
PO Box 280, Elkhart IN 46515-0280. 219/264-2125.

ETS
1916 South Main Street, South Bend IN 46613-2306. 219/234-0600.

Fargo Assembly Company
800 Cleveland Street, Mishawaka IN 46544-4861. 219/259-3728.

Global Components Corporation
3429 Knobs Valley Drive, Floyds Knobs IN 47119-9665. 812/923-1000.

Intec Group Inc.
2295 E State Road, Suite 114, Morocco IN 47963-8107. 219/285-2231.

Kauffman Engineering Inc.
PO Box 150, Lebanon IN 46052-0150. 765/482-5640.

Mid-American Electro-Cords
11555 Harter Drive, Middlebury IN 46540-9663. 219/825-9466.

Precision Wire Assemblies
551 East Main Street, Hagerstown IN 47346-1421. 765/489-6302.

PTS Electronics
PO Box 272, Bloomington IN 47402-0272. 812/824-9331.

Raytheon Systems Company
US Highway 30, County Rd 600, Columbia City IN 46725. 219/248-2501.

SEMICONDUCTORS AND RELATED DEVICES

CTS Microelectronics
1201 Cumberland Avenue, Lafayette IN 47906-1317. 765/463-2565.

Siemens Electromechanical Components
1200 East Broadway Street, Princeton IN 47670-3102. 812/386-2487.

SWITCHGEAR AND SWITCHBOARD APPARATUS

ABB Power T&D Company
300 North Curry Pike, Bloomington IN 47404-2503. 812/332-4421.

For more information on career opportunities in the electronic/industrial electrical equipment industry:

Associations

AMERICAN CERAMIC SOCIETY
P.O. Box 6136, Westerville OH 43086-6136. 614/890-4700. World Wide Web address: http://www.acers.org. Provides ceramics futures information. Membership required.

ELECTROCHEMICAL SOCIETY
10 South Main Street, Pennington NJ 08534. 609/737-1902. World Wide Web address: http://www.electrochem.org. An international society which holds bi-annual meetings internationally and periodic meetings through local sections.

ELECTRONIC INDUSTRIES ASSOCIATION
2500 Wilson Boulevard, Arlington VA 22201. 703/907-7500. World Wide Web address: http://www.eia.org.

ELECTRONICS TECHNICIANS ASSOCIATION
602 North Jackson Street, Greencastle IN 46135. 765/653-8262. World Wide Web address: http://www.eta-sda.com. Offers published job-hunting advice from the organization's officers and members.

FABLESS SEMICONDUCTOR ASSOCIATION
Galleria Tower I, 13355 Noel Road, Dallas TX 75240-6636. 972/239-5119. Fax: 972/774-4577. World Wide Web address: http://www.fsa.org. A semiconductor industry association.

INSTITUTE OF ELECTRICAL AND ELECTRONICS ENGINEERS (IEEE)
345 East 47th Street, New York NY 10017. 212/705-7900. Toll-free customer service line: 800/678-4333. World Wide Web address: http://www.ieee.org.

INTERNATIONAL SOCIETY OF CERTIFIED ELECTRONICS TECHNICIANS
2708 West Berry Street, Fort Worth TX 76109. 817/921-9101. World Wide Web address: http://www.iscet.org.

NATIONAL ELECTRONICS SERVICE DEALERS ASSOCIATION
2708 West Berry Street, Fort Worth TX 76109. 817/921-9101. World Wide Web address: http://www.nesda.com. Provides newsletters and directories to members.

SEMICONDUCTOR EQUIPMENT AND MATERIALS INTERNATIONAL
805 East Middlefield Road, Mountain View CA 94043-4080. 650/964-5111. E-mail address: semihq@semi.org. World Wide Web address: http://www.semi.org. An international trade association concerned with the semiconductor and flat-panel display industries. Membership required.

ENVIRONMENTAL AND WASTE MANAGEMENT SERVICES

The United States is the largest producer and consumer of environmental goods and services in the world. The industry continues to expand as a result of increasing public concern for the environment and the passing of both the Clean Air and Clean Water Acts. Global environmental revenues are expected to increase 33 percent by the year 2000. The Water Quality Association reports that Americans spent more than $1.3 billion on the filtration and purification of household water in 1995, and that number is expected to increase 70 percent by the year 2000.

Solid waste management remains the largest of the environmental business segments. Waste Management is a leader in the industry with the company's two main rivals, Browning-Ferris Industries and USA Waste, gaining ground. Job opportunities will continue to be found primarily in the areas of environmental protection, natural resources, and education.

A.T.C. ASSOCIATES
5150 East 65th Street, Indianapolis IN 46220. 317/577-0612. **Contact:** Human Resources. **World Wide Web address:** http://www.atc-enviro.com. **Description:** An environmental consulting services firm. **Common positions include:** Accountant/Auditor; Environmental Engineer; Geotechnical Engineer; Manager of Information Systems; Materials Engineer. **Educational backgrounds include:** Environmental Science; Geotechnology.

BROWNING-FERRIS INDUSTRIES (BFI)
2017 North Fares Avenue, Evansville IN 47711-3967. 812/424-3345. **Contact:** Human Resources. **World Wide Web address:** http://www.bfi.com. **Description:** Browning-Ferris Industries is primarily engaged in waste collection and disposal services. The company has worldwide operations at more than 500 facilities. **Corporate headquarters location:** Houston TX. **Other U.S. locations:** Nationwide. **Number of employees nationwide:** 40,000. **Number of employees worldwide:** 50,000.

ECOSEARCH ENVIRONMENTAL RESOURCES, INC.
9365 Counselors Row, Suite 104, Indianapolis IN 46240. 317/574-8830. **Contact:** Human Resources Department. **World Wide Web address:** http://www.ecosearch.net. **Description:** Provides supplemental, site assessment services including environmental reports and information gathering.

INDIANA RECYCLING SERVICES, INC.
865 Wheeler Street, Crown Point IN 46307. 219/922-4800. **Contact:** Human Resources Department. **Description:** A leading provider of waste management and recycling services. Founded in 1989.

WASTE MANAGEMENT OF NW INDIANA, INC.
2000 Domby Road, Portage IN 46368. 219/763-2502. **Fax:** 219/764-1344. **Contact:** Sally Phillips, Human Resources Department. **World Wide Web address:** http://www.wastemanagement.com. **Description:** Waste Management of NW Indiana provides waste collection, removal, and disposal services to its residential, commercial, and industrial customers. **Corporate headquarters location:** Oak Brook IL. **Other U.S. locations:** Nationwide. **Number of employees nationwide:** 67,200.

Note: *Because addresses and telephone numbers of smaller companies can change rapidly, we recommend you call each company to verify the information below before inquiring about job opportunities. Mass mailings are not recommended.*

Additional small employers:

SANITARY SERVICES

Browning-Ferris Industries
PO Box 36098, Indianapolis IN 46236-0098. 317/823-6881.

EA2 Systems
1931 Allens Lane, Evansville IN 47720-1312. 812/421-2130.

Environmental Services
3113 Riverside Drive, South Bend IN 46628. 219/277-8515.

Heckman Sani-Service
PO Box 2234, Fort Wayne IN 46801-2234. 219/747-4117.

Langsdale Recycling
832 Langsdale Avenue, Indianapolis IN 46202-1150. 317/926-5492.

Pollution Control Industries
4343 Kennedy Ave, East Chicago IN 46312-2723. 219/397-3951.

Ray's Recycling Plant
PO Drawer I, Clayton IN 46118-4909. 317/539-2024.

For more information on career opportunities in environmental and waste management services:

Associations

AIR & WASTE MANAGEMENT ASSOCIATION
One Gateway Center, 3rd Floor, Pittsburgh PA 15222. 412/232-3444. World Wide Web address: http://www.awma.org. A nonprofit, technical and educational organization providing a neutral forum where all points of view regarding environmental management issues can be addressed.

AMERICAN ACADEMY OF ENVIRONMENTAL ENGINEERS
130 Holiday Court, Suite 100, Annapolis MD 21401. 410/266-3311. World Wide Web address: http://www.enviro.engrs.org. Publishes the *Environmental Engineering Selection Guide*, a directory of engineering firms and educational institutions.

ENVIRONMENTAL INDUSTRY ASSOCIATIONS
4301 Connecticut Avenue NW, Suite 300, Washington DC 20008. 202/244-4700. World Wide Web address: http://www.envasns.org.

INSTITUTE OF CLEAN AIR COMPANIES
1660 L Street NW, Suite 1100, Washington DC 20036. 202/457-0911. World Wide Web address: http://www.icac.com. A national association of companies involved in stationary source air pollution control.

WATER ENVIRONMENT FEDERATION
601 Wythe Street, Alexandria VA 22314. 703/684-2400. World Wide Web address: http://www.wef.org. Subscription to jobs newsletter required for career information.

Magazines

JOURNAL OF AIR AND WASTE MANAGEMENT ASSOCIATION
One Gateway Center, 3rd Floor, Pittsburgh PA 15222. Toll-free phone: 800/275-5851. World Wide Web address: http://www.awma.org.

Online Services

ECOLOGIC
http://www.eng.rpi.edu/dept/union/pugwash/ecojobs.htm. This Website provides links to a variety of environmental job resources. This site is run by the Rensselaer Student Pugwash.

ENVIRONMENTAL JOBS SEARCH PAGE/UBIQUITY
http://ourworld.compuserve.com/homepages/ubikk/env4.htm. This Website includes internships, tips, and links to other databases of environmental job openings.

INTERNATIONAL & ENVIRONMENTAL JOB BULLETINS
http://www.sas.upenn.edu/African_Studies/Publications/International_Environmental_16621.html. Provides a wealth of information on bulletins, magazines, and resources for jobseekers who are looking to get into the environmental field. Most of these resources are on a subscription basis and provide job openings and other information. This information was compiled by Dennis F. Desmond.

LINKS TO SOURCES OF INFORMATION ON ENVIRONMENTAL JOBS
http://www.utexas.edu/ftp/student/scb/joblinks.html. Provides links to numerous sites that offer job openings and information in the environmental field.

FABRICATED/PRIMARY METALS AND PRODUCTS

The fabricated metals industry is on the rebound after a rough time in the early '90s. In 1996, domestic steel consumption reached 106 million tons, a 33 percent increase from the mid-'80s. U.S. Industry and Trade Outlook 1998 *reported that employment in the steel industry remains stable. Steel makers have managed to cut costs and increase productivity while at the same time keeping employment levels steady. Forecasters predicted that in 1998, shipments of steel mill products should increase by 2 percent as a result of demand from automobile manufacturers and the construction market. However, competition overseas could affect profits for U.S. companies.*

In 1998, aluminum supply was expected to remain low with prices remaining solid. The transportation sector was expected to increase demand for metal castings, and commercial aircraft deliveries still had a heavy reliance on plate products.

ATZ MECHANICAL CONTRACTORS
P.O. Box 362, East Chicago IN 46312. 219/977-1090. **Physical address:** 2801 West Ninth Avenue, Gary IN. **Contact:** Human Resources. **Description:** A steel fabricator.

ALCOA (ALUMINUM COMPANY OF AMERICA)
P.O. Box 10, Newburgh IN 47629. 812/853-6111. **Contact:** Human Resources. **World Wide Web address:** http://www.alcoa.com. **Description:** A leading producer of aluminum and alumina. Alcoa serves customers in the packaging, automotive, aerospace, construction, and other markets with a variety of fabricated and finished products. The company is organized into 22 business units, with 169 operating and sales locations in 26 countries.

ALLTRISTA CORPORATION
P.O. Box 5004, Muncie IN 47307-5004. 765/281-5000. **Contact:** Devona Coffey, Human Resources. **Description:** Alltrista is a diversified manufacturer doing business in a number of product and service areas including a line of home food preservation products, such as consumer canning jars, jar closures, and related food products; high-barrier, multilayer, co-extruded plastic products, including sheet-formed containers and retort containers; copper-plated zinc penny blanks, cans for use in zinc/carbon batteries, and other industrial zinc products; protective coating application and decorative lithography services; tin-plated steel aluminum and light-gauge rolled products; thermoformed plastic refrigerator door liners, separators, and evaporator trays; injection molded plastics products; and software and hardware for non-destructive inspection systems. **Corporate headquarters location:** This Location.

AMERICAN STEEL FOUNDRIES
3761 Canal Street, East Chicago IN 46312. 219/397-0246. **Contact:** Personnel Department. **Description:** Manufactures steel castings for industrial use and products for the transportation industry.

BETHLEHEM STEEL CORPORATION
P.O. Box 248, Chesterton IN 46304. 219/787-3291. **Fax:** 219/787-2597. **Contact:** Human Resources. **World Wide Web address:** http://www.bethsteel.com. **Description:** Manufactures and sells a wide variety of steel mill products, such as sheet and tin mill products, plates, bars, and rods. Operations of Bethlehem Steel also include marine construction and repair, and the mining and sale of raw materials. **Common positions include:** Blue-Collar Worker Supervisor;

Electrical/Electronics Engineer; Industrial Production Manager; Manufacturing Engineer; Mechanical Engineer; Metallurgical Engineer; Operations Manager; Production Manager; Project Manager; Typist/Word Processor. **Educational backgrounds include:** Engineering. **Office hours:** Monday - Friday, 7:30 a.m. - 4:00 p.m. **Other area locations:** Burns Harbor IN. **Other U.S. locations:** Sparrows Point MD; Lackawanna NY; Steelton PA. **Number of employees at this location:** 6,000.

CHICAGO STEEL & TINPLATE INC.
700 Chase Street, Gary IN 46404. 219/949-1111. **Contact:** Human Resources. **Description:** Engaged in tension leveling steel for other companies. Services also include cleaning, drying, degreasing, and recoiling. **Number of employees at this location:** 120.

CROWN CORK & SEAL COMPANY
400 North Walnut Street, Crawfordsville IN 47933. 765/362-3200. **Contact:** Human Resources. **Description:** This location manufactures metal bottle caps. Overall, Crown Cork & Seal manufactures cans, plastic bottles, metal and plastic closures, machinery for the packaging industry, and disposable medical devices and closures. **International locations:** Worldwide.

DALTON CORPORATION
P.O. Box 1388, Warsaw IN 46581-1388. 219/267-8111. **Contact:** Director of Human Resources. **World Wide Web address:** http://www.daltonfoundries.com. **Description:** A premium supplier of gray iron castings for the air conditioning and refrigeration, engine, gear box, stationary transmission, auto, heavy-duty truck transmission, marine, motor frame, and municipal water industries worldwide. **Common positions include:** Blue-Collar Worker Supervisor; Customer Service Representative; Electrician; Industrial Engineer; Mechanical Engineer; Metallurgical Engineer; Operations/Production Manager. **Educational backgrounds include:** Business Administration; Engineering; Sales. **Benefits:** 401(k); Dental Insurance; Disability Coverage; Life Insurance; Medical Insurance; Pension Plan; Profit Sharing; Tuition Assistance. **Corporate headquarters location:** This Location. **Other area locations:** Kendallville IN. **Other U.S. locations:** Ashland OH. **Operations at this facility include:** Manufacturing; Sales; Service. **Listed on:** Privately held. **Number of employees at this location:** 1,100.

DAV-CON STEEL PROCESSING CORPORATION
6799 East Dunes Highway, Gary IN 46403. 219/939-0142. **Contact:** Human Resources. **Description:** Engaged in steel processing, including mechanical descaling.

DIETRICH INDUSTRIES INC.
1435 165th Street, Hammond IN 46320. 219/931-3741. **Contact:** Human Resources. **Description:** Manufactures steel stubs.

DODGE ROCKWELL AUTOMATION
500 South Union Street, Mishawaka IN 46544. 219/256-4304. **Contact:** Human Resources Manager. **World Wide Web address:** http://www.rockwell.com. **Description:** Operates a gray and ductile iron foundry and manufactures conveyor-belt motors.

FABRICATORS CORPORATION
P.O. Box 838, Shererville IN 46375. 219/949-1300. **Contact:** Human Resources. **Description:** Engaged in steel fabrication.

HARRISON STEEL CASTINGS COMPANY
P.O. Box 60, Attica IN 47918. 765/762-2481. **Contact:** Human Resources. **Description:** Operates a steel works and blast furnace.

HAYNES INTERNATIONAL, INC.
P.O. Box 9013, Kokomo IN 46904-9013. 765/456-6122. **Toll-free phone:** 800/428-8857. **Fax:** 765/456-6155. **Contact:** Jane Ortman, Employment Representative. **Description:** Haynes International, Inc. is one of the world's leading manufacturers of nickel- and cobalt-based, heat-resistant, and corrosion-resistant alloys. **NOTE:** Entry-level positions and second and third shifts are offered. **Common positions include:** Account Manager; Blue-Collar Worker Supervisor;

Chemical Engineer; Chemist; Chief Financial Officer; Computer Programmer; Controller; Credit Manager; Customer Service Representative; Database Manager; Electrical/Electronics Engineer; Electrician; Environmental Engineer; General Manager; Human Resources Manager; Industrial Engineer; Librarian; Manufacturing Engineer; Marketing Manager; Marketing Specialist; Purchasing Agent/Manager; Quality Control Supervisor; Sales Executive; Sales Manager; Sales Representative; Secretary; Transportation/Traffic Specialist; Typist/Word Processor. **Educational backgrounds include:** Accounting; Business Administration; Chemistry; Computer Science; Engineering; Finance; Marketing. **Benefits:** 401(k); Disability Coverage; Life Insurance; Medical Insurance; Pension Plan; Profit Sharing; Savings Plan; Tuition Assistance. **Corporate headquarters location:** This Location. **Other U.S. locations:** Anaheim CA; Windsor CT; Arcadia LA; Houston TX. **International locations:** Openshaw, England; Paris, France; Zurich, Switzerland. **Operations at this facility include:** Administration; Manufacturing; Research and Development; Sales; Service. **Annual sales/revenues:** More than $100 million. **Number of employees at this location:** 950. **Number of employees nationwide:** 960.

IMS SURFACE CONDITIONING
One North Buchanan Street, Gary IN 46402. 219/881-0155. **Contact:** Human Resources. **Description:** Engaged in steel scarfing.

INDUSTRIAL STEEL CONSTRUCTION COMPANY INC.
86 North Bridge Street, Gary IN 46404. 219/885-5610. **Contact:** Human Resources. **Description:** Engaged in steel processing, including plate cutting.

INLAND STEEL
3210 Watling Street, East Chicago IN 46312. 219/399-1200. **Contact:** Human Resources. **Description:** A major diversified steelmaker. **Subsidiaries include:** Joseph T. Ryerson & Son, Inc. and J.M. Tull Industries, Inc. are major steel service businesses with 56 locations nationwide. These subsidiaries provide clients in the manufacturing industry with a variety of carbon, alloy, stainless steel, aluminum, nickel, brass, copper, and plastic products. Inland Steel also manufactures sheet, strip, and bar materials for the automotive, machinery, and appliance industries.

KENWAL STEEL COMPANY
201 Mississippi Street, Suite 3, Gary IN 46402. 219/881-1600. **Contact:** Human Resources. **Description:** A steel company that processes and sells coils which are used in a variety of applications including tubing and the automotive industry.

LTV STEEL
INDIANA HARBOR WORKS
3001 Dickey Road, East Chicago IN 46312. 219/391-2000. **Contact:** Employment. **Description:** A large, fully-integrated U.S. steel manufacturer, whose principal products include hot-rolled, cold-rolled, and coated steel sheets, as well as tubular and tin mill products serving the automotive, appliance, and electrical equipment industries. LTV operates two integrated mills in Ohio and Indiana. LTV also operates various finishing and processing facilities and tubular and tin mill plants.

LOBDELL EMERY CORPORATION
2190 Landmark Avenue, Corydon IN 47112. 812/738-7436. **Fax:** 812/738-4029. **Contact:** Human Resources. **Description:** A full-service supplier of metal stampings and welded assemblies, primarily to the automotive industry. Lobdell Emery maintains four plants in Indiana and one in Michigan. **Common positions include:** Blue-Collar Worker Supervisor; Buyer; Human Resources Manager; Industrial Engineer; Industrial Production Manager; Mechanical Engineer; Operations/Production Manager. **Educational backgrounds include:** Business Administration; Engineering. **Benefits:** 401(k); Dental Insurance; Disability Coverage; Life Insurance; Medical Insurance; Pension Plan; Tuition Assistance. **Corporate headquarters location:** Alma MI. **Subsidiaries include:** Winchester Fabrication. **Operations at this facility include:** Administration; Manufacturing. **Listed on:** Privately held. **Number of employees at this location:** 360. **Number of employees nationwide:** 2,000.

McGILL MANUFACTURING
909 North Lafayette Street, Valparaiso IN 46383. 219/465-2200. **Contact:** Human Resources. **Description:** A manufacturer of fabricated wire products.

MIDAMERICA EXTRUSIONS
4925 Aluminum Drive, Indianapolis IN 46218. 317/545-1221. **Contact:** Shirley Phillips, Controller. **Description:** Engaged in aluminum extrusions. **Common positions include:** Accountant/Auditor; Blue-Collar Worker Supervisor; Credit Manager; General Manager; Human Resources Manager; Industrial Engineer; Manufacturer's/Wholesaler's Sales Rep. **Educational backgrounds include:** Accounting; Business Administration; Engineering; Finance; Marketing. **Benefits:** 401(k); Dental Insurance; Disability Coverage; Life Insurance; Medical Insurance; Pension Plan; Savings Plan; Tuition Assistance. **Corporate headquarters location:** Danbury CT. **Parent company:** Metalmark. **Operations at this facility include:** Manufacturing. **Listed on:** New York Stock Exchange.

NATIONAL STEEL CORPORATION
4100 Edison Lakes Parkway, Mishawaka IN 46545. 219/273-7000. **Contact:** Ron Freeman, Human Resources Manager. **Description:** One of the largest domestic integrated steel companies. Products include flat-rolled carbon steel for automobiles, metal buildings, and containers; and hot and cold rolled steel for the pipe and tube industry and independent steel service centers. **Corporate headquarters location:** This Location. **Listed on:** New York Stock Exchange.

NIAGRA LASALLE STEEL COMPANY
1412 150th Street, Hammond IN 46327. 219/853-6006. **Contact:** Personnel. **Description:** A national producer of cold-finished and special-purpose steel bar products. The automotive industry is the major user of the company's steel bar products for making component parts which include shafts, gears, pins, rods, plug shells, and other automotive parts. This location's cold drawn facilities produce more than 200 standard carbon and alloy grades. In addition, these facilities offer specially-developed and trademarked high-strength steels that eliminate the need for heat treating in many part applications which cuts processing costs and saves energy. Surface Operations is responsible for the company's line of precision surface steel bars. The fluid power facility, located in Griffith IN, produces a line of induction-hardened chrome-plated steel bars for piston rods and hydraulic cylinders. **Common positions include:** Accountant/Auditor; Administrator; Advertising Clerk; Blue-Collar Worker Supervisor; Branch Manager; Buyer; Chemical Engineer; Claim Representative; Computer Programmer; Credit Manager; Customer Service Representative; Draftsperson; Electrical/Electronics Engineer; Financial Analyst; Human Resources Manager; Management Trainee; Manufacturer's/Wholesaler's Sales Rep.; Marketing Specialist; Mechanical Engineer; Metallurgical Engineer; Operations/Production Manager; Purchasing Agent/Manager; Quality Control Supervisor; Systems Analyst; Transportation/Traffic Specialist. **Benefits:** Dental Insurance; Disability Coverage; Life Insurance; Medical Insurance; Pension Plan; Profit Sharing; Savings Plan; Stock Option; Tuition Assistance; Vision Insurance. **Corporate headquarters location:** Houston TX. **Parent company:** Quanex Corporation. **Operations at this facility include:** Divisional Headquarters. **Listed on:** American Stock Exchange.

NUCOR STEEL
Rural Route 2, Box 311, Crawfordsville IN 47933. 765/364-1323. **Contact:** Human Resources. **World Wide Web address:** http://www.ns-ind.com. **Description:** Part of Nucor Corporation's Nucor Steel Division, which produces bars, angles, light structural, sheet, and special steel products. **Parent company:** Nucor Corporation is a manufacturer of steel products, whose other divisions include Vulcraft, one of the nation's largest producers of steel joists and joist girders; Nucor Cold Finish, which produces cold-finished steel bars used extensively for shafting and machined precision parts; Nucor Grinding Balls, which produces steel grinding balls in Utah for the mining industry; Nucor Fastener, a steel bolt-making facility; Nucor Bearing Products, Inc., which produces steel bearings and machined steel parts; and Nucor Building Systems, which produces metal buildings and components.

OLIN BRASS/INDIANAPOLIS
1800 South Holt Road, Indianapolis IN 46241. 317/244-2461. **Contact:** Personnel. **Description:** A fabricated metals company engaged in the rolling, drawing, and extruding of copper.

PHELPS DODGE MAGNET WIRE COMPANY
One Technology Center, 2131 South Coliseum Boulevard, Fort Wayne IN 46803. 219/421-5400. **Contact:** Human Resources. **World Wide Web address:** http://www.pdmw.com. **Description:** Manufactures magnet wire and houses the company's technology center.

PORTLAND FORGE
P.O. Box 905, Portland IN 47371. 219/726-8121. **Contact:** Marc Pendel, Vice President of Human Resources. **Description:** Manufactures carbon and alloy steel forgings. **Common positions include:** Accountant/Auditor; Biomedical Engineer; Blue-Collar Worker Supervisor; Buyer; Ceramics Engineer; Computer Programmer; Cost Estimator; Designer; Electrical/Electronics Engineer; Electrician; Human Resources Manager; Industrial Engineer; Materials Engineer; Mechanical Engineer; Metallurgical Engineer; Purchasing Agent/Manager; Quality Control Supervisor; Systems Analyst. **Benefits:** 401(k); Dental Insurance; Disability Coverage; Life Insurance; Medical Insurance; Pension Plan; Stock Option; Tuition Assistance. **Corporate headquarters location:** Los Angeles CA. **Parent company:** Teledyne Industries is a diversified producer of industrial and aviation machines, machine tools, aviation and electronics equipment, specialty metals, and consumer products. Major products of industrial segments are internal combustion engines, including air- and water-cooled, gasoline, and diesel fuel engines. **Listed on:** New York Stock Exchange. **Number of employees at this location:** 355. **Number of employees nationwide:** 20,000.

REPUBLIC ENGINEERED STEELS, INC.
4000 East Seventh Avenue, Gary IN 46403. 219/939-3400. **Contact:** Human Resources. **Description:** Produces stainless steel, alloy steel, billets, bar, rod, wire, special shapes, and nickel-based alloys.

SILGAN CONTAINER CORPORATION
2501 165th Street, Hammond IN 46320. 219/845-1500. **Contact:** Human Resources. **Description:** Manufactures metal food cans, aluminum food containers, and convenience ends for food cans.

SILGAN CONTAINER CORPORATION
2201 West Maryland Street, Evansville IN 47712. 812/425-6221. **Contact:** Human Resources. **Description:** This location manufactures metal lids. Overall, the company manufactures metal food cans, aluminum food containers, and convenience ends for food cans.

TELEDYNE CASTING SERVICE
P.O. Box 488, La Porte IN 46352. 219/362-1000. **Contact:** Personnel. **Description:** Manufactures gray and ductile iron castings.

U.S. STEEL GROUP GARY WORKS
One North Broadway, Gary IN 46402. 219/888-3355. **Contact:** Human Resources. **Description:** A steel mill. **Parent company:** U.S. Steel.

WABASH ALLOYS
P.O. Box 466, Wabash IN 46992. 219/563-7461. **Fax:** 219/563-5997. **Contact:** Bill Chaflin, Vice President of Human Resources. **Description:** Wabash Alloys is engaged in the smelting of secondary aluminum. **Common positions include:** Accountant/Auditor; Blue-Collar Worker Supervisor; Budget Analyst; Buyer; Computer Programmer; Credit Manager; Customer Service Representative; Draftsperson; Electrician; Environmental Engineer; Financial Analyst; General Manager; Human Resources Manager; Industrial Engineer; Industrial Production Manager; Management Trainee; Materials Engineer; Metallurgical Engineer; Operations/Production Manager; Purchasing Agent/Manager; Quality Control Supervisor; Software Engineer; Systems Analyst. **Educational backgrounds include:** Accounting; Computer Science; Engineering; Marketing. **Benefits:** 401(k); Dental Insurance; Disability Coverage; Life Insurance; Medical Insurance; Pension Plan; Profit Sharing; Savings Plan; Tuition Assistance. **Corporate headquarters location:** Boston MA. **Other U.S. locations:** Nationwide. **Parent company:** Connell Limited Partnership. **Operations at this facility include:** Divisional Headquarters; Manufacturing; Sales. **Listed on:** Privately held.

***Note:** Because addresses and telephone numbers of smaller companies can change rapidly, we recommend you call each company to verify the information below before inquiring about job opportunities. Mass mailings are not recommended.*

Additional small employers:

ALUMINUM

Alcoa Closure Systems International
2485 Director's Road,Suite A, Indianapolis IN 46241. 317/390-5000.

Southern Containers Manufacturing Corp.
1701 Williamsburg Pike, Richmond IN 47374-1492. 765/983-9200.

ALUMINUM FOUNDRIES

Aluminum Foundries Incorporated
PO Box 69, Winchester IN 47394-0069. 765/584-6501.

Bohn Aluminum Inc.
PO Box 80, Butler IN 46721-0080. 219/868-2168.

Casting Technology Company
1450 Musicland Drive, Franklin IN 46131-7922. 317/738-0282.

CMI Precision Mold
PO Box 659, Bristol IN 46507. 219/825-9457.

CMI-Wabash Cast Inc.
PO Box 668, Wabash IN 46992-0668. 219/563-8371.

Fort Wayne Foundry Corporation
4910 Lima Road, Fort Wayne IN 46808-1208. 219/483-1171.

Ward Aluminum Casting Incorporated
642 Growth Avenue, Fort Wayne IN 46808-3712. 219/426-8700.

COATING, ENGRAVING, AND ALLIED SERVICES

Conforma Clad Inc.
501 Park East Boulevard, New Albany IN 47150-7252. 812/948-2118.

Craddock Finishing Corporation
PO Box 269, Evansville IN 47702-0269. 812/425-2691.

Erler Industries Inc.
PO Box 219, North Vernon IN 47265-0219. 812/346-4421.

I/N-Kote
30755 Edison Road, New Carlisle IN 46552-9728. 219/654-1000.

Industrial Coating Services
6233 Brookville Road, Indianapolis IN 46219-8213. 317/322-7450.

Industrial Coating Services
5345 Lexington Avenue, Indianapolis IN 46219-7025. 317/351-0052.

Ken-Koat Group Corporation
PO Box 1027, Huntington IN 46750-1027. 219/356-4192.

Paint & Assembly Corp.
11700 N State Road 37, Elwood IN 46036-9024. 765/552-0851.

Roll Coater Inc.
PO Box 326, Kingsbury IN 46345-0326. 219/393-3561.

Roll Coater Inc.
PO Box 787, Greenfield IN 46140-0787. 317/462-7761.

DIECASTINGS

DuPage Die Casting of Indiana
410 Weatherhead Street, Angola IN 46703-1025. 219/665-9481.

Madison Precision Products
94 E 400 N, Madison IN 47250-9599. 812/273-4702.

ELECTROMETALLURGICAL PRODUCTS

Hoskin's Manufacturing Company
71103 County Road 23, New Paris IN 46553-9146. 219/831-2965.

FABRICATED METAL PRODUCTS

GKN Sinter Metals Inc.
PO Box 312, Salem IN 47167-0312. 812/883-3381.

Magnequench International Inc.
6435 Scatterfield Road, Anderson IN 46013-9619. 765/648-5000.

Motion Control
PO Box 1327, Logansport IN 46947-5327. 219/753-6391.

Perfecto Manufacturing Inc.
20975 Creek Rd, Noblesville IN 46060-9383. 317/773-6627.

Reelcraft Industries Inc.
PO Box 248, Columbia City IN 46725-0248. 219/248-8188.

Schwab Corp.
PO Box 70, Cannelton IN 47520-0070. 812/547-7041.

Ugimagnet Corporation
405 Elm St, Valparaiso IN 46383-3620. 219/462-3131.

Voyager Inc.
53468 Ada Dr, Elkhart IN 46514-9211. 219/264-9504.

FABRICATED STRUCTURAL METAL PRODUCTS

Active Products Corporation
PO Box 479, Marion IN 46952-0479. 765/664-9084.

Amerimark Building Products
PO Box 107, Bourbon IN 46504-0107. 219/342-3315.

Amfab Limited
PO Box 4124, Elkhart IN 46514-0124. 219/264-2190.

Bright Sheet Metal Company
2749 Tobey Drive, Indianapolis IN 46219-1417. 317/895-3939.

Brock Manufacturing
PO Box 2000, Milford IN 46542-2000. 219/658-4191.

Challenge Door Company
PO Box 259, Ligonier IN 46767-0259. 219/894-7111.

Galbreath Incorporated
PO Box 220, Winamac IN 46996-0220. 219/946-6631.

Girtz Industries Inc.
5262 N East Shafer Drive, Monticello IN 47960-7313. 219/278-7510.

Heat Transfer Specialties Incorporated
1202 Port Road, Jeffersonville IN 47130-8437. 812/288-5889.

Imperial Products Inc.
PO Box 368, Richmond IN 47375-0368. 765/966-0322.

Kennedy Tank & Manufacturing Company
PO Box 47070, Indianapolis IN 46247-0070. 317/787-1311.

La Grange Products Incorporated
PO Box 658, Fremont IN 46737-0658. 219/495-3025.

Linel Signature
101 Linel Drive, Mooresville IN 46158-8254. 317/831-5314.

Master Fit Manufacturing
1853 Ludlow Avenue, Indianapolis IN 46201-1064. 317/639-4404.

MI Home Products Inc.
PO Box 160, Brazil IN 47834-0160. 812/443-4631.

Micrometal Corporation
3419 Roosevelt Avenue, Indianapolis IN 46218-3761. 317/543-5980.

Milbank Manufacturing Company Inc.
PO Box 754, Kokomo IN 46903-0754. 765/452-5694.

Modern Door Corporation
PO Box 137, Walkerton IN 46574-0137. 219/586-3117.

Modine Manufacturing Company
PO Box 630, Logansport IN 46947-0630. 219/722-2211.

Ottenweller Company Incorporated
3011 Congressional Parkway, Fort Wayne IN 46808-1395. 219/484-3166.

Padgett Inc.
PO Box 1375, New Albany IN 47151-1375. 812/945-1299.

Phoenix Fabricators & Erectors
182 S County Road 900 E, Indianapolis IN 46234-8973. 317/271-7002.

Ran-Paige Company Inc.
PO Box B, Sellersburg IN 47172-0902. 812/246-3339.

SPI
PO Box 23, Logansport IN 46947-0023. 219/753-6323.

Stewart-Warner Southwind
PO Box 40, Troy IN 47588-0040. 812/547-7071.

Vern's Quality Products Incorporated
PO Box 4543, Elkhart IN 46514-0543. 219/262-9998.

Vincennes Steel Corporation
PO Box 236, Vincennes IN 47591-0236. 812/882-4550.

Wayne Metal Products Co.
400 East Logan Street, Markle IN 46770-9512. 219/758-3121.

Wiley Metal Fabricating Inc.
PO Box 1246, Marion IN 46952-7646. 765/674-9707.

FABRICATED WIRE PRODUCTS

Barber Manufacturing Company Inc.
PO Box 2454, Anderson IN 46018-2454. 765/643-6905.

Matthew-Warren Inc.
PO Box 7008, Logansport IN 46947-7008. 219/722-8200.

No Sag Products
2225 Production Road, Kendallville IN 46755-3255. 219/347-2600.

Winamac Coil Springs Inc.
PO Box 278, Kewanna IN 46939-0278. 219/653-2186.

IRON AND STEEL FOUNDRIES

ABC Rail Corporation
705 East School Street, Anderson IN 46012-1461. 765/642-4991.

Aero Metals Inc.
402 Darlington Street, La Porte IN 46350-2510. 219/326-1976.

Atlas Foundry Company Incorporated
PO Box 688, Marion IN 46952-0688. 765/662-2525.

Auburn Foundry Inc.
PO Box 471, Auburn IN 46706-0471. 219/925-0900.

Dalton Corporation
PO Box 271, Kendallville IN 46755-0271. 219/347-1820.

Gartland Foundry Company Inc.
PO Box 1564, Terre Haute IN 47808-1564. 812/232-0226.

Golden Casting Corporation
1616 Tenth Street, Columbus IN 47201-5932. 812/372-3701.

Grady Foundries Inc.
2700 Plum Street, New Castle IN 47362-3045. 765/521-8000.

Intat Precision Inc.
PO Box 488, Rushville IN 46173-0488. 765/932-5323.

Kokomo Tube Company
PO Box 28, Peru IN 46970-0028. 765/472-3951.

Noblesville Casting Inc.
PO Box 278, Noblesville IN 46061-0278. 317/773-3313.

North Manchester Foundry Incorporated
PO Box 345, North Manchester IN 46962-0345. 219/982-2191.

Omco Cast Metals
900 North Main Street, Winchester IN 47394-8208. 765/584-4000.

Rochester Metal Products Corp.
PO Box 318, Rochester IN 46975-0318. 219/223-3164.

Sibley Machine & Foundry Corp.
PO Box 40, South Bend IN 46624-0040. 219/288-4611.

Union Electric Steel Corporation
PO Box 29, Valparaiso IN 46384-0029. 219/464-1031.

Waupaca Foundry Inc.
PO Box 189, Tell City IN 47586-0189. 812/547-0705.

METAL FASTENERS

Nucor Fasteners
PO Box 6100, Saint Joe IN 46785-6100. 219/337-5611.

Ohio Rod Products Company
PO Box 416, Versailles IN 47042-0416. 812/689-6565.

Textron Inc.
4366 N Old US Highway 31, Rochester IN 46975-8322. 219/223-3131.

METAL FORGINGS

Eaton Corporation
2930 Foundation Drive, South Bend IN 46628-4337. 219/288-4446.

Impact Forge Inc.
PO Box 1847, Columbus IN 47202-1847. 812/342-4437.

Omni Forge Inc.
PO Box 67, Remington IN 47977-0067. 219/261-2115.

NONFERROUS ROLLING AND DRAWING OF METALS

8020 Company
1701 S 400 E, Columbia City IN 46725-8753. 219/248-8030.

Alcan Rolled Products
PO Box 1607, Terre Haute IN 47808-1607. 812/462-2287.

Alumax Inc.
206 Kesco Drive, Bristol IN 46507-9497. 219/848-7431.

Alumnitec Incorporated
PO Box 808, Jeffersonville IN 47131-0808. 812/282-8256.

Bundy Tubing
PO Box 397, Ashley IN 46705-0397. 219/587-6100.

Easco Aluminum
1500 East Murden Street, Kokomo IN 46901-5667. 765/457-1117.

Easco Aluminum
23841 Reedy Drive, Elkhart IN 46514-8315. 219/262-2667.

Ramco Manufacturing Company
1101 Oren Dr, Auburn IN 46706-2674. 219/925-7700.

Rea Magnet Wire Company Inc.
2800 Concord Rd, Lafayette IN 47905-3307. 765/474-3455.

Wells Aluminum Corporation
PO Box 519, North Liberty IN 46554-0519. 219/656-8111.

PRIMARY METAL PRODUCTS

Helsel Inc.
PO Box 68, Campbellsburg IN 47108-0068. 812/755-4501.

Kobelco Metal Powder of America
1625 Bateman Drive, Seymour IN 47274-1833. 812/522-3033.

Mascotech Sintered Components
3100 N State Highway, Suite 3, North Vernon IN 47265. 812/346-1566.

SCREW MACHINE PRODUCTS

Adapto Inc.
23246 Keller Road, South Bend IN 46628-5337. 219/233-1101.

GSC of Indiana
PO Box 681488, Indianapolis IN 46268-7488. 317/290-9400.

Jessen Manufacturing Company Inc.
PO Box 1729, Elkhart IN 46515-1729. 219/295-3836.

Mitchel & Scott Machine Company
1841 Ludlow Avenue, Indianapolis IN 46201-1035. 317/639-5331.

MKM Machine Tool Company Inc.
PO Box 2307, Clarksville IN 47131-2307. 812/282-6627.

Precision Machine Company Inc.
10930 E 59th St, Indianapolis IN 46236-8337. 317/826-2936.

SMELTING AND REFINING OF NONFERROUS METALS

Quemetco Inc.
7870 W Morris Street, Indianapolis IN 46231-1365. 317/247-1303.

STEEL PIPE AND TUBES

Bock Industries Inc.
PO Box 1027, Elkhart IN 46515-1027. 219/295-8070.

Indiana Tube Corporation
PO Box 3005, Evansville IN 47730-3005. 812/424-9028.

Lock Joint Tube Inc.
1400 Riverside Drive, South Bend IN 46616-1600. 219/233-9358.

Plymouth Tube Company
735 W 11th St, Winamac IN 46996-8907. 219/946-6191.

STEEL SHEET, STRIP, AND BARS

Cold Metal Products Inc.
PO Box 51530, Indianapolis IN 46251-0530. 317/248-6600.

Steel Technologies Inc.
5830 Southport Rd, Portage IN 46368-1289. 219/763-1500.

Worthington Steel Company Inc.
100 Worthington Dr, Porter IN 46304-8812. 219/929-4000.

STEEL WIRE, NAILS, AND SPIKES

Indiana Steel and Wire Corporation
PO Box 2647, Muncie IN 47307-0647. 765/288-3601.

Laclede Steel
PO Box 629, Fremont IN 46737-0629. 219/495-5360.

Michelin North America Inc.
PO Box 357, Scottsburg IN 47170-0357. 812/752-5909.

Mid-States Wire
PO Box 392, Crawfordsville IN 47933-0392. 765/362-2200.

STEEL WORKS, BLAST FURNACES, AND ROLLING MILLS

Allegheny Ludlum Corporation
PO Box 309, New Castle IN 47362-0309. 765/529-9570.

Avesta Sheffield Plate Inc.
PO Box 370, New Castle IN 47362-0370. 765/529-0120.

Beta Steel Corporation
6600 U.S. Highway 12, Portage IN 46368-1281. 219/787-8200.

National Steel Corporation
PO Box 220, Portage IN 46368-0220. 219/762-3131.

Nucor Building Systems
305 Industrial Parkway, Waterloo IN 46793-9438. 219/837-8361.

Steel Dynamics Inc.
4500 County Road 59, Butler IN 46721-9747. 219/868-8000.

WHOLESALE METALS SERVICE CENTERS AND OFFICES

Edgecomb Metals Company
PO Box 1053, Indianapolis IN 46206-1053. 317/823-1004.

Industrial Steel Company
2415 Bryant Street, Elkhart IN 46516-5536. 219/294-2502.

J&F Steel Corporation
310 Tech Drive, Chesterton IN 46304-8843. 219/764-3500.

Metro Metals Corporation
345 Salmon Drive, Portage IN 46368-1375. 219/787-8100.

Oneal Steel Inc.
PO Box 480, Shelbyville IN 46176-0480. 317/421-1200.

Tinplate Partners International
700 Chase St, Ste 300, Gary IN 46404-1211. 219/949-8829.

Westfield Steel Inc.
530 State Road 32 W, Westfield IN 46074-9349. 317/896-5587.

For more information on career opportunities in the fabricated/primary metals and products industries:

Associations

ASM INTERNATIONAL: THE MATERIALS INFORMATION SOCIETY
9639 Kinsman Road, Materials Park OH 44073. 800/336-5152. World Wide Web address: http://www.asm-intl.org. Gathers, processes, and disseminates technical information to foster the understanding and application of engineered materials.

AMERICAN FOUNDRYMEN'S SOCIETY
505 State Street, Des Plaines IL 60016. 847/824-0181. World Wide Web address: http://www.afsinc.org.

AMERICAN WELDING SOCIETY
550 NW LeJeune Road, Miami FL 33126. 305/443-9353. World Wide Web address: http://www.aws.org.

Directories

DIRECTORY OF STEEL FOUNDRIES IN THE UNITED STATES, CANADA, AND MEXICO
Steel Founders' Society of America, 455 State Street, Des Plaines IL 60016. 847/299-9160. World Wide Web address: http://www.sfsa.org.

Magazines

IRON & STEEL ENGINEER
Association of Iron and Steel Engineers, 3 Gateway Center, Suite 1900, Pittsburgh PA 15222-1004. 412/281-6323. World Wide Web address: http://www.aise.org.

MODERN METALS
Trend Publishing, 625 North Michigan Avenue, Suite 1500, Chicago IL 60611. 312/654-2300.

FINANCIAL SERVICES

Riding on the waves of a steady economy, the future appears solid for the financial services sector. Merrill Lynch & Co. had a strong year in 1997, posting over $1 trillion in customer assets. Attempting to match Merrill Lynch's success, Morgan Stanley and Dean Witter merged and Discover & Co. purchased Salomon Inc. with the help of Travelers Group.

Foreign investors are taking interest in American stocks. According to the Federal Reserve, at the end of the third quarter in 1997, foreigners had channeled $52 billion into U.S. equities. More and more investors are choosing U.S. stocks as the economy is strong, especially in contrast to the turmoil in Asia.

Despite all the good news, economists worry that the runaway U.S. stock market could be peaking, and fears of inflation are causing a downturn in the bond market, which could prompt the Federal Reserve to raise interest rates. The best opportunities through the end of the decade will be for investment managers, specifically those with experience in high-technology, natural resources, and emerging markets.

AMERICAN GENERAL FINANCE
P.O. Box 59, Evansville IN 47701. 812/468-5677. **Physical address:** 601 NW Second Street, Evansville IN 47708. **Fax:** 812/468-5119. **Recorded jobline:** 812/468-5600. **Contact:** Employment Department. **Description:** A large consumer lending and finance company with over 1,400 branches in 41 states. The company's subsidiaries are engaged in the consumer finance, credit card, and insurance businesses. Founded in 1920. **Common positions include:** Accountant/Auditor; Actuary; Attorney; Budget Analyst; Computer Programmer; Credit Manager; Economist; Electrical/Electronics Engineer; Financial Analyst; Human Resources Manager; Industrial Engineer; Management Analyst/Consultant; Management Trainee; Market Research Analyst; Mathematician; Mechanical Engineer; MIS Specialist; Statistician; Systems Analyst. **Educational backgrounds include:** Accounting; Business Administration; Computer Science; Economics; Engineering; Finance; Liberal Arts; Marketing; Mathematics. **Benefits:** 401(k); Dental Insurance; Disability Coverage; Life Insurance; Medical Insurance; Pension Plan; Profit Sharing; Savings Plan; Tuition Assistance. **Corporate headquarters location:** This Location. **Other U.S. locations:** Nationwide. **Subsidiaries include:** MorEquity. **Parent company:** American General Corporation. **Operations at this facility include:** Administration; Regional Headquarters; Sales. **Annual sales/revenues:** More than $100 million. **Number of employees at this location:** 1,300. **Number of employees nationwide:** 10,000.

CROWN MORTGAGE COMPANY
8313 Calumet Avenue, Suite D, Munster IN 46321. 219/836-0400. **Contact:** Human Resources Department. **Description:** Specializes in mortgage services.

GENERAL ACCEPTANCE CORPORATION
1025 Acuff Road, Bloomington IN 47404. 812/337-6000. **Contact:** Human Resources. **Description:** Purchases and services automobile installment sales contracts secured by used automobiles. **Number of employees nationwide:** 120.

IRWIN FINANCIAL CORPORATION
500 Washington Street, Columbus IN 47201. 812/376-1020. **Contact:** Human Resources. **World Wide Web address:** http://www.irwinunion.com. **Description:** A diversified financial services

company with operations in commercial banking, credit card services, insurance services, mortgage banking, investment services, and other financial activities.

IRWIN MORTGAGE CORPORATION
P.O. Box 6089, Indianapolis IN 46206. 317/844-7788. **Contact:** Human Resources. **World Wide Web address:** http://www.irwinmortgage.com. **Description:** A financial services company specializing in the refinancing of loans.

UNION ACCEPTANCE CORPORATION
P.O. Box 1083, Indianapolis IN 46206. 317/231-6400. **Contact:** Human Resources. **Description:** Purchases, collects, and services motor vehicle retail installment contracts.

Note: *Because addresses and telephone numbers of smaller companies can change rapidly, we recommend you call each company to verify the information below before inquiring about job opportunities. Mass mailings are not recommended.*

Additional small employers:

CREDIT AGENCIES AND INSTITUTIONS

EFS Inc.
8425 Woodfield Crossing Blvd, Indianapolis IN 46240-2495. 317/469-2000.

Tranex Credit Corp.
7602 Woodland Drive, Indianapolis IN 46278-2706. 317/872-6000.

USA Funds
PO Box 7039, Indianapolis IN 46207-7039. 317/849-6510.

USA Group Loan Services Incorporated
30 South Meridian Street, Indianapolis IN 46204-3503. 317/842-9669.

INVESTMENT ADVISORS

Natcity Investments Incorporated
251 N Illinois St, Suite 500, Indianapolis IN 46204-1930. 317/635-4551.

Oxford Financial Advisors Corp.
11711 North Meridian Street, Carmel IN 46032-4534. 317/843-5678.

MANAGEMENT INVESTMENT OFFICES

Linimac
200 East Berry Street, Fort Wayne IN 46802. 219/455-2753.

MORTGAGE BANKERS

Custom Capital
1712 N Meridian Street, Indianapolis IN 46202-1404. 317/920-5400.

Homegold
8555 N River Road, Suite 250, Indianapolis IN 46240-4304. 317/580-4866.

Waterfield Financial Corporation
PO Box 1289, Fort Wayne IN 46801-1289. 219/434-8411.

SECURITY BROKERS AND DEALERS

A.G. Edwards & Sons
1477 East 83rd Avenue, Merrillville IN 46410-6307. 219/738-6400.

Aviation Financial Group Incorporated
3950 Priority Way, Suite 106, Indianapolis IN 46240. 317/573-3830.

Charles Schwab & Co.
PO Box 388, Fishers IN 46038-0388. 317/596-4312.

City Securities Corporation
PO Box 44992, Indianapolis IN 46244-0992. 317/634-4400.

Hilliard-Lyons Inc.
PO Box 98, Evansville IN 47701-0098. 812/426-1481.

Merrill Lynch
PO Box 130, Fort Wayne IN 46801-0130. 219/424-2424.

Morgan Stanley Dean Witter
11611 North Meridian Street, Carmel IN 46032-6953. 317/843-5011.

Paine Webber Incorporated
8888 Keystone Crossing, Indianapolis IN 46240-4609. 317/816-0800.

Prudential Securities Inc.
8888 Keystone Crossing, Indianapolis IN 46240-4609. 317/844-4850.

Salomon Smith Barney Incorporated
8900 Keystone Crossing, Indianapolis IN 46240-2146. 317/581-5200.

TRUSTS

Barth Foundation Inc.
1934 N Illinois Street, Indianapolis IN 46202-1319. 317/924-6226.

Indiana University Foundation
PO Box 500, Bloomington IN 47402-0500. 812/855-8311.

McCartin Foundation
4508 Columbia Avenue, Hammond IN 46327-1665. 219/931-6600.

For more information on career opportunities in financial services:

Associations

FINANCIAL EXECUTIVES INSTITUTE
P.O. Box 1938, Morristown NJ 07962-1938. 973/898-4600. World Wide Web address: http://www.fei.org. Fee and membership required. Publishes biennial member directory. Provides member referral service.

INSTITUTE OF FINANCIAL EDUCATION
55 West Monroe Street, Suite 2800, Chicago IL 60603-5014. 312/364-0100. World Wide Web address: http://www.theinstitute.com. Offers career development programs.

NATIONAL ASSOCIATION FOR BUSINESS ECONOMICS
1233 20th Street NW, Suite 505, Washington DC 20036. 202/463-6223. World Wide Web address: http://www.nabe.com. Offers a newsletter and Website that provide a list of job openings.

NATIONAL ASSOCIATION OF CREDIT MANAGEMENT
8815 Centre Park Drive, Suite 200, Columbia MD 21045-2158. 410/740-5560. World Wide Web address: http://www.nacm.org. Publishes a business credit magazine.

NATIONAL ASSOCIATION OF TAX PRACTITIONERS
720 Association Drive, Appleton WI 54914-1483. Toll-free phone: 800/558-3402. E-mail address: natp@natptax.com. World Wide Web address: http://www.natptax.com. A membership organization that offers newsletters and nationwide workshops.

PUBLIC SECURITIES ASSOCIATION
40 Broad Street, 12th Floor, New York NY 10004. 212/809-7000. Contact: Caroline Binn, extension 427. Publishes an annual report and several newsletters.

SECURITIES INDUSTRY ASSOCIATION
120 Broadway, 35th Floor, New York NY 10271. 212/608-1500. World Wide Web address: http://www.sia.com. Contact: Phil Williams, Membership. Publishes a security industry yearbook. Membership required.

TREASURY MANAGEMENT ASSOCIATION
7315 Wisconsin Avenue, Suite 600-W, Bethesda MD 20814. 301/907-2862. World Wide Web address: http://www.tma-net.org/treasury.

Directories

DIRECTORY OF AMERICAN FINANCIAL INSTITUTIONS
Thomson Business Publications, 6195 Crooked Creek Road, Norcross GA 30092. 770/448-1011. Sales: 800/321-3373.

MOODY'S BANK AND FINANCE MANUAL
Moody's Investor Service, 99 Church Street, New York NY 10007. 212/553-0300. World Wide Web address: http://www.moodys.com.

Magazines

BARRON'S: NATIONAL BUSINESS AND FINANCIAL WEEKLY
Barron's, 200 Liberty Street, New York NY 10281. 212/416-2700.

FINANCIAL PLANNING
40 West 57th Street, 11th Floor, New York NY 10019. 212/765-5311.

FINANCIAL WORLD
1328 Broadway, 3rd Floor, New York NY 10001. 212/594-5030.

FUTURES: THE MAGAZINE OF COMMODITIES AND OPTIONS
250 South Wacker Drive, Suite 1150, Chicago IL 60606. 312/977-0999. World Wide Web address: http://www.futuresmag.com.

INSTITUTIONAL INVESTOR
488 Madison Avenue, 12th Floor, New York NY 10022. 212/303-3300.

Online Services

FINANCIAL/ACCOUNTING/INSURANCE JOBS PAGE
http://www.nationjob.com/financial. This Website provides a list of financial, accounting, and insurance job openings.

JOBS IN CORPORATE FINANCE
http://www.cob.ohio-state.edu/dept/fin/jobs/corpfin.htm.

NATIONAL BANKING NETWORK: RECRUITING FOR BANKING AND FINANCE
http://www.banking-financejobs.com. Offers a searchable database of job openings in financial services and banking.

FOOD AND BEVERAGES/AGRICULTURE

The food and beverages industry constitutes the nation's largest sector of manufacturing, and the demand for processed food and beverages should increase moderately as the market becomes more globalized. With the popularity of pre-cooked meals, supermarkets have increased spending on prepared foods; Technomic Inc., a food industry consulting firm, forecasted that these sales would rise by about 7 percent in 1998.

According to Business Week, *about 15 percent of packaged food industry jobs were eliminated between 1996 and 1998. The trend in the packaged food business is toward cutbacks in the number of brands offered as well as less coupons for consumers. By reducing the number of brands, food companies are able to spend less money on marketing and focus on top-selling products. General Mills, for example, has eliminated all but its more profitable cereals.*

Overall, the U.S. Department of Labor projects a slow decline in food industry employment through the year 2005, particularly for those occupations hurt by rising operating costs, including food processors and butchers. Agricultural careers are also expected to decline through 2005. However, the dairy sector should see about 3 percent annual growth over the next five years, due mainly to strong demand for reduced fat milk, natural cheese, and frozen desserts.

AMERICAN BOTTLING
One North Bridge Street, Gary IN 46404. 219/882-3100. **Contact:** Human Resources. **Description:** Produces, packages, and distributes a variety of soft drink and juice products.

CALUMET BREWERIES
6536 Osborne Avenue, Hammond IN 46320. 219/845-2337. **Contact:** Human Resources. **Description:** A beverage distributor.

CENTRAL SOYA COMPANY
P.O. Box 1400, Fort Wayne IN 46801-1400. **Contact:** Human Resources. **Description:** Manufactures soy proteins, lecithins, and feed. **NOTE:** This firm does not accept unsolicited resumes. Please only respond to advertised openings.

CERESTAR
1100 Indianapolis Boulevard, Hammond IN 46320. 219/659-2000. **Contact:** Laura Cosel, Human Resources Manager. **Description:** A leading manufacturer and marketer of corn and tobacco products. The corn processing business produces a wide variety of products ranging from sweeteners, such as corn syrup, to food starches. The tobacco products business manufactures and markets cigars with brand names such as Swisher Sweets, King Edward, Optimo, Bering, and a variety of smokeless tobacco products including Silver Creek and Redwood moist snuff; Navy and Railroad Mills dry snuff; and Chattanooga Chew, Lancaster, and Mail Pouch chewing tobaccos. **Corporate headquarters location:** Stamford CT. **Other U.S. locations:** Decatur AL; Dimmitt TX.

COUNTRYMARK COOPERATIVE, INC.
1200 Refinery Road, Mount Vernon IN 47620. 812/838-4341. **Contact:** Human Resources. **Description:** Manufactures, purchases, distributes, markets, and sells agricultural inputs and products.

DOLLY MADISON BAKERY
INTERSTATE BRANDS CORPORATION
3060 National Road, Columbus IN 47201. 812/372-4443. **Contact:** Gary Spiker, Personnel Manager. **Description:** A manufacturer and wholesaler of bread products. **Benefits:** Dental Insurance; Disability Coverage; Employee Discounts; Life Insurance; Medical Insurance; Pension Plan; Savings Plan. **Corporate headquarters location:** Kansas City MO.

FARBEST FOODS INC.
P.O. Box 240, Huntingburg IN 47542. 812/683-4200. **Fax:** 812/683-4226. **Contact:** Judy Jochem-Nino, Human Resources Manager. **Description:** A turkey processing plant. **Common positions include:** Agricultural Engineer; Blue-Collar Worker Supervisor; Clerical Supervisor; Electrical/Electronics Engineer; Food Scientist/Technologist; Human Resources Manager; Industrial Engineer; Manufacturer's/Wholesaler's Sales Rep.; Mechanical Engineer; Operations/Production Manager; Wholesale and Retail Buyer. **Educational backgrounds include:** Agricultural Science; Engineering. **Benefits:** 401(k); Dental Insurance; Disability Coverage; Employee Discounts; Life Insurance; Medical Insurance. **Corporate headquarters location:** This Location. **Operations at this facility include:** Administration; Manufacturing; Sales. **Listed on:** Privately held. **Annual sales/revenues:** $11 - $20 million. **Number of employees at this location:** 575.

FAVORITE BRANDS INTERNATIONAL
151 West Ohio Street, Kendallville IN 46755. 219/347-1300. **Contact:** Human Resources. **Description:** Manufactures caramel candies.

FRITO-LAY INC.
323 South County Road 300 West, Frankfort IN 46041. 765/659-1831. **Contact:** Human Resources. **World Wide Web address:** http://www.fritolay.com. **Description:** An office location of the worldwide manufacturer and wholesaler of snack products, which nationally markets a full-line of snack products including Fritos Corn Chips, Lays Potato Chips, Doritos Tortilla Chips. **Corporate headquarters location:** Plano TX. **Parent company:** PepsiCo (Purchase NY) operates within two industry segments: beverages and snack foods. The beverage segment markets and manufactures concentrates for its brands for sale to franchised bottlers worldwide. The segment also operates bottling plants and distribution facilities of its own located in the U.S. and key international markets and distributes ready-to-drink Lipton tea products under a joint-venture agreement. In addition, under separate distribution and joint-venture agreements, the segment distributes certain previously-existing, as well as jointly-developed, Ocean Spray juice products. The international snack food business includes major operations in Mexico, the United Kingdom, and Canada. **Number of employees nationwide:** 29,000.

INTERSTATE BRANDS CORPORATION
2929 North Shadeland Avenue, Indianapolis IN 46219. 317/547-9421. **Contact:** Human Resources. **World Wide Web address:** http://www.irin.com/ibc. **Description:** This location operates as part of a national wholesale bakery. Overall, Interstate Brands is engaged in the production and distribution of a line of bread and cake products with brand names including Wonder Bread and Hostess. **Benefits:** Dental Insurance; Disability Coverage; Life Insurance; Medical Insurance; Pension Plan; Savings Plan; Tuition Assistance.

PERDUE FARMS, INC.
P.O. Box 539, Washington IN 47501. 812/254-0536. **Contact:** John Tranum, Human Resources Director.**World Wide Web address:** http://www.perdue.com. **Description:** One of the largest suppliers of fresh poultry products in the United States. **Benefits:** 401(k); Disability Coverage; Employee Discounts; Life Insurance; Medical Insurance; Pension Plan; Tuition Assistance. **Special programs:** Internships. **Corporate headquarters location:** Salisbury MD. **Number of employees nationwide:** 18,000.

PILLSBURY COMPANY
707 Pillsbury Lane, New Albany IN 47150. 812/944-8411. **Contact:** Human Resources. **Description:** Manufactures and markets food products for consumer, industrial, and international markets.

PREMIERE CANDY
604 Hoffman Street, Hammond IN 46325. 219/932-2400. **Contact:** Human Resources. **Description:** Manufactures, packages, and distributes candy products.

SCOTT SEED COMPANY
709 East Fourth Street, New Albany IN 47150. 812/945-0229. **Contact:** Larry Bergamini, Human Resources Director. **Description:** Specializes in distributing forage and turf grass seed varieties including corn, alfalfa, forage seed, farm grasses, bird food, pet food, and small grains. Scott Seed Company's sales are made through wholesale farm seed distributors serving independent operators, dealers, garden centers, farmers, and other companies. **Parent company:** ABT (AgriBioTech, Inc.) is a specialized distributor of forage and turf grass seed. The company distributes the following non-seed products: Bloatenz Plus, a bloat preventative administered to the drinking water of cattle, permitting them to graze on alfalfa safely; and PDS-1000, marketed in conjunction with Bloatenz Plus, a microprocessor-controlled, precision dispensing system designed to dispense solutions into the drinking water of livestock at a preset dosage rate. Other subsidiaries of ABT include: Halsey Seed Company; Hobart Seed Company; Seed Resource, Inc.; and Sphar & Company.

SEAGRAM'S
7 Ridge Avenue, P.O. Box 7, Lawrenceburg IN 47025. 812/537-0700. **Contact:** Human Resources. **Description:** A large producer of distilled spirits and wines.

TYSON FOODS, INC.
P.O. Box 430, Corydon IN 47112. 812/738-3217. **Contact:** Dixie Cockerell, Human Resources Manager. **World Wide Web address:** http://www.tyson.com. **Description:** Manufactures and sells poultry products, luncheon meats, egg products, and frozen entrees to customers in the fast food, restaurant, warehouse club, institutional, and supermarket businesses. The company owns and operates facilities involved in the resale of purchased products, distribution, manufacturing, food processing, packaging, and marketing industries. **Benefits:** 401(k); Dental Insurance; Disability Coverage; Life Insurance; Medical Insurance; Savings Plan; Stock Option; Tuition Assistance. **Corporate headquarters location:** Springdale AR. **Listed on:** New York Stock Exchange. **Number of employees nationwide:** 8,500.

U.S. FOODSERVICE
P.O. Box 1049, Fort Wayne IN 46801. 219/432-0621. **Physical address:** 7235 Vicksburg Pike, Fort Wayne IN. **Toll-free phone:** 800/348-4910. **Fax:** 219/432-3376. **Contact:** Human Resources. **World Wide Web address:** http://www.usfoodservice.com. **Description:** An institutional food production and distribution company with clients in the restaurant and health care industries. **Corporate headquarters location:** Columbia MD.

UNIVERSAL FLAVORS
5600 West Raymond Street, Indianapolis IN 46241. 317/243-3521. **Contact:** Director of Human Resources. **Description:** A manufacturer of flavors for the food and beverage industry.

WYANDOT, INC.
125 Peacely Street, Jeffersonville IN 47130. 812/283-3528. **Contact:** John Holzapfel, Human Resources Manager. **Description:** Manufactures potato chips, corn chips, and other snack foods.

Note: *Because addresses and telephone numbers of smaller companies can change rapidly, we recommend you call each company to verify the information below before inquiring about job opportunities. Mass mailings are not recommended.*

Additional small employers:

ALCOHOL WHOLESALE

Cameron Springs Water Co.
PO Box 1602, Indianapolis IN 46206-1602. 317/636-6092.

Monarch Beverage Company Inc.
PO Box 438, Indianapolis IN 46206-0438. 317/821-1300.

North Coast Distributing Incorporated
PO Box 1123, Valparaiso IN 46384-1123. 219/464-2337.

Olinger Distributing Company
PO Box 151, Indianapolis IN 46206-0151. 317/876-1188.

ANIMAL SPECIALTY SERVICES

Indiana Packers Corporation
PO Box 318, Delphi IN 46923-0318. 765/564-3680.

Perdue Farms Incorporated
4586 N US Highway 52, Thorntown IN 46071-9287. 765/436-7990.

BAKERY PRODUCTS

Alpha Baking Company Inc.
360 N Fail Road, La Porte IN 46350-8811. 219/324-7440.

BIK Inc.
2618 E U.S. Highway 52, Morristown IN 46161-9798. 765/763-6114.

Dawn Food Products Frozen Division
1300 E Summit Street, Crown Point IN 46307-2744. 219/662-3296.

Holsum of Fort Wayne Inc.
PO Box 11468, Fort Wayne IN 46858-1468. 219/456-2130.

KBW Inc.
4201 Industrial Boulevard, Indianapolis IN 46254-2515. 317/297-2000.

Kreamo Bakers
1910 Lincoln Way Way, South Bend IN 46628-2622. 219/234-0188.

Lewis Brothers Bakeries
500 N Fulton Avenue, Evansville IN 47710-1571. 812/425-4642.

Lewis Brothers Bakeries
3114 Old Decker Road, Vincennes IN 47591-6109. 812/886-6533.

Lewis Brothers Bakeries
PO Box 426, La Porte IN 46352-0426. 219/362-4561.

New Horizons Baking Company
PO Box 695, Fremont IN 46737-0695. 219/495-9834.

Nickle's Bakery Indiana Inc.
600 Harrison Street, Suite 14, Elkhart IN 46516-2706. 219/293-0608.

Perfection Bakeries Inc.
350 Pearl St, Fort Wayne IN 46802-1508. 219/424-8245.

BEVERAGES

7-Up Bottling Company
8258 Zionsville Road, Indianapolis IN 46268-1627. 317/875-4900.

Alcatraz Brewing Company
49 W Maryland Street, Indianapolis IN 46204-3522. 317/488-1230.

Coca-Cola Bottling Company of Fort Wayne
PO Box 10750, Fort Wayne IN 46853-0750. 219/747-1084.

Coca-Cola Bottling Company of Indianapolis
5000 W 25th Street, Indianapolis IN 46224-3378. 317/243-3771.

Del Monte Foods
506 North Street, Plymouth IN 46563-1022. 219/936-3131.

Pepsi-Cola General Bottlers
PO Box 717, Fort Wayne IN 46801-0717. 219/423-1485.

Pepsi-Cola General Bottlers
9300 Calumet Ave, Munster IN 46321-2810. 219/836-1800.

Pepsi-Cola Metro Bottling Company Inc.
3110 Old Decker Rd, Vincennes IN 47591-6109. 812/885-1500.

Pluto Corporation
PO Box 391, French Lick IN 47432-0391. 812/936-9988.

Royal Crown Bottling Corp.
1100 Independence Ave, Evansville IN 47714-4549. 812/424-7978.

CHIPS AND SNACKS

Seyfert Foods Inc.
PO Box 8606, Fort Wayne IN 46898-8606. 219/483-9521.

CORN

Pioneer Hi-Bred International
7900 Pine Rd, Plymouth IN 46563-8881. 219/936-3243.

DAIRY PRODUCTS

Allen Dairy Products
PO Box 10419, Fort Wayne IN 46852-0419. 219/483-6436.

Burger Dairy Company
PO Box 8, New Paris IN 46553-0008. 219/831-2141.

Dean Foods Company of Indiana
PO Box 258, Rochester IN 46975. 219/223-2141.

Edy's Grand Ice Cream
3426 N Wells Street, Fort Wayne IN 46808-4001. 219/483-3102.

Good Humor-Breyers Ice Cream
PO Box 619, Huntington IN 46750-0619. 219/356-9530.

Ice Cream Specialties Inc.
PO Box 679, Lafayette IN 47902-0679. 765/474-2989.

Pace Dairy Foods of Indiana
PO Box 629, Crawfordsville IN 47933-0653. 765/364-5200.

Schenkel's All-Star Dairy Inc.
PO Box 642, Huntington IN 46750-0642. 219/356-4225.

Wayne Dairy Products Inc.
PO Box 250, Richmond IN 47375-0250. 765/935-7521.

DOG AND CAT FOOD

Hills Pet Nutrition
PO Box 2146, Richmond IN 47375-2146. 765/935-7071.

FOOD CROPS

Campbell Soup
Rural Route 3, Box 492, Howe IN 46746-9803. 219/367-2112.

FOOD PREPARATIONS

Ameri-Qual Foods
18200 Highway 41 North, Evansville IN 47711-8588. 812/867-1444.

Hulman & Company
PO Box 150, Terre Haute IN 47808-0150. 812/232-9446.

KB Specialty Foods
PO Box 289, Greensburg IN 47240-0289. 812/663-8184.

Orville Redenbacher Popcorn
463 Highway 30 E, Valparaiso IN 46383. 219/464-9602.

FOOD WHOLESALE

Alliant Foodservice
PO Box 280, Noblesville IN 46061-0280. 317/773-2290.

Banquet Dairy
PO Box 42099, Indianapolis IN 46242-0099. 317/244-2481.

Bonnie Lee Popcorn
PO Box 395, Van Buren IN 46991-0395. 765/934-2101.

Caito Foods Service Inc.
3120 N Post Road, Indianapolis IN 46226-6514. 317/897-2009.

Clark Foodservice Inc.
PO Box 3848, South Bend IN 46619-0848. 219/234-5011.

CSDC
PO Box 1799, Richmond IN 47375-1799. 765/962-8521.

Frito-Lay Inc.
8690 Louisiana Street, Merrillville IN 46410-6349. 219/736-1107.

Golden Stream Quality Foods Company
11899 Exit 5 Parkway, Fishers IN 46038-9627. 317/845-5534.

Hunt-Wesson Inc.
750 E Drexel Parkway, Rensselaer IN 47978-7294. 219/866-3020.

Indianapolis Fruit Company
4501 Massachusetts Avenue, Indianapolis IN 46218-3160. 317/546-2425.

J. Winkler & Sons Inc.
PO Box 68, Dale IN 47523-0068. 812/937-4421.

McFarling Foods Inc.
PO Box 2207, Indianapolis IN 46206-2207. 317/635-2633.

Otis Spunkmeyer Inc.
5757 West 85th Street, Indianapolis IN 46278-1330. 317/824-0540.

Piazza Produce Inc.
PO Box 68931, Indianapolis IN 46268-0931. 317/872-0101.

Royal Crown Company Inc.
PO Box 6930, Evansville IN 47719-0930. 812/423-4483.

Sysco
PO Box 248, Indianapolis IN 46206-0248. 317/291-2020.

Tree of Life Midwest
PO Box 2629, Bloomington IN 47402-2629. 812/333-1511.

Troyer Foods Inc.
PO Box 608, Goshen IN 46527-0608. 219/533-0302.

Wabash Coffee
PO Box 576, Vincennes IN 47591-0576. 812/882-6066.

GRAIN MILL PRODUCTS

A.E. Staley Manufacturing Company
PO Box 1398, Lafayette IN 47902-1398. 765/448-7123.

Azteca Milling Company
PO Box 23550, Evansville IN 47724-1550. 812/867-3190.

DCA Modern Maid
1515 Park Street, Evansville IN 47710-2259. 812/464-9151.

Royal Food Products
PO Box 19325, Indianapolis IN 46219-0325. 317/353-2131.

MEAT AND POULTRY PROCESSING

Armour Swift Eckrich
1711 West 18th Street, Anderson IN 46016-3803. 765/642-8071.

Berliner & Marx Inc.
PO Box 1166, South Bend IN 46624-1166. 219/291-8325.

Hinsdale Farms Ltd.
PO Box 1399, Bristol IN 46507-1399. 219/848-0344.

Iowa Beef Processors
2125 S County Road 125 W, Logansport IN 46947-8477. 219/753-6121.

Marburger Foods
PO Box 387, Peru IN 46970-0387. 765/473-3086.

Mariah Foods LP
PO Box 548, Columbus IN 47202-0548. 812/378-3366.

National Foods
PO Box 2327, Indianapolis IN 46206-2327. 317/637-5093.

Plumrose USA Inc.
PO Box 160, Elkhart IN 46515-0160. 219/295-8190.

Swift & Company
PO Box 1, Worthington IN 47471-0001. 812/875-2021.

POULTRY AND EGGS

Cort Acres
PO Box 1250, Seymour IN 47274-3850. 812/522-3964.

Culver Duck Farm Incorporated
PO Box 910, Middlebury IN 46540-0910. 219/825-9537.

Maple Leaf Duck Farms Incorporated
PO Box 308, Milford IN 46542-0308. 219/658-4121.

Rose Acre Farms Inc.
PO Box 1250, Seymour IN 47274-3850. 812/497-2557.

PREPARED FEEDS AND INGREDIENTS FOR ANIMALS

Windy Hill
PO Box 909, Portland IN 47371-0909. 219/726-7163.

PRESERVED FRUITS AND VEGETABLES

Curtice Burns Foods
PO Box 157, Mount Summit IN 47361-0157. 765/836-4801.

Henry's Pickle Company Incorporated
1430 Western Avenue, Plymouth IN 46563-1030. 219/936-4061.

Morgan Foods Inc.
90 West Morgan Street, Austin IN 47102-1741. 812/794-1170.

Olympic Food Products Incorporated
519 West Spraker Street, Kokomo IN 46901-2134. 765/452-4008.

Red Gold Inc.
PO Box 83, Elwood IN 46036-0083. 765/754-7527.

Rykoff Sexton Manufacturing
PO Box 1531, Indianapolis IN 46206-1531. 317/786-1415.

Sundor Brands Inc.
2050 N Oak Rd, Plymouth IN 46563-3407. 219/936-3138.

SUGAR AND CONFECTIONERY PRODUCTS

Zachary Confections Inc.
PO Box 219, Frankfort IN 46041-0219. 765/659-4751.

TOBACCO AND TOBACCO PRODUCTS WHOLESALE

Eby-Brown Company LLP
5820 Fortune Circle West, Indianapolis IN 46241-5503. 317/230-6300.

For more information on career opportunities in the food, beverage, and agriculture industries:

Associations

AMERICAN ASSOCIATION OF CEREAL CHEMISTS (AACC)
3340 Pilot Knob Road, St. Paul MN 55121. 612/454-7250. World Wide Web address: http://www.scisoc.org/aacc. Dedicated to the dissemination of technical information and continuing education in cereal science.

AMERICAN CROPS PROTECTION ASSOCIATION
1156 15th Street NW, Suite 400, Washington DC 20005. 202/296-1585. World Wide Web address: http://www.acpa.org.

AMERICAN FROZEN FOOD INSTITUTE
2000 Corporate Ridge, Suite 1000, McLean VA 22102. 703/821-0770. Fax: 703/821-1350. World Wide Web address: http://www.affi.com. A national trade association representing the interests of the frozen food industry.

AMERICAN SOCIETY OF AGRICULTURAL ENGINEERS
2950 Niles Road, St. Joseph MI 49085-9659. 616/429-0300. Contact: Julie Swim. World Wide Web address: http://www.asae.org.

AMERICAN SOCIETY OF BREWING CHEMISTS
3340 Pilot Knob Road, St. Paul MN 55121. 612/454-7250. World Wide Web address: http://www.scisoc.org/ asbc.

CIES - THE FOOD BUSINESS FORUM
5549 Lee Highway, Arlington VA 22209. 703/534-8880. World Wide Web address: http://www.ciesnet.com. A global food business network. Membership is on a company basis.

DAIRY MANAGEMENT, INC.
10255 West Higgins Road, Suite 900, Rosemont IL 60018. 847/803-2000. World Wide Web address: http://www.dairyinfo.com.

INTERNATIONAL ASSOCIATION OF FOOD INDUSTRY SUPPLIERS
1451 Dolley Madison Boulevard, McLean VA 22101. 703/761-2600. Fax: 703/761-4334. Contact: Dorothy Brady. E-mail address: info@iafis.org. World Wide Web address: http://www.iafis.org. A trade association whose members are suppliers to the food, dairy, liquid processing, and related industries.

MASTER BREWERS ASSOCIATION OF THE AMERICAS (MBAA)
2421 North Mayfair Road, Suite 310, Wauwatosa WI 53226. 414/774-8558. World Wide Web address: http://www.mbaa.com. Promotes, advances, improves, and protects the professional interests of brew and malt house production and technical personnel. Disseminates technical and practical information.

NATIONAL BEER WHOLESALERS' ASSOCIATION
1100 South Washington Street, Alexandria VA 22314-4494. 703/683-4300. Fax: 703/683-8965. Contact: Karen Craig.

NATIONAL FOOD PROCESSORS ASSOCIATION
1401 New York Avenue NW, Suite 400, Washington DC 20005. 202/639-5900. World Wide Web address: http://www.nfpa-food.org.

NATIONAL SOFT DRINK ASSOCIATION
1101 16th Street NW, Washington DC 20036. 202/463-6732. World Wide Web address: http://www.nsda.org.

USA POULTRY AND EGG EXPORT COUNCIL
2300 West Park Place Boulevard, Stone Mountain GA 30087. 770/413-0006. Fax: 770/413-0007. E-mail address: info@usapeec.org. World Wide Web address: http://www.usapeec.org.

Directories

THOMAS FOOD INDUSTRY REGISTER
Thomas Publishing Company, Five Penn Plaza, New York NY 10001. 212/695-0500. World Wide Web address: http://www.thomaspublishing.com.

Magazines

BEVERAGE WORLD
Keller International Publishing Corporation, 150 Great Neck Road, Great Neck NY 11021. 516/829-9210. E-mail address: kellpub@worldnet.att.net.

FROZEN FOOD AGE
Progressive Grocer Associates, 23 Old Kings Highway South, Darien CT 06820. 203/325-3500.

GOVERNMENT

Choosing a job in politics or government has never been for the faint of heart. But even with all the controversy that continues to surround the White House, the government remains the nation's largest employer. Be advised however, that the number of federal jobs is on the decline. The Defense Department is expected to reduce the size of its workforce through attrition over the next decade. The outlook for state and local government workers is somewhat better. While opportunities vary from state to state, the Bureau of Labor Statistics forecasts a 16 percent increase in state and local positions through 2005.

The U.S. Postal Service delivered the best profits in 1997, recorded at over $1 billion for the third straight year. This phenomenal success is a result of cost cuts, the elimination of 23,000 administrative jobs, improved delivery times, and last summer's United Parcel Service strike. In order remain competitive, the U.S. Postal Service is looking for ways to increase first-class mail business which has been sharply reduced by the convenience and efficiency of electronic mail, faxes, and teleconferencing.

There will be a growing need for correctional officers and prison guards as many leave due to low salaries and unattractive rural locations. Positions in fire departments and police departments will be hardest to come by as the number of candidates will exceed new openings.

The Armed Forces are reducing personnel as a result of relative international peace. As of 1997, the number of active duty personnel remained constant with decreased recruiting levels and tougher advancement standards. However, there are still opportunities for persons wishing to enter the military in the late '90s. These candidates will finish their first enlistments in 2000 when personnel reductions will be complete. It is estimated that there will then be a need for 190,000 enlisted personnel and 15,000 officers to replace retirees and those who have completed their enlistments.

DEMOCRATIC/MAJORITY CAUCUS OF THE HOUSE OF REPRESENTATIVES
INDIANA HOUSE OF REPRESENTATIVES
200 West Washington, Indianapolis IN 46204. 317/232-9794. **Contact:** Tim Jeffers, Staffing Manager. **World Wide Web address:** http://www.indiana.gov. **Description:** The legislative caucus organization of the state's Democratic Party.

HOOSIER NATIONAL FOREST/BROWNSTONE DISTRICT
U.S. FOREST SERVICE
811 Constitution Avenue, Bedford IN 47421. 812/275-5987. **Contact:** Human Resources. **Description:** Directs the management of approximately 100,000 acres of national forestland. Founded in 1891.

INDIANA DEPARTMENT OF ENVIRONMENTAL MANAGEMENT (IDEM)
P.O. Box 6015, Indianapolis IN 46206-6015. 317/232-8144. **Toll-free phone:** 800/451-6027. **Fax:** 317/233-6339. **Contact:** Dawnya Taylor, Human Resources Director. **Description:** A governmental agency. IDEM's mission is to improve the state of the environment and its resources by providing relevant services to the community.

INDIANA DEPARTMENT OF TRANSPORTATION
100 North Senate Avenue, Room N-750, Indianapolis IN 46204. 317/232-5186. **Contact:** Human Resources. **World Wide Web address:** http://www.ai.org/jobs. **Description:** A state agency involved in the construction and maintenance of all interstate and state highways in Indiana. **Common positions include:** Accountant/Auditor; Administrative Manager; Attorney; Budget Analyst; Buyer; Civil Engineer; Computer Programmer; Draftsperson; Financial Analyst; Public Relations Specialist; Purchasing Agent/Manager; Statistician; Surveyor; Systems Analyst; Transportation/Traffic Specialist. **Benefits:** Dental Insurance; Disability Coverage; Life Insurance; Medical Insurance; Pension Plan; Tuition Assistance. **Special programs:** Internships. **Corporate headquarters location:** This Location. **Operations at this facility include:** Administration; Research and Development; Service. **Number of employees nationwide:** 6,000.

INDIANA WORKFORCE DEVELOPMENT SERVICES
1776 West 37th Avenue, Gary IN 46408-2000. 219/981-1520. **Fax:** 219/884-5148. **Contact:** Human Resources. **Description:** A state employment office that offers job placement, individual skill/needs assessment, counseling, skills training, unemployment insurance protection, and labor market information. **Corporate headquarters location:** Indianapolis IN.

NAVAL SURFACE WARFARE CENTER
NSWC Crane Division, Code 0642, 300 Highway 361, Crane IN 47522. 812/854-2260. **Recorded jobline:** 812/854-3529. **Contact:** Teresa Callahan, Personnel Specialist. **World Wide Web address:** http://www.crane.navy.mil. **Description:** Provides engineering, technical, and material support to the Navy Fleet. **NOTE:** Entry-level positions are offered. **Common positions include:** Chemical Engineer; Chemist; Civil Engineer; Electrical/Electronics Engineer; Mechanical Engineer. **Educational backgrounds include:** Chemistry; Engineering; Physics. **Benefits:** Disability Coverage; Life Insurance; Medical Insurance; Pension Plan; Savings Plan. **Corporate headquarters location:** Washington DC. **Operations at this facility include:** Research and Development. **Number of employees at this location:** 3,200.

***Note:** Because addresses and telephone numbers of smaller companies can change rapidly, we recommend you call each company to verify the information below before inquiring about job opportunities. Mass mailings are not recommended.*

Additional small employers:

ADMINISTRATION OF ECONOMIC PROGRAMS

Department of Commerce
1 N Capitol Avenue, Suite 700, Indianapolis IN 46204-2026. 317/232-8800.

ADMINISTRATION OF PUBLIC HEALTH PROGRAMS

Comprehensive Mental Health Services
2401 W University Avenue, Muncie IN 47303-3428. 765/288-2032.

Department of Mental Health
402 West Washington Street, Indianapolis IN 46204-2739. 317/232-7800.

Department of Public Health
3838 N Rural Street, 8th Floor, Indianapolis IN 46205-2930. 317/541-2000.

Department of Public Health
1330 W Michigan Street, Indianapolis IN 46202-2829. 317/383-6400.

Department of Public Health
2 N Meridian Street, Indianapolis IN 46204-3003. 317/233-1325.

State Emergency Management
State Office Bldg, Rm 208, Indianapolis IN 46204-2728. 317/232-3980.

ADMINISTRATION OF SOCIAL AND MANPOWER PROGRAMS

Department of Family & Children
PO Box 154, Evansville IN 47701-0154. 812/421-5500.

Department of Welfare
PO Box 4638, South Bend IN 46634-4638. 219/236-5377.

Disability Determination
PO Box 7069, Indianapolis IN 46207-7069. 317/232-6014.

Family and Social Services Administration
402 W Washington Street, Indianapolis IN 46204-2739. 317/232-4379.

Madison County Division of Family & Children
220 E 10th Street, Suite D, Anderson IN 46016-1721. 765/649-0142.

Public Welfare Division
1200 Madison St, Clarksville IN 47129-7725. 812/283-8469.

U.S. Department of Labor
402 W Washington St,

Indianapolis IN 46204-2739. 317/232-2663.

Workforce Development Department
10 N Senate Ave, Indianapolis IN 46204-2201. 317/233-5661.

ADMINISTRATION OF VETERANS' AFFAIRS

VA Regional Office
575 N Pennsylvania St, Indianapolis IN 46204-1526. 317/226-7866.

COURTS

Vigo County Courthouse
33 S 3rd St, Terre Haute IN 47807-3430. 812/462-3000.

Wabash County Court House
1 W Hill St, Wabash IN 46992-3167. 219/563-0661.

EXECUTIVE, LEGISLATIVE, AND GENERAL GOVERNMENT

Army National Guard
PO Box 551, Greenfield IN 46140-0551. 317/462-1027.

Auditor's Office
101 W Main Street, Delphi IN 46923-1566. 765/564-3172.

Benton, County of
700 E 5th Street, Fowler IN 47944-1557. 765/884-0527.

Board of Commissioners
300 E Main Street, Suite 103, Madison IN 47250-3599. 812/265-8944.

Census Bureau
1201 E 10th Street, Room 145, Jeffersonville IN 47132-0001. 812/288-3300.

Clark, County of
501 E Court Avenue, Suite 137, Jeffersonville IN 47130-4029. 812/285-6244.

Clerk's Office
414 Main Street, Hobart IN 46342-4444. 219/942-1940.

Clinton County Commissioner's Office
180 Court House Square, Frankfort IN 46041. 765/659-6302.

Columbus, City of
123 Washington Street, Columbus IN 47201-6773. 812/376-2510.

County Commissioner's Office
440 3rd Street, Columbus IN 47201-6798. 812/379-1515.

Daviess, County of
County Courthouse, Washington IN 47501. 812/254-8662.

Dearborn, County of
215 W High Street, Suite B, Lawrenceburg IN 47025-1909. 812/537-1040.

DeKalb County Treasurer
100 S Main Street, Auburn IN 46706-2361. 219/925-1392.

Delaware County Commissioner's Office
100 W Main Street, Room 103, Muncie IN 47305-2827. 765/747-7717.

Dubois, County of
One Court House, Jasper IN 47546-3032. 812/481-7000.

Elkhart, City of
229 S 2nd Street, Elkhart IN 46516-3112. 219/294-5471.

Elkhart, County of
101 N Main St, Suite 204, Goshen IN 46526-3232. 219/534-3541.

Evansville, City of
One NW Martin Luther King Blvd, Evansville IN 47708. 812/426-5494.

Fayette, County of
PO Box 607, Connersville IN 47331-0607. 765/825-1813.

Fishers, Town of
1 Municipal Dr, Fishers IN 46038-1574. 317/595-3100.

Floyd, County of
311 West First Street, New Albany IN 47150-3570. 812/948-5433.

Garrett, City of
130 South Randolph Street, Garrett IN 46738-1468. 219/357-3836.

Gary, City of
455 Massachusetts Street, Gary IN 46402-1314. 219/881-5235.

General Assembly
200 W Washington St, Suite 302, Indianapolis IN 46204. 317/232-9561.

Goshen, City of
111 East Jefferson Street, Goshen IN 46528-3739. 219/533-8621.

Grant County Commissioner's Office
401 South Adams Street, Marion IN 46953-2037. 765/668-8871.

Green County Clerk's Office
Main Washington Street, Bloomfield IN 47424. 812/384-2005.

Griffith, Town of
111 North Broad Street, Griffith IN 46319-2218. 219/924-7500.

Hammond Water Department
5925 Calumet Avenue, Hammond IN 46320-2556. 219/853-6301.

Hancock, County of
9 E Main Street, Suite 208, Greenfield IN 46140-2320. 317/462-1109.

Henry County Board of Commissioners
101 South Main Street, New Castle IN 47362-4219. 765/529-4705.

Henry County Clerk
PO Box B, New Castle IN 47362-1044. 765/529-6401.

Howard, County of
117 South Main Street, Kokomo IN 46901-4648. 765/456-2211.

Jackson, County of
Main Street, Brownstown IN 47220. 812/358-6122.

Jeffersonville, City of
501 E Court Avenue, Jeffersonville IN 47130-4029. 812/285-6400.

Kosciusko, County of
100 W Center Street, Warsaw IN 46580-2846. 219/267-4444.

La Porte, City of
801 Michigan Avenue, La Porte IN 46350-3502. 219/362-3175.

La Porte, County of
813 E Lincolnway, La Porte IN 46350-3947. 219/326-6808.

Lafayette, City of
20 N 6th Street, Lafayette IN 47901-1412. 765/476-8404.

Lake Station, City of
3701 Fairview Street, Lake Station IN 46405-2371. 219/962-3111.

Lake, County of
2293 North Main Street, Crown Point IN 46307-1885. 219/755-3088.

Lawrence, City of
4455 McCoy Street, Indianapolis IN 46226-3980. 317/549-4804.

Lebanon, City of
201 E Main Street, Lebanon IN 46052-2686. 765/482-1201.

Madison, City of
101 W Main Street, Madison IN 47250-3777. 812/265-8300.

Madison, County of
16 E 9th Street, Anderson IN 46016-1508. 765/641-9474.

Marion, City of
301 S Branson Street, Marion IN 46952-4052. 765/662-9931.

Marion, County of
200 E Washington Street, Indianapolis IN 46204-3307. 317/327-3001.

Mayor's Office
201 Vigo Street, Vincennes IN 47591-1140. 812/882-7285.

Mayor's Office
One NW MLK Street, Room 302, Evansville IN 47708. 812/426-5581.

Mayor's Office
PO Box 280, Franklin IN 46131-0280. 317/736-3601.

Mayor's Office
601 E Broadway, Room 200, Logansport IN 46947-3156. 219/753-2551.

Monroe, County of
PO Box 547, Bloomington IN 47402-0547. 812/349-2600.

Montgomery, County of
PO Box 768, Crawfordsville IN 47933-0768. 765/362-2425.

Morgan, County of
180 S Main Street, Suite 104, Martinsville IN 46151-1979. 765/342-1002.

Muncie, City of
300 N High Street, Muncie IN 47305-1644. 765/747-4828.

Munster, Town of
1005 Ridge Rd, Munster IN 46321-1849. 219/836-8810.

Noble, County of
101 North Orange Street, Albion IN 46701-1049. 219/636-7877.

Perry, Township of
4925 Shelby St, Ste 300, Indianapolis IN 46227-4281. 317/788-4815.

Peru, City of
35 S Broadway, Peru IN 46970-2231. 765/472-2344.

Porter, County of
155 Indiana Ave, Valparaiso IN 46383-5502. 219/465-3440.

Pulaski, County of
Main Street Court House, Winamac IN 46996. 219/946-3653.

Putnam County Treasurer's Office
Court House Square, Greencastle IN 46135. 765/653-4510.

Shelbyville, City of
PO Box 568, Shelbyville IN 46176-0568. 317/392-5103.

South Bend, City of
227 W Jefferson Blvd, South Bend IN 46601-1830. 219/235-9742.

Tippecanoe, County of
20 N 3rd St, Lafayette IN 47901-1214. 765/423-9326.

Vigo, County of
201 Cherry St, Terre Haute IN 47807-2940. 812/462-3367.

FINANCE, TAXATION, AND MONETARY POLICY BODIES

Department of Revenue
100 N Senate Avenue, Room N248, Indianapolis IN 46204-2211. 317/232-2170.

Internal Revenue Service
575 N Pennsylvania Street, Indianapolis IN 46204-1526. 317/226-6016.

U.S. Customs Service
PO Box 68905, Indianapolis IN 46268-0905. 317/298-1220.

HOUSING AND URBAN DEVELOPMENT PROGRAMS

Department of Housing and Urban Development
410 N Meridian Street, Indianapolis IN 46204-1741. 317/634-2361.

Department of Housing and Urban Development
151 N Del Street, Suite 1200, Indianapolis IN 46204. 317/226-6303.

LAND, MINERAL, AND WILDLIFE CONSERVATION PROGRAMS

Bloomington Parks and Recreation Department
PO Box 100, Bloomington IN 47402-0100. 812/339-2261.

Johnson County Department of Parks & Recreation
86 W Court Street, Franklin IN 46131-2345. 317/736-3689.

Lafayette Department of Parks & Recreation
1915 Scott Street, Lafayette IN 47904-2929. 765/447-9351.

Nappanee Department of Parks & Recreation
PO Box 29, Nappanee IN 46550-0029. 219/773-2112.

South Bend Parks Department
301 S Saint Louis Blvd, South Bend IN 46617-3011. 219/235-9401.

Vincennes Department of Parks & Recreation
PO Box 242, Vincennes IN 47591-0242. 812/882-6426.

Washington Water Works
101 Northeast 3rd Street, Washington IN 47501-2937. 812/254-6143.

PUBLIC ENVIRONMENTAL QUALITY PROGRAMS

Department of Natural Resources
402 West Washington Street, Indianapolis IN 46204-2739. 317/232-4160.

Department of Public Works
151 S East Street, Indianapolis IN 46202-4027. 317/327-1600.

Gary Sanitary District
PO Box 388, Gary IN 46402-0388. 219/944-0595.

PUBLIC ORDER AND SAFETY

Allen County Police Department
12535 Lima Road, Fort Wayne IN 46818-8903. 219/428-7431.

Attorney General's Office
IGCS 402 W Washington Street, Indianapolis IN 46204. 317/232-6201.

Branchville Correctional Facility
PO Box 500, Tell City IN 47586-0500. 812/843-5921.

City Fire Department
307 Murray Street, Fort Wayne IN 46803-2336. 219/427-1170.

Columbus Sheriff's Department
PO Box 447, Columbus IN 47202-0447. 812/379-1650.

Crawfordsville Police Department
PO Box 329, Crawfordsville IN 47933-0329. 765/364-5150.

Department of Corrections
IGC South E334, Indianapolis IN 46204. 317/232-5766.

Department of Fire & Building Services
402 West Washington Street, Indianapolis IN 46204-2739. 317/232-1921.

East Chicago Police Department
2301 E Columbus Drive, East Chicago IN 46312-2806. 219/391-8400.

Elkhart Fire Department
500 East Street, Elkhart IN 46516-3610. 219/293-8931.

Evansville Police Department
15 West Mill Road, Suite K, Evansville IN 47710-4051. 812/426-5564.

FBI
P O Box 1186, Indianapolis IN 46206-1186. 317/639-3301.

Franklin Township Fire & Emergency Department
8845 Southeastern Avenue, Indianapolis IN 46239-1340. 317/862-3700.

Gary Fire Department
200 East 5th Avenue, Gary IN 46402-1309. 219/883-2797.

Gary Police Department
1301 Broadway, Gary IN 46407-1326. 219/881-1201.

Hammond City Fire Department
6110 Calumet Avenue, Hammond IN 46320-2525. 219/853-6418.

Hammond Police Department
5925 Calumet Avenue, Hammond IN 46320-2556. 219/853-6544.

Indiana State Prison
PO Box 41, Michigan City IN 46361-0041. 219/874-7258.

Indiana Women's Prison
401 N Randolph Street, Indianapolis IN 46201-3060. 317/639-2671.

Indianapolis Fire Department
200 East Washington Street, Indianapolis IN 46204-3307. 317/327-5200.

Jefferson County Sheriff's Department
300 E Main Street, Madison IN 47250-3590. 812/265-8900.

Knox County Sheriff's Department
PO Box 906, Vincennes IN 47591-0906. 812/885-2521.

Kokomo Fire Department
115 West Superior Street, Kokomo IN 46901-4638. 765/456-7400.

Marion County Juvenile Detention Center
2451 North Keystone Avenue, Indianapolis IN 46218-3503. 317/924-4841.

Muncie Police Department
300 N High Street, Muncie IN 47305-1644. 765/747-4838.

Noblesville Sheriff's Department
1 Hamilton County Sq, Noblesville IN 46060-2228. 317/776-9618.

Sheriff of Madison County
720 Central Ave, Anderson IN 46016-1548. 765/646-9290.

State Police Department
100 N Senate Ave, Indianapolis IN 46204-2211. 317/232-8241.

Tippecanoe County Sheriff's Department
2640 Duncan Rd, Lafayette IN 47904-1045. 765/423-9388.

Valparaiso Sheriff's Department
157 Franklin St, Valparaiso IN 46383-5631. 219/465-1515.

Wabash Valley Correctional Facility
PO Box 500, Carlisle IN 47838-0500. 812/398-5030.

Washington Township Fire Department
1595 E 86th St, Indianapolis IN 46240-2392. 317/251-6658.

Westville Correctional Center
PO Box 473, Westville IN 46391-0473. 219/785-2511.

REGULATORY ADMINISTRATION OF TRANSPORTATION

Bureau of Motor Vehicles
100 N Senate Ave, Room 410B, Indianapolis IN 46204-2211. 317/232-2800.

Crawford County Highway Department
312 S Court Street, English IN 47118-3606. 812/338-2802.

FAA
1850 South Sigsbee Street, Indianapolis IN 46241-3640. 317/247-2324.

Lawrence County Highway Department
916 15th Street, Room 28, Bedford IN 47421-3852. 812/275-3111.

UNITED STATES POSTAL SERVICE

United States Postal Service
2727 E 55th Street, Indianapolis IN 46220-3658. 317/464-6220.

United States Postal Service
3210 East 10th Street, Bloomington IN 47408-2400. 812/331-4554.

United States Postal Service
275 Medical Drive, Carmel IN 46032-2924. 317/846-1566.

United States Postal Service
2525 Independence Drive, Fort Wayne IN 46808-4418. 219/427-7308.

United States Postal Service
450 Jackson Street, Columbus IN 47201-6783. 812/378-2089.

United States Postal Service
601 S Main Street, Elkhart IN 46515-9000. 219/293-5502.

United States Postal Service
2719 S Webster Street, Kokomo IN 46902-3414. 765/455-8341.

United States Postal Service
1701 E Edgewood Ave, Indianapolis IN 46227-4797. 317/464-6227.

United States Postal Service
2690 S High School Road, Indianapolis IN 46241-4922. 317/464-6251.

United States Postal Service
2700 Valparaiso St, Valparaiso IN 46383-9998. 219/462-2189.

United States Postal Service
424 South Michigan St, South Bend IN 46624-4000. 219/282-8482.

United States Postal Service
4200 Bureau Road N, Terre Haute IN 47802-8128. 812/238-1531.

For more information about career opportunities in the government:

Online Services

FEDERAL JOB OPPORTUNITIES BOARD
http://fjob.opm.gov. A Telnet bulletin board that allows jobseekers to search for government jobs by department, agency, or state. The site includes information about the application process as well as opportunities overseas.

FEDERAL JOBS CENTRAL
http://www.fedjobs.com. This resourceful site has only one drawback: Its services require a fee. Federal Jobs Central offers a subscription to a 64-page biweekly publication containing over 3,500 job listings; online listings that are accessible by occupation, salary, and location; and a service that pairs you with the job you are seeking.

FEDERAL JOBS DIGEST
http://www.jobsfed.com. An excellent site for jobseekers hoping to work for the government, this site offers over 3,500 opportunities in fields such as engineering, medical, administration, management, secretarial, computer services, and law enforcement. The site also includes employment links to government agencies. For a fee, you can let *FJD*'s matching service perform the job hunt for you.

FEDWORLD
http://www.fedworld.gov. Provides a wealth of information on all aspects of the government. Besides an employment link to federal job opportunities, this site also offers access to all government agencies and many government documents.

JOBS IN GOVERNMENT
http://www.jobsingovernment.com. E-mail address: info@jobsingovernment.com. A helpful search engine for individuals seeking employment in government or the public sector. The site offers profile based searches for thousands of open positions, the ability to post and e-mail resumes, and information about current topics and resources in government.

LIBRARY JOB LEADS/GOVERNMENT JOB LISTINGS
http://www.emporia.edu/S/www/slim/resource/jobs/GovJob.htm. This Website provides many links to sites that post government job openings and information for jobseekers.

HEALTH CARE: SERVICES, EQUIPMENT, AND PRODUCTS

The rising cost of health care in the United States is influencing the move from the traditional fee-for-service plans to more cost-conscious managed care plans. Cost control is also creating a more demanding nation of health care customers who want the most for their money. In 1996, the average cost of health care per person was $3,760. Overall, spending increases have stabilized from rising at an average annual rate of 13.6 percent between 1975 and 1980 to approximately 6 percent between 1996 and 1997. If managed care continues to revolutionize the industry, the nation can expect a 6 to 7 percent average annual rate of growth through 2000. Cost-cutting improvements in the field are beginning to take shape with the advent of new technology such as the use of telemedicine. This process allows electronic images of X-rays and test results to be transmitted anywhere in the world for further consultation and diagnosis.

Consolidation is still a dominant factor in the industry. Small, independent hospitals are being purchased by large corporations to form multi-hospital enterprises. Recently, Columbia/HCA (an industry powerhouse) has been targeted in one of the largest federal investigations of health care fraud ever. Industry analysts expect the company will be sold, renamed, and split into four new smaller companies in an attempt to restructure and boost stock prices.

Health care services are still a major source of job creation in the economy. That distinction is not expected to change as the population over the age of 85 continues to grow faster than the nation's total population. With a growing elderly population, the number of home health care agencies has doubled since 1992.

Industry trends point to a stronger demand for primary care physicians, rather than specialists. Non-traditional forms of medicine such as acupuncture and home-infusion therapy are gaining acceptance by consumers, as well as insurers, which should create more job opportunities. Overall, occupations in health care will account for one-fifth of the nation's job growth from 1998 through 2005.

ANCILLA SYSTEMS, INC.

1000 South Lake Park Avenue, Hobart IN 46342. 219/947-8500. **Contact:** Toni Mola, Human Resources. **Description:** A multi-institutional, nonprofit health care corporation. Ancilla Systems, Inc. is sponsored by the Poor Handmaids of Jesus Christ. The company operates seven hospitals in Illinois and Indiana, and a home health care affiliate. The system also manages a community hospital in Indiana. Founded in 1857. **Common positions include:** Accountant; Administrative Assistant; Chief Financial Officer; Computer Operator; Computer Programmer; Controller; EEG Technologist; EKG Technician; Finance Director; Financial Analyst; Human Resources Manager; Pharmacist; Physical Therapist; Physician; Public Relations Specialist; Radiological Technologist; Registered Nurse; Respiratory Therapist; Secretary; Social Worker; Surgical Technician; Systems Analyst. **Educational backgrounds include:** Accounting; Business Administration; Computer Science; Finance; Health Care. **Benefits:** 401(k); 403(b); Dental Insurance; Disability Coverage;

Employee Discounts; Life Insurance; Medical Insurance; Pension Plan; Tuition Assistance. **Corporate headquarters location:** This Location. **Subsidiaries include:** Harbor Health Services, Inc.; Lakeshore Health Systems Incorporated; Michiana Community Hospital, Inc.; St. Elizabeth's Hospital of Chicago, Inc.; St. Joseph Medical Center of Fort Wayne; St. Joseph Mishawaka Health Services, Inc.; St. Mary's Hospital of East St. Louis, Inc. **Listed on:** Privately held. **Number of employees at this location:** 135. **Number of employees nationwide:** 4,800.

BALL MEMORIAL HOSPITAL
2401 University Avenue, Muncie IN 47303. 765/747-3007. **Recorded jobline:** 765/747-3636. **Contact:** Human Resources. **Description:** A 550-bed teaching hospital and medical referral center for east central Indiana. The hospital has comprehensive rehabilitation services and a full-service laboratory. **Common positions include:** Computer Programmer; Dietician/Nutritionist; EEG Technologist; EKG Technician; Health Services Manager; Human Service Worker; Licensed Practical Nurse; Medical Records Technician; Nuclear Medicine Technologist; Occupational Therapist; Pharmacist; Physical Therapist; Physicist; Radiological Technologist; Recreational Therapist; Registered Nurse; Respiratory Therapist; Social Worker; Speech-Language Pathologist; Surgical Technician; Systems Analyst. **Educational backgrounds include:** Health Care. **Benefits:** Dental Insurance; Disability Coverage; Employee Discounts; Life Insurance; Medical Insurance; Paid Sick Child Care; Pension Plan; Savings Plan; Tuition Assistance; Wellness Program. **Special programs:** Internships. **Operations at this facility include:** Administration; Research and Development; Service. **Listed on:** Privately held. **Number of employees at this location:** 2,500.

BIOMET, INC.
P.O. Box 587, Warsaw IN 46580. 219/267-6639. **Contact:** Darlene Whaley, Human Resources Director. **World Wide Web address:** http://www.biomet.com. **Description:** Designs, manufactures, and markets products used by orthopedic medical specialists in both surgical and non-surgical therapy. Products include reconstructive and trauma devices, electrical bone growth stimulators, orthopedic support devices, operating room supplies, powered surgical instruments, general surgical instruments, arthroscopy products, and oral-maxillofacial implants and instruments. Biomet's products are distributed worldwide. **Common positions include:** Accountant/Auditor; Financial Analyst; Marketing Specialist; Research Scientist; Sales Representative. **Corporate headquarters location:** This Location. **International locations:** Worldwide. **Number of employees nationwide:** 1,360.

BLOOMINGTON HOSPITAL
601 West Second Street, Bloomington IN 47403. 812/336-9535. **Fax:** 812/335-5447. **Contact:** Human Resources Department. **World Wide Web address:** http://www.bloomhealth.org. **Description:** A 314-bed, nonprofit, acute care hospital. **Common positions include:** Accountant/Auditor; Computer Programmer; Dietician/Nutritionist; EEG Technologist; EKG Technician; Electrician; Emergency Medical Technician; Financial Analyst; Licensed Practical Nurse; Medical Records Technician; Occupational Therapist; Pharmacist; Physical Therapist; Psychologist; Public Relations Specialist; Purchasing Agent/Manager; Radiological Technologist; Recreational Therapist; Registered Nurse; Respiratory Therapist; Social Worker; Speech-Language Pathologist; Surgical Technician; Systems Analyst. **Educational backgrounds include:** Health Care. **Benefits:** Daycare Assistance; Dental Insurance; Disability Coverage; Employee Discounts; Life Insurance; Medical Insurance; Pension Plan. **Listed on:** Privately held. **Number of employees at this location:** 2,200.

BOEHRINGER MANNHEIM CORPORATION
9115 Hague Road, Indianapolis IN 46250. **Contact:** Human Resources. **Description:** Produces medical diagnostic equipment and supplies. **NOTE:** This firm does not accept unsolicited resumes. Please only respond to advertised openings. **Parent company:** Corange.

BOSTON SCIENTIFIC CORPORATION
780 Brookside Drive, Spencer IN 47460. 812/829-4877. **Contact:** Darryl Curson, Human Resources Director. **World Wide Web address:** http://www.bsci.com. **Description:** This location manufactures disposable medical devices, such as catheters. Overall, Boston Scientific Corporation is a worldwide developer, manufacturer, and marketer of medical devices used in a broad range of interventional medical procedures including cardiology, gastroenterology, pulmonary medicine,

radiology, urology, and vascular surgery. Boston Scientific's products are used by physicians to perform less invasive procedures. **Corporate headquarters location:** Natick MA. **Other U.S. locations:** Mansfield MA; Milford MA. **Number of employees nationwide:** 2,840.

CHARTER BEHAVIORAL HEALTH SYSTEM OF INDIANAPOLIS
5602 Caito Drive, Indianapolis IN 46226. 317/545-2111. **Fax:** 317/549-0838. **Contact:** Judy Ware, Human Resources Director. **Description:** A psychiatric hospital that provides a full range of services and a wide variety of treatment options for adults, adolescents, and children. Charter Behavioral Health System offers care for depression, drug and alcohol problems, anxiety, obsessive-compulsive behaviors, and many other emotional illnesses. Treatment options include an intensive outpatient program, partial hospitalization, and inpatient treatments. **NOTE:** Entry-level positions and second and third shifts are offered. **Common positions include:** Psychiatrist; Registered Nurse. **Educational backgrounds include:** Health Care. **Benefits:** 401(k); Dental Insurance; Disability Coverage; Medical Insurance; Tuition Assistance. **Corporate headquarters location:** Atlanta GA. **Number of employees at this location:** 200.

CHARTER BEHAVIORAL HEALTH SYSTEM OF NORTHWEST INDIANA
101 West 61st Avenue, Hobart IN 46342. 219/947-4464. **Contact:** Human Resources. **Description:** A psychiatric hospital that provides a full range of services and a wide variety of treatment options for adults, adolescents, and children. Charter offers care for depression, drug and alcohol problems, anxiety, obsessive-compulsive behaviors, and many other emotional illnesses. Treatment options include an intensive outpatient program, partial hospitalization, and inpatient treatments.

CLARIAN HEALTH PARTNERS
1801 North Capital Avenue, Indianapolis IN 46202. 317/278-2980. **Contact:** Human Resources. **World Wide Web address:** http://www.clarian.com. **Description:** A hospital. **Number of employees at this location:** 5,000.

CLARK MEMORIAL HOSPITAL
1220 Missouri Avenue, Jeffersonville IN 47130. 812/283-2128. **Recorded jobline:** 812/283-2213. **Contact:** Judy Johnson, Employment Manager. **World Wide Web address:** http://www.jhhs.org. **Description:** Affiliated with Jewish Hospital HealthCare Services since 1992, the hospital provides services including CompCare occupational medicine program, emergency care, maternal-child health, inpatient psychiatric care, pediatrics, home health, and cardiology. Founded in 1922. **NOTE:** Entry-level positions and second and third shifts are offered. **Common positions include:** Certified Nurses Aide; Licensed Practical Nurse; Medical Records Technician; MIS Specialist; Nuclear Medicine Technologist; Occupational Therapist; Pharmacist; Physical Therapist; Radiological Technologist; Registered Nurse; Respiratory Therapist; Secretary; Social Worker; Speech-Language Pathologist; Surgical Technician. **Educational backgrounds include:** Health Care. **Benefits:** 403(b); Dental Insurance; Disability Coverage; Employee Discounts; Financial Planning Assistance; Life Insurance; Medical Insurance; Pension Plan; Savings Plan; Tuition Assistance. **Special programs:** Co-ops; Internships; Summer Jobs; Training. **Annual sales/revenues:** $21 - $50 million. **Number of employees at this location:** 1,400. **Number of projected hires for 1998 - 1999 at this location:** 300.

THE COMMUNITY HOSPITAL
901 MacArthur Boulevard, Munster IN 46321. 219/836-1600. **Contact:** Personnel Department. **Description:** A 305-bed hospital with a staff of over 1,900 employees, offering a wide range of medical services. The hospital operates one of the area's most advanced neonatal intensive care units, as well as a state-of-the-art oncology center. Founded in 1973.

DEPUY INC.
P.O. Box 988, Warsaw IN 46581-0988. 219/267-8143. **Contact:** Mark Ardington, Human Resources Manager. **World Wide Web address:** http://www.depuy.com. **Description:** A medical device manufacturing company specializing in orthopedic products, including total joint replacement and fracture management devices. **Common positions include:** Accountant/Auditor; Biological Scientist; Biomedical Engineer; Blue-Collar Worker Supervisor; Buyer; Computer Programmer; Credit Manager; Customer Service Representative; Draftsperson; Financial Analyst;

Human Resources Manager; Industrial Engineer; Marketing Specialist; Mechanical Engineer; Metallurgical Engineer; Operations/Production Manager; Purchasing Agent/Manager; Quality Control Supervisor; Systems Analyst; Technical Writer/Editor. **Educational backgrounds include:** Accounting; Biology; Business Administration; Computer Science; Engineering; Finance; Marketing. **Benefits:** Dental Insurance; Disability Coverage; Employee Discounts; Life Insurance; Medical Insurance; Pension Plan; Tuition Assistance. **Special programs:** Internships. **Corporate headquarters location:** This Location. **Other U.S. locations:** Jackson MI; Albuquerque NM. **Operations at this facility include:** Administration; Divisional Headquarters; Manufacturing; Research and Development; Service. **Number of employees nationwide:** 785.

EVANSVILLE STATE HOSPITAL
3400 Lincoln Avenue, Evansville IN 47714. 812/473-2222. **Contact:** Personnel. **Description:** A psychiatric hospital.

FLOYD MEMORIAL HOSPITAL AND HEALTH SERVICES
1850 State Street, New Albany IN 47150. 812/944-7701. **Recorded jobline:** 812/949-5660. **Contact:** Human Resources. **Description:** An acute care hospital offering 24-hour adult and pediatric emergency care. Floyd Memorial Hospital and Health Services also has an oncology unit, a critical care cardiac unit, and a full surgery center.

FRANKLIN UNITED METHODIST COMMUNITY
1070 West Jefferson Street, Franklin IN 46131. 317/736-1107. **Fax:** 317/736-1150. **Contact:** Mr. Pat Forbes, Human Resources Director. **Description:** A continuing care, retirement community. Founded in 1957. **Common positions include:** Food Service Manager; Housekeeper; Registered Nurse. **Benefits:** 403(b); Daycare Assistance; Dental Insurance; Disability Coverage; Employee Discounts; Life Insurance; Medical Insurance; On-Site Daycare; Pension Plan; Savings Plan; Tuition Assistance. **Office hours:** Monday - Friday, 8:00 a.m. - 4:30 p.m. **President/CEO/Owner:** Joseph Trueblood, Executive Director. **Annual sales/revenues:** $5 - $10 million. **Number of employees at this location:** 280.

GEMINUS CORPORATION
5281 Fountain Drive, Crown Point IN 46307. 219/791-2300. **Contact:** Personnel. **World Wide Web address:** http://www.geminus.org. **Description:** Owns and operates Cedars Academy, an inpatient mental health facility for adolescents. Geminus also operates Head Start programs, and performs accounting, marketing, and human resource functions for Southlake Mental Health (an inpatient and outpatient mental health center) and Tri-City Mental Health (a primarily outpatient mental health center). **Common positions include:** Claim Representative; Counselor; Medical Records Technician; Physician; Psychologist; Recreational Therapist; Registered Nurse; Social Worker; Teacher/Professor. **Educational backgrounds include:** Psychiatry; Psychology; Social Work. **Benefits:** Dental Insurance; Disability Coverage; Employee Discounts; Life Insurance; Medical Insurance; Pension Plan; Profit Sharing; Tuition Assistance. **Special programs:** Internships. **Corporate headquarters location:** This Location. **Operations at this facility include:** Service. **Listed on:** Privately held. **Number of employees at this location:** 550.

GOOD SAMARITAN HOSPITAL
GOOD SAMARITAN HEART CENTER
520 South Seventh Street, Vincennes IN 47591. 812/882-5220. **Fax:** 812/885-3961. **Contact:** Human Resources. **Description:** A 262-bed, acute care facility. The hospital provides a full range of services including cardiovascular surgery; neurosurgery; Women and Infants Center; cancer program; physical, occupational, and speech therapy; and hemodialysis. Good Samaritan Hospital also provides mental health and home health care services to the community. Good Samaritan Heart Center (also at this location; 812/885-3243) offers prevention, diagnosis, intervention (balloon angioplasty and pacemakers), surgery, and rehabilitation for a variety of heart ailments. **Common positions include:** Certified Nurses Aide; Licensed Practical Nurse; Medical Records Technician; Pharmacist; Physical Therapist; Physician; Psychologist; Registered Nurse; Respiratory Therapist; Secretary; Social Worker; Speech-Language Pathologist; Surgical Technician. **Educational backgrounds include:** Health Care. **Benefits:** Dental Insurance; Disability Coverage; Employee Discounts; Life Insurance; Medical Insurance; Pension Plan; Profit Sharing; Tuition Assistance.

GUIDANT CORPORATION
P.O. Box 44906, Indianapolis IN 46244. 317/971-2000. **Physical address:** 111 Monument Circle, 29th Floor, Indianapolis IN 46204. **Fax:** 317/971-2040. **Contact:** Human Resources. **World Wide Web address:** http://www.guidant.com. **Description:** Designs, develops, manufactures, and markets a broad range of products for use in cardiac rhythm management, coronary artery disease intervention, and other forms of minimally-invasive surgery. **Corporate headquarters location:** This Location.

HILLENBRAND INDUSTRIES, INC.
1025 East Pearl Street, Batesville IN 47006. 812/934-7000. **Contact:** Joyce Gagne, Human Resources. **World Wide Web address:** http://www.hillenbrand.com. **Description:** Manufactures electric-powered hospital beds, wound therapy systems, and home infusion therapy products. **Subsidiaries include:** SSI Medical Services, BLOCK Medical, and Medeco Security Locks, Inc. provide health care products and services. Through this health care division, the company provides rental equipment and manufactures pumps and locks; Batesville Casket Company manufactures caskets and sells them to funeral home directors through a marketing force in the U.S., Australia, Puerto Rico, Canada, and other areas. Batesville operates 68 North American service centers and owns a fleet of trucks; Forethought Group provides life insurance which is aimed at covering funeral and burial expenses. **Listed on:** New York Stock Exchange.

HOLY CROSS HEALTH SYSTEM
3606 East Jefferson Boulevard, South Bend IN 46615. 219/233-8558. **Contact:** Mr. Miller, Vice President of Human Resources. **Description:** A hospital management company. **Number of employees nationwide:** 18,360.

HOME HOSPITAL
2400 South Street, Lafayette IN 47904. 765/447-6811. **Contact:** Larry Strawser, Human Resources. **World Wide Web address:** http://www.homehospital.com. **Description:** A 365-bed hospital with surgery facilities, a recovery unit, Ambulatory Surgery Center, Critical Care Center, Neonatal Intensive Care Nursery, and Hook Rehabilitation Center. **Number of employees nationwide:** 1,400.

HOWARD COMMUNITY HOSPITAL
3500 South Lafountain Street, Kokomo IN 46902. 765/453-8560. **Fax:** 765/453-8380. **Recorded jobline:** 765/453-8185. **Contact:** Manager of Human Resources. **Description:** A 125-bed, nonprofit, community-based medical facility. The hospital also operates as a regional mental health center. **Common positions include:** Biomedical Engineer; Computer Operator; Computer Programmer; Counselor; Dietician/Nutritionist; Emergency Medical Technician; Licensed Practical Nurse; Medical Records Technician; Nuclear Medicine Technologist; Pharmacist; Physician; Psychologist; Registered Nurse; Social Worker; Surgical Technician. **Educational backgrounds include:** Computer Science; Health Care. **Benefits:** 403(b); Dental Insurance; Disability Coverage; Employee Discounts; Life Insurance; Medical Insurance; Paid Vacation; Pension Plan; Profit Sharing; Tuition Assistance. **Number of employees at this location:** 850.

ITO & KOBY DENTAL STUDIO
6402 Castleplace Drive, Indianapolis IN 46250. 317/849-5143. **Contact:** Human Resources. **Description:** A dental laboratory. **Benefits:** 401(k); Incentive Plan; Stock Option. **Corporate headquarters location:** Wayland MA. **Parent company:** National Dentex Corporation is one of the largest operators of dental laboratories in the United States. National Dentex serves an active customer base of approximately 9,000 dentists through its 27 full-service labs in 19 states. These dental laboratories provide a full range of custom-made dental prosthetic appliances, divided into three main groups: restorative products (crowns and bridges); reconstructive products (partial and full dentures); and cosmetic products (porcelain veneers and ceramic crowns). **Listed on:** NASDAQ. **Number of employees nationwide:** 1,000.

JOHNS DENTAL LABORATORY INC.
P.O. Box 606, Terre Haute IN 47808. 812/232-6026. **Physical address:** 423 South 13th Street, Terre Haute IN. **Contact:** Human Resources. **World Wide Web address:** http://www.johnsdental.com. **Description:** A full-service dental laboratory.

KING SYSTEMS
15011 Herriman Boulevard, Noblesville IN 46060. 317/776-6823x359. **Fax:** 317/776-6827. **Contact:** Diana Russell, Human Resources Director. **Description:** Manufactures plastic disposable breathing circuits used for the delivery of anesthesia in the operating room. **NOTE:** Entry-level positions and second and third shifts are offered. **Common positions include:** Administrative Assistant; Blue-Collar Worker Supervisor; Customer Service Representative; Manufacturing Engineer; Production Manager; Quality Control Supervisor. **Educational backgrounds include:** Engineering. **Benefits:** 401(k); Dental Insurance; Life Insurance; Medical Insurance; Tuition Assistance. **Special programs:** Summer Jobs. **Office hours:** Monday - Friday, 8:00 a.m. - 5:00 p.m. **Corporate headquarters location:** This Location. **Listed on:** Privately held. **President/Owner:** Flois Burrow. **Facilities Manager:** Bret Burrow. **Annual sales/revenues:** $21 - $50 million. **Number of employees at this location:** 350. **Number of projected hires for 1998 - 1999 at this location:** 25.

KING'S DAUGHTER'S HOSPITAL
One King's Daughter's Drive, Madison IN 47250. 812/265-5211. **Contact:** Debbie Temple, Human Resources Director. **Description:** A hospital that offers a fully equipped surgery unit with outpatient capabilities; an obstetrics unit that offers several birthing options; specialized areas for pediatrics and geriatrics; laser surgery; emergency services; an ICU; radiology; diagnostic services; oncology; respiratory care; home health care; and physical therapy. Founded in 1915.

LOGANSPORT STATE HOSPITAL
1098 State Road 25 South, Logansport IN 46947. 219/722-4141. **Contact:** Human Resources. **Description:** A district psychiatric hospital serving 24 counties in northwest and north central Indiana. **Parent company:** Indiana Family and Social Services Administration.

MARION GENERAL HOSPITAL
441 North Wabash Avenue, Marion IN 46952. 765/662-1441. **Contact:** Human Resources. **Description:** A hospital.

MEMORIAL HEALTH SYSTEM
615 North Michigan Street, South Bend IN 46601. 219/234-9041. **Contact:** Human Resources. **World Wide Web address:** http://www.qualityoflife.org. **Description:** A 525-bed, general medical and surgical hospital.

PARKVIEW MEMORIAL HOSPITAL
2200 Randallia Drive, Fort Wayne IN 46805. 219/484-6636. **Fax:** 219/480-5972. **Recorded jobline:** 219/480-5000. **Contact:** Human Resources. **World Wide Web address:** http://www.parkview.com. **Description:** A nonprofit health system which consists of several hospitals, a health plan, a foundation of employed physicians, and a managed services organization. Offerings include cardiopulmonary services (endoscopy, pulmonary rehabilitation, and respiratory care); corporate health services (industrial rehabilitation and occupational medicine); critical care center; diagnostic imaging; dietetics and food service; laboratory; Lindenview Regional Behavioral Center; Parkside Fitness Center; regional diabetes care center; regional heart center; regional neurology center (neurology unit, occupational therapy, physical therapy, rehabilitation services, and speech pathology); regional oncology center; regional orthopedic center; regional trauma center; senior health services; social services; surgical care center; and women and children's health services (fertility center, genetics lab, new life center, pediatric care, and women's health center). **Common positions include:** Accountant/Auditor; Biological Scientist; Biomedical Engineer; Clerical Supervisor; Clinical Lab Technician; Computer Programmer; Dietician/Nutritionist; EEG Technologist; EKG Technician; Emergency Medical Technician; Financial Analyst; Food Scientist/Technologist; Health Services Manager; Human Resources Manager; Human Service Worker; Librarian; Library Technician; Licensed Practical Nurse; Medical Records Technician; Nuclear Medicine Technologist; Occupational Therapist; Pharmacist; Physical Therapist; Physician; Preschool Worker; Psychologist; Recreational Therapist; Registered Nurse; Respiratory Therapist; Social Worker; Speech-Language Pathologist; Surgical Technician; Systems Analyst. **Educational backgrounds include:** Biology; Business Administration; Chemistry; Health Care. **Benefits:** 403(b); Daycare Assistance; Dental Insurance; Disability Coverage; Fitness Program; Life Insurance; Medical Insurance; Pension Plan; Tuition

Assistance. **Special programs:** Internships. **Operations at this facility include:** Administration; Divisional Headquarters; Regional Headquarters; Research and Development; Service. **Listed on:** Privately held. **Number of employees at this location:** 3,500.

PORTER MEMORIAL HOSPITAL SYSTEM
814 La Porte Avenue, Valparaiso IN 46383. 219/465-4600. **Contact:** Jim Pingatore, Human Resources Director. **Description:** Offers a growing number of health care services. The hospital's specialties include family practice, obstetrics, pediatrics, and cardiology. **Number of employees at this location:** 280.

REHABILITATION HOSPITAL OF INDIANA
4141 Shore Drive, Indianapolis IN 46254. 317/329-2233. **Fax:** 317/329-2238. **Recorded jobline:** 317/290-7441. **Contact:** Human Resources. **Description:** An 89-bed, nonprofit, physical rehabilitation facility. Rehabilitation Hospital of Indiana provides both in- and outpatient specialized care services for patients who have experienced spinal cord and head injuries, stroke, amputation, orthopedic problems, neuromuscular disease, and related disabilities. **Common positions include:** Accountant/Auditor; Claim Representative; Counselor; Dietician/Nutritionist; Education Administrator; Financial Analyst; Food Scientist/Technologist; Human Resources Manager; Medical Records Technician; Occupational Therapist; Pharmacist; Physical Therapist; Physician; Psychologist; Public Relations Specialist; Radiological Technologist; Recreational Therapist; Registered Nurse; Respiratory Therapist; Restaurant/Food Service Manager; Social Worker; Speech-Language Pathologist; Systems Analyst. **Educational backgrounds include:** Health Care. **Benefits:** Dental Insurance; Disability Coverage; Employee Discounts; Life Insurance; Medical Insurance; Pension Plan; Tuition Assistance. **Operations at this facility include:** Administration; Service. **Number of employees at this location:** 400.

ST. ANTHONY MEDICAL CENTER
1201 South Main Street, Crown Point IN 46307. 219/663-8120. **Recorded jobline:** 219/757-6177. **Contact:** Human Resources. **Description:** An acute care hospital. **NOTE:** Jobseekers are asked to call the jobline to hear a list of current openings before sending a resume. **Common positions include:** Accountant/Auditor; Buyer; Claim Representative; Clerical Supervisor; Credit Manager; Dietician/Nutritionist; EEG Technologist; EKG Technician; Electrician; Emergency Medical Technician; Food Scientist/Technologist; Human Resources Manager; Librarian; Licensed Practical Nurse; Medical Records Technician; Nuclear Medicine Technologist; Occupational Therapist; Pharmacist; Physical Therapist; Preschool Worker; Public Relations Specialist; Purchasing Agent/Manager; Radiological Technologist; Respiratory Therapist; Restaurant/Food Service Manager; Social Worker; Speech-Language Pathologist. **Benefits:** Dental Insurance; Life Insurance; Medical Insurance; Pension Plan; Tuition Assistance. **Number of employees at this location:** 1,340.

ST. JOSEPH HOSPITAL & HEALTH CENTER
1907 West Sycamore Street, Kokomo IN 46904-9010. 765/456-5403. **Fax:** 765/456-5823. **Contact:** Human Resources. **World Wide Web address:** http://www.stjhhc.org. **Description:** A medical center. **Common positions include:** Clinical Lab Technician; Computer Programmer; Emergency Medical Technician; Librarian; Licensed Practical Nurse; Pharmacist; Registered Nurse; Respiratory Therapist; Social Worker. **Educational backgrounds include:** Business Administration; Computer Science; Health Care; Liberal Arts; Marketing. **Benefits:** Daycare Assistance; Dental Insurance; Disability Coverage; Employee Discounts; Life Insurance; Medical Insurance; Pension Plan; Savings Plan; Tuition Assistance. **Operations at this facility include:** Administration. **Number of employees at this location:** 1,000.

ST. JOSEPH MEDICAL CENTER
700 Broadway, Fort Wayne IN 46802. 219/425-3016. **Fax:** 219/425-3013. **Contact:** Cheryl Hamed, Employment Coordinator. **Description:** A nonprofit, medical center offering primary and secondary acute care, neighborhood clinics, preventative outreach programs, and a satellite surgery center. Founded in 1869. **NOTE:** Second and third shifts are offered. **Common positions include:** Account Manager; Account Representative; Administrative Assistant; Administrative Manager; Blue-Collar Worker Supervisor; Buyer; Certified Nurses Aide; Chief Financial Officer; Claim Representative; Clerical Supervisor; Clinical Lab Technician; Controller; Customer Service

Representative; Dietician/Nutritionist; EEG Technologist; Emergency Medical Technician; Finance Director; Financial Analyst; Human Resources Manager; Licensed Practical Nurse; Management Analyst/Consultant; Marketing Manager; Marketing Specialist; Medical Records Technician; Nuclear Medicine Technologist; Nurse Practitioner; Occupational Therapist; Operations Manager; Pharmacist; Physical Therapist; Physician; Project Manager; Purchasing Agent/Manager; Radiological Technologist; Registered Nurse; Respiratory Therapist; Secretary; Social Worker; Speech-Language Pathologist; Surgical Technician; Systems Analyst; Typist/Word Processor. **Educational backgrounds include:** Accounting; Business Administration; Chemistry; Communications; Economics; Finance; Health Care; Liberal Arts; Marketing; Mathematics; Nutrition; Public Relations. **Benefits:** 403(b); Dental Insurance; Disability Coverage; Employee Discounts; Flexible Schedule; Life Insurance; Medical Insurance; Pension Plan; Savings Plan; Tuition Assistance. **Corporate headquarters location:** Hobart IN. **Other U.S. locations:** Chicago IL; St. Louis MO. **Parent company:** Ancilla Systems. **Listed on:** Privately held. **CEO:** John Farrell. **Annual sales/revenues:** $11 - $20 million. **Number of employees at this location:** 1,100. **Number of projected hires for 1998 - 1999 at this location:** 50.

ST. MARY'S MEDICAL PLAZA
2515 East Jefferson Boulevard, South Bend IN 46615. 219/282-3113. **Recorded jobline:** 219/284-2434. **Contact:** Human Resources. **Description:** Comprised of an outpatient medical center and St. Mary's Community Hospital, a 107-bed, acute care hospital. **Common positions include:** Claim Representative; Clinical Lab Technician; Credit Manager; Customer Service Representative; EEG Technologist; EKG Technician; Emergency Medical Technician; Medical Records Technician; Pharmacist; Physical Therapist; Physician; Registered Nurse; Respiratory Therapist; Social Worker; Surgical Technician. **Educational backgrounds include:** Business Administration; Health Care; Nursing. **Benefits:** Dental Insurance; Disability Coverage; Employee Discounts; Life Insurance; Medical Insurance; Pension Plan; Retirement Plan; Tuition Assistance. **Corporate headquarters location:** Donaldson IN. **Parent company:** Ancilla Systems. **Operations at this facility include:** Administration. **Number of employees at this location:** 350.

STAFF BUILDERS HOME HEALTH
3737 North Meridian, Suite 203, Indianapolis IN 46208. 317/882-4330. **Contact:** Human Resources. **World Wide Web address:** http://www.staffbuilders.com. **Description:** A home health care agency. **Common positions include:** Home Health Aide; Licensed Practical Nurse; Registered Nurse. **Corporate headquarters location:** Lake Success NY. **Other U.S. locations:** Nationwide.

TIPTON COUNTY MEMORIAL HOSPITAL
1000 South Main Street, Tipton IN 46072. 765/675-8500. **Contact:** J. Neal Shockney, Vice President of Human Resources. **Description:** A nonprofit community hospital. **NOTE:** Entry-level positions and second and third shifts are offered. **Common positions include:** Account Manager; Account Representative; Administrative Assistant; Certified Nurses Aide; Chief Financial Officer; Claim Representative; Clinical Lab Technician; Dietician/Nutritionist; EEG Technologist; EKG Technician; Electrician; Human Resources Manager; Licensed Practical Nurse; Medical Records Technician; Occupational Therapist; Pharmacist; Physical Therapist; Physician; Purchasing Agent/Manager; Radiological Technologist; Registered Nurse; Secretary; Speech-Language Pathologist; Surgical Technician; Typist/Word Processor. **Educational backgrounds include:** Business Administration; Liberal Arts; Public Relations. **Benefits:** 403(b); Dental Insurance; Disability Coverage; Employee Discounts; Flexible Schedule; Life Insurance; Medical Insurance; Pension Plan; Tuition Assistance. **Corporate headquarters location:** This Location. **CEO:** Al Gajmaitan. **Annual sales/revenues:** $21 - $50 million. **Number of employees at this location:** 350. **Number of projected hires for 1998 - 1999 at this location:** 100.

UNION HOSPITAL
1606 North Seventh Street, Terre Haute IN 47804. 812/238-7000. **Contact:** Human Resources. **Description:** A hospital.

ZIMMER INC.
BRISTOL-MYERS SQUIBB COMPANY
P.O. Box 708, Warsaw IN 46581-0708. 219/267-6131. **Contact:** Employment Office. **Description:** Develops, manufactures, and markets orthopedic products for human implant and patient care.

Zimmer's primary customers are hospitals. **NOTE:** Jobseekers must contact the employment office to receive a list of candidate criteria and to obtain application procedures. **Common positions include:** Accountant/Auditor; Buyer; Computer Programmer; Financial Analyst; Human Resources Manager; Mechanical Engineer; Product Manager. **Educational backgrounds include:** Business Administration; Engineering; Finance. **Benefits:** Dental Insurance; Disability Coverage; Employee Discounts; Life Insurance; Medical Insurance; Pension Plan; Prescription Drugs; Savings Plan; Tuition Assistance. **Corporate headquarters location:** This Location. **Operations at this facility include:** Administration; Divisional Headquarters; Manufacturing; Research and Development.

Note: Because addresses and telephone numbers of smaller companies can change rapidly, we recommend you call each company to verify the information below before inquiring about job opportunities. Mass mailings are not recommended.

Additional small employers:

DOCTORS' OFFICES AND CLINICS

Atwater Eye Care
800 E Atwater Ave, Bloomington IN 47405-3680. 812/855-2902.

BMH Health Strategies
3813 S Madison Street, Muncie IN 47302-5758. 317/751-3300.

Butler Clinic
1316 East 7th Street, Auburn IN 46706-2523. 219/925-4600.

Elkhart Clinic LLC
PO Box 201, Elkhart IN 46515-0201. 219/296-3200.

Fort Wayne Cardiology Inc.
PO Box 5603, Fort Wayne IN 46895-5603. 219/481-4850.

Fort Wayne Orthopaedics LLC
PO Box 2526, Fort Wayne IN 46801-2526. 219/436-8383.

Four County Counseling Center
1015 Michigan Avenue, Logansport IN 46947-1526. 219/722-5151.

Hammond Clinic LLC
7905 Calumet Avenue, Munster IN 46321-1215. 219/836-5800.

Heart Group PC
415 W Columbia Street, Evansville IN 47710-1656. 812/464-9133.

Indiana Hand Center
PO Box 80434, Indianapolis IN 46280-0434. 317/875-9105.

Indiana Heart Physicians Inc.
112 N 17th Avenue, Suite 300, Beech Grove IN 46107-1228. 317/783-8800.

Indianapolis Cardiology
1400 N Ritter Avenue, Indianapolis IN 46219-3052. 317/355-1500.

Medical Consultants PC
2525 W University Avenue, Muncie IN 47303-3409. 765/281-2000.

Medical Group-Michigan City PC
1225 E Coolspring Avenue, Michigan City IN 46360-6312. 219/879-6531.

Medical Specialists PC
761 45th Avenue, Suite 103, Munster IN 46321-2899. 219/922-3002.

Memorial Clinic
PO Box 88380, Indianapolis IN 46208-0380. 317/924-6131.

Metro Health Greenwood
7551 Shelby Street, Indianapolis IN 46227-5980. 317/888-7595.

Metro Health Maxicare
2310 E 62nd Street, Indianapolis IN 46220-2316. 317/251-6474.

Nasser Smith Pinkerton Cardiology
8333 Naab Road, Suite 400, Indianapolis IN 46260-1992. 317/338-6666.

Northern Indiana Family Physicians PC
3610 Brooklyn Avenue, Fort Wayne IN 46809-1313. 219/747-6171.

Northside Cardiology
8333 Naab Road, Suite 200, Indianapolis IN 46260-1983. 317/338-5050.

Select Specialty Hospital
3232 N Meridian St, Indianapolis IN 46208-4646. 317/931-1676.

South Bend Clinic
PO Box 1755, South Bend IN 46634-1755. 219/237-9201.

Unity Physician Group Inc.
1155 W 3rd St, Bloomington IN 47404-5016. 812/333-2731.

Valparaiso Medical Arts Center
2102 Evans Ave, Valparaiso IN 46383-4008. 219/462-1242.

Valparaiso Physician & Surgery
1201 S Main St, Crown Point IN 46307-8481. 219/738-2100.

White County Foot & Ankle Care
1101 O'Connor Blvd, Monticello IN 47960-1666. 219/583-7111.

HEALTH AND ALLIED SERVICES

Brennan Holdings LLC
2250 E Pointe Road, Bloomington IN 47401-9041. 812/824-4040.

Indiana Medical Management
8180 Clearvista Pkwy, Ste 200, Indianapolis IN 46256. 317/588-7500.

HOME HEALTH CARE SERVICES

Adams County Home Health
PO Box 151, Decatur IN 46733-0151. 219/724-2145.

Advanced Home Health Care
333 E Miller Drive, Bloomington IN 47401-6557. 812/336-4492.

BMH Homecare Services Inc.
4000 West Woodway Drive, Muncie IN 47304-4264. 765/284-4445.

Care At Home Indiana Inc.
5435 Emerson Way, Suite 200, Indianapolis IN 46226-1466. 317/591-1001.

Caregivers Inc.
4755 Kingsway Dr, Suite 336, Indianapolis IN 46205-1541. 317/252-5958.

Carestar Home Health Care Services
612 E 11th Street, Rushville IN 46173-1319. 765/932-4127.

Carestar Inc.
326 Walnut Street, Lawrenceburg IN 47025-1842. 812/537-3200.

Interim Healthcare-Fort Wayne
2310 Cass Street, Fort Wayne IN 46808-3110. 219/482-9405.

Olsten Health Services
303 N Alabama St, Suite 310, Indianapolis IN 46204-2152. 317/269-2660.

Olsten Health Services
9302 N Meridian Street, Indianapolis IN 46260-1873. 317/580-6830.

Preferred Companies Inc.
5250 E U.S. Highway 36, Danville IN 46122-9199. 317/745-5500.

Preferred Home Health Care-Vincennes
PO Box 725, Vincennes IN 47591-0725. 812/886-9646.

Riverfront Home Health Inc.
PO Box 681, Vincennes IN 47591-0681. 812/885-2767.

St. Margaret's Mercy Home Health Care
5454 Hohman Ave, Hammond IN 46320-1931. 219/933-6663.

Staff Builders Home Health Care
1512 W 96th Ave, Crown Point IN 46307-2218. 219/662-3500.

Tendercare Home Health Service
4954 E 56th St, Ste 9, Indianapolis IN 46220-5769. 317/251-0700.

Visiting Nurse Association
PO Box 7, Elwood IN 46036-0007. 765/552-3393.

Visiting Nurse Association
600 S 1st Street, Terre Haute IN 47807-4643. 812/232-7611.

Visiting Nurse Association of NW Indiana
201 West 89th Avenue, Merrillville IN 46410-6283. 219/844-1410.

Visiting Nurse Association of Porter
501 Marquette St, Valparaiso IN 46383-2508. 219/462-5195.

Visiting Nurse Association of SW Indiana
610 East Walnut Street, Evansville IN 47713-2460. 812/425-3561.

Visiting Nurse Health Care
PO Box 30, Anderson IN 46015-0030. 765/643-7371.

Western Medical
3404 North Janney Avenue, Muncie IN 47304-2066. 765/281-1133.

HOSPITALS AND MEDICAL CENTERS

Amisub Culver Union Hospital
1710 Lafayette Road, Crawfordsville IN 47933-1033. 765/362-2800.

Bedford Regional Medical Center
2900 16th Street, Bedford IN 47421-3583. 812/279-3581.

Behavioral Healthcare Corporation
1800 N Oak Road, Plymouth IN 46563-3406. 219/936-3784.

Behavioral Healthcare of Lebanon
1711 Lafayette Avenue, Lebanon IN 46052-1089. 765/482-3711.

Blackford County Hospital
503 E Van Cleve Street, Hartford City IN 47348-1836. 765/348-0300.

Cameron Memorial Community Hospital
416 E Maumee Street, Angola IN 46703-2015. 219/665-2141.

Caylor-Nickel Medical Center
One Caylor Nickel Square, Bluffton IN 46714-2529. 219/824-3500.

Charter Beacon Hospital
1720 Beacon Street, Fort Wayne IN 46805-4749. 219/423-3651.

Charter Behavioral Health Systems-Evansville
7200 E Indiana Street, Evansville IN 47715-2753. 812/476-7200.

Charter Hospital of Lafayette
PO Box 5969, Lafayette IN 47903-5969. 765/448-6999.

Charter Hospital of South Bend
6704 N Main Street, Granger IN 46530-7401. 219/272-9799.

Charter Medical of Vigo County
1400 E Crossing Boulevard, Terre Haute IN 47802-5316. 812/299-4196.

Clay County Hospital
1206 East National Avenue, Brazil IN 47834-2718. 812/448-2675.

Clinton County Hospital
PO Box 669, Frankfort IN 46041. 765/659-4731.

Columbus Regional Hospital
2400 17th Street, Columbus IN 47201-5351. 812/379-4441.

Community Hospital of Bremen
411 South Whitlock Street, Bremen IN 46506-1626. 219/546-2211.

Community Hospital South
1402 E County Line Road, Indianapolis IN 46227-0963. 317/887-7000.

Community Hospital-Anderson/Madison
1515 N Madison Avenue, Anderson IN 46011-3453. 765/642-8011.

Community Hospitals of Indiana
1500 N Ritter Avenue, Indianapolis IN 46219-3027. 317/355-1411.

Continental Rehabilitation
501 East St. Anthony Drive, Terre Haute IN 47802. 812/235-5656.

Deaconess Hospital
600 Mary Street, Evansville IN 47710-1658. 812/426-3000.

Dearborn County Hospital
600 Wilson Creek Road, Lawrenceburg IN 47025-2751. 812/537-1010.

Decatur County Memorial Hospital
720 N Lincoln Street, Greensburg IN 47240-1327. 812/663-4331.

Duke Memorial Hospital
Grant Boulevard, Peru IN 46970. 765/473-6621.

Dunn Memorial Hospital
1600 23rd Street, Bedford IN 47421-4704. 812/275-3331.

Elkhart General Hospital
PO Box 1329, Elkhart IN 46515-1329. 219/294-2621.

Fairbanks Hospital Inc.
8102 Clearvista Parkway, Indianapolis IN 46256-1661. 317/849-8222.

Gallahue Mental Health
7 East Hendricks Street, Shelbyville IN 46176-2124. 317/392-2564.

Gibson General Hospital Inc.
1808 Sherman Drive, Princeton IN 47670-1043. 812/385-3401.

Goshen General Hospital
PO Box 139, Goshen IN 46527-0139. 219/533-2141.

Greene County General Hospital
Rural Route 1, Box 1000, Linton IN 47441-9482. 812/847-2281.

Hamilton Center Inc.
PO Box 4323, Terre Haute IN 47804-0323. 812/231-8323.

Hancock Memorial Hospital & Health Services
PO Box 827, Greenfield IN 46140-0827. 317/462-5544.

Harrison County Hospital
245 Atwood Street, Corydon IN 47112-1738. 812/738-4251.

Hawley Army Community Hospital
Building 300, Indianapolis IN 46216. 317/546-9211.

HealthSouth
829 N Dixon Road, Kokomo IN 46901-1795. 765/452-6700.

Healthwin Hospital
20531 Darden Road, South Bend IN 46637-2915. 219/272-0100.

Hendricks Community Hospital
PO Box 409, Danville IN 46122-0409. 317/745-4451.

Henry County Memorial Hospital
PO Box 490, New Castle IN 47362-0490. 765/521-0890.

Intensiva Hospital of NW Indiana
PO Box 189, Hammond IN 46325-0189. 219/937-9900.

Jackson County Memorial Hospital
PO Box 2349, Seymour IN 47274-5000. 812/522-2349.

Jasper County Hospital
1104 E Grace Street, Rensselaer IN 47978-3211. 219/866-5141.

Jay County Hospital
500 W Votaw Street, Portland IN 47371-1322. 219/726-7131.

Jefferson Hospital
2700 River City Park Road, Jeffersonville IN 47130-5989. 812/284-3400.

Jennings Community Hospital
301 Henry Street, North Vernon IN 47265-1030. 812/346-6200.

Kendrick Memorial Hospital
1201 Hadley Road, Mooresville IN 46158-1737. 317/831-1160.

Kosciusko Community Hospital
2101 Dubois Drive, Warsaw IN 46580-3210. 219/267-3200.

La Porte Hospital Auxiliary
PO Box 50, B Street, La Porte IN 46350-4926. 219/326-1234.

Lafayette Home Hospital Inc.
2400 South Street, Lafayette IN 47904-3027. 765/447-6811.

Larue D. Carter Memorial Hospital
1315 West 10th Street, Indianapolis IN 46202-2802. 317/634-8401.

Lindenview Regional Behavioral Center
1909 Carew Street, Fort Wayne IN 46805-4707. 219/482-6513.

Lutheran Hospital of Indiana
7950 West Jefferson Boulevard, Fort Wayne IN 46804-4140. 219/435-7001.

Madison Hospital Corporation
403 E Madison Street, South Bend IN 46617-2322. 219/234-0061.

Madison State Hospital
711 Green Road, Madison IN 47250-2143. 812/265-2611.

Major Hospital
PO Box 10, Shelbyville IN 46176-0010. 317/392-3211.

Margaret Mary Community Hospital
PO Box 226, Batesville IN 47006-0226. 812/934-6624.

Mary Sherman Hospital
PO Box 10, Sullivan IN 47882-0010. 812/268-4311.

Memorial Hospital
PO Box 7013, Logansport IN 46947-7013. 219/753-7541.

Memorial Hospital & Health Care Center
800 W 9th Street, Jasper IN 47546-2516. 812/482-2345.

Memorial Hospital of Michigan City
5th & Pine Street, Michigan City IN 46360. 219/879-0202.

Methodist Hospital-Northlake Campus
600 Grant Street, Gary IN 46402-6001. 219/886-4000.

Morgan County Memorial Hospital
PO Box 1717, Martinsville IN 46151-0717. 765/342-8441.

Muscatatuck State Developmental Center
PO Box 77, Butlerville IN 47223-0077. 812/346-4401.

New Castle State Developmental Center
PO Box 34, New Castle IN 47362-0034. 765/529-0900.

Noble County Emergency Medical Services
PO Box 249, Kendallville IN 46755-0249. 219/347-1100.

Oaklawn Psychiatric Center
PO Box 809, Goshen IN 46527-0809. 219/533-1234.

Orange County Hospital
PO Box 499, Paoli IN 47454-0499. 812/723-2811.

Pulaski Memorial Hospital
PO Box 279, Winamac IN 46996-0279. 219/946-6131.

Putnam County Hospital
1542 S Bloomington St, Greencastle IN 46135-2212. 765/653-5121.

Randolph County Hospital
PO Box 407, Winchester IN 47394-0407. 765/584-9001.

Rehabilitation Hospital of Fort Wayne
7970 W Jefferson Blvd, Fort Wayne IN 46804-4140. 219/436-2644.

Reid Hospital & Health Care Services
1401 Chester Boulevard, Richmond IN 47374-1908. 765/983-3000.

Richmond State Hospital
498 NW 18th St, Richmond IN 47374-2851. 765/966-0511.

Riverview Hospital
PO Box 220, Noblesville IN 46061-0220. 317/773-0760.

Rush Memorial Hospital
1300 North Main Street, Rushville IN 46173-1116. 765/932-4111.

Scott County Memorial Hospital
PO Box 430, Scottsburg IN 47170-0430. 812/752-3456.

Southern Indiana Rehabilitation Hospital
3104 Blackiston Boulevard, New Albany IN 47150. 812/941-8300.

St. Anthony Hospital
301 West Homer Street, Michigan City IN 46360-4358. 219/879-8511.

St. Elizabeth Medical Center
PO Box 7501, Lafayette IN 47903-7501. 765/423-6011.

St. Joseph Hospital of Marshall
PO Box 670, Plymouth IN 46563-0670. 219/936-3181.

St. Joseph's Hospital of Huntingburg
1900 Medical Arts Dr, Huntingburg IN 47542-9521. 812/683-2121.

St. Joseph's Medical Center
PO Box 1935, South Bend IN 46634-1935. 219/237-7111.

St. Jude Children's Respiratory Hospital
PO Box 1313, New Albany IN 47151-1313. 812/948-1404.

St. Margaret's Mercy Healthcare Centers
24 Joliet St, Dyer IN 46311-1705. 219/865-2141.

St. Margaret's Mercy Healthcare Centers
5454 Hohman Ave, Hammond IN 46320-1931. 219/932-2300.

St. Mary Medical Center Inc.
1500 S Lake Park Ave, Hobart IN 46342-6638. 219/942-0551.

St. Mary's Hospital
3700 Washington Ave, Evansville IN 47714-0542. 812/485-4000.

St. Mary's Warrick
PO Box 629, Boonville IN 47601-0629. 812/897-4800.

St. Vincent Carmel Hospital
PO Box 40970, Indianapolis IN 46240-0970. 317/338-2345.

St. Vincent Mercy Hospital Inc.
1331 S A St, Elwood IN 46036-1942. 765/552-4600.

St. Vincent Williamsport Hospital
412 North Monroe St, Williamsport IN 47993-1049. 765/762-2496.

Starke Memorial Hospital
102 E Culver Rd, Knox IN 46534-2216. 219/772-6231.

Terre Haute Regional Hospital
3901 S 7th St, Terre Haute IN 47802-5709. 812/232-0021.

The Huntington Center
1215 Etna Ave, Huntington IN 46750-3637. 219/356-3000.

The Medical Center of Southern Indiana
PO Box 69, Charlestown IN 47111-0069. 812/256-3301.

The Methodist Hospitals Inc.
8701 Broadway, Merrillville IN 46410-7035. 219/738-5500.

Todd-Aikens Health Care Center
PO Box 549, Franklin IN 46131-0549. 317/736-3300.

Tri-State Regional Rehabilitation Hospital
PO Box 5349, Evansville IN 47716-5349. 812/476-9983.

VA Medical Center
1700 E 38th St, Marion IN 46953-4568. 765/674-3321.

VA Medical Center
1481 W 10th St, Indianapolis IN 46202-2803. 317/635-7401.

VA Medical Center
2121 Lake Ave, Fort Wayne IN 46805-5100. 219/426-5431.

Valle Vista Hospital
898 E Main St, Greenwood IN 46143-1407. 317/887-1348.

Vencor Inc.
1700 W 10th St, Indianapolis IN 46222-3802. 317/636-4400.

Vencor Inc.
898 E Main St, Greenwood IN 46143-1407. 317/888-8155.

Wabash County Hospital
PO Box 548, Wabash IN 46992-0548. 219/563-3131.

Wabash Valley Hospital Inc.
2900 N River Rd, Lafayette IN 47906-3744. 765/463-2555.

Wells Community Hospital
1100 S Main St, Bluffton IN 46714-3615. 219/824-3210.

Westview Hospital
PO Box 22650, Indianapolis IN 46222-0650. 317/924-6661.

Whitewater Valley Care Pavilion
1941 Virginia Ave, Connersville IN 47331-2833. 765/825-5131.

Whitley Memorial Hospital
353 North Oak Street, Columbia City IN 46725-1623. 219/244-6191.

William N. Wishard Memorial Hospital
1001 West 10th Street, Indianapolis IN 46202-2859. 317/639-6671.

Winona Memorial Hospital
3232 North Meridian St, Indianapolis IN 46208-4646. 317/924-3392.

Witham Memorial Hospital
PO Box 1200, Lebanon IN 46052-3005. 765/482-2700.

Women's Hospital-Indianapolis
PO Box 80430, Indianapolis IN 46280-0430. 317/875-5994.

Woodlawn Hospital
1400 East 9th Street, Rochester IN 46975-8931. 219/223-3141.

MEDICAL EQUIPMENT

BAS
2701 Kent Avenue, West Lafayette IN 47906-1350. 765/463-4527.

Bayer Corporation
PO Box 2004, Mishawaka IN 46546-2004. 219/256-3200.

Biosound Esaote Inc.
PO Box 50858, Indianapolis IN 46250-0858. 317/849-1793.

Cook Incorporated
6600 W McNeeley Street, Ellettsville IN 47429-9444. 812/876-7887.

Cook Urological
PO Box 277, Spencer IN 47460-0277. 812/829-4891.

Gibeck Inc.
PO Box 36430, Indianapolis IN 46236-0430. 317/823-6866.

Heraeus Kulzer Inc.
4315 South Lafayette Boulevard, South Bend IN 46614-2517. 219/291-0661.

Othy Inc.
486 West County Road 350 North, Warsaw IN 46580. 219/267-8700.

Sofamor/Danek Manufacturing
100 Publishers Dr, Winona Lake IN 46590-1355. 219/267-6801.

Sroufe Manufacturing Inc.
PO Box 347, Ligonier IN 46767-0347. 219/894-4171.

MEDICAL EQUIPMENT AND SUPPLIES WHOLESALE

Henry Schein Inc.
5010 West 81st Street, Indianapolis IN 46268-1638. 317/876-7800.

NURSING AND PERSONAL CARE FACILITIES

Americana Healthcare Center
1345 N Madison Avenue, Anderson IN 46011-1215. 765/644-2888.

Americana Healthcare Center
3518 S Lafountain Street, Kokomo IN 46902-3803. 765/453-4666.

Americana Healthcare Center
8549 Madison Avenue, Indianapolis IN 46227-6153. 317/881-9164.

Anderson Health Care Center
1809 N Madison Avenue, Anderson IN 46011-2145. 765/644-0903.

Beech Grove Health Care Center
2002 Albany Street, Beech Grove IN 46107-1408. 317/783-2911.

Bethany Village Nursing Home
3518 Shelby Street, Indianapolis IN 46227-3226. 317/783-4042.

Betz Nursing Home Inc.
3009 County Road 38, Auburn IN 46706-9558. 219/925-3814.

Beverly Health Care of Bloomington
3305 Odell Drive, Suite 37, Bloomington IN 47401. 812/332-4437.

Beverly Nursing Rehabilitation Center
2860 Churchman Avenue, Indianapolis IN 46203-4619. 317/787-3451.

Brethren Healthcare Corp.
801 West Columbia Street, Flora IN 46929-9216. 219/967-4571.

Brighton Hall Nursing Center
1201 Daly Drive, New Haven IN 46774-1891. 219/749-0413.

Brookview Rehabilitation
7145 East 21st Street, Indianapolis IN 46219-1715. 317/356-0977.

Brown County Community Care Center
PO Box 667, Nashville IN 47448-0667. 812/988-6666.

Brownsburg Health Care Center
1010 Hornaday Road, Brownsburg IN 46112-1972. 317/852-3123.

Byron Health Center
12101 Lima Road, Fort Wayne IN 46818-8903. 219/637-3166.

Camelot Care Centers
1555 Commerce Drive, Logansport IN 46947-1555. 219/753-0404.

Carmel Care Center
118 Medical Drive, Carmel IN 46032-2923. 317/844-4211.

Carriage Manor
2400 College Avenue, Goshen IN 46528-5010. 219/533-0351.

Century Villa Healthcare
705 N Meridian Street, Greentown IN 46936-1246. 765/628-3377.

Clark Nursing Rehabilitation Center LLP
1964 Clark Road, Gary IN 46404-2550. 219/949-5600.

Clifty Falls Health Rehabilitation Center
950 Cross Street, Madison IN 47250-2002. 812/273-4640.

Colonial Oaks
4625 South Colonial Oaks Drive, Marion IN 46953. 765/674-9791.

Columbia Health Care Center
621 W Columbia Street, Evansville IN 47710-1619. 812/428-5678.

Community Nursing & Rehabilitation
5600 East 16th Street, Indianapolis IN 46218-5012. 317/356-0911.

Countryside Manor Healthcare Center
205 Marine Drive, Anderson IN 46016-5937. 765/649-4558.

Countryside Place
1700 I Street, La Porte IN 46350-5750. 219/362-6234.

Coventry Village
8400 Clear Vista Place, Fishers IN 46038. 317/845-0464.

Covington Manor
1600 Liberty Street, Covington IN 47932-1715. 765/793-4818.

Covington Manor Nursing Center
5700 Wilkie Drive, Fort Wayne IN 46804-1662. 219/432-7556.

Crestview
3801 Old Bruceville Road, Vincennes IN 47591-3889. 812/882-1783.

Cypress Grove Rehabilitation
4255 Medwell Drive, Newburgh IN 47630-2528. 812/853-2993.

Dillsboro Manor Nursing Home
PO Box 37, Dillsboro IN 47018-0037. 812/432-5227.

Dyer Nursing
601 Sheffield Avenue, Dyer IN 46311-1029. 219/322-2273.

East Point Rehabilitation Hospital
4301 Washington Avenue, Evansville IN 47714-0678. 812/477-8971.

English Estates Health Care
1585 Perry Worth Road, Lebanon IN 46052-9635. 765/482-6391.

Fairway Nursing & Rehabilitation Center
650 Fairway Drive, Evansville IN 47710-3306. 812/425-5243.

Forest Del Convalescent Home
1020 Vine Street, Princeton IN 47670-1164. 812/385-5238.

Forest Park Healthcare Center
2233 W Jefferson Street, Kokomo IN 46901-4121. 765/457-9175.

Fountainview Place Corporation
609 Tanglewood Lane, Mishawaka IN 46545-2625. 219/277-2500.

Fountainview Place Corporation
315 West Jefferson Boulevard, South Bend IN 46601-1512. 219/236-4000.

Fountainview Terrace
1900 Andrew Avenue, La Porte IN 46350-6337. 219/362-7014.

Foutainview Place Corporation
3175 Lancer Street, Portage IN 46368-4407. 219/762-9571.

Franciscan Homes & Community Services
203 Franciscan Drive, Crown Point IN 46307-4802. 219/757-6083.

Glenburn Home
Rural Route 2, Box 208, Linton IN 47441-9664. 812/847-2221.

Golden Years Homestead Inc.
8300 Maysville Road, Fort Wayne IN 46815-6619. 219/749-9655.

Good Samaritan Home Inc.
210 North Gibson Street, Oakland City IN 47660-1308. 812/749-4774.

Good Samaritan Home Inc.
PO Box 2788, Evansville IN 47728-0788. 812/476-4912.

Grace Village Retirement Community
PO Box 337, Winona Lake IN 46590-0337. 219/372-6200.

Green Valley Convalescent Center
3118 Green Valley Road, New Albany IN 47150-4213. 812/945-2341.

Greenbriar Rehabilitation Center
8181 Harcourt Road, Carmel IN 46032. 317/872-7261.

Greencroft Nursing Center Inc.
PO Box 819, Goshen IN 46527-0819. 219/537-4000.

Greenwood Convalescent Center
937 Fry Road, Greenwood IN 46142-1820. 317/881-3535.

Hanover Nursing Center
410 W LaGrange Road, Hanover IN 47243-9439. 812/866-2625.

Healthcare of Indiana Inc.
1350 North Todd Drive, Scottsburg IN 47170-7755. 812/752-5663.

Heritage House of Connersville
281 S County Road, Suite 200 E, Connersville IN 47331-8220. 765/825-2148.

Heritage House of Greensburg
410 Park Road, Greensburg IN 47240-1953. 812/663-7543.

Heritage House of Seymour Inc.
707 S Jackson Park Drive, Seymour IN 47274-2627. 812/522-2416.

Heritage House of Shelbyville
2309 South Miller Street, Shelbyville IN 46176-9350. 317/398-9781.

Hillcrest Nursing Home
203 Sparks Avenue, Jeffersonville IN 47130-3732. 812/283-7918.

Holiday Health Care
1202 W Buena Vista Road, Evansville IN 47710-5178. 812/429-0700.

Holly Hill Health Care Facility
PO Box 130, Brazil IN 47834-0130. 812/446-2636.

Hoosier Christian Village
PO Box 172, Brownstown IN 47220-0172. 812/358-2504.

Hooverwood
7001 Hoover Road, Indianapolis IN 46260-4169. 317/251-2261.

Hospitality House
PO Box 1347, Bedford IN 47421-1347. 812/279-4437.

Houston Companies
PO Box 661, Crawfordsville IN 47933-0661. 765/362-0905.

Huntingburg Convalescent Center
1712 Leland Drive, Huntingburg IN 47542-9348. 812/683-4090.

Indian Creek Health & Rehabilitation Center
PO Box 208, Corydon IN 47112-0208. 812/738-8127.

Integrated Health Services
8530 Township Line Road,

Indianapolis IN 46260-1927. 317/876-9955.

Ironwood Health & Rehabilitation
1950 Ridgedale Road, South Bend IN 46614-2243. 219/291-6722.

Kennedy Living Center
PO Box 1676, Martinsville IN 46151-0676. 765/342-6636.

Lakeview Manor Inc.
45 Beachway Drive, Indianapolis IN 46224-8501. 317/243-3721.

Lakeview Nursing & Rehabilitation Center
500 Maple Ave, Terre Haute IN 47804-2733. 812/234-7702.

Life Care Center of Lagrange
770 N 075 E, Lagrange IN 46761-9359. 219/463-7445.

Life Care Center of Michigan City
802 E U.S. Highway 20, Michigan City IN 46360-7424. 219/872-7251.

Life Care Center of Rochester
PO Box 188, Rochester IN 46975-0188. 219/223-4331.

Life Care Center of Valparaiso
PO Box B1039, Valparaiso IN 46383. 219/462-1023.

Lifecare Centers of America
5016 South Plaza Drive, Newburgh IN 47630-3066. 812/858-1218.

Lincoln Hills Health Center-New Albany
326 Country Club Drive, New Albany IN 47150-4618. 812/948-1311.

Lowell Healthcare Center
710 Michigan Avenue, Lowell IN 46356-1849. 219/696-7791.

Lutheran Community Home
PO Box 810, Seymour IN 47274-0810. 812/522-5927.

Lutheran Community Services
502 West Jackson Street, Mulberry IN 46058-9538. 765/296-2911.

Lutheran Homes-Concord Village
6701 St. Anthony Boulevard, Fort Wayne IN 46816-2012. 219/447-1591.

Mariner Health Care of Fort Wayne
4430 Elsdale Drive, Fort Wayne IN 46835-2277. 219/485-8157.

Marion County Health Care Center
11850 Brookville Road, Indianapolis IN 46239-9695. 317/862-6631.

McCurdy Residential Center
101 Southeast 1st Street, Evansville IN 47708-1406. 812/425-1041.

Meadowvale Health & Rehabilitation Center
1529 Lancaster Street, Bluffton IN 46714-1507. 219/824-4320.

Medco Center-Evansville West
25 S Boehne Camp Road, Evansville IN 47712-3101. 812/423-7468.

Medco Center-Mount Vernon
1415 Country Club Road, Mount Vernon IN 47620-9301. 812/838-6554.

Middleview Health & Rehabilitation
900 Anson Street, Salem IN 47167-1982. 812/883-4681.

Midtown Nursing & Rehabilitation
1700 N Illinois Street, Indianapolis IN 46202-1316. 317/924-1325.

Miller's Merry Manor
500 Walkerton Trail, Walkerton IN 46574-1300. 219/586-3133.

Miller's Merry Manor
640 W Ellsworth Street, Columbia City IN 46725-2302. 219/248-8101.

Miller's Merry Manor
PO Box 1143, Huntington IN 46750-1143. 219/356-5713.

Miller's Merry Manor
1630 S County Farm Road, Warsaw IN 46580-8248. 219/267-8196.

Miller's Merry Manor
PO Box 89, Lagrange IN 46761-0089. 219/463-2172.

Miller's Merry Manor
PO Box 480, Logansport IN 46947-0480. 219/722-4006.

Miller's Merry Manor
2901 W 37th Avenue, Hobart IN 46342-1727. 219/942-2170.

Miller's Merry Manor
PO Box 124, Peru IN 46970-0124. 765/473-4426.

Miller's Merry Manor
259 W Harrison Street, Mooresville IN 46158-1634. 317/831-6272.

Milner Community Health Care
PO Box 15, Rossville IN 46065-0015. 765/379-2112.

Mitchell Manor
PO Box 338, Mitchell IN 47446-0338. 812/849-2221.

Muncie Health Care Center
PO Box 112, Muncie IN 47308-0112. 765/282-0053.

Munster Med-In
7935 Calumet Avenue, Munster IN 46321-1215. 219/836-8300.

New Castle Healthcare Center
990 N 16th Street, New Castle IN 47362-4317. 765/529-0230.

New Horizons Development Center
PO Box 419, Arcadia IN 46030-0419. 317/984-3555.

Newburgh Health Care Center
10466 Pollack Avenue, Newburgh IN 47630-9289. 812/853-2931.

Noblesville Health Care Center
295 Westfield Road, Noblesville IN 46060-1424. 317/773-3760.

North Lake Nursing & Rehabilitation
601 W 61st Avenue, Merrillville IN 46410-2519. 219/980-5950.

Northern Indiana State Developmental Center
1234 North Notre Dame Avenue, South Bend IN 46617-1345. 219/234-2101.

Northwest Manor Health Care Center
6440 W 34th Street, Indianapolis IN 46224-1138. 317/293-4930.

Northwood Good Samaritan
PO Box 1047, Jasper IN 47547-1047. 812/482-1722.

Norton Health Care
2010 North Capitol Avenue, Indianapolis IN 46202-1222. 317/924-5821.

Oak Ridge Rehabilitation & Specialty Care
1042 Oak Drive, Richmond IN 47374-1916. 765/966-7788.

Odd Fellows Home
1021 E Central Avenue, Greensburg IN 47240-2244. 812/663-8553.

Our Lady of the Holy Cross
7520 S Highway 421, San Pierre IN 46374. 219/828-4111.

Parkview Care Center
2819 Saint George Rd, Evansville IN 47711-2558. 812/424-2941.

Parkwood Health Care Center
1001 N Grant St, Lebanon IN 46052-1944. 765/482-6400.

Peabody Retirement Community
400 W 7th St, North Manchester IN 46962-1199. 219/982-8616.

Pine Tree Manor
1302 Lesley Ave, Indianapolis IN 46219-3144. 317/353-8061.

Plainfield Health Care Center
PO Box 7, Indianapolis IN 46206-0007. 317/839-6577.

Pro-Care Development Center
PO Box 159, Gaston IN 47342-0159. 765/358-3324.

Rawlins House
300 JH Walker Dr, Pendleton IN 46064-8730. 765/778-1501.

Regency Place
5226 East 82nd Street, Indianapolis IN 46250-1628. 317/842-6668.

Regency Place
377 Westridge Boulevard, Greenwood IN 46142-2137. 317/888-4948.

Regency Place of South Bend
52654 Ironwood Road, South Bend IN 46635-1123. 219/277-8710.

Ritter Healthcare Center
1301 N Ritter Ave, Indianapolis IN 46219-3024. 317/353-9465.

Riverbend Learning Center
221 N Washington St, Marion IN 46952-2707. 765/664-0612.

Riverview Care Center
2827 Northgate Blvd, Fort Wayne IN 46835-2903. 219/485-9691.

Riverview Home Care
4701 N Keystone Ave, Indianapolis IN 46205-1554. 317/722-8200.

Rosewood Terrace
1001 W Hively Ave, Elkhart IN 46517-1742. 219/294-7641.

Sacred Heart Home
515 N Main St, Avilla IN 46710-9601. 219/897-2841.

Sage Services
215 SE 4th Street, Evansville IN 47713-1201. 812/422-7774.

Shakamak Good Samaritan Center
800 E Ohio St, Jasonville IN 47438-1607. 812/665-2226.

Sherwood Healthcare Corp.
1302 Sherwood Dr, Greenfield IN 46140-1140. 317/462-6493.

Southlake Care Center
8800 Virginia Place, Gary IN 46410-7109. 219/736-1310.

Southwood Health Rehabilitation Center
2222 Margaret Avenue, Terre Haute IN 47802-3339. 812/232-2223.

St. Anne Home Retirement Community
1900 Randallia Dr, Fort Wayne IN 46805-4632. 219/484-5555.

St. Anthony Health Care Inc.
1205 N 14th St, Lafayette IN 47904-2024. 765/423-4861.

St. Joseph Care Morningside
18325 Bailey Avenue, South Bend IN 46637-5304. 219/272-6410.

St. Joseph's Care Center West
4600 W Washington St, South Bend IN 46619-2320. 219/282-1294.

Swiss Village Inc.
1350 W Main St, Berne IN 46711-1741. 219/589-3173.

The Lawton Nursing Home
1649 Spy Run Ave, Fort Wayne IN 46805-4032. 219/422-8520.

Timbercrest
PO Box 501, North Manchester IN 46962-0501. 219/982-2118.

Transitional Health Services South Bend
5024 W Western Ave, South Bend IN 46619-2312. 219/288-1464.

United Methodist Memorial Home
PO Box 326, Warren IN 46792-0326. 219/375-2201.

University Heights Convalescent Home
1380 E County Line Rd, Indianapolis IN 46227-0962. 317/885-7050.

University Nursing Center
4700 E Jackson St, Muncie IN 47303-4468. 765/282-9904.

Valparaiso Care Center LLC
606 Wall St, Valparaiso IN 46383-2513. 219/464-4976.

Vantage Healthcare Corporation
30 E Chandler Ave, Evansville IN 47713-1631. 812/423-6019.

Village Christian Parke Inc.
675 S Ford Rd, Zionsville IN 46077-1825. 317/873-5205.

Washington Nursing Center Inc.
603 E National Highway, Washington IN 47501-4118. 812/254-5117.

Wedgewood Health Care Center
101 Potters Lane, Clarksville IN 47129-1017. 812/948-0808.

Wernle Children's Home Inc.
PO Box 386, Richmond IN 47374-5634. 765/966-2506.

Wesleyan Health Care Center Inc.
729 W 35th St, Marion IN 46953-4215. 765/674-3371.

West Side Health Care Center
PO Box 389, Gary IN 46402-0389. 219/886-7070.

Westminster Village Kentuckiana
2200 Greentree N, Clarksville IN 47129-8965. 812/282-9691.

Westminster Village North Inc.
11050 Presbyterian Dr, Indianapolis IN 46236-2982. 317/823-6841.

Westview Manor
1510 Clinic Dr, Bedford IN 47421-3530. 812/279-4494.

Whispering Pines Health Care Center
3301 Calumet Ave, Valparaiso IN 46383-2614. 219/462-0508.

Williamsburg Health Care
PO Box 661, Crawfordsville IN 47933-0661. 765/364-0363.

Willow Manor Convalescent Center
1321 Willow St, Vincennes IN 47591-4205. 812/882-1136.

Willows Rehabilitation Center
1000 Elizabeth St, Valparaiso IN 46383-4326. 219/464-4858.

Windsor Estates Nursing Rehab. Center
429 W Lincoln Rd, Kokomo IN 46902-3508. 765/453-5600.

Windsor Manor Healthcare
7465 Madison Ave, Indianapolis IN 46227-6564. 317/787-1108.

Woodlands Convalescent Center
PO Box 400, Newburgh IN 47629-0400. 812/853-9567.

Woodview Healthcare Center
3420 E State Blvd, Fort Wayne IN 46805-5605. 219/484-3120.

Yorktown Health Care Center
PO Box 188, Yorktown IN 47396-0188. 765/759-7740.

OFFICES AND CLINICS OF HEALTH PRACTITIONERS

Healthcare Therapy Services Inc.
5214 S East St, Building D1, Indianapolis IN 46227-1917. 317/780-3737.

Nur-Staff Inc.
PO Box 10772, Merrillville IN 46411-0772. 219/738-1867.

Occupational Health Service
1713 N Post Road, Indianapolis IN 46219-1924. 317/355-3113.

Physical Medicine Associates
5610 Crawfordsville Rd, Indianapolis IN 46224-3714. 317/247-4419.

RESIDENTIAL CARE

Ability Services
PO Box 808, Crawfordsville IN 47933-0808. 765/362-4020.

Adec Resource for Independence
PO Box 398, Bristol IN 46507-0398. 219/295-3167.

Community Alternatives
12955 Old Meridian Street, Carmel IN 46032-7106. 317/573-8050.

Cross Road
2525 Lake Avenue, Fort Wayne IN 46805-5407. 219/484-4153.

Damar Homes Inc.
PO Box 41, Camby IN 46113-0041. 317/856-5201.

Evansville Protestant Home
3701 Washington Avenue, Evansville IN 47714-0544. 812/476-3360.

Four Seasons Retirement Center
1901 Taylor Road, Columbus IN 47203-3908. 812/372-8481.

GA Industries
PO Box 252 S B St, Richmond IN 47374-5632. 765/966-0502.

GCARC
PO Box 5, Princeton IN 47670-0005. 812/386-6312.

Greenbush Industries
PO Box 6449, Lafayette IN 47903-6449. 765/423-5531.

Greenwood Village South
295 Village Lane, Greenwood IN 46143-2440. 317/881-2591.

Hoosier Village Retirement Home
5300 W 96th Street, Indianapolis IN 46268-3905. 317/873-3349.

Indiana Soldiers & Sailors Children's Home
10892 North State Road 140, Knightstown IN 46148-9769. 765/345-5141.

Indiana United Methodists Children's Home
PO Box 747, Lebanon IN 46052-0747. 765/482-5900.

Indiana Veterans' Home
3851 N River Road, Lafayette IN 47906-3762. 765/463-1502.

Michigan City Health Care
1101 E Coolspring Avenue, Michigan City IN 46360-6310. 219/874-5211.

Normal Life of Indiana
PO Box 2099, Terre Haute IN 47802-0099. 812/234-3454.

Options For Better Living Inc.
PO Box 1732, Bloomington IN 47402-1732. 812/332-9615.

Pleasant Run Inc.
2400 N Tibbs Avenue, Indianapolis IN 46222-2458. 317/693-9222.

St. Paul's Retirement Community
3602 S Ironwood Dr, South Bend IN 46614-2453. 219/291-8205.

The Havan Center
2325 South Miller Street, Shelbyville IN 46176-9350. 317/392-3287.

Townhouse Health Care
2209 Saint Joe Center Road, Fort Wayne IN 46825. 219/483-3116.

Trade Winds Rehabilitation Center
PO Box 6308, Gary IN 46406-0308. 219/949-4000.

Vernon Manor Children's Home
1955 Vernon St, Wabash IN 46992-4026. 219/563-8438.

Westminster Village Muncie
5801 W Bethel Ave, Muncie IN 47304-9549. 765/288-2155.

White's Residential Family Services Inc.
5233 S 50 E, Wabash IN 46992-8011. 219/563-1158.

SPECIALTY OUTPATIENT FACILITIES

ALS
3811 Parnell Avenue, Fort Wayne IN 46805-1409. 219/482-4651.

Gary Community Mental Health Center
1100 West 6th Avenue, Gary IN 46402-1711. 219/885-4264.

Lifespring Mental Health Services
207 W 13th Street, Jeffersonville IN 47130-3707. 812/283-4491.

Madison Center Inc.
PO Box 80, South Bend IN 46624-0080. 219/234-0061.

Northeastern Center Inc.
PO Box 817, Kendallville IN 46755-0817. 219/347-4400.

Porter-Starke Counseling Center
601 Wall St, Valparaiso IN 46383-2512. 219/464-8541.

Rehabilitation Center & Developmental Services
3701 Bellemeade Ave, Evansville IN 47714-0137. 812/479-1411.

Silvercrest Children's Development Center
PO Box 99, New Albany IN 47151-0099. 812/945-5287.

South Central Community Mental Health
645 South Rogers St, Bloomington IN 47403-2353. 812/339-1691.

Southlake Center For Mental Health
8555 Taft St, Merrillville IN 46410-6123. 219/769-4005.

The Bowen Center
PO Box 497, Warsaw IN 46581-0497. 219/267-7169.

Tri-County Mental Health
PO Box 1129, Carmel IN 46032-6129. 317/574-0055.

For more information on career opportunities in the health care industry:

Associations

ACCREDITING COMMISSION ON EDUCATION FOR HEALTH SERVICES ADMINISTRATION
1911 North Fort Myer Drive, Suite 503, Arlington VA 22209. 703/524-0511.

AMBULATORY INFORMATION MANAGEMENT ASSOCIATION BAY VALLEY MEDICAL GROUP
27212 Calaroga Avenue, Hayward CA 94545. 510/293-5688. World Wide Web address: http://www.aim4.org. E-mail address: info@aim4.org.

AMERICAN ACADEMY OF ALLERGY, ASTHMA, AND IMMUNOLOGY
611 East Wells Street, Milwaukee WI 53202. 414/272-6071. World Wide Web address: http://www.aaaai.org.

AMERICAN ACADEMY OF FAMILY PHYSICIANS
8880 Ward Parkway, Kansas City MO 64114. 816/333-9700. World Wide Web address: http://www.aafp.org. Promotes continuing education for family physicians.

AMERICAN ACADEMY OF PEDIATRIC DENTISTRY
211 East Chicago Avenue, Suite 700, Chicago IL 60611-2626. 312/337-2169. World Wide Web address: http://www.aapd.org.

AMERICAN ACADEMY OF PERIODONTOLOGY
737 North Michigan Avenue, Suite 800, Chicago IL 60611-2690. 312/573-3218. World Wide Web address: http://www.perio.org.

AMERICAN ACADEMY OF PHYSICIAN ASSISTANTS
950 North Washington Street, Alexandria VA 22314-1552. 703/836-2272. World Wide Web address: http://www.aapa.org. Promotes the use of physician assistants.

AMERICAN ASSOCIATION FOR CLINICAL CHEMISTRY
2101 L Street NW, Suite 202, Washington DC 20037-1526. 202/857-0717. World Wide Web address: http://www.aacc.org. A nonprofit association for clinical, chemical, medical, and technical doctors.

AMERICAN ASSOCIATION FOR ORAL AND MAXILLOFACIAL SURGEONS
9700 West Bryn Mawr Avenue, Rosemont IL 60018-5701. 847/678-6200. World Wide Web address: http://www.aaoms.org.

AMERICAN ASSOCIATION FOR RESPIRATORY CARE
11030 Ables Lane, Dallas TX 75229-4593. 972/243-2272. World Wide Web address: http://www.aarc.org. Promotes the art and science of respiratory care, while focusing on the needs of the patients.

AMERICAN ASSOCIATION OF COLLEGES OF OSTEOPATHIC MEDICINE
5550 Friendship Boulevard, Suite 310, Chevy Chase MD 20815. 301/968-4190. World Wide Web address: http://www.aacom.org. Provides application processing services for colleges of osteopathic medicine.

AMERICAN ASSOCIATION OF COLLEGES OF PODIATRIC MEDICINE
1350 Piccard Drive, Suite 322, Rockville MD 20850. 301/990-7400. World Wide Web address: http://www.aacpm.org. Provides applications processing services for colleges of podiatric medicine.

AMERICAN ASSOCIATION OF DENTAL SCHOOLS
1625 Massachusetts Avenue NW, Suite 600, Washington DC 20036-2212. 202/667-9433. Fax: 202/667-0642. E-mail address: aads@aads.jhu.edu. World Wide Web address: http://www.aads.jhu.edu.

Represents all 54 of the dental schools in the U.S. as well as individual members. This organization works to expand postdoctoral training and increase the number of women and minorities in the dental field.

AMERICAN ASSOCIATION OF HEALTHCARE CONSULTANTS
11208 Waples Mill Road, Suite 109, Fairfax VA 22030. 703/691-2242. World Wide Web address: http://www.aahc.net.

AMERICAN ASSOCIATION OF HOMES AND SERVICES FOR THE AGING
901 E Street NW, Suite 500, Washington DC 20001. 202/783-2242. World Wide Web address: http://www.aahsa.org.

AMERICAN ASSOCIATION OF MEDICAL ASSISTANTS
20 North Wacker Drive, Suite 1575, Chicago IL 60606. 312/899-1500. World Wide Web address: http://www.aama-ntl.org.

AMERICAN ASSOCIATION OF NURSE ANESTHETISTS
222 South Prospect Avenue, Park Ridge IL 60068-4001. 847/692-7050. World Wide Web address: http://www.aana.com

AMERICAN CHIROPRACTIC ASSOCIATION
1701 Clarendon Boulevard, Arlington VA 22209. 703/276-8800. World Wide Web address: http://www.amerchiro.org. A national, nonprofit professional membership organization offering educational services (through films, booklets, texts, and kits), regional seminars and workshops, and major health and education activities that provide information on public health, safety, physical fitness, and disease prevention.

AMERICAN COLLEGE OF HEALTHCARE ADMINISTRATORS
325 South Patrick Street, Alexandria VA 22314. 703/549-5822. World Wide Web address: http://www.achca.org. A professional membership society for individual long-term care professionals. Sponsors educational programs, supports research, and produces a number of publications, including the *Journal of Long-Term Care Administration* and *The Long-Term Care Administrator.*

AMERICAN COLLEGE OF HEALTHCARE EXECUTIVES
One North Franklin Street, Suite 1700, Chicago IL 60606-3491. 312/424-2800. World Wide Web address: http://www.ache.org. Offers credentialing and educational programs. Publishes *Hospital & Health Services Administration* (a journal), and *Healthcare Executive* (a magazine).

AMERICAN COLLEGE OF MEDICAL PRACTICE EXECUTIVES
104 Inverness Terrace East, Englewood CO 80112-5306. 303/397-7869. World Wide Web address: http://www.mgma.com/acmpe.

AMERICAN COLLEGE OF OBSTETRICIANS AND GYNECOLOGISTS
409 12th Street SW, P.O. Box 96920, Washington DC 20090-6920. World Wide Web address: http://www.acog.org.

AMERICAN COLLEGE OF PHYSICIAN EXECUTIVES
4890 West Kennedy Boulevard, Suite 200, Tampa FL 33609-2575. 813/287-2000. Fax: 813/287-8993. World Wide Web address: http://www.acpe.org.

AMERICAN DENTAL ASSOCIATION
211 East Chicago Avenue, Chicago IL 60611. 312/440-2500. World Wide Web address: http://www.ada.org.

AMERICAN DENTAL HYGIENISTS ASSOCIATION
444 North Michigan Avenue, Suite 3400, Chicago IL 60611. 312/440-8900. World Wide Web address: http://www.adha.org.

AMERICAN DIETETIC ASSOCIATION
216 West Jackson Boulevard, Suite 800, Chicago IL 60606-6995. 312/899-0040. Toll-free phone: 800/877-1600. Promotes optimal nutrition to improve public health and well-being.

AMERICAN HEALTH INFORMATION MANAGEMENT ASSOCIATION
919 North Michigan Avenue, Suite 1400, Chicago IL 60611. 312/787-2672. World Wide Web address: http://www.ahima.org.

AMERICAN HOSPITAL ASSOCIATION
One North Franklin Street, 27th Floor, Chicago IL 60606. 312/422-3000. World Wide Web address: http://www.aha.org.

AMERICAN MEDICAL ASSOCIATION
515 North State Street, Chicago IL 60610. 312/464-5000. World Wide Web address: http://www.ama.org. An organization for medical doctors.

AMERICAN MEDICAL INFORMATICS ASSOCIATION
4915 St. Elmo Avenue, Suite 401, Bethesda MD 20814. 301/657-1291. World Wide Web address: http://www.amia2.amia.org.

AMERICAN MEDICAL TECHNOLOGISTS
710 Higgins Road, Park Ridge IL 60068. 847/823-5169.

AMERICAN MEDICAL WOMEN'S ASSOCIATION
800 North Fairfax Street, Suite 400, Alexandria VA 22314. 703/838-0500. Fax: 703/549-3864. E-mail address: director@amwa-doc.org. World Wide Web address: http://www.amwa-doc.org. Supports the advancement of women in medicine.

AMERICAN NURSES ASSOCIATION
600 Maryland Avenue SW, Suite 100W, Washington DC 20024-2571. 202/554-4444. World Wide Web address: http://www.nursingworld.org.

AMERICAN OCCUPATIONAL THERAPY ASSOCIATION
4720 Montgomery Lane, P.O. Box 31220, Bethesda MD 20824-1220. 301/652-2682. Toll-free phone: 800/377-8555. Fax: 301/652-7711. World Wide Web address: http://www.aota.org.

AMERICAN OPTOMETRIC ASSOCIATION
243 North Lindbergh Boulevard, St. Louis MO 63141. 314/991-4100. Offers publications, discounts, and insurance programs for members.

AMERICAN ORGANIZATION OF NURSE EXECUTIVES
One North Franklin Street, 34th Floor, Chicago IL 60606. 312/422-2800. World Wide Web address: http://www.aone.org.

AMERICAN ORTHOPAEDIC ASSOCIATION
6300 North River Road, Suite 300, Rosemont IL 60018. 847/318-7330. World Wide Web address: http://www.aoassn.org.

AMERICAN PHYSICAL THERAPY ASSOCIATION
111 North Fairfax Street, Alexandria VA 22314. 703/684-2782. World Wide Web address: http://www.apta.org. Small fee required for information.

AMERICAN PODIATRIC MEDICAL ASSOCIATION
9312 Old Georgetown Road, Bethesda MD 20814-1698. 301/571-9200. World Wide Web address: http://www.apma.org.

AMERICAN PSYCHIATRIC ASSOCIATION
World Wide Web address: http://www.psych.org. Professional association for mental health professionals.

AMERICAN PUBLIC HEALTH ASSOCIATION
1015 15th Street NW, Suite 300, Washington DC 20005. 202/789-5600. World Wide Web address: http://www.apha.org.

AMERICAN SOCIETY OF ANESTHESIOLOGISTS
520 North NW Highway, Park Ridge IL 60068. 847/825-5586. World Wide Web address: http://www.asahq.org.

AMERICAN SPEECH-LANGUAGE-HEARING ASSOCIATION
10801 Rockville Pike, Rockville MD 20852. Toll-free phone: 800/498-2071. World Wide Web address: http://www.asha.org. Professional, scientific, and credentialing association for audiologists, speech-language pathologists, and speech, language, and hearing, scientists.

AMERICAN SUBACUTE CARE ASSOCIATION
1720 Kennedy Causeway, Suite 109, North Bay Village FL 33141. 305/864-0396. World Wide Web address: http://members.aol.com/ascamail/index.htm.

AMERICAN VETERINARY MEDICAL ASSOCIATION
1931 North Meacham Road, Suite 100, Schaumburg IL 60173-4360. 847/925-8070. World Wide Web address: http://www.avma.org. Provides a forum for the discussion of important issues in the veterinary profession.

ASSOCIATION OF AMERICAN MEDICAL COLLEGES
2450 N Street NW, Washington DC 20037-1126. 202/828-0400. World Wide Web address: http://www.aamc.org.

ASSOCIATION OF MENTAL HEALTH ADMINISTRATORS
60 Revere Drive, Suite 500, Northbrook IL 60062. 847/480-9626.

ASSOCIATION OF UNIVERSITY PROGRAMS IN HEALTH ADMINISTRATION
1110 Vermont Avenue, Suite 220, Washington DC 20005. 202/822-8550.

BAYER QUALITY NETWORK
11511 West 73rd Place, Burr Ridge IL 60525. Toll-free phone: 888/BAYERNET. World Wide Web address: http://www.bayerquality.org. A cooperative educational forum for health care professionals.

HEALTH INFORMATION AND MANAGEMENT SYSTEMS SOCIETY
230 East Ohio Street, Suite 500, Chicago IL 60611-3201. 312/664-4467. World Wide Web address: http://www.himss.org.

HEALTHCARE FINANCIAL MANAGEMENT ASSOCIATION
2 Westbrook Corporate Center, Suite 700, Westchester IL 60154. 708/531-9600. World Wide Web address: http://www.hfma.org.

NATIONAL ASSOCIATION FOR CHIROPRACTIC MEDICINE
15427 Baybrook Drive, Houston TX 77062. 281/280-8262. World Wide Web address: http://www.chiromed.org.

NATIONAL COALITION OF HISPANIC HEALTH AND HUMAN SERVICES ORGANIZATIONS
1501 16th Street NW, Washington DC 20036. 202/387-5000. World Wide Web address: http://www.cossmho.org. Strives to improve the health and well-being of Hispanic communities throughout the United States.

NATIONAL HOSPICE ORGANIZATION
1901 North Moore Street, Suite 901, Arlington VA 22209. 703/243-5900. World Wide Web address: http://www.nho.org. Educates and advocates for the principles of hospice care to meet the needs of the terminally ill.

NATIONAL MEDICAL ASSOCIATION
1012 10th Street NW, Washington DC 20001. 202/347-1895.

Magazines

AMERICAN MEDICAL NEWS
American Medical Association, 515 North State Street, Chicago IL 60605. 312/464-5000.

HEALTH CARE EXECUTIVE
American College of Health Care Executives, One North Franklin, Suite 1700, Chicago IL 60606-3491. 312/424-2800.

MODERN HEALTHCARE
Crain Communications, 740 North Rush Street, Chicago IL 60611. 312/649-5374. World Wide Web address: http://www.modernhealthcare.com.

NURSEFAX
Springhouse Corporation, 1111 Bethlehem Pike, P.O. Box 908, Spring House PA 19477. 215/646-8700. World Wide Web address: http://www.springnet.com. This is a jobline service designed to be used in conjunction with *Nursing* magazine. Please call to obtain a copy of a magazine or the *Nursing* directory.

Online Services

ACADEMIC PHYSICIAN AND SCIENTIST
Gopher://aps.acad-phy-sci.com/. A great resource for jobseekers interested in administrative or clinical positions at teaching hospitals.

HEALTH CARE JOBS ONLINE JOB BULLETIN BOARD
http://www.hcjobsonline.com/bbs.html. This Website is for jobseekers who are looking for job opportunities in the health care industry. This site is maintained by Images, Ink.

MEDSEARCH AMERICA
http://www.medsearch.com. Site geared for medical professionals and a definite "must see" for those seeking positions in this area, *Medsearch America* offers national and international job searches, career forums, a resume builder, resume posting, recruiters' sites, listings of professional associations, and employer profiles. Precise and extensive searches can be done by job category, association or company name, keyword, or location.

MEDZILLA
E-mail address: info@medzilla.com. World Wide Web address: http://www.medzilla.com. Lists job openings for professionals in the fields of biotechnology, health care, medicine, and science related industries.

NURSING NETWORK FORUM
Go: Custom 261. A CompuServe bulletin board for nurses that provides periodic "live" discussions with special guests.

SALUDOS WEB CAREER GUIDE: HEALTH CARE
http://www.saludos.com/cguide/hcguide.html. Provides information for jobseekers looking in the health care field. The site includes links to several health care associations and other sites that are sources of job openings in health care. This site is run by Saludos Hispanos.

HOTELS AND RESTAURANTS

Employment in the hotel and restaurant industry has increased from 1.66 million workers in 1993 to 1.85 million workers in 1998. Hotels are doing considerable business with a shortage of new lodging facilities (many are under construction) and the booming economy. As a result, room rates have risen more than 12 percent over the past two years and were expected to rise another 5.3 percent in 1998. This will be offset by new construction which will increase the number of rooms faster than the demand. This is especially true in cities such as Las Vegas, where the construction of more than 10,000 new rooms since 1997 will outpace demand. U.S. Industry and Trade Outlook 1998 *reports that numerous U.S. cities are banking on the success of business meetings and conventions and are making significant investments in new and expanded convention facilities.*

Jobs are plentiful for candidates with degrees in hotel or restaurant management. Meanwhile, a shortage of young adult workers between 16 and 24 years of age to fill many of the industry's entry-level positions is causing hotels to rely more heavily on computer-based property management and check-in systems that require fewer employees.

According to the National Restaurant Association, 44 percent of every dollar Americans spend on food goes toward dining out. Nine million people are employed in food services and that number is expected to climb to 11 million in the year 2005. Across the industry, fast-food chains are experiencing tremendous growth and are moving into less traditional sites such as airports and college campuses.

ASSOCIATED HOSTS INC.
8910 Purdue Road, Suite 315, Indianapolis IN 46268. 317/876-3290. **Contact:** Human Resources. **Description:** Operates 78 restaurants under various names throughout the country and also maintains a number of hotels.

CONSOLIDATED PRODUCTS, INC.
36 South Pennsylvania Street, Suite 500, Indianapolis IN 46204. 317/633-4100. **Fax:** 317/633-4106. **Contact:** Robert L. Grimm, Vice President of Human Resources. **World Wide Web address:** http://www.steaknshake.com. **Description:** Owns and operates Steak n Shake restaurants. Founded in 1934. **NOTE:** Entry-level positions and second and third shifts are offered. **Common positions include:** District Manager; Division Manager; Management Trainee; Store Manager. **Educational backgrounds include:** Business Administration; Computer Science; Marketing. **Benefits:** Disability Coverage; Employee Discounts; Flexible Schedule; Life Insurance; Medical Insurance; Profit Sharing; Public Transit Available; Savings Plan. **Special programs:** Training. **Other U.S. locations:** Nationwide. **Listed on:** New York Stock Exchange. **Stock exchange symbol:** COP. **President/CEO/Owner:** Alan B. Gilman, CEO. **Annual sales/revenues:** More than $100 million. **Number of employees at this location:** 250. **Number of employees nationwide:** 12,000.

LEE'S INNS OF AMERICA
P.O. Box 86, North Vernon IN 47265. 812/346-5072. **Physical address:** 130 North State Street, North Vernon IN. **Fax:** 812/346-7521. **Contact:** Jim Pratt, Vice President of Operations. **Description:** Owns and operates 21 limited-service hotels throughout Indiana, Illinois, Michigan,

and Ohio. **NOTE:** Entry-level positions are offered. **Educational backgrounds include:** Business Administration; Hotel Administration. **Benefits:** Disability Coverage; Employee Discounts; Incentive Plan; Life Insurance; Medical Insurance. **Special programs:** Internships; Training. **Corporate headquarters location:** This Location. **Listed on:** Privately held.

McDONALD'S RESTAURANTS
One Woodside Drive, Suite L101, Richmond IN 47374. 765/962-7413. **Contact:** Human Resources. **Description:** Develops, operates, franchises, and services a worldwide system of restaurants which process, package, and sell a variety of fast foods. McDonald's is one of the largest restaurant operations in the United States and the world. The company operates more than 14,000 McDonald's restaurants in all 50 states and in 58 other countries.

McDONALD'S RESTAURANTS
YANCY SYSTEMS, INC.
1820 North National Road, Columbus IN 47201. 812/376-0552. **Contact:** Human Resources. **Description:** A franchisee of McDonald's Restaurants that operates 11 restaurants in Indiana. Overall, McDonald's Restaurants develops, operates, franchises, and services a worldwide system of restaurants which process, package, and sell a variety of fast foods. McDonald's is one of the largest restaurant operations in the United States and the world. The company operates more than 14,000 McDonald's restaurants in all 50 states and in 58 other countries.

NOBLE ROMAN'S, INC.
One Virginia Avenue, Suite 800, Indianapolis IN 46204. 317/634-3377. **Contact:** Human Resources. **Description:** Owns, operates, manages, and franchises pizza restaurants.

QUALITY DINING, INC.
4220 Edison Lakes Parkway, Mishawaka IN 46545. 219/271-4600. **Contact:** Human Resources. **Description:** A franchiser of restaurants. The company operates 48 quick-service Burger King Restaurants, eight casual dining restaurants under the trade name of Chili's, three bakeries under the trade name Bruegger's Fresh Bakery, and one casual dining restaurant under the name Spageddie's. **Other U.S. locations:** DE; MI; NJ; OH; PA.

SIGNATURE INNS, INC.
250 East 96th Street, Suite 450, Indianapolis IN 46240. 317/581-1111. **Contact:** Human Resources. **World Wide Web address:** http://www.signatureinns.com. **Description:** Manages and operates franchised Signature Inn hotels. **Corporate headquarters location:** This Location.

Note: Because addresses and telephone numbers of smaller companies can change rapidly, we recommend you call each company to verify the information below before inquiring about job opportunities. Mass mailings are not recommended.

Additional small employers:

DRINKING PLACES

Indianapolis Original Sports Bar
39 Jackson Place, Indianapolis IN 46225-1050. 317/972-1093.

World Mardi Gras
49 W Maryland St, Indianapolis IN 46204-3522. 317/630-5483.

EATING PLACES

Applebee's
5046 W Pike Plaza Road, Indianapolis IN 46254-3001. 317/290-1940.

Applebee's
1251 US Highway 31 North, Greenwood IN 46142-4503. 317/888-0744.

Arby's
3550 Park Place, Mishawaka IN 46545. 219/277-7540.

Bandido's Restaurant
6060 E State Boulevard, Fort Wayne IN 46815-7639. 219/493-0607.

Beef House Inc.
16501 N State Road 63, Covington IN 47932-7042. 765/793-3947.

Beef-N-Boards Dinner Theatre
9301 North Michigan Road, Indianapolis IN 46268-3108. 317/872-9664.

Brown County Inn Inc.
PO Box 128, Nashville IN 47448-0128. 812/988-2291.

Burger King Restaurant
2 W 240 Street, Suite B, Lafayette IN 47905-6301. 765/474-0054.

Captain D's Seafood Restaurant
311 S Green River Road, Evansville IN 47715-7311. 812/476-3865.

Carlisle Restaurant
1877 Center Street, Portage IN 46368-1644. 219/762-2105.

Carlos O'Kelly's
549 E Coliseum Boulevard, Fort Wayne IN 46805-1215. 219/483-0080.

Casa Gallardo
1446 E 82nd Avenue, Merrillville IN 46410-6324. 219/769-2675.

Cheddar's Restaurant
305 W Coliseum Boulevard, Fort Wayne IN 46805-1008. 219/484-4631.

Chi-Chi's Mexican Restaurant
1000 N Green River Road, Evansville IN 47715-2421. 812/473-4433.

Chi-Chi's Mexican Restaurant
6102 W 38th Street, Indianapolis IN 46254-2927. 317/299-8081.

Chi-Chi's Mexican Restaurant
867 U.S. Highway 31 North, Greenwood IN 46142-4402. 317/888-2886.

Chi-Chi's Mexican Restuarant
6110 E 82nd Street, Indianapolis IN 46250-1500. 317/842-4597.

Chili's Grill & Bar
3960 E 82nd Street, Indianapolis IN 46240-2467. 317/577-0309.

Chili's Grill & Bar
6943 W 38th Street, Indianapolis IN 46254-3905. 317/328-1767.

Chili's Grill & Bar
1281 U.S. Highway 31 North, Greenwood IN 46142-4502. 317/881-6991.

Chili's Grill and Bar
317 E Coliseum Boulevard, Fort Wayne IN 46805-1003. 219/471-2979.

Cooker Bar & Grill
8601 Keystone Crossing, Indianapolis IN 46240-2107. 317/574-0790.

Cooker Bar & Grille
2801 Lake Circle Drive, Indianapolis IN 46268-4205. 317/471-1111.

Dalt's Classic American Grill
8702 Keystone Crossing, Indianapolis IN 46240-7621. 317/846-7226.

Darryl's Restaurant
501 N Green River Road, Evansville IN 47715-2411. 812/474-1920.

Das Dutchman Essenhaus
PO Box 2608, Middlebury IN 46540-2608. 219/825-9471.

Derby Dinner Playhouse
525 Marriott Drive, Clarksville IN 47129-3053. 812/288-2632.

Dick Clark's American Bandstand Restaurant
3550 East 86th Street, Indianapolis IN 46240-2424. 317/848-2002.

Don Pablo's Mexican Restaurant
8150 U.S. Highway 31 South, Indianapolis IN 46227-0994. 317/888-0363.

Don Pablo's Mexican Restaurant
6929 West 38th Street, Indianapolis IN 46254-3905. 317/293-2178.

Enzo's Pizza
29 E McCarty Street, Suite 100, Indianapolis IN 46225-3307. 317/638-0357.

Ernie's Pizza
505 South Adams Street, Versailles IN 47042-9002. 812/689-7480.

Hacienda
186 Easy Shopping Plaza, Elkhart IN 46516-3535. 219/294-6597.

Hacienda
711 N 1st Avenue, Evansville IN 47710-1631. 812/423-6355.

Hacienda
990 S Green River Road, Evansville IN 47715-4108. 812/473-5080.

Hacienda
5836 Grape Road, Mishawaka IN 46545-1248. 219/277-1318.

Hacienda
1290 Scottsdale Mall, South Bend IN 46614-3471. 219/291-2566.

Hacienda
2006 S Plate Street, Kokomo IN 46902-5734. 765/452-8231.

Houlihan's
6101 N Keystone Avenue, Indianapolis IN 46220-2431. 317/257-3285.

Italiannis
1605 Southlake Mall, Merrillville IN 46410-6449. 219/736-1977.

Italiannis
10343 Indianapolis Boulevard, Highland IN 46322-3509. 219/922-9785.

Jonathan Byrd's Cafeteria
PO Box 413, Greenwood IN 46142-0413. 317/881-8888.

Kilroy's
502 E Kirkwood Avenue, Bloomington IN 47408-4059. 812/339-3006.

Lee's Recipe Country Chicken
206 East Collins Road, Fort Wayne IN 46825-5304. 219/484-0119.

Little Caesar's Enterprises Inc.
2810 Maplecrest Road, Fort Wayne IN 46815-7016. 219/486-4723.

Logan's Roadhouse Inc.
970 East State Road 131, Clarksville IN 47129-2214. 812/288-9789.

Lone Star Steakhouse & Saloon
405 Sagamore Parkway South, Colburn IN 47905-4700. 765/449-4907.

McDonald's
1885 Weslynn Drive, Indianapolis IN 46228-3057. 317/253-0855.

McDonald's
9611 North By Northeast Blvd, Fishers IN 46038-9785. 317/578-2028.

Miguel's Mexican Restaurant
1531 Goshen Avenue, Fort Wayne IN 46808-2037. 219/483-7214.

Montgomery Inn
8580 Allison Pointe Boulevard, Indianapolis IN 46250-4268. 317/570-9400.

Mountain Jack
5910 East 82nd Street, Indianapolis IN 46250-1567. 317/842-5225.

O'Charley's Inc.
1440 Vaxter Avenue, Clarksville IN 47129-7721. 812/284-9646.

Ogden Entertainment Inc.
12880 East 146th Street, Noblesville IN 46060-9582. 317/776-0712.

Ogden Entertainment Inc.
501 W Maryland Street, Indianapolis IN 46225-1041. 317/693-0329.

Ogden Entertainment Inc.
300 East Market Street, Indianapolis IN 46204-2603. 317/634-4121.

Old Chicago Steakhouse
222 South Michigan Street, South Bend IN 46601-2002. 219/234-5200.

Old Spaghetti Factory
210 S Meridian Street, Indianapolis IN 46225-1019. 317/635-6325.

Olive Garden
6130 E 82nd St, Indianapolis IN 46250-1500. 317/842-6321.

Olive Garden
1274 US Highway 31 N, Greenwood IN 46142-4501. 317/887-3030.

Olive Garden
4118 S Scatterfield Road, Anderson IN 46013-2627. 765/642-9980.

Olive Garden
3820 S U.S. Highway 41, Terre Haute IN 47802-4108. 812/235-5177.

Olive Garden
6410 Grape Road, Mishawaka IN 46545-1103. 219/277-6503.

Olive Garden
4015 South Lafountain Street, Kokomo IN 46902-6913. 765/455-2038.

Outback Steakhouse
3454 W 86th St, Indianapolis IN 46268-1929. 317/872-4329.

Pizza Express Inc.
PO Box 6955, Bloomington IN 47407-6955. 812/339-2256.

Planet Hollywood International
130 S Illinois St, Indianapolis IN 46225-1006. 317/822-9222.

Rally's Hamburgers Inc.
7311 W 10th St, Indianapolis IN 46214-2515. 317/271-1174.

Rally's Restaurant
325 S Green River Rd, Evansville IN 47715-7311. 812/479-8647.

Red Lobster
2617 E 3rd St, Bloomington IN 47401-5396. 812/332-9712.

Red Lobster
4605 Bellemeade Ave, Evansville IN 47714-0621. 812/477-9227.

Red Lobster
3501 Dixie Bee Rd, Terre Haute IN 47802. 812/234-7727.

Red Lobster
5806 S Scatterfield Rd, Anderson IN 46013-3147. 765/643-7663.

Red Lobster
1752 N Shadeland Ave, Indianapolis IN 46219-2734. 317/352-1679.

Rick's Cafe Boatyard
4050 Dandy Trail, Indianapolis IN 46254-9741. 317/290-9300.

Ruby Tuesday
515 E Southway Blvd, Kokomo IN 46902-3821. 765/453-0396.

Shapiro's Deli
808 S Meridian St, Indianapolis IN 46225-1335. 317/631-4041.

Southwest Mesquite Grills Bar
2005 State St, New Albany IN 47150-4921. 812/945-0177.

Steak N Shake Inc.
101 W Maryland St, Indianapolis IN 46225-1013. 317/634-8703.

Strongbow Turkey Inn Inc.
2405 US Highway 30, Valparaiso IN 46383-8362. 219/462-3311.

Subway Sandwiches
4280 W Jonathan Moore Pike, Columbus IN 47201-9585. 812/342-2120.

Teibel's Restaurant
1775 US Highway 41, Schererville IN 46375-1647. 219/865-2000.

Texas Roadhouse
2941 S 3rd St, Terre Haute IN 47802-3707. 812/234-3378.

TGI Friday's
3502 E 82nd St, Indianapolis IN 46240-2474. 317/844-3355.

TGI Friday's
501 W Washington St, Indianapolis IN 46204-2706. 317/685-8443.

Turoni's Pizza
408 N Main St, Evansville IN 47711-5418. 812/424-9871.

Weinbach's Inc.
1 N Weinbach Ave, Evansville IN 47711-6003. 812/476-1323.

Wendy's
4227 S Michigan St, South Bend IN 46614-2547. 219/291-6171.

Wendy's
8939 Technology Dr, Fishers IN 46038-2801. 317/841-0909.

Wendy's
310 S Dixie Way, South Bend IN 46637-3320. 219/271-9777.

Wendy's
3530 W Jefferson Blvd, Fort Wayne IN 46802-4952. 219/436-2779.

Wendy's
6816 Lincoln Highway E, Fort Wayne IN 46803-3248. 219/493-1106.

Wendy's
433 W Coliseum Blvd, Fort Wayne IN 46805-1010. 219/484-8348.

Wendy's
2215 Maplecrest Rd, Fort Wayne IN 46815-7627. 219/749-0858.

HOTELS AND MOTELS

Adam's Mark Hotel
2544 Executive Drive, Indianapolis IN 46241-5013. 317/248-2481.

Argosy Casino
777 E Arogsy, Lawrenceburg IN 47025. 812/539-8000.

Caesar's of Indiana
405 N Capitol Ave, Suite 102, Corydon IN 47112-1552. 812/738-3848.

Courtyard Downtown Indianapolis
501 W Washington Street, Indianapolis IN 46204-2706. 317/635-4443.

Crawfordsville Holiday Inn
2500 Lafayette Road, Crawfordsville IN 47933-1049. 765/362-8700.

Crowne Plaza
PO Box 2186, Indianapolis IN 46206-2186. 317/631-2221.

Embassy Suites Downtown
110 W Washington Street, Indianapolis IN 46204-3423. 317/236-1800.

Embassy Suites North
3912 Vincennes Road, Indianapolis IN 46268-3005. 317/872-7700.

Evansville Airport Marriott
7101 Highway 41 North, Evansville IN 47711-1713. 812/867-7999.

Fourwinds-Resort & Marina
9301 South Fairfax Road, Bloomington IN 47401-8962. 812/824-9904.

Hilton Fort Wayne Convention Center
PO Box 12049, Fort Wayne IN 46862-2049. 219/420-1100.

Hilton Inn At The Airport
PO Box 51316, Indianapolis IN 46251-0316. 317/244-3361.

Holiday Inn
4101 Highway 41 North, Evansville IN 47711-2822. 812/424-6400.

Holiday Inn
3300 Dixie Bee Road, Terre Haute IN 47802. 812/232-6081.

Holiday Inn
300 E Washington Boulevard, Fort Wayne IN 46802-3124. 219/422-5511.

Holiday Inn
3330 W Coliseum Boulevard, Fort Wayne IN 46808-1008. 219/484-7711.

Holiday Inn
505 Marriott Drive, Clarksville IN 47129-3053. 812/283-4411.

Holiday Inn
2480 W Jonathan Moore Pike, Columbus IN 47201-9254. 812/372-1541.

Holiday Inn
3850 Depauw Boulevard, Indianapolis IN 46268-1144. 317/872-9790.

Holiday Inn
515 N Dixie Way, South Bend IN 46637-3315. 219/272-6600.

Holiday Inn
5501 National Road East, Richmond IN 47374-2615. 765/966-7511.

Holiday Inn
PO Box 6, Jasper IN 47547-0006. 812/482-5555.

Hyatt
1 S Capitol Avenue, Indianapolis IN 46204-3400. 317/632-1234.

Indianapolis Marriott Hotel
7202 E 21st Street, Indianapolis IN 46219-1717. 317/352-1231.

Majestic Star Casino
One Buffington Harbor Drive, Gary IN 46406. 219/977-7823.

New Harmony Inn
PO Box 581, New Harmony IN 47631-0581. 812/682-4491.

Quality Inn-East
3525 N Shadeland Ave, Indianapolis IN 46226-5708. 317/549-2222.

Radisson Hotel At Star Plaza
800 E 81st Ave, Merrillville IN 46410-5646. 219/769-6311.

Radisson Plaza & Suite Hotel
8787 Keystone Crossing, Indianapolis IN 46240-2108. 317/846-2700.

Ramada Hotels Corporation
2500 S High School Rd, Indianapolis IN 46241-4943. 317/244-3361.

Ramada Inn
700 W Riverside Dr, Jeffersonville IN 47130-3122. 812/284-6711.

River City Executive Inn
PO Box 3246, Evansville IN 47731-3246. 812/424-8000.

Seasons Lodge & Conference Center
PO Box 187, Nashville IN 47448-0187. 812/988-2284.

Showboat Mardi Gras Casino
PO Box 777, East Chicago IN 46312-0777. 219/378-3000.

South Bend Marriott Hotel
123 North St. Joseph St, South Bend IN 46601-1624. 219/234-2000.

The Brickyard Crossing Inn
4400 West 16th Street, Indianapolis IN 46222-2512. 317/241-2500.

The Marten House
1801 West 86th Street, Indianapolis IN 46260-2001. 317/872-4111.

University Place Hotel
850 West Michigan St, Indianapolis IN 46202-2800. 317/269-9000.

For more information on career opportunities in hotels and restaurants:

Associations

AMERICAN HOTEL AND MOTEL ASSOCIATION
1201 New York Avenue NW, Suite 600, Washington DC 20005-3931. 202/289-3100. World Wide Web address: http://www.ahma.com. Provides lobbying services and educational programs, maintains and disseminates industry data, and produces a variety of publications.

THE EDUCATIONAL FOUNDATION OF THE NATIONAL RESTAURANT ASSOCIATION
250 South Wacker Drive, Suite 1400, Chicago IL

60606. 312/715-1010. World Wide Web address: http://www.edfound.org. Offers educational products, including textbooks, manuals, instruction guides, manager and employee training programs, videos, and certification programs.

NATIONAL RESTAURANT ASSOCIATION
1200 17th Street NW, Washington DC 20036. 202/331-5900. World Wide Web address: http://www.restaurant.org.

Directories

DIRECTORY OF CHAIN RESTAURANT OPERATORS
Business Guides, Inc., Lebhar-Friedman, Inc., 3922 Coconut Palm Drive, Suite 300, Tampa FL 33619-8321. 813/664-6700. World Wide Web address: http://www.lf.com.

DIRECTORY OF HIGH-VOLUME INDEPENDENT RESTAURANTS
Lebhar-Friedman, Inc., 3922 Coconut Palm Drive, Tampa FL 33619-8321. 813/664-6800. World Wide Web address: http://www.lf.com.

Magazines

CORNELL HOTEL AND RESTAURANT ADMINISTRATION QUARTERLY
Cornell University School of Hotel Administration, Statler Hall, Ithaca NY 14853-6902. 607/255-9393. World Wide Web address: http://www.cornell.edu.

INNKEEPING WORLD
P.O. Box 84108, Seattle WA 98124. 206/362-7125.

NATION'S RESTAURANT NEWS
Lebhar-Friedman, Inc., 3922 Coconut Palm Drive, Tampa FL 33619. 813/664-6700.

Online Services

COOLWORKS
http://www.coolworks.com/. This Website provides links to 22,000 job openings at resorts, summer camps, ski areas, river areas, ranches, fishing areas, and cruise ships. This site also includes information on volunteer openings.

HOSPITALITY NET VIRTUAL JOB EXCHANGE
http://www.hospitalitynet.nl/job. This site allows jobseekers to search for job opportunities worldwide in the hospitality industry including accounting, food and beverage, marketing and sales, and conference and banqueting positions. Jobseekers can also post resume information and a description of the job they want.

JOBNET: HOSPITALITY INDUSTRY
http://www.westga.edu/~coop/hospitality.html. This Website provides links to job openings and information for hotels.

INSURANCE

Shaped by a changing marketplace of consolidation and competitive pressures, the insurance industry will face a tough year. According to Business Week, *after record earnings in 1997, analysts expected that pretax operating income for insurance companies would drop to $26.3 billion in 1998, down from $35.5 billion in 1997. This was due in part to lower projected margins and higher projected claims.*

Property/casualty insurance is likely to see poor sales growth, and industry analysts blame this on companies' diminishing financial reserves from prior years that tend to boost earnings. More consolidations are also expected in this sector. Homeowner insurers are also doing poorly, while automobile insurers are faring better, but Business Week *projected that increases in car premiums would slow in 1998.*

In contrast, the life insurance sector is stable, driven by increased consumer demand due to increasing consumer savings and an aging population.

ACORDIA, INC.
111 Monument Circle, Suite 3200, Indianapolis IN 46204. 317/488-2500. **Contact:** Human Resources. **World Wide Web address:** http://www.acordia.com. **Description:** Acordia includes a growing network of companies which meet the employees' benefits, managed health care, life, and property and casualty insurance brokerage needs of companies and individuals. **Parent company:** The Associated Group.

AMERICAN UNITED LIFE INSURANCE COMPANY
One American Square, P.O. Box 368, Indianapolis IN 46206-0368. 317/263-1444. **Fax:** 317/263-1931. **Recorded jobline:** 317/263-4444. **Contact:** Dawn Peace, Employment Support Specialist. **E-mail address:** aul_employment@aol.com. **World Wide Web address:** http://www.aul.com. **Description:** A provider of insurance, annuities, reinsurance, and investments. **Common positions include:** Accountant/Auditor; Actuary; Adjuster; Claim Representative; Computer Programmer; Customer Service Representative; Financial Analyst; Insurance Agent/Broker; Management Analyst/Consultant; Property and Real Estate Manager; Systems Analyst; Underwriter/Assistant Underwriter. **Educational backgrounds include:** Computer Science; Mathematics. **Benefits:** 401(k); Dental Insurance; Disability Coverage; Employee Discounts; Life Insurance; Medical Insurance; Pension Plan; Profit Sharing; Savings Plan; Tuition Assistance. **Office hours**: Monday - Friday, 8:00 a.m. - 5:00 p.m. **Corporate headquarters location:** This Location. **Subsidiaries include:** State Life Insurance. **Operations at this facility include:** Administration; Sales. **Listed on:** Privately held. **CEO:** Jerry Semler. **Annual sales/revenues:** $21 - $50 million. **Number of employees at this location:** 1,400.

ANTHEM INSURANCE COMPANIES INC.
120 Monument Circle, Suite 200, Indianapolis IN 46204. 317/488-6000. **Contact:** Human Resources Department. **World Wide Web address:** http://www.anthem-inc.com. **Description:** An insurance company that provides all lines of personal and commercial insurance. **Corporate headquarters location:** This Location.

COMMERCIAL UNION INSURANCE COMPANIES
300 North Meridian Street, Suite 1400, P.O. Box 44230, Indianapolis IN 46204. 317/632-1451. **Contact:** Donald Whitesell, Administration Manager. **World Wide Web address:** http://www.cuusa.com. **Description:** Comprised of the U.S. property, casualty, and life insurance subsidiaries of Commercial Union Corporation, a wholly-owned subsidiary of Commercial Union plc of London, England. The principal operating companies are Commercial Union Insurance

Company, American Employers' Insurance Company, The Employers' Fire Insurance Company, The Northern Assurance Company of America, American Central Insurance Company, CU Homeland Insurance Company, Commercial Union Midwest Insurance Company, Commercial Union Life Insurance Company of America, and CU Life Insurance Company of New York. **Common positions include:** Administrative Assistant; Auditor; Claim Representative; Customer Service Representative; Marketing Specialist; Secretary; Typist/Word Processor; Underwriter/ Assistant Underwriter. **Educational backgrounds include:** Business Administration; Communications; Marketing. **Benefits:** 401(k); Dental Insurance; Disability Coverage; Employee Discounts; Life Insurance; Medical Insurance; Pension Plan; Profit Sharing; Savings Plan; Tuition Assistance. **Corporate headquarters location:** Boston MA. **International locations:** Worldwide. **Parent company:** Commercial Union Corporation. **Annual sales/revenues:** More than $100 million. **Number of employees at this location:** 160.

THE CONSECO COMPANIES
11815 North Pennsylvania Street, Carmel IN 46032. 317/817-6100. **Contact:** Human Resources Department. **World Wide Web address:** http://www.conseco.com. **Description:** The Conseco Companies is a life and health insurance company. **Corporate headquarters location:** This Location.

GOLDEN RULE INSURANCE COMPANY
7440 Woodland Drive, Indianapolis IN 46278. 317/297-4123. **Contact:** Human Resources Department. **World Wide Web address:** http://www.goldenrule.com. **Description:** Golden Rule Insurance Company provides life, health, and group insurance nationwide. **Number of employees nationwide:** 1,300.

GUARANTY NATIONAL CORPORATION
7400 North Shadeland Avenue, Suite 210, Indianapolis IN 46250. 317/577-0895. **Fax:** 317/849-9827. **Contact:** Human Resources Department. **Description:** Guaranty National Corporation offers standard and specialty property and casualty insurance and nonstandard personal automobile insurance through independent agents. Its coverages are sold throughout most of the United States. **NOTE:** Please send resumes to Human Resources, P.O. Box 3329, Englewood CO 80155. **Corporate headquarters location:** Englewood CO. **Other U.S. locations:** Phoenix AZ; Salem OR; Salt Lake City UT; Richmond VA. **Subsidiaries include:** Colorado Casualty Insurance Company; Guaranty National Insurance Company; Guaranty National Insurance Company of California; Landmark American Insurance Company; Peak Property and Casualty Insurance Company.

LINCOLN NATIONAL CORPORATION
P.O. Box 7829, Fort Wayne IN 46801. 219/455-1332. **Fax:** 219/455-7556. **Contact:** Human Resources Department. **Description:** Lincoln National Corporation is an insurance holding company whose four businesses sell insurance and investment products. **Common positions include:** Accountant/Auditor; Actuary; Insurance Agent/Broker; Investment Manager. **Educational backgrounds include:** Accounting; Finance; Liberal Arts; Marketing. **Corporate headquarters location:** This Location. **Subsidiaries include:** Employers Health Insurance Company (small group life and health); Lincoln National Life Insurance Company (individual life, annuities, and pensions); Lincoln National Reinsurance Companies (life and health reinsurance). **Operations at this facility include:** Administration; Divisional Headquarters; Regional Headquarters; Service. **Listed on:** American Stock Exchange; NASDAQ; New York Stock Exchange.

MERIDIAN MUTUAL INSURANCE COMPANY
P.O. Box 1980, Indianapolis IN 46206-1980. 317/931-7173. **Fax:** 317/931-7263. **Recorded jobline:** 317/931-7180. **Contact:** John Boles, Human Resources. **Description:** A regional property and casualty insurance company. **Common positions include:** Accountant/Auditor; Adjuster; Administrative Manager; Attorney; Budget Analyst; Claim Representative; Clerical Supervisor; Computer Programmer; Financial Analyst; Human Resources Manager; Insurance Agent/Broker; Systems Analyst; Underwriter/Assistant Underwriter. **Educational backgrounds include:** Accounting; Business Administration; Communications; Computer Science; Finance; Liberal Arts;

Marketing. **Benefits:** 401(k); Bonus Award/Plan; Dental Insurance; Disability Coverage; Life Insurance; Medical Insurance; Pension Plan; Tuition Assistance. **Corporate headquarters location:** This Location. **Other U.S. locations:** Louisville KY; Lansing MI. **Operations at this facility include:** Administration; Divisional Headquarters. **Listed on:** NASDAQ. **Number of employees at this location:** 400. **Number of employees nationwide:** 500.

SAFECO/AMERICAN STATES INSURANCE
500 North Meridian Street, Indianapolis IN 46204. 317/262-6262. **Contact:** Linda VanKirk, Human Resources Director. **World Wide Web address:** http://www.safeco.com. **Description:** Provides a range of insurance coverage including commercial, personal, and small business. **Parent company:** SAFECO Corporation.

Note: Because addresses and telephone numbers of smaller companies can change rapidly, we recommend you call each company to verify the information below before inquiring about job opportunities. Mass mailings are not recommended.

Additional small employers:

INSURANCE AGENTS, BROKERS, AND SERVICES

Adminastar Federal Inc.
PO Box 50454, Indianapolis IN 46250-0454. 317/841-4400.

CNA Insurance
PO Box 7016, Indianapolis IN 46207-7016. 317/575-5200.

Edward B. Morris Associates
PO Box 50440, Indianapolis IN 46250-0440. 317/842-4747.

Gardner & White Corporation
8902 North Meridian Street, Indianapolis IN 46260-5369. 317/581-1580.

JF Molloy & Associates Incorporation
4040 Vincennes Circle, Indianapolis IN 46268-3027. 317/879-4040.

K&K Insurance Group Incorporation
PO Box 2338, Fort Wayne IN 46801-2338. 219/459-5000.

The Nyhart Company Inc.
PO Box 88187, Indianapolis IN 46208-0187. 317/923-2391.

Wausau Insurance Companies
PO Box 1187, Indianapolis IN 46206-1187. 317/576-9654.

INSURANCE COMPANIES

Acordia, Inc.
5451 West Drive, Indianapolis IN 46236-2716. 317/298-6600.

Acordia Healthcare Solutions
5451 Lakeview Parkway South, Indianapolis IN 46268-4115. 317/387-5520.

Aetna US Healthcare
3500 E Coliseum Boulevard, Fort Wayne IN 46805. 219/496-5400.

Allstate Insurance Company
8900 Keystone Crossing, Indianapolis IN 46240-2146. 317/843-8100.

American Health Network
10333 N Meridian Street, Indianapolis IN 46290-1074. 317/580-6300.

American Reliance Inc.
PO Box 1736, Indianapolis IN 46206-1736. 317/253-1431.

Anthem Blue Cross
6720 Parkdale Place, Indianapolis IN 46254-4668. 317/290-2800.

Anthem Blue Cross Blue Shield
3760 Guion Road, Indianapolis IN 46222-1618. 317/921-7000.

Anthem Blue Cross Blue Shield
4040 Vincennes Circle, Indianapolis IN 46268-3027. 317/228-7356.

Anthem Blue Cross Blue Shield
2002 Wellesley Boulevard, Indianapolis IN 46219-2457. 317/322-5300.

Anthem, Inc.
5730 W 74th Street, Indianapolis IN 46278-1754. 317/290-4100.

Baldwin & Lyons Inc.
1099 N Meridian Street, Indianapolis IN 46204-1075. 317/636-9800.

Bankers National Life Insurance Company
PO Box 1911, Carmel IN 46032-4911. 317/817-2893.

Brotherhood Mutual Insurance Company
PO Box 2227, Fort Wayne IN 46801-2227. 219/482-8668.

Capitol American Life Insurance Company
11825 N Pennsylvania Street, Carmel IN 46032-4555. 317/817-4300.

Forethought Life Insurance Company
Forethought Center, Batesville IN 47006. 812/934-7139.

Grain Dealers Mutual Insurance Company
PO Box 1747, Indianapolis IN 46206-1747. 317/923-2453.

Great West Casualty Company
PO Box 4555, Bloomington IN 47402-4555. 812/337-0300.

Hoosier Insurance Company
8500 Keystone Crossing, Indianapolis IN 46240-2456. 317/722-3838.

Indiana Farmers Mutual Insurance Company
PO Box 527, Indianapolis IN 46206-0527. 317/846-4211.

Indianapolis Life Insurance Company
PO Box 1230, Indianapolis IN 46206-1230. 317/927-6500.

ITT Hartford
PO Box 68930, Indianapolis IN 46268-0930. 317/876-7076.

Lafayette Life Insurance Company
PO Box 7007, Lafayette IN 47903-7007. 765/477-7411.

Liberty Mutual Insurance Company
PO Box 768, Mishawaka IN 46546-0768. 219/258-4400.

M-Plan Inc.
8802 N Meridian Street, Indianapolis IN 46260-5371. 317/571-5300.

Medical Protective Company Inc.
5814 Reed Road, Fort Wayne IN 46835-3568. 219/485-9622.

Monroe Guaranty Insurance Company
11590 N Meridian Street, Carmel IN 46032-6954. 317/571-3000.

National Insurance Association
PO Box 6070, Indianapolis IN 46206-6070. 317/816-3400.

Partners National Health Plans of Indiana
100 E Wayne St, Ste 502, South Bend IN 46601-2354. 219/233-4899.

Sagamore Health Network Inc.
11555 N Meridian St, Carmel IN 46032-6934. 317/573-2900.

Sagamore Insurance Company
1099 N Meridian St, Indianapolis IN 46204-1075. 317/636-6300.

United Farm Family Life Insurance Co.
PO Box 1250, Indianapolis IN 46206-1250. 317/692-7200.

United Presidential Life Insurance Co.
PO Box 9006, Kokomo IN 46904. 765/453-0602.

VASA Brougher Inc.
PO Box 6037, Indianapolis IN 46206-6037. 317/238-5600.

Zurich Group Companies
8900 Keystone Crossing, Ste 300, Indianapolis IN 46204. 317/587-7500.

For more information on career opportunities in insurance:

Associations

ALLIANCE OF AMERICAN INSURERS
1501 Woodfield Road, Suite 400 West, Schaumburg IL 60173-4980. 847/330-8500. World Wide Web address: http://www.allianceai.org.

HEALTH INSURANCE ASSOCIATION OF AMERICA
555 13th Street NW, Suite 600E, Washington DC 20004. 202/824-1600. World Wide Web address: http://www.hiaa.org.

INSURANCE INFORMATION INSTITUTE
110 William Street, 24th Floor, New York NY 10038. 212/669-9200. World Wide Web address: http://www.iii.org.

NATIONAL ASSOCIATION OF PROFESSIONAL INSURANCE AGENTS
400 North Washington Street, Alexandria VA 22314. 703/836-9340. World Wide Web address: http://www.pianet.com.

SOCIETY OF ACTUARIES
475 North Martingale Road, Suite 800, Schaumburg IL 60173-2226. 847/706-3500. World Wide Web address: http://www.soa.org.

Directories

AMERICAN ASSN. OF HEALTH PLANS
Managed Health Care Directory, 1129 20th Street NW, Suite 600, Washington DC 20036. 202/778-3200. World Wide Web address: http://www.aahp.org.

INSURANCE ALMANAC
Underwriter Printing and Publishing Company, 50 East Palisade Avenue, Englewood NJ 07631. 201/569-8808. Hardcover annual, 639 pages, $115.00. Available at libraries.

INSURANCE PHONE BOOK AND DIRECTORY
Reed Reference Publishing, 121 Chanlon Road, New Providence NJ 07974. Toll-free phone: 800/521-8110.

Magazines

BEST'S REVIEW
A.M. Best Company, A.M. Best Road, Oldwick NJ 08858-9988. 908/439-2200. World Wide Web address: http://www.ambest.com. Monthly.

INSURANCE JOURNAL
Wells Publishing, 9191 Towne Centre Drive, Suite 550, San Diego, CA 92122-1231 619/455-7717. World Wide Web address: http://www.insurancejrnl.com. A biweekly magazine covering the insurance industry.

Online Services

THE INSURANCE CAREER CENTER
http://connectyou.com/talent/. Offers job openings, career resources, and a resume database for jobseekers looking to get into the insurance field.

INSURANCE NATIONAL SEARCH
http://www.insurancerecruiters.com/insjobs/jobs.htm.

LEGAL SERVICES

Prospective lawyers will continue to face intense competition through the year 2005, due to the overabundance of law school graduates. Consequently, fewer lawyers are working for major law firms, working instead for smaller firms, corporations, and associations, according to the U.S. Department of Commerce. Firms have reduced their support staffs, while large corporations are establishing in-house legal departments to avoid paying for expensive, big-name law offices.

Paralegals comprise the fastest-growing profession in legal services, and the U.S. Department of Labor projects that opportunities will continue to expand rapidly through 2005. Paralegals are taking on more responsibilities in areas such as real estate and trademark law. Private law firms will hire the most paralegals, but a vast array of other organizations also employ them, including insurance companies, real estate firms, and banks.

BAKER & DANIELS
300 North Meridian Street, Suite 2700, Indianapolis IN 46204-1750. 317/237-0300. **Contact:** Jim Murray, Personnel Director. **Description:** A legal services firm.

BARNES & THORNBURG
11 South Meridian Street, Indianapolis IN 46204. 317/638-1313. **Contact:** Mrs. LaNell D. Black, Personnel Director. **Description:** A legal firm practicing most types of law including international, trade, business, utility, taxes, and real estate.

HARRIS & HARRIS
222 North Buffalo Street, Warsaw IN 46580. 219/267-2111. **Contact:** Recruitment. **World Wide Web address:** http://www.lawyers.com/harrislaw. **Description:** A law firm specializing in areas such as corporate, banking, taxation, real estate, environmental, family/domestic, bankruptcy, and estate planning.

LOCKE REYNOLDS BOYD & WEISELL
1000 Capital Center South, 201 North Illinois Street, Indianapolis IN 46204. 317/237-3800. **Contact:** Thomas Schultz, Hiring Attorney. **Description:** A full-service law firm.

SPANGLER, JENNINGS & DOUGHERTY
8396 Mississippi Street, Merrillville IN 46410. 219/769-2323. **Contact:** David Abel, Hiring Attorney. **Description:** A law firm.

Note: *Because addresses and telephone numbers of smaller companies can change rapidly, we recommend you call each company to verify the information below before inquiring about job opportunities. Mass mailings are not recommended.*

Additional small employers:

LEGAL SERVICES

Andrews Harrell Mann Chapman & Coyne
PO Box 2639, Bloomington IN 47402-2639. 812/332-4200.

Baker & Daniels
111 E Wayne Street, Suite 800, Fort Wayne IN 46802-2603. 219/424-8000.

Barnes & Thornburg
101 W Washington Street, Indianapolis IN 46204-3407. 317/231-7528.

Barnes & Thornburg
600 First Source Bank Center, South Bend IN 46601. 219/233-1171.

Barrett & McNagny
PO Box 2263, Fort Wayne IN 46801-2263. 219/423-9551.

Bingham Summers Welsh Spilman
2700 Market Tower, 27th Floor, Indianapolis IN 46204. 317/635-8900.

Bose McKinney & Evans
135 N Pennsylvania Street, Indianapolis IN 46204-2400. 317/684-5000.

Bowers Harrison Kent & Miller
PO Box 1287, Evansville IN 47706-1287. 812/426-1231.

Bowman Heintz Boscia and Vician PC
8605 Broadway, Merrillville IN 46410-7033. 219/769-6671.

Burke Murphy Costanza & Cuppy
8585 Broadway, Suite 600, Merrillville IN 46410-5660. 219/769-1313.

Dann Pecar Newman & Kleiman PC
PO Box 82008, Indianapolis IN 46282. 317/632-3232.

G. Pearson Smith Jr.
135 N Pennsylvania Street, Indianapolis IN 46204-2400. 317/684-5118.

Harrison & Moberly LLC
135 North Pennsylvania Street, Indianapolis IN 46204-2400. 317/639-4511.

Hepner Wagner & Evans
PO Box 2357, Valparaiso IN 46384-2357. 219/464-4961.

Ice Miller Donadio & Ryan
1 American Square, 34th Floor, Indianapolis IN 46282-0001. 317/236-2100.

Kightlinger and Gray
151 N Delaware St, Suite 660, Indianapolis IN 46204-2513. 317/638-4521.

Krieg Devault Alexander & Capehart
One Indiana Square, Suite 2800, Indianapolis IN 46204-2017. 317/636-4341.

Lowe Gray Steele & Darco
111 Monument Cir, Suite 4600, Indianapolis IN 46204-5146. 317/236-8020.

McHale Cook & Welch
320 N Meridian Street, Indianapolis IN 46204-1719. 317/634-7588.

Pence Johnson Smith
1 Indiana Square, Ste 1800, Indianapolis IN 46204-2007. 317/634-9777.

Sommer Barnard Attorneys At Law PC
PO Box 44363, Indianapolis IN 46244-0363. 317/630-4000.

State Public Defender
1 N Capitol Ave, Ste 800, Indianapolis IN 46204-2052. 317/232-2475.

Stewart & Irwin Professional Corp.
251 E Ohio St, Ste 1100, Indianapolis IN 46204-2147. 317/639-5454.

Wooden & McLaughlin
201 N Illinois St, Indianapolis IN 46204-1904. 317/639-6151.

For more information on career opportunities in legal services:

Associations

AMERICAN BAR ASSOCIATION
750 North Lake Shore Drive, Chicago IL 60611. 312/988-5000. World Wide Web address: http://www.abanet.org.

FEDERAL BAR ASSOCIATION
1815 H Street NW, Suite 408, Washington DC 20006-3697. 202/638-0252. World Wide Web address: http://www.fedbar.org.

NATIONAL ASSOCIATION OF LEGAL ASSISTANTS
1516 South Boston Avenue, Suite 200, Tulsa OK 74119-4013. 918/587-6828. World Wide Web address: http://www.nala.org. An educational association. Offers the National Voluntary Association Exam. Memberships are available.

NATIONAL FEDERATION OF PARALEGAL ASSOCIATIONS
P.O. Box 33108, Kansas City MO 64114-0108. 816/941-4000. World Wide Web address: http://www.paralegals.org. Offers magazines, seminars, and Internet job listings.

NATIONAL PARALEGAL ASSOCIATION
P.O. Box 406, Solebury PA 18963. 215/297-8333.

Directories

MARTINDALE-HUBBELL LAW DIRECTORY
121 Chanlon Road, New Providence NJ 07974. 800/526-4902. World Wide Web address: http://www.martindale.com. A directory consisting exclusively of the names of legal employers. In all, listings for over 900,000 lawyers and law firms are available.

Newsletters

LAWYERS WEEKLY USA
Lawyers Weekly, Inc., 41 West Street, Boston MA 02111. 617/451-7300. World Wide Web address: http://www.lawyersweekly.com. A newsletter that profiles law firms, provides general industry information, and provides information on jobs nationwide.

Online Services

COURT REPORTERS FORUM
Go: CrForum. A CompuServe networking forum that includes information from the *Journal of Court Reporting*.

LEGAL EXCHANGE
Jump to: Legal Exchange. A debate forum for lawyers and other legal professionals, offered through Prodigy.

LEGAL INFORMATION NETWORK
Keyword: LIN. An America Online networking resource for paralegals, family law specialists, social security specialists, and law students.

MANUFACTURING: MISCELLANEOUS CONSUMER

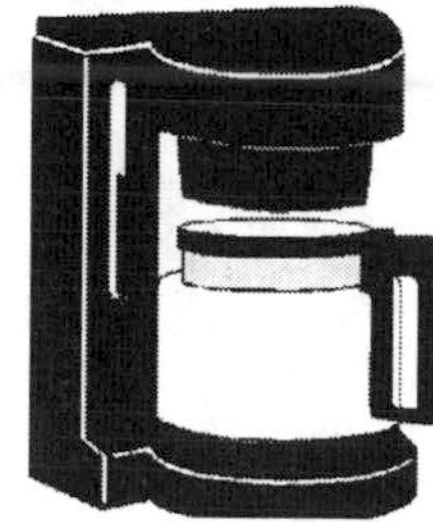

Greater globalization is the trend in consumer manufacturing as worldwide and regional trade agreements reduce barriers and provide more uniform trade standards. Demand for household goods is cyclical and depends on the state of the economy and the disposable income of consumers. Now, the distribution of these goods is more dependent on large discount retailers. Household appliance shipments were expected to grow by 2 percent in 1998.

The best opportunities for jobseekers will be in the manufacture of home entertainment products. Baby boomers are reaching their peak earning potential and spending money on big-screen televisions and upgraded sound equipment for home stereos. There is also a renewed interest overseas in "Made in the U.S.A." products such as Harley-Davidson motorcycles, golfing equipment, fishing boats, and mountain bikes.

In general, manufacturing jobs in the United States will continue to disappear as the economy continues shifting toward service industries. Factory automation -- including wireless communications, distributed intelligence, and centralized computer control -- is one major cause for the loss of manufacturing jobs. Growing competition has forced some companies to streamline production by replacing workers with computers in the areas of inventory tracking, shipping, and ordering. Individuals who have a working knowledge of these software applications will have an edge over less technically experienced jobseekers.

ALLTRISTA CORPORATION
P.O. Box 5004, Muncie IN 47307-5004. 765/281-5000. **Contact:** Devona Coffey, Human Resources. **Description:** Engaged in the manufacture of a line of home food preservation products, such as consumer canning jars, jar closures, and related food products; high-barrier, multilayer, co-extruded plastic products, including sheet-formed containers and retort containers; copper-plated zinc penny blanks, cans for use in zinc/carbon batteries, and other industrial zinc products; protective coating application and decorative lithography services; tin-plated steel aluminum and light-gauge rolled products; thermoformed plastic refrigerator door liners, separators, and evaporator trays; injection molded plastics products; and software and hardware for non-destructive inspection systems. **Corporate headquarters location:** This Location.

ATAPCO CUSTOM PRODUCTS DIVISION
1414 Crawford Drive, Crawfordsville IN 47933. 765/362-6733. **Contact:** Deb Walter, Human Resources. **World Wide Web address:** http://www.crawford-industries.com. **Description:** Manufactures polyurethane office binders. **Other U.S. locations:** Bristol PA. **Subsidiaries include:** Crawford Industries.

BATESVILLE CASKET COMPANY
One Batesville Boulevard, Batesville IN 47006. 812/934-7500. **Contact:** Human Resources. **World Wide Web address:** http://www.batesville.com. **Description:** A leading producer of protective metal and hardwood burial caskets. The company also manufactures a line of cremation urns and caskets. **Corporate headquarters location:** This Location.

CHILDCRAFT INDUSTRIES
P.O. Box 444, Salem IN 47167. 812/883-3111. **Contact:** Human Resources. **World Wide Web address:** http://www.childcraftind.com. **Description:** Manufactures children's beds and related accessories.

CHROMCRAFT REVINGTON, INC.
1100 North Washington Street, P.O. Box 238, Delphi IN 46923-0238. 765/564-3500. **Contact:** Personnel Director. **Description:** A national designer, manufacturer, and seller of casual dining, commercial, and occasional furniture sold under the Chromcraft, Peters-Revington, and Silver Furniture brand names. **Other U.S. locations:** Sentobia MS; Knoxville TN. **Number of employees nationwide:** 1,500.

COLGATE-PALMOLIVE COMPANY
P.O. Box CS-9, Jeffersonville IN 47131. **Contact:** Human Resources. **Description:** Manufactures and markets a wide variety of products in the U.S. and around the world in two distinct business segments: Oral, Personal, and Household Care; and Specialty Marketing. Oral, Personal, and Household Care products include toothpaste, oral rinses, toothbrushes, bar and liquid soaps, shampoos, conditioners, deodorants and antiperspirants, baby and shaving products, laundry and dishwashing detergents, fabric softeners, cleansers and cleaners, and bleach. Specialty Marketing products include pet dietary care products, crystal tableware, and portable fuel for warming food. **NOTE:** This firm does not accept unsolicited resumes. Please only respond to advertised openings.

ESCALADE SPORTS
817 Maxwell Avenue, Evansville IN 47711. 812/467-1200. **Contact:** Ms. Robyn Taylor, Human Resources. **World Wide Web address:** http://www.escaladesports.com. **Description:** Manufactures and sells a variety of sporting goods, such as table tennis tables and accessories, archery equipment, basketball backboards, goals, and home fitness accessories. **Parent company:** Escalade, Inc.

GENERAL ELECTRIC COMPANY
301 North Curry Pike, Bloomington IN 47402. 812/334-9500. **Contact:** Manager of Human Resources. **World Wide Web address:** http://www.ge.com. **Description:** This location manufactures side-by-side refrigerators. Overall, General Electric Company operates in the following areas: aircraft engines (jet engines, replacement parts, and repair services for commercial, military, executive, and commuter aircraft); appliances; broadcasting (NBC); industrial (lighting products, electrical distribution and control equipment, transportation systems products, electric motors and related products, a broad range of electrical and electronic industrial automation products, and a network of electrical supply houses); materials (plastics, ABS resins, silicones, superabrasives, and laminates); power systems (products for the generation, transmission, and distribution of electricity); technical products and systems (medical systems and equipment, as well as a full range of computer-based information and data interchange services for both internal use and external commercial and industrial customers); and capital services (consumer services, financing, and specialty insurance). **Number of employees worldwide:** 230,000.

GENERAL HOUSEWARES CORPORATION
P.O. Box 4066, Terre Haute IN 47804. 812/232-1000. **Physical address:** 1536 Beech Street, Terre Haute IN 47804. **Toll-free phone:** 800/457-2665. **Fax:** 800/330-9263. **Contact:** Carolyn Swick, Human Resources Manager. **World Wide Web address:** http://www.ghc.com. **Description:** Engaged in the manufacture and marketing of cookware, cutlery, kitchen tools, commercial knives, and garden tools. **Common positions include:** Accountant/Auditor; Blue-Collar Worker Supervisor; Ceramics Engineer; Computer Programmer; Credit Manager; Customer Service Representative; Department Manager; Draftsperson; Human Resources Manager; Industrial Engineer; Manufacturer's/Wholesaler's Sales Rep.; Marketing Specialist; Mechanical Engineer; Operations/Production Manager; Purchasing Agent/Manager; Quality Control Supervisor; Systems Analyst; Transportation/Traffic Specialist. **Educational backgrounds include:** Accounting; Business Administration; Communications; Computer Science; Economics; Engineering; Finance; Liberal Arts; Marketing. **Benefits:** Dental Insurance; Disability Coverage; Employee Discounts; Life Insurance; Medical Insurance; Pension Plan; Savings Plan; Stock Option; Tuition Assistance. **Special programs:** Internships. **Corporate headquarters location:** This Location. **Operations at**

this facility include: Administration; Manufacturing; Research and Development; Sales; Service. **Listed on:** New York Stock Exchange.

KELLER MANUFACTURING COMPANY
P.O. Box 8, Corydon IN 47112-0008. 812/738-2222. **Contact:** Human Resources. **Description:** Manufactures a wide variety of household furniture.

KOCH ORIGINALS, INC.
110 Main Street, Evansville IN 47708. 812/421-5600. **Contact:** Cindy Witte, Human Resources Manager. **World Wide Web address:** http://www.koch-originals.com. **Description:** Manufactures brass-plated, metal furnishings for resale.

LEVER BROTHERS COMPANY
1200 Calumet Avenue, Hammond IN 46320. 219/659-3200. **Contact:** Human Resources Department. **World Wide Web address:** http://www.lever.com. **Description:** This location produces a variety of soap and detergent products. Overall, Lever Brothers Company is an international manufacturer and distributor of soaps and cleaning products, specialty foods, toothpastes, and detergents.

MAJESTIC PRODUCTS COMPANY
1000 East Market Street, Huntington IN 46750. 219/356-8000. **Fax:** 219/358-9265. **Contact:** Human Resources. **World Wide Web address:** http://www.majesticproducts.com. **Description:** Manufactures gas and wood fireplaces. **Common positions include:** Accountant/Auditor; Blue-Collar Worker Supervisor; Buyer; Credit Manager; Customer Service Representative; Designer; Draftsperson; General Manager; Human Resources Manager; Industrial Production Manager; Purchasing Agent/Manager; Quality Control Supervisor; Systems Analyst. **Educational backgrounds include:** Business Administration. **Benefits:** 401(k); Dental Insurance; Disability Coverage; Employee Discounts; Life Insurance; Medical Insurance. **Corporate headquarters location:** This Location. **Other U.S. locations:** Austin TX. **Operations at this facility include:** Administration; Manufacturing. **Number of employees at this location:** 350. **Number of employees nationwide:** 580.

MATTEL
P.O. Box 6700, Fort Wayne IN 46896-0700. 219/424-1400. **Contact:** Human Resources. **Description:** This location manufactures battery-operated vehicles for children to ride. Overall, Mattel is a toy manufacturer.

NBS IMAGING SYSTEMS
1530 Progress Road, Fort Wayne IN 46808. 219/484-8611. **Contact:** Human Resources. **World Wide Web address:** http://www.nbstech.com. **Description:** Manufactures photographic equipment and supplies.

OMNI FILTER CORPORATION
2500 165th Street, Hammond IN 46320. 219/989-9800. **Contact:** Human Resources. **Description:** Manufactures water filters.

THE SELMER COMPANY
P.O. Box 310, Elkhart IN 46515. 219/522-1675. **Contact:** Human Resources Department. **World Wide Web address:** http://www.selmer.com. **Description:** Manufactures and distributes musical instruments and related accessories.

WHIRLPOOL CORPORATION
5401 U.S. 41 North, Evansville IN 47727. 812/426-4000. **Contact:** Human Resources Department. **World Wide Web address:** http://www.whirlpool.com. **Description:** Manufactures and markets home appliances. The company has manufacturing locations in 11 countries. Products are marketed in more than 120 countries under brand names such as Whirlpool, KitchenAid, Roper, Estate, Bauknecht, Ignis, Laden, and Inglis. Whirlpool is also the principal supplier of major home appliances to Sears, Roebuck and Company under the Kenmore brand name.

WHIRLPOOL CORPORATION
1801 Kalberer Road, West Lafayette IN 47906. 765/463-0900. **Contact:** Human Resources. **World Wide Web address:** http://www.whirlpool.com. **Description:** Manufactures and markets home appliances. The company has manufacturing locations in 11 countries. Products are marketed in more than 120 countries under brand names such as Whirlpool, KitchenAid, Roper, Estate, Bauknecht, Ignis, Laden, and Inglis. Whirlpool is also the principal supplier of major home appliances to Sears, Roebuck and Company under the Kenmore brand name. **Number of employees worldwide:** 39,600.

Note: *Because addresses and telephone numbers of smaller companies can change rapidly, we recommend you call each company to verify the information below before inquiring about job opportunities. Mass mailings are not recommended.*

Additional small employers:

BATTERIES

C&D Technologies Inc.
PO Box 279, Attica IN 47918-0279. 765/762-2461.

Exide Corporation
PO Box 2098, Muncie IN 47307-0098. 765/747-9980.

HAND AND EDGE TOOLS

Atlas Chem-Milling
2000 Middlebury Street, Elkhart IN 46516-5521. 219/295-0050.

Seymour Manufacturing Co. Inc.
PO Box 248, Seymour IN 47274-0248. 812/522-2900.

HOUSEHOLD APPLIANCES

Patton Electric Company Inc.
15012 Edgerton Road, New Haven IN 46774-9636. 219/493-3564.

Patton Electric Company Inc.
1070 Industrial Parkway, Peru IN 46970-9589. 765/472-3564.

The Kent Company
PO Box 1665, Elkhart IN 46515-1665. 219/293-8661.

HOUSEHOLD AUDIO AND VIDEO EQUIPMENT

Columbia House
PO Box 1100, Terre Haute IN 47811-1100. 812/466-8111.

E&H Partners
1200 E Broadway Street, Princeton IN 47670-3102. 812/386-3200.

Harman-Motive Inc.
1201 South Ohio Street, Martinsville IN 46151-2914. 765/342-5551.

Onkyo America Inc.
3030 Barker Dr, Columbus IN 47201-9611. 812/342-0332.

Pyle Manufacturing LLC
501 Center St, Huntington IN 46750-2523. 219/356-1300.

Sanyo-Verbatim CD Company LLC
1767 Sheridan St, Richmond IN 47374-1811. 765/935-7574.

Thompson Consumer Electronics
PO Box 1976, Indianapolis IN 46206-1976. 317/587-3000.

HOUSEHOLD FURNITURE

Arden Paradise
2701 S Coliseum Boulevard, Fort Wayne IN 46803-2950. 219/422-3351.

Best Chair Recliner Division
PO Box 158, Ferdinand IN 47532-0158. 812/367-1761.

Classico Seating
PO Box 48, Peru IN 46970-0048. 765/473-6691.

Design Institute America Incorporated
919 East 14th Street, Jasper IN 47546-2230. 812/482-4632.

Dolly Madison Industries
12 DMI Lane, Plant 12, Huntingburg IN 47542. 812/683-3165.

Dubois Wood Products Inc.
PO Box 186, Huntingburg IN 47542-0186. 812/683-3613.

Heritage Hills
PO Box 199, Santa Claus IN 47579-0199. 812/937-4581.

Jasper Corporation
PO Box 360, Jasper IN 47547-0360. 812/482-8426.

Jordan Manufacturing Company
721 N 1st Street, Monticello IN 47960-1779. 219/583-6008.

Karges By Hand
PO Box 6517, Evansville IN 47719-0517. 812/425-2291.

Keller Manufacturing Company Inc.
1010 Keller Drive NE, New Salisbury IN 47161-7884. 812/366-3122.

Mobel Incorporated
2130 Industrial Park Road, Ferdinand IN 47532-9470. 812/367-1214.

OFS
602 W 12th Street, Huntingburg IN 47542-9335. 812/683-0251.

Peters-Revington Corporation
PO Box 238, Delphi IN 46923-0238. 765/564-2586.

Simmons Upholstered Furniture Corp.
PO Box 226, Paoli IN 47454-0226. 812/723-4702.

Smith Brothers Berne Inc.
PO Box 270, Berne IN 46711-0270. 219/589-2131.

Styline Industries Inc.
908 N Chestnut St, Dale IN 47523. 812/683-0231.

W.C. Redmon Co.
PO Box 7, Peru IN 46970-0007. 765/473-6683.

Wabash Valley Manufacturing
PO Box 5, Silver Lake IN 46982-0005. 219/352-2102.

Woodmaster Inc.
PO Box 127, Saint Anthony IN 47575-0127. 812/326-2626.

JEWELRY, SILVERWARE, AND PLATED WARE

Herff-Jones
PO Box 68956, Indianapolis IN 46268-0956. 317/297-3740.

LAWN AND GARDEN TRACTORS AND RELATED EQUIPMENT

Earthway Products Inc.
PO Box 547, Bristol IN 46507-0547. 219/848-7491.

MISC. FURNITURE AND FIXTURES

Cooper Industries Inc.
PO Box 827, Middlebury IN 46540-0827. 219/825-9591.

Hill-Rom Company Inc.
1069 State Route 46 East, Batesville IN 47006-9164. 812/934-7777.

Kimball Lodging Group
1180 E 16th Street, Jasper IN 47546-2234. 812/482-8090.

Lafayette Venetian Blind Inc.
PO Box 2838, West Lafayette IN 47996-2838. 765/742-8418.

SAI Inc.
7676 Zionsville Road, Indianapolis IN 46268-2173. 317/872-2000.

MUSICAL INSTRUMENTS

Fox Products Corporation
PO Box 347, South Whitley IN 46787-0347. 219/723-4888.

Gemeinhardt Company Inc.
PO Box 788, Elkhart IN 46515-0788. 219/295-5280.

King-Armstrong
PO Box 727, Elkhart IN 46515-0727. 219/522-3392.

Vincent Bach Co.
500 Industrial Parkway, Elkhart IN 46516-5416. 219/295-6730.

OFFICE AND ART SUPPLIES

Southern Cylinder Manufacturing
1000 Bales Boulevard, Jeffersonville IN 47129-7714. 812/283-4600.

POWER-DRIVEN HAND TOOLS

Ingersoll-Rand Company
1105 Williams Street, Angola IN 46703-1213. 219/665-2175.

ITW Ramset/Redhead
PO Box 364, Michigan City IN 46361-0364. 219/874-4217.

Wen Products Inc.
PO Box 516, Akron IN 46910-0516. 219/893-4181.

TOYS AND SPORTING GOODS

Cosco Inc.
2525 State Street, Columbus IN 47201-7443. 812/372-0141.

International Machinery Corporation
1302 Port Road, Jeffersonville IN 47130. 812/283-4624.

Warren Industries Inc.
3200 South St, Lafayette IN 47904-3157. 765/447-2151.

WATCHES, CLOCKS, AND RELATED PARTS

Nascorp
275 Northridge Drive, Shelbyville IN 46176-8851. 317/421-2220.

For more information on career opportunities in consumer manufacturing:

Associations

ASSOCIATION FOR MANUFACTURING EXCELLENCE
380 West Palatine Road, Wheeling IL 60090. 847/520-3282. World Wide Web address: http://www.ame.org.

ASSOCIATION FOR MANUFACTURING TECHNOLOGY
7901 Westpark Drive, McLean VA 22102. 703/893-2900. World Wide Web address: http://www.mfgtech.org. Offers research services.

ASSOCIATION OF HOME APPLIANCE MANUFACTURERS
20 North Wacker Drive, Suite 1231, Chicago IL 60606. 312/984-5800. World Wide Web address: http://www.aham.org.

NATIONAL ASSOCIATION OF MANUFACTURERS
1331 Pennsylvania Avenue NW, Suite 600, Washington DC 20004. 202/637-3000. World Wide Web address: http://www.nam.org. A lobbying association for manufacturers.

NATIONAL HOUSEWARES MANUFACTURERS ASSOCIATION
6400 Schafer Court, Suite 650, Rosemont IL 60018. 847/292-4200. World Wide Web address: http://www.housewares.org. Offers shipping discounts and other services.

SOCIETY OF MANUFACTURING ENGINEERS
P.O. Box 930, One SME Drive, Dearborn MI 48121. 313/271-1500. World Wide Web address: http://www.sme.org. Offers educational events and educational materials on manufacturing.

Directories

AMERICAN MANUFACTURER'S DIRECTORY
5711 South 86th Circle, P.O. Box 37347, Omaha NE 68127. 800/555-5211. Made by the same company that created *American Big Business Directory*, *American Manufacturer's Directory* lists over 531,000 manufacturing companies of all sizes and industries.

The directory contains product and sales information, company size, and a key contact name for each company.

APPLIANCE MANUFACTURER ANNUAL DIRECTORY
Appliance Manufacturer, 5900 Harper Road, Suite 105, Solon OH 44139. 216/349-3060. $25.00.

HOUSEHOLD AND PERSONAL PRODUCTS INDUSTRY BUYERS GUIDE
Rodman Publishing Group, 17 South Franklin Turnpike, Ramsey NJ 07446. 201/825-2552. World Wide Web address: http://www.happi.com. $12.00.

Magazines

APPLIANCE
1110 Jorie Boulevard, Oak Brook IL 60522-9019. 630/990-3484. World Wide Web address: http://www.appliance.com. Monthly. $70.00 for a one-year subscription.

COSMETICS INSIDERS REPORT
Advanstar Communications, 131 West First Street, Duluth MN 55802. Toll-free phone: 800/346-0085. World Wide Web address: http://www.advanstar.com. $189.00 for a one year subscription; 24 issues annually. Features timely articles on cosmetics marketing and research.

Online Services

CAREER PARK - MANUFACTURING JOBS
http://www.careerpark.com/jobs/manulist.html. This Website provides a list of current job openings in the manufacturing industry. The site is run by Parker Advertising Service, Inc.

MO'S GATEWAY TO MANUFACTURING-RELATED JOBS LISTINGS
http://www.chesapk.com/mfgjobs.html. Provides links to sites that post job openings in manufacturing.

MANUFACTURING: MISCELLANEOUS INDUSTRIAL

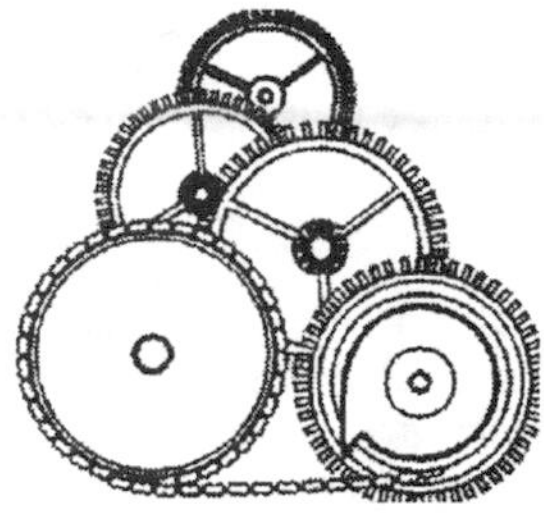

Industrial manufacturing is rising at a surprising rate in an attempt to keep up with foreign demand which has been strengthened by improving growth abroad. Industrial production in January 1997 rose 4.7 percent from the previous year, while the output of business equipment rose 0.8 percent. According to Business Week, *industrial machinery has seen the greatest increase in amount of exports, specifically to South America and Mexico.*

However, rising productivity and a strong economy are not indicative of an increase in jobs. Manufacturers are choosing to put money into technology rather than an increased workforce. On the whole, employment in industrial manufacturing is on the decline, as the national economy continues to shift its focus from producing goods to providing services. Companies that specialize in equipment for thriving industries, such as health care and construction, will show the most gains in the future.

AIRGUARD INDUSTRIES, INC.
2234 East Market Street, New Albany IN 47150. 812/944-6793. **Contact:** Gloria Dunlap, Human Resources. **Description:** Manufactures commercial and industrial air-filtration equipment.

ALLISON ENGINE COMPANY
P.O. Box 420, Indianapolis IN 46206-0420. 317/230-2000. **Contact:** Salaried Employment Director. **Description:** Manufactures precision bearings, locomotive parts, and gas turbine engines for automotive, marine, and aircraft applications. **Common positions include:** Aerospace Engineer; Industrial Engineer; Mechanical Engineer; Metallurgical Engineer. **Educational backgrounds include:** Engineering. **Benefits:** Dental Insurance; Disability Coverage; Employee Discounts; Life Insurance; Medical Insurance; Pension Plan; Profit Sharing; Savings Plan; Tuition Assistance. **Parent company:** General Motors. **Operations at this facility include:** Administration; Divisional Headquarters; Manufacturing; Research and Development; Sales; Service.

ANACOMP, INC.
P.O. Box 40888, Indianapolis IN 46240. 317/844-9666. **Contact:** Eric Whinston, Director of Human Resources Department. **World Wide Web address:** http://www.anacomp.com. **Description:** Anacomp, Inc. is a producer of computer output microfilm products, ranging from duplicate microfilm to microfilm readers and printers. The company also makes magnetic media products, such as computer tapes and cartridges, as well as various other data processing-related products. Anacomp also performs maintenance services for users of its equipment, and provides micrographics services such as microfilming through data service centers. **Number of employees nationwide:** 4,500.

ARVIN INDUSTRIES, INC.
One Noblitt Plaza, Columbus IN 47201. 812/379-3603. **Contact:** Raymond P. Mack, Vice President of Human Resources. **World Wide Web address:** http://www.arvin.com. **Description:** Arvin Industries has 11 operating companies engaged in manufacturing exhaust systems (OEM and aftermarket) and ride control products that serve the automotive, consumer, and industrial markets. **Common positions include:** Accountant/Auditor; Administrator; Computer Programmer; Department Manager; Electrical/Electronics Engineer; Financial Analyst; General Manager;

Human Resources Manager; Industrial Engineer; Industrial Production Manager; Management Trainee; Manufacturer's/Wholesaler's Sales Rep.; Mechanical Engineer; Metallurgical Engineer; Operations/Production Manager; Purchasing Agent/Manager; Quality Control Supervisor; Systems Analyst. **Educational backgrounds include:** Accounting; Business Administration; Computer Science; Economics; Engineering; Finance; Liberal Arts; Marketing. **Benefits:** Dental Insurance; Disability Coverage; Life Insurance; Medical Insurance; Pension Plan; Savings Plan; Stock Option; Tuition Assistance. **Corporate headquarters location:** This Location. **Operations at this facility include:** Administration; Manufacturing; Service. **Listed on:** New York Stock Exchange. **Number of employees nationwide:** 12,000.

AVERY DENNISON CORPORATION
650 West 67th Place, Schererville IN 46375. 219/322-5030. **Contact:** Jeff Botrorff, Human Resources Manager. **World Wide Web address:** http://www.averydennison.com. **Description:** A manufacturing plant for the national corporation, which is a leader in pressure-sensitive adhesives, office products, labels, tags, retail systems, and specialty chemicals. The company specializes in producing a wide variety of labels, especially clear labels, for use in packaging products including apparel, motor oil, liquid soap, and automobiles. Labels are marketed under the Avery and Fasson brand names. The company also produces product identification and control systems. **Corporate headquarters location:** Pasadena CA. **International locations:** Worldwide.

AVIS INDUSTRIAL CORPORATION
P.O. Box 548, Upland IN 46989. 765/998-8100. **Fax:** 765/998-8111. **Contact:** Judith E. Owen, Human Resources Director. **Description:** This location houses administrative offices for 12 subsidiaries nationwide. Overall, Avis Industrial Corporation and its subsidiaries manufacture industrial equipment, construction equipment, steel tubing, forgings, and metal fasteners. Founded in 1959. **Common positions include:** Accountant/Auditor; Administrative Assistant; Chief Financial Officer; Human Resources Manager; Industrial Engineer; Manufacturing Engineer; MIS Specialist; Secretary. **Educational backgrounds include:** Accounting; Business Administration; Computer Science; Engineering; Finance. **Benefits:** 401(k); Dental Insurance; Disability Coverage; Life Insurance; Medical Insurance; Profit Sharing; Tuition Assistance. **Corporate headquarters location:** This Location. **Other U.S. locations:** Nationwide. **Subsidiaries include:** Badger Equipment Company, Airport Industrial Park, P.O. Box 798, Winona MN 55987. 507/454-1563; Burro Crane, Airport Industrial Park, P.O. Box 798, Winona MN 55987. 507/454-8549; Crankshaft Machine Company, 314 North Jackson Street, P.O. Box 1127, Jackson MI 49201. 517/787-3791; Edgerton Forge, Inc., 257 East Morrison, Edgerton OH 43517. 419/298-2333; Hurd Corporation, 503 Bohannon Avenue, P.O. Box 1450, Greeneville TN 37743. 423/787-8800; James Steel & Tube Company, 29774 Stephenson Highway, Madison Heights MI 48071. 810/547-4200; Little Giant Corporation, 1601 NE 66th Avenue, Des Moines IA 50313. 515/289-2112; Melling Forging Company, 1709 Thompson Street, Lansing MI 48906. 517/482-0791; Pacific Forge, Inc., 10641 Etiwanda Avenue, Fontana CA 92337. 909/390-0701; The American Baler Company, 800 East Center Street, P.O. Box 29, Bellevue OH 44811. 419/483-5790; The Pierce Company, Inc., 201 North Eighth Street, P.O. Box 2000, Upland IN 46989. 317/998-2712; The Tobin Corporation, 35544 Lorain Road, North Ridgeville OH 44039. 216/327-4244; U.S. Broach, Inc., 378 East By-Pass, P.O. Box 1649, Sumter SC 29151. 803/775-2357; Winpower Generators, 201 North Eighth Street, Upland IN 46989. 317/998-2712. **Listed on:** Privately held. **Annual sales/revenues:** More than $100 million. **Number of employees at this location:** 30. **Number of employees nationwide:** 1,300.

BALL CORPORATION
345 South High Street, Muncie IN 47305. **Contact:** Human Resources. **Description:** Ball Corporation produces metal and glass packaging products, primarily for foods and beverages, and provides aerospace and communications products and services to government and commercial customers. **NOTE:** This firm does not accept unsolicited resumes. Please only respond to advertised openings. **Corporate headquarters location:** This Location.

BEMIS COMPANY INC.
FILM DIVISION
1350 North Fruitridge Avenue, Terre Haute IN 47804. 812/466-2213. **Contact:** Human Resources. **Description:** Bemis is a diversified producer of consumer and industrial packaging materials, film

products, and business products. Packaging products manufactured include tapes, paper bags, and packaging for pharmaceuticals, candy, toilet paper, and detergents. The company also produces sheetprint stock, roll labels, laminates, and adhesive products. **Corporate headquarters location:** Minneapolis MN.

BERRY BEARING COMPANY INC.
3620 Calumet Avenue, Hammond IN 46320. 219/931-3010. **Contact:** Human Resources Department. **Description:** Berry Bearing Company Inc. is a local distributor of industrial machinery parts including belts, pulleys, bearings, and other power transmission parts. **Parent company:** Motion Industries.

BRYAN BOILERS
P.O. Box 27, Peru IN 46970. 765/473-6651. **Contact:** Human Resources. **World Wide Web address:** http://www.bryanboilers.com. **Description:** Manufactures and sells oil boilers, gas boilers, electrically-fired boilers, commercial water heaters, and swimming pool heaters. The company also manufactures and sells a small number of storage tanks and other vessels for use with its boilers.

BUCCICONI ENGINEERING COMPANY
899 Grant St., Gary IN 46402. 219/882-4233. **Contact:** Human Resources. **Description:** Manufactures magnetic conveyors and stackers.

CATERPILLAR, INC.
LARGE ENGINE CENTER
3701 State Road 26 East, Lafayette IN 47905. 765/448-5000. **Contact:** Human Resources Department. **Description:** Caterpillar, Inc.'s Large Engine Center is a global leader in the production of large diesel and natural gas engines and engine systems that satisfy a wide variety of power needs for marine, petroleum, and construction equipment. Additionally, the company has developed electric power generating systems that power areas inaccessible to online power such as isolated communities, and provided emergency power to hospitals, schools, and airports. Caterpillar maintains almost 40 manufacturing facilities throughout the United States. **International locations:** Australia; Belgium; Brazil; Canada; Chile; China; Denmark; France; Germany; Great Britain; Hungary; India; Indonesia; Ireland; Italy; Japan; Korea; Malaysia; Mexico; Netherlands; Norway; Poland; Portugal; Russia; Singapore; Spain; Sweden; Switzerland; United Kingdom.

CELOTEX CORPORATION
P.O. Box 157, Lagro IN 46941. 219/563-2154. **Contact:** Human Resources. **Description:** Manufactures molded acoustical ceiling tile and mineral wool. **Common positions include:** Accountant/Auditor; Blue-Collar Worker Supervisor; Buyer; Customer Service Representative; Electrical/Electronics Engineer; Human Resources Manager; Industrial Production Manager; Operations/Production Manager; Purchasing Agent/Manager; Quality Control Supervisor; Transportation/Traffic Specialist. **Educational backgrounds include:** Accounting; Business Administration; Communications; Engineering; Finance. **Benefits:** Dental Insurance; Disability Coverage; Employee Discounts; Life Insurance; Medical Insurance; Pension Plan; Profit Sharing; Savings Plan; Tuition Assistance. **Corporate headquarters location:** Tampa FL. **Parent company:** Jim Walter Corporation. **Operations at this facility include:** Manufacturing. **Number of employees at this location:** 104.

CHORE-TIME BROCK
P.O. Box 2000, Milford IN 46542-2000. 219/658-4101. **Contact:** Human Resources Department. **World Wide Web address:** http://www.ctbinc.com. **Description:** Manufactures farm machinery and related equipment. Chore-Time Brock's products include watering, feeding, and ventilation equipment.

DELTA FAUCET COMPANY
1425 West Main, P.O. Box 47, Greensburg IN 47240. 812/663-4433. **Contact:** Human Resources. **Description:** Manufactures faucets and other plumbing fixtures.

DRESSER INDUSTRIES
ROOTS DIVISION
900 West Mount Street, Connersville IN 47331. 765/827-9200. **Contact:** Personnel Department. **World Wide Web address:** http://www.rootsblower.com. **Description:** The Roots Division supplies blowers and vacuum pumps to a variety of customers. Overall, Dresser Industries is a supplier of technology, products, and services to worldwide energy, natural resources, and industrial markets. Operations include petroleum, energy processing and conversion, mining and construction, and general industry. The company markets its products and services in more than 100 countries. **Common positions include:** Accountant/Auditor; Branch Manager; Buyer; Computer Programmer; Credit Manager; Customer Service Representative; Department Manager; Draftsperson; Electrical/Electronics Engineer; Human Resources Manager; Industrial Engineer; Manufacturer's/Wholesaler's Sales Rep.; Marketing Specialist; Operations/Production Manager; Purchasing Agent/Manager; Quality Control Supervisor; Systems Analyst; Transportation/Traffic Specialist. **Educational backgrounds include:** Accounting; Business Administration; Engineering; Marketing. **Benefits:** Dental Insurance; Disability Coverage; Employee Discounts; Life Insurance; Medical Insurance; Pension Plan; Savings Plan; Tuition Assistance. **Corporate headquarters location:** Dallas TX. **Operations at this facility include:** Administration; Divisional Headquarters; Manufacturing; Research and Development; Sales; Service.

DuPONT PHOTOMASKS, INC.
P.O. Box 4088, Kokomo IN 46904-4088. 765/457-8311. **Contact:** Evelyn Braden, Human Resources Manager. **Description:** DuPont Photomasks's activities include the manufacturing of biomedical, industrial, and consumer products (such as photographic, data-recording, and video devices); the production of man-made fiber products (with applications in a variety of consumer and commercial industries); polymer products (such as plastic resins, elastomers, and films); agricultural and industrial chemicals (such as herbicides and insecticides, pigments, fluorochemicals, petroleum additives, and mineral acids); the exploration and production of crude oil and natural gas; the refining, marketing, and downstream transportation of petroleum; and the mining and distribution of steam and metallurgical coals. Industries served include aerospace, agriculture, apparel, transportation, health care, printing, and publishing.

EATON CORPORATION
CONTROLS DIVISION
703 West South Street, North Manchester IN 46962. 219/982-2161. **Contact:** Human Resources. **World Wide Web address:** http://www.eaton.com. **Description:** This location manufactures timers for washing machines. Overall, Eaton Corporation designs, manufactures, and sells electronic and electromechanical devices to automotive, appliance, and air conditioning and refrigeration manufacturers.

EXIDE CORPORATION
P.O. Box 748, Frankfort IN 46041. 765/654-8561. **Contact:** Human Resources. **Description:** Produces lead acid storage batteries for a wide variety of uses including consumer, industrial, and automotive applications.

FABWELL INC.
P.O. Box 1366, Elkhart IN 46515. 219/522-8473. **Contact:** Matt Carboneau, Human Resources Director. **World Wide Web address:** http://www.fabwell.com. **Description:** Produces and supplies exterior components to the building and construction, manufactured housing, recreational vehicle, and transportation/cargo industries.

FORD METER BOX COMPANY
P.O. Box 443, Wabash IN 46992-0443. 219/563-3171. **Contact:** Human Resources. **World Wide Web address:** http://www.fordmeterbox.com. **Description:** Manufactures automatic controls and regulators.

FRENCH LICK FURNITURE
P.O. Box 352, French Lick IN 47432. 812/936-9200. **Contact:** Human Resources. **Description:** Manufactures office furniture. **Parent company:** Kimball International is a leading supplier of wood furnishings for offices, hotels, resorts, and health care facilities. A *Fortune* 500 company

with over 7,500 employees internationally, its business and consumer products include office furniture, systems, and seating under the Kimball, National, and Harpers brand names; Kimball and Bosendorfer pianos; Kimball hospitality furniture; Kimball health care furniture; Harmony Woods home office furniture; and Kimball Victorian and French furniture reproductions. As a contract/OEM manufacturer, Kimball also produces, through its subsidiaries, electronic assemblies, cabinetry, molded plastics, carbide cutting tools, and metal stampings, and also produces a variety of brand name products in addition to home electronics that are marketed by other companies.

GE MOTORS
1412 13th Street, Tell City IN 47586. 812/547-2311. **Contact:** Human Resources. **Description:** This location manufactures motors and industrial systems as part of the diversified manufacturer. Overall, General Electric Company operates in the following areas: aircraft engines (jet engines, replacement parts, and repair services for commercial, military, executive, and commuter aircraft); appliances; broadcasting (NBC); industrial (lighting products, electrical distribution and control equipment, transportation systems products, electric motors, and electrical and electronic industrial automation products); materials (plastics, ABS resins, silicones, superabrasives, and laminates); power systems (products for the generation, transmission, and distribution of electricity); technical products and services (medical systems and equipment, as well as computer-based information and data interchange services for both internal use and external commercial and industrial customers); and capital services (consumer services, financing, and specialty insurance).

GENCORP
One General Street, P.O. Box 507, Wabash IN 46992. 219/563-1121. **Contact:** Human Resources. **World Wide Web address:** http://www.gencorp.com. **Description:** An international corporation with varied business interests including rubber products, plastics, industrial products, wall coverings, athletic products, rocket propulsion ordnance systems, and electronic sensors. **Corporate headquarters location:** Fairlawn OH.

GENERAL ELECTRIC COMPANY
1635 Broadway, Fort Wayne IN 46802. 219/439-2000. **Contact:** Manager of Human Resources. **World Wide Web address:** http://www.ge.com. **Description:** This location manufactures motors and transformers. Overall, General Electric operates in the following areas: aircraft engines (jet engines, replacement parts, and repair services for commercial, military, executive, and commuter aircraft); appliances; capital services (consumer services, financing, and specialty insurance); industrial (lighting products, electrical distribution and control equipment, transportation systems products, electric motors and related products, and a broad range of electrical and electronic industrial automation products); technical products and services (medical systems and equipment sold worldwide to hospitals and medical facilities, as well as a full range of computer-based information and data interchange services for both internal use and external commercial and industrial customers); broadcasting (NBC); materials (plastics, ABS resins, silicones, and superabrasives); and power systems (products for the generation, transmission, and distribution of electricity). **Number of employees worldwide:** 230,000.

HOWMET CORPORATION
1110 East Lincoln Way, La Porte IN 46350. 219/326-7400. **Contact:** Human Resources. **World Wide Web address:** http://www.howmet.com. **Description:** Manufactures high-temperature engines for the automotive and aerospace industries. Howmet is 67 percent-owned by Pechiney, a diversified international corporation that has operations in packaging, aluminum, turbine components, and related industrial sectors.

ITW FINISHING SYSTEMS AND PRODUCTS
4141 West 54th Street, Indianapolis IN 46254. 317/298-5000. **Contact:** Lois Christopher, Human Resources Director. **Description:** Designs and sells powder coating equipment. ITW Finishing Systems also manufactures and sells wheel-balancing systems.

INDUSTRIAL COMBUSTION ENGINEER, INC.
7000 West 21st Avenue, Gary IN 46406. 219/949-5066. **Fax:** 219/944-7683. **Contact:** Human Resources. **World Wide Web address:** http://www.indcomb.com. **Description:** Designs and manufactures industrial heaters, ovens, furnaces, and electrical panels.

JOHNSON CONTROLS, INC.
1302 East Monroe Street, Goshen IN 46526. 219/533-2111. **Contact:** Don DeLay, Human Resources Director. **World Wide Web address:** http://www.johnsoncontrols.com. **Description:** This location manufactures refrigeration controls and flow control values. Overall, Johnson Controls, Inc. conducts operations in four business units: Automotive, Controls, Plastics, and Battery. The automotive business produces complete seat systems, seating components, and interior trim systems for cars, light trucks, and vans. The controls segment is involved in the installation and service of facility management and control systems, retrofitting and service of mechanical equipment and lighting systems in non-residential buildings, and on-site management of facility operations and maintenance. The plastics unit manufactures plastic containers for beverages, food, personal care, and household items, as well as manufacturing, installing, and servicing plastics blow molding machinery systems. The battery segment manufactures automotive batteries for the replacement and original equipment markets and specialty batteries for telecommunications and uninterruptible power supply (UPS) applications. Founded in 1885.

KIMBALL INTERNATIONAL, INC.
1600 Royal Street, Jasper IN 47549. 812/482-1600. **Contact:** Selena Vonderheide, Corporate Recruitment. **Description:** A leading supplier of high-quality wood furnishings for offices, hotels, resorts, and health care facilities. Its business and consumer products include office furniture and seating under the Kimball, National, and Harpers brand names; Kimball and Bosendorfer pianos; Kimball hospitality furniture; Kimball health care furniture; Harmony Woods home office furniture; and Kimball Victorian and French furniture reproductions. Kimball operates as a contract/OEM manufacturer through its subsidiaries which produce electronic assemblies, cabinetry, molded plastics, carbide cutting tools, and metal stampings, and also produce a variety of brand name products marketed by other companies in industries as diverse as home entertainment and furnishings, consumer electronics, marine, and automotive. **Common positions include:** Accountant/Auditor; Customer Service Representative; Electrical/Electronics Engineer; Financial Analyst; Industrial Engineer; Mechanical Engineer; Systems Analyst. **Educational backgrounds include:** Accounting; Computer Science; Engineering; Finance; Marketing. **Benefits:** 401(k); Dental Insurance; Disability Coverage; Life Insurance; Medical Insurance; Profit Sharing. **Special programs:** Internships. **Corporate headquarters location:** This Location. **Operations at this facility include:** Administration. **Listed on:** NASDAQ. **Number of employees at this location:** 500. **Number of employees nationwide:** 7,000.

LANDIS & GYR UTILITIES
3601 Sagamore Parkway North, Lafayette IN 47904-1070. 765/742-1001. **Contact:** Nick Fletcher, Human Resources Director. **Description:** This location manufactures meter bases for utilities. Overall, Landis & Gyr designs, manufactures, and installs computer-based heating and cooling controls for non-residential buildings. The company's integrated building systems manage energy usage, HVAC, fire safety, and security for nonresidential buildings.

LINCOLN FOODSERVICE PRODUCTS, INC.
P.O. Box 1229, Fort Wayne IN 46801. 219/432-9511. **Contact:** Human Resources. **Description:** Designs, manufactures, and markets commercial and institutional food service cooking equipment and kitchenware supplies.

MORRISON CONSTRUCTION CO.
1834 Summer Street, Hammond IN 46320-2236. 219/932-5036. **Contact:** Human Resources. **Description:** Manufactures and services pipe fittings for blast furnaces and boiler makers.

NTN-BCA
987 North U.S. Highway 421, Greensburg IN 47240. 812/663-3361. **Contact:** Human Resources. **Description:** Manufactures ball bearings which are used in the automotive and agriculture industries. NTN-BCA was formerly known as Federal-Mogul Corporation.

NIBCO, INC.
1516 Middlebury Street, Elkhart IN 46515-1167. 219/295-3000. **Contact:** Cathy Nafe, Senior Staffing Manager. **World Wide Web address:** http://www.nibco.com. **Description:** Manufactures flow control solutions, fittings, and valves. **NOTE:** Entry-level positions are offered. **Common**

positions include: Industrial Engineer; Mechanical Engineer; MIS Specialist; Operations/Production Manager; Systems Analyst. **Educational backgrounds include:** Engineering. **Benefits:** 401(k); Disability Coverage; Life Insurance; Medical Insurance; Pension Plan; Profit Sharing; Savings Plan; Tuition Assistance. **Special programs:** Internships. **Corporate headquarters location:** This Location. **Other U.S. locations:** Nationwide. **Operations at this facility include:** Administration; Divisional Headquarters; Manufacturing; Regional Headquarters. **Listed on:** Privately held. **Number of employees nationwide:** 3,500.

NORTH AMERICAN PRODUCTS CORPORATION
P.O. Box 647, Jasper IN 47547. 812/482-2000. **Physical address:** 1180 Wernsing Road, Jasper IN. **Contact:** Dave Smith, Director of Human Resources. **World Wide Web address:** http://www.napco.com. **Description:** Manufactures and services carbide-tipped cutting tools for the wood and metal industries. **Common positions include:** Accountant/Auditor; Blue-Collar Worker Supervisor; Buyer; Credit Manager; Customer Service Representative; Draftsperson; General Manager; Industrial Engineer; Industrial Production Manager; Mechanical Engineer; Services Sales Representative; Systems Analyst. **Educational backgrounds include:** Accounting; Business Administration; Computer Science; Engineering; Finance; Marketing. **Benefits:** 401(k); Dental Insurance; Life Insurance; Medical Insurance; Profit Sharing; Savings Plan. **Corporate headquarters location:** This Location. **Other U.S. locations:** Nationwide. **Operations at this facility include:** Administration; Manufacturing; Regional Headquarters; Sales; Service. **Listed on:** Privately held. **Number of employees at this location:** 480.

OSRAM-SYLVANIA, INC.
1231 A Avenue North, Seymour IN 47274. 812/523-5200. **Contact:** Human Resources. **World Wide Web address:** http://www.sylvania.com. **Description:** This location formerly operated as a division of GTE. OSRAM-SYLVANIA Inc. functions within the following divisions: Coated Coil Operation, which involves the production of tungsten filaments coated with high-performance insulator aluminum oxide used in television electron guns; Special Refractory Products, which manufactures products made from refractory metals that are used as furnace hardware; The Ceramics Department, which produces various types of steatite ceramic electrical insulators used in bases of light bulbs; and The Quartz Department, which produces and finishes quartz crucibles for use by the semiconductor industry. **Corporate headquarters location:** Danvers MA.

OTIS ELEVATOR COMPANY
1331 South Curry Pike, Bloomington IN 47402. 812/339-2281. **Contact:** John Korzac, Director of Human Resources. **World Wide Web address:** http://www.nao.otis.com. **Description:** Produces and distributes a line of elevators and escalators for commercial and industrial use. **Parent company:** United Technologies Corporation provides high-technology products and support services to customers in the aerospace, building, military, and automotive industries worldwide. Products include large jet engines, temperature control systems, elevators and escalators, helicopters, and flight systems.

PPG INDUSTRIES
424 East Inglefield Road, Evansville IN 47711. 812/867-6601. **Contact:** Human Resources. **World Wide Web address:** http://www.ppg.com. **Description:** A supplier of products for manufacturing, building, automotive, processing, and numerous other world industries. The Pittsburgh-based company makes decorative and protective coatings, flat glass and fabricated glass products, continuous-strand fiber glass, and industrial and specialty chemicals. Founded in 1883. **International locations:** Canada; China; France; Germany; Ireland; Italy; Mexico; Portugal; Spain; Taiwan; the Netherlands; United Kingdom.

RAYBESTOS PRODUCTS COMPANY
1204 Darlington Avenue, Crawfordsville IN 47933. 765/362-3500. **Contact:** Richard Dubish, Human Resources Director. **Description:** Manufactures friction products, such as transmission plates, which are used in automobile and tractor engines.

REXAM CLOSURES
3245 Kansas Road, Evansville IN 47711. 812/867-6671x223. **Fax:** 812/867-6289. **Contact:** Scott Harrell, Manager of Employment. **Description:** Designs, develops, manufactures, and markets

closure systems for the packaging industry. The company's products include child-resistant closures, dispensers, screw caps, and tamper-evident systems. Customers include pharmaceutical companies; over-the-counter drug companies; food and cosmetic companies; household, industrial, and agricultural chemical companies; swimming pool chemical companies; and packagers of household cleaners, automotive aftermarket products, and beverages. Founded in 1953. **Common positions include:** Accountant/Auditor; Blue-Collar Worker Supervisor; Customer Service Representative; Designer; Human Resources Manager; Mechanical Engineer; Operations/ Production Manager; Plastics Engineer. **Educational backgrounds include:** Accounting; Business Administration; Communications; Engineering. **Benefits:** 401(k); Dental Insurance; Disability Coverage; Life Insurance; Medical Insurance; Savings Plan; Tuition Assistance. **Corporate headquarters location:** This Location. **Other U.S. locations:** Princeton IN. **Parent company:** Rexam. **Operations at this facility include:** Administration; Divisional Headquarters; Manufacturing; Research and Development; Sales. **Annual sales/revenues:** $51 - $100 million. **Number of employees at this location:** 325. **Number of employees nationwide:** 400.

SCHAFER GEAR WORKS
814 South Main Street, South Bend IN 46601. 219/234-4116. **Fax:** 219/234-4115. **Contact:** Carol Senour, Human Resources Manager. **World Wide Web address:** http://www.schafergear.com. **Description:** A manufacturer of precision gears of all types, employing CNC lathe, CNC hobbing, shaping, shaving and grinding machines, and various manual machines. **Common positions include:** Accountant/Auditor; Industrial Engineer; Mechanical Engineer. **Educational backgrounds include:** Accounting; Business Administration; Engineering. **Benefits:** 401(k); Life Insurance; Medical Insurance; Tuition Assistance. **Corporate headquarters location:** This Location. **Other area locations:** Elkhart IN; Fort Wayne IN. **Operations at this facility include:** Administration; Manufacturing; Sales. **Number of employees at this location:** 70. **Number of employees nationwide:** 90.

SIEBE APPLIANCE CONTROLS
P.O. Box 423, Kendallville IN 46755. 219/347-1000. **Contact:** Human Resources. **World Wide Web address:** http://www.eaton.com. **Description:** Manufactures control switches for appliances including pressure switches for washers and infinite switches for ranges. SIEBE Appliance Controls was formerly known as the Eaton Corporation.

STERLING PEERLESS
P.O. Box 7026, Indianapolis IN 46207. 317/925-9661. **Contact:** Human Resources. **Description:** Manufactures industrial pumps and related products.

TRW
P.O. Box 60, Lafayette IN 47902. 765/423-5377. **Contact:** Gary Hale, Director of Personnel. **Description:** This location manufactures manual and power steering gears and components for trucks, farm equipment, construction and industrial equipment, low-speed high-torque hydraulic motors, and gear pumps. Overall, TRW is a diversified technology firm with operations in electronics and space systems; car and truck equipment for both original equipment manufacturers and the replacement market; and a wide variety of industrial and energy components, including aircraft parts, welding systems, and electromechanical assemblies. **Corporate headquarters location:** Cleveland OH. **Listed on:** New York Stock Exchange.

3M
TAPE DIVISION
0304 South 075 East, Hartford City IN 47348. 765/348-3200. **Contact:** Human Resources. **World Wide Web address:** http://www.3m.com. **Description:** This location manufactures label stock, microcapsule, and electrical specialties tape. Overall, 3M manufactures products in three sectors: Industrial and Consumer; Information, Imaging, and Electronic; and Life Sciences. The Industrial and Consumer Sector includes a variety of products under brand names including 3M, Scotch, Post-it, Scotch-Brite, and Scotchgard. The Information, Imaging, and Electronic Sector is a leader in several high-growth global industries including telecommunications, electronics, electrical, imaging, and memory media. The Life Science Sector serves two broad market categories: health care, and traffic and personal safety. In the health care market, 3M is a leading provider of medical and surgical supplies, drug-delivery systems, and dental products; in traffic and personal safety,

3M is a leader in products for transportation safety, worker protection, vehicle and sign graphics, and out-of-home advertising. **Corporate headquarters location:** St. Paul MN. **International locations:** Worldwide.

WHITE INDUSTRIES
8804 Bash Street, Suite A, Indianapolis IN 46256. 317/849-6830. **Contact:** Human Resources. **Description:** An industrial and commercial machinery manufacturer specializing in the production of cutting tools and machine tools.

Note: Because addresses and telephone numbers of smaller companies can change rapidly, we recommend you call each company to verify the information below before inquiring about job opportunities. Mass mailings are not recommended.

Additional small employers:

BALL AND ROLLER BEARINGS

Bremen Bearings Inc.
1342 W Plymouth Street, Bremen IN 46506-1954. 219/546-2311.

Faultless Caster
1421 North Garvin Street, Evansville IN 47711-4653. 812/425-1011.

Link Belt Bearing
PO Box 85, Indianapolis IN 46206-0085. 317/273-5500.

McGill Manufacturing Company Inc.
705 N 6th Street, Monticello IN 47960-1711. 219/583-9171.

Standard Locknut Inc.
PO Box 780, Westfield IN 46074-0780. 317/867-0100.

COMMERCIAL FURNITURE AND FIXTURES

Adnik Manufacturing
53236 County Road 13, Elkhart IN 46514-9628. 219/262-3400.

Artec Manufacturing
PO Box 460, Jasper IN 47549-0001. 812/482-8517.

Carr Metal Products Inc.
3735 N Arlington Avenue, Indianapolis IN 46218-1867. 317/542-0691.

Do More Group Inc.
2400 Sterling Avenue, Elkhart IN 46516-4906. 219/293-0621.

Dygert Seating Inc.
53381 Marina Drive, Elkhart IN 46514-8327. 219/262-4675.

Eaton Corporation
800 South Romy Street, Eaton IN 47338-8822. 765/396-3548.

Executive Furniture Inc.
PO Box 167, Huntingburg IN 47542-0167. 812/683-3334.

Flexsteel Industries Inc.
PO Box 129, New Paris IN 46553-0129. 219/831-4050.

General Seating of America
2298 West State Road 28, Frankfort IN 46041-9185. 765/659-4781.

Indiana Furniture Industries
PO Box 12, Dubois IN 47527-0012. 812/678-3351.

Inwood Office Furniture Inc.
PO Box 646, Jasper IN 47547-0646. 812/482-6121.

Jasper Seating Company
PO Box 231, Jasper IN 47547-0231. 812/482-3204.

Jofco Inc.
PO Box 71, Jasper IN 47547-0071. 812/482-5154.

Kimball Office Furniture Manufacturing
PO Box C, Borden IN 47106-0903. 812/967-2041.

Meg Division of Steelworks
PO Box 240, Cambridge City IN 47327-0240. 765/478-3141.

Modernfold Inc.
PO Box 310, New Castle IN 47362-0310. 765/529-1450.

National Office Funiture
PO Box 209, Santa Claus IN 47579-0209. 812/937-4585.

OFS
1002 N Chestnut Street, Huntingburg IN 47542-9721. 812/536-4848.

Paoli Inc.
PO Box 30, Paoli IN 47454-0030. 812/723-2791.

RM Wieland Co.
PO Box 1000, Grabill IN 46741-1000. 219/627-3686.

Steelcase Wood
67742 Country Road 23, New Paris IN 46553. 219/831-4811.

Syndicate Systems Incorporated
PO Box 70, Middlebury IN 46540-0070. 219/825-9561.

Wood Tek
PO Box 698, Elkhart IN 46515-0698. 219/293-0641.

COMPRESSORS

Sullair Corporation
3700 E Michigan Blvd, Michigan City IN 46360-6527. 219/879-5451.

CONSTRUCTION MACHINERY AND EQUIPMENT

Envirex Inc.
2753 Michigan Road, Madison IN 47250-1812. 812/273-1484.

Lift-All
PO Box 9738, Fort Wayne IN 46899-9738. 219/747-0526.

Teco Inc.
PO Box 9247, Fort Wayne IN 46899-9247. 219/747-1631.

CONVEYORS AND CONVEYING EQUIPMENT

C&M Inc.
PO Box 379, Mitchell IN 47446-0379. 812/849-5647.

Shuttleworth North America
10 Commercial Rd, Huntington IN 46750-8805. 219/356-8500.

United Pentek Inc.
8502 Brookville Rd, Indianapolis IN 46239-9427. 317/359-3858.

ENGINE PARTS

Federal-Mogul Powertrain Systems
3605 W Cleveland Rd Extension, South Bend IN 46628-9779. 219/272-5900.

Granning Air Suspensions
PO Box 600, Brookston IN 47923-0600. 219/279-2801.

PHD
PO Box 9070, Fort Wayne IN 46899-9070. 219/747-6151.

Zollner Pistons
2425 S Coliseum Blvd, Fort Wayne IN 46803-2939. 219/426-8081.

FANS, BLOWERS, AND AIR PURIFICATION EQUIPMENT

American Air Filter
210 N Enterprise Boulevard, Lebanon IN 46052-8192. 765/482-6040.

Bayley Fan Group
PO Box 646, Lebanon IN 46052-0646. 765/482-3650.

ECS Wire Division
201 West Carmel Drive, Carmel IN 46032-2527. 317/846-3438.

Lau Industries
PO Box 646, Lebanon IN 46052-0646. 765/482-0055.

Lau Industries
9522 East 30th Street, Indianapolis IN 46229-1026. 317/899-3900.

The New York Blower Company
171 Factory St, La Porte IN 46350-2622. 219/362-1531.

FARM MACHINERY AND EQUIPMENT

Farm Fans
5900 Elmwood Avenue, Indianapolis IN 46203-6033. 317/787-6341.

RG Applegate Steel Co. Inc.
PO Box 68, Saratoga IN 47382-0068. 765/584-4631.

Universal Manufacturing
PO Box 115, Goshen IN 46527-0115. 219/533-3131.

GASKETS, PACKING, AND SEALING DEVICES

American Rubber Products
PO Box 190, La Porte IN 46352-0190. 219/326-1315.

Hoosier Gasket Corporation
3333 Massachusetts Avenue, Indianapolis IN 46218-3754. 317/545-2000.

Jeans Extrusion Inc.
PO Box 307, Salem IN 47167-0307. 812/883-2581.

HEATING EQUIPMENT

Stewart-Warner Corporation
5701 Fortune Cir S, Indianapolis IN 46241-5534. 317/243-7367.

INDUSTRIAL AND COMMERCIAL MACHINERY AND EQUIPMENT

Ahaus Tool & Engineering Inc.
PO Box 280, Richmond IN 47375-0280. 765/962-3571.

Anderson Tool & Engineering Company
PO Box 1158, Anderson IN 46015-1158. 765/643-6691.

Cerden & Son Inc.
PO Box 368, Frankton IN 46044-0368. 765/754-7711.

Fulton Industries Inc.
PO Box 290, Rochester IN 46975-0290. 219/223-4387.

Hardigg Industries Inc.
2405 Norcross Drive, Columbus IN 47201-8844. 812/342-0139.

Hi-Tech Corporation
PO Box 30, Albion IN 46701-0030. 219/636-3040.

Major Tool & Machine Inc.
1458 E 19th Street, Indianapolis IN 46218-4228. 317/636-6433.

Wolfe & Swickard Machine Co.
PO Box 42817, Indianapolis IN 46242-0817. 317/241-2589.

INDUSTRIAL PROCESS FURNACES AND OVENS

Rogers Engineering & Manufacturing Co.
112 S Center St, Cambridge City IN 47327-1243. 765/478-5444.

Wellman Thermal Systems Corp.
1 Progress Rd, Shelbyville IN 46176-1837. 317/398-4411.

MEASURING AND CONTROLLING EQUIPMENT

Dwyer Instruments Inc.
PO Box 73, Michigan City IN 46360-2426. 219/879-8868.

Endress & Hauser Instruments
PO Box 246, Greenwood IN 46142-0246. 317/535-7138.

JFW Industries Inc.
5134 Commerce Square Drive, Indianapolis IN 46237-9738. 317/887-1340.

Pyromation Inc.
PO Box 5601, Fort Wayne IN 46895-5601. 219/484-2580.

Tokheim Corporation
227 Front St, Washington IN 47501-2533. 812/254-7400.

Trilithic Inc.
9202 E 33rd St, Indianapolis IN 46235-4200. 317/895-3600.

METAL CUTTING OR FORMING TOOLS

Air-Way Manufacturing Co.
PO Box 868, Auburn IN 46706-0868. 219/925-3584.

Capitol Technologies
PO Box 3626, South Bend IN 46619-0626. 219/232-3311.

City Machine Tool & Die Co.
PO Box 2607, Muncie IN 47307-0607. 765/288-4431.

Mosey Manufacturing Co. Inc.
262 Fort Wayne Avenue,

Richmond IN 47374-2328. 765/983-8800.

Wabash MPI
PO Box 298, Wabash IN 46992-0298. 219/563-1184.

METAL HARDWARE

Accuride International Inc.
4300 Olive Road, South Bend IN 46628. 219/280-4300.

American Metal Products
PO Box 87, La Porte IN 46352-0087. 219/362-3126.

Brammall Inc.
PO Box 208, Angola IN 46703-0208. 219/665-3176.

Glynn Johnson
PO Box 6023, Indianapolis IN 46206-6023. 317/897-9944.

Lectron Products of Indiana
2855 E Bellefontaine Road, Hamilton IN 46742-9667. 219/488-3521.

METALWORKING MACHINERY

Micro-Precision Textron
525 Berne Street, Berne IN 46711-1246. 219/589-2136.

MISC. INDUSTRIAL MACHINE TOOLS

Regal Cutting Tools
5100 South Meridian Road, Mitchell IN 47446-8300. 812/849-4700.

MISC. INDUSTRIAL MACHINERY AND EQUIPMENT

Amatrol Inc.
PO Box 2697, Jeffersonville IN 47131-2697. 812/288-8285.

Dana Corporation
PO Box 356, Mitchell IN 47446-0356. 812/849-3993.

Firestone Industrial Products
12650 Hamilton Crossing Blvd, Carmel IN 46032. 317/818-8659.

FSI
PO Box 735, Michigan City IN 46361-0735. 219/879-3307.

Osram Sylvania Inc.
PO Box 275, Westfield IN 46074-0275. 317/867-6000.

MISC. PIPE FITTINGS AND/OR VALVES

Biddle Manufacturing Corp.
800 South Georgia Street, Sheridan IN 46069-1408. 317/758-4451.

Daman Products Company Inc.
1811 N Home Street, Mishawaka IN 46545-7267. 219/259-7841.

Elkhart Products Corporation
PO Box 1008, Elkhart IN 46515-1008. 219/264-3181.

L&L Fittings
PO Box 11324, Fort Wayne IN 46857-1324. 219/747-9200.

Regin Manufacturing Inc.
PO Box 50654, Indianapolis IN 46250-0654. 317/579-6700.

MOTORS AND GENERATORS

AO Smith Corporation
Willow Creek Road, Paoli IN 47454. 812/723-5005.

Dodge/Rockwell Automation
1225 7th Street, Columbus IN 47201-5901. 812/378-2403.

Electric Motors & Specialties
PO Box 180, Garrett IN 46738-0180. 219/357-4141.

Hansen Corporation
901 South First Street, Princeton IN 47670-2369. 812/385-3000.

Hurst Manufacturing
PO Box 326, Princeton IN 47670-0326. 812/385-2564.

PLUMBING FIXTURE FITTINGS AND TRIM

Delta Faucet Company
PO Box 40980, Indianapolis IN 46240-0980. 317/848-0652.

POWER TRANSMISSION EQUIPMENT

Comet Industries
358 NW F Street, Richmond IN 47374-2230. 765/966-8161.

MB Manufacturing Inc.
213 S State Road 49, Valparaiso IN 46383-7834. 219/477-3800.

NTN Driveshaft Inc.
8251 S International Drive, Columbus IN 47201-9329. 812/342-7000.

PUMPS AND PUMPING EQUIPMENT

Flint & Walling
95 N Oak Street, Kendallville IN 46755-1772. 219/347-1600.

International Fuel Systems
980 Hurricane Road, Franklin IN 46131-9501. 317/738-9202.

Wayne Combustion Systems
801 Glasgow Ave, Fort Wayne IN 46803-1344. 219/425-9200.

ROLLING MILL MACHINERY AND EQUIPMENT

Continental Machine & Engineering Company
PO Box 270, East Chicago IN 46312-0270. 219/398-7300.

WOODWORKING MACHINERY

Wood-Mizer Products Inc.
8180 W 10th St, Indianapolis IN 46214-2430. 317/271-1542.

Wood-Mizer Products Inc.
8829 E State Road 46, Greensburg IN 47240-7449. 812/663-5257.

For more information on career opportunities in industrial manufacturing:

Associations

ASSN. FOR MANUFACTURING EXCELLENCE
380 West Palatine Road, Wheeling IL 60090. 847/520-3282. World Wide Web address: http://www.trainingforum.com/asn/ame.

ASSOCIATION FOR MANUFACTURING TECHNOLOGY
7901 Westpark Drive, McLean VA 22102. 703/893-2900. A trade association. World Wide Web address: http://www.mfgtech.org.

INSTITUTE OF INDUSTRIAL ENGINEERS
25 Technology Park, Norcross GA 30092-2988. 770/449-0460. World Wide Web address: http://www.iienet.org. A nonprofit organization with 27,000 members. Conducts seminars and offers reduced rates on its books and publications.

NATIONAL ASSOCIATION OF MANUFACTURERS
1331 Pennsylvania Avenue NW, Suite 1500, Washington DC 20004. 202/637-3000. World Wide Web address: http://www.nam.org. A lobbying association.

NATIONAL SCREW MACHINE PRODUCTS ASSOCIATION
6700 West Snowville Road, Brecksville OH 44141. 440/526-0300. Provides resource information.

NATIONAL TOOLING AND MACHINING ASSOCIATION
9300 Livingston Road, Fort Washington MD 20744. 301/248-1250. World Wide Web address: http://www.ntma.org. Reports on wages and operating expenses, produces monthly newsletters, and offers legal advice.

SOCIETY OF MANUFACTURING ENGINEERS
P.O. Box 930, One SME Drive, Dearborn MI 48121. 313/271-1500. World Wide Web address: http://www.sme.org. Offers educational events and educational materials on manufacturing.

Directories

AMERICAN MANUFACTURER'S DIRECTORY
5711 South 86th Circle, P.O. Box 37347, Omaha NE 68127. 800/555-5211. Made by the same company that created *American Big Business Directory*, *American Manufacturer's Directory* lists over 531,000 manufacturing companies of all sizes and industries. The directory contains product and sales information, company size, and a key contact name for each company.

Online Services

CAREER PARK - MANUFACTURING JOBS
http://www.careerpark.com/jobs/manulist.html. This Website provides a list of current job openings in the manufacturing industry. The site is run by Parker Advertising Service, Inc.

MO'S GATEWAY TO MANUFACTURING-RELATED JOBS LISTINGS
http://www.chesapk.com/mfgjobs.html. Provides links to sites that post job openings in manufacturing.

Special Programs

BUREAU OF APPRENTICESHIP AND TRAINING
U.S. Department of Labor, 200 Constitution Avenue NW, Room N4649, Washington DC 20210. 202/219-5921.

MINING/GAS/PETROLEUM/ENERGY RELATED

Crude oil prices have fallen 28 percent since October 1997 due to ailing economies in the Far East, mild winters in the U.S. and Europe, and a growing supply. The average price per barrel for crude oil was $4 lower in 1997 than 1996 and industry experts expect that to drop another $1 in 1998. The trend is likely to continue with Asia in turmoil and a surplus of commodities from heating oil to gasoline. This is good news for consumers who have benefited from lower prices. Business Week *reports that nationwide, the average price of regular unleaded gasoline has dropped to $1.12 per gallon, down more than 8 percent from 1997.*

What does all this mean for the industry as a whole? Analysts expected profits to rise by a mere 5 percent in 1998 (half the rate of 1997). Oil companies likely saw profits drop by 2 percent. Other sectors were expected to remain steady, specifically service companies and drillers. These companies will continue spending on exploration and production projects, and projections indicated that a majority of gas exploration companies intended to increase domestic spending in 1998.

In other mining sectors, the average price of gold has remained stable in recent years with a slight dip toward the end of 1996 and early 1997. Lime production has been reaching higher levels since 1993 and this growth was predicted through 1998. The coal mining industry has undergone some changes in order to regain profits. Total coal production is expected to rise 1 percent yearly through 2002. Factors that may negatively affect this sector include higher transportation costs, labor disruptions, and government restrictions.

AMOCO OIL COMPANY
2815 Indianapolis Boulevard, Whiting IN 46394. 219/473-7700. **Contact:** Human Resources. **Description:** Manufactures, transports, and markets petroleum products. **Parent company:** Amoco Corporation is engaged in the exploration, production, and transportation of crude oil and natural gas, and in the manufacturing, transporting, and marketing of petroleum and chemical products. Amoco also has interests in minerals and real estate, and is among the top 10 United States companies in assets controlled. The company is also active in more than 40 other countries. Petroleum operations are also conducted by the following subsidiaries: Amoco Production Company, which is engaged in worldwide exploration and production and Amoco Chemicals Corporation, which supervises the company's worldwide chemical operations. **Other U.S. locations:** Towson MD; Salt Lake City UT.

DEISTER CONCENTRATOR COMPANY
901 Glasgow Avenue, Fort Wayne IN 46803. **Toll-free phone:** 800/926-6453. **Fax:** 219/420-3252. **Contact:** Human Resources. **Description:** Manufactures mineral recovery equipment. Founded in 1906.

GENERAL PETROLEUM
PO Box 10688, Fort Wayne IN 46853. 219/489-8504. **Fax:** 219/489-6468. **Contact:** Human Resources Department. **Description:** General Petroleum is engaged in the wholesale distribution of a variety of lubricants. **Corporate headquarters location:** This Location. **Other area locations:** Indianapolis IN.

MIDWEST COAL COMPANY
CHINOOK MINE
11498 Bloomington Road, Brazil IN 47834. 812/894-2385. **Contact:** Human Resources. **Description:** A coal mining company.

WELSH OIL INC.
800 East 86th Street, Merrillville IN 46410-6270. 219/791-4321. **Contact:** Human Resources. **Description:** An oil wholesaler.

Note: *Because addresses and telephone numbers of smaller companies can change rapidly, we recommend you call each company to verify the information below before inquiring about job opportunities. Mass mailings are not recommended.*

Additional small employers:

COAL MINING

Black Beauty Mining Company
5526 E French Drive, Pimento IN 47866-9543. 812/495-6410.

Black Beauty Mining Company
PO Box 172, Switz City IN 47465-0172. 812/659-2417.

Kindill Mining Inc.
PO Box 338, Oakland City IN 47660-0338. 812/721-5250.

Kindill Mining Inc.
1890 N County Road, Sullivan IN 47882. 812/648-2236.

Peabody Coal Company
PO Drawer 56B2, Carlisle IN 47838. 812/659-3392.

Peabody Coal Company
PO Box 7, Lynnville IN 47619-0007. 812/922-3271.

Squaw Creek Co.
PO Box 111, Boonville IN 47601-0111. 812/925-3362.

LUBRICATING OILS AND GREASES

Metalworking Lubricants Co.
1509 South Senate Avenue, Indianapolis IN 46225-1573. 317/632-2043.

For more information on career opportunities in the mining, gas, petroleum, and energy industries:

Associations

AMERICAN ASSOCIATION OF PETROLEUM GEOLOGISTS
P.O. Box 979, Tulsa OK 74101. 918/584-2555. World Wide Web address: http://www.aapg.org. International headquarters for petroleum geologists.

AMERICAN GEOLOGICAL INSTITUTE
4220 King Street, Alexandria VA 22302-1502. 703/379-2480. World Wide Web address: http://www.agiweb.org. Scholarships available. Publishes monthly *Geotimes*. Offers job listings.

AMERICAN NUCLEAR SOCIETY
555 North Kensington Avenue, La Grange Park IL 60526. 708/352-6611. World Wide Web address: http://www.ans.org. Offers educational services.

AMERICAN PETROLEUM INSTITUTE
1220 L Street NW, Suite 900, Washington DC 20005. 202/682-8000. World Wide Web address: http://www.api.org. A trade association.

GEOLOGICAL SOCIETY OF AMERICA
3300 Penrose Place, P.O. Box 9140, Boulder CO 80301. 303/447-2020. World Wide Web address: http://www.geosociety.org. Membership of over 17,000. Offers sales items and publications. Also conducts society meetings.

NUCLEAR ENERGY INSTITUTE
1776 I Street NW, Suite 400, Washington DC 2006-3708. 202/739-8000. World Wide Web address: http://www.nei.org. Provides a wide variety of information on nuclear energy issues and offers complimentary educational packets for students and teachers.

SOCIETY FOR MINING, METALLURGY, AND EXPLORATION, INC.
P.O. Box 625002, Littleton CO 80162-5002. 303/973-9550. World Wide Web address: http://www.smenet.org.

SOCIETY OF EXPLORATION GEOPHYSICISTS
P.O. Box 702740, Tulsa OK 74170-2740. 918/493-3516. World Wide Web address: http://www.seg.org. A membership association. Offers publications.

SOCIETY OF PETROLEUM ENGINEERS
222 Palisades Creek Drive, Richardson TX 75080. 972/952-9393. World Wide Web address: http://www.spe.org.

Directories

BROWN'S DIRECTORY OF NORTH AMERICAN AND INTERNATIONAL GAS COMPANIES
Advanstar Communications, 7500 Old Oak

Boulevard, Cleveland OH 44130. Toll-free phone: 800/225-4569. World Wide Web address: http://www.advanstar.com.

OIL AND GAS DIRECTORY
Geophysical Directory, Inc., P.O. Box 130508, Houston TX 77219. 713/529-8789.

Magazines

AMERICAN GAS
1515 Wilson Boulevard, Arlington VA 22209. 703/841-8686.

GAS INDUSTRIES
Gas Industries News, Inc., 6300 North River Road, Suite 505, Rosemont IL 60018. 847/696-2394.

NATIONAL PETROLEUM NEWS
Adams Business Media, 2101 South Arlington Heights Road, Suite 150, Arlington Heights IL 60005. 847/427-9512. Fax: 847/427-2006. World Wide Web address: http://www.petroretail.net.

OIL AND GAS JOURNAL
PennWell Publishing Company, 1421 South Sheridan Road, P.O. Box 74112, Tulsa OK 74101. 918/835-3161. World Wide Web address: http://www.ogjonline.com.

Online Services

NATIONAL CENTRE FOR PETROLEUM GEOLOGY AND GEOPHYSICS
http://www.ncpgg.adelaide.edu.au/ncpgg.html. This Website provides links to sites that post job openings in mining, petroleum, energy, and related fields.

PETROLEUM & GEOSYSTEMS ENGINEERING
http://www.pe.utexas.edu/Dept/Reading/pejb.html. Offers a vast list of links to sites that are posting current job openings in petroleum and geosystems engineering and related fields. The site is run by the University of Texas at Austin. Links to many relevant associations are also offered.

PAPER AND WOOD PRODUCTS

Despite an increased demand for U.S. market pulp, employment growth in this sector should be relatively sluggish. According to the U.S. Department of Commerce, while the pulp sector is expected to enjoy higher sales through the year 2002, overseas shipment growth should be slower, at 1.8 percent annually.

A rebound was forecasted in 1998 for the paper and paperboard mills sector as global demand increases, and shipments should continue steady annual growth for the next several years. At the same time, shipments of corrugated boxes should be even stronger.

Automation is causing a decline in employment opportunities for precision woodworkers and woodworking machine operators, according to the U.S. Department of Labor. However, woodworkers who specialize in furniture, cabinets, moldings, and fixtures should find more opportunities. A significant upswing in the demand for household furniture should result in improved employment prospects.

AMERICAN STATIONERY COMPANY, INC.
300 North Park Avenue, Peru IN 46970. 765/473-4438. **Contact:** Human Resources Director. **E-mail address:** amerstat@iquest.net. **Description:** Manufactures stationery products.

INLAND CONTAINER CORPORATION
4030 Vincennes Road, Indianapolis IN 46268. 317/879-4222. **Contact:** Human Resources. **World Wide Web address:** http://www.iccnet.com. **Description:** Manufactures corrugated shipping containers and boxes. **Corporate headquarters location:** This Location.

MEAD PAPER
7575 Georgetown Road, Indianapolis IN 46268. 317/876-1676. **Contact:** Human Resources. **Description:** Manufactures carbonless copy paper rolls. Mead's primary customers are printers of business forms. **Parent company:** Mead International manufactures, sells, and markets pulp, paper, paperboard, shipping containers, packaging, lumber, school and office supplies, stationery products, and electronic publishing and information retrieval systems.

PRINT PACK
1505 West Main Street, Greensburg IN 47240. 812/663-5091. **Contact:** Human Resources. **Description:** Manufactures a variety of paper products, plastic tableware, and retail packaging products such as cartons, bags, and wraps. Paper products include tissues, towels, business and correspondence paper, coated papers for catalogs, and premium printing papers.

WABASH FIBRE BOX COMPANY
P.O. Box 238, Terre Haute IN 47808-0238. 812/232-0521. **Contact:** Human Resources. **Description:** A paperboard mill.

DAVID R. WEBB COMPANY, INC.
P.O. Box 8, Edinburgh IN 46124. 812/526-2601. **Contact:** Vince Ryan, Human Resources. **Description:** Produces hardwood veneer and plywood.

***Note:** Because addresses and telephone numbers of smaller companies can change rapidly, we recommend you call each company to verify the information below before inquiring about job opportunities. Mass mailings are not recommended.*

Additional small employers:

COATED AND LAMINATED PAPER

Avery Dennison
270 Westmeadow Place, Lowell IN 46356-1678. 219/696-7777.

CONVERTED PAPER AND PAPERBOARD PRODUCTS

Columbus Converting
983 S Marr Road, Columbus IN 47201-7439. 812/378-0308.

PM Company
8525 E 33rd St, Indianapolis IN 46226-6506. 317/899-5100.

DIE-CUT PAPER AND PAPER PRODUCTS

Universal Diecutters Corp. Inc.
8480 Highway 66, Wadesville IN 47638-9702. 812/985-5942.

LUMBER AND WOOD WHOLESALE

Cannon Valley Woodwork
1701 N Market Street, Kokomo IN 46901-2367. 765/868-0790.

Carter Lee Lumber Company Inc.
1717 W Washington Street, Indianapolis IN 46222-4542. 317/639-5431.

Davidson Lumber Company
PO Box 800, Franklin IN 46131-0800. 317/738-3211.

Hall & House Lumber Company Inc.
18030 U.S. Route 31 North, Westfield IN 46074. 317/896-2375.

KA Components
8606 Allisonville Rd, Ste 103, Indianapolis IN 46250. 317/595-6585.

Robert Weed Plywood Corp.
PO Box 487, Bristol IN 46507-0487. 219/848-4408.

MILLWORK, PLYWOOD, AND STRUCTURAL MEMBERS

Adorn Inc.
1808 W Hively Avenue, Elkhart IN 46517-4026. 219/295-5223.

American Millwork Corporation
4840 Beck Drive, Elkhart IN 46516-9569. 219/295-4158.

Benchmark Mouldings
PO Box 1502, Elkhart IN 46515-1502. 219/264-3129.

BL Curry & Sons Inc.
PO Box 439, New Albany IN 47151-0439. 812/945-6623.

Cana Inc.
29194 Phillips Street, Elkhart IN 46514-1050. 219/262-4664.

Door Craft of Indiana
2526 Western Avenue, Plymouth IN 46563-1050. 219/936-2183.

Indiana Veneers Corporation
1121 E 24th Street, Indianapolis IN 46205-4425. 317/926-2458.

Jasper Wood Products Company Inc.
PO Box 271, Jasper IN 47547-0271. 812/482-3454.

Koetter Woodworking Inc.
533 Louis Smith Road, Borden IN 47106-8100. 812/923-8875.

Middlebury Hardwood Products
PO Box 1429, Middlebury IN 46540-1429. 219/825-9524.

Mobilcraft Wood Products
PO Box 638, Elkhart IN 46515-0638. 219/293-0521.

Norstam Veneers Inc.
PO Box 32, Mauckport IN 47142-0032. 812/732-4391.

Premdor Corp.
PO Box 1, Walkerton IN 46574-0001. 219/586-3192.

Rockwell Window Co. Inc.
PO Box 130, Knox IN 46534-0130. 219/772-2955.

Stiles Inc.
PO Box 1807, Elkhart IN 46515-1807. 219/262-3671.

PAPER BAGS

Independent Packaging
303 N Curry Pike, Bloomington IN 47404-2502. 812/339-9294.

KCL Corporation
PO Box 629, Shelbyville IN 46176-0629. 317/392-2521.

PAPER MILLS

Beveridge Paper Company
717 West Washington Street, Indianapolis IN 46204-2709. 317/635-4391.

Chinet Company
6629 Indianapolis Boulevard, Hammond IN 46320-2833. 219/844-8950.

Fort James Corporation
301 S Progress Drive E, Kendallville IN 46755-3266. 219/347-5912.

Inland Paperboard & Packaging
PO Box 428, Newport IN 47966-0428. 765/492-3341.

Jefferson Smurfit Corporation
301 S Butterfield Road, Muncie IN 47303-4317. 765/289-7391.

Nice-Pak Products Inc.
One Nice Pak Road, Mooresville IN 46158-1367. 317/831-6800.

Westvaco Envelope Company
PO Box 1166, Indianapolis IN 46206-1166. 317/787-3361.

PAPERBOARD CONTAINERS AND BOXES

Artistic Carton Company
PO Box 547, Auburn IN 46706-0547. 219/925-6060.

Barger Packaging Corporation
PO Box 249, Elkhart IN 46515-0249. 219/295-6605.

Bell Packaging Marion
3112 S Boots Street, Marion IN 46953-4016. 765/664-1261.

Box USA Group Inc.
PO Box 270, Hartford City IN 47348-0270. 765/348-3000.

Corrugated Paper Products Inc.
PO Box 1326, Mishawaka IN 46546-1326. 219/259-7981.

Creative Expressions Group
3500 N Arlington Avenue,

Indianapolis IN 46218-1805. 317/546-9281.

Fibre Form Corporation
PO Box 211, Columbia City IN 46725-0211. 219/244-6169.

Flashfold Carton
1140 Hayden Street, Fort Wayne IN 46803-2040. 219/423-9431.

Grace Packaging
7950 Allison Avenue, Indianapolis IN 46268-1612. 317/876-4100.

Inland Paperboard & Packaging
PO Box 508, Crawfordsville IN 47933-0508. 765/362-4010.

Inland Paperboard & Packaging
2135 Stoutfield Drive East, Indianapolis IN 46241. 317/390-3300.

Jefferson Smurfit Containers
804 Hazlett Street, Anderson IN 46016-2324. 765/644-7705.

Jefferson Smurfit Containers
1201 E Lincolnway, La Porte IN 46350-3955. 219/326-5089.

Paper Art
PO Box 7700, Indianapolis IN 46277-4000. 317/841-9999.

Stone Container Corporation
PO Box 570, Mishawaka IN 46546-0570. 219/259-7881.

Stone Container Corporation
PO Box 867, Columbus IN 47202-0867. 812/372-8873.

Stone Container Corporation
1535 Fieldhouse Ave, Elkhart IN 46517-1404. 219/293-4941.

Tenneco Packaging Inc.
520 S 1st St, Gas City IN 46933-1727. 765/674-9781.

Tetra Pak Materials
5201 Investment Dr, Fort Wayne IN 46808-3650. 219/484-7734.

Tri-Wall Containers
2626 County Road 71, Butler IN 46721-9406. 219/868-2151.

Wabash Fibre Box
PO Box 9310, Fort Wayne IN 46899-9310. 219/747-9111.

WOOD MILLS

Dale Wood Manufacturing
PO Box 317, Dale IN 47523-0317. 812/937-4483.

Frank Miller Lumber Company Inc.
1690 Frank Miller Road, Union City IN 47390. 765/964-3196.

GAF Corporation
901 Givens Road, Mount Vernon IN 47620-8200. 812/838-1492.

WOOD PRESERVING

Universal Forest Products
PO Box 129, Granger IN 46530-0129. 219/277-7670.

WOOD PRODUCTS

Exide Corporation
3430 Cline Road Northwest, Corydon IN 47112-6908. 812/738-8274.

For more information on career opportunities in the paper and wood products industries:

Associations

FOREST PRODUCTS SOCIETY
2801 Marshall Court, Madison WI 53705-2295. 608/231-1361. World Wide Web address: http://www.supranet.com/forestprod.

NATIONAL PAPER TRADE ASSOCIATION
111 Great Neck Road, Great Neck NY 11021. 516/829-3070. World Wide Web address: http://www.papertrade.com. Offers management services to paper wholesalers, as well as books, seminars, and research services.

PAPERBOARD PACKAGING COUNCIL
201 North Union Street, Suite 220, Alexandria VA 22314. 703/836-3300. Offers statistical and lobbying services.

TECHNICAL ASSOCIATION OF THE PULP AND PAPER INDUSTRY
P.O. Box 105113, Atlanta GA 30348. 770/446-1400. World Wide Web address: http://www.tappi.org.

Directories

DIRECTORY OF THE WOOD PRODUCTS INDUSTRY
Miller Freeman, Inc., 600 Harrison Street, San Francisco CA 94107. 415/905-2200. World Wide Web address: http://www.woodwideweb.com.

LOCKWOOD-POST'S DIRECTORY OF THE PULP, PAPER AND ALLIED TRADES
Miller Freeman, Inc., 600 Harrison Street, San Francisco CA 94107. 415/905-2200. World Wide Web address: http://www.pulp-paper.com/lpdisk.htm.

POST'S PULP AND PAPER DIRECTORY
Miller Freeman, Inc., 600 Harrison Street, San Francisco CA 94107. 415/905-2200. World Wide Web address: http://www.pulp-paper.com.

Magazines

PAPERBOARD PACKAGING
Advanstar Communications, 131 West First Street, Duluth MN 55802. 218/723-9200. World Wide Web address: http://www.advanstar.com.

PULP AND PAPER WEEK
Miller Freeman, Inc., 600 Harrison Street, San Francisco CA 94107. 415/905-2200. World Wide Web address: http://www.mfi.com.

WOOD TECHNOLOGIES
Miller Freeman, Inc., 600 Harrison Street, San Francisco CA 94107. 415/905-2200. World Wide Web address: http://www.woodtechmag.com.

PRINTING AND PUBLISHING

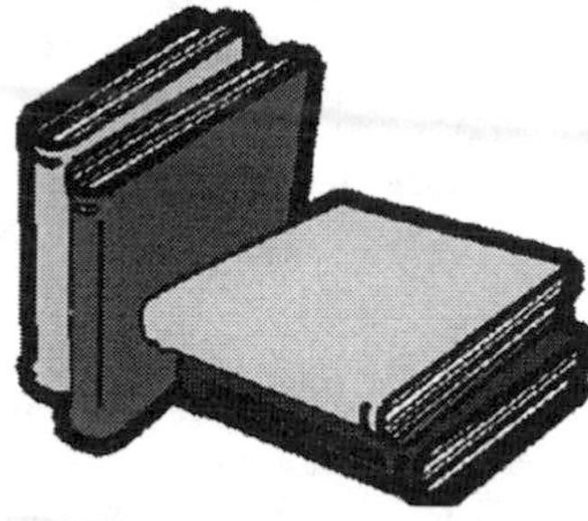

Digital technology took the book publishing industry by storm in 1997. New printing production and editorial systems, Web publishing software, and digital color proofs are just a few of the high-tech offerings. At this point, technology is outpacing the industry and analysts think it will take a few years before these new technologies are fully integrated into book publishing.

A recent survey by Arthur Andersen reveals that industry mergers may be a continuing trend. Results showed that 79 percent of book publishing executives are considering a merger or acquisition transaction. There are already several well-known companies on the market including Bender, Mosby, and Waverly. According to Publishers Weekly, *many other companies are restructuring and cutting loose smaller divisions that do not fit into their core businesses. The Arthur Andersen survey also indicates that publishers are motivated to agree to these deals in order to broaden product lines and increase market share in the industry. It seems more efficient for publishers to expand through mergers/acquisitions versus international expansion.*

Children's titles are the fastest growing segment of book publishing, with U.S. sales rising 30 percent from 1990 - 1997. According to the Association of American Publishers, the best book sales in 1997 were in education and professional book publishing. Another area that will be looking to expand is travel publishing. The World Tourism Organization predicts that by 2020 travel will be one of the leading industries in the United States. Look for publishers to expand their selections of travel books in an attempt to capture very specific audiences.

Newspaper publishers are on the rebound thanks in large part to lower paper prices, a healthy economy, and online services. MSNBC reports that more than half of the nation's Internet users now regularly obtain news from the World Wide Web and that nearly one-quarter of these individuals use it on a daily basis. Job seekers with Internet experience should look to Web publishing as a career possibility.

Consolidation of magazine wholesalers caused distribution problems in the mid-'90s. As a result, publishers will actively pursue foreign markets such as Asia and Latin America for their wares. Photographic and digital imaging professionals will see little employment growth leading into 1999.

COURIER KENDALLVILLE, INC.
2500 Marion Drive, Kendallville IN 46755. 219/347-3044. **Contact:** Kelly Walkup, Human Resources Director. **Description:** Courier is a manufacturer of books, religious products, reference texts, software manuals, and technical documentation. The company also provides electronic prepress and fulfillment services. **Corporate headquarters location:** Lowell MA. **Other U.S. locations:** North Chelmsford MA; Stoughton MA; Westford MA; Philadelphia PA. **Parent company:** Courier Corporation.

CURTIS MAGAZINE GROUP
INDIANA BUSINESS MAGAZINE
1000 Waterway Boulevard, Indianapolis IN 46202. 317/692-1200. **Contact:** Eric Servaas, Publisher. **Description:** A monthly statewide business publication. Curtis Magazine Group also issues a business directory of Indiana's top 2,500 firms. **Common positions include:** Administrator; Advertising Clerk; Editor; Sales Executive; Writer. **Educational backgrounds include:** Journalism; Liberal Arts. **Benefits:** Life Insurance; Medical Insurance. **Corporate headquarters location:** This Location. **Operations at this facility include:** Administration; Sales; Service.

DISCOUNT LABELS, INC.
P.O. Box 709, New Albany IN 47151-0709. 812/945-2617. **Fax:** 812/949-3810. **Contact:** Human Resources Department. **World Wide Web address:** http://www.discountlabels.com. **Description:** Discount Labels is a leading provider of labels for the quick-print market and one of the largest short-run label printers in the U.S. Products include self-adhesive labels, rubber stamps, and other related products such as laser labels, bumper stickers, barcode labels, and hot stamp labels. **Common positions include:** Accountant/Auditor; Blue-Collar Worker Supervisor; Clerical Supervisor; Computer Programmer; Construction Contractor; Customer Service Representative; Electrician; General Manager; Human Resources Manager; Industrial Production Manager; Management Trainee; Operations/Production Manager; Purchasing Agent/Manager. **Educational backgrounds include:** Accounting; Business Administration; Computer Science; Finance; Liberal Arts. **Benefits:** 401(k); Daycare Assistance; Dental Insurance; Disability Coverage; Employee Discounts; Life Insurance; Medical Insurance; Profit Sharing. **Corporate headquarters location:** Atlanta GA. **Parent company:** American Business Products. **Operations at this facility include:** Administration; Divisional Headquarters; Manufacturing; Sales. **Listed on:** New York Stock Exchange. **Number of employees at this location:** 500. **Number of employees nationwide:** 1,500.

R.R. DONNELLEY & SONS COMPANY
1009 Sloan Street, Crawfordsville IN 47933. 765/362-1300. **Contact:** Human Resources. **World Wide Web address:** http://www.rrd.com. **Description:** This location performs various manufacturing, printing, and publishing functions. Also known as The Lakeside Press, R.R. Donnelley & Sons is a world leader in managing, reproducing, and distributing print and digital information for publishing, merchandising, and information technology customers. The company is one of the largest commercial printers in the world, producing catalogs, inserts, magazines, books, directories, computer documentation, and financial printing. Principal services offered by the company are conventional and digital prepress operations, computerized printing and binding, and sophisticated pool shipping and distribution services for printed products; information repackaging into multiple formats (print, magnetic, and optical media); database management, list rental, list enhancement, and direct mail production services; turnkey computer documentation services (outsourcing, translation, printing, binding, diskette replication, kitting, licensing, republishing, and fulfillment); reprographics and facilities management; creative design and communication services; and digital and conventional map creation and related services. Founded in 1864. **Corporate headquarters location:** Chicago IL. **Other U.S. locations:** Nationwide. **International locations:** Worldwide. **Listed on:** New York Stock Exchange. **Stock exchange symbol:** DNY. **Annual sales/revenues:** More than $100 million. **Number of employees nationwide:** 30,000. **Number of employees worldwide:** 35,000.

R.R. DONNELLEY & SONS COMPANY
2801 West Old Road 30, Warsaw IN 46580. 219/267-7101. **Contact:** Human Resources Department. **World Wide Web address:** http://www.rrd.com. **Description:** This location is involved in catalog printing. Also known as The Lakeside Press, R.R. Donnelley & Sons is a world leader in managing, reproducing, and distributing print and digital information for publishing, merchandising, and information technology customers. The company is one of the largest commercial printers in the world, producing catalogs, inserts, magazines, books, directories, computer documentation, and financial printing. Principal services offered by the company are conventional and digital prepress operations, computerized printing and binding, and sophisticated pool shipping and distribution services for printed products; information repackaging into multiple

formats (print, magnetic, and optical media); database management, list rental, list enhancement, and direct mail production services; turnkey computer documentation services (outsourcing, translation, printing, binding, diskette replication, kitting, licensing, republishing, and fulfillment); reprographics and facilities management; creative design and communication services; and digital and conventional map creation and related services. Founded in 1864. **Corporate headquarters location:** Chicago IL. **Other U.S. locations:** Nationwide. **International locations:** Worldwide. **Listed on:** New York Stock Exchange. **Stock exchange symbol:** DNY. **Annual sales/revenues:** More than $100 million. **Number of employees nationwide:** 30,000. **Number of employees worldwide:** 35,000.

THE HERALD-PRESS
7 North Jefferson Street, Huntington IN 46750. 219/356-6700. **Contact:** Personnel. **World Wide Web address:** http://www.h-ponline.com. **Description:** A community newspaper with a weekday circulation of 8,800 (excluding Thursday, which has a circulation of 14,000) and a Sunday circulation of 9,200. Founded in 1848.

INDIANAPOLIS NEWSPAPERS
307 North Pennsylvania Street, Indianapolis IN 46204. 317/633-1240. **Contact:** Nicole Reid, Human Resources. **World Wide Web address:** http://www.starnews.com. **Description:** Publishes newspapers. *Indianapolis Star* is a morning newspaper with a Monday through Saturday circulation of more than 228,000, and a Sunday circulation of more than 391,000. *Indianapolis News* is an evening newspaper with a Monday through Saturday circulation of more than 41,000. **Special programs:** Internships.

MACMILLAN PUBLISHING USA
201 West 103rd Street, Indianapolis IN 46290. 317/581-3500. **Toll-free phone:** 800/545-5914. **Fax:** 317/581-4960. **Contact:** Human Resources Department. **World Wide Web address:** http://www.macmillanusa.com. **Description:** Macmillan Publishing USA is the reference division of Simon & Schuster (New York NY), the publishing operation of Viacom, Inc. Macmillan Publishing USA is also one of the world's largest computer book publishers and a leader in the home and library reference markets. The company creates and distributes information in traditional media such as books, audio books, and videotape as well as new media including CD-ROM and online formats. **Common positions include:** Computer Programmer; Customer Service Representative; Editor; Financial Analyst; Graphic Designer; Managing Editor; Marketing Manager; MIS Specialist; Online Content Specialist; Public Relations Specialist; Sales Executive; Systems Manager; Technical Writer/Editor; Webmaster. **Benefits:** 401(k); Dental Insurance; Disability Coverage; Employee Discounts; Flexible Schedule; Life Insurance; Medical Insurance; Pension Plan; Tuition Assistance. **Special programs:** Internships. **Number of employees at this location:** 1,500.

HOWARD W. SAMS
2647 Waterfront Parkway East Drive, Indianapolis IN 46214-2041. 317/298-5611. **Toll-free phone:** 800/255-6989. **Fax:** 317/298-5604. **Contact:** Melissa Carolan, Human Resources. **E-mail address:** dchein@in.net. **World Wide Web address:** http://www.hwsams.com. **Description:** A technical publisher. **NOTE:** Second and third shifts are offered. **Common positions include:** Administrative Assistant; Graphic Artist; Human Resources Manager; Managing Editor; Marketing Specialist; Project Manager; Sales Engineer; Sales Manager; Sales Representative; Systems Analyst; Technical Writer/Editor. **Educational backgrounds include:** Art/Design; Communications; Engineering; English; Liberal Arts; Marketing. **Benefits:** 401(k); Dental Insurance; Disability Coverage; Employee Discounts; Life Insurance; Medical Insurance; Tuition Assistance. **Corporate headquarters location:** This Location. **Number of employees at this location:** 300.

SOUTH BEND TRIBUNE
225 West Colfax, South Bend IN 46626. 219/235-6161. **Contact:** Human Resources. **World Wide Web address:** http://www.sbtinfo.com. **Description:** A newspaper with a daily circulation of nearly 80,000, and a Sunday circulation of more than 113,000. **Number of employees at this location:** 400.

TRIBUNE-STAR PUBLISHING COMPANY
P.O. Box 149, Terre Haute IN 47808. 812/231-4200. **Contact:** Human Resources. **World Wide Web address:** http://www.tribstar.com. **Description:** Publishes *The Terre Haute Tribune-Star* newspaper with a daily circulation of 36,000 and a Sunday circulation of 47,000.

Note: *Because addresses and telephone numbers of smaller companies can change rapidly, we recommend you call each company to verify the information below before inquiring about job opportunities. Mass mailings are not recommended.*

Additional small employers:

BLANK BOOKS AND BOOKBINDING

Heckman Bindery Inc.
PO Box 89, North Manchester IN 46962-0089. 219/982-2107.

BOOKS, PERIODICALS, AND NEWSPAPERS WHOLESALE

Golden Books Publishing Company
803 N Englewood Drive, Crawfordsville IN 47933-9741. 765/362-5125.

BOOKS: PUBLISHING AND/OR PRINTING

Addison Wesley Longman Incorporated
5851 Guion Rd, Indianapolis IN 46254-1519. 317/293-3660.

Houghton Mifflin Company
2700 N Richardt Avenue, Indianapolis IN 46219-1117. 317/359-5585.

IDG Books
7260 Shadeland Station, Indianapolis IN 46256-3917. 317/596-5266.

Jackson Press Inc.
5804 Churchman Bypass, Indianapolis IN 46203-6109. 317/791-1122.

Little, Brown & Company
121 N Enterprise Boulevard, Lebanon IN 46052-8193. 765/483-9900.

Pictorial Inc.
PO Box 68520, Indianapolis IN 46268-0520. 317/872-7220.

Simon & Schuster Inc.
5550 West 74th Street, Indianapolis IN 46268-4183. 317/293-9384.

BUSINESS FORMS

Moore Business Forms & Systems
PO Box 900, Angola IN 46703-0900. 219/665-9421.

Moore Business Forms & Systems
PO Box 568, Rochester IN 46975-0568. 219/223-4351.

The Reynolds and Reynolds Co.
PO Box 558, Goshen IN 46527-0558. 219/533-0361.

The Reynolds and Reynolds Co.
PO Box 310, Lebanon IN 46052-0310. 765/482-4700.

Wise Business Forms Inc.
PO Box 8550, Fort Wayne IN 46898-8550. 219/489-1561.

COMMERCIAL ART AND GRAPHIC DESIGN

Alexander Production Services
125 N East Street, Indianapolis IN 46204-2626. 317/634-2206.

Chromasource Inc.
2701 S Coliseum Boulevard, Fort Wayne IN 46803-2950. 219/420-3000.

EP Graphics Inc.
169 South Jefferson Street, Berne IN 46711-2157. 219/589-2145.

Graphic Arts Center
PO Box 68110, Indianapolis IN 46268-0110. 317/293-1500.

Graphic Resource Center
7536 Miles Drive, Indianapolis IN 46231-3344. 317/481-4000.

COMMERCIAL PRINTING

Abbey Press
270 Hill Drive, Saint Meinrad IN 47577. 812/357-6611.

Allison Payment Systems
PO Box 102, Indianapolis IN 46206-0102. 317/808-2400.

Clarke American
PO Box 1389, Jeffersonville IN 47131-1389. 812/283-9598.

Data Label Inc.
1000 Spruce Street, Terre Haute IN 47807-2125. 812/232-0408.

EPI Printers Inc.
7502 E 86th Street, Indianapolis IN 46256-1210. 317/579-4870.

Foster Printing Service Inc.
PO Box 2089, Michigan City IN 46361-8089. 219/879-8366.

Indiana Ticket Company
PO Box 823, Muncie IN 47308-0823. 765/288-8301.

Innovative Packaging Solutions
1405 W Missouri Street, Evansville IN 47710-1841. 812/428-2350.

Ivy Hill Packaging
PO Box 3189, Terre Haute IN 47803-3189. 812/466-9851.

Mossberg & Company Inc.
PO Box 210, South Bend IN 46624-0210. 219/289-9253.

Multi-Color Corporation
2281 Highway 31 South, Scottsburg IN 47170. 812/752-3187.

Rhodes Inc.
PO Box 157, Charlestown IN 47111-0157. 812/256-3396.

RR Donnelly Seymour Inc.
PO Box 385, Seymour IN 47274-0385. 812/523-1800.

The Standard Register Co.
PO Box 689, Shelbyville IN 46176-0689. 317/392-3235.

Wertz Novelty Co.
PO Box 2278, Muncie IN 47307-0278. 765/288-8825.

GREETING CARDS

Sunrise Publications Inc.
PO Box 4699, Bloomington IN 47402-4699. 812/336-9900.

MISC. PUBLISHING

At-A-Glance
PO Box 68944, Indianapolis IN 46268-0944. 317/388-1212.

George F. Cram Company Inc.
PO Box 426, Indianapolis IN 46206-0426. 317/635-5564.

Heartland Technical Publishing
125 North East Street, Indianapolis IN 46204-2626. 317/634-6758.

Leed Selling Tools Corporation
PO Box 68, Ireland IN 47545-0068. 812/482-7888.

Medi-Span Inc.
PO Box 40930, Indianapolis IN 46240-0930. 317/469-5200.

NEWSPAPERS: PUBLISHING AND/OR PRINTING

Calumet Herald Newspapers
3161 E 84th Place, Merrillville IN 46410-6401. 219/942-0521.

Chronicle-Tribune
PO Box 309, Marion IN 46952-0309. 765/664-5111.

Daily Journal
PO Box 699, Franklin IN 46131-0699. 317/736-7101.

Daily Reporter
22 W New Road, Greenfield IN 46140-1090. 317/462-5528.

Editorial Inc.
406 N Central Avenue, Connersville IN 47331-1926. 765/825-0588.

Elkhart Truth
PO Box 487, Elkhart IN 46515-0487. 219/294-1661.

Evansville Courier
PO Box 268, Evansville IN 47702-0268. 812/424-7711.

Fisher's Sun Herald
PO Box 1478, Noblesville IN 46061-1478. 317/598-6397.

Hendricks County Flyer
PO Box 6, Plainfield IN 46168-0006. 317/839-5129.

Herald-Republican Ltd.
PO Box 180, Angola IN 46703-0180. 219/665-3117.

Jasper Herald Company
PO Box 31, Jasper IN 47547-0031. 812/482-2424.

Journal Review Inc.
PO Box 512, Crawfordsville IN 47933-0512. 765/362-1200.

Kokomo Tribune
PO Box 9014, Kokomo IN 46904-9014. 765/459-3121.

Martinsville Daily Reporter
PO Box 1636, Martinsville IN 46151-0636. 765/342-3311.

Michigan City News Dispatch
121 W Michigan Boulevard, Michigan City IN 46360-3274. 219/874-7211.

New Castle Courier Times
PO Box 369, New Castle IN 47362-0369. 765/529-1111.

News-Banner Publications Inc.
PO Box 436, Bluffton IN 46714-0436. 219/824-0224.

Palladium-Item Newspaper
PO Box 308, Richmond VA 47375. 765/962-1575.

Penny Saver/Times
PO Box 326, South Bend IN 46624-0326. 219/282-4400.

Pharos-Tribune
PO Box 210, Logansport IN 46947-0210. 219/722-5000.

Post & Mail Newspaper Incorporated
PO Box 837, Columbia City IN 46725-0837. 219/625-3879.

Post-Tribune
1065 Broadway, Gary IN 46402-2907. 219/881-3000.

Rensselaer Republican
PO Box 298, Rensselaer IN 47978-0298. 219/866-5113.

Seymour Daily Tribune
PO Box 447, Seymour IN 47274-0447. 812/522-4871.

Star-Press
PO Box 2408, Muncie IN 47307-0408. 765/747-5700.

The Evening News
221 Spring St, Jeffersonville IN 47130-3353. 812/283-6636.

The Goshen News
PO Box 569, Goshen IN 46527-0569. 219/533-2151.

The Journal Gazette Co.
701 S Clinton St, Ste 104, Fort Wayne IN 46802-1806. 219/461-8202.

The News-Sentinel
PO Box 100, Fort Wayne IN 46801-0100. 219/461-8444.

The News-Sun
PO Box 39, Kendallville IN 46755-0039. 219/347-0400.

The Republic
333 2nd St, Columbus IN 47201-6709. 812/372-7811.

The Shelbyville News
PO Box 750, Shelbyville IN 46176-0750. 317/398-6631.

The Times
601 45th Ave, Munster IN 46321-2875. 219/933-3200.

Times-Union
PO Box 1448, Warsaw IN 46581-1448. 219/267-3111.

PERIODICALS: PUBLISHING AND/OR PRINTING

House of White Birches Inc.
306 E Parr Road, Berne IN 46711-1138. 219/589-8741.

Medical Education Foundation
PO Box 567, Indianapolis IN 46206-0567. 317/636-8881.

PHOTOGRAPHIC EQUIPMENT AND SUPPLIES

Advance Products
PO Box 137, Warsaw IN 46581-0137. 219/267-8101.

For more information on career opportunities in printing and publishing:

__Associations__

AMERICAN BOOKSELLERS ASSOCIATION
828 South Broadway, Tarrytown NY 10591. 914/591-2665. World Wide Web address: http://www.bookweb.org. Publishes *American Bookseller*, *Bookselling This Week*, and *Bookstore Source Guide*.

AMERICAN INSTITUTE OF GRAPHIC ARTS
164 Fifth Avenue, New York NY 10010. 212/807-1990. World Wide Web address: http://www.aiga.org. A 36-chapter, nationwide organization sponsoring programs and events for graphic designers and related professionals.

AMERICAN SOCIETY OF COMPOSERS, AUTHORS, AND PUBLISHERS (ASCAP)
One Lincoln Plaza, New York NY 10023. 212/621-6000. World Wide Web address: http://www.ascap.com. A membership association which licenses members' work and pays members' royalties. Offers showcases and educational seminars and workshops. The society also has an events hotline: 212/621-6485. Many events listed are free.

AMERICAN SOCIETY OF NEWSPAPER EDITORS
11690-B Sunrise Valley Drive, Reston VA 20191. 703/453-1122. World Wide Web address: http://www.asne.org.

ASSOCIATION OF AMERICAN PUBLISHERS, INC.
71 Fifth Avenue, New York NY 10001. 212/255-0200. Fax: 212/255-7007. World Wide Web address: http://www.publishers.org. A national trade association for the book publishing industry that provides industry updates and news of upcoming events.

ASSOCIATION OF GRAPHIC COMMUNICATIONS
330 Seventh Avenue, 9th Floor, New York NY 10001-5010. 212/279-2100. World Wide Web address: http://www.agcomm.org. Offers educational classes and seminars.

BINDING INDUSTRIES OF AMERICA
70 East Lake Street, Suite 300, Chicago IL 60601. 312/372-7606. Offers credit collection, government affairs, and educational services.

THE DOW JONES NEWSPAPER FUND
P.O. Box 300, Princeton NJ 08543-0300. 609/520-4000. World Wide Web address: http://www.dowjones.com.

GRAPHIC ARTISTS GUILD
90 John Street, Suite 403, New York NY 10038. 212/791-3400. World Wide Web address: http://www.gag.org. A union for artists.

THE GRAPHIC ARTS TECHNICAL FOUNDATION
P.O. Box 1020, Sewickley PA 15143. 412/741-6860. World Wide Web address: http://www.gatf.org. Provides information, services, and training to those in graphic arts professions.

MAGAZINE PUBLISHERS ASSOCIATION
919 Third Avenue, 22nd Floor, New York NY 10022. 212/752-0055. World Wide Web address: http://www.magazine.org. A membership association.

NATIONAL ASSOCIATION OF PRINTERS AND LITHOGRAPHERS
780 Pallisade Avenue, Teaneck NJ 07666. 201/342-0700. World Wide Web address: http://www.napl.org. Membership required. Offers consulting services and a publication.

THE NATIONAL NEWSPAPER ASSOCIATION
1010 North Glebe Road, Arlington VA 22201. 703/907-7900. World Wide Web address: http://www.oweb.com/nna.

NATIONAL PRESS CLUB
529 14th Street NW, 13th Floor, Washington DC 20045. 202/662-7500. World Wide Web address: http://npc.press.org. Offers professional seminars, career services, and conference facilities, as well as members-only restaurants and a health club.

NEWSPAPER ASSOCIATION OF AMERICA
1921 Gallows Road, Suite 600, Vienna VA 22182. 703/902-1600. World Wide Web address: http://www.naa.org. The technology department publishes marketing research.

PRINTING INDUSTRIES OF AMERICA
100 Dangerfield Road, Alexandria VA 22314. 703/519-8100. World Wide Web address: http://www.printing.org. Members are offered publications and insurance.

TECHNICAL ASSOCIATION OF THE GRAPHIC ARTS
68 Lomb Memorial Drive, Rochester NY 14623. 716/475-7470. World Wide Web address: http://www.taga.org. Conducts an annual conference and offers newsletters.

WRITERS GUILD OF AMERICA WEST
7000 West Third Street, Los Angeles CA 90048. 310/550-1000. World Wide Web address: http://www.wga.org. A membership association which registers scripts.

__Directories__

EDITOR & PUBLISHER INTERNATIONAL YEARBOOK
Editor & Publisher Company Inc., 11 West 19th Street, New York NY 10011. 212/675-4380. World Wide Web address: http://www.mediainfo.com. $100.00. Offers newspapers to editors in both the United States and foreign countries.

GRAPHIC ARTS BLUE BOOK
A.F. Lewis & Company, 245 Fifth Avenue, Suite

2201, New York NY 10016. 212/679-0770. $80.00. Manufacturers and dealers.

JOURNALISM CAREER AND SCHOLARSHIP GUIDE
The Dow Jones Newspaper Fund, P.O. Box 300, Princeton NJ 08543-0300. 609/520-4000.

Magazines

AIGA JOURNAL
American Institute of Graphic Arts, 164 Fifth Avenue, New York NY 10010. 212/807-1990. World Wide Web address: http://www.aiga.org.

THE EDITOR & PUBLISHER
Editor & Publisher Co., 11 West 19th Street, New York NY 10011. 212/675-4380. World Wide Web address: http://www.mediainfo.com. A periodical focusing on the newspaper publishing industry.

GRAPHIS
141 Lexington Avenue, New York NY 10016. 212/532-9387. $89.00. Magazine covers portfolios, articles, designers, advertising, and photos.

PRINT
104 Fifth Avenue, 19th Floor, New York NY 10011. 212/463-0600. Offers a graphic design magazine. $55.00 for subscription.

PUBLISHERS WEEKLY
245 West 17th Street, New York NY 10011. 212/645-9700. World Wide Web address: http://www.bookwire.com.

Special Book and Magazine Programs

CENTER FOR BOOK ARTS
626 Broadway, 5th Floor, New York NY 10012. 212/460-9768. Offers bookbinding, printing, and papermaking workshops.

EMERSON COLLEGE WRITING AND PUBLISHING PROGRAM
100 Beacon Street, Boston MA 02116. 617/824-8236. World Wide Web address: http://www.emerson.edu.

THE NEW YORK UNIVERSITY SUMMER PUBLISHING PROGRAM
11 West 42nd Street, Room 400, New York NY 10003. 212/790-3232.

THE RADCLIFFE PUBLISHING COURSE
6 Ash Street, Cambridge MA 02138. 617/495-8678.

RICE UNIVERSITY PUBLISHING PROGRAM
6100 Main Street, MS 550, Houston TX 70005-1892. 713/527-4803. World Wide Web address: http://www.rice.edu/scs.

THE STANFORD PROFESSIONAL PUBLISHING COURSE
Box PW, Stanford Alumni Association, Stanford CA 97305-4005. 650/725-6259. Fax: 650/725-9712. E-mail address: publishing.courses@stanford.edu.

UNIVERSITY OF DENVER PUBLISHING INSTITUTE
2075 South University Boulevard, #D-114, Denver CO 80210. 303/871-2570.

Online Services

BOOKS AND WRITING
Jump to: Books and Writing BB. A bulletin board service, available through Prodigy, that allows writers to discuss issues in publishing and gain advice on writing style.

JOURNALISM FORUM
Go: Jforum. A CompuServe discussion group for journalists in print, radio, or television.

PHOTO PROFESSIONALS
Go: Photopro. A CompuServe forum for imaging professionals.

PROPUBLISHING FORUM
Go: Propub. CompuServe charges a fee for this forum which caters to publishing and graphic design professionals.

REAL ESTATE

It's smooth sailing in the real estate sector. Employment has risen from 7.96 million in 1993 to 9.14 million in 1997. With the healthy condition of the economy, sales of single-family homes were projected to reach 4.11 million by the end of 1998. Low interest rates and strong consumer confidence are causing a surge in home buying. Office vacancy rates are down and rental rates of commercial real estate will remain stable.

The trend that is sweeping the industry is ownership of real estate investments trusts (REITs). REITs are companies that own, manage, and develop a number of diversified properties. These companies must follow strict guidelines and in the end remain exempt from corporate taxation. The REIT industry has seen profits soar from $8 billion in 1990 to $120 billion at the end of 1997.

The best opportunities for investment and sales are in office space. Industry analysts say that suburbs and downtowns, specifically in the Boston, Chicago, New York, San Francisco, and Seattle areas, will be the hot-spots for new construction. Forecasters predicted the development of 190 million square feet of office space in 1998, a 10 percent gain over the previous year.

Business Week *reported that the retail sector may have been the hardest hit in 1998. Overbuilding and changes in shopping habits have produced a glutted market of malls and shopping centers. Another negative is a potential overabundance in apartment space most noticeably in the Sunbelt.*

CB RICHARD ELLIS
National City Center, 115 West Washington Street, Indianapolis IN 46204-3421. 317/269-1000. **Fax:** 317/637-4404. **Contact:** Human Resources. **World Wide Web address:** http://www.cbrichardellis.com. **Description:** A real estate services company offering property sales and leasing; property and facility management; mortgage banking; and investment management services. **Corporate headquarters location:** Los Angeles CA. **Other U.S. locations:** Nationwide. **Listed on:** New York Stock Exchange. **Stock exchange symbol:** CBG. **Number of employees worldwide:** 9,000.

CB RICHARD ELLIS
ROBERT BRADLEY AND ASSOCIATES
501 East Monroe Street, Suite 350, South Bend IN 44601. 219/237-6000. **Fax:** 219/237-6001. **Contact:** Human Resources. **World Wide Web address:** http://www.cbrichardellis.com. **Description:** A real estate services company offering property sales and leasing; property and facility management; mortgage banking; and investment management services. **Corporate headquarters location:** Los Angeles CA. **Listed on:** New York Stock Exchange. **Stock exchange symbol:** CBG. **Number of employees worldwide:** 9,000.

COLDWELL BANKER
710 Eads Parkway, Lawrenceburg IN 47025-1139. 812/537-5700. **Contact:** Personnel. **Description:** One of the largest residential real estate companies in the United States and Canada. Coldwell Banker is also a leader in meeting corporate America's specialized relocation needs on a worldwide basis.

DUKE REALTY INVESTMENTS
8888 Keystone Crossing, Suite 1200, Indianapolis IN 46240. 317/846-4700. **Contact:** Human Resources. **World Wide Web address:** http://www.dukereit.com. **Description:** Duke Realty

Investments is a self-administered real estate investment trust which provides leasing, management, development, construction, and other tenant-related services for its properties and for about 12 million square feet of properties owned by third parties. **Common positions include:** Accountant/Auditor; Attorney; Construction Contractor; Financial Analyst; Paralegal; Property and Real Estate Manager; Real Estate Agent. **Educational backgrounds include:** Accounting; Business Administration; Finance; Real Estate. **Benefits:** 401(k); Dental Insurance; Disability Coverage; Life Insurance; Medical Insurance; Profit Sharing. **Corporate headquarters location:** This Location. **Operations at this facility include:** Administration; Sales. **Listed on:** New York Stock Exchange. **Annual sales/revenues:** More than $100 million. **Number of employees at this location:** 225. **Number of employees nationwide:** 455.

HARCOURT MANAGEMENT CO.
3901 West 86th Street, Suite 470, Indianapolis IN 46268. 317/872-0044. **Contact:** Personnel. **Description:** Manages several real estate properties.

JUSTUS RENTAL PROPERTY MANAGEMENT INC.
1398 North Shadeland Avenue, Indianapolis IN 46219-3652. 317/852-4091. **Contact:** Personnel. **Description:** Manages real estate properties.

F.C. TUCKER CO. INC. REALTORS
10116 East Washington Street, Indianapolis IN 46229-2626. 317/897-3300. **Contact:** Personnel. **Description:** A real estate agency. **Other area locations:** Carmel IN.

Note: Because addresses and telephone numbers of smaller companies can change rapidly, we recommend you call each company to verify the information below before inquiring about job opportunities. Mass mailings are not recommended.

Additional small employers:

REAL ESTATE AGENTS AND MANAGERS

Carpenter Better Homes and Gardens Realtor
6945 E 77th Street, Indianapolis IN 46250-2068. 317/842-1000.

DMSI
135 North Pennsylvania Street, Indianapolis IN 46204-2400. 317/684-3333.

Heritage Financial Group Inc.
120 W Lexington Avenue, Elkhart IN 46516. 219/522-8000.

L-B Residential Management Company
8901 E 5th Avenue, Gary IN 46403-3304. 219/938-1600.

NHP Incorporated
9200 Keystone Crossing, Indianapolis IN 46240-2121. 317/817-7500.

REAL ESTATE OPERATORS

Altenheim Community
3525 E Hanna Avenue, Indianapolis IN 46237-1230. 317/788-4261.

Amalgamated Management Corporation
9135 N Meridian Street, Indianapolis IN 46260-1815. 317/844-8825.

Canterbury Green Apartments
2615 Abbey Drive, Fort Wayne IN 46835-3109. 219/485-1687.

Community Reinvestment Foundation Inc.
8355 Rockville Road, Indianapolis IN 46234-2722. 317/271-9829.

First Richmond Realtor
PO Box 238, Richmond IN 47375-0238. 765/966-7653.

Methodist Associates Ltd.
1801 N Senate Ave, Suite 750, Indianapolis IN 46202-1206. 317/929-5770.

Robin Run Village
5354 W 62nd St, Indianapolis IN 46268-4491. 317/293-5500.

The Edward Rose Companies
PO Box 24007, Indianapolis IN 46224-0007. 317/297-3060.

Wesley Manor Inc.
1555 N Main St, Frankfort IN 46041-1167. 765/659-1811.

For more information on career opportunities in real estate:

Associations

INSTITUTE OF REAL ESTATE MANAGEMENT
430 North Michigan Avenue, P.O. Box 109025, Chicago IL 60610-9025. 312/661-1930. World Wide Web address: http://www.irem.org. Dedicated to educating and identifying real estate managers who are committed to meeting the needs of real estate owners and investors.

INTERNATIONAL ASSOCIATION OF CORPORATE REAL ESTATE EXECUTIVES
440 Columbia Drive, Suite 100, West Palm Beach FL 33409. 561/683-8111. World Wide Web address: http://www.nacore.com. An international association of real estate brokers.

INTERNATIONAL REAL ESTATE INSTITUTE
8383 East Evans Road, Scottsdale AZ 85260. 602/998-8267. Fax: 602/998-8022. Offers seminars on issues relating to the real estate industry.

NATIONAL ASSOCIATION OF REAL ESTATE INVESTMENT TRUSTS
1129 20th Street NW, Suite 305, Washington DC 20036. 202/785-8717. World Wide Web address: http://www.nareit.com. Contact: Matt Lentz, Membership. Membership required.

NATIONAL ASSOCIATION OF REALTORS
430 North Michigan Avenue, Chicago IL 60611. 312/329-8200. World Wide Web address: http://www.realtor.com. A membership organization compiling statistics, advising the government, and publishing several magazines including *Real Estate Today*, and *Today's Realtor*.

Magazines

JOURNAL OF PROPERTY MANAGEMENT
Institute of Real Estate Management, 430 North Michigan Avenue, Chicago IL 60610. 312/661-1930. World Wide Web address: http://www.irem.org.

NATIONAL REAL ESTATE INVESTOR
PRIMEDIA Intertec, 6151 Powers Ferry Road NW, Suite 200, Atlanta GA 30339. 770/955-2500. World Wide Web address: http://www.intertec.com.

Online Services

JOBS IN REAL ESTATE
http://www.cob.ohio-state.edu/dept/fin/jobs/realest.htm. This Website provides resources for jobseekers who are looking to work in the real estate field.

REAL JOBS
http://www.real-jobs.com/. This Website is designed to help real estate professionals who are looking for jobs.

RETAIL

Online buying is the new option in retailing. Internet shoppers were expected to spend an estimated $4.8 billion in 1998, double the sales of 1997. Computers and high-tech wares seem to be the most popular items and the sale of these items was expected to increase by 85 percent in 1998. Despite this, the growth of sales in the retail industry overall will slow to about 2 percent annually through 2002. With a glutted market of malls and shopping centers, increasing competition for expendable income, retail purchases are losing profits to entertainment and travel spending. Low unemployment rates and a hike in the minimum wage is good news for discounters like Wal-Mart, Kmart, and Target, as low-end consumers have more money in their pockets. Discount retailers posted a 10 percent sales gain in 1997. On the opposite end of the spectrum, luxury goods are expected to boast sales gains as long as the stock market is flourishing. Supermarkets are reaping the benefits of lower food prices but facing increased competition.

In order to see profits continue to rise, retailers will need to consistently offer lower, fair prices. Stores that also provide consumers with added incentives and reward benefits will draw more customers. Jobs for retail salespersons and cashiers will continue to increase significantly through 2005.

BARNES & NOBLE BOOKSTORES
3748 East 82nd Street, Indianapolis IN 46240. 317/594-7525. **Contact:** Manager. **World Wide Web address:** http://www.barnesandnoble.com. **Description:** A discount bookstore chain operating nationwide. This location has a cafe and music department in addition to its comprehensive book departments.

FINISH LINE INC.
3308 North Mitthoeffer Road, Indianapolis IN 46236. 317/899-1022. **Contact:** Human Resources. **World Wide Web address:** http://www.thefinishline.com. **Description:** Finish Line Inc. operates retail stores which offer a broad selection of current men's, women's, and children's brand name athletic and leisure footwear, activewear, and accessories. **Number of employees nationwide:** 1,825.

JOHN C. GROUB COMPANY
P.O. Box 1004, Seymour IN 47274-1004. 812/522-1374. **Contact:** Human Resources. **Description:** Operator of a chain of supermarkets operating under the names JC Food, Foods Plus, and Rulers.

MARSH SUPERMARKETS, INC.
9800 Crosspoint Boulevard, Indianapolis IN 46256. 317/594-2100. **Contact:** David Redden, Director of Human Resources. **Description:** A major regional food retailer. Through three divisions, the company operates 80 Marsh Supermarkets, seven LoBill Foods, 177 Village Pantry Convenience Stores in Indiana and Ohio, and CSDC, a convenience store distribution company serving 1,300 unrelated stores in eight states. Founded in 1931. **Corporate headquarters location:** This Location.

PAUL HARRIS STORES INC.
6003 Guion Road, Indianapolis IN 46254. 317/293-3900. **Fax:** 317/298-6958. **Contact:** Ms. Sandy Gilbert, Executive Director of Human Resources. **World Wide Web address:**

http://www.paulharrisstores.com. **Description:** A specialty retailer of women's clothing, selling the Paul Harris Design private label brand. The company currently operates 225 stores in 26 states and the District of Columbia. **Common positions include:** Accountant/Auditor; Wholesale and Retail Buyer. **Educational backgrounds include:** Accounting; Art/Design; Business Administration; Fashion; Merchandising. **Corporate headquarters location:** This Location. **Other U.S. locations:** Nationwide. **Listed on:** NASDAQ. **Number of employees at this location:** 125. **Number of employees nationwide:** 2,500.

SHOE CARNIVAL, INC.
805 North Green River Road, Evansville IN 47715. 812/867-6471. **Contact:** Human Resources. **World Wide Web address:** http://www.shoecarnival.com. **Description:** Operates specialty shoe stores.

SUPERVALU INC.
FOOD MARKETING DIVISION
4815 Executive Boulevard, Fort Wayne IN 46808. 219/483-2146. **Contact:** Human Resources. **Description:** One of the nation's largest food retailers and distribution companies, supplying grocery, health and beauty aids, and general merchandise products to over 4,000 customers. In the corporate retail sector, SUPERVALU operates over 300 stores under the following names: bigg's, Cub Foods, Shop 'n Save, Save-A-Lot, Scott's Foods, Laneco, and Hornbachers. **Corporate headquarters location:** Eden Prairie MN. **Subsidiaries include:** Hazelwood Farms Bakeries, which manufactures frozen bakery products. **Listed on:** New York Stock Exchange. **Stock exchange symbol:** SVU. **Number of employees at this location:** 500.

Note: Because addresses and telephone numbers of smaller companies can change rapidly, we recommend you call each company to verify the information below before inquiring about job opportunities. Mass mailings are not recommended.

Additional small employers:

AUTO DEALERS

Allen County Motors Incorporated
PO Box 2310, Fort Wayne IN 46801-2310. 219/436-3673.

Bales Motor Company
630 Broadway Street, Jeffersonville IN 47130-3526. 812/282-4356.

Bill Estes Chevrolet Incorporated
4105 West 96th Street, Indianapolis IN 46268-1112. 317/872-3315.

Blossom Chevrolet Incorporated
PO Box 19366, Indianapolis IN 46219-0366. 317/357-1121.

D. Patrick Jeep/Eagle
PO Box 5186, Evansville IN 47716-5186. 812/473-6500.

Dan Young Honda
PO Box 40319, Indianapolis IN 46240-0319. 317/846-6666.

DeFouw Chevrolet Inc.
PO Box 4907, Lafayette IN 47903-4907. 765/449-2800.

Don Ayre's Pontiac/Honda
4740 Lima Road, Fort Wayne IN 46808-1204. 219/484-0551.

Hubler Chevrolet Inc.
PO Box 17040, Indianapolis IN 46217-0040. 317/882-4389.

Johnny Morris Chevrolet Incorporated
4101 West Clara Lane, Muncie IN 47304-5466. 765/284-6702.

Jordan Ford
PO Box 370, Mishawaka IN 46546-0370. 219/259-1981.

Kelley Chevrolet Inc.
PO Box 5015, Fort Wayne IN 46895-5015. 219/484-5566.

Pedigo Chevrolet
5101 West 38th Street, Indianapolis IN 46254-3325. 317/297-4040.

Uebelhor & Sons Chevrolet
PO Box 630, Jasper IN 47547-0630. 812/482-2222.

CATALOG AND MAIL-ORDER HOUSES

BMG Direct Marketing
6550 East 30th Street, Indianapolis IN 46219-1102. 317/542-6338.

Brylane
37 South Park Boulevard, Greenwood IN 46143-8838. 317/885-5600.

JCPenney
6501 Grape Road, Suite 200, Mishawaka IN 46545-1008. 219/277-6000.

Time-Life Books & Music
5240 West 76th Street, Indianapolis IN 46268-4137. 317/872-0678.

Touch of Class Catalog
PO Box 237, Huntingburg IN 47542-0237. 812/683-3707.

COMPUTER AND SOFTWARE STORES

Creative Computers Inc.
7710 E 96th Street, Indianapolis IN 46256. 317/845-5800.

CONSUMER ELECTRONICS STORES

Best Buy Store
3249 E Lincoln Highway, Merrillville IN 46410-5808. 219/942-9447.

Best Buy Store
9977 E Washington Street, Indianapolis IN 46229-3039. 317/897-3941.

Best Buy Store
929 North Green River Road, Evansville IN 47715-2418. 812/473-4843.

Best Buy Store
6502 Grape Road, Suite 710, Mishawaka IN 46545-1102. 219/273-1866.

Best Buy Store
5820 E 82nd Street, Indianapolis IN 46250-1550. 317/841-0711.

Best Buy Store
5402 West 38th Street, Indianapolis IN 46254-2918. 317/290-1330.

Best Buy Store
562 Fry Road, Greenwood IN 46142-4138. 317/881-0898.

Best Buy Store
4320 Coldwater Road, Fort Wayne IN 46805-1112. 219/471-5501.

HH Gregg
4151 East 96th Street, Indianapolis IN 46240-1442. 317/848-8710.

Incredible Universe
9820 Kincaid Drive, Fishers IN 46038-9535. 317/596-3400.

CONSUMER SUPPLY STORES

Autozone
3827 S East Street, Indianapolis IN 46227-1326. 317/780-8681.

Menard Inc.
6050 W Ridge Road, Gary IN 46408-1701. 219/838-6134.

DEPARTMENT STORES

Ayr-Way Stores
2209 State Street, New Albany IN 47150-4924. 812/945-5046.

Big Kmart
9550 Wicker Avenue, Saint John IN 46373-9488. 219/365-8545.

Big Kmart
2801 Calumet Avenue, Valparaiso IN 46383-2605. 219/464-1091.

Big Kmart
2003 East Tipton Street, Seymour IN 47274-3567. 812/522-5996.

Big Kmart
101 West Lincoln Highway, Gary IN 46410-5451. 219/769-4221.

Big Kmart
305 Sagamore Parkway West, Lafayette IN 47906-1503. 765/463-7556.

Big Kmart
804 South 13th Street, Decatur IN 46733-1804. 219/728-2010.

Big Kmart
3802 Illinois Road, Fort Wayne IN 46804-1202. 219/432-8545.

Big Kmart
820 N Coliseum Boulevard, Fort Wayne IN 46805-5516. 219/426-4546.

Big Kmart
750 Indian Boundary Road, Chesterton IN 46304-1519. 219/926-7521.

Big Kmart
7530 U.S. 27 S Anthony Blvd, Fort Wayne IN 46816. 219/447-3594.

Big Kmart
1805 E Markland Avenue, Kokomo IN 46901-6235. 765/457-8281.

Big Kmart
7925 Indianapolis Boulevard, Hammond IN 46324-3348. 219/845-7493.

Big Kmart
1460 West State Road 2, La Porte IN 46350-4602. 219/326-7755.

Carson Pirie Scott & Company
1995 Southlake Mall, Gary IN 46410-6434. 219/738-2600.

Carson Pirie Scott & Company
6600 Indianapolis Boulevard, Hammond IN 46320-2812. 219/844-2525.

Carson Pirie Scott & Company
305 W U.S. Highway 20, Michigan City IN 46360-7399. 219/879-6511.

Elder-Beerman Store
2104 25th Street, Columbus IN 47201-3203. 812/372-1700.

Elder-Beerman Store
3501 N Granville Avenue, Muncie IN 47303-1263. 765/286-5040.

Elder-Beerman Store
601 E Main Street, Richmond IN 47374-4309. 765/966-7641.

Elder-Beerman Store
3701 South Main Street, Elkhart IN 46517-3106. 219/875-8571.

Elder-Beerman Store
1250 S Green River Road, Evansville IN 47715-6806. 812/477-9000.

Elder-Beerman Store
2101 South Scatterfield Road, Anderson IN 46016-5736. 765/644-0954.

Elder-Beerman Store
1540 E Boulevard, Kokomo Mall, Kokomo IN 46902. 765/459-0180.

Elder-Beerman Store
North Park Mall, Marion IN 46952. 765/662-0001.

Famous-Barr Department Store
6101 N Keystone Avenue, Indianapolis IN 46220-2431. 317/255-6611.

Famous-Barr Department Store
3201 N Granville Avenue, Muncie IN 47303. 765/286-0011.

Famous-Barr Department Store
2210 Southlake Mall, Merrillville IN 46410-6441. 219/769-9100.

Famous-Barr Department Store
2812 East 3rd Street, Bloomington IN 47401-5423. 812/333-8781.

Famous-Barr Department Store
10202 E Washington Street, Indianapolis IN 46229-2629. 317/899-4411.

Famous-Barr Department Store
6501 Grape Road, Mishawaka IN 46545-1007. 219/277-2950.

Famous-Barr Department Store
2000 Elmwood Avenue, Lafayette IN 47904-2226. 765/447-2141.

Famous-Barr Department Store
1251 U.S. 31 North, Greenwood IN 46142. 317/881-6781.

Famous-Barr Department Store
4201 Coldwater Road, Fort Wayne IN 46805-1113. 219/484-1561.

Famous-Barr Department Store
7800 St. Anthony Boulevard, Fort Wayne IN 46816. 219/447-3511.

Hill's Department Store
1801 W McGalliard Road, Muncie IN 47304-2210. 765/289-4363.

Hudson Department Store
6501 Grape Road, Mishawaka IN 46545-1007. 219/271-6100.

Hudson Department Store
4201 Coldwater Road, Fort Wayne IN 46805-1113. 219/480-5100.

JCPenney
3501 N Granville Avenue, Muncie IN 47303-1263. 765/288-8891.

JCPenney
1890 Southlake Mall, Merrillville IN 46410-6433. 219/738-2155.

JCPenney
10202 E Washington Street, Indianapolis IN 46229-2629. 317/899-4900.

JCPenney
800 N Green River Road, Evansville IN 47715-2492. 812/477-7222.

JCPenney
2415 Sagamore Parkway South, Lafayette IN 47905-5124. 765/447-3161.

JCPenney
6020 E 82nd Street, Suite 700, Indianapolis IN 46250-4572. 317/849-6500.

JCPenney
3900 Lafayette Road, Indianapolis IN 46254-2503. 317/291-1490.

JCPenney
1251 U.S. Highway 31 North, Greenwood IN 46142-4503. 317/882-7339.

JCPenney
1718 E Boulevard, Kokomo IN 46902-2454. 765/457-8121.

JCPenney
2101 S Scatterfield Road, Anderson IN 46016-5736. 765/644-0965.

JCPenney
201 W U.S. Highway 20, Michigan City IN 46360-7339. 219/879-8341.

Kmart
7425 E Washington Street, Indianapolis IN 46219-6706. 317/357-8556.

Kmart
1807 N Broadway Street, Greensburg IN 47240-8217. 812/663-0880.

Kmart
4111 S Walnut Street, Muncie IN 47302-5687. 765/289-7136.

Kmart
1501 E McGalliard Road, Muncie IN 47303. 317/282-3434.

Kmart
3150 National Road West, Richmond IN 47374-4414. 317/966-2561.

Kmart
2715 Madison Avenue, Indianapolis IN 46225-2112. 317/783-6621.

Kmart
52401 Interchange Drive, Elkhart IN 46514-5700. 219/262-0711.

Kmart
2828 Broadway Street, Anderson IN 46012-1339. 765/649-5524.

Kmart
7201 Pendleton Pike, Indianapolis IN 46226-5131. 317/545-5386.

Kmart
1320 James Avenue, Bedford IN 47421-3592. 812/275-3022.

Kmart
PO Box 458, Washington IN 47501-0458. 812/254-1613.

Kmart
3501 S Main Street, Elkhart IN 46517-3123. 219/293-6556.

Kmart
2601 Hart Street, Vincennes IN 47591-6212. 812/882-1424.

Kmart
5101 E Thompson Road, Indianapolis IN 46237-2084. 317/786-1421.

Kmart
975 N Green Street, Brownsburg IN 46112-1032. 317/852-6555.

Kmart
6200 E Lloyd Expressway, Evansville IN 47715-2718. 812/471-8200.

Kmart
420 W McKinley Avenue, Mishawaka IN 46545-5522. 219/259-6361.

Kmart
2500 N Oak Road, Plymouth IN 46563-3409. 219/936-4000.

Kmart
1004 North Main Street, Monticello IN 47960-1503. 219/583-9131.

Kmart
6780 West Washington Street, Indianapolis IN 46241-2935. 317/247-4771.

Kmart
4600 High Street, South Bend IN 46614-3200. 219/291-8089.

Kmart
4850 W Western Avenue, South Bend IN 46619-2308. 219/234-6096.

Kmart
3860 N High School Road, Indianapolis IN 46254-2709. 317/293-7305.

Kmart
2500 N Park Road, Connersville IN 47331-3040. 765/825-5102.

Kmart
815 E 53rd Street, Anderson IN 46013-1730. 765/642-4911.

Kmart
705 N Dixon Road, Kokomo IN 46901-1755. 317/457-1111.

Kmart
860 U.S. Highway 31 South, Greenwood IN 46143-2403. 317/882-2271.

Kmart
2394 25th Street, Columbus IN 47201-3719. 812/372-7863.

Kmart
2020 Burton Lane, Martinsville IN 46151-3010. 765/349-1867.

Kmart
305 East Highway 131, Clarksville IN 47129-1725. 812/945-9117.

Kohl's
5660 Crawfordsville Road, Indianapolis IN 46224-3713. 317/244-7666.

Kohl's
1601 Southlake Mall, Merrillville IN 46410-6449. 219/791-9141.

Kohl's
2005 E Greyhound Pass, Carmel IN 46033-7729. 317/844-3996.

Kohl's
9999 E Washington Street, Indianapolis IN 46229-3039. 317/897-9822.

Kohl's
4410 Grape Road, Mishawaka IN 46545-2691. 219/273-6266.

Kohl's
2415 Sagamore Parkway South, Lafayette IN 47905-5124. 765/448-6504.

Kohl's
835 E Coliseum Boulevard, Fort Wayne IN 46805-1221. 219/483-0564.

Kohl's
7800 St. Anthony Boulevard, Fort Wayne IN 46816-2598. 219/447-2551.

Kohl's
10353 Indianapolis Boulevard, Highland IN 46322-3509. 219/924-0337.

Lazarus-Castleton
6020 E 82nd Street, Indianapolis IN 46250-4572. 317/842-8880.

Lazarus-Evansville
800 N Green River Road, Evansville IN 47715-2492. 812/473-9244.

Lazarus-Greenwood
1251 U.S. Highway 31 North, Greenwood IN 46142-4503. 317/882-6244.

Lazarus-Washington Square
10202 E Washington Street, Indianapolis IN 46229-2629. 317/899-6213.

Meijer
1425 W Carmel Drive, Carmel IN 46032-8722. 317/573-8300.

Meijer
150 S Marlin Drive, Greenwood IN 46142-1451. 317/885-3000.

Meijer
10841 E U.S. 36 Rockville Road, Plainfield IN 46168. 317/273-6000.

Meijer
6260 W McGalliard Road, Muncie IN 47304-9413. 765/281-7800.

Meijer
11351 E Washington Street, Indianapolis IN 46229-3101. 317/894-6700.

Meijer
4522 Elkhart Road, Goshen IN 46526-5822. 219/875-3000.

Meijer
5325 E Southport Road, Indianapolis IN 46237-9336. 317/859-2200.

Meijer
5020 Grape Road, Mishawaka IN 46545-8705. 219/273-3500.

Meijer
3600 Portage Road, South Bend IN 46628-6037. 219/273-3400.

Meijer
3610 S Bremen Highway, Mishawaka IN 46544-6500. 219/254-2500.

Meijer
10301 State Road 37, Fort Wayne IN 46815. 219/492-1300.

Meijer
5349 W Pike Plaza Road, Indianapolis IN 46254-3008. 317/387-2400.

Meijer
5909 Illinois Road, Fort Wayne IN 46804-1159. 219/434-3900.

Meijer
2301 E Markland Avenue, Kokomo IN 46901-6245. 765/454-7800.

Montgomery Ward & Company Inc.
8203 Broadway, Gary IN 46410-6216. 219/738-4700.

Montgomery Ward & Company Inc.
10202 E Washington Street, Indianapolis IN 46229-2629. 317/899-0990.

Montgomery Ward & Company Inc.
3701 S Main Street, Elkhart IN 46517-3106. 219/875-6541.

Montgomery Ward & Company Inc.
1390 E Ireland Road, South Bend IN 46614-3451. 219/291-7910.

Montgomery Ward & Company Inc.
Lafayette & 38th Street, Indianapolis IN 46254. 317/290-0902.

Montgomery Ward & Company Inc.
1531 U.S. Highway 31 South, Greenwood IN 46143-2418. 317/885-8001.

Montgomery Ward & Company Inc.
8005 Calumet Avenue, Hammond IN 46321-1217. 219/836-5950.

Sears
PO Box 468, Columbus IN 47202-0468. 812/379-1400.

Sears
2300 Southlake Mall, Merrillville IN 46410-6443. 219/738-5000.

Sears
3801 National Rd E, Richmond IN 47374-3636. 765/962-7545.

Sears
PO Box 549, Bloomington IN 47402-0549. 812/333-5800.

Sears
1100 S Green River Rd, Evansville IN 47715-6804. 812/473-8200.

Sears
6501 Grape Rd, Mishawaka IN 46545-1007. 219/271-6500.

Sears
3401 S US Highway 41, Terre Haute IN 47802-4154. 812/231-5700.

Sears
6020 E 82nd St, Ste 200, Indianapolis IN 46250-4571. 317/579-2700.

Sears
4050 Lafayette Rd, Indianapolis IN 46254-2527. 317/228-6400.

Sears
7800 S Anthony Blvd, Fort Wayne IN 46816-2598. 219/441-4100.

Sears
1235 S Reed Rd, Kokomo IN 46902-1904. 765/452-5401.

Sears
3902 E Market St, Logansport IN 46947-2239. 219/753-4911.

Sears
226 E Main St, North Manchester IN 46962-1823. 219/982-8514.

Sears
3501 N Granville Ave, Muncie IN 47303-1263. 765/747-8300.

Sears
2109 S State Road 9, Anderson IN 46016-5734. 765/644-5541.

Sears
757 E Highway 131, Ste 702, Clarksville IN 47129-7414. 812/288-5311.

Service Merchandise
5501 Coldwater Rd, Fort Wayne IN 46825-5448. 219/484-1134.

Target
US 40 & Perimeter Rd, Plainfield IN 46168. 317/839-4027.

Target
1300 E 86th Street, Indianapolis IN 46240-1990. 317/846-7731.

Target
8101 E Washington St, Indianapolis IN 46219-6813. 317/898-3636.

Target
2985 N National Rd, Columbus IN 47201-3215. 812/372-0216.

Target
5302 N Keystone Ave, Indianapolis IN 46220-3611. 317/257-6525.

Target
2661 E US Highway 30, Gary IN 46410-5898. 219/942-0402.

Target
601 S College Mall Rd, Bloomington IN 47401-5456. 812/332-4487.

Target
8811 Hardegan St, Indianapolis IN 46227-6362. 317/882-9311.

Target
154 W Hively Ave, Elkhart IN 46517-2160. 219/293-2550.

Target
5501 S Scatterfield Rd, Anderson IN 46013-3140. 765/649-2521.

Target
4000 N 1st Ave, Evansville IN 47710-3614. 812/426-2218.

Target
730 S Green River Rd, Evansville IN 47715-4104. 812/477-6411.

Target
1225 S High School Rd, Indianapolis IN 46241-3126. 317/247-8471.

Target
3512 Cedar St, South Bend IN 46615-3302. 219/289-7041.

Target
8448 Center Run Dr, Indianapolis IN 46250-4505. 317/845-9823.

Target
6925 W 38th St, Indianapolis IN 46254-3905. 317/329-1034.

Target
4000 W Bethel Ave, Muncie IN 47304-5442. 765/286-5144.

Target
2080 North Jefferson St, Huntington IN 46750-1353. 219/356-7823.

Target
3801 Coldwater Rd, Fort Wayne IN 46805-1101. 219/484-9591.

Target
7601 S Anthony Blvd, Fort Wayne IN 46816-2513. 219/447-2511.

Target
10451 Indianapols Blvd, Highland IN 46322-3511. 219/924-1527.

Target
1500 Greentree Blvd, Clarksville IN 47129-2208. 812/282-8446.

The May Department Stores Co.
800 N Green River Rd, Evansville IN 47715-2492. 812/471-8888.

Value City
6002 E 38th St, Indianapolis IN 46226-5602. 317/547-9691.

Value City
5110 W Pike Plaza Rd, Indianapolis IN 46254-3003. 317/297-8808.

Value City
700 Eastern Blvd, Clarksville IN 47129-2356. 812/283-4481.

Venture
2500 N 1st Ave, Evansville IN 47710-2950. 812/422-7677.

Venture
101 N Green River Rd, Evansville IN 47715-2403. 812/474-9644.

Venture
5802 Grape Rd, Mishawaka IN 46545-1248. 219/277-3011.

Venture
6650 W Washington St, Indianapolis IN 46241-3002. 317/243-0393.

Wal-Mart
2202 Pleasant St, Noblesville IN 46060-3630. 317/773-5212.

Wal-Mart
1149 N National Rd, Columbus IN 47201-5586. 812/372-0227.

Wal-Mart
567 Ivy Tech Dr, Madison IN 47250-1882. 812/273-4993.

Wal-Mart
1850 N Main St, Rushville IN 46173-9316. 765/932-2133.

Wal-Mart
2110 N State Highway 3, North Vernon IN 47265. 812/346-5100.

Wal-Mart
1501 E Tipton St, Seymour IN 47274-3557. 812/522-1212.

Wal-Mart
4801 W Clara Ln, Muncie IN 47304-5548. 765/284-7181.

Wal-Mart
1800 E State Road 44, Shelbyville IN 46176-1814. 317/392-4940.

Wal-Mart
2100 N Park Rd, Connersville IN 47331-2902. 765/827-1255.

Wal-Mart
1600 N Meridian St, Portland IN 47371-9301. 219/726-3682.

Wal-Mart
3601 E Main St, Richmond IN 47374-5934. 765/935-9158.

Wal-Mart
2001 E 151st St, Carmel IN 46033-7737. 317/844-0096.

Wal-Mart
3201 W State Highway 45, Bloomington IN 47403. 812/337-0002.

Wal-Mart
2649 16th St, Bedford IN 47421-3581. 812/275-0335.

Wal-Mart
RR 4 Box 24, Spencer IN 47460-9556. 812/829-2251.

Wal-Mart
7245 US Highway 31 S, Indianapolis IN 46227-8538. 317/888-7906.

Wal-Mart
10617 E Washington St, Indianapolis IN 46229-2611. 317/895-0065.

Wal-Mart
3875 N Newton St, Jasper IN 47546-8016. 812/634-1233.

Wal-Mart
730 US Highway 66 E, Tell City IN 47586-2758. 812/547-8434.

Wal-Mart
650 Kimmell Rd, Vincennes IN 47591-6341. 812/886-6728.

Wal-Mart
820 W Main St, Boonville IN 47601-3004. 812/897-5962.

Wal-Mart
2304 Lincolnway E, Goshen IN 46526-6421. 219/534-8586.

Wal-Mart
2700 W Broadway St, Princeton IN 47670-9418. 812/386-6620.

Wal-Mart
4551 University Dr, Evansville IN 47712-6578. 812/424-5475.

Wal-Mart
401 N Burkhardt Rd, Evansville IN 47715-2733. 812/473-1815.

Wal-Mart
2150 E National Ave, Brazil IN 47834-2831. 812/443-0667.

Wal-Mart
PO Box 329, Clinton IN 47842-0329. 765/832-3533.

Wal-Mart
8300 E 96th St, Fishers IN 46038-9795. 317/578-4336.

Wal-Mart
2505 N Oak Rd, Plymouth IN 46563-3410. 219/935-9000.

Wal-Mart
Rural Route 2, Box 485, Sullivan IN 47882-9802. 812/268-3381.

Wal-Mart
3861 State Road 26 E, Lafayette IN 47905-4872. 765/449-4155.

Wal-Mart
3660 Commerce Dr, Warsaw IN 46580-3927. 219/269-7811.

Wal-Mart
905 S College Ave, Rensselaer IN 47978-3006. 219/866-0266.

Wal-Mart
1540 N Morton St, Franklin IN 46131-1256. 317/738-4399.

Wal-Mart
1501 N Wayne St, Angola IN 46703-2352. 219/665-7313.

Wal-Mart
4024 Elkhart Rd, Ste 2, Goshen IN 46526-5801. 219/875-6601.

Wal-Mart
25 Putnam County Plaza, Greencastle IN 46135-9418. 765/653-2481.

Wal-Mart
505 Touring Dr, Auburn IN 46706-2054. 219/925-8080.

Wal-Mart Store
402 W Plaza Dr, Columbia City IN 46725-1019. 219/244-4060.

Wal-Mart
629 N 13th St, Decatur IN 46733-1203. 219/724-9990.

Wal-Mart
2401 E Wabash St, Frankfort IN 46041-9400. 765/654-5528.

Wal-Mart
2800 Wal-Mart Dr, Huntington IN 46750-7977. 219/358-8311.

Wal-Mart
510 Fairview Blvd, Kendallville IN 46755-2922. 219/347-4300.

Wal-Mart
9 Cherry Tree Plaza, Washington IN 47501-4501. 812/254-6681.

Wal-Mart
4420 S Scatterfield Rd, Anderson IN 46013-2600. 765/642-5025.

Wal-Mart
1675 N State St, Greenfield IN 46140-1068. 317/462-8850.

Wal-Mart
3221 W 86th St, Indianapolis IN 46268-3606. 317/875-0273.

Wal-Mart
970 E Washington St, Winchester IN 47394-9221. 765/584-2199.

Wal-Mart
1710 Apple Glen Blvd, Fort Wayne IN 46804-1725. 219/436-0113.

Wal-Mart
5311 Coldwater Rd, Fort Wayne IN 46825-5444. 219/484-4198.

Wal-Mart
1920 East Markland Ave, Kokomo IN 46901-6236. 765/456-3550.

Wal-Mart
709 S Memorial Dr, New Castle IN 47362-4954. 765/529-5990.

Wal-Mart
3919 US Highway 24 E, Logansport IN 46947-2249. 219/732-0221.

Wal-Mart
3240 S Western Ave, Marion IN 46953-3967. 765/662-0809.

Wal-Mart
2440 N Lebanon St, Lebanon IN 46052-1100. 765/482-6070.

Wal-Mart
1800 S Ohio St, Martinsville IN 46151-3320. 765/342-3591.

Wal-Mart
2100 Main St, Ste 1, Rochester IN 46975-2653. 219/223-9481.

Wal-Mart
1550 N Cass St, Wabash IN 46992-9435. 219/563-5536.

Wal-Mart
888a Green Blvd, Aurora IN 47001-1508. 812/926-1151.

Wal-Mart
2575 E Main St, Plainfield IN 46168-2713. 317/839-2261.

Wal-Mart
2363 Highway 135 NW, Corydon IN 47112-2068. 812/738-4551.

Wal-Mart
4301 Franklin Street, Michigan City IN 46360-7806. 219/879-3620.

Wal-Mart
951 East Highway 131, Clarksville IN 47129-7400. 812/284-9926.

DRUG STORES

Care Pharmaceutical Services
139 South Broad Street, Griffith IN 46319-2232. 219/924-6671.

Revco Drug Store
7047 East 10th Street, Indianapolis IN 46219-4903. 317/356-7337.

GROCERY AND CONVENIENCE STORES

ALS Grocery Store
702 E Lincolnway, La Porte IN 46350-3838. 219/879-2191.

Austin's Superfoods
3400 Grantline Road, New Albany IN 47150. 812/944-5839.

Buehler's Buy Low
1018 James Ave, Bedford IN 47421-6104. 812/275-2522.

Buehler's Buy Low
Highway 50 West, Washington IN 47501. 812/254-6644.

Buehler's Buy Low
212 E Highway 66, Rivergate Plaza, Tell City IN 47586. 812/547-4751.

Buehler's Buy Low
602 N Main Street, Princeton IN 47670-1502. 812/385-5324.

Buehler's Buy Low
Broadway & 5th Avenue, RR 3, Princeton IN 47670. 812/386-7664.

Buehler's Buy Low
4635 N First Avenue, Evansville IN 47710-3625. 812/467-7258.

Buehler's Buy Low
200 N Main Street, Evansville IN 47711-5451. 812/421-5860.

Buehler's Buy Low
2220 E Morgan Avenue, Evansville IN 47711-4314. 812/475-6730.

Buehler's Buy Low
4851 Pennsylvania Street, Evansville IN 47712-6520. 812/426-7080.

Buehler's Buy Low
1550 Vann Avenue, Evansville IN 47714-3359. 812/471-7575.

Buehler's Buy Low
5480 E Indiana Street, Evansville IN 47715-2857. 812/474-2965.

Carter's Supermarkets Inc.
840 E Jefferson Street, Tipton IN 46072-8750. 765/675-2373.

Costa's Foods Supermarket Inc.
PO Box 2297, Valparaiso IN 46384-2297. 219/464-3571.

County Market
4650 S U.S. Highway 41, Terre Haute IN 47802-5404. 812/234-2611.

Crawfordsville County Market
PO Box 1206, Crawfordsville IN 47933-0694. 765/362-8822.

Cub Foods
7901 U.S. Highway 31 South, Indianapolis IN 46227-5906. 317/888-8900.

Cub Foods
5651 Castleton Corner Way, Indianapolis IN 46250-4521. 317/841-4350.

Cub Foods
6316 Covington Road, Fort Wayne IN 46804-7314. 219/432-2511.

Flying J
1720 W Thompson Road, Indianapolis IN 46217-9350. 317/783-5543.

Foods Plus
1541 East Tipton Street, Seymour IN 47274-3557. 812/522-4799.

Great Scott Market
1100 Locust Street, Terre Haute IN 47807-1642. 812/235-6091.

Harold's Dixie Plaza Market
PO Box 663, Vincennes IN 47591-0663. 812/882-0191.

JC Ruler and Food Supply
4290 W Jonathan Moore Pike, Columbus IN 47201-9585. 812/342-4226.

Jewel Food Stores
770 Indian Boundary Road, Chesterton IN 46304-1519. 219/926-7172.

Jewel Food Stores
1276 Main Street, Crown Point IN 46307-2717. 219/662-0080.

Jewel Food Stores
101 Joliet Street, Dyer IN 46311-1707. 219/865-6507.

Jewel Food Stores
716 Ridge Road, Munster IN 46321-1612. 219/836-1118.

Jewel Food Stores
3839 45th Street, Highland IN 46322-3009. 219/924-3300.

Jewel Food Stores
3535 Franklin Street, Michigan City IN 46360-7010. 219/872-1816.

Key Markets
12 Ridge Road, Munster IN 46321-1518. 219/836-8286.

Kroger's
200 New Albany Plaza, New Albany IN 47150. 812/948-2817.

Kroger's
3110 N National Road, Columbus IN 47201-3106. 812/376-9451.

Kroger's
2629 E 65th Street, Indianapolis IN 46220-1507. 317/255-1498.

Kroger's
1930 E Main Street, Plainfield IN 46168-1859. 317/839-7961.

Kroger's
5718 Crawfordsville Road, Indianapolis IN 46224-3704. 317/241-1880.

Kroger's
1175 S College Mall Road, Bloomington IN 47401-6177. 812/333-5766.

Kroger's
528 S College Avenue, Bloomington IN 47403-1517. 812/339-3351.

Kroger's
4401 E 10th Street, Indianapolis IN 46201-2754. 317/359-1166.

Kroger's
6025 Madison Avenue, Indianapolis IN 46227-4769. 317/783-4947.

Kroger's
130 W Hively Avenue, Elkhart IN 46517-2113. 219/522-7051.

Kroger's
209 N Chicago Avenue, Goshen IN 46526-2311. 219/674-6479.

Kroger's
906 S Merrifield Avenue, Mishawaka IN 46544-2807. 219/256-1229.

Kroger's
2330 Hickory Road, Mishawaka IN 46545-3013. 219/255-4488.

Kroger's
75 Meadows Court, Terre Haute IN 47803-2378. 812/232-4519.

Kroger's
2140 Fort Harrison Road, Terre Haute IN 47804-1522. 812/466-6861.

Kroger's
2001 N Michigan Street, Plymouth IN 46563-1020. 219/936-2040.

Kroger's
916 N Main Street, Monticello IN 47960-1501. 219/583-7896.

Kroger's
5173 W Washington Street, Indianapolis IN 46241-2205. 317/244-2290.

Kroger's
1217 E Ireland Road, South Bend IN 46614-3448. 219/291-0666.

Kroger's
4526 W Western Avenue, South Bend IN 46619-2302. 219/288-0471.

Kroger's
909 N Bendix Drive, South Bend IN 46628-1833. 219/288-0055.

Kroger's
6325 University Commons, South Bend IN 46635-1475. 219/277-8200.

Kroger's
8707 Hardegan Street, Indianapolis IN 46227-7211. 317/888-3300.

Kroger's
172 Logan St, Noblesville IN 46060-1437. 317/776-3342.

Kroger's
6108 East 46th Street, Indianapolis IN 46226-3500. 317/545-7145.

Kroger's
4202 N Sheridan Ave, Indianapolis IN 46226-3623. 317/786-3304.

Kroger's
4202 S East St, Indianapolis IN 46227-1416. 317/781-4246.

Kroger's
10450 E Washington St, Indianapolis IN 46229-2657. 317/895-2245.

Kroger's
785 E Main St, Danville IN 46122-1941. 317/745-8020.

Kroger's
1700 Northwood Plaza, Franklin IN 46131-1036. 317/736-6004.

Kroger's
821 Lincoln Highway W, New Haven IN 46774-2139. 219/749-4939.

Kroger's
324 E State Blvd, Fort Wayne IN 46805-3224. 219/420-3343.

Kroger's
7101 E 10th St, Indianapolis IN 46219-4905. 317/352-1722.

Kroger's
5466 E 82nd Street, Indianapolis IN 46250-1519. 317/842-7780.

Kroger's
5615 W 38th Street, Indianapolis IN 46254-2921. 317/299-6780.

Kroger's
1571 N State Street, Greenfield IN 46140-1066. 317/462-3451.

Kroger's
46th Arlington, Indianapolis IN 46226. 317/545-8095.

Kroger's
2550 Lake Circle Drive, Indianapolis IN 46268-4220. 317/879-2460.

Kroger's
218 E Pettit Avenue, Fort Wayne IN 46806-3005. 219/745-7800.

Kroger's
3100 Meridian Park Drive, Greenwood IN 46142-9424. 317/887-5745.

Kroger's
930 W Main Street, Peru IN 46970-1741. 765/472-1449.

Kroger's
2420 N Lebanon Street, Lebanon IN 46052-1183. 765/482-7274.

Kroger's
530 S Indiana Street, Mooresville IN 46158-1712. 317/831-0241.

Kroger's
706 E Highway 131, Suite C, Clarksville IN 47129-2245. 812/282-2833.

Marsh Supermarket
3075 25th Street, Columbus IN 47203-2434. 812/375-5555.

Marsh Supermarket
3633 Kentucky Avenue, Indianapolis IN 46221-2702. 317/381-4141.

Marsh Supermarket
7400 Fishers Station Drive, Fishers IN 46038-2323. 317/577-5325.

Marsh Supermarket
1033 Indianapolis Road, Greencastle IN 46135-2407. 765/653-4171.

Martin's Supermarket
1200 Nappanee Street, Elkhart IN 46514. 219/264-4425.

Martin's Supermarket
3267 Northview Drive, Elkhart IN 46514-6750. 219/264-6505.

Martin's Supermarket
555 E Jackson Boulevard, Elkhart IN 46516-3528. 219/293-6659.

Martin's Supermarket
926 Erkskine Plaza, South Bend IN 46614. 219/291-3571.

Martin's Supermarket
4401 W Western Avenue, South Bend IN 46619-2640. 219/288-4854.

Martin's Supermarket
1302 Elwood Avenue, South Bend IN 46628-2761. 219/233-8229.

Martin's Supermarket
2081 South Bend Avenue, South Bend IN 46635. 219/272-6922.

Mr. D's Food Market
512 S College Mall Road, Bloomington IN 47401-6314. 812/331-2823.

O'Malia Food Markets Inc.
2342 W 86th Street, Indianapolis IN 46260-1906. 317/875-7810.

O'Malia Food Markets Inc.
7405 West 10th Street, Indianapolis IN 46214-2517. 317/271-1441.

Owens North
2718 Guilford St, Huntington IN 46750-9701. 219/356-1811.

Owen's Super Markets Inc.
PO Box 877, Warsaw IN 46581-0877. 219/267-8848.

Payless Super Market
PO Box 639, Anderson IN 46015-0639. 765/649-3446.

Pick N Save
College Ave, Rensselaer IN 47978. 219/866-8080.

Richmond County Market
2300 National Rd W, Richmond IN 47374-4625. 765/962-7676.

Ross Supermarkets
1900 S Hoyt Ave, Muncie IN 47302-3041. 765/284-1441.

Schnuck Store
3700 N 1st Ave, Evansville IN 47710-3324. 812/464-3920.

Schnuck Store
4500 W Lloyd Expressway, Evansville IN 47712-6515. 812/422-6325.

Schnuck Store
4600 Washington Ave, Evansville IN 47714-0895. 812/473-0151.

Scott's
580 Fairview Blvd, Kendallville IN 46755-2969. 219/347-9155.

Scott's
496 W Plaza Dr, Columbia City IN 46725-1019. 219/625-4724.

Scott's
5725 Coventry Ln, Fort Wayne IN 46804-7146. 219/432-0485.

Scott's
3905 E State Blvd, Fort Wayne IN 46805-4948. 219/483-8126.

Scott's
4120 N Clinton St, Fort Wayne IN 46805-1210. 219/484-7021.

Scott's
710 E DuPont Rd, Fort Wayne IN 46825. 219/489-6973.

Scott's
4522 Maplecrest Road, Fort Wayne IN 46835-3970. 219/485-0640.

Scott's
350 Auburn Dr, Auburn IN 46706. 219/925-4785.

Scott's
496 West Plaza Dr, Columbia City IN 46725-1019. 219/244-7018.

Scott's
4020 Upper Huntington Rd, Fort Wayne IN 46804. 219/432-2591.

Skico Inc.
865 E Jefferson St, Plymouth IN 46563-1847. 219/936-4081.

Sterk's Super Foods
4725 Indianapolis Blvd, East Chicago IN 46312-3327. 219/397-2620.

Sterk's Super Foods
6529 Columbia Ave, Hammond IN 46320-2749. 219/932-4958.

Sterk's Super Foods
31 Sibley St, Hammond IN 46320-1725. 219/937-4350.

Town and Country Market
6020 Central Ave, Portage IN 46368-3501. 219/762-9518.

Tysen's Country Grocery Inc.
PO Box 77, Demotte IN 46310-0077. 219/987-2141.

Ultra Foods
8401 Indianapolis Blvd, Highland IN 46322-1557. 219/972-0254.

Ultra Foods
7760 E 37th Ave, Hobart IN 46342. 219/962-1115.

Wesselman's-North Park
4624 N 1st Ave, Evansville IN 47710-3626. 812/423-5829.

Wilco Foods
2080 E Commercial Ave, Lowell IN 46356-2116. 219/696-6633.

Wiseway Food Center
2168 US Highway 30, Valparaiso IN 46385-5437. 219/462-5147.

Wiseway Food Center
6010 W Ridge Rd, Gary IN 46408-1701. 219/923-8107.

MISC. GENERAL MERCHANDISE STORES

Sam's Club
5805 Rockville Rd, Indianapolis IN 46224-9120. 317/248-3577.

Sam's Club
3205 W State Rd 45, Bloomington IN 47403-5107. 812/331-0003.

Sam's Club
10859 E Washington St,

Indianapolis IN 46229-2615. 317/897-0135.

Sam's Club
5101 Vogel Rd, Evansville IN 47715-7817. 812/477-0138.

Sam's Club
4350 S US Highway 41, Terre Haute IN 47802. 812/235-5660.

Sam's Club
3819 State Route 26 E, Lafayette IN 47905. 765/449-4607.

Sam's Club
8100 E 96th St, Fishers IN 46038-9793. 317/849-9409.

Sam's Club
3015 West 86th Street, Indianapolis IN 46268-3602. 317/871-7135.

Sam's Club
488 W Muskegon Dr, Greenfield IN 46140-3057. 317/467-0497.

Sam's Club
6610 Lima Rd, Fort Wayne IN 46818-1120. 219/489-1603.

Sam's Club
1917 E Markland Ave, Kokomo IN 46901-6237. 765/868-7025.

RETAIL BAKERIES

Parco Foods
502 W US Highway 20, Michigan City IN 46360-6836. 219/879-4431.

RV DEALERS

Stout's RV Sales Inc.
303 Sheek Rd, Greenwood IN 46143-9713. 317/881-7670.

Tom Raper Inc.
PO Box 1365, Richmond IN 47375-1365. 765/966-8361.

SPORTING GOODS STORES

Galyan's Trading Company Inc.
2437 East Main Street, Plainfield IN 46168-2715. 317/532-0200.

Galyan's Trading Company Inc.
2003 East Greyhound Pass, Carmel IN 46033. 317/573-7777.

Galyan's Trading Company Inc.
7609 Shelby Street, Indianapolis IN 46227-5989. 317/887-9220.

Knollwood Pro Shop
16633 Baywood Lane, Granger IN 46530-6953. 219/277-2620.

For more information on career opportunities in retail:

<u>Associations</u>

INTERNATIONAL ASSOCIATION OF CHAIN STORES
5549 Lee Highway, Arlington VA 22207. 703/534-8880. Fax: 703/534-9080.

INTERNATIONAL COUNCIL OF SHOPPING CENTERS
665 Fifth Avenue, New York NY 10022-5370. 212/421-8181. World Wide Web address: http://www.icsc.org. Offers conventions, research, education, a variety of publications, and awards programs.

NATIONAL AUTOMOTIVE DEALERS ASSOCIATION
8400 Westpark Drive, McLean VA 22102. 703/821-7000. World Wide Web address: http://www.nadanet.com.

NATIONAL INDEPENDENT AUTOMOTIVE DEALERS ASSOCIATION
2521 Brown Boulevard, Suite 100, Arlington TX 76006. 817/640-3838. World Wide Web address: http://www.niada.com.

NATIONAL RETAIL FEDERATION
325 7th Street NW, Suite 1000, Washington DC 20004. 202/783-7971. World Wide Web address: http://www.nrf.com. Provides information services, industry outlooks, and a variety of educational opportunities and publications.

<u>Directories</u>

AUTOMOTIVE NEWS MARKET DATA BOOK
Automotive News, Crain Communication, 1400 Woodbridge Avenue, Detroit MI 48207-3187. 313/446-6000.

<u>Online Services</u>

THE INTERNET FASHION EXCHANGE
http://www.fashionexch.com. An excellent site for those industry professionals interested in apparel and retail. The extensive search engine allows you to search by job title, location, salary, product line, industry, and whether you want a permanent, temporary, or freelance position. The Internet Fashion Exchange also offers career services such as recruiting, and outplacement firms that place fashion and retail professionals.

RETAIL JOBNET
http://www.retailjobnet.com. Sponsored by Retail Search Consultants, Inc. and Barnes & Associates Retail Search, this site is geared toward recruiting professionals for the retail industry. The resume database has a fee of $15 for three months or $25 for six months.

STONE, CLAY, GLASS, AND CONCRETE PRODUCTS

Largely dependent on the success of the construction market, the stone, clay, glass, and concrete industry was expected to experience steady demand in 1998, as new construction projects began nationwide. Manufacturers of float glass (a raw material used in producing windows, windshields, and door panes) were projected to see flat sales in 1998 until increases in vehicle demand and non-residential construction picked up later in the year. Six of the largest float glass plants are located in the United States. Among these are Guardian Industries, PPG Industries, and Ford Motor Company's glass division.

The primary market for clay and brick is in the construction of single-family housing; the demand should grow at an average of less than 1 percent annually through 2002. By the end of the decade, ceramic tile imports are likely to increase due to Mexico's duty-free access to the U.S. market and a projected 10 percent cut in tariffs.

ANCHOR GLASS CONTAINER CORPORATION
603 East North Street, Winchester IN 47394. 765/584-6101. **Contact:** Howard Sheets, Human Resources. **Description:** Manufactures and sells a diversified line of household, hardware, and packaging products including glassware, commercial and institutional chinaware, decorative and convenience hardware, glass containers, and metal and plastic closures. Operations encompass over 20 divisions and subsidiaries with 40 plants and distribution centers located in the United States and abroad.

BALL-FOSTER GLASS CONTAINER CORPORATION
1509 South Macedonia Avenue, Muncie IN 47302. 765/741-7000. **Contact:** Human Resources Department. **Description:** A packaging company that produces glass bottles. **Other U.S. locations:** Nationwide.

BALL-FOSTER GLASS CONTAINER CORPORATION
524 East Center Street, Dunkirk IN 47336. 765/768-7891. **Contact:** Human Resources Department. **Description:** A packaging company that produces glass bottles. **Other U.S. locations:** Nationwide.

HAMMOND GROUP, INC.
5231 Hohman Avenue, Hammond IN 46320. 219/931-9360. **Contact:** Human Resources. **World Wide Web address:** http://www.hmndgroup.com. **Description:** This location houses administrative offices. Overall, Hammond Group manufactures lead chemicals and products, under the name Hammond Lead Products, including lead carbonates, silicates, and sulfates for a variety of industries. The company also developed and manufactures a dedusted granular litharge called 400Y. **Corporate headquarters location:** This Location.

INDIANA GLASS COMPANY
717 E Street, Box 171, Dunkirk IN 47336. 765/768-6789. **Contact:** Human Resources Department. **Description:** Indiana Glass company manufactures glass housewares and containers such as glasses, mugs, and ashtrays.

KNAUF FIBER GLASS
240 Elizabeth Street, Shelbyville IN 46176. 317/398-4434. **Contact:** Larry Stagner, Human Resources Director. **World Wide Web address:** http://www.knauffiberglass.com. **Description:** Manufactures fiber glass for both commercial and residential uses.

OWENS-BROCKWAY GLASS INC.
P.O. Box 368, Lapel IN 46051. 765/534-3121. **Contact:** Human Resources. **Description:** One of several area divisions of the diversified manufacturer of packaging products. Principal products are glass containers, although the company also produces and sells containerboard, corrugated containers, printing plates and ink, plywood and dimension lumber, blown plastic containers, plastic beverage bottles, plastic drums, metal and plastic closures, tamper-resistant closures, plastic and glass prescription containers, pharmaceutical items, labels, and multipack plastic carriers for containers. Specialized glass products made and sold by the company include Libbey Tumblers, stemware, and decorative glassware; television bulbs for picture tubes; and Kimble scientific and laboratory ware. Some overseas affiliates also manufacture flat glass and related products.

***Note:** Because addresses and telephone numbers of smaller companies can change rapidly, we recommend you call each company to verify the information below before inquiring about job opportunities. Mass mailings are not recommended.*

Additional small employers:

ASPHALT

Asphalt Materials Inc.
PO Box 68123, Indianapolis IN 46268-0123. 317/872-6010.

Globe Building Materials Incorporated
2207 Schrage Avenue, Whiting IN 46394-2108. 219/659-7420.

CEMENT

Essroc Cement Corporation
PO Box 219, Jeffersonville IN 47131-0219. 812/246-5472.

Essroc Cement Corporation
3084 W County Road, Suite 225, Logansport IN 46947-8476. 219/753-5121.

Lone Star Industries Incorporated
PO Box 482, Greencastle IN 46135-0482. 765/653-9766.

CRUSHED AND BROKEN STONE

Evansville Materials
PO Box 3596, Evansville IN 47734-3596. 812/424-5583.

CUT STONE AND STONE PRODUCTS

Cameo Marble
540 Central Court, New Albany IN 47150-7223. 812/944-5055.

EARTH AND MINERALS

American Art Clay Company
4717 West 16th Street, Indianapolis IN 46222-2516. 317/244-6871.

International Mill Service
PO Box M824, Gary IN 46401-0824. 219/885-5728.

The Levy Co.
PO Box 540, Portage IN 46368-0540. 219/787-8666.

GLASS AND GLASS PRODUCTS

Anchor Resolution Corporation
200 W Belleview Road, Lawrenceburg IN 47025-1337. 812/537-1655.

Ball-Foster Glass Company
PO Box 249, Marion IN 46952-0249. 765/668-1200.

D&W Inc.
941 Oak Street, Elkhart IN 46514-2207. 219/264-9674.

Dacra Glass Inc.
7126 North State Road 3, Montpelier IN 47359-9613. 765/348-2190.

Guardian Industries
860 West U.S. Route 6, Ligonier IN 46767. 219/894-7750.

Hamilton Glass Products
PO Box 317, Vincennes IN 47591-0317. 812/882-2680.

Hehr International
PO Box 219, Plymouth IN 46563-0219. 219/935-5122.

Lawson Mardon Wheaton Inc.
PO Box 617, Westport IN 47283-0617. 812/591-2332.

MINERAL WOOL

Jet Composites Inc.
300 W 100 S, Bluffton IN 46714-9760. 219/824-6200.

Johns Manville
PO Box 428, Richmond IN 47375-0428. 765/973-5300.

Thermafiber
3711 Mill St, Wabash IN 46992-7778. 219/563-2111.

TILE

General Shale Products Corp.
PO Box 159, Mooresville IN 46158-0159. 317/831-3317.

KPT Inc.
PO Box 468, Bloomfield IN 47424-0468. 812/384-3563.

For more information on career opportunities in stone, clay, glass, and concrete products:

Associations

THE AMERICAN CERAMIC SOCIETY
P.O. Box 6136, Westerville OH 43086-6136. 614/890-4700. World Wide Web address: http://www.acers.org. Offers a variety of publications, meetings, information, and educational services. Also operates

Ceramic Futures, an employment service with a resume database.

NATIONAL GLASS ASSOCIATION
8200 Greensboro Drive, Suite 302, McLean VA 22102. 703/442-4890. World Wide Web address: http://www.glass.org.

Magazines

GLASS MAGAZINE
National Glass Association, 8200 Greensboro Drive, McLean VA 22102. 703/442-4890.

ROCK PRODUCTS
MacLean Hunter Publishing Company, 29 North Wacker Drive, Chicago IL 60606. 312/726-2805.

TRANSPORTATION/TRAVEL

All sectors of the transportation industry appear stable, particularly the domestic airline sector, which boasted record profits in 1997 that were expected to be topped in 1998. Brian D. Harris of Lehman Brothers Inc. suggested that the 11 largest airlines could post a 5 percent increase in profits and revenues. Despite an increase in labor costs and high fuel prices, air carriers have maintained high profits due to strong consumer demand coupled with high ticket prices.

Both Congress and the Transportation Department are proposing bills that would potentially spark more competition among airlines by seizing some of the takeoff and landing rights from larger airlines and granting them to smaller airlines, reports Business Week. *As safety and security issues have loomed larger in recent years, government demands for security upgrades on existing aircraft will be a growing priority for the next few years.*

A locomotive shortage may have hindered some railroads in 1998, but mergers between companies such as Union Pacific Corporation and Southern Pacific Rail Corporation should have benefited the industry, according to industry analyst James J. Valentine.

Rising labor costs and deregulation have forced the trucking industry to lower operating costs, but the U.S. Department of Commerce forecasts that industrial and commercial shipments should increase by about 17 percent annually until 2005.

AIR ROAD EXPRESS
P.O. Box 66056, Indianapolis IN 46266. 317/390-6500. **Physical address:** 3150 Chief Lane, Indianapolis IN 46241. **Toll-free phone:** 800/899-3812. **Contact:** Human Resources. **World Wide Web address:** http://www.airroad.com. **Description:** An air transportation company.

AMERICAN COMMERCIAL BARGE LINE COMPANY
1701 East Market Street, Jeffersonville IN 47130. 812/288-0100. **Fax:** 812/288-0294. **Contact:** Larry Weas, Director of Human Resources. **World Wide Web address:** http://www.acbl.net. **Description:** A transportation company. **Benefits:** 401(k); Dental Insurance; Disability Coverage; Life Insurance; Medical Insurance; Pension Plan; Savings Plan; Tuition Assistance. **Special programs:** Internships. **Corporate headquarters location:** This Location. **Subsidiaries include:** American Commercial Marine Services Company. **Parent company:** CSX Corporation. **Operations at this facility include:** Administration. **Number of employees at this location:** 300. **Number of employees nationwide:** 2,585.

AMERICAN COMMERCIAL MARINE SERVICES COMPANY
P.O. Box 610, Jeffersonville IN 47130. 812/288-0162. **Contact:** Robert P. Herre, Vice President of Engineering. **Description:** Manufactures and repairs ships. **Common positions include:** Design Engineer; Draftsperson; Manufacturing Engineer; Mechanical Engineer; Naval Architect. **Parent company:** American Commercial Barge Line Company (Jeffersonville IN).

AMERICAN TRANS AIR, INC.
P.O. Box 51609, Indianapolis IN 46251. 317/248-8308. **Recorded jobline:** 317/240-7106. **Contact:** Corporate Employment. **World Wide Web address:** http://www.ata.com. **Description:** ATA is one of the largest charter airlines in North America, providing capacity to U.S. and European tour operators, as well as to the United States military. ATA's scheduled service takes

passengers to 20 destinations from gateways in Indianapolis, Chicago-Midway, Milwaukee, Boston, and St. Louis. **Common positions include:** Accountant/Auditor; Advertising Clerk; Aerospace Engineer; Aircraft Mechanic/Engine Specialist; Blue-Collar Worker Supervisor; Budget Analyst; Buyer; Claim Representative; Clerical Supervisor; Computer Programmer; Customer Service Representative; Economist; Financial Analyst; Human Resources Manager; Mechanical Engineer; Public Relations Specialist; Purchasing Agent/Manager; Quality Control Supervisor; Software Engineer; Structural Engineer; Systems Analyst; Technical Writer/Editor; Travel Agent. **Educational backgrounds include:** Accounting; Business Administration; Computer Science; Engineering; Finance; Marketing; Mathematics. **Benefits:** 401(k); Dental Insurance; Disability Coverage; Employee Discounts; Life Insurance; Medical Insurance; Travel Allowance; Tuition Assistance. **Corporate headquarters location:** This Location. **Parent company:** Amtran, Inc. was founded in 1973 and operates a fleet of Lockheed L-1011, Boeing 757, and Boeing 727 aircraft. **Operations at this facility include:** Administration; Divisional Headquarters; Sales; Service. **Listed on:** New York Stock Exchange. **Number of employees at this location:** 2,600. **Number of employees nationwide:** 4,200.

ATLAS VAN LINES, INC.
1212 St. George Road, Evansville IN 47711. 812/424-4326. **Fax:** 812/421-7125. **Contact:** Patricia Walter, Assistant Vice President of Human Resources. **World Wide Web address:** http://www.atlasvanlines.com. **Description:** Atlas Van Lines is a worldwide common carrier, principally engaged in the transportation of used household goods, general commodities, special products, and freight forwarding. **Common positions include:** Accountant/Auditor; Adjuster; Budget Analyst; Claim Representative; Clerical Supervisor; Computer Operator; Computer Programmer; Customer Service Representative; Department Manager; Dispatcher; Financial Manager; Insurance Agent/Broker; Order Clerk; Payroll Clerk; Public Relations Specialist; Receptionist; Secretary; Systems Analyst; Transportation/Traffic Specialist; Travel Agent; Typist/Word Processor. **Educational backgrounds include:** Accounting; Business Administration; Communications; Computer Science; Finance; Liberal Arts; Marketing; Mathematics. **Benefits:** Dental Insurance; Disability Coverage; Life Insurance; Medical Insurance; Pension Plan; Tuition Assistance. **Corporate headquarters location:** This Location. **Operations at this facility include:** Administration; Sales; Service. **Number of employees at this location:** 430.

BURLINGTON MOTOR CARRIERS
14611 West Commerce Road, Daleville IN 47334. 765/378-0261. **Contact:** Deb Condon, Director of Human Resources. **World Wide Web address:** http://www.bmtr.com. **Description:** Provides trucking transportation services for manufacturers of consumer products, pharmaceuticals, building materials, automobile parts, produce, food, and beverage containers.

CELADON GROUP, INC.
9503 East 33rd Street, Indianapolis IN 46236. 317/972-7000. **Fax:** 317/890-9414. **Contact:** Diana Bean, Human Resources Director. **World Wide Web address:** http://www.celadontrucking.com. **Description:** Celadon Group is a transportation company that primarily offers trucking and freight forwarding services. The company's trucking business, operating through Celadon Trucking, specializes in long-haul, full truckload transportation services between the United States and Mexico. The company's freight forwarding business, operating through Celadon/Jacky Maeder, provides a full line of air, ocean, import, and customs brokerage services internationally. Other businesses include Celadon Logistics, specializing in handling; Celadon Express, a rapid package delivery business; and Celadon Travel, a full-service travel agency that specializes in group and corporate travel. **Corporate headquarters location:** This Location. **Other U.S. locations:** Kearny NJ.

GD LEASING COMPANY
2399 East 15th Avenue, Gary IN 46402. 219/881-0215. **Contact:** Human Resources. **Description:** A truck driving company servicing 48 states and Canada.

INDIANA HARBOR BELT RAILROAD
2721 161st Street, Hammond IN 46323-1099. 219/989-4703. **Contact:** Personnel. **Description:** A railroad company.

JEFFBOAT, INC.
1030 East Market Street, Jeffersonville IN 47130. 812/288-0200. **Contact:** Human Resources. **Description:** Engaged in shipbuilding and repair services.

MORGAN DRIVE AWAY, INC.
P.O. Box 1168, Elkhart IN 46515-1168. 219/295-2200. **Contact:** Human Resources. **World Wide Web address:** http://www.morgrp.com. **Description:** Arranges transportation services for the movement and delivery of manufactured houses and recreational vehicles. Morgan Drive Away also arranges the movement of commercial vehicles, office trailers, automobiles, buses, and other vehicles and freight. The company operates a network of about 1,900 independent owner-operators and drivers, and 1,100 part-time drive-away employees in 108 offices in 36 states. **Subsidiaries include:** Interstate Indemnity; Morgan Finance. **Parent company:** The Morgan Group, Inc.

NORTH AMERICAN VAN LINES, INC.
P.O. Box 988, Fort Wayne IN 46801-0988. 219/429-2511. **Contact:** Human Resources. **Description:** A motor carrier.

SHOUP BUSES, INC.
P.O. Box 271, Middlebury IN 46540. 219/825-9405. **Contact:** Tom Clark, Human Resources. **Description:** A transport company consisting of three divisions: Cardinal Charters & Tours, a charter bus business; Tri State Coach, covering northwest Indiana and the South Chicago area; and United Limo, Inc., a limousine service.

STARCRAFT MONARCH MARINE
201 Starcraft Drive, P.O. Box 517, Topeka IN 46571. 219/593-2500. **Contact:** Human Resources. **Description:** Manufactures marine products including power motors and pleasure boating equipment.

THUNDERBIRD PRODUCTS CORPORATION
2200 West Monroe Street, P.O. Box 1003, Decatur IN 46733. 219/724-9111. **Contact:** Human Resources. **World Wide Web address:** http://www.thunderbirdboats.com. **Description:** Engaged in boat building and repair services.

UNION TANK CAR COMPANY
300 West 151st Street, East Chicago IN 46312. 219/392-1500. **Contact:** Personnel. **Description:** Manufacturers of railroad tank cars.

Note: Because addresses and telephone numbers of smaller companies can change rapidly, we recommend you call each company to verify the information below before inquiring about job opportunities. Mass mailings are not recommended.

Additional small employers:

AIR TRANSPORTATION AND SERVICES

Airborne Express
7740 Johnson Road, Indianapolis IN 46250-2079. 317/842-1373.

American International Freight
520 S Airport Street, Terre Haute IN 47803-9706. 812/877-7100.

AMR Combs Inc.
PO Box 51568, Indianapolis IN 46251-0568. 317/248-4900.

Bombardier Aerospace Services
PO Box 51320, Indianapolis IN 46251-0320. 317/390-8100.

Federal Express Corporation
5301 Lincoln Way West, South Bend IN 46628-5520. 219/236-7400.

Indianapolis Airport Authority
2500 S High School Road, Indianapolis IN 46241-4943. 317/487-9594.

Landair Services Inc.
4711 W Morris Street, Indianapolis IN 46241-3519. 317/243-2366.

Purdue University Airport
Airport Operations Terminal Bldg, West Lafayette IN 47906. 765/743-3442.

Towne Air Freight Inc.
6430 Airway Dr, Indianapolis IN 46241-6400. 317/856-5405.

UFS Inc.
4819 Lincoln Way W, South Bend IN 46628-5525. 219/233-4511.

United Airlines
8929 W Washington St, Indianapolis IN 46231-1281. 317/757-7007.

United Airlines
320 W 8th St, Ste 116, Bloomington IN 47404-3700. 812/355-0155.

US Airways Express
2500 S High School Rd, Indianapolis IN 46241-4943. 317/484-6000.

COURIER SERVICES

Special Dispatch Inc.
PO Box 171, Indianapolis IN 46206-0171. 317/638-0608.

United Parcel Service Inc.
3147 169th Parrish Avenue, Hammond IN 46320. 219/845-0834.

United Parcel Service Inc.
2727 Independence Dr, Fort Wayne IN 46808-1331. 219/483-5966.

United Parcel Service Inc.
PO Box 7023, Indianapolis IN 46207-7023. 317/927-6352.

United Parcel Service Inc.
1901 W 26th St, Muncie IN 47302-9403. 765/289-3797.

United Parcel Service Inc.
100 Industrial Parkway, Waterloo IN 46793-9438. 219/837-7851.

LOCAL AND INTERURBAN PASSENGER TRANSIT

Anderson Transit System Inc.
1500 W 2nd Street, Anderson IN 46016-2438. 765/643-3494.

Fort Wayne Community Schools Transportation
301 Cook Road, Fort Wayne IN 46825. 219/425-7280.

Gary Public Transportation Corporation
2101 West 35th Avenue, Gary IN 46408-1406. 219/884-6100.

Indygo
PO Box 2383, Indianapolis IN 46206-2383. 317/635-2100.

Transpo
PO Box 1437, South Bend IN 46624-1437. 219/232-9901.

US Airways Inc.
2349 Aviation Drive, Indianapolis IN 46241-3729. 317/486-2002.

MAINTENANCE FACILITIES FOR MOTOR FREIGHT TRANSPORTATION

ANR Freight
1101 Harding Court, Indianapolis IN 46217-9531. 317/788-4766.

Consolidated Freightways Corporation
PO Box 738, Fremont IN 46737-0738. 219/833-3850.

Roadway Express Inc.
2530 South Tibbs Ave, Indianapolis IN 46241-5347. 317/243-3291.

USF Holland Inc.
4320 Merchant Road, Fort Wayne IN 46818-1252. 219/489-5502.

PACKING AND CRATING

Ameriqual Packaging
225 W Morgan Avenue, Evansville IN 47710-2515. 812/421-4876.

J&J Packaging Inc.
8031 Golden Road, Brookville IN 47012-9703. 765/647-2571.

PASSENGER TRANSPORTATION ARRANGEMENT SERVICES

Ace Rent-A-Car
PO Box 8039, Fort Wayne IN 46898-8039. 219/489-2776.

RCI Travel Inc.
3502 Woodview Terrace, Indianapolis IN 46268-1195. 317/871-9462.

Rosenbluth International Incorporated
State Road 32 W, Crawfordsville IN 47933. 765/364-2223.

RRD Direct Seymour
709 A Ave E, Seymour IN 47274-3234. 812/523-0106.

RAILROAD EQUIPMENT

Hadady Corporation
1832 Lake Street, Dyer IN 46311-1547. 219/322-7417.

RAILROAD TRANSPORTATION

Amtrak Material Control
202 Walter Barrick Way, Beech Grove IN 46107. 317/263-0400.

Conrail Big Four Yard
2491 N Dan Jones Road, Plainfield IN 46168-9605. 317/838-3381.

CSX
2710 Dixie Flyer Road, Evansville IN 47712-4668. 812/465-1701.

CSX Transportation Inc.
301 North Randolph Street, Garrett IN 46738-1059. 219/357-3900.

EJ&E Railway Company
PO Box 899, Gary IN 46402-0899. 219/883-4208.

Norfolk and Western Railway Company
8111 Nelson Road, Fort Wayne IN 46803-1992. 219/493-5303.

Norfolk Southern Corporation
220 East Garfield Avenue, Princeton IN 47670-3472. 812/385-5031.

SHIP/BOAT BUILDING AND REPAIRING

Brunswick Marine
PO Box 530, Nappanee IN 46550-0530. 219/773-2401.

Godfrey Marine
PO Box 1158, Elkhart IN 46515-1158. 219/522-8381.

Rinker Boat Company Inc.
300 W Chicago St, Syracuse IN 46567-1545. 219/457-5731.

Sea Nymph Aluminum Boats
PO Box 337, Syracuse IN 46567-0337. 219/457-3131.

Smoker-Craft
PO Box 65, New Paris IN 46553-0065. 219/831-2103.

TRANSPORTATION EQUIPMENT

Reese Products Inc.
PO Box 1706, Elkhart IN 46515-1706. 219/264-7564.

TRUCKING

AG Trucking Inc.
PO Box 453, Goshen IN 46527-0453. 219/642-3351.

Allied Holdings
PO Box 520, Roanoke IN 46783-0520. 219/672-2166.

Astro Enterprises Inc.
6015 Pendleton Avenue, Anderson IN 46013-9725. 765/642-0346.

Atlantic Inland Carriers Inc.
PO Box 21337, Indianapolis IN 46221-0337. 317/634-9340.

Bestway Express Inc.
PO Box 728, Vincennes IN 47591-0728. 812/882-6448.

Bestway Trucking Inc.
PO Box 339, Jeffersonville IN 47131-0339. 812/285-5515.

Central Trucking Inc.
11930 N Hartman Drive, Edinburgh IN 46124-9548. 812/526-9737.

Certified Transport Inc.
2415 W Thompson Road, Indianapolis IN 46217-9365. 317/791-1212.

CF Motor Freight
3915 W Morris Street, Indianapolis IN 46241-2619. 317/241-2842.

CF Motor Freight
PO Box 738, Fremont IN 46737-0738. 219/833-1366.

CLM Freight Lines Inc.
PO Box 19333, Indianapolis IN 46219-0333. 317/353-8344.

CNF Transportation Inc.
3915 W Morris Street, Indianapolis IN 46241-2619. 317/484-9870.

Coast Midwest Transport Incorporated
229 America Place A, Jeffersonville IN 47130-4271. 812/282-5191.

Collins Transportation Company
PO Box 2588, Kokomo IN 46904-2588. 765/457-6648.

Customized Transportation Inc.
800 Perry Road, Plainfield IN 46168-7637. 317/839-9299.

DE Willoughby Trucking Inc.
PO Box 1522, Columbus IN 47202-1522. 812/526-9774.

DP Cartage Inc.
PO Box 6171, Indianapolis IN 46206-6171. 317/549-9281.

Eck Miller Transportation Corporation
PO Box 248, Rockport IN 47635-0248. 812/649-5001.

Free Enterprise Systems
1254 S West Street, Indianapolis IN 46225-1544. 317/634-9293.

Gainey Transportation Services of Indiana
PO Box 3836, South Bend IN 46619-0836. 219/271-0401.

Heritage
1626 Research Way, Indianapolis IN 46231-3352. 317/241-9406.

Hiner Transport Inc.
PO Box 621, Huntington IN 46750-0621. 219/356-8218.

Icon Transportation Company Inc.
PO Box 450, Remington IN 47977-0450. 219/261-2166.

Jet Transport
PO Box 460, Middlebury IN 46540-0460. 219/825-0522.

Jones Trucking Inc.
PO Box 64, Paragon IN 46166-0064. 765/537-2279.

KAT Inc.
PO Box 2198, Chesterton IN 46304-0298. 219/926-3413.

Knight Transportation Inc.
3702 W Minnesota Street, Indianapolis IN 46241-4554. 317/486-1770.

Laker Express Inc.
PO Box 681215, Indianapolis IN 46268-7215. 317/873-6181.

Mount Trucking Inc.
460 Jonesville Road, Columbus IN 47201-7513. 812/376-7726.

National Distributors Inc.
PO Box 255, Sellersburg IN 47172-0255. 812/246-6306.

Ormsby Trucking Inc.
PO Box 67, Uniondale IN 46791-0067. 219/543-2233.

Overnite Transportation Company
3747 West Morris St, Indianapolis IN 46241-2705. 317/244-3744.

Pegasus Transportation Inc.
PO Box 1571, Jeffersonville IN 47131-1571. 812/282-5510.

Preston Trucking Company Inc.
4209 West Morris St, Indianapolis IN 46241-2501. 317/247-0151.

Preston Trucking Company Inc.
1300 South Walnut St, South Bend IN 46619-4308. 219/287-3335.

RAD Transport Inc.
1020 Kent St, Elkhart IN 46514-1702. 219/266-1330.

Safeway Moving Systems Incorporated
2828 N Emerson Ave, Indianapolis IN 46218-3238. 317/545-7533.

Sodrel Truck Lines Inc.
1 Sodrel Dr, Jeffersonville IN 47129-2859. 812/282-7941.

Stone Transport Inc.
5225 New Haven Ave, Fort Wayne IN 46803-3026. 219/749-6144.

Tandem Transport Corporation
PO Box 2038, Michigan City IN 46361-8038. 219/874-6271.

Triple Crown Service Company
6920 Pointe Inverness Way, Fort Wayne IN 46804-7926. 219/434-3600.

Underwood Truck Lines Inc.
PO Box 100, Brazil IN 47834-0100. 812/448-8861.

Wabash Valley Transportation
PO Box 351, Remington IN 47977-0351. 219/261-2101.

Wheaton World Wide Moving
PO Box 50800, Indianapolis IN 46250-0800. 317/849-7900.

Yellow Freight System Inc.
Drawer 41307, Indianapolis IN 46241. 317/241-9261.

Zipp-Express Inc.
PO Box 1326, Indianapolis IN 46206-1326. 317/782-9665.

WAREHOUSING AND STORAGE

Aldi
PO Box 1398, Valparaiso IN 46384-1398. 219/464-2500.

Commercial Warehouse & Cartage
200 E Superior Street, Fort Wayne IN 46802-1205. 219/422-9889.

DMI Distribution Inc.
PO Box 426, Winchester IN 47394-0426. 765/584-3234.

FB Distro Inc.
1901 East State Rd, Suite 240, Greencastle IN 46135-7825. 765/653-7500.

Genco Return Centers
7901 W 21st Street, Indianapolis IN 46214-2306. 317/273-0000.

Genova Products Inc.
9501 Airport Drive, Fort Wayne IN 46809-3001. 219/478-1639.

Indco Dry Warehouse
1740 Stout Field East Drive, Indianapolis IN 46241-4007. 317/248-0427.

Jenn-Air
2525 N Shadeland Avenue, Indianapolis IN 46219-1787. 317/545-2271.

Marsh Warehouse
9511 W Depot Street, Yorktown IN 47396-1532. 765/759-4240.

Nabco Inc.
600 Broadway Street, Anderson IN 46012-2922. 765/644-8457.

Power Logistics
3333 N Franklin Rd, Indianapolis IN 46226-6314. 317/895-9506.

Warehouse Services Inc.
PO Box 608, Mount Vernon IN 47620-0608. 812/831-4053.

For more information on career opportunities in transportation and travel industries:

Associations

AIR TRANSPORT ASSOCIATION OF AMERICA
1301 Pennsylvania Avenue NW, Suite 1100, Washington DC 20004. 202/626-4000. World Wide Web address: http://www.air-transport.org. A trade association for the major U.S. airlines.

AMERICAN BUREAU OF SHIPPING
2 World Trade Center, 106th Floor, New York NY 10048. 212/839-5000. World Wide Web address: http://www.eagle.org.

AMERICAN SOCIETY OF TRAVEL AGENTS
1101 King Street, Suite 200, Alexandria VA 22314. 703/739-2782. World Wide Web address: http://www.astanet.com. For information, send a SASE with $.75 postage to the attention of the Fulfillment Department.

AMERICAN TRUCKING ASSOCIATION
2200 Mill Road, Alexandria VA 22314-4677. 703/838-1700. World Wide Web address: http://www.trucking.org. A national federation of the trucking industry representing all types of trucking companies. ATA is affiliated with 51 independent state trucking associations and 14 national conferences. The association also publishes *Transport Topics*, a weekly trade newspaper.

ASSOCIATION OF AMERICAN RAILROADS
50 F Street NW, Washington DC 20001. 202/639-2100. World Wide Web address: http://www.aar.com.

INSTITUTE OF TRANSPORTATION ENGINEERS
525 School Street SW, Suite 410, Washington DC 20024-2797. 202/554-8050. World Wide Web address: http://www.ite.org. Scientific and educational association, providing for professional development of members and others.

MARINE TECHNOLOGY SOCIETY
1828 L Street NW, Suite 906, Washington DC 20036. 202/775-5966.

NATIONAL MOTOR FREIGHT TRAFFIC ASSOCIATION
2200 Mill Road, Alexandria VA 22314-4654. 703/838-1810. World Wide Web address: http://www.truckline.com. Works towards the improvement and advancement of the interests and welfare of motor common carriers.

NATIONAL TANK TRUCK CARRIERS
2200 Mill Road, Alexandria VA 22314. 703/838-1700.

Books

FLIGHT PLAN TO THE FLIGHT DECK: STRATEGIES FOR A PILOT CAREER
Cage Consulting, Inc., P.O. Box 460327, Aurora CO 80046-0327. Toll-free phone: 888/899-CAGE. Fax: 303/799-1998. World Wide Web address: http://www.cageconsulting.com.

WELCOME ABOARD! YOUR CAREER AS A FLIGHT ATTENDANT
Cage Consulting, Inc., P.O. Box 460327, Aurora CO 80046-0327. Toll-free phone: 888/899-CAGE. Fax: 303/799-1998. World Wide Web address: http://www.cageconsulting.com.

Directories

MOODY'S TRANSPORTATION MANUAL
Moody's Investors Service, Inc., 99 Church Street, New York NY 10007. 212/553-0300. $12.95 per year with weekly updates.

NATIONAL TANK TRUCK CARRIER DIRECTORY
National Tank Truck Carriers, 2200 Mill Road, Alexandria VA 22314. 703/838-1700.

OFFICIAL MOTOR FREIGHT GUIDE
CNC Publishing, 1700 West Courtland Street, Chicago IL 60622. 773/278-2454.

Magazines

AMERICAN SHIPPER
Howard Publications, P.O. Box 4728, Jacksonville FL 32201. 904/355-2601. Monthly.

FLEET OWNER
Intertech Publishing, 707 Westchester Avenue, White Plains NY 10604-3102. 914/949-8500.

HEAVY DUTY TRUCKING
Newport Communications, P.O. Box W, Newport Beach CA 92658. 714/261-1636.

ITE JOURNAL
Institute of Transportation Engineers, 525 School Street SW, Suite 410, Washington DC 20024-2797. 202/554-8050. World Wide Web address: http://www.ite.org. One year subscription (12 issues): $50.00.

MARINE DIGEST AND TRANSPORTATION NEWS
Marine Publishing, Inc., P.O. Box 3905, Seattle WA 98124. 206/682-3607.

SHIPPING DIGEST
Geyer-McAllister Publications, 51 Madison Avenue, New York NY 10010. 212/689-4411.

TRAFFIC WORLD MAGAZINE
529 14th Street NW, Washington DC 20045-2200. 202/783-1101.

TRANSPORT TOPICS
National Tank Truck Carriers, 2200 Mill Road, Alexandria VA 22314. 703/838-1772. World Wide Web address: http://www.ttnews.com.

Newsletters

AIR JOBS DIGEST
World Air Data, Department 700, P.O. Box 42360, Washington DC 20015. World Wide Web address: http://www.tggh.net/wad. This monthly resource provides current job openings in aerospace, space, and aviation industries. Subscription rates: $96.00 annually, $69.00 for six months, and $49.00 for three months.

Online Services

THE AIRLINE EMPLOYMENT ASSISTANCE CORPS.
http://www.avjobs.com. Site for aviation jobseekers providing worldwide classified ads, resume assistance, publications, and over 350 links to aviation-related Websites and news groups. Certain resources are members-only access.

COOLWORKS
http://www.coolworks.com. This Website provides links to 22,000 job openings on cruise ships, at national parks, summer camps, ski areas, river areas, ranches, fishing areas, and resorts. This site also includes information on volunteer openings.

JOBNET: HOSPITALITY INDUSTRY
http://www.westga.edu/~coop/joblinks/subject/hospitality.html. Provides links to job openings and information for airlines and cruise ships.

1-800-DRIVERS
http://rwa.metronetworks.com/800drivers.html. Designed to help job hunters find employment as a driver. This site offers an online job application, job listings, and links to various trucking companies.

TRAVEL PROFESSIONALS FORUM
Go: Travpro. To join this CompuServe forum, you will need to send an e-mail to the sysop for permission.

UTILITIES: ELECTRIC/GAS/WATER

Deregulation has greatly increased competition throughout all segments of the utilities industry. For example, many states now permit independent power producers to build electric power generating plants. In an effort to lower prices and compete with the new entrants, many existing electric utilities have resorted to layoffs and other cost-cutting measures. Although the utilities industry as a whole is expected to continue to grow, the U.S. Department of Labor forecasted that job growth would be only 12 percent in the period from 1992 to 2005, a rate much slower than the average for all industries.

AMERICAN ELECTRIC POWER (AEP)
P.O. Box 60, Fort Wayne IN 46801. 219/425-2111. **Contact:** Personnel. **World Wide Web address:** http://www.aep.com. **Description:** An electric utility company. This location formerly operated under the name Indiana Michigan Power Company. **Common positions include:** Accountant/Auditor; Attorney; Automotive Mechanic; Buyer; Chemical Engineer; Civil Engineer; Computer Programmer; Customer Service Representative; Draftsperson; Editor; Electrical/ Electronics Engineer; Electrician; Human Resources Manager; Mechanical Engineer; Nuclear Engineer; Purchasing Agent/Manager; Real Estate Agent; Systems Analyst. **Educational backgrounds include:** Accounting; Engineering; Marketing. **Benefits:** 401(k); Dental Insurance; Disability Coverage; Employee Discounts; Life Insurance; Medical Insurance; Pension Plan; Savings Plan; Tuition Assistance. **Corporate headquarters location:** This Location. **Operations at this facility include:** Administration.

BLOOMINGTON CITY UTILITIES
1969 South Henderson Street, Bloomington IN 47401-6567. 812/339-1444. **Contact:** Human Resources. **Description:** A public utility that provides water and sewer services.

CITIZENS GAS & COKE UTILITY
2020 North Meridian Street, Indianapolis IN 46202. **Contact:** Human Resources. **Description:** A utility company that provides gas services to residents in Marion County. **NOTE:** This firm does not accept unsolicited resumes. Please only respond to advertised openings.

CITIZENS GAS & COKE UTILITY
2950 Prospect Street, Indianapolis IN 46203. 317/264-8707. **Contact:** Human Resources. **Description:** A utility company that provides gas services to its customers.

INDIANA ENERGY, INC.
1630 North Meridian Street, Indianapolis IN 46202-1496. 317/926-3351. **Contact:** Human Resources. **World Wide Web address:** http://www.indiana-energy.com. **Description:** A holding company involved with natural gas and electric power. **Subsidiaries include:** Indiana Gas Company, Inc., a public utility which distributes natural gas to 477,000 customers in Indiana; IEI Services, LLC, an administrative unit; and IEI Investments, Inc., manager of a portfolio of industry-related investments which support Indiana Energy, Inc. In September 1998, Reliant Services, a cooperative venture between Cinergy Corp. and Indiana Energy, Inc., reportedly became involved in the underground facilities market through the purchase of two area companies.

INDIANAPOLIS POWER & LIGHT COMPANY
2102 North Illinois Street, Indianapolis IN 46202-1330. 317/261-8222. **Recorded jobline:** 800/735-8515. **Contact:** Human Resources. **Description:** A utility company. **NOTE:** Please call the jobline for current openings and application procedures.

INDIANAPOLIS WATER COMPANY (IWC)
1220 Waterway Boulevard, Indianapolis IN 46202. 317/639-1501. **Contact:** Human Resources. **Description:** A holding company with subsidiaries that own and operate waterworks systems, which supply water for residential, commercial, and industrial use.

NORTHEAST INDIANA WATER CO.
650 Madison Street, P.O. Box M-486, Gary IN 46401. 219/886-3770. **Contact:** Human Resources. **Description:** A water company.

NORTHERN INDIANA PUBLIC SERVICE COMPANY (NIPSCO)
5265 Hohman Avenue, Hammond IN 46320. 219/853-5200. **Contact:** Robert Frankowiak, Human Resources Executive. **World Wide Web address:** http://www.nipsco.com. **Description:** Northern Indiana Public Service Company (NIPSCO) is a gas and electric public utility company. NIPSCO provides energy to the northern third of Indiana. **Common positions include:** Accountant/Auditor; Administrator; Advertising Clerk; Biological Scientist; Blue-Collar Worker Supervisor; Buyer; Chemical Engineer; Chemist; Claim Representative; Computer Programmer; Department Manager; Economist; Editor; Electrical/Electronics Engineer; Financial Analyst; Forester/Conservation Scientist; General Manager; Human Resources Manager; Industrial Engineer; Management Trainee; Marketing Specialist; Mechanical Engineer; Operations/Production Manager; Public Relations Specialist; Purchasing Agent/Manager; Reporter; Services Sales Representative; Statistician; Systems Analyst. **Educational backgrounds include:** Accounting; Biology; Business Administration; Chemistry; Computer Science; Economics; Engineering; Finance; Liberal Arts; Marketing; Mathematics. **Benefits:** Dental Insurance; Life Insurance; Medical Insurance; Pension Plan; Savings Plan; Tuition Assistance. **Corporate headquarters location:** This Location. **Parent company:** NIPSCO Industries. **Operations at this facility include:** Administration; Regional Headquarters; Sales; Service. **Listed on:** New York Stock Exchange. **Number of employees at this location:** 800. **Number of employees nationwide:** 4,300.

PSI ENERGY, INC.
1000 East Main Street, Plainfield IN 46168. **Contact:** Human Resources. **Description:** An electric utility. **NOTE:** This firm does not accept unsolicited resumes. Please only respond to advertised openings. **Parent company:** Synergy.

SOUTHERN INDIANA GAS AND ELECTRIC COMPANY (SIGECO)
P.O. Box 569, Evansville IN 47741. 812/465-5300. **Contact:** Rodney C. Penfield, Director of Human Resources. **World Wide Web address:** http://www.sigcorpinc.com. **Description:** Generates and distributes electricity to over 120,000 customers and purchases, transports, and distributes natural gas to over 104,000 customers. The service area covers 10 counties in southwestern Indiana. SIGECO also sells power to municipalities and to other companies and public utilities. **Parent company:** SIGCORP.

Note: Because addresses and telephone numbers of smaller companies can change rapidly, we recommend you call each company to verify the information below before inquiring about job opportunities. Mass mailings are not recommended.

Additional small employers:

COMBINATION UTILITY SERVICES

Logansport Municipal Utilities
601 E Broadway, Suite 101, Logansport IN 46947-3156. 219/753-6231.

Northern Indiana Public Service Company
801 E 86th Ave, Gary IN 46410-6271. 219/647-4750.

ELECTRIC SERVICES

American Electric Power
2791 Highway 231 North, Rockport IN 47635. 812/649-9171.

Clifty Creek Station
PO Box 97, Madison IN 47250-0097. 812/265-8700.

Dean H. Mitchell Station
PO Box H720, Gary IN 46401. 219/977-5023.

Gallagher Generating Station
PO Box 409, New Albany IN 47151-0409. 812/944-8471.

Hoosier Energy Rural Electric Co-op
PO Box 908, Bloomington IN 47402-0908. 812/876-2021.

HT Pritchard Generating Station
4040 Blue Bluff Road, Martinsville IN 46151-7887. 765/342-3163.

I&M Electric
400 N High Street, Muncie IN 47305-1643. 765/288-7701.

Peru Utilities
PO Box 67, Peru IN 46970-0067. 765/473-6681.

PSI Energy Inc.
PO Box 25, Jeffersonville IN 47131-0025. 812/282-0342.

PSI Energy Inc.
PO Box 960, Terre Haute IN 47808-0960. 812/234-3726.

PSI Energy Inc.
PO Box 3039, Kokomo IN 46904-3039. 765/454-6171.

Richmond Light & Power
PO Box 908, Richmond IN 47375-0908. 765/973-7200.

Wabash River Generating Station
450 Bolton Road, West Terre Haute IN 47885-9563. 812/535-3156.

GAS AND/OR WATER SUPPLY

Public Works & Utilities
1201 N Nappanee Street, Elkhart IN 46514-1733. 219/293-2572.

GAS UTILITY SERVICES

Northern Indiana Public Service Company
PO Box 77, Goshen IN 46527. 219/535-0218.

Northern Indiana Public Service Company
300 East Main Street, Fort Wayne IN 46802-1908. 219/460-2300.

For more information on career opportunities in the utilities industry:

Associations

AMERICAN PUBLIC GAS ASSOCIATION
11094-D Lee Highway, Suite 102, Fairfax VA 22030. 703/352-3890. World Wide Web address: http://www.apga.org. Publishes a weekly newsletter.

AMERICAN PUBLIC POWER ASSOCIATION (APPA)
2301 M Street NW, Suite 300, Washington DC 20037. 202/467-2900. World Wide Web address: http://www.appanet.org. Represents publicly-owned utilities. Provides many services including government relations, educational programs, and industry-related information publications.

AMERICAN WATER WORKS ASSOCIATION
6666 West Quincy Avenue, Denver CO 80235. 303/794-7711.

NATIONAL RURAL ELECTRIC COOPERATIVE ASSOCIATION
4301 Wilson Boulevard, Arlington VA 22203. 703/907-5500. World Wide Web address: http://www.nreca.org.

Directories

MOODY'S PUBLIC UTILITY MANUAL
Moody's Investors Service, Inc., 99 Church Street, New York NY 10007. 212/553-0300. World Wide Web address: http://www.moodys.com. Annually available at libraries.

Magazines

PUBLIC POWER
American Public Power Association, 2301 M Street NW, Washington DC 20037. 202/467-2900.

MISCELLANEOUS WHOLESALING

According to the U.S. Department of Commerce, the need to cut costs is increasing as wholesaling and distributing businesses become more global and competitive, leading to changes in manufacturer-distributor working relationships. The most significant of these is an improved efficiency in inventory management, whereby the distributor manages inventory at the customer's site.

Wholesaling has evolved into an industry driven by customer needs, and while companies now prefer to do business with fewer suppliers, they still expect quality services. Smaller wholesaling companies, therefore, are concentrating on offering specialized services that address customers' specific needs.

H.W.I.
P.O. Box 868, Fort Wayne IN 46801-0868. 219/748-5300. **Fax:** 219/748-5608. **Contact:** Dan Federspiel, Human Resources Manager. **E-mail address:** hwicorp@aol.com. **Description:** A cooperative wholesale supplier of hardware, lumber, and building materials. **Common positions include:** Advertising Clerk; Blue-Collar Worker Supervisor; Buyer; Clerical Supervisor; Computer Programmer; Customer Service Representative; Manufacturer's/Wholesaler's Sales Rep.; MIS Specialist; Services Sales Representative. **Educational backgrounds include:** Business Administration; Computer Science; Liberal Arts; Marketing. **Benefits:** Dental Insurance; Disability Coverage; Employee Discounts; Life Insurance; Medical Insurance; Pension Plan; Profit Sharing; Tuition Assistance. **Corporate headquarters location:** This Location. **Other U.S. locations:** Nationwide. **Operations at this facility include:** Administration; Sales; Service. **Annual sales/revenues:** More than $100 million. **Number of employees at this location:** 460. **Number of employees nationwide:** 1,060.

LASALLE-BRISTOL COMPANY, INC.
P.O. Box 98, Elkhart IN 46515. 219/295-4400. **Physical address:** 601 County Road 17, Elkhart IN 46516. **Contact:** Human Resources. **Description:** A wholesaler of furniture, lighting, flooring, and plumbing supplies.

LEISURE DISTRIBUTORS INC.
4220 East Morgan Avenue, Evansville IN 47715. 812/473-9684. **Contact:** Human Resources. **Description:** Distributes patio and fireplace equipment including gas grills, fireplaces, gas logs, and similar products.

For more information on career opportunities in the wholesaling industry:

<u>Associations</u>

NATIONAL ASSOCIATION OF WHOLESALERS (NAW)
1725 K Street NW, Washington DC 20006. 202/872-0885. Offers publications on industry trends and how to operate a wholesaling business.

EMPLOYMENT SERVICES

Many people turn to temporary agencies, permanent employment agencies, or executive recruiters to assist them in their respective job searches. At their best, these resources can be a valuable friend -- it's comforting to know that someone is putting his or her wealth of experience and contacts to work for you. At their worst, however, they are more of a friend to the employer, or to more experienced recruits, than to you personally, and it is best not to rely on them exclusively.

That said, there are several types of employment services for jobseekers to check out as part of their job search efforts:

TEMPORARY EMPLOYMENT AGENCIES

Temporary or “temp” agencies can be a viable option. Often these agencies specialize in clerical and support work, but it’s becoming increasingly common to find temporary assignments in other areas like accounting or computer programming. Working on temporary assignments will provide you with additional income during your job search and will add experience to your resume. It may also provide valuable business contacts or lead to permanent job opportunities.

Temporary agencies are listed in your local telephone directory and in *The JobBank Guide to Employment Services* (Adams Media Corporation), found in your local public library. Send a resume and cover letter to the agency, and call to schedule an interview. Be prepared to take a number of tests at the interview.

PERMANENT EMPLOYMENT AGENCIES

Permanent employment agencies are commissioned by employers to find qualified candidates for job openings. The catch is that their main responsibility is to meet the employer's needs -- not necessarily to find a suitable job for the candidate.

This is not to say that permanent employment agencies should be ruled out altogether. There are permanent employment agencies specializing in specific industries that can be useful for experienced professionals. However, permanent employment agencies are not always a good choice for entry-level jobseekers. Some will try to steer inexperienced candidates in an unwanted direction or offer little more than clerical placements to experienced applicants. Others charge a fee for their services -- a condition that jobseekers should always ask about up front.

Some permanent employment agencies dispute the criticisms mentioned above. As one recruiter puts it, "Our responsibilities are to the applicant and the employer equally, because without one, we'll lose the other." She also maintains that entry-level people are desirable, saying that "as they grow, we grow, too, so we aim to move them up the ranks."

In short, as that recruiter states, "All services are not the same." If you decide to register with an agency, your best bet is to find one that is recommended by a friend or associate. Barring that, names of agencies across the country can be found in *The Adams Executive Recruiters Almanac* (Adams Media Corporation) or *The JobBank Guide to Employment Services* (Adams Media Corporation). Or you can contact:

National Association of Personnel Services (NAPS)
3133 Mount Vernon Avenue
Alexandria VA 22305
703/684-0180

Be aware that there are an increasing number of bogus employment service firms, often advertising in newspapers and magazines. These "services" promise even inexperienced jobseekers top salaries in exciting careers -- all for a sizable fee. Others use expensive 900 numbers that jobseekers are encouraged to call. Unfortunately, most people find out too late that the jobs they have been promised do not exist.

As a general rule, most legitimate permanent employment agencies will never guarantee a job and will not seek payment until after the candidate has been placed. Even so, every agency you are interested in should be checked out with the local chapter of the Better Business Bureau (BBB). Find out if the agency is licensed and has been in business for a reasonable amount of time.

If everything checks out, call the firm to find out if it specializes in your area of expertise and how it will go about marketing your qualifications. After you have selected a few agencies (three to five is best), send each one a resume with a cover letter. Make a follow-up phone call a week or two later, and try to schedule an interview. Once again, be prepared to take a battery of tests at the interview.

Above all, do not expect too much. Only a small portion of all professional, managerial, and executive jobs are listed with these agencies. Use them as an addition to your job search campaign, not a centerpiece.

EXECUTIVE SEARCH FIRMS

Also known as "headhunters," these firms consist of recruiters who are paid by client companies that hire them to fill a specific position. Executive search firms seek out and carefully screen (and weed out) candidates for high-salaried technical, executive, and managerial positions and are paid by the employer. The prospective employee is generally not charged a fee. Unlike permanent employment agencies, they often approach viable candidates directly, rather than waiting for candidates to approach them. Some prefer to deal with already employed candidates. Whether you are employed or not, do not contact an executive search firm if you aren't ready to look for a job. If a recruiter tries to place you right away and finds out you are not really looking yet, it is unlikely they will spend much time with you in the future.

Many search firms specialize in particular industries, while generalist firms typically provide placements in a wide range of industries. Look for firms that specialize in your field of interest or expertise, as well as generalist firms that conduct searches in a variety of fields. While you should concentrate on firms in your geographic area, you do not have to limit yourself to these as many firms operate nationally or internationally.

There are two basic types of executive search firms -- retainer-based and contingency-based. Note, however, that some firms conduct searches of both types. Essentially, retainer firms are hired by a client company for a search and paid a fee by the client company regardless of whether or not a placement is made. Conversely, contingency firms receive payment from the client company only when their candidate is hired. Fees are typically based on the position's first-year salary. The range is usually between 20 and 35 percent, and retainer firm fees tend to be at the higher end of that scale, according to Ivan Samuels, President of Abbott's of Boston, an executive search firm that conducts both types of searches.

Generally, companies use retainer firms to fill senior-level positions, with salaries over $60,000. In most cases, a company will hire only one retainer firm to fill a given position, and part of the process is a thorough, on-site visit by the search firm to the client company so that the recruiter may check out the operation. These search firms are recommended for a highly experienced professional seeking a job in his or her current field. Confidentiality is more secure with these firms, since a recruiter may only use your file in consideration for one job at a time, and most retainer firms will not freely circulate your resume without permission. This is particularly important to a jobseeker who is currently employed and insists on absolute discretion. If that's the case, however, make sure you do not contact a retainer firm used by your current employer.

Contingency firms make placements that cover a broader salary range, so these firms are more ideal for someone seeking a junior or mid-level position. Unlike retainer firms, contingency firms may be competing with other firms to fill a particular opening. As a result, these firms can be quicker and more responsive to your job search. In addition, a contingency firm will distribute your resume more widely. Some firms require your permission before sending your resume to any given company, while others ask that you trust their discretion. You should inquire about this with your recruiter at the outset, and choose according to your needs.

That said, once you've chosen the specific recruiter or recruiters that you will contact, keep in mind that recruiters are working for the companies that hire them, not for you, the jobseeker. Attempting to fill a position -- especially amongst fierce competition with other firms -- means your best interests may not be the recruiter's only priority. For this reason, you should contact as many search firms as possible in order to increase your chances of finding your ideal position.

A phone call is your first step, during which you should speak with a recruiter and exchange all relevant information. Ask lots of questions to determine the firm's credibility, whether they operate on a retainer or contingency basis (or both), and any and all questions you have regarding the firm's procedures. Offer the recruiter information about your employment history, as well as what type of work you are seeking. Make sure you sound enthusiastic, but not pushy. The recruiter will ask that you send a resume and cover letter as soon as possible.

Occasionally, the recruiter will arrange to meet with you, but most often this will not occur until he or she has received your resume and has found a potential match. James E. Slate, President of F-O-R-T-U-N-E Personnel Consultants in Topsfield, Massachusetts, advises that you generally not expect an abundance of personal attention at the beginning of the relationship with your recruiter, particularly with a large firm that works nationally and does most of its work over the phone. You should, however, use your recruiter's inside knowledge to your best advantage. Some recruiters will help coach you before an interview and many are open about giving you all the facts they know about a client company.

Not all executive search firms are licensed, so make sure those you plan to deal with have solid reputations and don't hesitate to check with the Better Business Bureau. Also keep in mind that it is common for recruiters to search for positions in other states. For example, recruiters in Boston sometimes look for candidates to fill positions in New York City, and the reverse is true as well. Names of search firms nationwide can be found in *The Adams Executive Recruiters Almanac* or *The JobBank Guide to Employment Services*, or by contacting:

American Management Association (AMA)/Management Services Department
135 West 50th Street, New York NY 10020. 212/586-8100.

Association of Executive Search Consultants (AESC)
500 Fifth Avenue, Suite 930, New York NY 10110. 212/398-9556.

Top Echelon, Inc.
World Wide Web address: http://www.topechelon.com.
A cooperative placement networking service of recruiting firms.

CONTRACT SERVICES FIRMS

Firms that place individuals on a contract basis commonly receive job orders from client companies that can last anywhere from a month to over a year. The function of these firms differs from that of a temporary agency in that the candidate has specific, marketable skills they wish to put to work, and the contract recruiter interviews the candidate extensively. Most often, contract services firms specialize in placing technical professionals, though some do specialize in other fields, including clerical and office support. The use of these firms is increasing in popularity, as jobseekers with technical skills recognize the benefit of utilizing and demonstrating their talents at a sampling of different companies, and establishing contacts along the way that could lead to a permanent position, if desired. Most contract services firms do not charge a fee to the candidate.

RESUME/CAREER COUNSELING/OUTPLACEMENT SERVICES

These firms are very diverse in the services they provide. Many nonprofit organizations -- colleges, universities, private associations -- offer free or very inexpensive counseling services. For-profit career/outplacement counseling services, on the other hand, can charge a broad range of fees, depending on what services they provide. Services offered include career counseling, outplacement, resume development/writing, interview preparation, assessment testing, and various workshops. Upon contacting one of these firms, you should ask about the specific services that firm provides. Some firms provide career counseling only, teaching you how to conduct your own job search, while others also provide outplacement services. The difference here is that those which provide outplacement will conduct a job search for you, in addition to the counseling services. Firms like these are sometimes referred to as "marketing firms."

According to a representative at Career Ventures Counseling Services in Salem, Massachusetts, fees for career counseling average about $85 per hour. Counseling firms located in major cities tend to be more expensive. Furthermore, outplacement fees can range from $170 to over $7,000! As results are not guaranteed, you may want to check on a firm's reputation through the local Better Business Bureau.
For more information on resume services, contact:

Professional Association of Resume Writers
3637 Fourth Street, Suite 330, St. Petersburg FL 33704.
Attention: Mr. Frank Fox, Executive Director.

Note: On the following pages, you will find employment services for this JobBank book's coverage area. Because contact names and addresses can change regularly, we recommend that you call each company to verify the information before inquiring about opportunities.

TEMPORARY EMPLOYMENT AGENCIES

ACCUSTAFF
7863 Broadway, Suite 112, Merrillville IN 46410. 219/769-3448. **Fax:** 219/756-0618. **Contact:** Georgina Segan, Manager. **Description:** A temporary agency. **Positions commonly filled include:** Accountant/Auditor; Bookkeeper; Clerk; Computer Operator; Computer Programmer; Customer Service Representative; Data Entry Clerk; Driver; Factory Worker; Legal Secretary; Light Industrial Worker; Medical Secretary; Purchasing Agent/Manager; Receptionist; Secretary; Statistician; Stenographer; Typist/Word Processor.

ACCUSTAFF
600 North Alabama Street, Suite 600A, Indianapolis IN 46204. 317/488-8367. **Fax:** 317/488-8403. **Contact:** Steve Frankovitz, Owner. **Description:** A temporary agency. **Specializes in the areas of:** Food; Industrial; Manufacturing; Publishing; Sales; Secretarial; Technical. **Positions commonly filled include:** Customer Service Representative; Typist/Word Processor.

ACCUSTAFF
711 East Highway 131, Clarksville IN 47129. 812/283-0915. **Fax:** 812/283-3412. **Contact:** Manager. **Description:** A temporary and temp-to-perm agency. **Specializes in the areas of:** Clerical; Industrial.

ACTION TEMPORARY SERVICE
1482 Executive Boulevard, Suite B, Jasper IN 47546. 812/482-7730. **Fax:** 812/482-1927. **Contact:** Manager. **Description:** A temporary agency. **Specializes in the areas of:** Industrial.

ACTION TEMPORARY SERVICE
P.O. Box 15398, Evansville IN 47716-0398. 812/479-8373. **Fax:** 812/473-1006. **Contact:** Manager. **Description:** A temporary agency. **Specializes in the areas of:** Industrial. **Positions commonly filled include:** Factory Worker; Warehouse/Distribution Worker.

ADECCO
1417 Coliseum Boulevard, Fort Wayne IN 46808. 219/482-2390. **Fax:** 219/482-1589. **Contact:** Branch Manager. **Description:** A temporary agency that also offers some temp-to-perm, long-term contract, and permanent placements. **Specializes in the areas of:** Clerical.

ADECCO
3500 West DePauw Boulevard, Suite 2041, Indianapolis IN 46268. 317/872-8091. **Fax:** 317/879-2388. **Contact:** Branch Manager. **Description:** A temporary agency that also offers some temp-to-perm placements. **Specializes in the areas of:** Administration; Secretarial; Word Processing.

CORPORATE STAFFING RESOURCES (CSR)
820 North Baldwin Avenue, Marion IN 46952. **Contact:** Debbie Weaver, Branch Manager. **World Wide Web address:** http://www.csronline.com. **Description:** A short- and long-term temporary placement firm. Founded in 1985. **Specializes in the areas of:** Personnel/Labor Relations. **Positions commonly filled include:** Blue-Collar Worker Supervisor; Branch Manager; Clerical Supervisor; Computer Programmer; Credit Manager; Customer Service Representative; Draftsperson; Financial Analyst; General Manager; Human Resources Manager; Human Service Worker; Industrial Engineer; Industrial Production Manager; Insurance Agent/Broker; Operations/Production Manager; Quality Control Supervisor; Securities Sales Representative; Systems Analyst; Typist/Word Processor; Underwriter/Assistant Underwriter. **Corporate headquarters location:** South Bend IN. **Average salary range of placements:** Less than $20,000. **Number of placements per year:** 200 - 499.

CORPORATE STAFFING RESOURCES (CSR)
100 East Wayne Street, Suite 100, South Bend IN 46601. 219/233-8209. **Fax:** 219/280-2653. **Contact:** Manager. **World Wide Web address:** http://www.csronline.com. **Description:** A temporary agency that also provides some contract technical placements. Founded in 1987. **Specializes in the areas of:** Accounting/Auditing; Administration; Computer Science/Software; Engineering; Industrial; Manufacturing; Technical. **Positions commonly filled include:** Accountant/Auditor; Administrative Manager; Architect; Biological Scientist; Buyer; Chemical Engineer; Chemist; Civil Engineer; Computer Programmer; Cost Estimator; Credit Manager; Customer Service Representative; Design Engineer; Designer; Draftsperson; Electrical/Electronics Engineer; Electrician; Environmental Engineer; Financial Analyst; Human Resources Manager; Industrial Engineer; Industrial Production Manager; Laboratory Technician; Mechanical Engineer; Metallurgical Engineer; MIS Specialist; Operations/Production Manager; Purchasing Agent/Manager; Quality Control Supervisor; Software Engineer; Structural Engineer; Systems Analyst; Technical Writer/Editor. **Corporate headquarters location:** This Location. **Other U.S. locations:** IN; MI; MO; OH. **Number of placements per year:** 1000+.

CORPORATE STAFFING RESOURCES (CSR)
3552 Commerce Drive, Warsaw IN 46580. 219/269-2149. **Fax:** 219/269-3465. **Recorded jobline:** 219/237-9675. **Contact:** Mary Joyner, Branch Manager. **World Wide Web address:** http://www.csronline.com. **Description:** A temporary agency that also provides some career/outplacement counseling. **Specializes in the areas of:** Administration; Computer Science/Software; Engineering; General Management; Industrial; Manufacturing; Sales; Technical. **Positions commonly filled include:** Agricultural Engineer; Biomedical Engineer; Blue-Collar Worker Supervisor; Buyer; Chemical Engineer; Chemist; Civil Engineer; Claim Representative; Clerical Supervisor; Computer Programmer; Customer Service Representative; Design Engineer; Draftsperson; Editor; Electrical/Electronics Engineer; Environmental Engineer; Financial Analyst; General Manager; Industrial Engineer; Industrial Production Manager; Mechanical Engineer; Metallurgical Engineer; Operations/Production Manager; Purchasing Agent/Manager; Quality Control Supervisor; Services Sales Representative; Software Engineer; Stationary Engineer; Systems Analyst; Technical Writer/Editor; Typist/Word Processor. **Corporate headquarters location:** South Bend IN. **Average salary range of placements:** Less than $20,000. **Number of placements per year:** 1000+.

CORPORATE STAFFING RESOURCES (CSR)
8656 Purdue Road, Indianapolis IN 46268. 317/228-1188. **Fax:** 317/228-4178. **Contact:** Manager. **World Wide Web address:** http://www.csronline.com. **Description:** A temporary agency. **Specializes in the areas of:** Clerical; Light Industrial. **Corporate headquarters location:** South Bend IN.

CORPORATE STAFFING RESOURCES (CSR)
310 North Michigan Street, Suite 100, Plymouth IN 46563. 219/935-0091. **Fax:** 219/935-0067. **Contact:** Manager. **World Wide Web address:** http://www.csronline.com. **Description:** A temp-to-perm employment agency. **Specializes in the areas of:** Industrial; Office Support. **Corporate headquarters location:** South Bend IN.

CROWN TEMPORARY SERVICES OF INDIANAPOLIS
4503C West 16th Street, Brickyard Plaza, Indianapolis IN 46222. 317/243-1999. **Fax:** 317/243-9130. **Contact:** Manager. **Description:** A temporary agency. **Specializes in the areas of:** Accounting/Auditing; Banking; Clerical; Engineering; Finance; Insurance; Legal; Manufacturing; Personnel/Labor Relations. **Positions commonly filled include:** Accountant/Auditor; Administrative Assistant; Advertising Clerk; Bookkeeper; Claim Representative; Clerk; Computer Operator; Computer Programmer; Construction Trade Worker; Customer Service Representative; Data Entry Clerk; Driver; Factory Worker; Legal Secretary; Light Industrial Worker; Marketing Specialist; Medical Secretary; Receptionist; Sales Representative; Secretary; Typist/Word Processor. **Number of placements per year:** 1000+.

DAVIS STAFFING
8039 Euclid Avenue, Munster IN 46321. 219/836-8966. **Fax:** 219/836-8968. **Contact:** Manager. **Description:** A temporary agency.

DUNHILL STAFFING SYSTEMS
5420 Southern Avenue, Suite 103, Indianapolis IN 46241. 317/247-1775. **Fax:** 317/241-4029. **Contact:** Manager. **Description:** A temporary agency that also provides some permanent placements. **Specializes in the areas of:** Clerical; Computer Science/Software; Light Industrial; Manufacturing; Secretarial; Technical. **Positions commonly filled include:** Blue-Collar Worker Supervisor; Branch Manager; Claim Representative; Clerical Supervisor; Computer Programmer; Customer Service Representative; Mechanical Engineer; Medical Records Technician; Systems Analyst. **Number of placements per year:** 1000+.

EMPLOYMENT PLUS
4629 East Morningside Drive, Bloomington IN 47408. 812/333-1070. **Fax:** 812/331-8017. **Contact:** Manager. **Description:** A temporary agency that also provides some temp-to-perm and permanent placements. **Specializes in the areas of:** Clerical; Light Industrial; Technical.

EXPRESS PERSONNEL
332 West U.S. Highway 30, Valparaiso IN 46385. 219/465-1868. **Fax:** 219/477-5915. **Contact:** Manager. **Description:** A temporary agency. **Specializes in the areas of:** Accounting/Auditing; Clerical; Finance; Industrial.

FLEXIBLE PERSONNEL
STAFFMARK MEDICAL STAFFING
1010 West Coliseum Boulevard, Suite E, Fort Wayne IN 46808. 219/482-3532. **Fax:** 219/471-1728. **Contact:** Manager. **Description:** A temporary agency that also offers temp-to-perm and permanent placements. **Specializes in the areas of:** Clerical; Health/Medical; Industrial.

INTERIM PERSONNEL
6089 Stoney Creek Drive, Fort Wayne IN 46825. 219/483-9590. **Fax:** 218/489-7889. **Contact:** Manager. **World Wide Web address:** http://www.interim.com. **Description:** A temporary agency. **Specializes in the areas of:** Industrial. **Corporate headquarters location:** Fort Lauderdale FL. **Other U.S. locations:** Nationwide.

INTERIM PERSONNEL
52 South Girls School Road, Indianapolis IN 46231. 317/273-4444. **Fax:** 317/273-4440. **Contact:** Manager. **Description:** A temporary agency. **Specializes in the areas of:** Administration; Industrial; Office Support; Word Processing. **Corporate headquarters location:** Fort Lauderdale FL.

KELLY SERVICES, INC.
3413 North Briarwood Lane, Muncie IN 47304-5210. 765/284-0897. **Fax:** 765/284-0655. **Contact:** Supervisor. **Description:** A temporary agency. **Specializes in the areas of:** Secretarial; Technical. **Positions commonly filled include:** Customer Service Representative; Typist/Word Processor. **Corporate headquarters location:** Troy MI. **International locations:** Worldwide.

MAC STAFFING
3500 DePauw Boulevard, Suite 1076, Indianapolis IN 46268. 317/872-5153. **Fax:** 317/876-7029. **Contact:** Ken Wetzel, President. **Description:** A temporary agency. **Specializes in the areas of:** Administration; Advertising; Art/Design; Computer Science/Software; Publishing. **Positions commonly filled include:** Designer; Draftsperson; Editor; Multimedia Designer; Technical Writer/Editor; Typist/Word Processor; Video Production Coordinator. **Number of placements per year:** 200 - 499.

MANPOWER TECHNICAL SERVICES
200 North Meridian Street, Suite 900, Indianapolis IN 46204. 317/262-2020. **Toll-free phone:** 800/366-0557. **Fax:** 317/262-2451. **Contact:** Connie Whisner, Technical Services Manager. **Description:** A temporary agency. **Specializes in the areas of:** Computer Science/Software; Engineering; Technical. **Positions commonly filled include:** Chemical Engineer; Civil Engineer; Computer Programmer; Design Engineer; Electrical/Electronics Engineer; Industrial Engineer; Mechanical Engineer; Metallurgical Engineer; MIS Specialist; Quality Control Supervisor;

Software Engineer; Structural Engineer; Systems Analyst. **Corporate headquarters location:** Milwaukee WI. **Average salary range of placements:** $30,000 - $50,000. **Number of placements per year:** 200 - 499.

NORRELL STAFFING SERVICES
201 South Emerson Avenue, Suite 140, Greenwood IN 46143. 317/885-9599. **Fax:** 317/885-9899. **Contact:** Manager. **Description:** A temporary agency. **Specializes in the areas of:** Industrial; Manufacturing; Personnel/Labor Relations; Secretarial. **Positions commonly filled include:** Accountant/Auditor; Administrative Manager; Advertising Clerk; Blue-Collar Worker Supervisor; Claim Representative; Clerical Supervisor; Clinical Lab Technician; Customer Service Representative; Human Resources Specialist; Librarian; Manufacturer's/Wholesaler's Sales Rep.; Purchasing Agent/Manager; Systems Analyst; Typist/Word Processor. **Corporate headquarters location:** Atlanta GA. **Other U.S. locations:** Nationwide. **Average salary range of placements:** Less than $20,000. **Number of placements per year:** 1000+.

NORRELL STAFFING SERVICES OF EVANSVILLE
500 North Congress Avenue, Evansville IN 47715. 812/473-3838. **Fax:** 813/473-3939. **Contact:** Manager. **Description:** A temporary agency. **Specializes in the areas of:** Clerical; Manufacturing. **Positions commonly filled include:** Bookkeeper; Clerk; Computer Operator; Draftsperson; Factory Worker; Legal Secretary; Light Industrial Worker; Medical Secretary; Receptionist; Secretary; Stenographer; Typist/Word Processor. **Corporate headquarters location:** Atlanta GA. **Other U.S. locations:** Nationwide.

OLSTEN STAFFING SERVICES
3005 25th Street, Columbus IN 47203. 812/372-2722. **Toll-free phone:** 800/789-1100. **Fax:** 812/372-2999. **Contact:** Tammy Finley, Branch Manager. **Description:** A temporary agency. **Specializes in the areas of:** Accounting/Auditing; Industrial; Legal; Manufacturing; Personnel/Labor Relations; Secretarial. **Positions commonly filled include:** Accountant/Auditor; Administrative Manager; Advertising Clerk; Blue-Collar Worker Supervisor; Clerical Supervisor; Computer Programmer; Customer Service Representative; Industrial Production Manager; Paralegal; Quality Control Supervisor; Restaurant/Food Service Manager; Systems Analyst; Typist/Word Processor. **Corporate headquarters location:** Melville NY. **Average salary range of placements:** Less than $20,000. **Number of placements per year:** 1000+.

PERSONNEL MANAGEMENT, INC. (PMI)
P.O. Box 322, Jeffersonville IN 47131. 812/284-3223. **Fax:** 812/285-6506. **Contact:** Manager. **Description:** A temporary agency. **Specializes in the areas of:** Industrial; Light Industrial; Retail; Secretarial. **Positions commonly filled include:** Account Representative; Administrative Assistant; Blue-Collar Worker Supervisor; Customer Service Representative; Secretary. **Benefits available to temporary workers:** 401(k); Life Insurance; Medical Insurance; Paid Holidays; Paid Vacation. **Corporate headquarters location:** 1499 Windhorst Way, Greenwood IN. **Other U.S. locations:** FL; GA; KY. **Average salary range of placements:** Less than $20,000. **Number of placements per year:** 1000+.

PERSONNEL MANAGEMENT, INC. (PMI)
1499 Windhorst Way, Suite 100, Greenwood IN 46143. 317/888-4400. **Fax:** 317/885-3755. **Contact:** Manager. **Description:** A temporary agency. **Corporate headquarters location:** This Location.

STAR STAFFING
332 Third Avenue, Suite 5, Jasper IN 47546. 812/482-6836. **Toll-free phone:** 800/551-6823. **Fax:** 812/482-2490. **Contact:** Manager. **Description:** Star Staffing is a temporary agency. Founded in 1961. **Specializes in the areas of:** Industrial; Manufacturing; Secretarial. **Positions commonly filled include:** Clerical Supervisor; Computer Programmer; Customer Service Representative; Management Trainee; MIS Specialist; Services Sales Representative; Software Engineer; Typist/Word Processor. **Benefits available to temporary workers:** Medical Insurance; Paid Holidays; Paid Vacation. **Corporate headquarters location:** South Bend IN. **Average salary range of placements:** Less than $20,000. **Number of placements per year:** 1000+.

TRC STAFFING SERVICES
8720 Castle Creek Parkway, Suite 112, Indianapolis IN 46250. 317/842-7779. **Fax:** 317/849-3166. **Contact:** Jennifer Barlow, Assistant Operations Manager. **Description:** A temporary agency. **Specializes in the areas of:** Computer Science/Software; Industrial; Secretarial; Technical. **Positions commonly filled include:** Administrative Assistant; Computer Operator; Customer Service Representative; MIS Specialist; Secretary; Software Engineer; Systems Analyst; Typist/Word Processor. **Benefits available to temporary workers:** 401(k); Paid Holidays; Paid Vacation; Referral Bonus Plan. **Corporate headquarters location:** Atlanta GA. **Other U.S. locations:** Nationwide. **Number of placements per year:** 200 - 499.

TOUSSAINT & COMPANY
9200 Keystone Crossing, Suite 250, Indianapolis IN 46240. 317/844-0900. **Fax:** 317/573-5074. **Contact:** Manager. **Description:** A temporary agency that also provides temp-to-perm and some permanent placements.

TRY TEMPS INC.
P.O. Box 339, Chandler IN 47610. 812/925-3903. **Fax:** 812/925-3920. **Contact:** Manager. **Description:** A temporary employment agency that also provides some permanent placements. **Specializes in the areas of:** Engineering; Industrial; Technical. **Positions commonly filled include:** Applications Engineer; Architect; Biomedical Engineer; Buyer; Chemical Engineer; Chemist; Chief Financial Officer; Civil Engineer; Computer Operator; Computer Programmer; Controller; Design Engineer; Draftsperson; Electrical/Electronics Engineer; Food Scientist/Technologist; General Manager; Graphic Designer; Human Resources Manager; Industrial Engineer; Industrial Production Manager; Management Analyst/Consultant; Manufacturing Engineer; Marketing Manager; Mechanical Engineer; Metallurgical Engineer; MIS Specialist; Operations Manager; Physical Therapist; Physician; Product Manager; Project Manager; Public Relations Specialist; Purchasing Agent/Manager; Quality Control Supervisor; Sales Manager; Secretary; Software Engineer; Systems Analyst; Technical Writer/Editor. **Benefits available to temporary workers:** Medical Insurance; Paid Holidays; Paid Vacation. **Average salary range of placements:** \$30,000 - \$50,000. **Number of placements per year:** 1 - 49.

VICTOR PERSONNEL
3601 Hobson Road, Suite 110, Fort Wayne IN 46815. 219/484-0611. **Fax:** 219/484-1046. **Contact:** Manager. **Description:** A temporary agency.

WESTAFF
512 Noble Drive, Fort Wayne IN 46825. 219/486-5649. **Fax:** 219/484-8877. **Contact:** Marcia Norris, Manager. **Description:** A temporary agency that also provides some permanent placements. **Specializes in the areas of:** Manufacturing; Secretarial. **Positions commonly filled include:** Accountant/Auditor; Blue-Collar Worker Supervisor; Clerical Supervisor; Computer Programmer; Customer Service Representative; Dental Assistant/Dental Hygienist; Electrical/Electronics Engineer; Mechanical Engineer; MIS Specialist; Paralegal; Systems Analyst; Typist/Word Processor. **Corporate headquarters location:** Walnut Creek CA. **Average salary range of placements:** Less than \$20,000. **Number of placements per year:** 200 - 499.

WIMMER TEMPORARIES AND DIRECT PLACEMENT
1415 West Jeffras Avenue, Marion IN 46956. 765/664-9550. **Fax:** 765/664-9553. **Contact:** Bill Wimmer, President. **E-mail address:** wimmer@comteck.com. **Description:** A temporary agency for professionals, engineers, and general managers. **Specializes in the areas of:** Computer Science/Software; Engineering; General Management; Industrial; Manufacturing; Personnel/Labor Relations; Technical. **Positions commonly filled include:** Accountant/Auditor; Administrative Manager; Agricultural Engineer; Blue-Collar Worker Supervisor; Buyer; Chemical Engineer; Clerical Supervisor; Customer Service Representative; Design Engineer; Draftsperson; Electrical/Electronics Engineer; Electrician; General Manager; Human Resources Manager; Industrial Engineer; Licensed Practical Nurse; Mechanical Engineer; Metallurgical Engineer; Operations/Production Manager; Paralegal; Purchasing Agent/Manager; Quality Control Supervisor; Registered Nurse; Typist/Word Processor. **Benefits available to temporary workers:** Life Insurance; Medical Insurance; Paid Holidays; Paid Vacation; Tuition Assistance. **Other area**

locations: Highland IN. **Average salary range of placements:** $20,000 - $29,999. **Number of placements per year:** 200 - 499.

PERMANENT EMPLOYMENT AGENCIES

ACCOUNTANTS ON CALL
111 Monument Circle, Bank One Tower, Indianapolis IN 46204. 317/686-0001. **Fax:** 317/686-0007. **Contact:** Manager. **Description:** An employment agency that provides both permanent and temporary placements. **Specializes in the areas of:** Accounting/Auditing.

AGRA PLACEMENTS, LTD.
55 South Wabash, P.O. Box 4, Peru IN 46970. 765/472-1988. **Fax:** 765/472-7568. **Contact:** Dave Lawrence, Manager. **Description:** A permanent employment agency. **Specializes in the areas of:** Agri-Business; Chemicals.

ALPHA RAE PERSONNEL, INC.
127 West Berry Street, Suite 200, Fort Wayne IN 46802. 219/426-8227. **Fax:** 219/426-1152. **Contact:** Rae Pearson, President. **Description:** A permanent employment agency. **Specializes in the areas of:** Computer Science/Software; Data Processing; Engineering; Legal; Sales; Software Engineering.

AMERICA WORKS
2021 North Meridian Street, Indianapolis IN 46208. 317/923-3600. **Fax:** 317/921-6877. **Contact:** Manager. **Description:** A permanent employment agency.

ANGOLA PERSONNEL SERVICES, INC.
901 North Wayne Street, Suite B, Angola IN 46703. 219/665-1162. **Fax:** 219/665-6997. **Contact:** Jeff Peters, President/Owner. **Description:** A permanent employment agency. **Specializes in the areas of:** Clerical; Engineering; Light Industrial; Manufacturing; Personnel/Labor Relations; Secretarial; Technical. **Positions commonly filled include:** Blue-Collar Worker Supervisor; Clerical Supervisor; Customer Service Representative; Design Engineer; Designer; General Manager; Human Resources Specialist; Industrial Engineer; Industrial Production Manager; Mechanical Engineer; Quality Control Supervisor. **Benefits available to temporary workers:** Paid Holidays; Paid Vacation. **Other area locations:** Auburn IN. **Other U.S. locations:** Archbold OH. **Average salary range of placements:** $20,000 - $29,999. **Number of placements per year:** 1000+.

BANE & ASSOCIATES
19 1/2 South Eighth Street, Richmond IN 47374. 765/966-5512. **Fax:** 765/966-2623. **Contact:** David Bane, Owner/CEO. **Description:** A permanent employment agency that also conducts some executive searches. **Specializes in the areas of:** Industrial.

BARRISTER PERSONNEL
155 East Market Street, Suite 701, Indianapolis IN 46204. 317/637-0123. **Fax:** 317/637-0163. **Contact:** Manager. **Description:** An employment agency that provides both permanent and temporary placements. **Specializes in the areas of:** Legal Secretarial.

BONE PERSONNEL, INC.
6424 Lima Road, Fort Wayne IN 46818. 219/489-3350. **Fax:** 219/489-0556. **Contact:** Manager. **Description:** A permanent employment agency. **Positions commonly filled include:** Accountant/Auditor; Administrative Manager; Advertising Clerk; Aerospace Engineer; Agricultural Scientist; Biomedical Engineer; Branch Manager; Budget Analyst; Buyer; Chemical Engineer; Chemist; Civil Engineer; Clerical Supervisor; Computer Programmer; Construction Contractor; Cost Estimator; Credit Manager; Designer; Draftsperson; Electrical/Electronics Engineer; Electrician; Financial Analyst; General Manager; Health Services Manager; Hotel

Manager; Industrial Engineer; Industrial Production Manager; Manufacturer's/Wholesaler's Sales Rep.; Mechanical Engineer; Metallurgical Engineer; Paralegal; Quality Control Supervisor; Restaurant/Food Service Manager; Science Technologist; Services Sales Representative; Software Engineer; Stationary Engineer; Structural Engineer; Systems Analyst. **Number of placements per year:** 1000+.

BILL CALDWELL EMPLOYMENT SERVICE
123 Main Street, Suite 307, Evansville IN 47708. 812/423-8006. **Fax:** 812/423-8008. **Contact:** Manager. **Description:** A permanent employment agency. **Specializes in the areas of:** Accounting/Auditing; Banking; Computer Science/Software; Engineering; Finance; General Management; Health/Medical; Industrial; Manufacturing; Retail; Sales. **Positions commonly filled include:** Accountant/Auditor; Actuary; Adjuster; Administrative Manager; Advertising Clerk; Agricultural Engineer; Architect; Attorney; Automotive Mechanic; Bank Officer/Manager; Biochemist; Biological Scientist; Biomedical Engineer; Blue-Collar Worker Supervisor; Branch Manager; Broadcast Technician; Brokerage Clerk; Budget Analyst; Buyer; Chemical Engineer; Chemist; Civil Engineer; Claim Representative; Clerical Supervisor; Clinical Lab Technician; Computer Programmer; Construction Contractor; Cost Estimator; Customer Service Representative; Design Engineer; Designer; Draftsperson; Economist; Editor; EEG Technologist; Electrical/Electronics Engineer; Electrician; Financial Analyst; Food Scientist/Technologist; General Manager; Health Services Manager; Human Resources Specialist; Industrial Engineer; Internet Services Manager; Librarian; Management Analyst/Consultant; Market Research Analyst; Materials Engineer; Mechanical Engineer; Metallurgical Engineer; Mining Engineer; Operations/Production Manager; Pharmacist; Physical Therapist; Public Relations Specialist; Quality Control Supervisor; Radio/TV Announcer/Broadcaster; Radiological Technologist; Real Estate Agent; Recreational Therapist; Restaurant/Food Service Manager; Services Sales Representative; Sociologist; Software Engineer; Statistician; Structural Engineer; Systems Analyst; Teacher/Professor; Telecommunications Manager; Typist/Word Processor; Underwriter/Assistant Underwriter.

CAREER CONSULTANTS, INC.
O.I. PARTNERS
107 North Pennsylvania, Suite 400, Indianapolis IN 46204. 317/639-5601. **Fax:** 317/634-0277. **Contact:** Manager. **Description:** A permanent employment agency. **Specializes in the areas of:** Accounting/Auditing; Computer Science/Software; Engineering; Food; Industrial; Information Systems; Manufacturing; Technical. **Positions commonly filled include:** Accountant/Auditor; Computer Programmer; Electrical/Electronics Engineer; Financial Analyst; Human Resources Manager; Industrial Engineer; Industrial Production Manager; Mechanical Engineer; Metallurgical Engineer; Purchasing Agent/Manager; Quality Control Supervisor; Software Engineer; Statistician; Systems Analyst; Technical Writer/Editor. **Number of placements per year:** 50 - 99.

CENTURY PERSONNEL INC.
11590 North Meridian Street, Suite 500, Carmel IN 46032. 317/580-8500. **Fax:** 317/580-8535. **Contact:** Manager. **Description:** A permanent employment agency. **Specializes in the areas of:** Accounting/Auditing; Data Processing; Engineering; Health/Medical; Technical.

CROWE, CHIZEK AND COMPANY
340 Columbia Street, P.O. Box 11208, South Bend IN 46634-0208. 219/232-3992. **Fax:** 219/236-8692. **Contact:** Janet Racht, Senior Manager. **Description:** A permanent employment agency. **Specializes in the areas of:** Accounting/Auditing; Banking; Finance; Manufacturing.

DATA ACCESS
5420 West Southern Avenue, Suite 201, Indianapolis IN 46241. 317/545-5882. **Contact:** Manager. **Description:** A permanent employment agency. **Specializes in the areas of:** Clerical; Engineering.

PAT DAY PERSONNEL INC.
6100 North Keystone, Suite 222, Indianapolis IN 46220. 317/257-1411. **Fax:** 317/257-1305. **Contact:** Manager. **Description:** A permanent employment agency. **Specializes in the areas of:** Clerical; Office Support; Restaurant; Retail; Sales. **Positions commonly filled include:** Restaurant/Food Service Manager; Retail Manager; Sales Representative.

DENTAL MEDICAL POWER INC.
6249 Southeast Street, Suite B, Indianapolis IN 46227. 317/337-1312. **Fax:** 317/781-0112. **Contact:** Manager. **Description:** An employment agency that provides both permanent and temporary placements. **Specializes in the areas of:** Health/Medical.

EMPLOYMENT MART INC.
7002 Graham Road, Suite 100, Indianapolis IN 46220. 317/842-8890. **Fax:** 317/842-8892. **Contact:** Manager. **Description:** A permanent employment agency. **Specializes in the areas of:** Engineering.

EMPLOYMENT RECRUITERS INC.
P.O. Box 1624, Elkhart IN 46515-1624. 219/262-2654. **Fax:** 219/262-0095. **Contact:** Suzanne Pedler, President. **Description:** A permanent employment agency that places professionals with manufacturers throughout the Midwest. Founded in 1982. **Specializes in the areas of:** Computer Science/Software; Engineering; General Management; Industrial; Manufacturing; Sales. **Positions commonly filled include:** Chemical Engineer; Chemist; Computer Programmer; Credit Manager; Customer Service Manager; Customer Service Representative; Design Engineer; Designer; Draftsperson; Electrical/Electronics Engineer; Environmental Engineer; Food Scientist/Technologist; General Manager; Industrial Engineer; Industrial Production Manager; Manufacturer's/Wholesaler's Sales Rep.; Market Research Analyst; Mathematician; Metallurgical Engineer; Mining Engineer; MIS Specialist; Operations/Production Manager; Purchasing Agent/Manager; Quality Control Supervisor; Safety Engineer; Science Technologist; Software Engineer; Stationary Engineer; Statistician; Strategic Relations Manager; Structural Engineer; Systems Analyst; Technical Writer/Editor. **Average salary range of placements:** $30,000 - $50,000. **Number of placements per year:** 1 - 49.

JOB PLACEMENT SERVICE INC.
5404 North Calumet Avenue, Valparaiso IN 46383. 219/462-7894. **Fax:** 219/462-9680. **Contact:** James S. Holycross, Vice President. **Description:** A permanent employment agency. **Specializes in the areas of:** Accounting/Auditing; Administration; Advertising; Architecture/Construction; Computer Science/Software; Engineering; Finance; General Management; Industrial; Insurance; Legal; Manufacturing; Nonprofit; Personnel/Labor Relations; Retail; Sales; Secretarial. **Positions commonly filled include:** Accountant/Auditor; Advertising Clerk; Architect; Automotive Mechanic; Blue-Collar Worker Supervisor; Branch Manager; Buyer; Chemist; Claim Representative; Clerical Supervisor; Clinical Lab Technician; Computer Programmer; Cost Estimator; Counselor; Credit Manager; Customer Service Representative; Design Engineer; Designer; Draftsperson; Economist; Editor; Electrical/Electronics Engineer; Electrician; Financial Analyst; General Manager; Hotel Manager; Human Resources Specialist; Industrial Engineer; Industrial Production Manager; Insurance Agent/Broker; Management Trainee; Operations/Production Manager; Paralegal; Services Sales Representative; Social Worker; Software Engineer; Systems Analyst; Typist/Word Processor. **Average salary range of placements:** Less than $20,000. **Number of placements per year:** 500 - 999.

KENDALL & DAVIS RESOURCES, INC.
415 East Cook Road, Suite 600, Fort Wayne IN 46825. 219/489-8014. **Toll-free phone:** 800/860-8014. **Fax:** 800/860-2982. **Contact:** Manager. **Description:** A permanent employment agency that also provides some contract services. **Specializes in the areas of:** Computer Science/Software. **Positions commonly filled include:** Computer Operator; Computer Programmer; MIS Specialist; Systems Analyst; Technical Writer/Editor; Telecommunications Manager. **Benefits available to temporary workers:** 401(k); Dental Insurance; Disability Coverage; Life Insurance; Medical Insurance; Profit Sharing. **Corporate headquarters location:** This Location. **Other U.S. locations:** Detroit MI. **Average salary range of placements:** More than $50,000. **Number of placements per year:** 200 - 499.

KRISE PROFESSIONAL PERSONNEL SERVICES
P.O. Box 53136, Indianapolis IN 46253. 317/299-3882. **Contact:** Randy Krise CPC/Owner. **Description:** A permanent employment agency specializing in engineering and technical

manufacturing management. **Specializes in the areas of:** Engineering; Manufacturing; Personnel/Labor Relations. **Positions commonly filled include:** Aerospace Engineer; Agricultural Engineer; Biomedical Engineer; Chemical Engineer; Civil Engineer; Electrical/Electronics Engineer; Human Resources Manager; Industrial Engineer; Industrial Production Manager; Mechanical Engineer; Metallurgical Engineer; Purchasing Agent/Manager; Quality Control Supervisor; Software Engineer; Stationary Engineer; Structural Engineer. **Average salary range of placements:** $30,000 - $50,000. **Number of placements per year:** 1 - 49.

DAN LANE PERSONNEL
8395 Keystone Crossing, Suite 213, Indianapolis IN 46240. 317/255-9632. **Contact:** Manager. **Description:** A permanent employment agency.

LIFE EMPLOYMENT SERVICE
600 Life Building, 300 Main Street, Lafayette IN 47901. 765/742-0278. **Fax:** 765/742-0270. **Contact:** Charles A. Hoovler, Manager. **E-mail address:** charlie@life-employment.com. **Description:** A permanent employment agency. **Specializes in the areas of:** Accounting/Auditing; Banking; Fashion; Finance; Food; General Management; Retail; Sales; Secretarial. **Positions commonly filled include:** Branch Manager; Buyer; Clerical Supervisor; Credit Manager; General Manager; Hotel Manager; Management Trainee; Manufacturer's/Wholesaler's Sales Rep.; Purchasing Agent/Manager; Restaurant/Food Service Manager; Securities Sales Representative; Services Sales Representative; Typist/Word Processor. **Average salary range of placements:** $30,000 - $50,000. **Number of placements per year:** 100 - 199.

MAYS & ASSOCIATES INC.
941 East 86th Street, Suite 109, Indianapolis IN 46240. 317/253-9999. **Fax:** 317/253-2749. **Contact:** Roger R. Mays, President. **Description:** A permanent employment agency. **Specializes in the areas of:** Computer Science/Software; Engineering; Manufacturing. **Positions commonly filled include:** Aerospace Engineer; Biomedical Engineer; Chemical Engineer; Computer Programmer; Designer; Electrical/Electronics Engineer; General Manager; Human Resources Manager; Industrial Engineer; Mechanical Engineer; Metallurgical Engineer; Purchasing Agent/Manager; Quality Control Supervisor; Software Engineer; Structural Engineer; Systems Analyst. **Number of placements per year:** 50 - 99.

P.R. PERSONNEL
537 West Jefferson Boulevard, Fort Wayne IN 46802. 219/422-4671. **Contact:** Manager. **Description:** A permanent employment agency.

PERRY PERSONNEL PLUS
200 West Pike Street, Goshen IN 46526. 219/533-7330. **Fax:** 219/533-1417. **Contact:** Manager. **Description:** Perry Personnel Plus is a permanent employment agency. **Specializes in the areas of:** Accounting/Auditing; Banking; General Management; Industrial; Manufacturing; Personnel/Labor Relations; Sales; Secretarial. **Positions commonly filled include:** Accountant/Auditor; Bank Officer/Manager; Blue-Collar Worker Supervisor; Branch Manager; Buyer; Clerical Supervisor; Computer Programmer; Credit Manager; Customer Service Representative; General Manager; Human Resources Specialist; Industrial Engineer; Industrial Production Manager; Management Trainee; Mechanical Engineer; MIS Specialist; Operations/Production Manager; Purchasing Agent/Manager; Quality Control Supervisor; Systems Analyst. **Corporate headquarters location:** Sturgis MI. **Other U.S. locations:** Goshen IN; Coldwater MI; Three Rivers MI.

PERSONNEL PARTNERS
828 East Jefferson, Suite 200, South Bend IN 46617. 219/234-2115. **Fax:** 219/234-2834. **Contact:** Manager. **Description:** A permanent employment agency. **Specializes in the areas of:** Light Industrial.

PRO RESOURCES
1728 Spy Run Avenue, Fort Wayne IN 46805. 219/420-2117. **Fax:** 219/420-1925. **Contact:** Manager. **Description:** A permanent employment agency that also offers some temporary placements. **Specializes in the areas of:** Light Industrial.

PYRAMIDS PERSONNEL
8910 Purdue Road, Suite 200, Indianapolis IN 46268-1155. 317/872-4960. **Fax:** 317/879-1233. **Contact:** Manager. **Description:** A permanent employment agency. **Specializes in the areas of:** Clerical; Office Support.

THE REGISTRY INC.
600 King Cole Building, 7 North Meridian Street, Indianapolis IN 46204-3033. 317/634-1200. **Fax:** 317/263-3845. **Contact:** Director of Operations. **Description:** A permanent employment agency. **Specializes in the areas of:** Accounting/Auditing; Administration; Bookkeeping; Clerical; Computer Science/Software; Health/Medical; Legal; Real Estate.

RELIABLE TECHNICAL SERVICES
P.O. Box 2126, Muncie IN 47307. 765/282-6907. **Fax:** 765/282-6292. **Contact:** Manager. **Description:** Reliable Technical Services is a permanent employment agency. **Specializes in the areas of:** Technical.

SNELLING PERSONNEL SERVICES
1000 East 80th Place, Suite 207, Merrillville IN 46410-5644. 219/769-2922. **Fax:** 219/755-0557. **Contact:** Cheri K. Elser, General Manager. **Description:** A permanent employment agency. Founded in 1985. **Specializes in the areas of:** Accounting/Auditing; Sales; Secretarial. **Positions commonly filled include:** Bookkeeper; Restaurant/Food Service Manager; Secretary; Services Sales Representative. **Number of placements per year:** 100 - 199.

STAFFMARK ACCOUNTANTS
1010 West Coliseum Boulevard, Fort Wayne IN 46808. 219/484-2903. **Toll-free phone:** 888/777-7129. **Fax:** 219/471-8101. **Contact:** Janet Hambrock, Branch Manager. **Description:** A permanent employment agency that also provides some temporary placements. **Specializes in the areas of:** Accounting/Auditing; Finance. **Positions commonly filled include:** Accountant; Auditor; Budget Analyst; Controller; Credit Manager; Finance Director; Financial Analyst. **Benefits available to temporary workers:** Paid Holidays; Paid Vacation; Referral Bonus Plan. **Other U.S. locations:** Nationwide. **Number of placements per year:** 100 - 199.

TIME SERVICES, INC.
P.O. Box 784, Kendallville IN 46755-0784. 219/347-3940. **Toll-free phone:** 800/837-8463. **Fax:** 219/347-9619. **Contact:** Melissa Carpenter, Branch Manager. **Description:** A permanent employment agency providing clerical, industrial, and technical placements. **Specializes in the areas of:** Industrial; Manufacturing; Secretarial. **Positions commonly filled include:** Blue-Collar Worker Supervisor; Customer Service Representative. **Benefits available to temporary workers:** Medical Insurance; Paid Holidays; Paid Vacation. **Corporate headquarters location:** Fort Wayne IN. **Other area locations:** Auburn IN. **Average salary range of placements:** Less than $20,000. **Number of placements per year:** 200 - 499.

EXECUTIVE SEARCH FIRMS

ABS-AARON BUSINESS SYSTEMS
8515 Cedar Place Drive, Suite 103B, Indianapolis IN 46240. 317/251-0125. **Fax:** 317/251-0127. **Contact:** Manager. **Description:** An executive search firm providing low- to middle-management placements. **Specializes in the areas of:** Sales.

ALEXANDER & ASSOCIATES
527 Park Place Court, Suite 100, Mishawaka IN 46545. 219/271-0594. **Fax:** 219/272-7566. **Contact:** Manager. **Description:** Alexander & Associates is an executive search firm. **Specializes in the areas of:** Manufacturing. **Positions commonly filled include:** General Manager; Human Resources Specialist; Product Engineer. **Average salary range of placements:** $30,000 - $50,000.

THE BENNETT GROUP
5640 Professional Circle, Indianapolis IN 46241. 317/247-1240. **Contact:** Manager. **Description:** An executive search firm. **Specializes in the areas of:** Electronics; Engineering; High-Tech.

CANIS MAJOR, INC.
HR QUEST
P.O. Box 742, Carmel IN 46032-0742. 317/581-8880. **Toll-free phone:** 800/536-4276. **Fax:** 317/581-8856. **Contact:** Carol Albright, President. **Description:** An executive search firm operating on a contingency basis. **Specializes in the areas of:** Administration; Computer Science/Software; Engineering; Industrial; Insurance; Manufacturing; MIS/EDP; Occupational Health/Safety; Personnel/Labor Relations; Safety. **Positions commonly filled include:** Adjuster; Claim Representative; Electrical/Electronics Engineer; Human Resources Manager; Industrial Engineer; Licensed Practical Nurse; Registered Nurse; Underwriter/Assistant Underwriter. **Average salary range of placements:** $30,000 - $50,000. **Number of placements per year:** 1 - 49.

CAREERS UNLIMITED INC.
1238 South Main Street, Elkhart IN 46516. 219/293-0659. **Fax:** 219/294-1254. **Contact:** Steve Berger, President/Owner. **Description:** An executive search firm operating on a contingency basis. The firm also provides some contract services. **Specializes in the areas of:** Computer Science/Software; Engineering; General Management; Industrial; Manufacturing. **Positions commonly filled include:** Computer Programmer; Electrical/Electronics Engineer; Industrial Engineer; Industrial Production Manager; Manufacturing Engineer; Mechanical Engineer; Production Manager; Systems Analyst. **Number of placements per year:** 1 - 49.

CHEVIGNY PERSONNEL AGENCY
P.O. Box 11342, Merrillville IN 46411-1342. 219/663-7801. **Fax:** 219/663-7819. **Contact:** Jule Chevigny, President. **Description:** An executive search firm operating on a contingency basis. **Specializes in the areas of:** Engineering; Industrial; Manufacturing; MIS/EDP. **Positions commonly filled include:** Accountant/Auditor; Bank Officer/Manager; Chemical Engineer; Civil Engineer; Computer Programmer; Design Engineer; Electrical/Electronics Engineer; Environmental Engineer; Hotel Manager; Industrial Engineer; Industrial Production Manager; Mechanical Engineer; Metallurgical Engineer; MIS Specialist; Operations/Production Manager; Petroleum Engineer; Purchasing Agent/Manager; Quality Control Supervisor; Restaurant/Food Service Manager; Structural Engineer; Systems Analyst.

COMPUSEARCH
1657 Commerce Drive, Suite 15B, South Bend IN 46628. 219/239-2970. **Fax:** 219/239-2980. **Contact:** Manager. **Description:** An executive search firm for computer professionals. **Specializes in the areas of:** Computer Hardware/Software.

THE CONSULTING FORUM, INC.
9200 Keystone Crossing, Suite 700, Indianapolis IN 46240. 317/580-4800. **Fax:** 317/580-4801. **Contact:** Don Kellner, President. **E-mail address:** admin@consultingforum.com. **Description:** An executive search firm operating on both retainer and contingency bases. **Specializes in the areas of:** Administration; Computer Science/Software; Information Systems. **Positions commonly filled include:** Computer Programmer; MIS Specialist; Software Engineer; Systems Analyst; Technical Writer/Editor. **Average salary range of placements:** $30,000 - $50,000. **Number of placements per year:** 100 - 199.

CREATIVE FINANCIAL STAFFING
340 Columbia Street, Suite 105, South Bend IN 46601. 219/236-7600. **Fax:** 219/239-7878. **Contact:** Manager. **Description:** An executive search firm. **Specializes in the areas of:** Finance.

THE CURARE GROUP, INC.
4001 East Third Street, Suite B, Bloomington IN 47401. 812/331-0645. **Fax:** 812/331-0659. **Contact:** David Witte, Senior Recruiter. **Description:** An executive search firm focusing on contingency recruitment of primary care physicians, including family practice, internal medicine,

pediatrics, and OB/GYN. Founded in 1991. **Specializes in the areas of:** Health/Medical. **Positions commonly filled include:** Physician. **Other U.S. locations:** New Orleans LA. **Average salary range of placements:** More than $50,000.

DATA FORCE
626 North Park Avenue, Indianapolis IN 46202. 317/636-9900. **Contact:** Manager. **E-mail address:** searchforce@ori.net. **Description:** An executive search firm. **Specializes in the areas of:** Information Systems.

DUNHILL OF BROWN COUNTY
P.O. Box 1068, Nashville IN 47448. 812/988-1944. **Contact:** George W. Rogers, President. **Description:** An executive search firm. **Specializes in the areas of:** Engineering; Health/Medical; Industrial; Manufacturing; Personnel/Labor Relations; Technical. **Positions commonly filled include:** Aerospace Engineer; Agricultural Engineer; Biomedical Engineer; Chemical Engineer; Chemist; Civil Engineer; Designer; Electrical/Electronics Engineer; Health Services Manager; Industrial Engineer; Industrial Production Manager; Mechanical Engineer; Metallurgical Engineer. **Number of placements per year:** 100 - 199.

DUNHILL PROFESSIONAL SEARCH
9918 Coldwater Road, Fort Wayne IN 46825. 219/489-5966. **Fax:** 219/489-6120. **Contact:** Office Manager. **E-mail address:** dunftwin@aol.com. **Description:** Dunhill Professional Search is an executive search firm operating on a contingency basis. **Specializes in the areas of:** Engineering; Industrial; Manufacturing; Technical. **Positions commonly filled include:** Chemical Engineer; Chemist; Design Engineer; General Manager; Industrial Engineer; Industrial Production Manager; Mechanical Engineer; Metallurgical Engineer; Operations/Production Manager; Quality Control Supervisor; Statistician. **Other U.S. locations:** Nationwide. **Average salary range of placements:** $30,000 - $50,000.

EXCELLENCE IN SEARCH
186 Amys Run Drive, Carmel IN 46032. 317/573-5222. **Fax:** 317/573-5223. **Contact:** Manager. **Description:** An executive search firm. **Specializes in the areas of:** Data Processing; Health/Medical.

EXECUSEARCH
105 East Jefferson Boulevard, Suite 800, South Bend IN 46601-1811. 219/233-9353. **Fax:** 219/236-4840. **Contact:** Manager. **Description:** An executive search firm. **Specializes in the areas of:** Accounting/Auditing; Administration; Advertising; Architecture/Construction; Banking; Chemicals; Communications; Computer Hardware/Software; Construction; Electrical; Engineering; Finance; Food; General Management; Health/Medical; Insurance; Legal; Manufacturing; Personnel/Labor Relations; Pharmaceuticals; Procurement; Publishing; Real Estate; Retail; Sales; Technical; Textiles; Transportation.

F-O-R-T-U-N-E PERSONNEL CONSULTANTS
347 West Berry Street, Suite 319, Fort Wayne IN 46802. 219/424-5159. **Fax:** 219/424-4201. **Contact:** Manager. **Description:** An executive search firm. **Specializes in the areas of:** Electronics; Plastics; Rubber. **Corporate headquarters location:** New York NY. **Other U.S. locations:** Nationwide.

GREAT LAKES SEARCH
1010 West Coliseum Boulevard, Fort Wayne IN 46808. 219/436-2534. **Fax:** 219/471-8101. **Contact:** Manager. **Description:** An executive search firm. **Specializes in the areas of:** Engineering; Finance; Manufacturing.

HMO EXECUTIVE SEARCH
8910 Purdue Road, Suite 200, Indianapolis IN 46268-1155. 317/872-1056. **Fax:** 317/879-1233. **Contact:** Dick Carroll, CPC/President. **Description:** An executive search firm. **Specializes in the areas of:** Health/Medical. **Positions commonly filled include:** Registered Nurse. **Number of placements per year:** 50 - 99.

ROBERT HALF INTERNATIONAL
OFFICETEAM/ACCOUNTEMPS
135 North Pennsylvania Avenue, Suite 2300, Indianapolis IN 46204. 317/687-3270. **Contact:** Manager. **World Wide Web address:** http://www.roberthalf.com. **Description:** An executive search firm. OfficeTeam (also at this location) provides temporary and permanent administrative placements. Accountemps (also at this location) provides temporary placements. **Specializes in the areas of:** Accounting/Auditing. **Corporate headquarters location:** Menlo Park CA. **Other U.S. locations:** Nationwide.

THE HART LINE INC.
P.O. Box 39, Brazil IN 47834. 812/448-3490. **Fax:** 812/442-5227. **Contact:** Eric V. Stearley, CPC/President. **Description:** An executive search firm. **Specializes in the areas of:** Engineering; Manufacturing. **Positions commonly filled include:** Electrical/Electronics Engineer; Industrial Engineer; Mechanical Engineer; Software Engineer. **Average salary range of placements:** $30,000 - $50,000. **Number of placements per year:** 50 - 99.

KEITH HAYES & ASSOCIATES
8420 Galley Court, Indianapolis IN 46236. 317/823-7100. **Contact:** Manager. **Description:** Keith Hayes & Associates is an executive search firm. **Specializes in the areas of:** Health/Medical; Pharmaceuticals.

HEALTH LINK
EXECUTIVE PLACEMENT SERVICES (EPS)
1321 North Meridian Street, Suite 209, Indianapolis IN 46202. 317/321-0200. **Fax:** 317/321-0213. **Contact:** Manager. **Description:** An executive search firm. Executive Placement Services (also at this location) provides computer and information technology placements. **Specializes in the areas of:** Health/Medical.

INSURANCE PEOPLE
4755 Kingsway Drive, Suite 315, Indianapolis IN 46205. 317/253-2128. **Contact:** Manager. **Description:** An executive search firm. **Specializes in the areas of:** Insurance.

JOHNSON BROWN ASSOCIATES
55 Monument Circle, Suite 1214, Indianapolis IN 46204. 317/237-4328. **Fax:** 317/237-4335. **Contact:** Dan Brown/Kim Johnson, Principals. **Description:** An executive search firm that operates on both retainer and contingency bases. **Specializes in the areas of:** Accounting/Auditing; Engineering; Industrial; Information Technology; Investment; Personnel/Labor Relations; Sales; Technical. **Positions commonly filled include:** Account Manager; Account Representative; Accountant; Administrative Assistant; Applications Engineer; Architect; Auditor; Budget Analyst; Buyer; Chief Financial Officer; Controller; Customer Service Representative; Design Engineer; Education Administrator; Financial Analyst; Fund Manager; General Manager; Human Resources Manager; Industrial Engineer; Industrial Production Manager; Manufacturing Engineer; Market Research Analyst; Marketing Manager; Marketing Specialist; Mechanical Engineer; Metallurgical Engineer; Operations Manager; Project Manager; Public Relations Specialist; Purchasing Agent/Manager; Quality Control Supervisor; Sales Engineer; Sales Executive; Sales Manager; Sales Representative; Systems Manager. **Corporate headquarters location:** This Location. **Average salary range of placements:** More than $50,000. **Number of placements per year:** 1 - 49.

MARY KENNEDY & ASSOCIATES
5987 East 71st Street, Suite 210, Indianapolis IN 46220. 317/579-6942. **Contact:** Mary Kennedy, Owner. **Description:** An executive search firm.

KEY SALES PERSONNEL
312 NW Martin Luther King Boulevard, Suite 100, Evansville IN 47708. 812/426-2244. **Contact:** George Krauss, Vice President. **Description:** An executive search firm. **Specializes in the areas of:** Sales. **Positions commonly filled include:** Manufacturer's/Wholesaler's Sales Rep.; Sales Engineer; Services Sales Representative.

LANGE & ASSOCIATES, INC.
107 West Market Street, Wabash IN 46992. 219/563-7402. **Fax:** 219/563-3897. **Contact:** Jim Lange, President. **Description:** An executive search firm that also operates as a contract services firm. **Specializes in the areas of:** Accounting/Auditing; Engineering; General Management; Manufacturing; Personnel/Labor Relations; Sales. **Positions commonly filled include:** Accountant/Auditor; Blue-Collar Worker Supervisor; Buyer; Chemical Engineer; Chemist; Cost Estimator; Design Engineer; Electrical/Electronics Engineer; Environmental Engineer; General Manager; Human Resources Manager; Industrial Engineer; Industrial Production Manager; Materials Engineer; Mechanical Engineer; Operations/Production Manager; Purchasing Agent/Manager; Quality Control Supervisor. **Number of placements per year:** 1 - 49.

THE MALLARD GROUP
3322 Oak Borough, Fort Wayne IN 46804. 219/436-3970. **Fax:** 219/436-7012. **Contact:** Director. **Description:** An executive search firm operating on a contingency basis. **Specializes in the areas of:** Computer Science/Software; Engineering; Manufacturing; Sales. **Positions commonly filled include:** Design Engineer; Electrical/Electronics Engineer; Human Resources Manager; Industrial Engineer; Mechanical Engineer; Metallurgical Engineer; Purchasing Agent/Manager; Software Engineer. **Number of placements per year:** 1 - 49.

MANAGEMENT RECRUITERS INTERNATIONAL, INC. (MRI)
P.O. Box 2234, Columbus IN 47202. 812/372-5500. **Fax:** 812/372-8292. **Contact:** Manager. **Description:** An executive search firm. **Specializes in the areas of:** Banking; Computer Programming; Engineering. **Corporate headquarters location:** Cleveland OH.

MANAGEMENT RECRUITERS INTERNATIONAL, INC. (MRI)
SALES CONSULTANTS
8200 Haverstick Road, Suite 240, Indianapolis IN 46240. 317/257-5411. **Fax:** 317/259-6886. **Contact:** Manager. **Description:** An executive search firm. **Specializes in the areas of:** Marketing; Sales; Technical. **Corporate headquarters location:** Cleveland OH.

MANAGEMENT RECRUITERS INTERNATIONAL, INC. (MRI)
15209 Herriman Boulevard, Noblesville IN 46060. 317/773-4323. **Fax:** 317/773-9744. **Contact:** H. Peter Isenberg, President. **Description:** An executive search firm. **Specializes in the areas of:** Administration; Computer Science/Software; Engineering; General Management; Industrial; Manufacturing; Sales. **Positions commonly filled include:** Computer Programmer; Designer; Draftsperson; Electrical/Electronics Engineer; Food Scientist/Technologist; Industrial Engineer; Industrial Production Manager; Manufacturer's/Wholesaler's Sales Rep.; Mechanical Engineer; Metallurgical Engineer; Pharmacist; Software Engineer; Systems Analyst. **Corporate headquarters location:** Cleveland OH. **Average salary range of placements:** More than $50,000. **Number of placements per year:** 1 - 49.

MANAGEMENT RECRUITERS OF EVANSVILLE (MRI)
101 Court Street, Riverside 1 Building, Suite 209, Evansville IN 47708. 812/464-9155. **Fax:** 812/422-6718. **Contact:** Manager. **Description:** An executive search firm. **Specializes in the areas of:** Accounting/Auditing; Administration; Advertising; Architecture/Construction; Banking; Chemicals; Communications; Computer Hardware/Software; Construction; Electrical; Engineering; Finance; Food; General Management; Health/Medical; Insurance; Legal; Manufacturing; Personnel/Labor Relations; Pharmaceuticals; Procurement; Publishing; Real Estate; Retail; Sales; Technical; Textiles; Transportation. **Corporate headquarters location:** Cleveland OH.

MANAGEMENT RECRUITERS OF INDIANAPOLIS
3905 Vincennes Road, Suite 202, Indianapolis IN 46268. 317/228-3300. **Fax:** 317/228-3317. **Contact:** Peggy Cusack, Administrative Manager. **Description:** An executive search firm. **Specializes in the areas of:** Accounting/Auditing; Administration; Advertising; Architecture/Construction; Banking; Chemicals; Communications; Computer Hardware/Software; Construction; Electrical; Engineering; Finance; Food; General Management; Health/Medical; Insurance; Legal; Manufacturing; Operations Management; Personnel/Labor Relations; Pharmaceuticals; Procurement; Publishing; Real Estate; Retail; Sales; Technical; Textiles; Transportation. **Positions commonly filled include:** Account Manager; Accountant; Adjuster;

Applications Engineer; Branch Manager; Buyer; Chemical Engineer; Civil Engineer; Claim Representative; Clinical Lab Technician; Computer Operator; Computer Programmer; Controller; Database Manager; Design Engineer; Editor; Electrical/Electronics Engineer; Environmental Engineer; Financial Analyst; General Manager; Graphic Artist; Human Resources Manager; Industrial Engineer; Industrial Production Manager; Insurance Agent/Broker; Management Analyst/Consultant; Manufacturing Engineer; Marketing Manager; Marketing Specialist; Mechanical Engineer; Metallurgical Engineer; MIS Specialist; Operations Manager; Production Manager; Project Manager; Public Relations Specialist; Purchasing Agent/Manager; Quality Control Supervisor; Sales Engineer; Sales Executive; Sales Manager; Sales Representative; Software Engineer; Systems Analyst; Systems Manager; Telecommunications Manager; Underwriter/Assistant Underwriter. **Corporate headquarters location:** Cleveland OH. **Other U.S. locations:** Nationwide. **International locations:** Worldwide. **Average salary range of placements:** $30,000 - $50,000. **Number of placements per year:** 50 - 99.

MANAGEMENT RECRUITERS OF RICHMOND
STAFFING SOLUTIONS OF RICHMOND
2519 East Main Street, Suite 101, Richmond IN 47374-5864. 765/935-3356. **Contact:** Mr. Rande Martin, Manager. **Description:** An executive search firm. **Specializes in the areas of:** Accounting/Auditing; Administration; Advertising; Architecture/Construction; Banking; Chemicals; Communications; Computer Hardware/Software; Construction; Electrical; Engineering; Finance; Food; General Management; Health/Medical; Insurance; Legal; Manufacturing; Operations Management; Personnel/Labor Relations; Pharmaceuticals; Procurement; Publishing; Real Estate; Retail; Sales; Technical; Textiles; Transportation. **Corporate headquarters location:** Cleveland OH.

MANAGEMENT SERVICES
P.O. Box 830, Middlebury IN 46540-0830. 219/825-3909. **Fax:** 219/825-7115. **Contact:** Office Manager. **Description:** An executive search firm operating on a contingency basis. The firm focuses on administrative, technical, and executive management placements. **Specializes in the areas of:** Computer Science/Software; Engineering; Manufacturing; Personnel/Labor Relations; Sales. **Positions commonly filled include:** Accountant/Auditor; Buyer; Chemical Engineer; Computer Programmer; Electrical/Electronics Engineer; Financial Analyst; General Manager; Human Resources Manager; Industrial Engineer; Industrial Production Manager; Landscape Architect; Mechanical Engineer; Metallurgical Engineer; MIS Specialist; Operations/Production Manager; Purchasing Agent/Manager; Quality Control Supervisor; Software Engineer; Systems Analyst; Transportation/Traffic Specialist. **Number of placements per year:** 1 - 49.

MAYHALL SEARCH GROUP INC.
4410 Executive Boulevard, Suite 1A, Fort Wayne IN 46808. 219/484-7770. **Fax:** 219/482-9397. **Contact:** Manager. **Description:** An executive search firm. **Specializes in the areas of:** Accounting/Auditing; Manufacturing; Sales.

MEDICAL RECRUITMENT SPECIALISTS
8910 Purdue Road, Indianapolis IN 46268. 317/875-6080. **Contact:** Gail Florey, Manager. **Description:** An executive search firm. **Specializes in the areas of:** Health/Medical. **Positions commonly filled include:** Marketing Specialist; Product Manager; Sales Manager. **Other U.S. locations:** Atlanta GA.

MICHIANA PERSONNEL SERVICE
1441 Northside Boulevard, South Bend IN 46615. 219/232-3364. **Contact:** Manager. **Description:** An executive search firm.

MILLER PERSONNEL
931 East 86th Street, Suite 103, Indianapolis IN 46240. 317/251-5938. **Toll-free phone:** 800/851-5938. **Fax:** 317/251-5762. **Contact:** Mark Miller, Owner/Manager. **Description:** An executive search firm operating on a contingency basis. **Specializes in the areas of:** Engineering; Manufacturing. **Positions commonly filled include:** Applications Engineer; Design Engineer; Electrical/Electronics Engineer; Industrial Engineer; Industrial Production Manager; Manufacturing Engineer; Mechanical Engineer; Operations Manager; Production Manager;

Purchasing Agent/Manager; Quality Control Supervisor; Sales Engineer; Software Engineer. **Other U.S. locations:** Nationwide. **Average salary range of placements:** More than $50,000. **Number of placements per year:** 50 - 99.

MONTE DENBO ASSOCIATES
127 North Front Street, Rising Sun IN 47040. 812/438-2400. **Fax:** 812/438-2567. **Contact:** Manager. **Description:** An executive search firm that places senior-level managers. **Specializes in the areas of:** Engineering.

MORLEY GROUP
8910 Purdue Road, Suite 670, Indianapolis IN 46268. 317/879-4770. **Fax:** 317/879-4787. **Contact:** Manager. **Description:** An executive search firm that also provides some contract and temporary placements. **Specializes in the areas of:** Banking; Clerical; Engineering; Finance; Health/Medical; Human Resources; Information Systems; Manufacturing.

NATIONAL RECRUITING SERVICE
P.O. Box 218, 1832 Hart Street, Dyer IN 46311. 219/865-2373. **Fax:** 219/865-2375. **Contact:** Stanley M. Hendricks II, Owner. **Description:** An executive search firm operating on both retainer and contingency bases. **Specializes in the areas of:** Metals; Plastics. **Positions commonly filled include:** General Manager; Industrial Engineer; Industrial Production Manager; Manufacturing Engineer; Marketing Manager; Mechanical Engineer; Metallurgical Engineer; Operations/Production Manager; Sales Engineer; Sales Executive; Sales Representative. **Average salary range of placements:** More than $50,000. **Number of placements per year:** 1 - 49.

OAKWOOD INTERNATIONAL INC.
3935 Lincoln Way East, Suite A, Mishawaka IN 46544. 219/255-9861. **Fax:** 219/257-8914. **Contact:** Scott Null, President. **E-mail address:** brent@mvillage.com. **World Wide Web address:** http://www.interact.withus.com/oakwood. **Description:** A contingency search firm. **Specializes in the areas of:** Administration; Computer Science/Software; Engineering; General Management; Manufacturing; Sales; Technical. **Positions commonly filled include:** Aerospace Engineer; Biomedical Engineer; Branch Manager; Chemical Engineer; Chemist; Civil Engineer; Computer Programmer; Design Engineer; Designer; Draftsperson; Electrical/Electronics Engineer; Industrial Engineer; Internet Services Manager; Mechanical Engineer; Metallurgical Engineer; MIS Specialist; Multimedia Designer; Quality Control Supervisor; Software Engineer; Structural Engineer; Systems Analyst; Technical Writer/Editor; Telecommunications Manager. **Average salary range of placements:** More than $50,000. **Number of placements per year:** 1 - 49.

OFFICEMATES5
8888 Keystone Crossing Boulevard, Suite 120, Indianapolis IN 46240. 317/843-2512. **Contact:** Manager. **Description:** An executive search firm. **Specializes in the areas of:** Accounting/Auditing; Administration; Advertising; Architecture/Construction; Banking; Chemicals; Communications; Computer Hardware/Software; Construction; Electrical; Engineering; Finance; Food; General Management; Health/Medical; Legal; Manufacturing; Personnel/Labor Relations; Pharmaceuticals; Procurement; Publishing; Real Estate; Retail; Sales; Technical; Textiles; Transportation.

OFFICEMATES5 OF INDIANAPOLIS
1099 North Meridian Street, Landmark Building, Suite 640, Indianapolis IN 46204. 317/237-2787. **Fax:** 317/237-2786. **Contact:** Manager. **Description:** An executive search firm. **Specializes in the areas of:** Accounting/Auditing; Administration; Advertising; Architecture/Construction; Banking; Chemicals; Communications; Computer Hardware/Software; Construction; Electrical; Engineering; Finance; Food; General Management; Health/Medical; Insurance; Legal; Manufacturing; Personnel/Labor Relations; Pharmaceuticals; Procurement; Publishing; Real Estate; Retail; Sales; Technical; Textiles; Transportation.

P.R.C.
3077 East 98th Street, Suite 210, Indianapolis IN 46280. 317/580-5730. **Contact:** Manager. **Description:** An executive search firm. **Specializes in the areas of:** Administration; Engineering.

PERSONNEL PLUS, INC.
300 West Jefferson Street, Plymouth IN 46563. 219/935-5727. **Fax:** 219/935-4521. **Contact:** Marcy Eckhoff, CPC/President. **Description:** An executive search firm focusing on placements in the automotive, HVAC, and engine cooling industries. The company operates on both retainer and contingency bases. Founded in 1976. **Specializes in the areas of:** Engineering; Technical; Transportation. **Positions commonly filled include:** Electrical/Electronics Engineer; Mechanical Engineer.

QUALITY SEARCH
1100 South Calumet Road, Suite One, Chesterton IN 46304. 219/926-8202. **Fax:** 219/926-3834. **Contact:** James L. Jeselnick, President. **E-mail address:** quality@staffing.net. **World Wide Web address:** http://www.niia.net/biz/quality. **Description:** A technical engineering recruiting firm that focuses on the placement of packaging professionals. **Specializes in the areas of:** Engineering; Food; General Management; Technical. **Positions commonly filled include:** Buyer; Chemical Engineer; Design Engineer; Designer; Industrial Engineer; Manufacturing Engineer; Mechanical Engineer; Production Manager; Purchasing Agent/Manager; Quality Control Supervisor. **Corporate headquarters location:** This Location. **Other U.S. locations:** Show Low AZ; Grand Rapids MI. **Average salary range of placements:** More than $50,000. **Number of placements per year:** 50 - 99.

QUIRING ASSOCIATES INC.
7321 Shadeland Station Way, Suite 150, Indianapolis IN 46256-3935. 317/841-7575x4. **Fax:** 317/577-8240. **Contact:** Patti Quiring, CPC/President. **E-mail address:** quiring@iquest.net. **World Wide Web address:** http://www.iquest.net/quiring. **Description:** A fee-free, human resources consulting firm, providing a full line of staffing services including temporary and permanent placements, and executive search and contract services. Quiring Associates Inc. also offers career/outplacement services. **Specializes in the areas of:** Computer Science/Software; Engineering; Health/Medical; Nonprofit; Personnel/Labor Relations; Sales; Secretarial. **Positions commonly filled include:** Account Manager; Account Representative; Accountant; Administrative Assistant; Applications Engineer; Biomedical Engineer; Chemical Engineer; Computer Operator; Computer Programmer; Consultant; Controller; Cost Estimator; Customer Service Representative; Database Manager; Design Engineer; Electrical/Electronics Engineer; Financial Analyst; Human Resources Manager; Industrial Engineer; Licensed Practical Nurse; Manufacturing Engineer; Marketing Manager; MIS Specialist; Operations Manager; Physician; Purchasing Agent/Manager; Quality Control Supervisor; Sales Manager; Sales Representative; Software Engineer; Systems Analyst; Systems Manager; Typist/Word Processor. **Average salary range of placements:** More than $50,000. **Number of placements per year:** 50 - 99.

SALES SEARCH
2420 North Coliseum Boulevard, Suite 220, Fort Wayne IN 46805. 219/485-0850. **Fax:** 219/482-1943. **Contact:** Manager. **Description:** An executive search firm. **Specializes in the areas of:** Sales.

SANFORD ROSE ASSOCIATES
P.O. Box 1106, Newburgh IN 47629. 812/853-9325. **Fax:** 812/853-1953. **Contact:** Ken Forbes, Director. **E-mail address:** kforbes@aol.com. **World Wide Web address:** http://www.sanfordrose.com. **Description:** An executive search firm operating on both retainer and contingency bases. **Positions commonly filled include:** Account Manager; Account Representative; Advertising Account Executive; Advertising Clerk; Graphic Artist; Graphic Designer; Human Resources Manager; Market Research Analyst; Marketing Manager; Marketing Specialist; Multimedia Designer; Operations Manager; Public Relations Specialist; Sales Executive; Sales Manager; Sales Representative. **Average salary range of placements:** $30,000 - $50,000. **Number of placements per year:** 1 - 49.

SANFORD ROSE ASSOCIATES
650 East Carmel Drive, Suite 450, Carmel IN 46032. 317/848-9987. **Fax:** 317/848-9979. **Contact:** Manager. **World Wide Web address:** http://www.sanfordrose.com. **Description:** An executive search firm. **Specializes in the areas of:** Finance; Insurance.

SMITH & SYBERG INC.
825 Washington Street, Suite 2A, Columbus IN 47201. 812/372-7254. **Contact:** Manager. **Description:** An executive search firm.

SOURCE SERVICES CORPORATION
111 Monument Circle, Suite 3930, Indianapolis IN 46204-5139. 317/631-2900. **Fax:** 317/682-6100. **Contact:** Manager. **Description:** An executive search firm. The divisions at this location include Source Consulting, Source EDP, Source Healthcare Staffing, and Accountant Source Temps. **Specializes in the areas of:** Accounting/Auditing; Computer Hardware/Software; Health/Medical; Information Technology.

STAFFMARK TECHNICAL
1010 West Coliseum Boulevard, Fort Wayne IN 46808. 219/436-3868. **Contact:** Manager. **Description:** An executive search firm. **Specializes in the areas of:** Technical.

STRATEGIC RESOURCE MANAGEMENT
3500 DePauw Boulevard, Suite 1034, Indianapolis IN 46268. 317/872-8900. **Contact:** Manager. **Description:** An executive search firm. **Specializes in the areas of:** Health/Medical. **Positions commonly filled include:** Certified Nurses Aide; Physical Therapist; Physician.

THE DOBIAS GROUP
130 West Main Street, Fort Wayne IN 46802. 219/436-6570. **Fax:** 219/432-7396. **Contact:** Manager. **Description:** An executive search firm. **Specializes in the areas of:** Hotel/Restaurant.

UNIQUE, INC.
9850 North Michigan Road, Carmel IN 46032. 317/875-8281. **Fax:** 317/875-3127. **Contact:** Jennifer Flora, President. **Description:** An executive search firm. **Specializes in the areas of:** Computer Science/Software; Data Processing; Food; General Management; High-Tech; Legal; Office Support; Personnel/Labor Relations; Publishing; Sales; Secretarial; Telecommunications. **Positions commonly filled include:** Branch Manager; Clerical Supervisor; Computer Programmer; Customer Service Representative; General Manager; Hotel Manager; Human Resources Manager; Management Trainee; Paralegal; Restaurant/Food Service Manager; Services Sales Representative; Software Engineer; Systems Analyst; Telecommunications Manager; Typist/Word Processor. **Number of placements per year:** 500 - 999.

CONTRACT SERVICES FIRMS

ADECCO/TAD TECHNICAL SERVICES
7007 Graham Road, Suite 207, Indianapolis IN 46220. 317/842-2870. **Fax:** 317/842-3085. **Contact:** Jane Moore, Branch Manager. **World Wide Web address:** http://www.tadresources.com. **Description:** A contract services firm. **Specializes in the areas of:** Administration; Architecture/Construction; Computer Science/Software; Engineering; Manufacturing; Technical. **Positions commonly filled include:** Aerospace Engineer; Architect; Biochemist; Biomedical Engineer; Blue-Collar Worker Supervisor; Buyer; Chemical Engineer; Chemist; Civil Engineer; Clinical Lab Technician; Computer Programmer; Design Engineer; Designer; Draftsperson; Electrical/Electronics Engineer; Industrial Engineer; Industrial Production Manager; Internet Services Manager; Mechanical Engineer; MIS Specialist; Multimedia Designer; Operations/Production Manager; Software Engineer; Structural Engineer; Systems Analyst; Technical Writer/Editor; Telecommunications Manager. **Average salary range of placements:** $30,000 - $50,000. **Number of placements per year:** 200 - 499.

ALLIANCE GROUP TECHNOLOGIES
8252 Virginia Street, Merrillville IN 46410. 219/736-3855. **Fax:** 219/736-3864. **Contact:** Manager. **Description:** A contract services firm. **Specializes in the areas of:** Engineering; Technical.

ALLIANCE GROUP TECHNOLOGIES
911 Broadripple Avenue, Suite B, Indianapolis IN 46220. 317/254-8285. **Fax:** 317/254-8339. **Contact:** Manager. **Description:** A contract services firm that also provides some permanent placements. **Specializes in the areas of:** Engineering; Technical.

ALLIANCE GROUP TECHNOLOGIES
P.O. Box 2314, Kokomo IN 46904-2314. 765/459-3931. **Fax:** 765/452-2091. **Contact:** Manager. **Description:** A contract services firm. **Specializes in the areas of:** Engineering; Technical. **Positions commonly filled include:** Engineer; Technician.

BELCAN TECHNICAL SERVICES
8355 Rockville Road, Suite 100, Indianapolis IN 46234. 317/273-6700. **Toll-free phone:** 800/967-5287. **Fax:** 317/273-6707. **Contact:** Michael G. Tribul, Branch Manager. **E-mail address:** techind@tech.belcan.com. **World Wide Web address:** http://www.belcan.com. **Description:** A contract services firm. **Specializes in the areas of:** Engineering; Industrial; Technical. **Positions commonly filled include:** Chemical Engineer; Chemist; Civil Engineer; Computer Operator; Database Manager; Design Engineer; Draftsperson; Electrical/Electronics Engineer; Environmental Engineer; Geologist/Geophysicist; Industrial Engineer; Internet Services Manager; Manufacturing Engineer; Mechanical Engineer; Metallurgical Engineer; MIS Specialist; Production Manager; Purchasing Agent/Manager; Quality Control Supervisor; Registered Nurse; Software Engineer; Systems Analyst; Systems Manager; Technical Writer/Editor; Telecommunications Manager. **Corporate headquarters location:** Cincinnati OH. **Other U.S. locations:** Nationwide. **Average salary range of placements:** $30,000 - $50,000. **Number of placements per year:** 200 - 499.

CMS MANAGEMENT SERVICES
5920 Castle Way West Drive, Suite 120, Indianapolis IN 46250. 317/842-5777. **Fax:** 317/577-3077. **Contact:** Manager. **Description:** A contract services firm that also offers some contract-to-hire and permanent placements. **Specializes in the areas of:** Accounting/Auditing; Engineering; Finance.

CONTINENTAL DESIGN COMPANY
2710 Enterprise Drive, Anderson IN 46013. 765/778-9999. **Toll-free phone:** 800/875-4557. **Fax:** 765/778-8590. **Contact:** Cathy Mellinger, Recruitment. **Description:** A contract services firm. **Specializes in the areas of:** Automotive; Design; Engineering; Manufacturing; Technical. **Positions commonly filled include:** Chemical Engineer; Computer Programmer; Design Engineer; Designer; Draftsperson; Electrical/Electronics Engineer; Industrial Engineer; Mechanical Engineer; Metallurgical Engineer; Quality Control Supervisor; Systems Analyst; Technical Writer/Editor. **Corporate headquarters location:** This Location. **Other U.S. locations:** Troy MI. **Average salary range of placements:** $30,000 - $50,000. **Number of placements per year:** 50 - 99.

POLLAK AND SKAN GROUP
9143 Indianapolis Boulevard, Highland IN 46322. 219/838-0004. **Contact:** Manager. **Description:** A contract services firm. **Specializes in the areas of:** Computer Hardware/Software; Engineering.

QCI TECHNICAL STAFFING
4705 Illinois Road, Suite 113, Fort Wayne IN 46804. 219/436-9797. **Fax:** 219/436-6228. **Contact:** William E. Quackenbush, President. **World Wide Web address:** http://www.qcitechstaffing.com. **Description:** A contract services firm. **Specializes in the areas of:** Administration; Computer Science/Software; Engineering; Technical. **Positions commonly filled include:** Computer Programmer; Design Engineer; Draftsperson; Electrical/Electronics Engineer; Electrician; Industrial Engineer; Manufacturing Engineer; Mechanical Engineer; Metallurgical Engineer; MIS Specialist; Project Manager; Purchasing Agent/Manager; Quality Control Supervisor; Software Engineer; Systems Analyst. **Benefits available to temporary workers:** Holiday Bonus; Paid Vacation. **Average salary range of placements:** $30,000 - $50,000. **Number of placements per year:** 100 - 199.

TECHNETICS CORPORATION
8383 Craig Street, Suite 200, Indianapolis IN 46250. 317/842-5377. **Toll-free phone:** 800/467-8324. **Fax:** 317/842-6992. **Contact:** Recruiter. **Description:** A contract services firm. **Specializes**

in the areas of: Architecture/Construction; Computer Science/Software; Engineering; Industrial; Manufacturing; Technical. **Positions commonly filled include:** Architect; Biomedical Engineer; Chemical Engineer; Civil Engineer; Computer Programmer; Design Engineer; Designer; Draftsperson; Editor; Electrical/Electronics Engineer; Electrician; Environmental Engineer; Industrial Engineer; Industrial Production Manager; Internet Services Manager; Mechanical Engineer; Metallurgical Engineer; MIS Specialist; Multimedia Designer; Operations/Production Manager; Purchasing Agent/Manager; Quality Control Supervisor; Science Technologist; Software Engineer; Structural Engineer; Systems Analyst; Technical Writer/Editor. **Average salary range of placements:** $30,000 - $50,000. **Number of placements per year:** 100 - 199.

H.L. YOH COMPANY
2345 South Lynhurst Drive, Suite 111, Indianapolis IN 46241. 317/381-7000. **Fax:** 317/244-3735. **Contact:** Manager. **Description:** A contract services firm that also provides some temporary and temp-to-hire placements. **Specializes in the areas of:** Administration; Computer Hardware/Software; Engineering; Technical.

RESUME/CAREER COUNSELING SERVICES

GREEN THUMB, INC.
P.O. Box 687, Seymour IN 47274. 812/522-7930. **Fax:** 812/522-7684. **Contact:** Manager. **Description:** Provides job training and skills training to individuals aged 55 or over.

JOB CORPS
504 Broadway, Suite 727, Gary IN 46402-1921. 219/882-2677. **Fax:** 219/882-6718. **Contact:** Counselor. **Description:** A career/outplacement counseling firm. **Positions commonly filled include:** Claim Representative; Clinical Lab Technician; Computer Programmer; Customer Service Representative; Dental Assistant/Dental Hygienist; Dietician/Nutritionist; Electrical/Electronics Engineer; Electrician; Hotel Manager; Licensed Practical Nurse; Medical Records Technician; Restaurant/Food Service Manager; Services Sales Representative; Typist/Word Processor. **Number of placements per year:** 1000+.

WARRICK COUNTY EMPLOYMENT & TRAINING CENTER
224 West Main Street, P.O. Box 377, Boonville IN 47601. 812/897-4700. **Fax:** 812/897-6352. **Contact:** Paul K. Wright, Executive Director. **Description:** A career/outplacement agency and training center. **NOTE:** Clients must be JTPA (Job Training Partnership Act) eligible. **Specializes in the areas of:** Industrial; Manufacturing; Retail; Sales; Secretarial; Transportation. **Positions commonly filled include:** Draftsperson; Electrician; Maintenance Technician. **Average salary range of placements:** $20,000 - $29,999. **Number of placements per year:** 50 - 99.

INDEX OF PRIMARY EMPLOYERS

NOTE: *Below is an alphabetical index of primary employer listings included in this book. Those employers in each industry that fall under the headings "Additional employers" are not indexed here.*

A

B

C

D

E

F

G

H

I

J

K

L

M

N

O

P

Q, R

S

T

U

V, W

Y

Z

Your Job Hunt
Your Feedback

Comments, questions, or suggestions? We want to hear from you! Please complete this questionnaire and mail it to:

The JobBank Staff
Adams Media Corporation
260 Center Street
Holbrook, MA 02343

or send us an e-mail at jobbank@adamsonline.com

Did this book provide helpful advice and valuable information which you used in your job search? Was the information easy to access?

Recommendations for improvements. How could we improve this book to help in your job search? No suggestion is too small or too large.

Would you recommend this book to a friend beginning a job hunt?

Name: ______________________________

Occupation: ______________________________

Which JobBank did you use? ______________________________

Address: ______________________________

Daytime phone: ______________________________